Citizen Politics
Research and Theory in
Canadian Political Behaviour

Edited by

Joanna Everitt and Brenda O'Neill

OXFORD
UNIVERSITY PRESS

UNIVERSITY OF WINNIPEG, 515 Portage Ave. Winnipeg, MB R3B 2E9 Canada

OXFORD

UNIVERSITY PRESS

70 Wynford Drive, Don Mills, Ontario M3C 1J9
www.oupcan.com

Oxford University Press is a department of the University of Oxford.
It furthers the University's objective of excellence in research, scholarship,
and education by publishing worldwide in

Oxford   New York

Athens   Auckland   Bangkok   Bogotá   Buenos Aires   Cape Town
Chennai   Dar es Salaam   Delhi   Florence   Hong Kong   Istanbul   Karachi
Kolkata   Kuala Lumpur   Madrid   Melbourne   Mexico City   Mumbai   Nairobi
Paris   São Paulo   Shanghai   Singapore   Taipei   Tokyo   Toronto   Warsaw

with associated companies in Berlin   Ibadan

Oxford is a trade mark of Oxford University Press
in the UK and in certain other countries

Published in Canada by Oxford University Press
Copyright © Oxford University Press Canada 2002

The moral rights of the author have been asserted

Database right Oxford University Press (maker)

First published 2002

National Library of Canada Cataloguing in Publication Data

Main entry under title:

Citizens politics : research and theory in Canadian political behaviour

Includes bibliographical references.
ISBN 0-19-541447-0

1. Political participation—Canada. 2. Political culture—Canada.
I. Everitt, Joanna Marie, 1964– II. O'Neill, Brenda Lee, 1964–

JL65.2001 C58 2001   324'.0971   C2001-901430-9

Cover design: Joan Dempsey

1 2 3 4 – 05 04 03 02

This book is printed on permanent (acid-free) paper ∞.

Printed in Canada

Contents

Preface

This is a book about Canadian political behaviour in all its facets. With it we hope to demonstrate that the subject extends beyond the traditional study of elections, voting, and political parties; while these are essential in any serious study of the field, they alone do not constitute its totality. Political culture, public opinion, political participation, interest groups, social movements, and élite activity represent additional and equally important research topics. Moreover, we hope to emphasize that political action is taking place in new venues, utilizing new approaches, and involving a broader mix of Canadians. Indeed, the use of the label 'political behaviour' is seen by some as too narrow for an approach that traverses several of the subfields of political science. The objective in developing the book was to put together a package of readings suitable for undergraduate students that would be both comprehensive in its review of existing research and theory and indicative of the wealth of current research that is in many ways pushing the boundaries of the discipline. The key to doing this, we reasoned, was to bring together established and active academics, who could provide the richness and foundation for the field, and younger scholars, whose work builds on those foundations and yet often re-examines its core assumptions and long-standing conclusions.

The idea to put together this collection resulted from necessity. Both of us were slated to teach courses on some element of political behaviour and each of us found little in the way of Canadian textbooks that could fill that need adequately. Plenty of teaching material exists for courses in Canadian politics generally and political parties more specifically. Several research treatments on voting exist, but their sophistication makes them difficult to employ as textbooks in undergraduate courses. Moreover, we knew that political behaviour included more than simply voting and elections. Each of us had only recently received our Ph.D.s, with doctoral dissertations falling within the Canadian political behaviour field, and found this deficiency hard to explain. We were well aware of the great research that had been and continues to be undertaken by Canadian academics on the subject. With little hesitation (perhaps too little!), we decided to edit a book that would collect this work and hopefully introduce others to a field of study that we both loved and continue to love. We believe that the result has been well worth the effort. In addition to putting together an important collection of pieces, we forged new acquaintances, strengthened existing ones, and developed a greater appreciation for the work of our peers.

We were extremely fortunate in having had the support of a number of individuals and institutions while putting together this collection. We must thank those individuals who agreed to be part of this project—the many contributors. The quality of your work is our blessing. We also thank the three universities that provided crucial institutional support—the University of Lethbridge, the University of Manitoba, and the University of New Brunswick at Saint John. The people we have worked with at Oxford University Press—Ric Kitowski, Len Husband, and Laura Macleod—were both supportive and patient with two very 'green' editors. We will always be grateful for your understanding and support, and we especially thank you for believing in two young academics. We would also like to thank the two anonymous Oxford referees for their comprehensive reviews of the manuscript; your comments improved the final product. Thanks as well to Richard Tallman, who did a comprehensive and vigorous job of copy-editing. And for their part in initiating and developing our love of this field of study, we would like to single out several individuals: Terrance G. Carroll, William D. Coleman, Richard Johnston, Sylvia Bashevkin, Elisabeth Gidengil, Larry LeDuc, Jon Pammett, and Scott Bennett. To you we owe a debt of gratitude.

Finally, we owe thanks to our families. Joanna would like to thank her parents, Bill and Doreen Everitt, and her brothers, David, Bruce, and John whose support and encouragement over the years have meant so much to her. Brenda wishes to thank her children, Rachel and Aidan Stewart, a constant source of tremendous pride and joy, and her husband, David Stewart, for his editorial help, unconditional love, and constant encouragement. It goes without saying that our lives are better for knowing and loving these people.

Joanna Everitt, Saint John
Brenda O'Neill, Winnipeg
February 2001

To our grandmothers,
from whom we have learned so much.

Part I

Behavioural Methods

Chapter 1

The Study of Canadian Political Behaviour: What Is It, How Do You Do It, and Why Bother?

BRENDA O'NEILL AND JOANNA EVERITT

The 2000 elections in both Canada and the United States were noteworthy for the questions they raised about the democratic nature of each country's electoral institutions. The American election will be remembered as much for the jargon it brought to public discussions (hanging chad, dimpled chad, pregnant chad, butterfly ballot) as for constitutional and procedural issues about citizen participation and equality in the voting process. At its conclusion, one point seemed etched on the minds of a majority of Americans: every vote counts. Although in not nearly as dramatic a fashion, the 2000 Canadian federal election also renewed discussions on the quality and character of the Canadian electoral system. The fractionalization of the Canadian party system and the limited ability of the electoral system to adequately accommodate regional interests have led to renewed calls for a re-examination of the first-past-the-post electoral system. Unlike in the past, however, many of these calls are coming from concerned citizens rather than primarily from academics and think-tanks.[1] Similarly, the continued decline in turnout in Canadian elections has initiated an examination of a long neglected topic: the nature, quality, and results of democratic participation.

As a result, this is an exciting time to be studying political behaviour. While the traditional questions of how, when, where, and why individuals become involved in politics remain, their importance has been heightened by the recent arrival of two phenomena fundamentally connected to democracy and citizen participation. The first is globalization, the other the Internet and the World Wide Web. The first limits the ability of states to respond to the demands of citizens in that a measure of political power is transferred to international, and often non-governmental, political actors and institutions. The increased communication potential resulting from Internet and Web access has been touted as a possible route to renewing democratic participation, and in particular, for countering the shifting power structure brought on by globalization. To grasp fully the implications of modern political issues such as these, it is imperative that students of politics understand the concepts, models, and questions occupying researchers within the field of politics often described as 'political behaviour'.

This introduction has three objectives. First, it describes the concept of political behaviour, as both a focus and a method of inquiry, to equip the reader with the tools required for understanding the chapters that follow. As a focus of inquiry, political behaviour concentrates on several specific topics as a result of assumptions it makes about the most important questions that political researchers should be asking. Shifts in this focus have occurred over time, some more substantial than others, and many in response to criticisms levelled at the field or the discipline more broadly (see the final chapter, this volume). As a method of inquiry, political behaviour adopts a specific approach to social science research with which students of the subject should acquaint themselves. Second, the chapter outlines the various methods employed in political behaviour research, both to equip the student with an understanding of the many possible ways in which the topic can be investigated and, perhaps of more immediate concern, to allow for some understanding of the tools employed by the authors in this book. Finally, and perhaps most importantly, the chapter develops an argument for continued research on Canadian political behaviour. The 'need' to justify our research reflects general trends in the public sector and elsewhere towards ensuring accountability. The importance of social science research has not escaped this 'value for money' inquisition. Luckily, the argument is an easy one to mount, and one that we hope will encourage a new generation of political science researchers to continue on with the task.

What Is Political Behaviour?

Politics is about social decision-making, and within liberal democracies there exists a desire to employ democratic means for reaching what are tremendously difficult decisions in light of conflict over values, interests, and a scarcity of resources. According to Heinz Eulau (1963: 3, 5), 'Politics is concerned with the conditions and consequences of human action' and the study of political behaviour concerns 'what man [sic] does politically and the meanings he attaches to his behaviour'. Political behaviour thus concentrates on individuals, on how they act and behave within social organizations, and on establishing explanations for their behaviour. Concentrating on the individual does not translate into a belief that political behaviour occurs in a vacuum. As Carmines and Huckfeldt (1996: 235) point out, the individual actor must be examined 'in the context of surrounding constraints and opportunities that operate on patterns of social interaction, the acquisition of political information, and the formulation of political choice'. As a result, the study of political behaviour includes the examination of organizations, such as political parties and social movements, to situate individual actions and attitudes within institutional structures, cultures, and goals. And within liberal democracies such as Canada, political behaviour research has been occupied by the individual citizen's ability and desire to function within the democracy system and the resultant ability of that system to succeed (ibid.).

The study of political behaviour, then, is about the many ways in which people 'act' politically, largely within the context and framework of social decision-making, that is, human activity directed at politics. As such, political behaviour includes behaviours and attitudes that are 'political'. Checking a name off on a ballot, waving a placard while shouting slogans, and writing a letter to an MP are some of the many ways in which citizens choose to act politically. Political attitudes are also a key element of political behaviour—how we choose to act reflects our many values, beliefs, and attitudes. As an example, writing a letter to an MP might stem from its author's belief that it will be read and perhaps influence social decision-makers, a belief that will undoubtedly reflect the prevailing political culture of the state. Similarly, joining a protest is often precipitated by strongly held attitudes on the issue or cause in question and by an acceptance that formal decision-making channels, for whatever reason, are not a viable option for bringing about change. Such attitudes are also likely to be firmly embedded in the political culture. While there currently exists a certain complacency surrounding democratic participation in Canada, recent events such as the demonstrations at the November 1997 APEC meting in Vancouver and the Canadian state's reactions to them should alert us to the fact that political participation, in its many forms, is the essence of the liberal democratic political system.

But what makes an act or attitude *political*? While at first this may seem like a naïve question, further reflection reveals that the definition political researchers have given to 'political' has changed in the past 30 years (see Burt, O'Neill, this volume). At its core, politics concerns the distribution of power, and traditional political research has focused on power within the formal public institutions of governance. But in light of the claims of the women's movement that 'the personal is political', for example, the definitions of 'politics' and 'political behaviour' have expanded.

In earlier days, political behaviour was easily described as the beliefs and activities of citizens in the formal political arena undertaken to influence social decision-making. These acts would have included those connected with the institutions of government, elections and voting, political parties, and interest groups as each represents a channel for effecting democratic change. In addition, attention would be directed to protest behaviour (signing petitions, taking part in boycotts, demonstrations, and strikes), activities designed to influence government's decisions from outside rather than inside formal channels of influence, and at times through illegal means. The chapters that follow reveal that the arenas for the study of political behaviour remain largely unchanged: political culture, public opinion, voting and elections, political participation, leaders and activists, and interest groups continue to occupy researchers working within the general field of political behaviour studies.[2] The one key exception is the addition of social movements, a topic added to the study of political activity in light of the growth and influence of environmental and feminist movements, among others.

Several notable changes can nevertheless be identified within each of these arenas that mirror those that have occurred in the study of political science more broadly. For one, the definition of what constitutes 'political' activity has expanded to include activity occurring in organizations outside the traditional organizations of governance, such as parent/teacher councils and food banks. Part of this shift reflects feminist critiques of the discipline and its previously narrow focus on activities dominated by men (for one such critique, see Vickers, 1997). It also reflects a growing awareness that participation in civil society is frequently linked to traditional forms of political activity (see Carbert, this volume). Another change has occurred in the focus of research concentrating on political institutions and processes. Far more attention is paid to the political behaviour of women and minorities by Canadian researchers than was the case even 10 years ago (see Black, Abu-Laban, this volume). Again, this reflects criticism levelled at traditional behavioural studies, but also the ascendancy of the issues of representation and citizenship within the field of political science (see, e.g., Kymlicka, 1995). And the scope of factors examined as possible determinants of political behaviour and attitudes has also grown due to the changed definition of politics, as well as from greater awareness of the degree to which long-standing assumptions narrowed the field of vision of many researchers regarding significant private and public influences on political behaviours and attitudes (see Burt, O'Neill, in this volume).

In light of such changes and shifts, for the purposes of this book 'political behaviour' is defined as the range of actions undertaken and attitudes held by individuals in connection with the social organization and decision-making structures of the state in both its formal and informal manifestations. Political behaviour research is devoted to the study of these actions and attitudes. More specifically, the aim of political behaviour research is 'firstly, to describe what people think and how they behave politically, and secondly, to explain why they think and behave as they do' (Erickson, 1998: 83).

Political Behaviour: Focus and Method

Political behaviour can refer to two distinct elements of the study of politics: political behaviour as a focus of study, that is, *what is studied*; and behaviouralism as an approach, that is, *how you study* (see Kavanagh, 1983; Sanders,1995). Both are key to understanding the choices and decisions made by political behaviour researchers. The early and continued reaction against this 'behavioural revolution' is best understood by noting that the approach began as a protest against the state of the discipline as it existed in the 1950s. Nevertheless, labelling it a 'revolution' reflected some wishful thinking on the part of its earliest proponents (Kavanagh, 1983: 2).

As a focus of study, political behaviour was a reaction to the tendency within the study of politics to concentrate on formal government institutions, most notably the constitution, to the neglect of political actors and processes, and to the normative and prescriptive bent within political philosophy.[3] In Canada, Robert MacGregor Dawson's *The Government of Canada* (1947) typified the institutional approach dominant at the time. Such work concentrated its inquiry on the main institutions of the state (primarily the constitution and the legislative branch of government) to the neglect of other actors, institutions, and groups, such as political parties and interest groups, and elections and communication processes. The emphasis in this early work was on description rather than causal analysis, although researchers often lapsed into normative prescriptions about the merits of one particular institutional structure over another, most notably liberal democratic systems (Erickson, 1998). As noted by Baxter-Moore et al. (1994: 5), this approach was more aptly described as 'the study of government rather than the study of politics'. Kavanagh (1983) suggests that events in the Soviet Union, Nazi Germany, and Italy in the interwar period confirmed that states did not always progress naturally towards the adoption of liberal democratic values, as earlier researchers had claimed. This awareness that politics and government are not subject to a natural and progressive evolutionary process revealed the importance of social and economic influences on political conditions and the flawed nature of traditional political research.

The response of the earliest proponents of the political behaviour approach was to redirect the discipline towards the study of political activity both within and outside of the formal institutions of the state. The result was a growth in the number of investigations of previously neglected institutions, including the executive and judicial branches, the public bureaucracy, political parties, and interest groups. The increased appreciation of the importance of individual political actors and the forces influencing them led to an explosion of research on voting and elections. The focus of the new branch of inquiry was the individual, but institutional constraints remained a core component of the social forces affecting individual behaviour.

The study of elections and voting had a long history, but the introduction of survey methodology, coinciding with a desire to achieve a more 'scientific' discipline than had previously been the case, fundamentally altered research in the subfield. The result was research distinguishable from other political studies subfields and from previous voting research. Empirical methods, primarily sampling and surveying techniques, and mathematical tools for analysis, were central to this new methodology. The behavioural focus on the individual as the core political actor and on voting as a key political act continues in the United States and elsewhere.[4]

Imported from the United States in the 1960s, the introduction of the behavioural approach in Canada resulted from a rapid growth in the number of Canadian universities established to accommodate increased enrolments due to the postwar baby boom. Political scientists trained in American universities filled many of the new academic positions because of the relative lack of suitable graduate programs in Canada; the result was the importation of American trends in the discipline (Trent and Stein, 1991: 72). But in keeping with trends towards independence from the 'sleeping elephant' to the south, the study of political behaviour in Canada never achieved a similar level of dominance among political researchers and even in its heyday came under significant criticism. The Canadian behavioural 'revolution' was mediated by strong adherence among a significant number of academics to neo-institutional and neo-Marxist approaches and by the continued support for public policy analysis (Baxter-Moore et al., 1994). The American influence was also tempered by a conscious desire to adopt a uniquely 'Canadian' approach to the discipline (see, e.g., Smiley, 1974; Cairns, 1975). The weaker record of the behavioural approach in Canada rests as well on its inability to deal effectively with a number of Canadian questions that were prominent in the 1960s and 1970s, including the place of Quebec in the Canadian state, Western alienation, constitutional reform, and the challenges of a multicultural society (Baxter-Moore et al., 1994: 17). More recent challenges have been added by feminist critiques and postmodern approaches. The result is that Canadian political behaviour continues to play a key, albeit challenged, role among several dominant fields in the discipline. For some, however, political behaviour is less seen as a core field in the study of politics than as an area of specialization that cuts across all fields.[5]

Work by Jean Laponce (1969), Robert Alford (1963), John Meisel (1964), John Courtney (1967), and Mildred Schwartz (1974), among others, represents the output of the first generation of Canadian political behaviouralists, which in many respects set the tone for much subsequent work in the field. But it also reveals the tendency of early work in the field to concentrate narrowly on voting, elections, and parties. It remains true that many more textbooks on Canadian political parties (e.g., Bickerton et al., 1999; Tanguay and Gagnon, 1996; Thornburn, 1996) and on voting and elections (e.g., Clarke et al., 1996; Johnston et al., 1992; Johnston et al., 1996; Wearing, 1991) exist than on other political behaviour topics or the field in general. Although Bashevkin's *Canadian Political Behaviour* (1985) filled the void identified earlier by Elkins and Blake (1975), the void has since reappeared as a result of that text no longer being in print. The choice of topics included in this book reflects the expansion of the study of political behaviour, beyond the 'ballot box' issues of voting, elections, and parties. Bashevkin (1985) chose to include separate sections for public opinion, political participation, political culture, and party and legislative élites in her edited volume on Canadian political behaviour. While significant overlap exists between her choices and the ones made for this book, a look at those chapters selected to reflect research currently being conducted in the field reveals the distance travelled in the field between then and now; the selection of women as independent political actors, the importance of the media for voting and elections, the uniqueness of immigrant and ethnic minority participation in Canadian politics, and new social movements are indicative of this shift.

But more than a simple shifting of the lens, work inspired by critiques of traditional approaches introduced a new set of assumptions regarding methodology and how research is conducted. The new set of assumptions was a reaction to the perceived disjointedness and lack of general theoretical development of the discipline. Critiques of the political philosophy and institutional approaches stemmed from the former's perceived myopia and the latter's lack of rigour (Erickson, 1998). Political philosophy concentrated on normative questions (*what ought to be*) to the neglect of empirical ones (*what is*) and institutional analysis often failed to move beyond mere description. In this sense, the critique was less about *what* was being studied and more about *how* it was being studied and to what end. Existing studies, it was argued, did little to provide students with key orienting concepts, criteria for selecting variables, and connections between different phenomena. Moreover, the traditional, descriptive approaches failed to provide explanations for political phenomena and as such were limited in their ability to predict events and outcomes. The idea, then, was to transform the study of politics into a *science*. The adoption of such a scientific approach within the discipline, it was thought, might provide the knowledge necessary for the development of better politics and a more successful society (Kavanagh, 1983).

One of the key proponents of this transformation was David Easton (1957). In an effort to bring the study of politics closer to that of a science, Easton advocated a search for a universal theoretical model that could assume the role of theories found in the natural sciences. In the quest for a general theoretical model of politics, Easton developed the *systems approach* as a tool for understanding the process that governs political systems and for explaining political decision-making. The model remains useful for its treatment of politics as a process constantly reacting to and evolving with a changing environment. Although the model continues to appear in many introductory textbooks (e.g., Jackson and Jackson, 2000: 35; Brodie, 1999: 78), it is for the most part dismissed as a useful explanatory theory because of the very generality it sought to achieve and instead has been relegated to the status of a useful heuristic tool. Similar searches for a general theory of politics resulted in the *structural functionalist approach* of politics (Almond and Powell, 1966).

The search for an overarching theory of politics has, for the most part, been abandoned (Kavanagh, 1983: 9), as political scientists come to realize that to encompass all political systems such models would have to be pitched at such a level of abstraction as to render them extremely limited in their ability to explain processes and behaviour at the micro level. Moreover, the search has been tempered by an acceptance that human behaviour is not akin to the subject matter of the natural sciences. Behaviouralism had argued for the search for theories such as existed in the natural sciences, reflecting a desire to render the study of politics more scientific. A key distinction, however, is that a complete understanding of human behaviour requires a move beyond the external social forces acting on political actors. Human behaviour is subject to free will and does not consistently and predictably respond to external stimuli in the manner found in the natural sciences. This element of political behaviour renders its study particularly difficult. According to one textbook on political behaviour:

> If you want to know why people act as they do, you must understand not only what they are like as people, but also the constraints of the situation in which they find themselves. Both environmental and personality factors must be considered in trying to understand the context in which any human behaviour takes place. (Woshinsky, 1995: 115)

And until science has mastered the topic of human psychology, the study of politics will not mirror the natural sciences in its development of general theories and models. However, it can and does aim to establish 'patterns of regularity in social life' that exist in spite of the tremendous diversity at the individual level (Babbie, 1998: 25).

Nevertheless, theory continues to play an extremely important role in behavioural research. As a method, behaviouralism emphasizes an approach to the study of politics heavily influenced by positivism and the scientific approach. As such, it adopts explicit assumptions and requirements for the manner in which research is conducted and for the search for knowledge. In this context, theory remains a core element of behavioural research.

In the first instance, positivism requires that research and the researcher remain objective, eschewing subjective, normative, or prescriptive evaluations. The requirement rests on a belief that the existence of an observable reality is discoverable only through a rational and logical examination of the evidence (ibid.). Researchers should be concerned with facts rather than values and remain emotionally uninvolved with the issues and subject matter of their investigations. The goals are to describe how things are and to explain why they are that way rather than how they should or ought to be. The ultimate objective remains scientific theory development. To become emotionally committed to the results of one's research, it is argued, reduces the possibility of objectively viewing evidence that counters one's preferred conclusions.

A serious challenge to these assumptions is found in post-modern approaches arguing that knowledge is socially constructed. For behaviouralists, however, knowledge is assumed to exist independently of the researcher and the researched. The researcher is better placed to discover knowledge than the researched because of his/her ability to adopt an objective distance from the evidence and data reviewed.

Knowledge development requires more, however, than simply the adoption of an objective stance; it also requires that theoretical propositions be both logically and empirically supportable (ibid.,18). As such, models, theories, and explanations must both make sense and correspond with our observations. The empirical requirement—that the only appropriate method for testing propositions is by testing the predictions they generate against observation—demands that support for propositions come from an examination of a large number of cases, or at least a randomly selected subsample of cases rather than a limited number of supportive illustrations (Sanders, 1995). Further, the empirical requirement demands that theoretical propositions be testable and capable of falsification (ibid.). And since conclusions based on setting values and social priorities cannot meet these requirements, they should not then occupy social scientists. The focus is on that which is observable and therefore knowable, leading to an approach that 'requires the formulation of testable hypotheses, and the marshalling of empirical data that can either confirm or fail to confirm the hypotheses' (Archer et al., 1998: 4).

The empirical requirement constitutes the most fundamental of political behaviour's assumptions. The only valid means for testing theoretical propositions is to assess them against observations. Empirical research is thus contrasted against that which relies singularly on appeals to logic, introspection, or the usefulness of theories to explain the world. Behaviouralism is also scientific in that it promotes the discovery of theoretical propositions that will explain behaviour at the general rather than the individual level. Thus, its objective is to explain the decisions of political participants rather than those of any one individual. For example, research on Canadian voting behaviour would outline the key forces acting upon Canadian voters, rather than what shapes the vote decision of Jane Doe from Pugwash, Nova Scotia.

Determinism constitutes a further cornerstone of the behaviouralist structure. The desire to explain patterns of human activity rests on the belief that such activities are at least partly the result of external social forces working on individual political actors. As such, hypotheses are predictions about the relationship between at least two variables—the effect (or activity) and the cause(s) of the effect. A requirement of any explanation is the existence of variation in both variables (hence the name). A hypothesis concerning why individuals engage in protest activity, for example, requires that some individuals choose not to engage in such activities. If all citizens join the protest over Alberta's Health Care Protection Bill (Bill 11), there ultimately is nothing to explain. But when some individuals choose to protest while others do not, the goal becomes to provide an explanation for this variation in political behaviour. Several alternative explanations, or hypotheses, are then outlined, each attempting to account for the observed patterns of behaviour. Their relative success is determined by the degree to which each helps to 'explain' that variation. The development of theories of causation is crucial to the ability to predict future behaviour.

A concern of behavioural research is to ensure that studies are capable of replication (Sanders, 1995: 68) and to guarantee 'intersubjectivity' (Babbie, 1998). Their importance lies in the desire among researchers to ensure that the conclusions they reach in their work be identical to those that would have been reached had other researchers studied the same evidence in the same manner. This relates to the concern for objectivity and leads to significant attention being paid to detail and to a demand for clarity at every stage of the research process.

Behavioural research formally proceeds in a prescribed manner beginning with the identification of a particular issue or problem (see Archer et al., 1998). The researcher then develops theoretical propositions (hypotheses) to identify the causes of the identified effect that are amenable to empirical testing. The researcher will normally rely on the work of earlier researchers at this stage to help identify possibilities based on the conclusions they reached. The next stage is to define clearly one's concepts to allow for the gathering of data to test the hypotheses identified in the previous stage. The researcher then tests these hypotheses against the data to assess the degree to which they help to explain the cause-effect relationship established in the theoretical propositions. This latter stage also requires the researcher to step back from his or her own research results to reflect on how they inform the theoretical conclusions previously reached. As such, it is hoped that individual studies will add to and direct the overall development of knowledge in the study of a general phenomenon by relying on past research and by informing future research.

The positivist foundation of behavioural research in political science has inspired a significant portion of criticisms levied at the field (see concluding chapter). It must be pointed out, however, that the foundational assumptions and prescriptions of positivism and empiricism are rarely adopted blindly by modern researchers. As an example, uncommon is the behaviouralist who purports to adopt a completely objective research stance. Instead, modern researchers acknowledge their potential biases and work to minimize their effects. While complete objectivity is conceded as an unattainable goal, the goal still is to be as objective as possible in one's research. Behaviouralism has modified its earlier claims in light of criticisms and also as a result of reflection by its proponents and practitioners.

Empirical Research Methods

While the empirical method sets a number of requirements for the researcher, a significant degree of latitude remains in the choice of specific method of inquiry to adopt in any research project. A key distinction lies in whether the chosen method is quantitative or qualitative in its approach.[6] Although both fit squarely within the empirical branch of social science research, each is distinguishable from the other in several important ways.

Quantitative analysis is driven by a desire to quantify evidence gathered on human behaviour in order to generalize from the sample to the larger population. Large, randomly drawn samples ensure that one's conclusions are not based on unrepresentative cases. The focus on large numbers also results in structured research to ensure comparability across cases. This research approach employs statistical analysis and the quantification of data to identify patterns and relationships among the many cases, and is characterized by its breadth rather than its depth. Quantitative analysis in particular strives to achieve the objectivity promoted by the quest for a more scientific study of politics.

A number of quantitative methods are employed in political research. Survey analysis dominates in investigating political behaviour and political attitudes primarily for its ability to tap into the beliefs and behaviours of a large sample of respondents relatively easily, quickly, and at modest cost (see chapters by Nevitte and Kanji, Fournier, Everitt, Blake, Martin and Nadeau, Blais et al., Jenkins, Leduc, Stewart, Black, Carbert, Cross, this volume). Content analysis is an additional quantitative method involving the systematic investigation of print and verbal communication for patterns in attitudes or in media coverage of politics (see Jenkins, this volume). Case studies are another, although these investigations focus on a smaller number of cases than is true of other quantitative methods. What sets them apart from case studies in other disciplines is that the goal is to use the case study to say something about patterns in behaviour beyond the few cases investigated. As described by Archer et al. (1998: 114–15):

> There is always a broader phenomenon lying at the back of the researcher's mind. This in turn ties into the theoretical nature of political science research. Describing the case is not enough; something must be done to fit the case into a larger theoretical

perspective or framework. Political science, therefore, drives from the specific to the general, from the case or sample to the population within which it is embedded.

The chapters by Young and Stefanick in this book employ the case study method for examining the feminist and environmental movements.

A final quantitative method employs secondary data gathered at an earlier point in time by researchers working on a distinct although often complementary research question. The use of secondary data is particularly challenging in that the operationalization of concepts and data collected may not correspond with the desires of subsequent users of the data. The benefit of employing secondary data lies in its easy access, often without cost, which is an important consideration during particularly lean years in universities. Many of the chapters in this book employ secondary data in their investigations. The chapters by Docherty and Black employ data from the Canadian Parliamentary Guide and the census, respectively, in their examinations of the political participation of parliamentarians; Eagles's chapter on ecological voting focuses on data from Statistics Canada and Elections Canada.

Qualitative analysis, on the other hand, is more concerned with an in-depth examination of fewer cases to provide a richer understanding of political behaviour than is possible with more quantitative methods. When compared to more quantitative approaches, qualitative analysis is characterized by its less structured method for collecting data. Where quantitative data are typified by numbers, qualitative data are rich in words, and words require greater subjective evaluation than numbers. Qualitative research is also less likely to follow the sequential steps in a research project identified earlier in this chapter. Instead, the use of grounded theory results in a more inductive examination of data with a constant re-evaluation and reformulation of theory as the research progresses (Archer et al., 1998).

Political scientists employ a number of qualitative research methods. The personal interview method provides a means for investigating political attitudes and behaviour where a structured self-administered survey is unlikely to provide a rich understanding of the respondent's views or when the sample of cases is small enough to allow for face-to-face interviewing. Although structured surveys can be administered face-to-face, a qualitative interview is allowed to deviate from the survey instrument, lacks closed-ended questions that force respondents to choose from a limited set of answers, and offers a more relaxed and personal interviewer-interviewee relationship. Finally, interviewing provides political researchers with a window into the thoughts and actions of political participants that is often not available through self-administered surveys. Carbert's chapter on the political behaviour of Ontario farm women is built on information collected in personal interviews and Stefanick, Young, and Cross interviewed members of environmental, feminist, and party organizations.

Observation provides a second qualitative tool for conducting political research. Such observation can occur unbeknownst to those being observed (covert observation) and/or by having the researcher join the organization or group (participant observation) (e.g., Flanagan, 1995). Although the method is more often employed in sociological studies, political science has adopted it as a means of studying political behaviour, in particular political parties and party nomination conventions (e.g., Carty, 1991; Carty et al., 2000; Courtney,1973, 1995).[7] A final qualitative approach to political research is the comparative method. The comparative method attempts to examine a relationship by assessing it in at least two different places or times (Archer et al., 1998: 136). As a goal of social science research is to generalize from the specific to the general, the comparative approach attempts to determine to what degree results are limited to particular countries, groups or generations. Lisa Young's chapter in this book employs the comparative method to examine social movements in the US and Canada to determine how they are shaped by the political institutions and structures in each country.

Thus various approaches can be employed to investigate political attitudes and behaviour. The selection of method should be directed by the goals and nature of the research question itself, by the nature of the cases and/or individuals under investigation, and by the availability of data and/or research funds. The choice may also reflect the beliefs of the researcher regarding the appropriateness of 'science' in political research and the positivist/empirical approach. Quantitative approaches tend more towards the science element of political science research. On the other hand:

> Qualitative analysis . . . has been particularly associated in recent years with a *verstehen* or interpretive approach to social science that rejects imitation of the standard science model and holds that knowledge of political life can only be derived from an understanding of a society's values and on the ways in which people subjectively interpret the meaning of their own and other people's actions. (Baxter-Moore et al., 1994: 3)

Critical and feminist researchers often adopt more qualitative research methods because of various concerns with and critiques of quantitative approaches (O'Neill, 1995). Such criticisms have included: the authority granted 'hard cold facts' over anecdotal evidence and other information sources; a rejection of the presumed desirability of disinterested researchers; skepticism regarding the supposed objectivity of quantitative research and researchers; and the exploitation of human beings in the data collection process. The use of triangulation (where more than one type of research method is adopted in a research project) provides an important opportunity for employing the best that each has to offer (Archer et al., 1998: 120). Many of the chapters in this book employ several methods at once in their research. In the end, an awareness of the assumptions, goals, weaknesses, and strengths of each method is fundamental to an objective, critical evaluation of the conclusions reached in research as it is for engaging in quality research oneself.

Why Study Political Behaviour?

Political researchers often face the task of justifying the value in their research and the subject matter they teach, especially in times of shrinking budgets, limited resources, and increasing cynicism directed at politicians and governments. The argument that knowledge should be sought for knowledge's sake alone remains a powerful one—universities are, after all, institutions of learning—but this argument is not limited to any discipline in particular. Why, then, should one study political behaviour?

The importance of the study of political behaviour is intimately connected with the democratic project. The core and prominent unit of investigation within democracies remains the citizen. Almost 30 years ago, in his book *The Behavioural Persuasion in Politics* (1963: 3) Heinz Eulau wrote:

> The root is man. I don't think it is possible to say anything meaningful about the governance of man without talking about the political behavior of man—his acts, goals, drives, feelings, beliefs, commitments, and values . . . Politics is the study of why man finds it necessary or desirable to build government, of how he adapts government to his changing needs or demands, of how and why he decides on public policies.

The argument remains a forceful one today (though the need for inclusiveness demands that 'woman' be added to the discourse).

Part of the value of research on political behaviour lies in its ability to say something about the process, quality, and stability of the democratic project of which the basic unit is the individual. Such research can tell us which systems are stable and which are not, and goes some distance towards explaining why stability varies across systems. The belief that the success of a modern democratic system rests squarely on the active and informed participation of its citizenry is commonly held. The level of participation and the knowledge required for that success nevertheless remain topics of debate.

An understanding of the causes of democratic success provides the possibility of structuring systems to promote their success. Yet a premature conclusion on the dominance of liberal democratic systems over alternative systems, based on events such as those in the former USSR and East Germany, is tempered by a simple accounting of the number of fledgling democracies around the world. Comparative research on political processes and institutions provides avenues for investigating the connections and causes of democratic stability and instability. As mentioned at the outset of this chapter, the impact on democracy and participation of new information technologies and the 'digital' revolution currently stands as an important research question within the field. Yet more remains to be done; the democratic ideal has yet to be reached in many, if not all, of the world's states where it has been adopted. And events in South Africa and elsewhere reveal that democratic success is neither easily achieved nor guaranteed.

The relative success of the democratic project in Canada is unquestionable—political violence is rare, turnover of legislative and executive offices is painless, citizen participation in politics remains at a respectable level. Within this context sits the Canadian citizen—key to the democratic project and yet for the most part individually powerless. The ability to shape social decisions in a liberal democratic system rests on one's perceived ability, actual ability, and desire to wield political power. The ability to wield power lies predominantly in the ability to gather support for one's positions and/or platforms. Yet, as a result of increased education levels and given their greater access to and the greater availability of information, Canadian citizens are better placed today than in earlier years to wield that power. Globalization and the arrival of worldwide Internet access provide exciting new twists to citizen participation in politics. This potential political empowerment, however, has not taken root among all Canadians. Canadians (and especially younger Canadians) appear to have moved away from traditional political institutions and processes and are increasingly cynical about politics and less trusting of politicians. An increased level of political cynicism and a falling voter turnout rate in the 2000 federal election suggest little has changed. The changes in political behaviour have been recorded in other advanced democracies (Putnam, 1993). Canadians nevertheless remain interested in politics and appear to be moving towards alternative avenues of participation (see Nevitte and Kanji, this volume; Nevitte, 1996). The changes have tremendous implications for democratic politics. Political parties, for example, have shifted to more democratic leadership selection processes at least in part to regain some of the ground that they have lost in light of increasing cynicism towards the traditional institutions of politics. In the end, the success of the Canadian democratic project depends on the values, beliefs, attitudes, choices, and participation or non-participation of individual Canadians. And this is the subject matter of the study of political behaviour.

But political behaviour remains more than a focus of inquiry. As a method or 'mood', behaviouralism embodies a commitment to adopting empirical, rigorous, and systematic methods in the study of politics (Dahl, 1969). Many, if not most, modern political researchers rarely question the requirement of providing empirical support for theoretical positions and arguments. In this sense, behaviouralism has been successful in turning a 'mood' into a standard. But it must be understood that the behavioural method constitutes the means, rather than the end, of political research. It provides the empirical foundation on which to render normative judgements. The democratic ideal requires an informed citizenry, but 'facts' in and of themselves cannot answer questions regarding what is of value and desirable in a society. Moreover, facts can be employed to buttress a preferred position rather than in the spirit of objective inquiry. Academic investigations of citizens' attitudes and behaviour provide an important counter to investigations conducted and disseminated by governments, think-tanks, and citizens' groups. Undertaking research to answer what is and why provides an important basis on which to answer questions of what ought to be and how we get there. And there are few more valuable questions to answer than these.

A Note on Organization

This text contains a collection of original essays designed to provide a foundation for the study of Canadian political behaviour, as well as several additional essays highlighting some of the research currently being undertaken on citizen politics. The text has been organized into sections that correspond to the subfields of research on political behaviour: political culture, public opinion, voting and elections, participation, leaders and activists, and interest groups and social movements. Within each of these sections, the first chapter provides a comprehensive introduction to the subfield. Each of these five chapters, written by recognized scholars in the field:

- provides a review of the key literature in the area;
- situates Canadian research within a comparative context;
- identifies the important questions and key challenges that have dominated research in the field;
- discusses the methodologies that have been used to address these questions; and
- attempts to indicate directions for future research in the area.

Each of these review chapters is followed by two or more chapters that specifically profile research currently being conducted in the area in Canada. These chapters are more focused than the review chapters and are meant to provide timely examples of the many ideas, methods, and issues found in the work of active researchers in the field of political behaviour. Many of these chapters are drawn from the authors' recent publications or ongoing research projects. Efforts were made in selecting these chapters to ensure a fairly accurate representation of the diversity of research questions and methodologies found in the field; they represent, however, only a small portion of the research conducted on Canadian political behaviour and students are encouraged to seek out additional studies written on these and other subjects in the field of political behaviour.

Notes

1. For example, Fair Vote Canada was founded on 1 Aug. 2000 'to provide concerned citizens, community leaders and activists with an organizational framework to build a nationwide grassroots civic education and electoral reform campaign in Canada' (see http://www.fairvotecanada.org/).
2. The study of elections and voting continues to dominate research on political behaviour, although less so than in the past.
3. For an early critique of traditional methods employed to study politics in Canada, see Cairns (1974).
4. In two reviews of the state of American political science research (Finifter, 1983, 1993), political behaviour (referred to as 'micropolitical behavior' and 'individual political behavior') is a primary focus. Similarly a recent text out of the UK on methods and theory in political science includes chapters on behavioural analysis (Marsh and Stoker, 1995).
5. A quick scanning of PhD programs at Canadian universities reveals that few provide students with the possibility of specializing in political behaviour as a core field, as was once the case.
6. Although qualitative and quantitative methods are often set up as separate and unique, it is beneficial to think of them as lying at separate ends of a methodological continuum (see Archer et al., 1998: 119; Jackson, 1999: 12).
7. For an excellent review of the use of the participant observation method in the study of politicians and politics, see Fenno (1990).

References

Alford, Robert. 1963. *Party and Society: The Anglo-American Democracies*. Chicago: Rand McNally.

Almond, Gabriel, and G. Bingham Powell. 1966. *Comparative Politics: A Developmental Approach*, 2nd edn. Boston: Little, Brown.

Archer, Keith, Roger Gibbins, and Loleen Youngman. 1998. *Explorations: A Navigator's Guide to Quantitative Research in Canadian Political Science*. Toronto: Nelson.

Babbie, Earl. 1998. *The Practice of Social Research*, 8th edn. Scarborough, Ont.: ITP Nelson Canada.

Bashevkin, Sylvia. 1985. *Canadian Political Behaviour: Introductory Readings*. Agincourt, Ont.: Methuen.

Baxter-Moore, Nicolas, Terrance Carroll, and Roderick Church. 1994. *Studying Politics: An Introduction to Argument and Analysis*. Toronto: Copp Clark, Longman.

Bickerton, James, Alain-G. Gagnon, and Patrick J. Smith. 1999. *Ties That Bind: Parties and Voters in Canada*. Toronto: Oxford University Press.

Brodie, Janine, ed. 1999. *Critical Concepts: An Introduction to Politics*. Scarborough, Ont.: Prentice-Hall Allyn and Bacon Canada.

Cairns, Alan. 1974. 'Review Article: Alternative Styles in the Study of Canadian Politics', *Canadian Journal of Political Science* 7, 1: 101–28.

———. 1975. 'Political Science in Canada and the Americanization Issue', *Canadian Journal of Political Science* 8, 2: 191–234.

Carmines, Edward G., and Robert Huckfeldt. 1996. 'Political Behaviour: An Overview', in Robert E. Goodin and Hans-Dieter Klingemann, eds, *A New Handbook of Political Science*. Toronto: Oxford University Press.

Carty, R.K. 1991. *Canadian Political Parties in the Constituencies*, vol. 23 of the research studies for the Royal Commission on Electoral Reform and Party Financing. Ottawa and Toronto: RCERPF/Dundurn.

———, William Cross, and Lisa Young. 2000. *Rebuilding Canadian Parties*. Vancouver: University of British Columbia Press.

Clarke, Harold D., Jane Jenson, Lawrence LeDuc, and Jon H. Pammett. 1996. *Absent Mandate: Canadian Electoral Politics in an Era of Restructuring*, 3rd edn. Vancouver: Gage.

Courtney, John, ed. 1967. *Voting in Canada*. Scarborough, Ont.: Prentice-Hall.

———. 1973. *The Selection of National Party Leaders in Canada*. Toronto: Macmillan of Canada.

———. 1995. *Do Conventions Matter? Choosing National Party Leaders in Canada*. Montreal and Kingston: McGill-Queen's University Press.

Dahl, Robert A. 1969. 'The Behavioral Approach in Political Science: Epitaph for a Monument to a Successful Protest', in Heinz Eulau, ed., *Behavioralism in Political Science*. New York: Atherton Press.

Dawson, Robert MacGregor. 1947. *The Government of Canada*. Toronto: University of Toronto Press.

Easton, David. 1957. 'An Approach to the Analysis of Political Systems', *World Politics* 9, 3: 383–400.

Elkins, David, and Donald Blake. 1975. 'Voting Research in Canada', *Canadian Journal of Political Science* 8, 2: 313–25.

Erickson, Lynda. 1998. 'Political Behaviour: Introduction', in Michael Howlett and David Laycock, eds, *The Puzzles of Power: An Introduction to Political Science*. Toronto: Oxford University Press.

Eulau, Heinz. 1963. *The Behavioral Persuasion in Politics*. Toronto: Random House.

Fenno, Richard. 1990. *Watching Politicians: Essays on Participant Observation*. Berkeley: Institute of Governmental Studies, University of California at Berkeley.

Finifter, Ada, ed. 1983. *Political Science: The State of the Discipline*. Washington: American Political Science Association.

———. 1993. *Political Science: The State of the Discipline II*. Washington: American Political Science Association.

Flanagan, Thomas. 1995. *Waiting for the Wave: The Reform Party and Preston Manning*. Don Mills, Ont.: Stoddart.

Jackson, Robert J., and Doreen Jackson. 2000. *An Introduction to Political Science: Comparative and World Politics*. Scarborough, Ont.: Prentice-Hall Allyn and Bacon Canada.

Jackson, Winston. 1999. *Methods: Doing Social Research*, 2nd edn, Scarborough, Ont.: Prentice-Hall Allyn and Bacon Canada.

Johnston, Richard, André Blais, Henry Brady, and Jean Crête. 1992. *Letting the People Decide: Dynamics of a Canadian Election*. Montreal and Kingston: McGill-Queen's University Press.

———, ———, Elisabeth Gidengil, and Neil Nevitte. 1996. *The Challenge of Direct Democracy: The 1992 Canadian Referendum*. Montreal and Kingston: McGill-Queen's University Press.

Kavanagh, Dennis. 1983. *Political Science and Political Behaviour*. Boston: Allen and Unwin.

Kymlicka, Will. 1995. *Multicultural Citizenship: A Liberal Theory of Minority Rights*. Oxford: Clarendon Press.

Laponce, Jean. 1969. *People vs. Politics*. Toronto: University of Toronto Press.

Marsh, David, and Gerry Stoker, eds. 1995. *Theory and Methods in Political Science*. London: Macmillan.

Meisel, John, ed. 1964. *Papers on the 1962 Election*. Toronto: University of Toronto Press.

Nevitte, Neil. 1996. *The Decline of Deference: Canadian Value Change in Cross-National Perspective*. Peterborough, Ont.: Broadview Press.

O'Neill, Brenda. 1995. 'The Gender Gap: Re-evaluating Theory and Method', in Sandra Burt and Lorraine Code, eds, *Changing Methods: Feminists Transforming Practice*. Peterborough: Ont.: Broadview Press.

Putnam, Robert. 1993. 'Bowling Alone', *Journal of Democracy* 6: 65–78.

Sanders, David. 1995. 'Behavioural Analysis', in David Marsh and Gerry Stoker, eds, *Theory and Methods in Political Science*. London: Macmillan.

Smiley, Donald. 1974. 'Must Canadian Political Science Be a Miniature Replica?', *Journal of Canadian Studies* 9, 1: 31–41.

Schwartz, Mildred. 1974. 'Canadian Voting Behaviour', in Richard Rose, ed., *Electoral Behavior: A Comparative Handbook*. New York: Free Press.

Tanguay, A. Brian, and Alain-G. Gagnon, eds. 1996. *Canadian Parties in Transition*, 2nd edn. Toronto: Nelson Canada.

Thorburn, Hugh G., ed. 1996. *Party Politics in Canada*, 7th edn. Scarborough, Ont.: Prentice-Hall Canada.

Trent, John E., and Michael Stein. 1991. 'The Interaction of the State and Political Science in Canada: A Preliminary Mapping', in David Easton, John G. Gunnell, and Luigi Graziano, eds, *The Development of Political Science*. New York: Routledge.

Vickers, Jill. 1997. *Reinventing Political Science: A Feminist Approach*. Halifax: Fernwood.

Wearing, Joseph, ed. 1991. *The Ballot and Its Message: Voting in Canada*. Toronto: Copp Clark Pitman.

Woshinsky, Oliver H. 1995. *Culture and Politics: An Introduction to Mass and Elite Behavior*. Englewood Cliffs, NJ: Prentice-Hall.

Part II

Political Culture

Chapter 2

Vanishing Points: Three Paradoxes of Political Culture Research

Ian Stewart

'Along with the novel, baseball on grass, and the family, political culture is often thought to be moribund, when it is thought about at all' (McDonough, 1993: 847). Given that its intellectual genealogy can be traced back to Toqueville's *Democracy in America*, to Burke's 'cake of custom', and even to Aristotle's 'state of mind', (Kavanagh, 1983: 48), this cavalier dismissal of the concept of political culture merits closer scrutiny. In its modern incarnation, political culture elbowed its way into the discipline's collective consciousness in the 1960s after 'national character' studies fell into bad odour because of their racist overtones. At that time, the study of mass beliefs was judged to be both feasible (with the advent of modern survey techniques) and desirable (as those inside the academy sought to redress the failings of the institutionalist paradigm and those outside the academy, especially American foreign policy-makers, sought to understand the social requisites of democratic stability) (Pye, 1973: 65–6). Thus, the comparative study of political culture, epitomized by Almond and Verba's (1965) famous analysis of *The Civic Culture*, came, for a time, to be 'on the cutting edge' of the discipline (Dittmer, 1977: 553). According to one ambitiously precise assessment, interest in political culture studies peaked in 1966 (Brint, 1991: 103); thereafter, the conceptual, methodological, and theoretical difficulties associated with the approach dampened the ardour of many political scientists. As a result, the study of political culture 'underwent first of all stagnation and then a gradual retreat during the 1970s' (Gibbins, 1989: 2). More colourfully, one observer has noted that political culture research was 'in the professional dog house for a generation' and that following in the footsteps of Almond and Verba had taken on 'the aura of working out anomalies in Ptolemaic astronomy' (Laitin, 1995: 169). New disciplinary enthusiasms, such as rational choice modelling, emerged as interest in political culture waned. By the start of the 1980s, it was apparently possible to detect only 'sporadic and spasmodic evidence' of renewed concern for the study of political culture (Gibbins, 1989: 11).

The passions of the academy, however, have a cyclical (or, perhaps, dialectical) quality. In the final decade of the twentieth century, political scientists increasingly used political culture to inform their analyses. The collapse of Marxism-Leninist ideologies in Eastern Europe and the re-emergence of long dormant national values in their stead gave many scholars pause. So, too, did the rise of Islam in many parts of Asia and Africa. Arguing that such beliefs were epiphenomenal, that they merely reflected more basic material interests, seemed to be increasingly untenable. Ronald Inglehart, whose work on the growth of post-materialism proved to be increasingly influential, wrote a much-cited article on 'The Renaissance of Political Culture' (1988; Jackman and Miller, 1996a). Robert Putnam's elegant analysis of modern Italian democracy gave further impetus to the discipline's renewed interest in the political culture approach. According to Putnam (1993: 157), the 'civic traditions' of Italy not only have 'remarkable staying power' but also may have 'powerful consequences for economic development and social welfare, as well as for institutional performance'.

In Canada, the cultural revival has also been apparent. Neil Nevitte's *The Decline of Deference* (1996), for example, argues that the values of Canadians changed during the turbulent decade of the 1980s. In particular, Canadians grew more interested in politics, less trusting in state élites, more willing to consider protest activities, and more supportive of environmentalism and other new social movements. Following on from Inglehart, Nevitte roots these changes in the emergence of a post-materialist society; historically unprecedented levels of affluence and education could not help but resonate throughout the Canadian political culture. What is particularly useful about Nevitte's analysis is the situating of the Canadian case in a broader comparative context. Canadian political orientations have not been evolving in an idiosyncratic fashion. On the contrary, concludes Nevitte, 'the direction, content, and style of Canadian value change has a great deal in common with the transformations taking place in other advanced industrial states' (Nevitte, 1996: 298).

The Clash of Rights, by Sniderman et al. (1996), also illustrates the renewed interest in Canadian political culture. The authors undertook a sophisticated scrutiny of the political orientations held not only by the broad mass of Canadians but also by different socio-political élites. Somewhat surprisingly, the latter were not revealed to be more committed than the former either to basic democratic values or to the recognition of particular group rights. One might have surmised that élite tolerance helps to bridge the Canadian cultural divide between Anglophones and Francophones. Yet Sniderman et al. discovered that party élites do not 'offer a markedly firmer basis of support for the rights of French Canadians than does the ordinary English Canadian' (ibid., 208). Much of their analysis demonstrates 'the inescapable and essential pluralism of values in liberal democracy' (ibid., 8). Political struggles are not mere artifacts of errors or misunderstandings; rather, they can be rooted in the contestability of even the most basic of liberal democratic values.

Interest in Canadian political culture may well be undergoing a 'renaissance'. To some, however, this field has always promised more than it has delivered. In this chapter, I maintain that the study of political culture illuminates many of the central features of Canadian politics. Consider voting, still the most fundamental form of political behaviour. In the absence of a concept such as political culture, how could one understand the electoral support given to the Bloc Québécois by the community of Quebec nationalists? Considerations of material interest (from increasing the proportion of Québécois in the Ottawa civil service to extracting, for Quebec, a greater share of federal largesse) undoubtedly form part of their voting calculus. But so, too, do concerns of pride and identity, of nationalism and perhaps even revenge, all of which are properly subsumed under the concept of political culture. In fact, even the material component of the Bloc Québécois vote can be argued to have cultural underpinnings. Matters of self-interest have to be perceived before they can be acted upon, and the perceptual lens through which the Quebec nationalist community becomes aware of its political self-interest is provided by political culture. In short, without some recourse to political culture, only the most stunted understanding of voting behaviour is possible.

Nevertheless, the practising political culturalist is likely to be bedevilled by three paradoxes:

1. *The nuance paradox.* The more nuanced the understanding of a particular political culture, the less useful that understanding will be in comparative analysis.
2. *The anchor paradox.* The more anchored the understanding of a particular political culture, the narrower the explanatory power of that understanding.
3. *The acceptance paradox.* The more accepted the understanding of a particular political culture, the more suspicious one should be of that understanding.

Conceptual Matters

Before confronting these paradoxes in some detail, however, some conceptual clarification is in order. A common flaw in comparative analysis is to impose conceptual homogenization on a heterogeneous field (Dogan and Pelassy, 1990: 151–9). Put less pedantically, this involves attaching the same conceptual label to political phenomena that are significantly, but not essentially, similar. Grouping the Cuban Communist Party and the British Columbia NDP under the rubric 'socialist party' affords an example of this problem. For some matters, such as a scrutiny of recurring ideological motifs, imposing the concept of 'socialist party' on both of these political actors might be legitimate. Yet for other purposes, such as an examination of electoral links with environmentalist interest groups, the conceptual elasticity required would be such as to render meaningless any findings. The comparative study of political culture is certainly not immune to this difficulty; at the same time, however, it might also be said to suffer from precisely the opposite failing: the conceptual heterogenization of a (potentially) homogeneous field. While most scholars in the area continue to employ the concept of 'political culture,' their understanding of what is meant by that concept varies widely. What began as a straightforward attempt to capture fundamental political orientations and assumptions has, in some instances, been embroidered beyond recognition. Consider, for example, the definition of political culture provided by Richard Wilson (1992: 97):

> A political culture is a social construction of meaning termed a compliance ideology, whose structure and content serve to reduce institutional transaction costs by delimiting obligations, expressed in positional and contractual terms that justify elite status and bolster group solidarity.

Or consider the understanding of Paul Nesbitt-Larking, who claims not to conceive of political culture as an 'abstracted element of an individuated role'. On the contrary, according to Nesbitt-Larking (1988: 7):

> Political culture is concerned with how people, both co-operatively and in conflict, come to conceive of and symbolize the distribution and uses of valued resources, and the making of rules. Political culture is practiced when people achieve symbolic manifestations of their places in those power-related contexts that are important to them.

Or, finally, consider those political scientists who employ the term in a normative, rather than analytic, sense and consequently doubt whether particular societies 'can be considered to possess a "political culture" at all' (Roberts, 1984: 425).

Formulations such as these are clearly not helpful. If the concept of political culture is to advance the cause of theory-building, it must capture, in basic terms, an important element of political reality. Here we shall conceptualize political culture, quite simply, as *a collectivity's fundamental orientations and assumptions about politics*. These can exist at the conscious or unconscious level, can be cognitive (i.e., knowledge about politics), evaluative (i.e., judgements about politics), or affective (i.e., feelings about politics), and can be directed at a wide range of political phenomena. Of course, this conception of political culture is not as straightforward as it might initially seem. On the contrary, it begs four questions, each of which must be confronted before the discussion can usefully move on.

1. Does political culture include political behaviour?

For most analysts of political culture, the answer has been unambiguously negative (Patrick, 1984: 281); the concept should be used to capture the psychological, rather than the behavioural, dimensions of politics. This interpretation has not, however, gone unchallenged, especially among students of communist politics. These scholars argue that Communist governments have been simultaneously attempting to remake not only the practices and behaviour of their citizens, but also their thoughts and beliefs. To attempt to draw a conceptual distinction between culture and behaviour, in this context at any rate, would miss the point of the exercise. As well, it is advanced that Communist scholars have generally been denied access to survey data and, hence, have insufficient purchase on the orientational dimensions of politics (Brown, 1984: 4). Yet neither of these objections is particularly compelling. With respect to the latter, it is unacceptable to make fundamental conceptual choices on the basis of methodological ease. As we shall subsequently see, there are many ways, aside from public opinion polls, to access orientations; including behaviour in the conceptualization of political culture on these grounds alone would be tantamount to endorsing lazy scholarship. As for the argument that Communist societies are attempting to re-engineer both the beliefs and practices of a 'new, socialist being', this also is unconvincing (even leaving aside the fact that the number of such societies is thankfully dwindling). Communist élites may have found it useful to blur their understanding of culture; members of the academy have no such rationale for embracing this astigmatism.

More difficult to refute are the arguments of cultural anthropologists, who see culture as something lived rather than merely held (Street, 1994: 103; Jancar, 1984: 76), and who argue that each generation is socialized into an interwoven web of values and behaviours (Mayer, 1972: 349–50). To separate the former from the later is both a practical impossibility and a scholarly dead end. Stephen Welch (1993: 104–5) points out that many activities, such as winking, are culturally impregnated; one might be able to describe such behaviour entirely in terms of its objective manifestations, but this does not enhance our understanding of the practice. Perhaps, but is effectively conflating the concepts of political culture and political behaviour likely to be any more productive? If institutions are conceived to be a type of patterned behaviour, then culture becomes 'everything except the biologically given' (Mayer, 1972: 349). And if 'political culture' becomes interchangeable with 'political phenomena', its explanatory power is all but spiked. In any case, it is a significant leap from arguing that political culture and political behaviour cannot be kept hermetically separated to arguing that they should therefore be subsumed under the same rubric. All theory-building in political science requires that the objects of analysis be more or less artificially segmented from the more or less seamless web of human activity of which they are a part. This segmentation occurs across space and over time as well as along a host of less obvious dimensions. It does not seem fair to hold political culturalists to a stricter standard than that which constrains others working in the discipline.

Let us be absolutely clear about what is at stake here. This textbook is predicated on the assumption that understanding Canadian political behaviour is a central part of the discipline. No such understanding is achievable, however, if political behaviour is subsumed under an unnecessarily expansive conception of political culture. Nor is it possible to explore the links between the 'internal' world of values, feelings, and beliefs and the 'external' world of behaviour if the two realms are conflated. This error must be avoided; in order for political culture to enhance our understanding of political behaviour, the two must be kept conceptually distinct.

2. How can political culture be distinguished from culture?

Political culture is a subset of culture, but the lines demarking the former are both indistinct and somewhat arbitrary. Not all scholars will agree where political culture ends and culture begins; even Almond and Verba, the intellectual godfathers of the concept, have been subject to criticism on this score (Lijphart, 1980). Compounding the difficulty is our expanding understanding of the political to include matters formerly regarded as purely private. Taken to the logical extreme, this could result in the leveraged takeover of 'culture' by 'political culture'.

Such an eventuality would be unfortunate. Even with the most inflated understanding of the 'political', some cultural orientations are only obliquely of interest to political scientists. Including these within 'political culture' would only serve to make the concept more cumbersome for the academy. As before, some segmentation (even if largely artificial at the margins) is necessary in order for political scientists to concentrate on those orientations directly linked to matters of politics, that is, those that revolve around power and the state.

3. Is political culture an aggregate or holistic concept?

Individuals have beliefs, values, and preferences; only collectivities can have culture. The nature of these collectivities, however, requires further specification. Are they merely aggregates of individuals or are they something holistic and indivisible? Most political culturalists implicitly rely on the former conceptualization. The unit of analysis remains the individual and political culture is just the sum total (or the average, range, or mode) of individual psychological attributes. Such an approach is not only conceptually simple; it also has the advantage of encouraging methodological simplicity.

Nevertheless, significant arguments have been raised against this conceptualization of political culture. Just as one cannot study macroeconomics through an aggregated analysis of microeconomics (Pye, 1973: 72), it has been suggested that

> Culture is an intersubjective, rather than a subjective phenomenon; consequently, culture cannot be read off from responses to individual-level analyses alone. Culture is much more than the sum total of abstracted thoughts about life. (Nesbitt-Larking, 1988: 13)

Consider, for example, the matter of political trust. It does not reside within individuals; rather, it exists between and among groups. In short, political trust is essentially a social phenomenon, and scrutinizing individuals will permit, at best, only partial access to that phenomenon. Notwithstanding some of the methodological difficulties engendered, there will be many occasions when political culture is most appropriately conceptualized as holistic.

4. How is political culture to be distinguished from public opinion?

Although both concepts attempt to capture popular values, political culture refers to a collectivity's orientational bedrock, while public opinion refers to a more volatile and ephemeral phenomenon. Nelson Wiseman (1996: 21) has provided us with a useful meteorological metaphor: political culture is to public opinion as climate is to weather. This is not to dismiss the significance of the short-term factor. Just as the behaviour of farmers, for example, is profoundly influenced by both climate and weather, so, too, are voters driven both by enduring attachments to particular values and by more transitory enthusiasms.

But do those enduring attachments actually exist? In the absence of such stability, the conceptual utility of political culture could legitimately be questioned. Almost all scholars in this area agree that most political cultures are gradually evolving. Before World War II, it was socially acceptable for Ontario shopkeepers to post signs reading 'Jews and Dogs Not Admitted' (Howe, 1988: 4). Sixty years on, such a practice would be overwhelmingly condemned. Nevertheless, there are limits to this cultural malleability. Most political culturalists agree that enduring 'cross-cultural differences exist' (Inglehart, 1988: 1207; Eckstein, 1988) and that 'inertia remains a powerful force for continuity in the political culture' (Martin and Stronach, 1992: ix).[1] Recent events in Eastern Europe provide ample fodder for this perspective. Since the demise of many communist regimes, it has become apparent that

> political cultures are not easily transformed. A sophisticated political movement ready to manipulate, penetrate, organize, indoctrinate, and coerce and given an opportunity to do so for a generation or longer ends up as much or more transformed than transforming. (Almond, 1990: 168; see also White, 1979: 166–7; Hahn, 1991)

Even allowing for some systemic quakes, the political culture of today is likely to resemble its counterpart from yesteryear (although post-Quiet Revolution Quebec provides an interesting exception to the rule).

Given that some orientations are enduring while others are ephemeral, political culturalists must develop the facility for tapping into the one but not the other. Not all are successful in this endeavour. In fact, even Almond and Verba included both orientations towards the regime and orientations towards the authorities in their initial conceptualization of political culture (1965: 14–16). Yet the latter would more usefully be considered as part of public opinion; extreme unhappiness with particular members of the political élite can thus coexist quite easily with widespread support for the institutions and processes of the political regime. Similarly, attempts to tap into underlying levels of political trust and political efficacy have sometimes strayed into matters more suited to a study of public opinion than of political culture (MacDermid, 1989). Maintaining this distinction may not always be straightforward; failure to do so, however, robs political culture of much of its utility.

In short, it is most useful to conceptualize political culture as: (1) *an orientational*, but not a behavioural, attribute; (2) that subset of culture which focuses on *power and the state*; (3) *holistic*, rather than merely aggregate, where necessary; and (4) consisting of *enduring*, rather than transitory, value attachments. Most of the landmark treatments of Canadian political culture have been guided by this conceptualization. Three, in particular, are worthy of note.

(1) Louis Hartz (1964) attempted to characterize the political culture of all 'New World' societies. According to Hartz, their original settlers did not represent the full range of their former homeland's ideological diversity. On the contrary, the founding (European) fragment was unusually homogeneous. In the case of New

France, the founding fragment was feudal in character; with respect to British North America, the founding fragment was essentially liberal. According to Hartzians, the orientations of the first immigrant group congealed (much like metaphysical bowls of jelly) into a dominant political culture. Subsequent generations and later waves of immigrants either conformed to the dominant social values or were marginalized. Finally, Hartz argued that the political culture of a 'New World' society could not undergo a process of dialectical change; lacking diverse ideological threads, such cultures were doomed to 'unfold' in a fashion profoundly constrained by the values of the founding fragment.

Many scholars have taken issue with the Hartzian approach to the study of Canadian political culture (Stewart, 1994a). Perhaps the most celebrated critique has been provided by Gad Horowitz (1968). While Horowitz accepted most of Hartz's analysis, he took issue with the purported ideological homogeneity of English Canada. To Horowitz, liberalism has indeed been the dominant thread in English-Canadian political culture. Liberalism has had to coexist, however, with minority strains of conservatism and socialism. The Hartzian model (especially as amended by Horowitz) has two chief virtues. First, it has sensitized students of Canadian political culture to the importance of the values brought to this country by the founding immigrant fragments. Second, the Hartzian model has called attention to the idiosyncratic cultural complexity of Canada. Not only were there two founding fragments (French and English), but the latter at least was atypically heterogeneous. For many, this throws light not only on the ongoing absence of a definitive national identity, but also on the willingness of Canadians to tolerate diversity.

(2) Unlike Louis Hartz, who placed Canadian political culture in a broad comparative context (including Australia, Latin America, and South Africa), Seymour Lipset has generally taken a continental approach. According to Lipset (1970, 1976, 1986), political cultures are profoundly shaped by 'formative events', which, like switches on a railroad siding, can shunt a culture indefinitely off in a new direction. For the political cultures of both Canada and the United States, Lipset maintains that the American War of Independence constituted just such a formative event. The American Revolution and the Canadian counter-revolution ensured that inhabitants of these two societies would thereafter hold significantly divergent views on such matters as the appropriate role of the state, the right to bear arms, and the need for social order. Admittedly, Lipset's analysis has been thoroughly critiqued (Truman, 1971). Nevertheless, his understanding that American political culture emphasizes 'life, liberty, and the pursuit of happiness', while its Canadian counterpart stresses 'peace, order, and good government', does illuminate one of the central differences between the two societies.

(3) Richard Simeon and David Elkins (1974) are renowned for their study of regional political cultures in Canada. While both Hartz and Lipset tended to blur the orientational diversity of Canada (or, at least, of English Canada) to facilitate cross-national comparisons, Simeon and Elkins sensitized us to the attendant

dangers of such an approach. Using a series of national election studies, Simeon and Elkins revealed, for example, that the Atlantic Canadian political culture could be characterized as 'disaffected' (since a disproportionate number of Atlantic Canadians neither trusted the state nor felt that they had the capacity to effect political change). In contrast, citizens who could be labelled 'supporters' (that is, who displayed high levels of both political trust and political efficacy) were disproportionately concentrated in the provinces of Ontario and British Columbia. Like that of Hartz and Lipset, the work of Simeon and Elkins has been widely critiqued (perversely, one of the hallmarks of path-breaking work on political culture is the amount of critical attention generated). Subsequent national election studies, for example, failed to confirm some of Simeon and Elkins's findings (Stewart, 1994b). Nevertheless, they should be credited with sensitizing us to the contribution of political culture to Canada's deep regional fissures.

The Three Paradoxes of Political Culture Study

Establishing a conceptual consensus on political culture (along the lines suggested earlier and, for the most part, in keeping with these landmark treatments of the subject) is essential. Even so, the student of political culture is by no means out of the woods. On the contrary, he or she is likely to confront the three paradoxes noted earlier.

The Nuance Paradox

When political scientists replaced 'national character' with 'political culture', they gained a much more sophisticated conceptualization of basic political orientations. National character studies had assumed that societies cohered around particular belief systems to which all members subscribed (White, 1979: 14). In contrast, political culture analyses have generally recognized that different and competing political orientations exist in all societies, that even where a dominant political culture holds sway it is constantly challenged by a number of minority or subordinate subcultures. Hence, modern-day Canadian attitudes towards governance can be shown to be confused and contradictory; enthusiasm for the present democratic regime is widespread, but it coexists uneasily with a cynical and contemptuous approach to politics.

Clearly, political culture permits a more nuanced appreciation of a society's basic political orientations than was afforded by the concept of national character. Unfortunately, this heightened complexity is not without analytic costs. Given that there is 'rarely a value consensus within a [political] culture' (Laitin, 1988: 589), political scientists will find it difficult to base differences in political behaviour across societies on underlying differences in political culture. Stephen Welch is particularly sensitive to this problem. Welch notes that political culture can be employed for purposes that are either comparative (that is, to explain differences across societies) or sociological (that is, to understand more completely any single society). Yet perversely, these two purposes are contradictory. As Welch (1993: 7) asserts:

A conflict between comparative and sociological uses for political culture arises from the fact that the more detailed and complex (therefore in a sense adequate) an account of political culture is the less comparable it is. Sociological sophistication . . . renders untenable the generalizations that are necessary for cross-national comparison.

A few examples will illustrate this problem more clearly.

Consider, for instance, the work of Yael Yishai, who attempts to root the abortion laws of Sweden (permissive) and Ireland (restrictive) in the two countries' political cultures. According to Yishai, the Swedes are committed to 'equality', while the Irish are attached to 'puritan[ism]'. The result is that 'Sweden has perceived abortion as a social benefit granted under the auspices of the welfare state; Ireland has defined abortion as a moral vice' (1993: 218).

While Yishai's tableau is not without intuitive appeal, it has clearly been painted with an exceedingly broad brush. Delving more deeply into the political cultures of Sweden and Ireland inevitably raises significant doubts about Yishai's thesis. Hence, it has been persuasively advanced that scholars familiar with the Nordic countries are much less likely to assume the cultural pre-eminence of egalitarianism and that despite an extensive welfare state, citizens of the Nordic countries 'do not hold particularly strong leftist views' (Listhaug, 1990: 231). As for Ireland, that country has witnessed the rise of minority strains of individualism, secularism, and liberalism since at least the 1960s (Girvin, 1989: 37). 'What may emerge', concludes one analysis, 'will be a political culture which while increasingly pluralistic and liberal, will also continue to reflect aspects of an older and more traditional set of values' (Girvin, 1993: 398). Yet if the Swedish and Irish political cultures are complex and contradictory, how do they translate straightforwardly into a particular set of legislative enactments?

Analyses of the pre-collapse Asian economic 'miracle' are similarly troubled. Some political culturalists have attempted to see the economic advances of Singapore, South Korea, Hong Kong, Taiwan, and Japan in terms of the long-standing Confucian and Buddhist traditions of these countries (Swank, 1996; Granato, et al., 1996: 608). Even though experts on Confucianism have pointed to the conflicting cues contained within that belief system (Jackman and Miller, 1996b: 709; Moody, 1994: 736), and even though experts on particular East Asian political cultures have identified subcultures at odds with any recognizable understanding of Confucianism (Martin and Stronach, 1992: 17), some scholars are unbowed. Hence, Ronald Inglehart (1988: 1229) continues to embrace Confucianism as East Asia's 'dominant religious or philosophic tradition', even though he acknowledges that it is 'a greatly oversimplified indicator of prevailing world views at a given time and place'. Without such oversimplification, Inglehart would be forced to confront almost unanswerable questions about the cause-and-effect relationship under scrutiny. How widely must a political orientation be held? How intensely must it be embraced? Such matters of thresholds and sufficiency are exceedingly complex, and are likely to be the source of much frustration. The nuance paradox pushes members of the discipline into an unattractive choice. Either they rely on a caricature of a particular political culture (in which case their theories will always be suspect) or they employ a richer characterization of said culture (in which case analytic sclerosis is likely to ensue).

The Anchor Paradox

All concepts are abstractions from reality. The concept of political culture, however, is doubly abstract, since it is an abstraction from an abstract portion of political reality. Unlike statute books, parliament buildings, cabinet ministers, and the like, political orientations cannot be perceived by the five basic senses. Their presence, therefore, can only be inferred from the existence of more tangible phenomena, such as public policy or political behaviour. Alas, such inferences are never easy.[2] In particular circumstances, the same orientation can generate different behavioural manifestations; unhappiness with a regime can generate either apathy or protest (Moisés, 1993). Conversely, the same behaviour can be the product of different underlying orientations; one would not attribute the same belief system to the westerners and the Quebeckers who supported Progressive Conservative candidates in the 1984 and 1988 general elections. Even at its most powerful, the influence of political culture on political behaviour is likely to be 'permissive rather than deterministic' (Simeon and Elkins, 1979: 133), and it is easy to uncover instances where a change in one is not linked to a change in the other (Gibbins, 1989: 11; Liska, 1974).

Nor is a reliance on survey research likely to provide more complete access to an underlying political culture. Recall the distinction made earlier between political culture and public opinion; surveys are much more likely to tap into the latter rather than the former (although Elisabeth Gidengil argues persuasively to the contrary in her contribution to this volume). Countless polls have revealed that notwithstanding their generalized distrust of the state, a majority of Americans support the introduction of a national health-care system (Jacobs, 1992; Feldman and Zaller, 1992). The links between culture and opinions is no less complex than those between culture and behaviour. Some opinions will be culturally driven, others will not. Even leaving aside the customary problems with respondent reactivity and prevarication, and leaving aside as well the methodological individualism of this approach, survey research will be unable to tap into the unconscious dimensions of political culture. Polls may uncover what is averred; they are likely to make little headway on what is assumed.

Quite sensibly, political scientists have responded to this interpretive ambiguity by turning to multiple measures. If we cannot confidently deduce the contours of a particular political culture from any single indicator (whether that indicator is a vote cast, a question answered, or whatever), inferences must be drawn from many different sources. Hence, we are advised to uncover political culture not only through survey instruments, public policy and electoral data, but also via leadership styles (Pye, 1993: 415), participant observation (Nesbitt-Larking, 1988: 22), literature (Wakeman, 1993: 134), conversational analysis (Welch, 1993: 164), political institutions (Elkins, 1987), and symbols (Dittmer, 1977: 583). The adept analyst will use a variety of methodologies; even though not all will point in the same direction there may be enough consistency to permit, by a process of triangulation, intelligent inferences about an underlying political culture.

Unfortunately, this need for multiple indicators is at the root of the anchor paradox. Tautologies have no place in sound scholarship; one cannot first deduce the existence of A from the presence of B and then subsequently employ A to explain B. Such circularity is not uncommon in political culture analyses (McAuley, 1984: 20–3; Jancar, 1984: 76). It is difficult to avoid, however, when one requires so many different types of evidence to infer the contours of a particular political culture. Consider Geoffrey Roberts's injunction that to tap adequately into the German political culture, one needs to use 'behavioural indicators, concerning attitudes, participation, preference, etc., or systemic indicators concerning, for example, the performance of the political system or its relative stability'. As well, a 'sensitive' analysis of political culture would require investigating 'the indicators concerning post-materialist values, . . . the comparative indicators of conventional and unconventional political participation, . . . (and) the indicators of electoral cleavage' (Roberts, 1984: 425). Yet if all these widely differing political phenomena are used to infer a particular pattern of political orientations, what is left for German political culture to explain? If all plausible dependent variables are to be used instead as indicators of political culture, the approach truly becomes 'a cause in search of an effect' (Simeon and Elkins, 1979). Or consider John Gibbins's analysis of British political culture. According to Gibbins (1989: 8–10), the decline of the civic culture in that country can be deduced from the dealignment of class and party, the end to deference, the rise of instrumentalist rationality, the appearance of new political movements, and many other indicators. Gibbins is quite convincing but his success in this regard is rather pyrrhic. For his skill in establishing an important feature of the modern British political culture has perversely robbed his finding of any non-tautological theoretical utility. As with the nuance paradox, the anchor paradox forces political culturalists to select between two equally unpalatable options. On the one hand, they may choose to do a slipshod job of establishing the outlines of a particular political culture by relying on only a few indicators of invariably dubious reliability in the hope that some of the remaining portions of political reality can be understood as cultural outcomes. Or, alternatively, they can recognize that inferring the existence of any political culture is an extremely complex undertaking that requires the employment of multiple and diverse measures, in which case, sadly, there will be almost nothing left for this robust understanding of political culture to explain.

The Acceptance Paradox

Many members of the academy fancy themselves as engaged in a piece-by-piece construction of an edifice of knowledge. Such a perspective assumes that each generation of scholars not only builds on the foundations established by the previous one, but also provides that basis for the next generation to add yet another level of knowledge. Political scientists are no strangers to this conceit, but at least with respect to political culture research, it is a difficult notion to sustain. Indeed, one could as easily argue the exact opposite; as more scholars embrace and employ a seemingly well-established understanding of a particular political culture, the sum total of knowledge actually contracts.

It is useful to scrutinize a specific example. Almost all writing on the political culture of Maritime Canada emphasizes its conservative and traditional character. This understanding may be attacked on empirical matters; there is much evidence that the Maritime provinces are less conservative and traditional than has heretofore been assumed (Stewart, 1994b). This understanding may also be questioned on conceptual grounds; members of the discipline have tended to use 'conservative' and 'traditionalist' interchangeably when the former should entail a conscious ideological mindset (of which dislike of change and suspicion of 'progress' are important components), while the latter should imply an assumed or even unconscious attachment to the familiar. The acceptance paradox indicates a third line of criticism. That so many political scientists accept that the Maritime political culture is conservative and traditional perversely heightens the likelihood that this view is built on insecure foundations.

To see how this is so requires a search for the academic genesis of this understanding. Tracing footnotes back from the present day, it becomes apparent that the image of Maritime political culture as traditional and conservative is rooted in five particular works: Hugh Thorburn's *Politics in New Brunswick* (1961); the chapters by Beck, MacKinnon, and Fitzpatrick on Nova Scotia, Prince Edward Island, and New Brunswick in *Canadian Provincial Politics* (1972); and David Bellamy's article on 'The Atlantic Provinces' (1976). When more recent analyses suggest that there 'is general agreement about the traditionalist Maritime political culture' (Stewart, 1992: 56), these five works, directly or indirectly, invariably are the source of the credo. Yet what is striking about these five pieces is that none of them provides any evidence as to the character of the Maritime political culture; the presence of traditionalism and conservatism is observed by the author but not demonstrated. What is provided, instead, are the putative causes of this phenomenon—the arrival of the United Empire Loyalists, the ongoing strength of rural communities, the relative absence of post-Confederation immigrants, and so on—as well as the putative effects. The type of political culture posited by Thorburn et al. is certainly consistent with the alleged causes and effects, but the skeptical reader will require more evidence of its existence. In short, the entire edifice of work on the Maritime political culture is constructed on shaky foundations; it is not inevitable that the initial characterizations of a given political culture will be light on evidence, but it is striking how frequently that turns out to be the case.

Compounding this problem is the lack of any disciplinary consensus (as implied by the anchor paradox) as to what constitutes a cultural indicator as distinct from a cultural effect. Hence, David Stewart (1992: 56) suggests that the Maritimes' political culture 'is *revealed* to be traditional by . . . the relative exclusion of women from prominent political roles, . . . as well as the persistence of patronage'. Yet for Adamson and Stewart (1991: 515) with respect to the former and for Beck (1981: 149) with respect to the latter, these are *effects* of the traditionalist political culture. Elsewhere, Adamson (1991: 78) notes that the ongoing strength of the Liberals and Progressive Conservatives serves to '*illustrate* the region's political traditionalism'. For Robb (1982: 99), by contrast, the weakness of third parties is the *result* of Maritime traditionalism. Similarly, Dyck (1991: 99) perceives 'a parochialism which bordered on the xenophobic' as indicative of a particular political culture (in this case, Prince Edward Island's), while Fitzpatrick (1972: 128) sees this hostility towards 'outsiders' as a cultural 'manifestation' (in this case, New Brunswick's).

This disciplinary inability to distinguish a cultural indicator from a cultural effect has profound consequences for the accumulation of knowledge. Even where individual political scientists are able to sidestep some of the most pernicious effects of the anchor paradox, the discipline as a whole can become hopelessly ensnared. The persistence of patronage, the exclusion of women, the continuation of religious voting, the weakness of third parties, the absence of innovation, and the suspicion of outsiders are, *in the aggregate*, taken to be *both* indicators and effects of a traditional political culture. Perversely, the acceptance paradox ensures that our most widely held understandings of political culture are those most likely to be tautological to the core. As each new political scientist establishes and employs the traditional character of the Maritime political culture, the tautological basis of that understanding is likely to become even more established. Irrespective of its intellectual elegance, such new work only subtracts, rather than adds, to the accumulated knowledge of our discipline.

Conclusion

The nuance, anchor, and acceptance paradoxes will bedevil political scientists irrespective of time and place, and thus students of political culture in Canada are likely to be as frustrated as their counterparts in other countries. There are, however, some particularly distinctive aspects to the study of Canadian political culture at the beginning of the twenty-first century. Three are especially worthy of note. First, neo-Hartzian analysis continues to be in vogue. Recall that Hartz claimed that a society's political culture was profoundly shaped by its initial group of immigrants (or 'founding fragment'). A recent assessment of provincial political cultures has incorporated this understanding; the result is an evocative group of images ranging from Newfoundland as 'Canada's Ireland and West Country England' to Manitoba as 'The Prairies' Ontario' (Wiseman, 1996: 36). In the United States, it has been suggested that Hartzian analysis 'shows little vitality' and 'is practically dead' (Forbes, 1987: 299). In Canada, by contrast, the atypically heterogeneous character of the founding fragment(s) has provided ample grist for the political culturalist's mill.

Second, students of Canadian political culture, following the lead of Simeon and Elkins, remain particularly sensitive to regional subcultures. Region is the most salient political cleavage in Canada; the results of the 2000 general election provide generous support for this truism. Even though there are geographic, economic, and institutional explanations for the pervasive strength of Canadian regionalism, a complete picture requires an awareness of cultural distinctiveness. Ironically, even with the objective erosion of some of these differences, the subjective perception of such differences remains dangerously (and in one sense, erroneously) high. The parochialism of regional political cultures has thus perversely been able to resist their apparent objective convergence (Stewart, 1994b).

Third, Canadian political culturalists have recently been turning their analytic attention to the impact of institutional change. Canada's chronic constitutional malaise has generated a staggering number of proposals for institutional reform. Most of these, admittedly, have been stillborn, but the passage of the Constitution Act, 1982 resulted in one dramatic structural change: the entrenchment of the Canadian Charter of Rights and Freedoms. Since 1982, it has been apparent that the Charter has generated 'a political culture increasingly sympathetic to constitutional participation by citizens' (Cairns, 1988). The terms of political discourse between political élites and ordinary Canadians have thus been irrevocably altered by the Charter.

Ultimately, political scientists must continue to employ the political culture approach, notwithstanding its conceptual, methodological, and theoretical frustrations. What accounts for the historical pattern of party support in Canada? Why have campaign strategists emphasized some themes, but not others? Why have federal and provincial governments enacted some laws, but not others? These and many other important questions simply cannot be answered satisfactorily without recourse to the concept of political culture. Only the most vulgar of materialists believes that culture is completely epiphenomenal, that orientations do not in some measure play an autonomous and determinant role in political affairs. Ideas, it is worth emphasizing, matter in politics. Why else would totalitarian regimes expend so many resources in attempting to recast the political orientations of their subjects? The frequency with which these attempts fall short, therefore, should serve not only as a comfort to all liberal democrats, but also as a spur to members of the academy. Students of political culture must think more deeply about the paradoxes that confound their analyses; the importance of the subject demands such attention.

Notes

1. Note, however, Stephen Welch's contention that 'in a social setting disrupted, for instance, by urbanization, social meanings do not simply press forward under their own steam, as they might mistakenly have been taken to do in the earlier stable setting.' On the contrary, phenomenologists emphasize the contingent character of 'inherited' political orientations; the 'activity of construction of meaning is continuous' (Welch, 1993: 111–12).
2. Some scholars seem less concerned about the interpretive ambiguity inherent in political culture studies. Lipset's *Continental Divide* (1990) provides a particularly confident example of this tendency.

References

Adamson, Agar. 1991. 'The Atlantic Provinces: An Enigma?', in Robert M. Krause and R.H. Wagenberg, eds, *Introductory Readings in Canadian Government and Politics*. Toronto: Copp Clark Pitman, 70–85.

———— and Ian Stewart. 1991. 'Party Politics in Atlantic Canada: Still the Mysterious East?', in Hugh G. Thorburn, ed., *Party Politics in Canada*, 6th edn. Scarborough: Ont.: Prentice-Hall, 507–21.

Almond, Gabriel A. 1990. *A Discipline Dividend: Schools and Sects in Political Science*. Newbury Park, Calif.: Sage.

———— and Sidney Verba. 1965. *The Civic Culture*. Boston: Little, Brown.

Beck, J. Murray. 1972. 'The Party System in Nova Scotia: Traditional Conservatism', in Martin Robin, ed., *Canadian Provincial Politics: The Party Systems of the Ten Provinces*. Scarborough, Ont.: Prentice-Hall, 168–97.

————. 1981. 'An Atlantic Region Political Culture: A Chimera', in David Jay Bercuson and Phillip A. Buckner, eds, *Eastern and Western Perspectives*. Toronto: University of Toronto Press, 147–68.

Bellamy, David. 1976. 'The Atlantic Provinces', in Bellamy, Jon H. Pammet, and Donald C. Rowat, eds, *The Provincial Political Systems: Comparative Essays*. Agincourt, Ont.: Methuen, 3–18.

Brint, Michael. 1991. *A Genealogy of Political Culture*. Boulder, Colo.: Westview Press.

Brown, Archie. 1984. 'Introduction', in Archie Brown, ed., *Political Culture and Communist Studies*. London: Macmillan, 1–12.

Cairns, Alan C. 1988. 'Citizens (Outsiders) and Governments (Insiders) in Constitution-Making: The Case of Meech Lake', *Canadian Public Policy* 14 (Supplement): 121–45.

Dittmer, Lowell. 1977. 'Political Culture and Political Symbolism: Toward a Theoretical Synthesis', *World Politics* 29: 553–83.

Dogan, Mattei, and Dominique Pelassy. 1990. *How to Compare Nations*, 2nd edn. Chatham, NJ: Chatham House.

Dyck, Rand. 1991. *Provincial Politics in Canada*, 2nd edn. Scarborough, Ont.: Prentice-Hall.

Eckstein, Harry. 1988. 'A Culturalist Theory of Political Change', *American Political Science Review* 82: 789–804.

Elkins, David. 1987. ' Electoral Reform and Political Culture in Australia and Canada', unpublished paper.

Feldman, Stanley, and John Zaller. 1992. 'The Political Culture of Ambivalence: Ideological Responses to the Welfare State', *American Journal of Political Science* 36: 268–307.

Fitzpatrick, P.J. 1972. 'New Brunswick: The Politics of Pragmatism', in Martin Robin, ed., *Canadian Provincial Politics: The Party Systems of the Ten Provinces*. Scarborough, Ont.: Prentice-Hall, 116–33.

Forbes, H.D. 1987. 'Hartz-Horowitz at Twenty: Nationalism, Toryism and Socialism in Canada and the United States', *Canadian Journal of Political Science* 21: 287–315.

Gibbins, John R. 1989. 'Introduction', in Gibbins, ed., *Contemporary Political Culture: Politics in a Postmodern Age*. London: Sage, 1–30.

Girvin, Brian. 1989. 'Change and Continuity in Liberal Democratic Political Culture', in John R. Gibbins, ed., *Contemporary Political Culture: Politics in a Postmodern Age*. London: Sage, 31–51.

———. 1993. 'Social Changes and Political Culture in the Republic of Ireland', *Parliamentary Affairs* 46: 380–98.

Granato, Jim, Ronald Inglehart, and David Leblang. 1996. 'The Effect of Cultural Values on Economic Development: Theory Hypotheses and Some Empirical Tests', *American Journal of Political Science* 40: 607–31.

Hahn, Jeffrey W. 1991. 'Continuity and Change in Russian Political Culture', *British Journal of Political Science* 21: 393–421.

Hartz, Louis, ed. 1964. *The Founding of New Societies*. New York: Harcourt, Brace and World.

Horowitz, Gad. 1968. *Canadian Labour in Politics*. Toronto: University of Toronto Press.

Howe, R. Brian. 1988. 'Political Culture and the Human Rights Commission: Roots of Conflict in the Development of Human Rights Policy in Ontario', paper presented to the annual meeting of the Canadian Political Science Association, Windsor.

Inglehart, Ronald. 1988. 'The Renaissance of Political Culture', *American Political Science Review* 82: 1203–30.

Jackman, Robert W., and Ross A. Miller. 1996a. 'A Renaissance of Political Culture?', *American Journal of Political Science* 40: 632–59.

——— and ———. 1996b. 'The Poverty of Political Culture', *American Journal of Political Science* 40: 697–716.

Jacobs, Lawrence R. 1992. 'Institutions and Culture: Health Policy and Public Opinion in the U.S. and Britain', *World Politics* 44: 179–209.

Jancar, Barbara. 1984. 'Political Culture and Political Change', *Studies in Comparative Communism* 17: 69–82.

Kavanagh, Dennis. 1983. *Political Science and Political Behaviour*. London: George Allen & Unwin.

Laitin, David. 1988. 'Political Culture and Political Preferences', *American Political Science Review* 82: 589–96.

———. 1995. 'The Civic Culture at 30', *American Political Science Review* 89: 168–73.

Lijphart, Arend. 1980. 'The Structure of Inference', in Gabriel Almond and Sidney Verba, eds, *The Civic Culture Revisited*. Boston: Little, Brown, 37–56.

Lipset, Seymour Martin. 1970. 'Revolution and Counterrevolution: The United States and Canada', in Orest M. Kruhlak, Richard Schultz, and Sidney I. Pobihushchy, eds, *The Canadian Political Process: A Reader*. Toronto: Holt, Rinehart and Winston, 13–38.

———. 1976. 'Radicalism in North America: A Comparative View of the Party Systems in Canada and the United States', *Transactions of the Royal Society of Canada*, Fourth Series 14: 19–55.

———. 1986. 'Historical Traditions and National Characteristics: A Comparative Analysis of Canada and the United States', *Canadian Journal of Sociology* 11: 113–55.

———. 1990. *Continental Divide*. New York: Routledge.

Liska, Allen E. 1974. 'Emergent Issues in the Attitude-Behavior Consistency Controversy', *American Sociological Review* 39: 261–72.

Listhaug, Ola. 1990. 'Macrovalues: The Nordic Countries Compared', *Acta Sociologica* 33: 219–34.

McAuley, Mary. 1984. 'Political Culture and Communist Politics: One Step Forward, Two Steps Back', in Archie Brown, ed., *Political Culture and Communist Studies*. London: Macmillan, 13–39.

MacDermid, R.H. 1989. 'Reviewing Political Efficacy', paper presented to the annual meeting of the Canadian Political Science Association, Quebec City.

McDonough, Peter. 1993. 'Book Review of Richard W. Wilson, *Compliance Ideologies: Rethinking Political Culture*', *Journal of Politics* 55: 847–49.

MacKinnon, Frank. 1972. 'Prince Edward Island: Big Engine, Little Body', in Martin Robin, ed., *Canadian Provincial Politics: The Party Systems of the Ten Provinces*. Scarborough, Ont.: Prentice-Hall, 240–61.

Martin, Curtis H., and Bruce Stronach. 1992. *Politics East and West: A Comparison of Japanese and British Political Culture*. Armonk, NY: M.E. Sharpe.

Mayer, Alfred G. 1972. 'Communist Revolutions and Cultural Change', *Studies in Comparative Communism* 5: 345–70.

Moisés, José Alvaro. 1993. 'Elections, Political Parties, and Political Culture in Brazil', *Journal of Latin American Studies* 28: 575–611.

Moody, Peter R., Jr. 1994. 'Trends in the Study of Chinese Political Culture', *China Quarterly* 139: 731–40.

Nesbitt-Larking, Paul. 1988. 'Toward a New Methodology for the Study of Canadian Political Culture', paper presented to the annual meeting of the Canadian Sociology and Anthropology Association, Windsor.

Nevitte, Neil. 1996. *The Decline of Deference*. Peterborough, Ont.: Broadview Press.

Patrick, Glenda M. 1984. 'Political Culture', in Giovanni Sartori, ed., *Social Science Concepts: A Systematic Analysis*. Beverly Hills, Calif: Sage, 265–314.

Putnam, Robert D. 1993. *Making Democracy Work: Civic Traditions in Modern Italy*. Princeton, NJ: Princeton University Press.

Pye, Lucian W. 1973. 'Culture and Political Science: Problems in the Evaluation of the Concept of Political Culture', in Louis Schneider and Charles M. Bonjean, eds, *The Idea of Culture in the Social Sciences*. London: Cambridge University Press, 65–76.

———. 1993. 'An Introductory Profile: Deng Xiaoping and China's Political Culture', *China Quarterly* 125: 412–43.

Robb, Andrew. 1982. 'Third Party Experience on the Island', in Verner Smitheram, David Milne, and Satadal Dagapusta, eds, *The Garden Transformed, 1945–1980*. Charlottetown, PEI: Ragweed Press.

Roberts, Geoffrey K. 1984. ' "Normal" or "Critical"?: Progress Reports on the Condition of West Germany's Political Culture', *European Journal of Political Research* 12: 423–31.

Simeon, Richard E.B., and David J. Elkins. 1974. 'Regional Political Cultures in Canada', *Canadian Journal of Political Science* 7: 397–437.

——— and ———. 1979. 'A Cause in Search of Its Effect, or What Does Political Culture Explain?', *Comparative Politics* 11: 127–45.

Sniderman, Paul, Joseph Fletcher, Peter Russell, and Philip Tetlock. 1996. *The Clash of Rights*. New Haven: Yale University Press.

Stewart, David K. 1992. ' "Friends and Neighbours": Patterns of Delegate Support at Maritime Liberal and Conservative Conventions', in R. Kenneth Carty, Lynda Erickson, and Donald E. Blake, eds, *Leaders and Parties in Canadian Politics: Experiences of the Provinces*. Toronto: Harcourt Brace Jovanovich, 56–79.

Stewart, Ian. 1994a. 'All the King's Horses: The Study of Canadian Political Culture', in Alain-G. Gagnon and James P. Bickerton, eds, *Canadian Politics: An Introduction to the Discipline*. Peterborough, Ont.: Broadview Press, 75–92.

————. 1994b. *Roasting Chestnuts: The Mythology of Maritime Political Culture*. Vancouver: University of British Columbia Press.

Street, John. 1994. 'Review Article: Political Culture—from Civic Culture to Mass Culture', *British Journal of Political Science* 24: 95–113.

Swank, Duane. 1996. 'Culture, Institutions, and Economic Growth: Theory, Recent Evidence, and the Role of Communication Politics', *American Journal of Political Science* 40: 660–79.

Thorburn, H.G. 1961. *Politics in New Brunswick*. Toronto: University of Toronto Press.

Truman, Tom. 1971. 'A Critique of Seymour M. Lipset's Article, Value Differences, Absolute or Relative: The English-speaking Democracies', *Canadian Journal of Political Science* 4: 497–525.

Wakeman, Frederic, Jr. 1993. 'The Civil Society and Public Sphere Debate: Western Reflections on Chinese Political·Culture', *Modern China* 19: 108–38.

Welch, Stephen. 1993. *The Concept of Political Culture*. London: Macmillan.

White, Stephen. 1979. *Political Culture and Soviet Politics*. London: Macmillan.

Wilson, Richard V. 1992. *Compliance Ideologies: Rethinking Political Culture*. Cambridge: Cambridge University Press.

Wiseman, Nelson. 1996. 'Provincial Political Cultures', in Christopher Dunn, ed., *Provinces: Canadian Provincial Politics*. Peterborough, Ont.: Broadview Press, 21–62.

Yishai, Yael. 1993. 'Public Ideas and Public Policy: Abortion Politics in Four Democracies', *Comparative Politics* 25: 207–28.

Chapter 3

Sugar and Spice? Political Culture and the Political Behaviour of Canadian Women

BRENDA O'NEILL

Canadian women and men live in different but overlapping worlds. An individual's gender is likely to determine the hours spent on household duties and tasks, the level of guilt experienced by a decision to pursue a career during the formative years of one's children's lives, and whether one's career is interrupted by a period spent caring for young children. The process of political socialization for women and men also differs, and the difference has direct implications for adult political behaviour. Gender influences the groups one is likely to join, the positions one is likely to hold in those groups, and the resources one will bring to the political arena. Evidence of these realities abounds. Political strategists, for example, are cognizant of the 'gender gap' in attitudes and voting and its implications for electoral success. The degree to which political scientists have accepted the importance of such factors in shaping women's and men's political experiences and behaviour, however, has been more guarded.

Such differences are of direct and immediate importance to the manner in which Canadians engage in politics since they determine the opportunities and resources that allow them to participate. Equally important is how values might differently shape political opinions and behaviour. I argue that there is significant mileage to be gained by understanding differences in Canadian women's and men's values as differences in political culture. Political culture consists of 'assumptions about the political world' (Elkins and Simeon, 1979: 127). As a determinant of political opinions and behaviour, political culture restricts the range of alternatives entertained by those within its collectivity. If the assumptions that women and men make about the political world and the range of alternatives they entertain vary, then their political opinions and behaviour are likely to reflect these varying perspectives.

The idea that women and men are socialized into unique private roles is not new. The necessary step is an acceptance that this *private socialization* plays a role in *public political behaviour*. This chapter suggests that gender differences in opinion, which cannot be fully explained by social circumstances or demographic factors, might be better understood by suggesting that Canadian women and men approach politics from within political cultures that differ in degree, rather than kind. The range of alternatives they consider and their assumptions about the political world vary; that is, their political values are not always identical. An appreciation of this cultural difference is essential for a complete understanding of gender differences in political opinion and behaviour.

Previous research has assumed that differences in political values indicate differences in political culture (Elkins and Simeon, 1979, 1980). Thus the investigative framework adopted here falls very much in line with previous evaluations of political culture in Canada. Applying it to gender differences in opinions and belief systems has not, however, preoccupied Canadian political scientists[1] (for some exceptions, see Vickers, 1988; Bashevkin, 1993). But such a strategy provides us with a useful theoretical tool since 'the analysis of subcultures remains important in understanding tensions and cleavages within particular societies' (McLean, 1996: 379–80).

Within the discipline of political science, Thelma McCormack was among the first to suggest that the notion of a Canadian women's political culture should be explored for its explanatory value: 'The alternative thesis is that women live in a different political culture from men, a culture based on differences in political socialization . . . , differences in political opportunity structures, and the way in which the media of communication define each of them' (1975: 25). More recently, Sylvia Bashevkin (1993) suggests that women's and men's differences in opinion on political interest, efficacy, party support, and selected political issues could be explained by the existence of a women's culture rather than by the lack of women's experience in politics. Despite such arguments, the concept has not taken root.[2]

The goal of this chapter is not to provide an accounting of gender differences in political behaviour in Canada. Instead, it seeks to provide a possible explanation for their existence. Although insufficient attention has been given to research on the political behaviour of women in Canada, that which does exist supports the conclusion that even as women's political involvement levels increasingly approach those of men, they are not mirroring their political behaviour in every respect. Evidence exists of gender gaps in support for the two women-led federal parties at the time of the 1993 election (O'Neill, 1998); in differentiated support for the major political parties at the federal level (Brodie, 1991; Wearing and Wearing, 1991); in the legislative behaviour of members of Parliament and legislative assemblies (Arscott and Trimble, 1997); in the opinions of party members at conventions (Brodie, 1988) and among the public (Everitt, 1998a, 1998b; O'Neill, 1995, 1996, 2001); and in levels of political efficacy and interest (Brodie, 1991). The latter, in particular, challenges the notion that women are politically parochial.

Gender differences in education and income account in part for some of the distinction in political behaviour patterns. Yet, while socio-demographic differences account for some of these gaps, an often significant portion of the variation between Canadian women's and men's attitudes and behaviour remains to be explained. Hence, there is ample reason for investigating the concept of a women's political culture as a possible explanation for such differences.

An emphasis on gendered subcultures is not meant to imply that the two cultures are not similar in many respects. The dominant political world equates almost completely to the male world. Despite recent gains made by women, men continue to dominate in traditional political institutions and, consequently, male values and beliefs permeate them[3] (Arscott and Trimble, 1997). Yet the political world is one in which women live and that shapes many elements of their lives. Women and men often choose to partner or marry and share their lives with each other, they live in the same cities, towns, and provinces, attend the same churches and universities, and are represented by the same members of Parliament. Moreover, focusing the investigation on Canada necessarily restricts the degree to which the political world views of men and women will and can differ. Canadian women and men share a number of political rights, freedoms, and benefits that significantly limit the extent to which their political values and, by extension, their political cultures differ. But persistent differences exist despite such similarities, which makes their investigation all the more necessary, and all the more interesting.

An emphasis on a women's political culture as distinct from men's is not meant to discount the existence of differences in political world views and life experiences *among women*.[4] In fact, differences in women's political beliefs and values are often larger than those found among men's, evidence that supports the argument that political cultures are differentiated by gender. Thus, the argument for the existence of a women's culture, derived by definition through a comparison of women and men, does not equate to an argument that women are somehow homogeneous in their attitudes and experiences. But neither should we discount the commonalities women share and how these differ from those of men. And neither should the comparison with men be interpreted as a normative evaluation of women's culture as 'parochial' or underdeveloped. 'Different' need not translate into a normative comparison of the 'better' or 'worse' type.

The chapter sets three goals in arguing for the use of culture as an explanation for differences in the political behaviour patterns of women and men. First, it presents evidence in support of the argument that a women's subculture—i.e., their political values—differs from the dominant male culture. The chapter then proceeds to examine briefly those factors that might account for this differentiated culture. Finally, the discussion turns to an examination of the dynamic nature of this culture, given the changes currently taking place among women in Canada.

A Women's Political Culture in Canada

According to Inglehart (1990:18), 'culture is a system of attitudes, values and knowledge that is widely shared within a society and transmitted from generation to generation.' As a concept within political science, political culture is often employed to explain patterns in policies, behaviour, and governance across states. As such, political culture is deemed worthy of study because it is assumed to have a direct impact on the means and ends of politics (Stewart, 1994).

The concepts employed in the study of political culture are many. *Values* constitute preferences and priorities held for their own sake, that provide a means for judging human activity. They are yardsticks by which activity and choices are measured. *Opinions*, on the other hand, are expressions of attitudes and beliefs that reflect the set of values held by individuals. Values are enduring and steeped in life experiences; attitudes and opinions are more fleeting and likely to shift with political events, but will nevertheless reflect the set of deeply held values (see Figure 3.1). A *political subculture* is a particular group within a culture whose values and opinions vary to some degree from those of the dominant culture. Employing the concept of a women's culture assumes that their political values differ somewhat from men's and that these differences will translate into divergent patterns of opinions and behaviour. As such, differing values can help explain differing opinions and behaviour. In all cases, however, these differences will not be complete; there will be a certain degree of overlap in Canadian women's and men's values, opinions and behaviour. The difficulty, made clear by Stewart in the previous chapter, is in amassing evidence of this difference in values, or world views, that is not inferred from that which we hope to explain.

The main goal, then, is to assess whether gender merits serious consideration as a culture-defining factor in Canadian politics. The focus in this chapter is on explicitly identifying a women's political culture that at some level deviates from the male culture. The male political culture is taken at face value to correspond to the values of the 'dominant' political culture. The female political culture, on the other hand, is less visible; the relative absence of women from formal politics and the dominance of male norms in the political arena itself make it particularly difficult for this women's culture to materialize.

Figure 3.1: Political Values as Determinants of Political Opinions and Behaviour

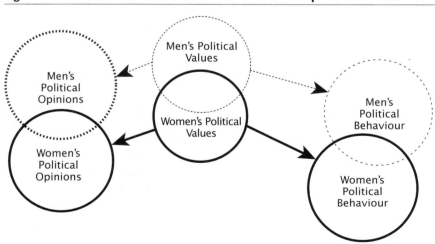

If political culture consists of the assumptions and orientations that individuals hold about politics, what evidence can be assembled to support women's overlapping yet differentiated subculture? Two avenues provide possible evidence of the existence of gendered political cultures: first, feminist research on differences in the *fundamental values* held by women and men; and second, research examining how these differences in fundamental values translate into gender gaps in *political values and attitudes*. Each shall be examined in turn.

While not directly 'political' in focus and largely American, Carol Gilligan's work presents an important starting point for an investigation of women's political culture in Canada. Despite its empirical imperfections,[5] her work, *In a Different Voice*, remains an influential and intuitively appealing account of the basic difference in the fundamental values of women and men. Psychological in focus, Gilligan's data were collected from interviews with three separate groups: the first, a group of 29 women each in her first-trimester of pregnancy and considering abortion as an option; the second, a group of 25 college students enrolled in a course on moral and political choice; and the third, a group of 144 males and females, aged 6 through 60. The goal in the interviews was to probe individuals 'on conceptions of self and morality, experiences of moral conflict and choice, and judgements of hypothetical moral dilemmas' (Gilligan, 1982: 3).

Gilligan concludes that when confronted with moral dilemmas, women and men interpret them differently, hence the title of her book. In brief, she posits that moral reasoning in women is based on the notion of responsibility—'the ethic of care'—rather than on the premise of rights. She argues that a central underlying value among women emphasizes connection and relationships—political 'collectivism' rather than 'individualism'—and placing the care of others before oneself. In contrast, male moral reasoning is said to be imbued with values directly connected to individualism. Individual rights, rather than responsibility for others, take precedence. Moral questions are interpreted as competitions between the rights of individuals, as disjointed rather than connected elements. While highlighting the degree of overlap between women and men in their moral reasoning, Gilligan nevertheless concludes that an ethic of care is more prevalent among women than men.

From an explicitly political perspective, Sandra Burt provides direct evidence that women and men conceive of politics and representative democracy in unique ways. In a small sample of intensive interviews with Canadian women and men, she questioned them on the meaning of politics, their reasons for participating in politics, and their conceptions of the 'ideal' citizen. Despite commonality in the responses to the first two sets of questions, on the final set a clear gender gap emerged in that women 'explicitly called for a more humanitarian approach from political leaders, more caring for others and more responsiveness to citizens' requests than exists' (Burt, 1986: 77). This suggests that at the most basic level differences exist in the values that women and men bring to bear on beliefs regarding politics and citizenship. And here as well, the evidence suggests greater concern for individual responsibilities and an ethic of care among Canadian women.

In a slightly different vein, Jill Vickers suggests a Canadian women's distinctive political culture based on first-hand accounts and views of their involvement in Canadian political life. Drawing on in-depth interviews with women involved in both non-traditional and traditional political activities, Vickers concludes that women's participation in political life takes place within dual spheres and with double vision. Formal politics and traditional political institutions of the state are dominated by men, and as such embody the values of conflict, individualism, and the acquisition of power. Men dominate that arena in part because they seek to 'get ahead'. Many more women, however, choose to engage in local informal politics, as many stated, 'because they wished to get things done' (Vickers, 1988: 12). Many women choose this less formal political arena because it is community-oriented and located close to home, and because these more informal structures are likely to embody values that women have a greater tendency to espouse: collectivism versus individualism, for instance. Politics, then, is suggested as an activity that women engage in specifically for the ends the process provides; men, on the other hand, are argued to become involved in politics as much for the process of power as for its outcomes.

Examples of women's uneasiness and 'unlikeness' in the traditional 'male' political arena are not difficult to collect. For instance, in her reflections on the House of Commons, Sheila Copps, Minister for Canadian Heritage in the present Liberal government, stated that 'from the moment you step inside, you sense that this place is foreign to women, alien to our spirit of cooperation, steeped in confrontation and simply not a place for traditional female virtues' (Copps, 1986: 93). Kim Campbell, former Conservative Prime Minister, outlined the difficulty she encountered in attempting to introduce 'inclusive justice' as a process of legal reform during her position as Justice Minister in the Mulroney government.[6] The key stumbling block for justice officials was the first principle of inclusive justice, which denies the universality and equality of justice, particularly as it applies to women (Campbell, 1996: 161). And Audrey McLaughlin (1997: 26), former leader of the federal New Democrats, noted: 'When a women enters the House of Commons, she enters what in significant ways is an old-fashioned men's club. There are all sorts of reminders—some subtle, some not so subtle—that this is not a woman's place.' The message that the political world is not 'a woman's place' may stem from an unconscious desire, on the part of many Canadians, to preserve the traditions of the political domain that until recently was populated only by men. It may also stem from women's political culture being sufficiently different from men's as to lead to some level of uneasiness in women who enter its preserve, even among those who have succeeded by traditional political standards.

Research on gender gaps in opinion provides a second branch of reinforcing evidence that women and men are political creatures of a different stripe. Unlike the previous research, however, this research more often *assumes* the existence of a women's culture than *proves* it. That is, differences in values are often suggested as possible explanatory factors for measured differences in voting and opinions, rather than measured in their own right. This weakness rests in part on the difficulty involved in attempting to measure values as opposed to voting behaviour and opinions and attitudes. Nevertheless, the evidence merits consideration because of the degree to which the recorded differences can be argued to fall in line with the differences in values outlined above.

Employing a more quantitative empirical method, Elisabeth Gidengil's (1995) analysis of survey data from the 1988 Canadian federal election reaches conclusions remarkably similar to those of Burt and Vickers. Her examination of the gender gap in opinion on the Free Trade Agreement with the United States, an issue central to debate during that election, revealed that men were far more supportive of the agreement than women. Gidengil concludes that an 'economic man-social woman' model goes some distance towards explaining this gender gap in opinion over free trade. This model falls in line with the distinctions between male and female values originally outlined by Gilligan. In Gidengil's model, the male emphasis on individual rights corresponds with a belief in the value of competition that has direct implications for economic policy: government involvement in the economy should be limited so as to allow for unfettered competition in the marketplace. This underlying value helps to explain men's greater support for free trade. A female emphasis on relationships and responsibilities means that egalitarianism is valued more highly than competition, and this translates into greater support for the welfare state. As such, women gave less support to free trade, particularly in light of the potential many argued the agreement held for undermining Canadian social welfare programs. And importantly, this difference in values accounted for a larger share of the gender gap in opinion on free trade than did differences in material advantage; that is, although women were less likely to support free trade because lower income levels increase their reliance on social programs, this difference in reliance explained less of the gap in opinion than did the differences in values. Importantly, however, the author argues that for such differences in opinion to occur, not only must a policy issue become salient; gender-related values and concerns also must be triggered, as they were in the 1988 debate on free trade. A women's culture matters, Gidengil suggests, but only under particular circumstances.

My own research into the gender gap has uncovered differences between women and men on two basic values: feminism and religious beliefs (O'Neill, 1996, 2001). An examination of survey data collected at the time of the 1988 Canadian federal election reveals that women in general are more committed to the traditional organized faiths, and this has clear implications for political behaviour and opinions in Canada.[7] Such differences continue to exist (O'Neill, 2001) and have been reported elsewhere (for the US, see Conover 1988; Poole and Zeigler, 1985). The central role of organized religion in female culture includes the use of the church (mosque, temple, synagogue) as an arena for community participation and an avenue for community 'good works', including visiting the sick and caring for the poor, and, given the role of the family in teaching faith to children, women's maternal role ensures in part their commitment to religion and religious faith (Bernard, 1981: 496–7). Religion plays a key role in many women's daily lives, a greater direct role in the determination of their values, and, hence, an indirect role in shaping their political opinions and behaviour.

While women as a group reveal themselves to be more religious than men, at the same time they reveal themselves to be more feminist, an equally relevant determinant of opinions. The gender gap in support of feminism has been relatively small and inconsistent; however, research suggests that the intensity of women's support for feminism is stronger (Everitt, 1998a) and that feminism plays a more central role in women's political belief systems (O'Neill, 1996). Examining the more distinct feminist consciousness, measured as the psychological identification with the group rather than simply agreement with feminist policies, suggests that gender differences are larger than previous research suggests (O'Neill, 2001). The suggestion that feminism differs between men and women has been made by a number of researchers and centres on the distinct roots of women's and men's feminism (Klein, 1984; Fulenwider, 1980). For some, women's feminism is rooted in their gender consciousness and self-interest while feminist belief among men is part of a more general ideological framework. Others argue that women's feminism is a central or core value, less dependent on self-interest and social status than is the case for men. Instead, it is rooted in women's existence as women. In either case, the research suggests that feminism plays a significant role in shaping opinions and behaviour, and importantly, in different ways for women and men.

Additional Canadian evidence on the gender gap in opinion suggests that women and men, based on their differing political values, have different political priorities and policy preferences. The issues on which gaps appear include nuclear weapons and defence, government spending, welfare policies, and the welfare system in general. Across a number of issues, women are more 'liberal' in their political outlook. They endorse programs of government spending to aid the poor and disadvantaged (see Everitt, this volume) and are more likely to adopt 'dovish' opinions on war and peace issues. Such differences have appeared among Canadians (Terry, 1984; O'Neill, 1995; Wearing and Wearing, 1991; Everitt, 1998a, and 1998b) and even among delegates to party conventions (Brodie, 1988).

This evidence supports the argument that women exhibit opinions that conform to a broad-gauged humanitarianism, or 'agape ethos' (Bernard, 1981: ch. 21). Their weaker commitment to a conservative ethos on a number of issues suggests a greater concern for the well-being of individuals than is generally true of men: women are less supportive of the capitalist system in general; they endorse a greater degree of government involvement in the economy; and they are less supportive of increasing economic ties with the United States. Such differences in opinions reveal that Gilligan's insight that moral decision-making in women constitutes an ethic of care may have validity with respect to their political opinions more broadly.

Such research reinforces the notion that the values women and men bring to bear on their political activity are not completely similar. Many women view politics as a relationship and a web of connections and responsibilities to others.

Women's involvement in the non-traditional political arena likely reflects this particular set of values, given the reciprocal relationship between values and external environment. The non-traditional political arena often eschews hierarchical organizational forms in favour of more grassroots involvement in decision-making (see Vickers, et al. 1993). Moreover, the goal and *raison d'être* of such organizations is often the provision of immediate help and care for those in need. Involvement in the traditional political arena, on the other hand, likely exposes participants to a decidedly contrasting set of values that focuses on relationships among independent actors connected within a hierarchy of rights and responsibilities. The decision by many women to engage in political activity in an alternative arena, with a different set of guiding principles, supports the notion of the existence of a particular ethic or value among them. Women's distinctive political priorities may help to explain their greater participation in organizations outside of dominant politics.

The Sources of Gendered Subcultures

According to David Bell (1992: 25), 'a culture—a set of ways of thinking about the world—means nothing. . . outside the material circumstances of its birth and development and the social arrangements that keep it alive'. It is not immediately clear how far back in time one must go to explain the 'birth' of a Canadian women's culture. Its roots may not necessarily exist on Canadian soil but rather in societies from which many Canadians emigrated. Common patterns of difference in public opinion and political participation among women and men in Western societies suggest perhaps some distant common beginning. The mileage gained, however, in determining a particular beginning to the Canadian women's political culture is limited; of greater weight are the factors that perpetuate it. A women's political culture, then, continues as a result of the social circumstances that reinforce patterns of difference between the sexes. Indeed, the very use of the term 'gender' is meant to emphasize 'the *socio-cultural* manifestations of being a man or woman' (Sapiro, 1983: 36, emphasis added). If gender shapes the values that Canadian women and men bring to bear on their political behaviour, then socialization into those particular gender roles is key to understanding the influence of gender. This socialization begins very early in life (for example, girls play and care for dolls while boys play with trucks) but continues into adulthood.

In the interest of parsimony, two factors will be highlighted for their role in perpetuating a Canadian women's political culture among adults: the institution of the family and motherhood. These two factors are neither independent of one another nor incidental. For many Canadian women, family and motherhood constitute primary forces in their adult lives. The traditional roles that society defines for women in families and as mothers provide significant insight into the existence of a subculture differentiated by its focus on relationships and responsibilities.

Societal pressures to conform to these roles are such that women who do not 'fit' these expectations (i.e., mothers and wives) nevertheless feel their weight.

Single women and those without children, for example, by virtue of their socialization as girls and women and the continuous reinforcement of the traditional stereotypes in the family, the media, and in political and educational institutions, are as likely to adopt the values that characterize the women's political culture. The present-day myths and culture that support a particular vision of woman as mother and care-giver are strong enough for all women to feel their effects. According to psychologist Shari Thurer (1994: xii), 'A sentimentalized image of the perfect mother casts a long, guilt-inducing shadow over real mother's lives.' The shadow is large enough, I would argue, to loom over most women's lives. Societal pressures, despite rhetorical pronouncements of the equality of the sexes in Canada, are such that many women find the decision to return to work, or to remain at home, following the birth of a child tremendously difficult. As Barb Burgess, a stay-at-home mother, declared, 'you're damned if you do [stay home] and you're damned if you don't'(Mitchell, 1999: A9). The difficulties and stresses faced by women, stay-at-home and employed alike, were recently made clear in the public discussions surrounding proposed tax changes in Alberta to benefit stay-at-home parents. Although many men also feel such pressures and stresses, their numbers do not equal women's, in part because society does not place the same expectations on men as fathers as it does on women as mothers. Societal pressures and socialization forces very likely have a tremendous influence in shaping the values that all women bring to their political behaviour.

Being socialized as a woman may translate into greater human compassion because of the continued emphasis placed on woman's maternal, nurturing qualities, the concentration of women in the domestic rather than the public sphere, and the expectation that women will assume much of the responsibility for the family and the home. According to Vickers, 'Rather than acting out of "rational" or "self-interested" relationships, most women are engaged in more **altruistic** relationships with their children, families and communities. Women are expected, and indeed trained, to act in self-sacrificing *not self-interested* ways, especially in their relationships with their children' (1997: 34, emphases in original). Societal expectations and the institutions of our daily lives directly shape the criteria employed to evaluate political positions and choices. For Canadian women, selflessness is expected. Indeed, societal expectations are such that it is often assumed that women will extend familial concerns into the public sphere, hence the predominance of women cabinet ministers in 'soft' ministries such as social welfare and family services.

The institution of the family is without a doubt a central force in many women's lives. It is the arena in which traditional adult gender roles are played out and the institution in which one finds the continued existence of the sexual division of labour. According to Sue Tolleson Rinehart (1992: 68), 'the "traditional" gender role ideology and its variations, to be found almost everywhere one looks, bears as its central dictum the privatization of women, their restriction to the domestic sphere.' The traditional role of the family is to provide 'affection, understanding, emotional support, and solace from a possibly harsh world' (McDaniel,

1988: 103), and in their roles as mothers, wives, daughters, and sisters, women are expected to provide these conditions. Beyond emotional support, women in families are also expected to assume the largest share of the unpaid work necessary for the family's well-being. Despite the fact that a significant number of women now work outside the home,[8] employed women spend approximately two more hours per day than employed men on domestic activities such as cooking, cleaning and laundry, child-care activities, and shopping (Statistics Canada, 1995: 70). The sexual division of labour in the home reinforces the ethic of care.

The traditional family gender role adopted by a number of women is personified by the 'homemaker'. The ascribed role of the homemaker has traditionally been that of the nurturing, gentle woman devoted to home and family. The acceptance of such a role implies an acceptance of the particular place of women within it, and as such is a source of value learning. Differences in opinion may result if women, as homemakers, adopt or exhibit the values specific to that role (e.g., nurturing and compassion for others). Moreover, the homemaking role most closely approximates cultural expectations of women, and, homemakers are expected to perform in the political system in stereotyped ways (Sapiro, 1983). The expectation is that homemakers will display socially defined 'feminine' characteristics: nurturance, concern for others, tolerance, co-operation rather than competition, and pacifism (Tolleson Rinehart, 1992: 11). The stereotype also extends to women as defenders of morality, stemming again from their responsibility as guardians of children.

According to the 1997 Canadian Election Study (CES), 13 per cent of all women respondents reported their employment status as 'homemaker', a significant number although down from the 21 per cent reported in the 1988 CES. Homemakers spend on average anywhere from three to nine hours a day on unpaid work, varying with the number of children in the home and the presence or absence of a spouse (Statistics Canada, 1995: 83). Many women, however, cannot choose the 'homemaker' role—the ability to devote full time care to home and family is a decision often only made possible by the existence of an alternative stable and sufficient source of income. Thus, that fewer women appear to be 'choosing' the homemaker role may have less to do with choice than with economic necessity. Many women who work outside the home may be 'homemakers' in spirit.

In addition to gender role socialization in the family, motherhood may account for the particular set of values found in women (see Ruddick, 1988). Pregnancy and childbirth are tremendously emotional and moving experiences, and may account in part for women's particular set of values. Besides the physical experience of childbirth, women are also more likely to take on the role of full-time caregiver to children. And it is also the case that the majority of single-parent families are headed by women—80 per cent in 1991. This results in part from custody more often being awarded to women by the courts; for example, in 1991 women were awarded custody in 74 per cent of all custody decisions settled in court that year (Statistics Canada, 1995: 18). The ethic of care, born perhaps of the experience of childbirth, is also likely to be reinforced by child-care and custody responsibilities.

A Culture in Transition

If a women's political culture exists, it is in transition. According to Inglehart (1990: 19), 'central parts of culture may be transformed, but they are much more apt to change through intergenerational population replacement than by the conversion of already socialized adults.' Younger generations of Canadian women reveal values at odds with previous generations of women, suggesting that differing socialization processes might result in changes in this women's culture as population replacement occurs.

The impact of feminism on the attitudes of younger cohorts of women, quite apart from whether these women consider themselves to be feminist, must be accounted for in discussions of cultural transition. In endorsing greater freedom for women and in providing women with the confidence to speak in 'a different voice', the feminist movement has influenced the values of many women. The culture reflected in women's values reveals a distinct pattern in belief: young women are generally more liberal than older women (Everitt, 1998a).

Indications of a cultural shift among women are also found in intergenerational differences in women's religious commitment. Younger women are less religious than older women (O'Neill, 1996). Although this difference is also apparent among men, the shift in beliefs among women has coincided with greater shifts in their attitudes and behaviour. The movement away from religion, combined with the increased salience of gender due partly to feminism's influence, may very well result in the discovery of larger generational gaps among women's opinions and behaviour in the future.

The lives of younger generations of women are not likely to mirror those of their mothers, and will certainly differ from those of their grandmothers. According to the Statistics Canada report, *Women in Canada* (1995), many more women are entering post-secondary institutions than ever before, and the rates at which they are earning their degrees is steadily increasing (Statistics Canada, 1995: 37). In fact, in the 1992–3 academic year, women made up 52 per cent of all university students (ibid., 54). Women are increasingly entering the paid workforce—in 1994, 52 per cent of all women aged 15 and over were employed outside the home, up from 42 per cent in 1976 (ibid., 64). Apart from work and educational changes among women, women's personal lives are also changing. Canadian women are waiting longer to marry; figures from 1992 reveal that average age at first marriage for women was 26.5 years, up from 22.1 in 1971 (ibid., 17). Canadian women are also giving birth less often: figures from 1991 reveal 56 births per 1,000 women between the ages of 15 and 49, significantly down from the 116 recorded in 1959 (ibid., 19). Fewer births means fewer children per family: in 1971 the average number of children per family stood at 1.8 but by 1991 this figure had dropped to 1.2 (ibid., 19).

The changes in younger women's lives seem likely to influence their values, and as these women come of age women's political culture will evolve. One might anticipate that the movement of women into the workforce and out of the home and the homemaker role would result in a shift in their values away from the ethic of care. However, such a conclusion may be somewhat premature. Evidence suggests that despite the movement of women into the workforce, women continue to be found in jobs that mirror the sexual division of labour, often referred to as the 'pink-collar ghetto'. If the movement of women out of the home and into the workforce serves to reinforce traditional gender role socialization, then it is unlikely that significant changes in the Canadian women's political culture will occur.

Conclusion

An adequate understanding of the political behaviour of Canadian women requires a complete understanding of the public and private forces in their lives and the degree to which such forces shape their political values. The study of political behaviour has traditionally ignored the private dimension of political behaviour, in part due to the difficulty of documenting private lives, but more often due to the belief that it was of little consequence for political action. As has been shown here, however, the private does influence the public.

The difference between women's and men's values indicates the existence of a women's political culture. Such a culture is distinctive in its political priorities and the degree to which an ethic of care and concern for responsibility permeate it. This culture exists by virtue of gender alone, shaped by societal forces and definitions of women's and men's roles that colour perceptions of what 'matters' and what is 'right'. It continues to exist perhaps as a result of women's lesser participation in the dominant political arena and because of the roles women continue to adopt in the family and as mothers. It seems certain that women's involvement in non-traditional political arenas allows it to flourish.

The concept of culture allows a fuller understanding of how political values and assumptions shape women's political behaviour. That women's political culture differs from men's helps to account for the many gender gaps discovered in political behaviour and attitudes. And importantly, changes in this culture and the concomitant effects on political behaviour provide an interesting and ongoing test of the degree to which culture matters.

Notes

1. It is important to point out that much more work has been completed on the political behaviour of women in the United States than in Canada, in part because of differences in the number of political scientists in each country. While arguments have been made for a women's political culture in the US (see, e.g., Carroll, 1992) and elsewhere, this chapter seeks to build a similar argument from exclusively Canadian evidence.

2. Several objections have been raised to the concept of a women's political culture, including the fear that the argument could be used to keep women out of the traditional political arena, and that it could be employed to further an essentialist argument, i.e., that women's values and behaviour are rooted in their biological makeup. The debate is ongoing and mirrors the debate taking place among feminists.

3. The dominant political arena and traditional politics have monopolized the study of politics, including but not limited to constitutions, legislatures, executives, political parties and interest groups. Informal politics, where women are more likely to dominate, takes places in the local community and outside of the formal organizations of the state. Feminist political science argues in part that the latter should be included in the core of the discipline's subject matter since it is where much of women's politics occurs (see Vickers, 1997).

4. The emphasis is also not meant to imply that there is little deviation among the world views of Canadian men, although this critique of gender comparison research is much less argued.

5. Gilligan's work has been critiqued on methodological and other grounds. See Kerber et al., 1986.

6. Inclusive justice is a process of four steps: 1) accept that the law does not treat everyone equally; 2) invite excluded individuals to discuss their reality; 3) invite those individuals to help in arriving at a solution to the problem; and 4) implement that solution.

7. For a recent look at the place of religious beliefs in Canadian political behaviour, see Mendelsohn and Nadeau (1997).

8. According to Statistics Canada (1995), 51.9 per cent of women were employed outside of the home in 1994.

References

Arscott, Jane, and Linda Trimble, eds. 1997. *In the Presence of Women: Representation in the Canadian Governments*. Toronto: Harcourt Brace.

Bashevkin, Sylvia. 1993. *Toeing the Lines: Women and Party Politics in English Canada*, 2nd edn. Toronto: Oxford University Press.

Bell, David V.J. 1992. *The Roots of Disunity: A Study of Canadian Political Culture*, rev. edn. Toronto: Oxford University Press.

Bernard, Jessie. 1981. *The Female World*. New York: Free Press.

Brodie, Janine. 1988. 'The Gender Factor and National Leadership Conventions in Canada', in George Perlin, ed., *Party Democracy in Canada*. Scarborough, Ont.: Prentice-Hall Canada.

———, with Celia Chandler. 1991. 'Women and the Electoral Process in Canada', in Kathy Megyery, ed., *Women in Canadian Politics*, Lortie Commission on Electoral Reform and Party Financing, vol. 6. Toronto: Dundurn Press.

Burt, Sandra. 1986. 'Different Democracies? A Preliminary Examination of the Political Worlds of Canadian Men and Women', *Women & Politics* 6: 57–79.

Campbell, Kim. 1996. *Time and Chance: The Political Memoirs of Canada's First Prime Minister*. Toronto: Doubleday Canada.

Carroll, Susan J. 1992. 'Women State Legislators, Women's Organizations, and the Representation of Women's Culture in the United States', in Jill M. Bystydzienski, ed., *Women Transforming Politics*. Bloomington: Indiana University Press.

Conover, Pamela Johnston. 1988. 'Feminists and the Gender Gap', *Journal of Politics* 50: 985–1010.

Copps, Sheila. 1986. *Nobody's Baby*. Toronto: Deneau.

Elkins, David, and Richard Simeon. 1979. 'A Cause in Search of Its Effect, or What Does Political Culture Explain?', *Comparative Politics* 11: 127-45.

——— and ———, eds. 1980. *Small Worlds: Provinces and Parties in Canadian Political Life*. Toronto: Methuen.

Everitt, Joanna. 1998a. 'Public Opinion and Social Movements: The Women's Movement and the Gender Gap in Canada', *Canadian Journal of Political Science* 31: 743-65.

———. 1998b. 'The Gender Gap in Canada: Now You See It, Now You Don't', *Canadian Review of Sociology and Anthropology* 35: 191-219.

Fulenwider, Claire Knoche. 1980. *Feminism in American Politics*. New York: Praeger.

Gidengil, Elisabeth. 1995. 'Economic Man-Social Woman? The Case of the Gender Gap in Support for the Canada-U.S. Free Trade Agreement', *Comparative Political Studies* 28: 384-408.

Gilligan, Carol. 1982. *In a Different Voice*. Cambridge, Mass: Harvard University Press.

Inglehart, Ronald. 1990. *Culture Shift in Advanced Industrial Society*. Princeton, NJ: Princeton University Press.

Kerber, L.K., C.G. Greeno, E. Maccoby, Z. Luria, C.B. Stack, and C. Gilligan. 1986. 'In a Different Voice: An Interdisciplinary Forum', *Signs* 11: 304-33.

Klein, Ethel. 1984. *Gender Politics*. Cambridge, Mass.: Harvard University Press.

McCormack, Thelma. 1975. 'Towards a Nonsexist Perspective on Social and Political Change', in Marci Millman and Rosabeth Moss, eds, *Another Voice: Feminist Perspectives on Social Life and Social Science*, Garden City, NY: Anchor Books.

McDaniel, Susan. 1988. 'The Changing Canadian Family: Women's Roles and the Impact of Feminism', in Sandra Burt, Lorraine Code, and Lindsay Dorney, eds, *Changing Patterns: Women in Canada*. Toronto: McClelland & Stewart.

McLaughlin, Audrey, with Rick Archbold. 1992. *A Woman's Place: My Life & Politics*. Toronto: Macfarlane Walter & Ross.

McLean, Iain, ed. 1996. *Oxford Concise Dictionary of Politics*. New York: Oxford University Press.

Mendelsohn, Matthew, and Richard Nadeau. 1997. 'The Religious Cleavage and the Media in Canada', *Canadian Journal of Political Science* 30: 129-46.

Mitchell, Alanna. 1999. 'The hard decisions of a stay-home mother', *Globe and Mail*, 13 Mar., A1, A9.

O'Neill, Brenda. 1995. 'The Gender Gap: Re-evaluating Theory and Method', in Sandra Burt and Lorraine Code, eds, *Changing Methods: Feminists Transforming Practice*. Peterborough, Ont.: Broadview Press.

———. 1996. 'Rethinking Political Thinking: Gender and Public Opinion in Canada', PhD dissertation, University of British Columbia.

———. 1998. 'The Relevance of Leader Gender to Voting in the 1993 Canadian National Election', *International Journal of Canadian Studies* 17: 105-30.

———. 2001. 'A Simple Difference of Opinion? Religious Beliefs and Gender Gaps in Public Opinion in Canada', *Canadian Journal of Political Science*.

Poole, Keith T., and L. Harmon Zeigler. 1985. *Women, Public Opinion and Politics*. New York: Longman.

Ruddick, Sara. 1988. *Maternal Thinking: Towards a Politics of Peace*. Boston: Beacon Press.

Sapiro, Virginia. 1983. *The Political Integration of Women*. Urbana: University of Illinois Press.

Statistics Canada. 1995. *Women in Canada: A Statistical Report*, 3rd edn. Ottawa: Minister of Industry.

Stewart, Ian. 1994. 'All the King's Horses: The Study of Canadian Political Culture', in James P. Bickerton and Alain G. Gagnon, eds, *Canadian Politics*, 2nd edn. Peterborough, Ont.: Broadview Press.

Terry, John. 1984. 'The Gender Gap: Women's Political Power', *Current Issues Review*. Ottawa: Library of Parliament.

Thurer, Shari L. 1994. *The Myths of Motherhood: How Culture Reinvents the Good Mother*. Toronto: Penguin Books.

Tolleson Rinehart, Sue. 1992. *Gender Consciousness and Politics*. New York: Routledge.

Vickers, Jill, ed. 1988. *Getting Things Done: Women's Views of their Involvement in Political Life*. Ottawa: Canadian Research Institute for the Advancement of Women.

————. 1997. *Reinventing Political Science: A Feminist Approach*. Halifax: Fernwood.

————, Pauline Rankin, and Christine Appelle. 1993. *Politics As If Women Mattered: A Political Analysis of the National Action Committee on the Status of Women*. Toronto: University of Toronto Press.

Wearing, Peter, and Joseph Wearing. 1991. 'Does Gender Make a Difference in Voting Behaviour?', in J. Wearing, ed., *The Ballot and Its Message: Voting in Canada*. Toronto: Copp Clark Pitman.

Chapter 4

Canadian Political Culture and Value Change

NEIL NEVITTE AND MEBS KANJI

What are Canadian values? Are they changing? And, if so, why, and what are the consequences of these changes? These questions have preoccupied Canadians for generations and they are important questions to ask, not least because values are the cornerstone of our collective identity. Shared values and collective assumptions provide a grounding for community. There are a variety of ways of going about answering these questions. One approach is to delve into written and oral histories to search for the common threads, for coherent elements of unity. Another might be to examine our traditions as revealed through poetry and art to fathom what makes Canadians unique and what sets them apart from others. An examination of Canadian laws and institutions might be another strategy for understanding the shape and texture of the Canadian community. The approach followed in this chapter relies more on one of the tools of contemporary social science—survey research evidence that comes from the World Values Surveys.

The World Values Survey data show that significant value changes have taken place in Canada. Canadians have become less parochial, more cosmopolitan. They want more involvement in workplace decisions, and families have become more egalitarian. This chapter begins by outlining three broad explanations for why these value changes may have taken place. We then explore the survey evidence to show the directions of value change and to see which particular interpretation of Canadian value change seems to be the most plausible.

Explanations for Value Change

There are at least three explanations for why Canadian values are changing, and each corresponds to a familiar image of Canadian society: that Canada is a nation of immigrants; that Canada is a North American state; and that Canada is an advanced industrial state.

Canada as an Immigrant Society

First, there is the possibility that Canadian value changes might be attributable to patterns of population replacement. Canada depends more on immigration for population replacement than any other country in the advanced industrial world except Australia. Patterns of population replacement are affected by a combination of factors, including fertility rates, longevity, immigration and emigration, attitudes about ideal family size, education, and the place of women in the paid workforce. Over the last 25 years or so there have been significant changes on each of these dimensions. For example, census data show that in 1965 Canada's fertility rate stood at about 3.1 births per woman, but by 1972 that rate had dropped below the replacement level of 2.1. By 1985, it had fallen yet again to just 1.7. Added to the reduced fertility rate is emigration: some 50,000 people emigrate from Canada each year. The combined effect of declining fertility rates and emigration means that Canada has to recruit some 175,000 immigrants a year just to maintain current population levels. One consequence of our heavy reliance on immigration as a source of population replacement is that some 16 per cent of Canada's population was not born in the country.

To focus only on the volume of immigration, however, misses one of the most dramatic features of Canada's population shift over the last decade and a half, namely, there has been a fundamental shift in immigrants' countries of origin. Between 1956 and 1960, immigrants came mainly from traditional, European points of origin; immigrants from these traditional sources outnumbered those coming from outside of Europe by a ratio of about 10:1. By 1980, that pattern had reversed; immigrants coming from non-European countries outnumbered those coming from Europe by a ratio of about 2:1 (Beaujot and Rappak, 1988).

A number of consequences flow from this dramatic shift in the patterns of population replacement. One is that Canada has become a far less 'European' society than ever before. Remarkably little is known about precisely what values immigrants bring to this country or about the adaptation of immigrants' values, but high volumes of immigration and shifting sources of immigration plainly have the potential to reshape the overall value trajectories of any country. In the absence of direct systematic evidence, it is impossible to demonstrate how, or even whether, the values of new Canadians differ significantly from those who are born in the country. Even so, immigration certainly stands as a plausible explanation for aggregate value change in this country for at least two reasons. First, the basic value orientations of immigrants are not, and by definition could not have been, rooted in the Canadian experience, and second, the volume of immigrants makes up a substantial portion of the Canadian population as a whole.

Canada as a North American State

A second plausible explanation for why Canadian values may have changed comes from a broader frame of comparison; it fixes attention on Canada as a North American state and, more particularly, on Canada's location as the northern neighbour of the United States. Understandably, there is a long-standing tradition of interpreting Canadian values through Canadian-American comparisons, and within that tradition there are vigorous debates about whether Canadian and American values are 'basically the same' or 'fundamentally different' (Lipset, 1990; Horowitz, 1973). Some observers, like Seymour Martin Lipset (1990), suggest that differences in Canadian-American values are reflected in, and contemporarily shaped by, variations in founding circumstances. Yet others suggest that contemporary value differences might be attributable to structural differences between the two countries. Irving Louis Horowitz (1973), for example, makes the case that when it comes to Canadian-American value differences, Canada qualifies as a case of 'lagged development'. The implication of that line of speculation is that as Canada and the United States become more alike in their economies and other structural characteristics, they will also become more similar in their value systems. By most measures, Canada and the United States have become structurally more similar with the passage of time.

Each school of thought has been able to muster intriguing arguments relying on a wide variety of qualitative, historical, contextual, historical, and structural evidence to support either conclusion. The possibility that Canadian values have changed because they have become increasingly Americanized is a concern that has haunted the guardians of Canadian culture for generations. Certainly, it is not difficult to find anecdotal evidence to fit that view. For instance, some observers interpret the adoption of the Charter of Rights and Freedoms, the changing role of the courts, the calls for an elected Senate, and the use of 'attack ads' during election campaigns as indications of the 'Americanization' of Canada's political culture. Added to these is evidence indicating that the once sharp cultural differences between the two countries may have become less pronounced over the last two decades. In the 1960s and 1970s it was common practice to point to Canada's bilingualism as a distinguishing feature separating Canadian culture from that of the United States. The contemporary picture is quite different. With some 30 million Hispanic peoples now calling the United States home, bilingualism has become a reality of the American domestic landscape, although not necessarily of its political institutions. Similarly, the racial divide once served as a benchmark differentiating the United States from Canada, but with the shifting patterns of immigration to Canada, race has moved from the margins of communal reality to become a part of normal discourse.

The most widely held explanation for Canadian value change, and for the Canadian-American value convergence, and one that fuelled vigorous opposition to Canada's free trade agreement with the United States, concerns Canada's geographic proximity to the United States. Canada and the United States are more interdependent than any other two countries in the world and that interdependence operates on multiple levels. In the economic realm, the volume of two-way trade between the two countries is huge; Canada and the United States are the largest trading dyad in the world. In addition to massive two-way trade and financial transactions, there are very substantial cross-border population and communications flows. Canada is more exposed to American cultural exports than any other country in the world; some 80 per cent of the Canadian population has access to all the major American television networks. And on yet another level, Canadians and Americans share common strategic interests in the defence of the continent.

That the combined effect of these kinds of multi-level transactions might produce value change is not a new idea. Forty years ago, Karl Deutsch and his colleagues suggested that high levels of cross-border transactions encourage greater similarities in 'main values' (Deutsch, 1957). There is little difficulty in documenting substantial increases in these kinds of cross-border transactions between Canada and the United States over the last 20 years, and so it is surely plausible that the rising volumes of transactions between Canada and the United States might encourage convergence between American and Canadian 'main values'. And, given the discrepancies in size between Canada and the United States, it is also plausible that American values could be leading to change in Canadian values.

Canada as an Advanced Industrial State

The third explanation for Canadian value change is more general still and focuses attention on the fact that Canada now qualifies as an advanced industrial state. Central to this perspective is the idea that significant changes in social and economic structures are usually accompanied by corresponding shifts in basic value orientations. Observers since the nineteenth century have noted that the economic, social, and political values prevalent during the feudal era were not the same as those associated with the industrial era (Tilly, 1988). Nor, following the same logic, is there reason to suppose that the values prevailing during early industrialism would be identical to mainstream values during late or advanced industrialism. Advanced industrial states share a number of characteristics that separate them from their early industrial counterparts. Typically, each has experienced a sustained period of prosperity in the postwar era; all have economies increasingly driven by the tertiary sector—financial capital, commerce, technology, and the service sector; each has undergone massive expansions of post-secondary education; and each has experienced the information revolution with the associated growth in communications-related technologies. Not surprisingly, these changes have been accompanied by social transformations that can be characterized most broadly as increases in the social, occupational, and geographic mobilities of populations. It would be remarkable indeed if these profound structural and social changes were not accompanied by equally profound shifts in public values—economic values, social values, and political values.

Investigators exploring the nature of the value shifts associated with the emergence of advanced industrialism do not all agree about what are the most important features of these value shifts to late industrialism, but there is agreement about the scope, content, and consequences of these broad value changes. Some characterize the most important features of these shifts as having to do with the rise of 'individualization', the fact that publics in late industrial states are more inclined to be directed by inner goals rather than externally defined ones (Huntington,

1974; Ester, et al., 1993). Others focus more on how the value changes associated with late industrialism have transformed attitudes towards authority, conformity, religiosity, and the work ethic (Flanagan, 1982; Naisbitt, 1982; Toffler, 1980), and these observations are particularly pertinent and provocative given that the vigorous debates about Canadian-American value similarities and differences have focused precisely on these particular value dimensions. Canadians, conventional wisdom has it, are supposed to be more conformist, more passive and inclined to accept authority, less religious, and less likely to take economic risks than their American counterparts (Lipset, 1968).

Not surprisingly, most observers argue that the value shifts associated with advanced industrialism have had enormous consequences for the economy, for the family, and for political life broadly understood. Workplaces have become more democratic and less hierarchical than ever before. Families have become smaller, less traditional, less patriarchal, and more fluid as women have moved into the paid workforce in huge numbers. According to Harding (1986), these value changes have produced a 'new morality', and on the political front the value shifts associated with the rise of advanced industrialism have also been associated with the transition from 'old politics' to 'new politics', a style of politics that places greater emphasis on the kinds of issues driven by political behaviours and priorities that reflect a new emphasis on such quality-of-life concerns as environmentalism (Miller and Levitin, 1976; Hildebrandt and Dalton, 1978).

Different analysts offer different explanations for precisely why these widespread value changes have taken place. Some identify these shifts with the changing class structures (Lipset, 1979) or with the inherent weaknesses of old welfare states (Offe, 1984). But perhaps the best documented explanations for the root causes of the value shifts associated with advanced industrialism are supplied by Inglehart (1971, 1990), who argues that the primarily 'materialist' preoccupations of those living under the conditions of earlier phases of industrialism have been replaced by 'post-materialist' orientations of publics living in advanced industrial environments. Inglehart observes that people place the greatest subjective value on those things that are in short supply and that, according to socialization theory, people's formative experiences are vital in shaping long-term value orientations. Thus citizens who were raised during conditions of material and physical insecurity, who experienced such traumas as the Depression and World War II, tend to give relatively high priority to such materialist orientations as economic and physical security. And following Maslow's observations about the hierarchy of needs (Maslow 1954), Inglehart speculates that younger generations, those born after 1945, were socialized under very different circumstances. These younger generations in advanced industrial states had no first-hand experience with material and physical insecurity. Instead, they were socialized during an unprecedentedly long period of affluence and for them economic security could be taken for granted (Inglehart, 1971: 991). Because postwar generations were no longer preoccupied with economic and physical security they give greater priority to aesthetic and intellectual needs and to the need for belonging.

Applied to the Canadian setting, this line of reasoning implies that Canadian value changes do not require a Canada-specific explanation. Rather, the value changes that Canadians have experienced share much in common with the kinds of value changes that have taken place throughout most advanced industrial states. In this scheme of things, Canada can be seen as another stage on which the rhythms of late industrialism are being played out.

The World Values Evidence

The World Values Surveys (WVS) are a valuable source of information for exploring the interpretations of value change outlined above for a combination of reasons. First, the WVS provide us with directly comparable evidence: the surveys were conducted in Canada in both 1981 and 1990; they asked the same survey questions about core values of a random sample of Canadians at both points in time and so we should be able to detect any significant value shifts by comparing the results from the two surveys.

Second, the very same surveys were also undertaken in a number of other countries, including the United States and most Western European countries. Consequently, the WVS data allow us to compare directly Canadians' values with those of representative samples of Americans as well as publics in other advanced industrial states. Moreover, the Canadian surveys included a survey item that identifies the language in which the surveys were conducted (English or French) and whether respondents were born in the country or not. Using these indicators, we should be able to see if the values of Canadian immigrants are similar to, or different from, those of Canadians who were born in the country.[1]

Third, unlike many other surveys, the WVS are deliberately designed to explore basic orientations towards a wide range of values. They not only probe people's political values, narrowly understood, but also explore a wide variety of social and economic values. Political values, of course, are important in their own right. But these value orientations do not exist in isolation and one unique strength of the WVS is that they allow us to look at the linkages between different kinds of values and to see if, and how, changes in political values might be connected to value shifts in other domains.

What the WVS Evidence Shows

As in nearly all of the countries included in the WVS, significant value changes have taken place in Canada. There are variations, of course; value shifts have been more rapid in some countries than in others. More impressive than the variations, though, is the scope and breadth of the transformations; they apply to all value domains—the social, economic, and political. It is not possible to present all of the data coming from the World Values Surveys,[2] but we can summarize some of the main findings that shed light on the three interpretations of Canadian value change with which we began. Each of those three interpretations produces somewhat different expectations about what we would expect to find in the WVS data. The point needs to be spelled out in more detail. Consider the case of Canada as an immigrant society. If Canadian values have changed because of high volumes of immigration, if the trajectories of Canadian value change are being shaped by the influx of 'new' Canadians, then we would expect to find significant and consistent differences between the values of Canadians not born in the country and those who were born in the country. There is no expectation that the values of all Canadians born in the country would be the same. Indeed, there are sound historical reasons for supposing that the value orientations of Francophone Canadians might be significantly different from those of Anglophone Canadians. If we take the average location of Francophone and Anglophone Canadians on any value dimension and consider these as the basic benchmarks, as an indication of the values held by most native-born Canadians of traditional European descent, then a simple empirical question to ask is: Are the values of new Canadians somewhere in between the value positions of Francophone and Anglophone Canadians born in the country or do they fall outside of that range?

With the WVS data we can examine this question in detail and do so across some 25 different value dimensions. When this immigrant society hypothesis of Canadian value change is tested on each of these dimensions the results are clear-cut and, perhaps, somewhat surprising. Taken as a group, the values of new Canadians are hardly ever significantly different from those of native-born Canadians. In short, little evidence supports the idea that Canadian value change is the result of the influx of new Canadians.[3]

What about the second possibility, namely, that Canadian value change is a consequence of proximity to the United States, and the multi-level cross-border transactions between the two countries, and reflects the Americanization of Canadian values? Once again, the WVS data can be used to examine this account of Canadian value change; a summary of the WVS results of this hypothesis is provided in Table 4.1. The lefthand column lists each of the 25 value dimensions under consideration, grouped into political, economic, and social orientations. The next column shows how Canadian and American values changed on each of these dimensions between 1981 and 1990. Here, the consistency between Americans and Canadians is quite striking—22 of the 25 dimensions, Canadian and American value changes were in the same direction. This demonstrates far greater consistency than one would expect by chance alone.

The next column indicates the net result of the value shifts, showing that on 19 of the 25 dimensions Canadian and American values were either converging or on a parallel course. Notice that in two out of the three cases where Canadian and American value shifts were moving in opposite directions—job satisfaction and financial satisfaction—the net result is that they were becoming more alike; they were converging. On only one dimension out of the 25, church attendance, were Canadians and Americans actually becoming less alike.

Another noteworthy finding concerns the evidence of Canadian-American value divergence. In the political domain, there is value divergence on two dimensions, cosmopolitanism and protest potential. Canadian and American values moved in the same direction but Americans were becoming more cosmopolitan in their outlooks

Table 4.1: Value Change in Canada and the United States, 1981–1990

Dimensions	Direction of North American Value Change	US–Canada Movement 1981–1990	Leader of Trend in 1990 (US or Canada)	Overall Leader of Trend in 1990 highest/lowest
Political Orientations				
Interest in politics	rising	parallel	Canada	W. Germany
Confidence in government institutions	falling	converging	Canada	Italy
Confidence in non-government institutions	falling	converging	Canada	Netherlands
Protest potential	rising	diverging	Canada	Italy
Civil permissiveness	rising	parallel	Canada	Belgium
General deference	falling	parallel	Canada	W. Germany
National pride	falling	parallel	Canada	W. Germany
Cosmopolitanism	rising	diverging	US	Italy
Economic Orientations				
Importance of work	falling	parallel	Canada	Belgium
Support for meritocracy	rising	converging	US	US
Pride in work	rising	parallel	US	US
Worker expressiveness	falling	parallel	Canada	France
Workplace obedience	falling	converging	Canada	Italy
Worker participation	rising	parallel	Canada	Spain
Job satisfaction	US (rising) Canada (falling)	converging	—	Denmark (highest) France (lowest)
Financial satisfaction	US (rising) Canada (falling)	converging	—	Netherlands (highest) France (lowest)

Table 4.1: *(continued)*

Dimensions	Direction of North American Value Change	US–Canada Movement 1981–1990	Leader of Trend in 1990 (US or Canada)	Overall Leader of Trend in 1990 highest/lowest
Social Orientations				
Importance of God	falling	parallel	Canada	Denmark
Church attendance	US (rising) Canada (falling)	diverging	—	Ireland (highest) Denmark (lowest)
Moral permissiveness	rising	diverging	Canada	Netherlands
Principle of tolerance	rising	diverging	Canada	Netherlands
Social intolerance	rising	parallel	US	US
Racial intolerance	rising	parallel	US	Belgium
Political intolerance	rising	parallel	US	W. Germany
Egalitarian spousal relations	rising	parallel	Canada	Canada
Egalitarian parent-child relations	rising	diverging	Canada	Denmark

Note: The dimensions in boldface are the six indicators of authority orientations.

Source: 1981 and 1990 World Values Surveys (see Inglehart et al., 1998).

at a slightly faster rate. The same applies to protest potential. Orientations moved in the same direction but Canadians became more protest-oriented at a faster rate. There is also divergence on three social dimensions—greater moral permissiveness, growing support for the principle of tolerance, and rising egalitarianism in child-parent relations. In each of these cases, the directions of change were also the same and Canadian value shifts took place somewhat more quickly than in the United States.

Overall, the WVS evidence indicates that Canadian and American values were becoming more alike during the decade; there was value convergence. But the results summarized in the next column provide the most telling test of the hypothesis that Canadian values have become Americanized. The notion that Canadian value changes reflect the Americanization of Canada implies that the United States provides Canada with a picture of its own future, that American values eventually become Canadian values. With data from two points in time it becomes possible to determine whether American value changes do in fact lead Canadian ones. The conclusion is clear, and contrary to the Americanization hypothesis. On balance, Canadian value changes lead American value changes, not the other way round. Canadian value changes lead American value changes on seven out of the eight political dimensions, on four out of six economic orientations, and on four out of seven social value dimensions.[4] In other words, the WVS data provide little support for the idea that Canadian value changes can be explained in terms of the Americanization of Canadian values, at least in regard to those values considered here.

What about the third perspective on value change, namely, that Canada is an advanced industrial state and the value shifts taking place in Canada are attributable to the rhythms of late industrialism? The plausibility of this interpretation hinges on two sets of considerations. First, we have to be able to determine the extent to which the value changes in advanced industrial states are synchronized. Are most countries moving in the same direction? And, if there is a pattern, how coherent is the pattern and to what extent is it replicated in the Canadian setting? The second set of considerations has to do with what lies behind these patterns. If the value changes taking place in advanced industrial states are driven by such structural factors as the shifting economy, the expansion of post-secondary education, and the information revolution, if they correspond to generational change, and if they are rooted in emerging post-materialist orientations, as Inglehart suggests, then we should see some systematic connections between these value changes and indicators of such background factors as education, age, and post-materialist values.

Table 4.2 reports WVS data that shed light on these questions. First, consider the extent of the similarities in the directions of value change across 12 advanced industrial states. The basic patterns are fairly clear: in most advanced industrial states the value changes were in the same direction. For example, interest in politics was rising among publics in all 12 countries. Likewise, in all 12 countries confidence in governmental institutions fell, support for a meritocracy grew, pride in work increased, and both spousal and parent-child relations became more egalitarian. In the overwhelming majority of cases, people's political and social orientations moved in the same direction, and in only a handful of cases (for example, workplace obedience and participation, and national pride) does the evidence indicate that the directions of change come even close to qualifying as random. The significant related point comes from a comparison of the direction of Canadian value change (Table 4.1) with the data from Table 4.2: the directions of Canadian value change correspond with the directions of value change in the other advanced industrial states.

The second piece of evidence is even more compelling. Analysis of the WVS data reveals an overwhelmingly consistent set of connections between such background factors as age, education, and post-materialist value type. With but one exception—support for the principle of tolerance—there is a consistent relationship between age and orientations to all of these value dimensions. There is, in other words, a generational gradient with systematic value differences between younger and older generations. That finding does not prove that the value changes are driven by generational factors but it is certainly consistent with that interpretation. Table 4.2 shows an entirely consistent relationship between education and all 25 value dimensions, and this underscores the relevance of structural factors to value change. Furthermore, the correlation between post-materialist orientations and each of the 25 value dimensions is also entirely consistent.

The implications of these findings are clear. Canadian value changes are very much like the value changes that have taken place in other advanced industrial states. The evidence is powerful: the directions of value change conform to an easily recognizable pattern and the connections between these changes and background factors are so strikingly systematic that these results cannot be plausibly interpreted as random.

Interpreting Value Change

To document systematically Canadian value change across multiple value dimensions with directly comparable evidence amounts to useful basic research. But what do these findings amount to? And what do they mean for the future? Answers to these questions are necessarily more speculative, but the WVS evidence does call for some interpretation. Some of the findings summarized here challenge conventional wisdom about what are, and what are not, Canadian values. One conventional belief is that Canada can be characterized as a tolerant society. Tolerance is a slippery concept, but there is nothing in the WVS data to suggest that Canada qualifies as a uniquely tolerant society. For example, the Dutch and Norwegians seem to rate as more tolerant than Canadians. In fact, of all the 25 value dimensions considered here, Canadians rate first out of 12 on only one dimension —egalitarianism in spousal relations (see Table 4.1).

Another conventional belief is that Canadians are a passive lot, conformist, risk-averse, and obedient to their élites. These images are sometimes projected by noting the contrasts between the revolutionary tradition of the United States and the counter-revolutionary tradition of early Canadian settlers, and by extrapolating from these conditions, with their foundational concepts of 'life, liberty, and the pursuit of happiness' and of 'peace, order, and good government', to present circumstances. Some ideas do not travel well, and this conventional bit of wisdom does not seem to

Table 4.2: Directions of Value Change in 12 Advanced Industrial Countries, 1981–1990

| | | | Correlated with: | |
| | | | | Post-materialist |
Dimensions	Direction of Change	Age	Education	Value Type
Political Orientations				
Interest in politics	rising	12/12	yes (+)	yes (∧)
Confidence in government institutions	falling	10/12	yes (−)	yes (−)
Confidence in non-government institutions	falling	10/12	yes (+)	yes (−)
Protest potential	rising	11/12	yes (+)	yes (+)
Civil permissiveness	rising	9/12	yes (+)	yes (+)
General deference	falling	10/12	yes (−)	yes (−)
National pride	rising	7/12	yes (−)	yes (−)
Cosmopolitanism	rising	8/12	yes (+)	yes (+)
Economic Orientations				
Importance of work	falling	9/11	yes (−)	yes (−)
Support for meritocracy	rising	12/12	yes (+)	yes (+)
Pride in work	rising	12/12	yes (∪)	yes (−)
Worker expressiveness	falling	7/12	yes (+)	yes (+)
Workplace obedience	falling	6/12	yes (−)	yes (−)
Worker participation	rising	6/12	yes (+)	yes (+)
Job satisfaction	falling	8/12	yes (+)	yes (−)
Financial satisfaction	falling	7/12	yes (−)	yes (−)

Table 4.2: *(continued)*

			Correlated with:	
Dimensions	Direction of Change	Age	Education	Post-materialist Value Type
Social Orientations				
Importance of God	falling	10/12	yes (+)	yes (−)	yes (−)
Church attendance	falling	10/12	yes (+)	yes (−)	yes (−)
Moral permissiveness	rising	10/12	yes (−)	yes (+)	yes (+)
Principle of tolerance	rising	12/12	weak	yes (+)	yes (+)
Social intolerance	rising	11/12	yes (+)	yes (−)	yes (−)
Racial intolerance	rising	9/12	yes (+)	yes (−)	yes (−)
Political intolerance	rising	11/12	yes (+)	yes (−)	yes (−)
Egalitarian spousal relations	rising	12/12	yes (−)	yes (+)	yes (+)
Egalitarian parent-child relations	rising	12/12	yes (−)	yes (+)	yes (+)

Note: The dimensions in boldface are the six indicators of authority orientations.

    + = positive relationship

    − = negative relationship

    ∧ = curvilinear relationship

Source: 1981 and 1990 World Values Surveys.

hold up either. The portrait emerging from the WVS is that contemporary Canadians are not politically passive. They are not more obedient than others to élites, nor are they peculiarly deferential to authority in general. In fact, Canadians are relatively frisky when it comes to these political orientations; they are more likely than Americans to engage in protest behaviours, and they score higher on measures of civil permissiveness. And Canadians are less deferential than Americans in regard to their orientations towards workplace and family hierarchies (see Table 4.1).

Authority is one theme that ties together many of the findings coming from the World Values Surveys. Authority orientations are profoundly political and they apply to the workplace and the family as well as to the polity. What is striking is that shifts in authority orientations have rippled through all of these domains and it turns out that the shifts in one domain, such as the family, are related to shifts in the polity and the workplace. What lies behind these transformations?

Providing a definitive answer to that question is difficult, but the WVS data provide some intriguing clues. Using more complicated statistical tools allows us to isolate the separate effects of different factors that contribute to orientations towards political authority. The estimates reported in Table 4.3 (see Methodological

Table 4.3: Regression Analysis: Predictors of Political Authority Orientations in Canada

Predictors		Standardized Beta Coefficients
Personal satisfaction	Life satisfaction	−.08**
	Financial satisfaction	−.08**
Broad-gauged shifts	Post-material orientations	.09**
	Cognitive mobilization	.19**
	Left libertarianism	.02
Authority orientations	Worker expressiveness	.06**
	Worker participation	.10**
	Spousal relations	.01
	Parent-child relations	.09**
Religiosity		−.12**
Socio-demographics	Age	−.19**
	Male	.08**
	Income	.09**
	Catholic	.05*
	Constant	.50**
	R-squared	.24

*significant at p <.05; **significant at p <.01.
Source: 1990 World Values Surveys (weighted results).

Appendix for the coding of the variables in the regression equation) indicate the relative importance of a variety of predictors. The simplest way to interpret these data is to examine the size and direction, positive or negative, of each of the coefficients. Here, the dependent variable in the regression equation is the lack of deference.

The most telling findings to emerge from these data are that a number of different factors help to predict political authority orientations. One powerful predictor of low deference is cognitive mobilization, a variable that combines interest in politics with level of formal education: those who are interested in politics and who have high levels of formal education are less likely than others to be deferential to authority (.19). Age is also important (–.19); older Canadians are more deferential than their younger counterparts. Both of these factors are related to structural changes of the sort that are associated with late industrialism, and the age effects may signify the impact of generational changes. Post-materialist value orientations are less powerful predictors, but they are also significant (.09); they have significant independent effects after all of the other factors have been taken into account. The important point to underscore, however, is that the shifting orientations towards authority seem to be a product of a combination of both value shifts and structural changes. Core values change slowly but structural shifts are slower still. One implication of these findings is that such short-term factors as temporary reversals in economic growth may well encourage correspondingly short-term changes in some value priorities. A temporary recession may make people feel less secure and hence more materialist. But it does not follow that a short-term economic reversal will also produce public reorientations towards authority. As the WVS data indicate, authority orientations are more firmly grounded in such resilient structural conditions as education. What matters to the future of these basic political orientations, in both Canada and other advanced industrial states, is the interaction of structural factors and values. What also matters is how institutions respond and adjust to the challenges that flow from these transformations.

Conclusion

We began this chapter by asking: What are Canadian values? And, are they changing? The core dimensions of Canadian political culture have been specified in a variety of ways. There is broad agreement that Canadians share many of the values central to those of other liberal democracies, including support for such principles as freedom and equality. There is less agreement on the matter of how and why Canadian values are changing.

Evidence from the World Values Surveys offers some useful insights to the matter of Canadian value change because these data allow us to place Canadian values in a broad context. The time period for which we have reliable direct evidence of value change, 1981–90, is relatively brief, so there are reasons to be cautious when interpreting these data. That said, strong parallels clearly exist between the value shifts identified in the Canadian setting and those found in other advanced industrial states. Citizens are becoming less parochial and more cosmopolitan. Interest in politics is rising. Confidence in governmental institutions is falling. The propensity to engage in protest behaviours is rising. Citizens are less satisfied with hierarchical structures regardless of whether those structures are found in the family, the workplace, or the polity. The same patterns are replicated in nearly all advanced industrial states, Canada included.

Equally impressive is the discovery that these same value shifts are linked to the same structural indicators, such as age and education, in almost precisely the same ways in different advanced industrial states. The value shifts appear to predominate among the young and the well-educated. Collectively, these shifts have been interpreted as signalling the emergence of a new political culture, one that has a number of recognizable components. In that new political culture, traditional notions of class seem to be less important. Single-issue politics is becoming more important and new social issues, particularly those concerning the environment, women's rights, and gay rights, are becoming more salient. Attachments to traditional political parties seem to have weakened and, at the same time, citizens seem more prepared to engage in direct action strategies to meet their political goals (Clark and Rempel, 1997). The indications are that Canadian political culture is moving in the same direction.

Notes

1. The surveys were designed to be cross-nationally comparative. They contain the same questions, the sampling designs operate from the same principles, and the data collection involved face-to-face interviews in all countries. The Canadian sample size is n = 1,730, and the margin of error slightly under $+/-$ 2 per cent.
2. A more detailed presentation of the results for Canada, the US, and 10 other advanced industrial states is in Nevitte (1996).
3. Note that this approach considers all new Canadians together; the sample sizes for any particular group of new Canadians is too small to be reliable.
4. On the remaining value dimensions the differences between who leads and who follows the value changes are not determinable because they are within the margins of statistical error.

References

Beaujot, Roderic, and Peter J. Rappak. 1988. *Immigration from Canada: Its Importance and Interpretation*. Population Working Paper No. 4, Policy Department. Ottawa: Employment and Immigration Canada.

Clark, Terry Nichols, and Michael Rempel. 1997. *Citizen Politics in Post-Industrial Societies*. Boulder, Colo.: Westview Press.

Deutsch, Karl W. 1957. *Political Community and the North Atlantic Area*. Princeton, NJ: Princeton University Press.

Ester, Peter, Loek Halman, and Ruud de Moor, eds. 1993. *The Individualizing Society: Value Change in Europe and North America*. Tilburg, Netherlands: Tilburg University Press.

Flanagan, Scott C. 1982. 'Changing Values in Advanced Industrial Societies: Inglehart's Silent Revolution from the Perspective of Japanese Findings', *Comparative Political Studies* 14: 403–44.

Harding, S. 1986. 'Contrasting Values in Western Europe: Some Methodological Issues Arising from the EVSSG European Values Project', paper presented at the Third Cross-National Research Seminar, Language and Culture in Cross-National Research, Aston University, Birmingham, UK.

Hildebrandt, Kai, and Russell Dalton. 1978. 'The New Politics', in Max Kaase and K. von Beyme, eds, *German Political Studies: Elections and Parties*, vol. 3. Beverly Hills, Calif.: Sage.

Horowitz, Irving Louis. 1973. 'The Hemispheric Connection', *Queen's Quarterly* 80, 3: 327–59.

Huntington, Samuel P. 1974. 'Post-Industrial Politics: How Benign Will It Be?', *Comparative Politics* 6: 147–77.

Inglehart, Ronald. 1971. 'The Silent Revolution in Europe: Intergenerational Change in Post-Industrial Societies', *American Political Science Review* 65: 991–1017.

———. 1990. *Culture Shift in Advanced Industrial Society*. Princeton, NJ: Princeton University Press.

———, Miguel Basanez, and Alejandro Mareno. 1998. *Human Values and Beliefs: A Cross-Cultural Sourcebook*. Ann Arbor: University of Michigan Press.

Lipset, Seymour Martin. 1968. *Revolution and Counterrevolution: Change and Persistence in Social Structures*. New York: Basic Books.

———. 1979. 'The New Class and the Professoriate', in B. Bruce-Briggs, ed., *The New Class?* New Brunswick, NJ: Transaction Books.

———. 1990. *Continental Divide: The Values and Institutions of the United States and Canada*. Ottawa: C.D. Howe Institute.

Maslow, Abraham. 1954. *Motivation and Personality*. New York: Harper.

Miller, Warren E., and Teresa Levitin. 1976. *Leadership and Change*. Boston: Winthrop.

Naisbitt, John. 1982. *Megatrends*. New York: Warner Books.

Nevitte, Neil. 1996. *The Decline of Deference: Canadian Value Change in Cross-National Perspective*. Peterborough, Ont.: Broadview Press.

Offe, Claus. 1984. *Contradictions of the Welfare State*. Cambridge, Mass.: MIT Press.

Tilly, Charles. 1988. 'Social Movements, Old and New', *Research in Social Movements: Conflicts and Change* 10: 1–18.

Toffler, Alvin. 1980. *The Third Wave*. New York: Morrow.

Methodological Appendix:

Operationalization of Variables Measuring Attitudes Towards Authority in the Polity, the Workplace, and the Family

Indicators of Attitudes Towards Authority in the Polity (Dependent variable—additive index):

1. Signing a petition: (have done or might do = 1; would never do = 0).
2. Joining in boycotts: (have done or might do = 1; would never do = 0).
3. Attending unlawful demonstrations: (have done or might do = 1; would never do = 0).

4. Joining unofficial strikes: (have done or might do = 1; would never do = 0).
5. Occupying buildings or factories: (have done or might do = 1; would never do = 0).
6. Non-confidence in armed forces: (not very much or not at all = 1; a great deal or quite a lot = 0).
7. Non-confidence in the police: (not very much or not at all = 1; a great deal or quite a lot = 0).
8. Non-confidence in parliament: (not very much or not at all = 1; a great deal or quite a lot = 0).
9. Non-confidence in the civil service: (not very much or not at all = 1; a great deal or quite a lot = 0).

Indicators of Attitudes Towards Worker Expressiveness:
10. An opportunity to use initiative on the job: (important = 1; not important = 0).
11. A job in which you feel you can achieve something: (important = 1; not important = 0).
12. A responsible job: (important = 1; not important = 0).
13. A job that is interesting: (important = 1; not important = 0).
14. A job that meets one's abilities: (important = 1; not important = 0).

Indicators of Workplace Participation:
15. (Opinion on how business or industry should be managed) Owners and the employees should participate in the selection of managers or the employees should own the business and should elect the managers: (select either statement = 1; select neither statement = 0).
16. (Opinion on following instructions at work) Must be convinced before following instructions at work or it depends (= 1); should follow instructions (= 0).

Indicators of Attitudes Towards Authority in Spousal Relations:
17. Mutual respect and appreciation makes for a successful marriage: (very important or rather important = 1; not very important = 0).
18. Understanding and tolerance makes for a successful marriage: (very important or rather important = 1; not very important = 0).
19. Sharing household chores makes for a successful marriage: (very important or rather important = 1; not very important = 0).

Indicators of Attitudes Towards Authority in Parent-Child Relations:
20. One does not have the duty to respect and love parents who have not earned it by their behaviour and attitudes: (agree = 1; disagree = 0).
21. Children should be encouraged to learn independence at home (important = 1; not important = 0).
22. Children should be encouraged to learn imagination at home (important = 1; not important = 0).
23. Children should be encouraged to learn obedience at home (important = 1; not important = 0).

Part III
_____

Public Opinion

Chapter 5

Bringing Politics Back In: Recent Developments in the Study of Public Opinion in Canada

ELISABETH GIDENGIL

In a memorable phrase, sociologist Allen Barton (1968: 1) once described the typical social survey as 'a sociological meatgrinder' that tore respondents from their social context. He went on to make a plea for 'bringing society back in' to survey research.[1] A similar charge could long have been levelled against surveys of political opinion. Too often survey respondents were abstracted from the political context, as if public opinion were a purely individual-level phenomenon (see Sniderman, 1993). This has changed dramatically in the past dozen years or so with the advent of new survey technologies. Marrying innovative methods to theoretical concerns, survey-based studies of public opinion have been bringing politics back in. As Sniderman et al. (1996: 55) state, 'Politics is about argument, about getting people who start off on one side of an issue to join your side or at least leave theirs. Where people start off politically matters, but what counts is where they wind up after the pushing and shoving of political argument.'

In this chapter, I will describe how advances in computer-assisted telephone interviewing (CATI) have enabled researchers to mimic this dynamic in the design of their surveys.[2] This chapter does not purport to offer a comprehensive survey of opinion research in Canada. Instead, the focus will be on two of the most important questions confronting the study of public opinion and how the advances in survey technology have been brought to bear on them. First, do citizens have authentic opinions about politics, and, second, how do citizens arrive at those opinions? As we shall see, answering both of those questions requires us to take the political context into account.

Setting the Agenda

In retrospect, Richard Johnston's (1986) wide-ranging study of public opinion for the Royal Commission on the Economic Union and Development Prospects for

Canada, popularly known as the Macdonald Commission, can be seen as having set the agenda for subsequent studies of public opinion in Canada, not least by putting politics firmly at its centre. Johnston's analyses revealed a striking pattern of contradictory findings. On a number of issues, the distribution of opinion depended very much on the question asked. When queried about commercial policy, for example, Canadians would typically reject protection in favour of making Canadian industry more competitive internationally, only to adopt a protectionist stance when asked about concrete cases like import quotas on Japanese cars.

Johnston could have dismissed such contradictions as artifactual, reflecting either 'non-attitudes' (Converse, 1964, 1970) or poorly worded questions. Philip Converse's seminal studies of mass belief systems in the United States revealed that many respondents appeared to lack genuine attitudes towards politically salient questions. This was indicated by the fact their responses to the same question were often unstable across time and correlated poorly with their responses to other questions on logically related issues. If non-attitudes are also prevalent in Canada, this would provide one possible explanation for the contradictory patterns of response that Johnston identified: many Canadians may have been responding to questions on matters about which they had thought little and cared even less. They would oblige the interviewer with an answer, but it would not represent a genuine attitude for the simple reason that they lacked such an attitude. On the other hand, it could be that they did have genuine attitudes, but the questions failed to elicit them because the questions were poorly constructed. Johnston acknowledged both possibilities, but raised an intriguing third possibility, namely, that for some of the respondents at least, the divergent responses to different questions on the same issue were real. These respondents were not simply responding more or less randomly to irrelevant and/or flawed questions.

But why should real attitudes be manifested in seemingly contradictory responses to survey questions? This is where Johnston brought politics back in. Variations in question wording mimic the attempts of politicians to control the agenda by framing the issue to their advantage. Far from being 'a self-directed force . . . opinion is something to be evoked and mobilized. Majorities are built or split by the framing of questions' (Johnston, 1986: 226). As we shall see, this 'rhetorical struggle' on the part of political élites was to become a central concern of the 1988 Canadian Election Study, which Richard Johnston headed.[3]

Assessing Johnston's third possibility empirically actually requires answers to three questions. First, how prevalent are non-attitudes? Second, do voters in fact respond to élites' rhetorical ploys? And finally, how do the rhetorical ploys work? As Johnston notes, to the extent that his third possibility is plausible, it has significant implications, not least for the quality of direct democracy. Because they tend to result in random choices, the effects of non-attitudes on the vote will usually (though not always) be self-cancelling. Thus the votes of those who do have real attitudes will usually be decisive.

'Non-Attitudes'

As we have just seen, Johnston readily recognized that some of the divergent response simply reflected non-attitudes. This is one of the most worrying issues in the study of public opinion: to what extent do our survey questions elicit authentic expressions of opinion? Studies of fictitious issues in the United States (Bishop et al., 1980; Schuman and Presser,1980) have provided abundant evidence that respondents will oblige interviewers by providing 'opinions' that they cannot possibly possess. Whether this is a matter of wanting to please the interviewer or of not wanting to appear ignorant is beside the point. What students of public opinion need is a way of detecting these 'non-attitudes'.

This is where CATI comes into its own. The new computer-assisted interviewing technologies have enabled researchers to assess the scope of the problem of non-attitudes and to identify those respondents who do not really have opinions on the matter at hand. With CATI, it is a straightforward task to embed experiments in the questionnaire. Which version of a question a respondent receives is determined randomly. This use of randomization enables the researcher to isolate the effects of the experiment since the only difference between the randomized sub-samples is the version heard.

André Blais and I (Blais and Gidengil, 1991) used question-wording experiments like these in our study of Canadians' opinions on electoral reform and party financing for the Lortie Commission. Based on our experiences with focus group discussions of the workings of the electoral system and the rules governing party financing, we suspected that many people were poorly informed about some aspects of these questions and had given them little, if any, thought. To guard against the possibility that respondents might in some cases be giving nothing more than top-of-the-head responses, we varied the order in which response options were offered, used different versions of the same question, or presented the same questions in a different order. Which version or which ordering a respondent received was determined randomly.

The most interesting of these randomizations involved the use of alternative forms of the same question, one presenting a positive argument and the other a negative argument. If respondents were expressing 'non-attitudes,' the distribution of responses would vary systematically from one version to the other, with the positively worded question eliciting higher levels of support for a given position than the negatively worded one. This pattern was illustrated dramatically by the responses to our question on third-party advertising. A random half of our sample was asked the question: 'Some say interest groups should be allowed to advertise to promote their positions on the election issues because that is their right in a democracy. Basically, do you agree or disagree with this view?' The other random half heard this version: 'Some say interest groups should not be allowed to advertise to promote their positions during campaigns, otherwise groups with lots of money will have too much influence on the election. Basically, do you agree or disagree with this view?' Support for allowing third-party advertising dropped from 76 per cent among those who received the positive argument to only 32 per cent among those who received the negative argument. With responses so sensitive to question wording, the conclusion has to be that many Canadians simply lacked opinions on the question. Provide an argument in favour of third-party advertising and a majority agrees with the practice. Provide an argument against and now a majority disagrees. If people had firm views on the issue, they would express the same opinion whatever the argument put to them.

This type of question-wording experiment can alert us to possible problems with non-attitudes, but it does not tell us *which* respondents are expressing these non-attitudes. If questionnaire length permits, challenges can be used to identify respondents who do not really have an opinion on the matter at hand. This technique involves asking people for their position and then presenting a counter-argument in an attempt to induce them to change that position. Joseph Fletcher and Marie-Christine Chalmers (1991) have shown quite convincingly that those who can be swayed away from their initial position were probably expressing non-attitudes. Their analysis was based on a question from the 1987 Charter Study (Sniderman et al., 1996) that dealt with the issue of employment quotas to promote gender equity: 'Do you think that large companies should have quotas to ensure a fixed percentage of women are hired, or should women get no special treatment?' Those who favoured quotas were challenged with a counter-argument invoking the merit principle, while those who opposed quotas were confronted with a challenge invoking the principle of equality. Fletcher and Chalmers compared the role of beliefs about equality and merit in structuring the initial responses of those who moved versus those who held firm in the face of a counter-argument. While the non-movers' responses were rooted in their endorsement of the values of equality or merit, the movers' responses to the initial quota question appeared to have been almost random. The inference had to be that they lacked genuine opinions on the issue of affirmative action.

This counter-argument technique seems to offer a reliable way of weeding out non-attitudes, but challenges have to be used sparingly. Incorporating challenges increases the number of questions that have to be asked on a given topic and that will usually mean fewer questions can be asked on other topics. There is also the possibility of a loss of rapport with respondents if their expressed opinions are challenged too often.

John Bassili and Joseph Fletcher (1991) have come up with an extremely imaginative and technically sophisticated method for weeding out non-attitudes without increasing questionnaire length or risking respondent wrath. It involves timing, within millisecond accuracy, how long it takes respondents to answer a given question. Used in conjunction with CATI, the process is not visible to respondents in any way. The logic is simple: if people have well-developed opinions, they will answer relatively quickly, whereas those who lack opinions will need time to improvise a response. This logic is supported by the authors' finding that simple factual questions about the respondents themselves typically took less than a second to answer and 'simple attitude questions' took between 1.4 and 2 seconds, but 'complex attitude questions' required between 2 and 2.6 seconds.

To determine whether longer response times are indeed indicative of non-attitudes, Bassili and Fletcher used a challenge to identify respondents who changed their minds when confronted with a counter-argument and then compared their response times for the original question with those of the 'non-movers' whose opinions stayed firm in the face of a challenge. The question dealing with the issue of employment quotas to promote gender equity was repeated from the Charter Study, this time with a student sample.[4] This is a 'complex attitude question' in the sense that it brings two values—equality and merit—into opposition. Bassili and Fletcher replicated the finding about the role of values in structuring the initial responses of non-movers, but not movers, with their student sample. They reasoned that the non-movers were not readily swayed because they had already resolved the value trade-off. If this were so, the non-movers should have been able to answer the initial question more quickly than the movers. They went on to show that the movers had indeed taken significantly longer to answer, supporting the argument that the movers lacked 'crystallized' attitudes and thus had had to figure out an 'attitude' on the spot.

Bassili and Fletcher do not just develop an ingenious method for identifying non-attitudes and those who hold them; they wed the method to theoretical concerns. Their response-time measurements enable them to adjudicate between two different theoretical positions on the cognitive processes underlying survey responses. If movers had proved to have the shorter initial response times, this would have supported the on-line information-processing interpretation, as opposed to the attitude-crystallization interpretation. According to the former view, it would be the non-movers who would have taken longer to respond to the initial quota question. In contrast to the quick, unthinking replies of the movers, the non-movers would have taken the time to resolve the value conflict 'on-line' and so their opinion on the question, once formed, would hold firm in the face of a challenge. The fact that their response times were not longer, but shorter, supports the alternative attitude-crystallization view. In other words, their responses to the initial quota question reflected the fact that they possessed coherent sets of beliefs and had already figured out the implications of an issue like quotas for their fundamental values.

Finally, Bassili and Fletcher's method potentially offers a way of identifying poorly worded questions. If respondents have difficulty understanding a question because it is ambiguous or confusing, they are likely to take longer to come up with an answer. Just trying to make sense of the question will take time. Again, the technical advance offers the potential to resolve a long-standing debate in opinion research (Feldman, 1990), this time over the source of attitude instability. Philip Converse's (1964, 1970) original non-attitude thesis had been prompted by the finding of considerable flux in opinion among respondents to a three-wave panel study. One possible explanation for this apparent attitude instability was non-attitudes, but another was measurement error. If questions are unclear or ambiguous, respondents may interpret them differently from one occasion to another. The result of such poor question wording will be response instability, even for respondents who possess genuine attitudes on the topic. In this case, however, the potential to resolve the debate has yet to be realized. The problem is that, empirically, the implications of non-attitudes and question-wording problems are the same in terms of response time. Both will lead to longer response times. As Bassili and Fletcher note, it was not possible with the data at hand to determine how much of the response time was taken up with just figuring out the question and how much with coming up with an answer.

Important—and theoretically grounded—as these questions relating to non-attitudes are, the technical advances in survey design really come into their own when they are used to understand how people arrive at their political opinions. These advances have been employed to particularly telling effect in the 1987 Charter Study and the 1988 Canadian Election Study,[5] both of which used a variety of these devices to mimic the dynamics of political argumentation.

Public Opinion and Rhetorical Ploys

Richard Johnston and his colleagues, André Blais, Henry Brady, and Jean Crête, set out to show that campaigns matter. Partisan élites seek to reinforce the loyalties of their supporters and induce defections from opposing parties, and they do this by employing a variety of rhetorical ploys. This 'rhetorical struggle' (Johnston 1986) was particularly evident in the 1988 federal election campaign. The election was precipitated by an impasse over ratification of the Canada-US Free Trade Agreement (FTA) and the campaign revolved very much around this one issue. Johnston and his colleagues sought to mimic the rhetoric of the campaign by embedding question wording experiments in the design of the 1988 Canadian Election Study, along with a number of challenges.

The opposition parties (the Liberals and the NDP) sought to undercut support for the FTA by capitalizing on voters' distrust of Conservative leader Brian Mulroney. They did this by referring to the agreement as 'the Mulroney trade deal'. One of the key experiments in the 1988 Canadian Election Study sought to assess the impact of this rhetorical ploy.[6] One random half-sample was asked: 'As you know, Canada has reached a free trade agreement with the United States. All things considered, do you support the agreement or do you oppose it?' The other random half-sample was asked exactly the same question, save for the substitution of 'the Mulroney government' for 'Canada'. The rolling cross-section design employed in the study made it possible to assess the effect of this experimental manipulation in dynamic fashion. This sampling design involves selecting a new sample each day of the campaign. Each sample should, in theory, be a microcosm of the electorate and so the only characteristic that distinguishes the daily samples is the day of interview. This design thus provides a powerful method for analysing opinion dynamics because it enables us to pinpoint when the shifts actually occur.[7]

The design enabled Johnston et al. (1992: 149–52) to show that the impact of their question-wording experiment was limited to the period before the televised leaders' debates. Until the debates, associating the agreement with Brian Mulroney did indeed lower support by about 10 percentage points. This effect vanished after the debates. As Johnston and his colleagues explain, voters no longer needed reminding of their doubts about the agreement's negotiator. The debates—and especially Liberal leader John Turner's accusation that Mulroney had sold the country out—had apparently succeeded in getting voters to make this connection themselves. The combination of a question-wording experiment and the rolling cross-section design thus enabled the 1988 election team to make a convincing case for the success of the opposition's strategy.

The 1988 study also used challenges as a way of assessing which side of the free trade issue enjoyed the rhetorical advantage (ibid., 152–5). Respondents who opposed the agreement were presented with a counter-argument in the agreement's favour and asked if this made them less opposed. Similarly, those who favoured the agreement received an argument against the agreement and were asked if it made them less supportive. The arguments against mirrored the opposition's predictions of job loss, threats to social programs, and loss of control over key economic sectors, while the arguments in favour were cast in terms of defending Canada against American protectionism and of lower prices for consumers. Which counter-argument opponents and supporters received was determined randomly. Again, it turned out that the opposition parties had the advantage, at least in terms of campaign rhetoric. The argument that served the opposition best was the possible threat to Canada's social programs. The impact of these opposing arguments diminished towards the end of the campaign. The authors' inference is that the counter-arguments no longer swayed so many erstwhile supporters because there were fewer 'soft' supporters left to persuade. In other words, the opposition parties had succeeded in moving 'soft' supporters into the opposition camp.

Clearly, the manipulation of question wording and the use of challenges enabled the 1988 Canadian Election Study team to buttress their central contention that campaigns matter and that one of the reasons campaigns matter is because of the role played by campaign rhetoric. They were able to show not just that opinion moved on free trade, but why: the opponents' rhetorical ploys succeeded by affecting the considerations (the identity of the negotiator, the agreement's predicted effects) that people brought to bear in forming their opinions.

Public Opinion and Value Pluralism

The 1987 Charter Study provides further insight into the way that people arrive at their opinions about politics and the importance of the way that issues are framed. The Charter Study was a Canada-wide survey conducted in 1987 to examine Canadians' attitudes toward a variety of issues bearing on matters of rights and liberties. The study was designed by Paul Sniderman, Joseph Fletcher, Peter Russell, and Philip Tetlock. Telephone interviews were conducted with a sample of the general population and with samples of decision-makers with legislative, executive, or legal responsibilities in the civil liberties area. Respondents also completed a mail-back questionnaire.

The theoretical underpinnings of the study are provided by Philip Tetlock's (1986) 'value pluralism' model of political reasoning. This model recognizes that people simultaneously subscribe to more than one value and that these values can come into conflict. This is not a matter of inconsistency or insincerity. People can quite consistently and sincerely hold values that collide in practice. It is quite reasonable, for example, to value equality of opportunity and individual achievement, and yet the one can surely undermine the other. Whether values such as these are mutually reinforcing or in conflict depends on the matter at hand. When the issue is pornography, liberty gets pitted against human dignity. When the issue is wire-tapping, on the other hand, liberty can run afoul of order (Fletcher, 1989). This value pluralism is the prime reason that rights clash. Claims to rights are contestable because they invoke competing values. And the abstract nature of rights opens the way for conflict over how those rights apply in concrete situations. A closer look at the Charter Study will demonstrate how the counter-argument technique comes into its own when competing values are invoked to challenge opinions on Charter issues. As we will see, this technique is only one among a number used to develop a damning critique of the notion that political élites are more reliable than ordinary citizens when it comes to upholding fundamental democratic rights.

The key point is that opinions about claims to rights depend on the context of those claims. In pursuit of this insight, Sniderman and his colleagues tried to bring the political context into the design of their study by using actual Charter cases as a basis for formulating their survey questions. This is not the only way that they sought to incorporate the real political world into the Charter Study. 'The world of actual politics', they argue, 'is a world of argument and counterargument', (Sniderman et al., 1996: 10), and this is the dynamic aspect that they set out to capture by exploiting the capabilities of CATI.

A number of experiments built around different Charter rights were incorporated into the survey design. The *'constitutional springboard experiment,'* for example, was used to explore support for Aboriginal rights, along with the Charter's role in civic education (ibid., 134–6). All respondents were asked the question: 'Should native peoples be treated just like any other Canadian, with no special rights, or should their unique rights be preserved?' For one randomly selected half-sample, though, this question was prefaced with the statement: 'Canada's constitution recognizes the unique rights of Canada's native peoples.' The idea was to determine whether the perceived legitimacy of a right is enhanced when it is explicitly linked to the Charter. It turns out that it is for political decision-makers, but not for the public at large.

Identity-substitution experiments were used to analyse double standards. Here, the question is whether people's support for a right depends on whose behalf it is being claimed. The experiments involve randomly varying the identity of the groups involved. In the *quota-beneficiary experiment,* for example, the topic is affirmative action and the substitution involves women versus French Canadians (Fletcher and Chalmers, 1991; Sniderman et al., 1996: 152–4). In the language rights experiments, the topics were minority-language education rights and access to government services in both official languages (Sniderman et al., 1989; 1996: 204–10). The *mobility rights experiment* took this identity-substitution one step further to explore norms of reciprocity, using a four-way experiment to determine how the identity of the beneficiary (a resident of the respondent's own province or not) interacted with the right being claimed (to equal or preferential treatment) (Sniderman et al., 1996: 225–8). In the *principle-policy experiment*, support for the override provision (Section 33 of the Charter, the 'notwithstanding' clause) in the abstract was compared with support for the provision in the context of a specific policy, and now the substitution involved controlling unions versus assisting poor people.

Finally, and most critically for their thesis, the Charter questionnaires included challenges to determine whether respondents could be swayed from their initial position on a question of rights by reminding them of a counter-argument. Some of these counter-arguments invoked competing values. The issues were support for anti-hate legislation and censorship of sexually explicit films, and the competing values invoked (depending on the initial response) were freedom of speech and tolerance and freedom of choice and human dignity, respectively (Sniderman et al., 1996: 62–78). Challenges were also used on the issue of minority-language education rights, but now the counter-arguments were cast, not in terms of competing values, but in terms of considerations like increased taxes, the risk of separatism, and Quebec's right to be a predominantly French-speaking community, depending on the response and whose rights were involved. Similarly, supporters and opponents of public funding of religious schools were challenged with reminders of the historical and social context.

The results of these experiments took Sniderman and his colleagues by surprise. They had begun the study confident of the conventional wisdom that political élites were the most reliable guardians of democratic rights. Contrary to this theory of democratic élitism, however, it turned out that political decision-makers can be as seemingly inconsistent as ordinary citizens when asked about these abstract principles in the context of specific controversies. This is especially so when social order is at stake. The various question-wording experiments enabled Sniderman and his colleagues to see that the inconsistency was due to value pluralism and the contestability of rights.

The central contribution of their published study, *The Clash of Rights*, is to shake the theory of democratic élitism to its foundations, but it also challenges the conventional wisdom about the democratic capabilities of the ordinary citizen, which had long been judged deficient. The authors caution against any optimistic assessment of those capabilities, but their study does cast the disjuncture between principle and practice in a new light. The gap between principle and practice is a familiar and long-standing finding in mass opinion research (see, e.g., McClosky, 1964). Respondents will happily endorse a principle like gender equality, but recoil from endorsing a policy (such as affirmative action) that will promote it (Fletcher and Chalmers, 1991). This slippage between abstract principles and policy preferences is typically attributed to a lack of understanding of what those principles entail. Sniderman and his colleagues remain less than sanguine on this score, but their findings open up the possibility that for at least some citizens the fundamental contestability of rights, rather than a simple failure of understanding, accounts for the principle-practice gap. As the authors themselves note (1996: 122), 'Citizens may not work out systematic answers to complex questions about conflicting conceptions of rights. But they nonetheless wrestle with some of the questions.'

The 'Ideological Possibility'

Recent findings about the so-called 'ideological possibility'[8] also point to at least a partial rehabilitation of the ordinary citizen. Underpinning the Charter Study is the assumption that fundamental values provide one means that ordinary citizens use to make sense of politics. Values are relatively enduring beliefs about what is good or right (see Williams, 1979; Rokeach, 1973; Feldman, 1988; Nevitte, 1996). They provide normative standards that can be brought to bear on the issues of the day. Policy proposals will be judged, at least to some extent in terms of their implications for these deeply held beliefs. This new focus on the ways in which values influence people's opinions provides a fresh perspective on the long-running debate in the study of Canadian opinion about whether Canadians think about politics in ideological terms. It turns out that while many Canadians may be unfamiliar with conventional ideological terms, their fundamental political beliefs are organized in ideologically meaningful ways.

The extent of ideological thinking has typically been inferred from voters' ability to understand and use left-right terminology appropriately. This narrow view of what qualifies as an ideological understanding of politics reflects the genesis of this tradition of analysis in Canada. The various studies that bear on this question were sparked by the anomalies revealed in analyses of the left-wing—right-wing semantic differential scale included in both the 1965 and 1968 Canadian National Election Studies.[9] This scale was included as part of a battery of items designed to tap party images. In other words, the left-wing-right-wing item was originally included for purposes quite other than drawing conclusions about the extent and nature of ideological thinking in the Canadian electorate. That it came to serve instead as a basis for such conclusions can be explained by the peculiarities observed in its empirical performance.

Noting the quite atypically high refusal rate on this item, John Meisel (1975) surmised that many Canadians either did not understand the meaning of the terms 'left wing' and 'right wing' or else were unable to reconcile them with politics as they knew it in Canada. Subsequent analyses suggested that many of those who *did* provide responses may not have understood the terms' meaning. Some of the perverse findings included the observation that *every* party's *own* identifiers placed their party farther to the right than did those who identified with other parties (Elkins, 1974), that even NDP supporters, on average, placed their ideal party slightly to the right of centre (ibid.), and that every party, including the NDP, consistently received more votes among those who perceived the party to be 'right wing,' a tendency that was accentuated when the party was perceived to be both 'right wing' *and* 'for the working class' (Kay, 1977). There appeared, in short, to be little meaningful left-right thinking on the part of Canadian voters. And yet respondents were too consistent in their behaviour (ibid.; Lambert and Hunter, 1979) to dismiss their ratings as merely random responses to meaningless questions.

Rick Ogmundson (1979) suggested one possible explanation for this puzzling pattern of findings: perhaps respondents were interpreting the term 'right' to mean 'correct', 'legitimate', or 'honest', and who would not want their ideal party to qualify as 'right'? Ronald Lambert (1983) took a different tack, dismissing the low level of ideological thinking as a methodological artifact. With the semantic differential format used a total of 65 times in each survey, he suspected a response set problem, whereby respondents fall into a pattern of answering questions in the same manner. This would encourage respondents to rate the parties even when they lacked the requisite knowledge, typically by choosing the midpoint as a neutral, non-committal way of answering. Based on his analysis of responses to the left-right semantic differential item in the 1979 Canadian National Election Study (which did not encourage a response set), Lambert concluded that there was evidence of meaningful left/right thinking within the Canadian electorate, despite the sizeable pockets of political illiteracy.

Lambert was one of the principal investigators for the 1984 Canadian National Election Study. Their survey included a number of questions designed to elicit the meaning that respondents attached to the concepts of 'left' and 'right'. Lambert et al. (1986: 547) were impressed that 'The overwhelming majority of respondents who attempted to define the concepts . . . did so in quite sensible ways—even if they did not always agree with the preferences of academics and journalists.' It bears emphasis, though, that only 40 per cent of respondents were willing or able to venture definitions and some of those definitions were merely evaluative, equating 'right', for example, with being honest or principled. Moreover, when Lambert and his colleagues went on to factor analyse respondents' self-ratings on the left-right scale, along with their positions on a battery of political attitude statements, they found little evidence of policy differences associated with left and right self-identifications.[10]

However we choose to read the findings, a larger question remains: Does evidence that voters fail to understand the terms 'left' and 'right' indicate a lack of ideological thinking? Elinor Scarbrough's (1984: 19) answer is a definitive 'no'. A lack of conceptual knowledge is more properly viewed as indicating a lack of political sophistication, and the fact that relatively few voters are politically sophisticated in this sense does not necessarily mean that few voters have an ideological understanding of politics. Indeed, given the limited extent to which the terms 'left' and 'right' have traditionally figured in our political discourse, we should not rush to label Canadian voters 'unsophisticated' for experiencing difficulty in defining and using these terms. Political élites in Canada have typically not organized their pronouncements into explicitly 'left-wing' or 'right-wing' packages for mass consumption.[11]

Adopting a broader conceptualization of what it means to think ideologically, recent analyses (Nevitte et al., 1999), using data from the 1997 Canadian Election Study, suggest that the level of ideological thinking among Canadians is higher than previously suspected. The analytical strategy was to ask whether Canadians' fundamental beliefs go together in ideologically interpretable ways. Factor analysis of responses to an array of questions tapping fundamental beliefs revealed that Canadians do indeed have coherently structured ideological orientations. What is critical for assessing the 'ideological possibility' is the emergence of two dimensions labelled 'beliefs about free enterprise' and 'moral traditionalism', respectively.[12] Beliefs about free enterprise serve to order people along the economic dimension that is at the heart of the 'old' left-right dimension, while moral traditionalism helps to locate them along the social dimension that is crucial to the 'new' left-right distinction. Beliefs about free enterprise embrace orientations towards the profit system, along with beliefs about individual responsibility, while moral traditionalism encompasses beliefs about women's place and perspectives about children and marriage that fall under the heading of 'family values'.

Not only were Canadians' values structured coherently and meaningfully along clearly identifiable ideological dimensions, but these dimensions were consequential for understanding their political positions. In particular, knowing where voters stood on these ideological dimensions played an important role in explaining how they voted. One of the intriguing findings to emerge from this study was the regional variation in the values that mattered to the vote. Moral traditionalism, for example, helped attract voters to the Reform Party in the West, but not in Ontario (Gidengil et al., 1999). Further study is required to determine whether there is similar variation among regions in the values that shape public opinion, but this finding serves as an important reminder that people do not all make up their minds the same way (see Kinder, 1983).

Heterogeneity in Public Opinion

This recognition that people arrive at their opinions by different routes is what Sniderman et al. (1991) term the 'heterogeneity assumption.' This emphasis on heterogeneity does not mean that students of public opinion are abandoning the search for recurring regularities in opinion formation. On the contrary, the focus is on identifying factors that *systematically* condition the considerations that different individuals bring into play in deriving their opinions.

Gender turns out to play just such a role. Indeed, differences in the considerations that shape opinion were at the root of the gender gap in opinion on the Canada-US Free Trade Agreement (Gidengil, 1995). The theoretical underpinnings for this study were provided by Carol Gilligan's (1982) work. Based on in-depth interviews, Gilligan counterposed a 'male voice' that emphasized the maximization of liberty, privacy, and self-development with a 'female voice' that valued attachment over individual autonomy. She also contrasted the male and female images of relationship as a hierarchy and relationship as a web. Drawing on Gilligan's work, I contrasted the models of 'economic man' and 'social woman'. They are, of course, just that—models—but they are nonetheless useful in understanding why men were so much readier than women to endorse the FTA. Men were indeed more likely than women to bring economic considerations and market arguments to bear, whereas women's opinions were shaped more by their commitment to the welfare state. Interestingly, cue-taking kept the gap in support for the agreement from being wider still. One reason was that feelings about leaders (the cue-givers) had more impact on women's opinions than on men's.

The heterogeneity argument has been most thoroughly developed with respect to the role of political information. In their study of political reasoning in the United States, Sniderman et al. (1991) developed a 'sophistication-interaction hypothesis'. Its central idea is that citizens will vary systematically in the type of information shortcuts—or 'heuristics'—that they use depending on their level of information. In particular, it is assumed that only the more politically sophisticated citizens will be able to bring abstract cognitive considerations, like fundamental values, to bear in forming their opinions. Less sophisticated citizens, on the other hand, are more likely to compensate for their information shortfalls by relying on their likes and dislikes of politically salient groups. Sniderman and his colleagues emphasize, though, that affect, or feelings, also plays a part in the reasoning of the well-informed.

This notion of reasoning chains has been explored in Canada in the context of the 1992 referendum on the Charlottetown Accord (Johnston et al., 1996b). It turned out that information did indeed make for more complex, hierarchical reasoning, and while ideas did matter more among the well-informed, feelings played a role in their reasoning, too. At the same time, the study cast new light on the role of cue-taking from agenda-setters and intervenors: those who were most in need of these cues to compensate for their information shortfalls were the least likely to receive them. The focus in exploring information effects, however, was on vote choice rather than opinion. A good deal more work needs to be done to explore the conditioning effect of information on opinion formation. What seems clear, though, is that rejecting the causal homogeneity assumption will prove crucial to unravelling the mystery of opinion formation.

Conclusion

Clearly, there have been important advances in the study of public opinion over the past dozen years or so. There is, as Sniderman (1993) put it, a 'new look in public opinion research'. Studies of Canadian public opinion have been instrumental in creating this new look. While the advances have been theoretically grounded, it is important to recognize the role that developments in computer-assisted telephone interviewing have played. Non-attitudes can be identified and weeded out. Equally important, the point and counterpoint of political argument can be brought into the survey instrument.

The role of values in shaping public opinion has been firmly established, but so, too, has the complexity of the ways in which values play into opinion formation. Values can and do come into conflict when concrete issues are under debate. The values that matter can differ in systematic ways from one respondent to another. And, while the new focus on the role of values should encourage us to revise our assessment of the extent to which Canadians think ideologically, how much values matter to opinion formation depends on voters' political sophistication.

The full ramifications of the heterogeneity assumption remain to be explored. There is evidence that gender systematically affects the values (and other considerations) that people bring to bear in arriving at their opinions, and there are indications that region may play a similar role. Age, religion, and ethnicity are all candidates for similar effects. Finally, much more work is required on the role of feelings in shaping opinion, especially in light of the finding both here and in the United States that even the well-informed rely on feelings about politically salient groups and individuals when making their political choices. And this reminds us that politics belongs at the centre of the study of public opinion.

Notes

1. Political scientists are also seeking to bring the socio-economic context back into the study of public opinion. For example, Donald Blake (1999) is examining the impact on opinion formation of the contexts in which people live and work, focusing on the impact of the economic context on opinion on environmental issues.

2. With CATI, interviewing takes place from one central location. The interviewers are seated in front of PCs, equipped with headsets. They read each question as it appears on their screen and then use their keyboard to record respondents' answers. The next question appears automatically. It is possible to program the software so that the question order and/or question wording is randomly varied. It is also possible to program the software so that respondents receive different questions depending on their answers to a prior question. The first large-scale Canadian survey to use CATI was the 1987 Charter Study, directed by Paul Sniderman, Joseph Fletcher, Peter Russell, and Philip Tetlock (see below). Canadian researchers have embraced the new technology with particular enthusiasm. This may partly reflect geographical imperatives: a relatively small population dispersed across a vast territory makes face-to-face interviews prohibitively expensive. Another factor may be the lack of an institutionalized structure for Canadian election studies (in contrast to, say, the National Election Studies in the US), which has made it easier to innovate.

3. The Canadian Election Studies have been conducted, by various academic-based research teams, for every federal election since 1965 (with the exception of 1972). For a full description of these studies, see Chapter 26 in this volume.

4. The timer has since been used on vote and/or party identification questions in the 1992 Referendum Study, the 1993 Canadian Election Study, and the 1997 Canadian Election Study.

5. The 1993 and 1997 Canadian Election Studies also incorporate a variety of question-wording and -ordering experiments.

6. A second question-wording experiment was used to examine support for the Meech Lake Accord. Four versions of this question were randomly administered. Three of the versions supplied possible considerations that might sway respondents' opinions: that the accord recognized Quebec as a distinct society, that the accord brought Quebec into the constitution, and that the accord strengthened the powers of provincial governments. The effect of mentioning the distinct society clause was quite dramatic (Johnston et al., 1992: 106).

Anglophone support dropped, while Francophone support rose, to produce an English-French cleavage of almost 40 percentage points (up from only 14 points when no consideration was supplied).

7. One drawback is that the daily samples are necessarily quite small. Other things being equal, the smaller the sample, the greater the risk that it may be unrepresentative. This problem can be countered by using what are called moving averages. Instead of using the actual daily value (say, the percentage who intend to vote Liberal), that value is averaged in with the values for the two previous days and the two following days.

8. The term is from Donald Kinder (1983).

9. A semantic differential scale requires survey respondents to place objects—in this case, the federal political parties—on a seven-point scale whose opposite ends are anchored by bipolar adjectives, such as dull-exciting, honest-dishonest.

10. Respondents who were university-educated *and* provided definitions of both left and right were an exception.

11. Arguably, Canadian politics has become more explicitly ideological in this sense in recent years, at least on the right of the spectrum, and it would be interesting to know whether voters are acquiring greater facility with the terminology of 'left' and 'right'.

12. The other value orientations that emerged outside Quebec were cynicism, orientations towards Quebec, orientations towards outgroups (e.g., racial minorities and Aboriginal peoples), and continentalism. In Quebec, sovereignty replaced orientations towards Quebec, while the outgroups factor split into two separate factors, one made up of orientations towards racial minorities and immigrants and the other made up of orientations towards Aboriginal peoples. For a similar analysis that looks at issue positions as well as basic values, see Johnston et al. (1996a).

References

Barton, Allen H. 1968. 'Bringing Society Back in: Survey Research and Macro-Methodology', *The American Behavioral Scientist* 12: 1–9.

Bassili, John N., and Joseph F. Fletcher. 1991. 'Response-Time Measurement in Survey Research: A Method for CATI and A New Look at Non-Attitudes', *Public Opinion Quarterly* 55: 331–46.

Bishop, George F., Robert W. Oldendick, Alfred Tuchfarber, and Stephen Bennett. 1980. 'Pseudo-Opinions on Public Affairs', *Public Opinion Quarterly* 44: 198–209.

Blais, André, and Elisabeth Gidengil. 1991. *Making Representative Democracy Work: The Views of Canadians*, vol. 17 of the Research Studies for the Royal Commission on Electoral Reform and Party Financing. Toronto: Dundurn Press.

Blake, Donald E. 1999. 'Economic Context and Public Opinion: The Case of Environmental Issues', paper presented at the annual meeting of the Canadian Political Science Association, Sherbrooke, Que.

Converse, Philip E. 1964. 'The Nature of Belief Systems in Mass Publics', in David E. Apter, ed., *Ideology and Discontent*. New York: Free Press, 106–61.

———. 1970. 'Attitudes and Non-Attitudes: Continuation of a Dialogue', in Edward R. Tufte, ed., *The Quantitative Analysis of Social Problems*. Reading, Mass.: Addison-Wesley, 168–89.

Elkins, David J. 1974. 'The Perceived Structure of the Canadian Party Systems', *Canadian Journal of Political Science* 7: 502–24.

Feldman, Stanley. 1988. 'Structure and Consistency in Public Opinion: The Role of Core Beliefs and Values', *American Journal of Political Science* 32: 416–40.

——. 1990. 'Measuring Issue Preferences: The Problem of Response Instability', in James A. Stimson, ed., *Political Analysis*. Ann Arbor: University of Michigan Press, 25–60.

Fletcher, Joseph F. 1989. 'Mass and Elite Attitudes about Wiretapping in Canada: Implications for Democratic Theory and Politics', *Public Opinion Quarterly* 53: 222–45.

—— and Marie Christine Chalmers. 1991. 'Attitudes of Canadians Toward Affirmative Action: Opposition, Value Pluralism, and Non-attitudes', *Political Behavior* 13: 67–95.

Gidengil, Elisabeth. 1995. 'Economic Man—Social Woman? The Case of the Gender Gap in Support for the Canada-US Free Trade Agreement', *Comparative Political Studies* 28: 384–408.

——, André Blais, Richard Nadeau, and Neil Nevitte, 1999. 'Making Sense of Regional Voting in the 1997 Federal Election: Liberal and Reform Support Outside Quebec', *Canadian Journal of Political Science* 32: 247–72.

Gilligan, Carol. 1982. *In a Different Voice: Psychological Theory and Women's Development*. Cambridge, Mass.: Harvard University Press.

Johnston, Richard. 1986. *Public Opinion and Public Policy in Canada: Questions of Confidence*. Toronto: University of Toronto Press.

——, André Blais, Henry E. Brady, and Jean Crête. 1992. *Letting the People Decide: Dynamics of a Canadian Election*. Montreal and Kingston: McGill-Queen's University Press.

——, ——, ——, Elisabeth Gidengil, and Neil Nevitte. 1996a. 'The 1993 Canadian Election: Realignment, Dealignment, or Something Else?', paper presented at the annual meeting of the American Political Science Association, Washington.

——, ——, Elisabeth Gidengil, and Neil Nevitte. 1996b. *The Challenge of Direct Democracy: The 1992 Canadian Referendum*. Montreal and Kingston: McGill-Queen's University Press.

Kay, Barry J. 1977. 'An Examination of Class and Left-Right Party Images in Canadian Voting', *Canadian Journal of Political Science* 10: 127–43.

Kinder, Donald. 1983. 'Diversity and Complexity in American Public Opinion', in Ada W. Finifter, ed., *Political Science: The State of the Discipline*. Washington: American Political Science Association.

Lambert, Ronald D. 1983. 'Question Design, Response Set and the Measurement of Left/Right Thinking in Survey Research', *Canadian Journal of Political Science* 16: 135–44.

——, James E. Curtis, Steven D. Brown, and Barry J. Kay. 1986. 'In Search of Left/Right Beliefs in the Canadian Electorate', *Canadian Journal of Political Science* 19: 541–63.

—— and Alfred A. Hunter. 1979. 'Social Stratification, Voting Behaviour, and Images of Canadian Federal Political Parties', *Canadian Review of Sociology and Anthropology* 16: 287–304.

McClosky, Herbert. 1964. 'Consensus and Ideology in American Politics', *American Political Science Review* 58: 361–82.

Meisel, John. 1975. 'Party Images in Canada: A Report on Work in Progress', in Meisel, ed., *Working Papers on Canadian Politics*, 2nd enlarged edn. Montreal and Kingston: McGill-Queen's University Press.

Nevitte, Neil. 1996. *The Decline of Deference: Canadian Value Change in Cross-National Perspective*. Peterborough, Ont.: Broadview Press.

———, André Blais, Elisabeth Gidengil, and Richard Nadeau. 1999. *Unsteady State: The 1997 Canadian Federal Election*. Toronto: Oxford University Press.

Ogmundson, R.L. 1979. 'A Note on the Ambiguous Meanings of Survey Research Measures Which Use the Words "Left" and "Right"', *Canadian Journal of Political Science* 12: 799–805.

Rokeach, Milton. 1973. *The Nature of Human Values*. New York: Free Press.

Scarbrough, Elinor. 1984. *Political Ideology and Voting: An Exploratory Study*. Oxford: Clarendon Press.

Schuman, Howard, and Stanley Presser. 1980. 'Public Opinion and Public Ignorance: The Fine Line between Attitudes and Nonattitudes', *American Journal of Sociology* 85: 1214–25.

Sniderman, Paul M. 1993. 'The New Look in Public Opinion Research', in Ada W. Finifter, ed., *Political Science: The State of the Discipline II*. Washington: American Political Science Association, 219–45.

———, Richard A. Brody, and Philip E. Tetlock. 1991. *Reasoning and Choice: Explorations in Political Psychology*. Cambridge: Cambridge University Press.

———, Joseph F. Fletcher, Peter H. Russell, and Philip E. Tetlock. 1989. 'Political Culture and the Problem of Double Standards: Mass and Elite Attitudes Toward Language Rights in the Canadian Charter of Rights and Freedoms', *Canadian Journal of Political Science* 22: 259–84.

———, ———, ———, and ———. 1996. *The Clash of Rights: Liberty, Equality, and Legitimacy in Pluralist Democracy*. New Haven: Yale University Press.

Tetlock, Philip E. 1986. 'A Value Pluralism Model of Ideological Reasoning', *Journal of Personality and Social Psychology* 50: 819–27.

Williams, Robin M., Jr. 1979. 'Change and Stability in Values and Value Systems: A Sociological Approach', in Milton Rokeach, ed., *Understanding Human Values: Individual and Societal*. New York: Free Press.

Chapter 6

The Uninformed Canadian Voter

PATRICK FOURNIER

Traditional democratic theory asserts that a strong and healthy democracy relies on an alert, attentive, responsive, and informed citizenry. We do not expect citizens to be well informed about the names of provincial lieutenant-governors, the positions of political parties on the protection of endangered species and their habitats, the stipulations of the public sector's collective bargaining agreements, the mobility rights provisions of the Charter of Rights and Freedoms, or the role of the Judicial Committee of the Privy Council in changing the balance of powers between the federal and provincial governments. In a representative democracy, citizens do not need to be experts on the intricacies of public management, policy-making, and federalism. But as designator of who runs government, controls the bureaucracy, and drives the elaboration of public policy, the voter must be aware of some basic political facts. 'He is supposed to know what the issues are, what their history is, what the relevant facts are, what alternatives are proposed, what the party stands for, what the likely consequences are' (Berelson et al., 1954: 308). Equipped with these facts, citizens become capable of effectively evaluating the respective merits of competing party platforms and selecting the option that best reflects their interests and preferences.

In the United States, research on the public's political information originated over a half-century ago. One can find report cards on Americans' knowledge of politics from the 1940s and 1950s. After an extended hiatus, interest in the subject has rejuvenated over the last two decades and political information has become a central concern in the field of political behaviour. Scholars have uncovered that information influences the decision-making, opinions, choices, and behaviour of individuals. North of the forty-ninth parallel, little attention had been allocated to political information prior to the recent resurgence of interest. As a result, we still do not know much about the political knowledge of Canadians.

To rectify the situation, this chapter surveys the work conducted on political information, replicating and expanding the body of evidence with Canadian data. Specifically, this chapter examines the level of information of Canadians, the determinants of their information level, and the effects of their information level on their political behaviour. It concludes that Canadians are largely uninformed, but not misinformed, about general political facts. Only a small minority of politically, socially, and economically privileged Canadians are quite knowledgeable about politics. This is of great consequence, since studies suggest that political information, beyond its considerable intrinsic value for citizens, has a direct impact on the direction of individuals' political attitudes, and it influences the effects on attitudes of other variables.

The Concept of Political Information

Political information can be defined as factual knowledge about politics stored in conscious memory (Delli Carpini and Keeter, 1996: 10).[1] This definition excludes unconscious cognitions and subjective political opinions, attitudes, and values. For example, knowing there are 10 provinces in Canada qualifies as political information, but the same cannot be said of believing the level of immigration should be cut back. Which political facts should citizens know? One could imagine that such a question might lead to very acrimonious debate. However, a survey of American political scientists came to quite similar conclusions: they recommend that institutions and processes, issues and policies, history, and current political alignments constitute four important topics (Delli Carpini and Keeter, 1993). Furthermore, notwithstanding some dissenting accounts (e.g., McGraw and Pinney, 1990), studies have found that political information is unidimensional rather than multidimensional: citizens are more generalists than specialists, so knowledge about one political subject captures reasonably well knowledge about all subjects (Delli Carpini and Keeter, 1993). Therefore, any short series of survey questions about 'what government is and does' adequately captures general factual knowledge about politics (ibid.; Luskin, 1987; Fiske et al., 1990; Zaller, 1990). Such questions are used in the following empirical analyses.

It should be noted that rationality is quite distinct from political information (Luskin, 1987; Smith, 1989). The extent to which a person's opinions are rational (i.e., correspond to his or her own interests) is not a criterion in the assessment of that person's level of political information. One could argue that informed citizens are more likely to have rational attitudes and preferences, but this is not necessarily the case. In fact, it is probably intrinsically irrational for most individuals to become very informed about politics, in light of the costs in time, effort, and money associated with acquiring political information and the weak gains provided by high levels of political knowledge (Downs, 1957). So there is a tension between democratic requirements and individual rationality: the former pushing for well-informed citizens, the latter pushing against it. The next section examines how this tension is resolved in the real world.

How Informed Is the Public?

The vast majority of the work on levels of political information comes from the United States. From the earliest statements, the picture that public opinion analysts drew of the electorate's political sophistication was quite bleak. The subjective impressions of authors such as Walter Lippmann (1922, 1925) were formally enshrined in compelling empirical evidence by the first major studies of voting behaviour. The seminal research of the Columbia School (Lazarsfeld et al., 1944; Berelson et al., 1954) and the Michigan School (Campbell et al., 1960; Converse, 1964) established that the American public possesses dismally low levels of political attention and information, a failing comprehension of abstract political concepts, unstable political preferences and attitudes, and unorganized belief systems. While there is still debate over the electorate's political conceptualization, stability, and consistency, the public's lack of political information has become a cornerstone of the study of public opinion. Recent studies have confirmed and detailed the scope and extent of Americans' ignorance about politics (Neuman, 1986; Luskin, 1987; Smith, 1989; Delli Carpini and Keeter, 1996).

Are Canadians different? We have almost no evidence about Canadians' level of political information. There are bits and pieces scattered among studies that are not concerned with documenting the knowledge of Canadians. For instance, one study thoroughly investigates the claims that aggregation and low information rationality allow citizens of differing levels of political information to get to the right position as effectively, but very little time is spent depicting the information of the Canadian electorate (Johnston et al., 1996). The sole study that directly tackles this question gathers little evidence—it examines only a single item: the ability to name the 10 provincial premiers (Lambert et al., 1988). The following analysis considers a much larger and more varied set of knowledge items.

Table 6.1 reports the percentage of correct, incorrect, and 'don't know' answers to various factual knowledge questions asked by the Canadian Election Studies during the 1990s.[2] The items are grouped under various subjects: general political facts, general economic facts, and major campaign promises and stands of political parties and intervenors. These subjects deal with basic facts about political players, their objectives, the rules of the game, and the relevant economic context (Delli Carpini and Keeter, 1996). A generous coding of every item was administered.[3]

The percentage of correct answers is generally quite low. Only five items out of 24 had a success rate of 50 per cent or higher. For the large majority of items, less than half of the sample could come up with the accurate response. The proportion of correct answers also varies across items. At one extreme, over eight out of 10 respondents correctly identified Bill Clinton as the current US President. Inversely, just over 10 per cent of the sample could say the New Democratic Party was the party that promised during the 1997 federal election campaign to cut the unemployment rate in half by 2001. An interesting pattern is that the ability to link a particular party with its main campaign promise fluctuates according to the apparent strength of the party. For instance, questions relating to the NDP, the least

Table 6.1: Knowledge of Various Political Facts

	Correct answer (%)	Wrong answer (%)	Don't know (%)
General Political Facts (1997)			
Current President of the US [B. Clinton]	83.5	1.9	14.5
Current Premier of the Respondent's Province	78.5	2.8	18.7
First Woman Prime Minister of Canada [K. Campbell]	40.4	5.3	54.3
Current Federal Minister of Finance [P. Martin]	37.1	6.2	56.6
General Economic Facts (1993)			
Size of the National Unemployment Rate,			
±2% [11.2%]	47.7	34.0	18.3
Size of the National Inflation Rate, ±1.5% [2.5%]	35.8	23.8	40.4
Size of the Federal Deficit, ±$20 billion [$40 b.]	21.9	40.0	38.1
Major Campaign Promises and Stands of Parties and Intervenors			
1992 Referendum			
Pierre Trudeau [Opponent]	62.7	15.4	21.9
Preston Manning [Opp.]	47.2	8.1	44.7
Business Community [Supporter]	45.3	20.4	34.3
Jean Allaire [Opp.]	40.9	9.2	49.9
Union Leaders [Sup./Opp.]*	40.6	16.2	43.2
Women's Movement [Opp.]	37.3	24.5	38.2
Peter Lougheed [Sup.]	27.0	9.4	63.6
Claude Castonguay [Sup.]	18.3	9.5	72.2
1993 Election			
Party promising to increase spending on public works [Lib.]	47.9	7.9	44.2
Party promising to eliminate deficit in 5 Years [PC]	44.7	23.5	31.8
Party promising to eliminate deficit in 3 Years [Ref.]	41.9	34.0	24.1
Party promising to do away with NAFTA [NDP]	22.6	41.1	36.3
Party supports the GST [PC]	62.2	9.7	28.1
Party opposes the GST [NDP, Lib.]	50.0	17.0	33.0
1997 Election			
Party against Quebec as distinct society [Ref.]	47.3	17.8	34.8
Party promising to lower income taxes by 10% [PC]	29.0	19.7	51.3
Party promising to cut unemployment in half by 2001 [NDP]	10.6	35.9	53.5
Average of All Items	42.5	18.1	39.4

*Differs in Quebec and the rest of Canada.

popular of the principal parties, are among those answered the least successfully. Moreover, the Progressive Conservatives' campaign promise question had a higher success rate in 1993, when the party was the incumbent governing party than in 1997, when the party's standing in the previous Parliament was limited to two seats. The contrast in visibility and coverage of the party between the two elections must be at play.

When respondents do not give the right answer, do they provide incorrect or 'don't know' responses? The two are quite different. Incorrect answers imply misinformation or guessing. 'Don't know' answers represent lack of information. The evidence generally exhibits many more uninformed than incorrect responses. In fact, for most items, the proportion of 'don't know' answers approaches or surpasses the percentage of correct answers. The average proportion of 'don't know' responses for all items (39 per cent) almost matches the average proportion of correct answers (43 per cent), and is twice the size of the average proportion of incorrect responses (18 per cent). Along with the relatively low percentage of accurate information, the high level of lack of information is the most pivotal conclusion stemming from the data.

The ratio of correct to incorrect answers is typically very high. Misinformation and/or guessing are not the norm. For instance, take the positions of intervenors in the 1992 Charlottetown Accord referendum. Here, respondents only have to choose between two options: whether the intervenor is for the constitutional accord, or against it. Yet, they seem to be getting the intervenors' positions right at a much higher degree than we would expect by chance alone (i.e., flipping a coin). So, the majority of respondents who choose to respond to a factual question do not guess the answer and do not provide misguided information. But the fact remains that a large portion of the electorate is not informed enough to answer these questions.

Incorrect responses are more frequent among questions about economic facts and campaign promises, especially those of smaller parties.[4] The NDP suffers particularly from a lack of recognition. In 1993, people who incorrectly attributed the NDP's main campaign promise about NAFTA to another party (41 per cent) were almost twice as many as those who answered accurately (23 per cent). In 1997, the erroneous attributions about the party promising to cut unemployment in half (36 per cent) outnumbered the correct ones (11 per cent) by a factor of more than three. It is possible that partisanship plays a role in this pattern. A person favourably disposed towards a party should be more likely to be exposed to the party's discourse and to accept it (Berelson et al., 1954). If partisans are the core source of correct attributions of a party's promise, then the NDP's weak partisan base could represent the major reason behind the low level of information about the party. It turns out, in analyses not reported here, that partisans are substantially more knowledgeable about their party's promises than other respondents. For instance, in 1997, 70 per cent of Reform partisans and 46 per cent of other respondents could associate opposition to distinct society status for Quebec as part of Reform's platform. Similarly, the success rate of NDP partisans in 1997 at identifying their party as the one that promised to cut unemployment in half

(19 per cent) was almost twice that of other respondents answering the same question (10 per cent), but it was still much lower than the success rate of other parties' identifiers with their party's promise. So the NDP's lack of recognition is not overwhelmingly due to its small following. It is probably attributable to the party's modest exposure and media coverage (Nadeau et al., 2000).[5]

The proportions of right, wrong, and uninformed answers say nothing about the collective distribution of political information among the Canadian electorate. On average, about 40 per cent of the sample is responding correctly to the knowledge items. Does this mean the same people (comprising approximately 40 per cent of the sample) consistently respond correctly while the rest consistently answer incorrectly? Does this mean all respondents are equally but distinctly informed, so that each individual responds accurately 40 per cent of the time to an item? Rather than a perfectly polarized or a perfectly single category distribution of information, a more plausible scenario is a bell curve distribution where few individuals are very informed or very uninformed, and most individuals are moderately informed. Such a distribution was found to characterize the collective political knowledge of Americans (Neuman, 1986; Delli Carpini and Keeter, 1996).

Table 6.2 describes the distribution of scales constructed from the items of Table 6.1 that relate to the same subject. The evidence does not corroborate either the polarized or the single-category scenarios. Information is distributed unequally across all respondents. Furthermore, as the number of items included in a scale increases, the distribution of information increasingly resembles the profile of a bell curve. Figure 6.1, for instance, illustrates the distribution of a scale containing all seven knowledge items from the 1997 Canadian Election Study (the general political facts and the parties' major campaign promises and stands). One finds few cases at the extremes—among the perfectly and dismally informed. The bulk of cases cluster around the centre, with slightly more cases among the low end of the information scale.[6] So most Canadians are neither highly informed nor highly uninformed about politics; rather, they are moderately knowledgeable.[7]

Table 6.2: Distribution of Subject Knowledge Scales (Percentage of Respondents)

	Number of questions correctly answered						
	0	*1*	*2*	*3*	*4*	*5*	*6*
General Political Facts (1997)	7.2	15.9	28.7	26.7	21.6		
General Economic Facts (1993)	37.9	28.0	22.0	12.0			
Major Campaign Promises and Stands of Parties and Intervenors							
1992	17.9	18.0	16.3	15.2	13.3	13.0	6.1
1993	17.4	13.0	15.7	17.2	14.4	13.4	8.9
1997	42.4	31.9	21.2	4.7			

Figure 6.1: Distribution of 1997 Overall Knowledge

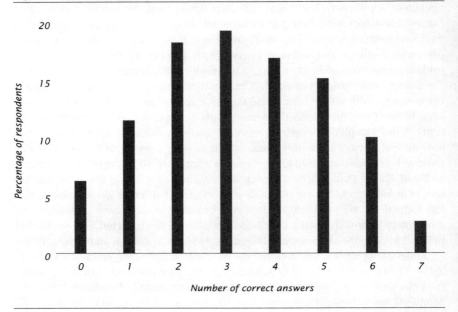

Who Is Informed?

Since individuals differ in the amount of political information they possess, it is logical to ask who is more informed and why are they more informed? Previous studies of the determinants of political information among Americans have identified several key variables: interest in politics, political activity, media exposure, education, and some socio-demographics, such as gender and race, that capture the 'residue of historical exclusion and discouragement' (Luskin, 1990: 337; Neuman, 1986; Smith, 1989; Luskin and Ten Barge, 1995; Delli Carpini and Keeter, 1996). Robert Luskin has proposed a useful model to classify and interpret these variables (Luskin, 1990; Luskin and Ten Barge, 1995). The model explains that any form of behaviour is promoted by three conditions: opportunity, ability, and motivation.

> Bedouins in the Sahara do not become champion swimmers; ordinary people who enjoy music do not compose great symphonies; professors with research assistants do not do their own leg work. They lack the opportunity, the ability, and the motivation, respectively. . . . To become highly sophisticated, we must encounter a certain quantity of political information, be intellectually able enough to retain and organize large portions of the information we encounter, and have reason enough to make this effort. (Luskin, 1990: 334–5)

Does this model apply to the Canadian case? Lambert et al. (1988) found that knowledge of the names of provincial premiers was related to education, media exposure, political activity, age, gender, income, and region; all factors that fit well with the model of opportunity, ability, and motivation. This study conducts a similar analysis with a more adequate measure of political information and a more complete set of explanatory variables.

Table 6.3 highlights some interesting group differences in the ability to answer correctly the 1997 knowledge items. Women's average success rate is 10 percentage points lower than men's. The proportion of correct answers among respondents who have attended university is, on average, 23 percentage points higher than among those who did not complete high school. The contrast between individuals of low and high political interest is similar. Although such group discrepancies are noteworthy, they do not allow us to gauge the real importance of these factors in accounting for the level of political information. For instance, education and interest are correlated, and thus there may exist a spurious relationship with information: highly educated persons may not be more knowledgeable because of their schooling but due to their higher interest in politics, and vice versa.

To ascertain the specific impact of each information determinant, holding all others constant, a multivariate regression analysis of the scale (0–7) containing all 1997 knowledge items has been performed. The analysis contains attitudinal variables: interest in politics, interest in the election, information sources, talking about the election, strength of partisanship, and a few indicators of efficacy and alienation. The analysis also includes socio-demographic variables: age, education, gender, income, region, language at home, and type of occupation. Finally, a context variable (day of interview) is introduced to capture the impact of the campaign on information levels.[8] For the sake of comparison, all variables are coded to vary from 0 to 1, except for age (18–101), day of interview (1–36), and the dependent variable (0–7), which retain their natural scales.[9]

Table 6.4 reports the results of an ordinary least squares regression. As indicated by the model fit statistic (adjusted R-squared), this set of variables does a good job at predicting the level of political information. No single variable possesses an impact that dwarfs all others, but several variables have comparably strong and significant effects on information. Among attitudes, these important variables include interest in politics (motivation), the source of election information (opportunity), talking to friends or relatives about the election (opportunity), and the belief that politics seems so complicated (ability). A shift between the extremes (0/1) on the most powerful variables generates a 1-point change in the dependent variable: for instance, respondents who are greatly interested in politics are likely to answer one more knowledge item (on the 7-item scale) than individuals who are not at all interested.[10] Even after controlling for these attitudes, some statistically significant socio-demographic differences in information level remain. Age, education, gender, income, and language spoken at home are the most important socio-demographics. Older, wealthier, and more educated respondents—

Table 6.3: Group Differences in Knowledge of 1997 Items (% correct)

	All	Gender			Education			Interest		
		Male	Female	Diff.	No High School	Univ.	Diff.	Low	High	Diff.
General Political Facts										
US President	83.5	87.1	80.4	**6.7**	70.8	93.4	**−22.6**	77.4	89.3	**−11.9**
Prov. Premier	78.5	83.5	73.9	**9.6**	69.5	88.6	**−19.1**	67.1	88.7	**−21.6**
Woman PM	40.4	43.1	38.0	**5.1**	22.8	56.5	**−33.7**	27.3	54.2	**−26.9**
Min. of Fin.	37.1	45.2	29.9	**15.3**	27.3	50.8	**−23.5**	22.8	56.4	**−33.6**
Campaign Promises										
Reform	47.3	56.3	39.1	**17.2**	28.4	67.8	**−39.4**	31.1	63.7	**−32.6**
PC	29.0	36.4	22.5	**13.9**	24.2	37.1	**−12.9**	17.4	43.4	**−26.0**
NDP	10.6	12.5	8.9	**3.6**	8.1	14.4	**− 6.3**	6.4	16.8	**−10.4**
Average difference:				**10.2**			**−22.5**			**−23.3**

Table 6.4: Determinants of the 1997 Overall Knowledge Scale (OLS Regression)

	Unstand. Coefficients	Standard Errors	T-Statistics
Attitudes			
Interest in politics	1.20	.13	8.97***
Interest in election	.06	.13	.47
Source of election information (missing = TV)			
Newspaper	.25	.07	3.59***
Family	−.51	.16	−3.18**
Friends	−1.10	.17	−6.67***
Talked to friends/relatives about election	.39	.10	4.10***
Elected lose touch with people	.52	.11	4.57***
Politics and gov. seem so complicated	−.86	.09	−9.40***
Politicians are ready to lie to get elected	.24	.11	2.14*
Strength of partisan identification	.17	.08	2.06*
Socio-demographics			
Age	.02	.00	8.60***
Education	1.67	.16	10.63***
Female	−.42	.06	−7.22***
Income	.43	.10	4.30***
Region (missing = Ontario)			
Atlantic	.05	.12	.46
Quebec	.24	.12	2.06*
West	.06	.07	.90
Language at home (missing = English)			
French	−.38	.12	−3.24**
Other	−.53	.12	−4.36***
Public-sector employee	.09	.07	1.31
Unemployed	−.14	.12	−1.17
Context			
Day of Interview	.01	.00	4.07***
(Constant)	.48	.21	2.36*
Number of Cases	2,661		
Adjusted R-squared	.34		

Statistical significance: * = p <.05; ** = p <.01; *** = p <.001

Note: the dependent variable ranges from 0 to 7, while all independent variables run from 0 to 1, except for age (18–101) and day of interview (1–36).

individuals who have encountered opportunities or possess abilities that favour becoming more informed—exhibit greater political information.[11] Like women and blacks in the United States, the Canadian citizenry also contains particular disadvantaged or disenfranchised groups who experience additional costs (in both opportunity and motivation) for the acquisition of political knowledge: women, Francophones, and allophones.[12] Interestingly, there are no occupational differences (public-sector employee, unemployed) and, unlike the findings of Lambert et al. (1988), the only significant difference between regions found here concerns Quebec, not the Atlantic provinces. Overall, the evidence confirms the model that individuals with greater opportunity, ability, and motivation demonstrate a higher level of political information.[13]

Besides individual characteristics, other factors contribute to the explanation of political information levels. While the public's overall political knowledge level remains relatively stable over time, knowledge of particular items can fluctuate as circumstances affect their complexity (Smith, 1989). As noted earlier, the relative popularity and visibility of the political parties affect the degree of recognition of their campaign promises: the Conservatives had much more notoriety as the incumbent governing party in 1993 than as an opposition party without official status in the House of Commons in 1997. There is also evidence of learning during campaigns (Bartels, 1988; Franklin, 1991; Johnston et al., 1992, 1996; Alvarez, 1996; Jenkins, 1998). As information is dispersed, citizens gain knowledge about parties, candidates, and intervenors, notably their stands on the major issues of the day. In Table 6.4, the 'day of interview' variable captures the positive gains in information that accompany the unfolding of the campaign as a result of increased political media coverage and/or increased public attention. But the effect of the campaign should not be consistent across all knowledge items. Figure 6.2 illustrates the dynamics of two knowledge items during the 1997 federal election campaign: knowledge of the first woman Prime Minister and knowledge of the party against distinct society status for Quebec. One would expect that these two subjects would not receive comparable amounts of coverage during the campaign. Attention to the major parties' central campaign stands should easily outweigh reporting on a dated political fact. As a result, the progress of the campaign should have a different impact on the evolution of knowledge of the two items. And this is exactly what the data reveal. As the campaign unfolded, respondents were increasingly capable of identifying Reform as the party opposed to distinct society status for Quebec, while knowledge of the first woman Prime Minister remained essentially unchanged.

What Are the Effects of Political Information?

Political information matters because it has an intrinsic utility for citizens. It 'assists citizens in discerning their individual and group interests, in connecting their interests to broader notions of the public good, and in effectively expressing these views through political participation' (Delli Carpini and Keeter, 1996: 1). Consequently, the more informed individuals and groups identified in the previous section are

Figure 6.2: Movement of Two Knowledge Items during the 1997 Federal Campaign

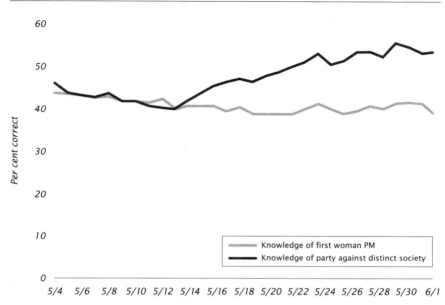

more likely to see their political wishes expressed and implemented. Inversely, 'the least advantaged socially and economically are least able to redress their grievances politically' (ibid.). For instance, since 90 per cent of the population was not aware that the New Democratic Party is the party that promised to cut the unemployment rate in half during the 1997 federal election campaign, then it is probable that many individuals who value job creation could not vote for the party championing this issue because they lacked knowledge about the parties' issue positions.

Also, recent research is increasingly recognizing the effects of political information on other forms of behaviour. American studies have shown that the more informed are more tolerant, participate more in politics, and have more consistent and stable attitudes than the less informed (ibid.). Canadian studies have provided major contributions to this area of research during the last few years. First, Canadian research has documented that information has a direct effect on the direction of political opinions. Johnston et al. (1996) reveal that, even after controlling for all other factors, greater levels of political information were correlated with greater support for the Charlottetown Accord. Berinsky and Cutler (1998) have confirmed that information has a conservative influence (in an ideological sense) on opinions about economic issues and a liberal influence on opinions about social issues, both in Canada and in the US. For instance, individuals with greater levels of information are less likely to favour increases in government services and spending, and they are more likely to favour access to abortion. What has yet to be explained is 'why knowing more about politics ... should affect the direction of a citizen's politically relevant opinions' (Berinsky and Cutler, 1998: 9).

Second, political information has been identified as a mediating variable that influences the effects of other variables on political attitudes, decisions, and behaviour. It has been argued that citizens do not reason the same way about politics: they rely on different considerations, or they give different weight to similar considerations (Sniderman et al., 1991). This research warns that when we estimate the behaviour of the 'average' citizen, we may systematically misconceive the behaviour of both sophisticated and unsophisticated citizens. For example, it is possible that a single coefficient for the relationship between attitudes towards an issue and the vote overestimates the relationship of some voters, underestimates the relationship of other voters, and effectively applies to very few individuals. Canadian scholars have demonstrated that political information is actually the driving source of this heterogeneity in decision-making (Johnston et al., 1996; Fournier, 2000). Furthermore, it has been shown that these differences between individuals decrease during a campaign, as political information is dispersed (Fournier, 2000).

Discussion and Conclusions

The evidence presented here reveals that Canadians are largely uninformed, but not misinformed, about general political facts. Most Canadians are not political junkies. They manage to get on with their lives without paying much attention to politics and without having much information about political matters. Nevertheless, they are not political ignoramuses or know-nothings, oblivious to anything political. Instead, they fall somewhere between these two extremes. This study has shown that, on average, approximately four out of 10 Canadians were able to provide correct information to the knowledge questions selected for examination. And in general, it appears that far fewer Canadians fake, guess, or provide misinformation to such questions than acknowledge their information limitations. On average, approximately two out of 10 respondents answered incorrectly, while four out of 10 admitted they did not know.

Canadian citizens, nevertheless, do not live up to the standards of traditional democratic theory. It may be, however, that the standards are unnecessarily high. Alternative models of democracy have been proposed, models that take as their starting point the public's low level of political information and claim that democracy can thrive without an informed electorate. On the one hand, it has been argued that affective and cognitive shortcuts help voters simplify political choices and act as if they were fully informed. Some scholars assert that uninformed citizens can identify the candidate whose issue positions are closest to their own issue preferences, and vote appropriately, by using cues such as public opinion polls and intervenor endorsements (McKelvey and Ordeshook, 1986; Lupia and McCubbins, 1998). Others claim that affective reasoning schemes, oversimplifications, and clever inference chains allow individuals to overcome their lack of political information and come up with opinions that are reasonable, given their personal belief systems (Popkin, 1991; Sniderman et al., 1991).

On the other hand, some scholars contend that, despite individual ignorance, instability, and inconsistency, collective public opinion is nevertheless rational and coherent, and corresponds to the electorate's fully informed preferences. 'The simple process of adding together or averaging many individuals' survey responses, for example, tends to cancel out the distorting effects of random errors in the measurement of individuals' opinions. Similarly, statistical aggregation tends to eliminate the effects of real but effectively random (i.e., offsetting) opinion changes by individuals' (Page and Shapiro, 1992: 14–15). Theoretically, the process of aggregation relies on generalizations of a statistical model that states that a group of individuals makes better decisions than any single individual (Miller, 1986; Lahda, 1992).

Johnston and his colleagues, however, have dealt a decisive blow to the empirical validity of these claims. Feelings, intervenor cues, polls, and aggregation "*did not close the gap, in translating interests into expressed preferences, between the poorly and the well-informed*" (Johnston et al., 1996: 250, emphasis in original). Both groups were effective in connecting their feelings with the vote, but only the well-informed supplemented their feelings with ideas. Intervenor cues did not help the less-informed, because the well-informed were more likely to be aware of these cues and to use them.[14] Polls did influence the less knowledgeable voters, but they led them away from the more knowledgeable, towards opposition to the Charlottetown Accord.[15] Finally, the bottom line is that the less informed voters did not behave like the more informed. Therefore, 'aggregationists arguments, claims that pooling information compensates for individual differences—in some cases, shortfalls—in cognitive capacity were not vindicated' (ibid., 249).[16]

Concerns regarding the incomplete political information of Canadians should not then be dismissed or assumed away. Information is a resource that is unevenly distributed among Canadians. Only a small minority—politically, socially, and economically privileged—is well equipped to deal with the complexity of politics, to deliberate conscientiously, to articulate their interests and preferences effectively, and to 'get what they want from government' (Smith, 1989: 6). Most Canadians stumble along in semi-darkness and manage to come up with reasonable political opinions and choices, we hope, more often than not.

Notes

The author benefited from the support of the Social Sciences and Humanities Research Council of Canada and the Izaak Walton Killam Foundation, and wishes to acknowledge André Blais, Richard Jenkins, Richard Nadeau, the editors, and an anonymous reviewer for helpful comments and suggestions.

1. Part of the significance of political information stems from the fact that it represents a pivotal dimension of the concept of political sophistication. Political sophistication refers to the size, range, and organization of a citizen's political belief system (Luskin, 1987). A highly sophisticated individual possesses substantial knowledge about politics that

covers a wide scope and is considerably interconnected. The term 'political sophistication' is effectively synonymous with other terms in the literature such as 'political attentiveness', 'political awareness', 'political competence', 'political engagement', 'political
expertise' and 'political involvement'. Although sophistication is a function of many
factors—some of which are difficult to measure (e.g., level of cognitive organization)—
empirically, the concept can be reduced to a more simple and straightforward phenomenon: political information (Luskin, 1987; Fiske et al., 1990; Zaller, 1990).

2. The co-investigators of these studies were Richard Johnston, André Blais, Elisabeth
Gidengil, and Neil Nevitte for the 1992 constitutional referendum; Johnston, Blais, Henry
Brady, Gidengil, and Nevitte for the 1993 federal election; and Blais, Gidengil, Richard
Nadeau, and Nevitte for the 1997 federal election.

3. For example, respondents only had to name one of the two parties opposed to the GST; a
large margin of error was permitted for the economic items; and since the position of union
leaders on the Charlottetown Accord differed in Quebec and the rest of Canada, 'both for
and against' answers were coded as correct. Also, refusals were excluded from the tabula-
tion; only explicit 'don't know' responses were coded as such.

4. Furthermore, there is evidence of substantial amounts of misinformation about specific
public policy issues: notably, HIV transmission (Price and Hsu, 1992), minority numeracy
(Nadeau et al., 1993; Nadeau and Niemi, 1995), racial inequality, environmental protection (Keeter, 1996), and welfare policy (Kuklinski et al., 2000). Knowledge about such
issue-relevant items is more likely to be coloured by political preferences, orientations,
and prejudices.

5. There is also evidence of the notable consequences that misinformation can have on the
political system. For instance, a study has established that there was widespread inaccuracy
about the recent evolution of the unemployment rate in Canada during the 1997 federal
election campaign, and that this misinformation cost the Liberal Party three percentage
points of the vote outside Quebec (Nevitte et al., 2000).

6. Other large-scale distributions, not reported here, also form a slightly positively skewed
bell shape.

7. Beyond comparing the performance of Canadians relative to theoretical expectations, it
would be interesting to know how Canadians rank with electorates of other democracies.
Unfortunately, data that would permit such comparative work are not yet available.

8. The 1997 Canadian Election Study, like those of 1988, and 1993, is a rolling cross-sectional design where a different small sample (80–140 cases) is interviewed each day of
the official campaign.

9. The general nature of the information scale precludes the inclusion of correlates of
knowledge about specific policy issues, such as issue importance and attitudinal and contextual cues (Nadeau and Niemi, 1995; Nadeau et al., 1995).

10. When interpreting the relationships between these variables, one must be careful about
attributing responsibility for cause and effect. The independent variables are not necessarily exogenous. Interest in politics can lead people to become informed about politics.
But the reverse is also true: the more a person knows about a subject, the more likely he
or she is to appreciate it and become even more interested in it. It is therefore best to talk
of these variables as correlates rather than sources of political information.

11. In studies where the impact of intelligence is controlled, education does not contribute anything to the explanation of political information (Luskin, 1990; Luskin and Ten Barge, 1995). Thus, the effect of education should be construed as a proxy for cognitive ability, rather than the result of erudition or training. Unfortunately, no Canadian data exist to corroborate this conclusion.

12. Although men are more politically informed than women, they are also more likely to guess and to answer incorrectly (Gidengil, 1995).

13. In analyses not reported here, I examined the determinants of campaign and general political knowledge separately. They were only minor differences between the two models. The most important variables had similar links to both types of knowledge. The fact that the same variables similarly account for campaign and general knowledge supports the notion that political information is essentially unidimensional: knowledge about one political subject represents well knowledge about all political subjects (Delli Carpini and Keeter, 1996).

14. For arguments and evidence about the perils associated with cues and other shortcuts, see Kuklinski and Hurley (1994).

15. 'Given that low-information voters were intrinsically less favourable to Quebec, this was not an inconsistent move' (Johnston et al., 1996: 282).

16. Bartels (1996) also demonstrates that less informed Americans do not vote as they would have voted under full information. Uninformed voters do not mimic the choices of informed voters with similar socio-demographic profiles. So all the means reportedly available to citizens to overcome informational disparities (polls, cues, and shortcuts) do not perform that role, at least not perfectly. Furthermore, at the aggregate level, these individual 'errors' are not random, they do not cancel each other out. This means that actual electoral outcomes do not correspond to hypothetical outcomes where the same electorate is fully informed. Bartels reports that, on average, American presidential incumbents receive five percentage points more than they would under full information, while Democratic presidential candidates receive two extra percentage points.

References

Alvarez, R. Michael. 1996. *Information and Elections*. Ann Arbor: University of Michigan Press.

Bartels, Larry. 1988. *Presidential Primaries and the Dynamics of Vote Choice*. Princeton, NJ: Princeton University Press.

———. 1996. 'Uninformed Votes: Information Effects in Presidential Elections', *American Journal of Political Science* 40: 194–230.

Berelson, Bernard R., Paul F. Lazarsfeld, and William N. McPhee. 1954. *Voting: A Study of Opinion Formation in a Presidential Campaign*. Chicago: University of Chicago Press.

Berinsky, Adam, and Fred Cutler. 1998. 'Political Information and Political Attitudes: Is There a Direct Link?', paper presented at the annual meeting of the Canadian Political Science Association, Ottawa.

Campbell, Angus, Philip E. Converse, Warren E. Miller, and Donald E. Stokes. 1960. *The American Voter*. New York: Wiley.

Converse, Philip E. 1964. 'The Nature of Belief Systems in Mass Publics', in David E. Apter, ed., *Ideology and Discontent*. New York: Free Press.

Delli Carpini, Michael X., and Scott Keeter. 1993. 'Measuring Political Knowledge: Putting First Things First', *American Journal of Political Science* 37: 1179–1206.

———— and ————. 1996. *What Americans Know about Politics and Why It Matters*. New Haven: Yale University Press.

Downs, Anthony. 1957. *An Economic Theory of Democracy*. New York: Harper & Row.

Fiske, Susan, Richard Lau, and Richard Smith. 1990. 'On the Varieties and Utilities of Political Expertise', *Social Cognition* 8: 31–48.

Fournier, Patrick. 2000. 'Heterogeneity in Political Decision-Making: The Nature, Sources, Extent, Dynamics, and Consequences of Interpersonal Differences in Coefficient Strength', Ph.D. thesis, University of British Columbia.

Franklin, Charles. 1991. 'Eschewing Obfuscation? Campaigns and the Perceptions of U.S. Senate Incumbents', *American Political Science Review* 85: 1193–1214.

Gidengil, Elisabeth. 1995. 'The Gender Gap in Opinion Expression', paper presented at the annual meeting of the American Political Science Association, Chicago.

Jenkins, Richard W. 1998. 'Reform's 1993 Insurgent Success: The Role of the Mass Media', paper presented at the annual meeting of the Canadian Political Science Association, Ottawa.

Johnston, Richard, André Blais, Henry Brady, and Jean Crête. 1992. *Letting the People Decide: Dynamics of a Canadian Election*. Montreal and Kingston: McGill-Queen's University Press.

————, ————, Elisabeth Gidengil, and Neil Nevitte. 1996. *The Challenge of Direct Democracy: The 1992 Canadian Referendum*. Montreal and Kingston: McGill-Queen's University Press.

Keeter, Scott. 1996. 'Origins of the Disjunction of Perception and Reality: The Cases of Racial Equality and Environmental Protection', paper presented at the annual meeting of the American Political Science Association, San Francisco.

Kuklinski, James H., and Norman L. Hurley. 1994. 'On Hearing and Interpreting Political Messages: A Cautionary Tale of Citizen Cue-Taking', *Journal of Politics* 56: 729–51.

————, Paul Quirk, Jennifer Jerit, David Schweider, and Robert Rich. 2000. 'Misinformation and the Currency of Democratic Citizenship', *Journal of Politics* 62: 790–816.

Lahda, Krishna K. 1992. 'The Condorcet Jury Theorem, Free Speech, and Correlated Votes', *American Journal of Political Science* 36: 617–34.

Lambert, Ronald, James Curtis, Barry Kay, and Steven Brown. 1988. 'The Social Sources of Political Knowledge', *Canadian Journal of Political Science* 21: 359–74.

Lazarsfeld, Paul F., Bernard R. Berelson, and Hazel Gaudet. 1944. *The People's Choice*. New York: Duell, Sloane, and Pierce.

Lippmann, Walter. 1922. *Public Opinion*. New York: Free Press.

————. 1925. *The Phantom Public*. New York: Harcourt, Brace.

Lupia, Arthur, and Mathew D. McCubbins. 1998. *The Democratic Dilemma: Can Citizens Learn What They Need to Know?* Cambridge: Cambridge University Press.

Luskin, Robert C. 1987. 'Measuring Political Sophistication', *American Journal of Political Science* 31: 856–99.

————. 1990. 'Explaining Political Sophistication', *Political Behaviour* 12: 331–61.

——— and Joseph C. Ten Barge. 1995. 'Education, Intelligence, and Political Sophistication', paper presented at the annual meeting of the Midwest Political Science Association, Chicago.

McGraw, Kathleen M., and Neil Pinney. 1990. 'The Effects of General and Domain Specific Expertise on Political Memory and Judgment', *Social Cognition* 8: 9–30.

McKelvey, Richard D., and Peter C. Ordeshook. 1986. 'Information, Electoral Equilibria, and the Democratic Ideal', *Journal of Politics* 48: 909–37.

Miller, Nicholas R. 1986. 'Information, Electorates and Democracy: Some Extensions and Interpretations of the Condorcet Jury Theorem', in B. Grofman and G. Owen, eds, *Information Pooling and Group Decision Making*. Greenwich, Conn.: JAI Press.

Nadeau, Richard, Neil Nevitte, André Blais, and Elisabeth Gidengil. 2000. 'Election Campaigns as Information Campaigns: The Dynamics of Information Gains, the Knowledge Gap, and Vote Intentions', unpublished typescript, Université de Montréal.

——— and Richard G. Niemi. 1995. 'Educated Guesses: Extending Theories of the Survey Response to Factual Questions', *Public Opinion Quarterly* 59: 323–46.

———, ———, and Timothy Amato. 1995. 'Emotions, Issues Salience and Political Learning', *American Journal of Political Science* 39: 558–74.

———, ———, and Jeffrey Levine. 1993. 'Innumeracy about Minority Populations', *American Journal of Political Science* 39: 558–74.

Neuman, W. Russell. 1986. *The Paradox of Mass Politics*. Cambridge, Mass.: Harvard University Press.

Nevitte, Neil, André Blais, Elisabeth Gidengil, and Richard Nadeau. 2000. *Unsteady State: The 1997 Canadian Federal Election*. Toronto: Oxford University Press.

Page, Benjamin I., and Robert Y. Shapiro. 1992. *The Rational Public*. Chicago: University of Chicago Press.

Popkin, Samuel L. 1991. *The Reasoning Voter*. Chicago: University of Chicago Press.

Price, Vincent, and Mei-Ling Hsu. 1992. 'Public Opinion about AIDS Policies: The Role of Misinformation and Attitudes toward Homosexuals', *Public Opinion Quarterly* 56: 29–52.

Smith, Eric R.A.N. 1989. *The Unchanging American Voter*. Berkeley: University of California Press.

Sniderman, Paul M., Richard A. Brody, and Philip E. Tetlock. 1991. *Reasoning and Choice: Explorations in Political Psychology*. Cambridge: Cambridge University Press.

Zaller, John R. 1990. 'Political Awareness, Elite Opinion Leadership, and the Mass Survey Response', *Social Cognition* 8: 125–53.

Chapter 7

Gender Gaps on Social Welfare Issues: Why Do Women Care?

JOANNA EVERITT

The second half of the twentieth century witnessed dramatic changes in the roles that women play in political life in Canada. Since gaining the vote in the early part of the century, women have become increasingly active at all levels of political activity. Studies show that differences between women's and men's participation in mass-level political activities (i.e., voting, paying attention to and discussing politics) have decreased substantially or disappeared since the mid-1960s (Brodie, with Chandler, 1991: 25). While women are still not participating in élite politics to the same degree as men (Bashevkin, 1993), the numbers of women in party élites, attending conventions, and running for office have increased steadily during the past few years.

Paradoxically, as women increasingly resemble men in their political participation, their political attitudes appear to be becoming more distinct. In recent years, social scientists have found intriguing differences between women's and men's attitudes on a variety of public policy issues (Shapiro and Mahajan, 1986; Carroll, 1988; Everitt, 1998). These so called 'gender gaps' have important implications for Canadian policy-makers and the study of political science since they represent stark cleavages in the policy priorities and support that Canadians exhibit for key issues. Their significance becomes even greater when they occur in the context of election campaigns (see Erickson and O'Neill, 2000; Gidengil et al., 2000).

One of the areas where the views of women and men diverge the most is in regard to social welfare policies (Dietch, 1988; Erie and Rein, 1988). Numerous studies indicate that women tend to attach greater importance than men to issues of social welfare and that they consistently display higher levels of support for social welfare programs (Lake, 1982; Gidengil, 1995; O'Neill, 1995; Rinehart, 1992; Shapiro and Mahajan, 1986; Terry, 1984; Wearing and Wearing, 1991). Furthermore, attitudes towards social welfare are among the most important predictors of women's voting behaviour during election campaigns (Gidengil et al., 2000). For these reasons it is of interest to researchers to learn more about the factors influencing these gender gaps.

This chapter examines gender differences in the frequency that Canadians identified issues of social welfare (as opposed to other issues such as unemployment or the economy) as the 'most important issue' in the 1997 election campaign. Employing a multivariate analysis, it attempts to unravel the puzzle of why women, as compared to men, continually view social welfare issues as a higher priority. Using data collected in the 1997 Canadian Election Study, it explores various explanations for these differing priorities, including personal social and economic circumstances, socialization, feminist consciousness, general economic evaluations, support for the welfare state, and partisanship. It concludes that next to a strong sympathy for the welfare state, gender is one of the most important variables influencing the level of priority given to social welfare issues. In other words, something related to being female, independent of women's social or economic situations, produces these attitudes among women. The influence of gender remains impressive even when the relevance of other factors is taken into account, making it difficult to answer the question of why women care.

Gender and Public Opinion on Social Welfare

The study of gender and public opinion constitutes a growing research area in the larger field of women and politics. Since the early 1980s, when gender gaps emerged in American support for presidential candidates, scholarly interest in attitudinal gender differences has increased (Bolce, 1985; Lake, 1982). This research, much of which was conducted in the United States, indicates that women are more likely than men to believe governments must ensure their citizens an adequate standard of living. For example, American women show consistently higher levels of support for social programs, including unemployment insurance, income equity, health care, and old-age assistance (Lake, 1982; Rinehart, 1992; Shapiro and Mahajan, 1986). Women are more supportive than men of government-provided unemployment insurance and job guarantees (Shapiro and Mahajan, 1986) and are more likely than men to agree with guaranteed annual income programs, income redistribution, and other economic policies to equalize wealth and help the poor (Lake and Breglio, 1992).

Strong support for social issues does not just appear among American women. Similar observations can be made about women in Western Europe and Canada. Research indicates that during election campaigns in the early 1980s, more British women than men felt that the most important campaign issues would be education, health, social services and housing; women were especially concerned with protecting these programs from budget cuts (Rogers, 1983; Welch and Thomas, 1988). Norris's work on Western Europe found that British women showed greater support than men for Labour Party proposals concerning the redistribution of wealth (Norris, 1985) and that Swedish women were more in favour of public medical care than Swedish men (Norris, 1988). She also discovered that European women in general were more inclined than their male counterparts to support work-sharing as a means of reducing unemployment (ibid., 1988).

While research on attitudinal differences in Canada is limited, some evidence exists of similar gender gaps in Canadian women's and men's responses to questions of social welfare policy. John Terry's analysis of mid-1980s Gallup surveys showed that more women than men believed that: (1) social programs should be expanded rather than reduced; (2) government should be responsible for ensuring adequate retirement income; and (3) women should not receive lower pensions because of their probability of living longer (Terry, 1984). O'Neill's work on the 1988 Canadian federal election showed women were more supportive of government intervention and less supportive of the free market and big business (O'Neill, 1992). Some commentators attribute gender gaps on the issue of free trade between Canada and the United States to women's fear that the agreement would endanger Canadian social welfare programs (Bashevkin, 1989). Others point to women's greater likelihood to rely on social versus economic concerns as the basis of their opinion on free trade (Gidengil, 1995). Studies have also found that Canadian women are less likely than Canadian men to support cutting social programs to reduce the deficit (Wearing and Wearing, 1991). However, despite this evidence, relatively little research has been published in Canada that specifically attempts to discover the factors contributing to Canadian women placing a greater priority on social welfare issues than men.

Contributors to the Gender Gap

Most of the gender and public opinion literature attributes gender gaps to the combined impact of changing socio-demographic characteristics, patterns of socialization, and the development of a gender consciousness among certain groups of women. These explanations are based on arguments grounded in self-interest, socialization, or group identity. For example, demographic variables such as education, marital status, employment status, and income may have an important influence on support for social welfare policies for a variety of reasons. As women become more educated and exposed to inequality through discrimination in the workplace and in other aspects of their lives, they may develop a greater awareness of their own economic and social interests. The phrase 'the feminization of poverty' appeared in the 1980s to describe the growing proportion of women living below the poverty line (Goldberg and Kremen, 1990). Because of wage differentials, marital breakdowns, child custody and support arrangements, and inadequate pensions, women often found themselves in more economically vulnerable positions than men. As Dietch noted, these experiences 'left increasing numbers of women economically dependent, in varying degrees, on welfare state programs for subsistence, for support services or for employment' (1988: 214; see also Erie and Rein, 1988). Socio-demographic factors may also contribute to gender gaps through the growing number of women taking on non-traditional roles. Women's greater labour force participation, rising levels of education, and increasing independence from men (whether due to delayed marriage or marital breakdown) may have caused specific groups of women to view issues in a different manner from men and women who lead more traditional lives. As Welch and Thomas (1988: 29) have argued, 'Faced with juggling household chores, part- or full-time paid employment and child raising, employed women may be even more eager than full-time housewives for government assistance in care-taking functions for the aged, handicapped and poor.'

Employment may be especially important since the welfare state in Canada serves as one of the primary sources of jobs for women. Fields such as health care, education, social work, and the civil service tend to be dominated by women (see Andrew, 1984: 677). Women's greater reliance on the state for their livelihood, as well as their daily contact with individuals who rely on the programs of the state, may encourage them to display higher levels of support than men for social welfare policies.

Alternatively, socialization explanations argue that attitudinal differences may have been influenced by the resurgence of the Canadian women's movement since the late 1960s, and by the various policy positions taken by women's organizations during this period. Over this period the women's movement has articulated demands for day care, pensions, social security, and access to health care. In doing so, the movement may have been able to heighten the awareness and support of the movement's goals, particularly among women in their mid-thirties to fifties whose formative years would have occurred at the height of second-wave feminist activity. These women would have been more exposed to the movement and its messages than men or than younger and older women whose socialization occurred in a different environment.

A final argument used to account for gender gaps relates to the development of a group identity or feminist consciousness among women. Many authors argue that women who have developed this feminist consciousness identify with other women and become more aware of how being female is linked to economic vulnerability (Conover, 1988; Gurin, 1985; Klein, 1984; Rinehart, 1992; Sapiro, 1990). While feminist women may never find themselves in the position of being single mothers or seniors living on inadequate pensions, they may be cognizant of the fact that this is a situation many women face.

While feminist researchers have tended to focus on these explanations to account for gender gaps, it is important to acknowledge that factors such as assessments of the state of the economy, orientations to the welfare state, and partisanship may also affect the priority Canadians attribute to social issues. Accordingly, this chapter explores the priority awarded to social welfare issues with the goal of determining which among these factors are most useful for explaining gender gaps on social welfare issues.

Priorities in the 1997 Election

The 1997 Canadian national election presents an excellent opportunity to explore gender differences in public opinion. The campaign allowed the five main

Canadian parties the opportunity to present political agendas ranging from arguments for tax cuts and debt reduction to the infusion of more money to support Canadian health care, social assistance, and employment insurance programs. While parties debated everything from national unity and gun control to the decline of the fish stocks in Atlantic Canada, the 1997 Canadian Election Study[1] enables the examination of the priority issues of Canadian voters. It included a question asking its survey respondents to identify the single election issue that mattered most to them. Responses to this question were diverse but can be divided into four broad categories; jobs and unemployment; economic concerns such as reducing the debt, transfer payments to the provinces, and interest rates; social issues such as cuts to health care, old-age pensions, and rising university tuition fees; and a more general category that included gun control, national unity, and the stability of government.

As Table 7.1 shows, the priority women and men placed on some of these issues varied dramatically. While there was little difference in their concern on the issue of jobs, clear gender gaps appeared on economic and social issues. Next to the job situation, women believed that social issues were the most important in the election campaign. On the other hand, next to jobs and unemployment, men felt that economic issues were most important. Other issues, such as national unity, fell close behind. These differing priorities were reflected in gender gaps of 19.1 percentage points on social issues and 11.1 points on economic issues. A difference of 8.5 points appeared in the 'other issues' category. A closer examination of these gender breakdowns reveals that differences in the priority on economic issues were the result of more men than women expressing specific concerns about deficit reduction and the general economy while gender gaps on social welfare issues were focused mostly on the issues of health care and education. There were no striking differences in the 'other' category, but the tendency was for men to be more concerned than women about issues of Quebec sovereignty and national unity.

These results clearly indicate that women place a much greater priority on social issues (and especially health care) than men. A gender gap of almost 20 percentage points is substantial and could have had important ramifications for the way people responded to the policy platforms of the different political parties.

Table 7.1: Gender Gaps on the 'Most Important Issue in the Campaign'

	% Women (N)	% Men (N)	Difference* (women-men)
Jobs	36.5 (582)	36.0 (537)	0.5
Economic Issues	17.0 (271)	28.1 (420)	−11.1
Social Issues	28.9 (461)	9.8 (146)	19.1
Other Issues	17.6 (281)	26.1 (390)	−8.5

*Differences are statistically significant at .000 level.

Indeed, examinations of the gender gap in party support during the 1997 election indicate that this is exactly what happened (Gidengil et al., 2000). This raises many questions about the causes of the gender gap. Is it linked to women's social and economic circumstances? Is it related to a feminist consciousness, or is it partisanship or an orientation to the role of the state that is driving them? Furthermore, are the factors that lead women to view social issues as a priority the same factors that influence men? In other words, are women's attitudes extensions of a moral reasoning based on connection, and are men's attitudes based on a moral reasoning that emphasizes separation and autonomy (Gidengil, 1995)?

To answer these questions it is necessary to use multiple regression analysis.[2] The benefit of this analysis is that it allows us to isolate the relative impact of each of these explanations. Because there are two separate questions being addressed, the analysis is broken into two different stages. The first stage, which includes both women and men, addresses the question of what factors other than sex are most closely connected to policy priorities and may account for gender gaps on social issues. The second stage, which is guided by a desire to explain whether priority on social welfare items is determined differently for women and men, conducts the same regression analysis separately by sex.

The dependent variable in this analysis is the priority of social welfare issues. The question asking respondents to identify the most important issue in the election campaign was recoded so that the value 1 represents those respondents who viewed a social issue as most important and 0 represents those who viewed an alternative issue as the most important. The independent variables examined help to demonstrate the relative impact of gender, social and economic condition, socialization, feminism, subjective opinions about the state of the Canadian economy, orientations to the welfare state, and partisanship on the dependent variable. (See Appendix for question wording and a description of the construction of indices).

The variables measuring social and economic conditions include measures of education, employment, marital status, and income. As indicated earlier, a self interest argument would suggest that those individuals with low incomes who are not in the paid labour market and who are separated or divorced would be most likely to rely on the services of the state. This may cause them to place a greater priority on social welfare issues than others. If gender gaps on these issues are related to the feminization of poverty, then the impact of gender should be reduced when these variables are included in the regression equation. At the same time, those with higher levels of education are more likely employed in the provision of social services, which may mean that controlling for this factor would also reduce the impact of gender on the priority assigned to social welfare. The education, marital status, and employment variables have all been transformed into dummy variables such that the condition identified by the variable label is coded as 1 and the alternative is coded as 0. Income has been recoded to range between 0 and 1, with 1 indicating those individuals with the highest incomes. This allows for the direct comparison of the impact of the different variables on the priority of social welfare issues.

The impact of socialization is measured by a series of birth cohorts encompassing those Canadians who came of age before, during, and after the appearance of the second-wave women's movement. Socialization arguments suggest that the women's movement cohort and post-movement cohorts would be those most likely to have been exposed to the messages of the movement and open to adopting the movement's highly supportive position on social welfare issues. To test this argument respondents were divided into four different cohorts designed to reflect the different social environment they would have encountered during their early adulthood. Again, these cohorts are represented by dummy variables in which the members of the cohort are coded as 1 and others are coded as 0.

Arguments suggesting that feminism is linked to support for social welfare issues (Klein, 1984; Sapiro, 1990) are examined by including a measure of feminist values. Those individuals who can be considered feminist are identified by an index composed of questions tapping sympathies for the women's movement or feminist policies. Again, this index ranges between 0 and 1 to allow for comparisons between variables.

Similarly, indices were developed to measure respondents' beliefs about the status of the Canadian economy or their orientation towards the welfare state. These composite measures allow us to determine whether support for social welfare programs is driven by concern about a poor economy in the months leading up to the election or by general beliefs that the federal government's role is to ensure an adequate standard of living for its citizens. The higher the respondents' score on the economic evaluations index the worse they believe the economic situation in Canada is, while the higher scores on the welfare state orientations index reflect greater support for the provision of social services by the government.

Finally, since Canadian elections are fought by political parties that put different levels of emphasis on social welfare issues, a control for partisanship is included in this equation as well. Women's greater support for social welfare issues may be related to their tendency to favour parties of the centre and left, such as the Liberals and the NDP, while men's lower levels of support may be related to their greater preference for the Reform Party or the Progressive Conservatives. By including dummy variables measuring support for these different parties we can ensure that the impact of partisanship is held constant.

Before conducting a multivariate analysis it is helpful to determine whether there are any important relationships between the various independent variables since it is possible that these different explanations may be linked to one another. A correlation matrix outlining the strength and direction of the relationships among all of these independent variables reveals some expected results. For example, university education is linked to higher levels of income, support for the welfare state is positively related to support for the NDP, and a feminist identification is negatively associated with support for the Reform Party. Gender was only moderately connected to the different independent variables. Women appeared more likely than men to hold feminist values and support the welfare state, while men were slightly more likely than women to be employed and to think that the economy had worsened in recent years. While these gender differences appeared statistically significant, they were not substantial and therefore were likely to have only a moderate effect in reducing the impact of gender in the general multivariate analysis. Nonetheless, these results suggest that different explanations may be more important for women or for men.

Table 7.2 reveals the results of the regression analysis. There are three main things to note in a regression table. The first is whether the different variables can be considered statistically significant and therefore generalizable to the population at large rather than just being indicative of the respondents under examination. This can be determined by the value of the measure of significance (identified by an asterisk). The smaller it is, the less likely it is that these results are due to chance. Only four of the variables in the general equation that includes all respondents meet the conventional cut-off level for significance of .05. These include

Table 7.2: Regression Analysis for Priority of Social Welfare Issues

	All Respondents	Women	Men
Female	188***		
University education	−.032	−.064	−.019
Married/partner	.077	.076	.021
Separated/divorced	.031	.035	−.010
Single	.036	.073	−.010
Employed	−.040	−.109*	.009
Income	.012	.138	−.007
Women's movement (1942–57)	.005	.008	−.006
Post movement (1958–72)	.092*	.175*	.018
Third wave (post-1973)	.207***	.327**	.128*
Feminist values	−.111	−.294*	−.027
Economic evaluations	.066	.182	.023
Welfare state orientations	.261***	.454**	.119
Liberal	.039	.067	.016
PC	−.016	−.066	.020
NDP	.093	.152	.050
Reform	.035	.107	−.005
Constant	−.147	−.095	.007
R	.371	.340	.175
R²	.137	.116	.031
N	847	377	470

Note: Entries are unstandardized regression (OLS) coefficients.
  *p <.05, **p <.01, ***p <.001

gender, the post-movement and third-wave cohorts, and the variable measuring orientations towards the welfare state. This implies that the relationship between these variables and the identification of social welfare as the most important issue in the 1997 election campaign is one that is likely to be found in the population at large. Other variables, such as education, income, marital status, feminist values, economic evaluations, and partisanship, failed to produce statistically significant results so are not considered to be truly influential in the selection of social welfare issues as priority issues, at least as they are measured in the model set out here.

Next, to determine which of these variables is most strongly related to the likelihood of identifying a social welfare issue as a priority issue we need to look at the size of the values of the unstandardized regression coefficients. It is possible to compare the regression coefficients with one another since they were all coded within the same range of 0 to 1. In this case, the larger the value, the stronger the relationship and the more important the variable. Three of the four variables stand out. As one might anticipate, those individuals who felt that the state has an important role to play in safeguarding and protecting its citizens were more likely than those who believed in the market principle to view social welfare as an election priority. Those who were not sympathetic to the welfare state were less likely to view these issues as the legitimate responsibilities of the state.

Following this index in importance is the variable representing the youngest generation under study. This is composed of Canadians born after 1973. This cohort, and to some extent the post-movement cohort (1958–72), came of age during a period in which the priority of the women's movement had shifted from a focus on liberal feminist issues of equal pay for equal work and the elimination of barriers to women's participation in politics and the economy, to a more socialist feminist focus on social welfare questions such as child care, old-age pensions, and social assistance to single-parent families. This shift of focus may have contributed the greater priority these generations had for social issues. Alternatively, it may be attributed to the fact that education issues were included among the social welfare issues and many of these young people might be concerned with access to post-secondary education and increasing tuition rates.

The third most important variable is gender. Female respondents were clearly more likely to select a social welfare issue as a priority than male respondents even when controlling for the influence of other factors. This is particularly important to note since even when controlling for alternative explanations, the difference in women's and men's priorities on social welfare issues has not been substantially diminished.

While the impact of gender is clearly demonstrated in the first column of Table 7.2, it is only by looking at the second and third columns that we can truly appreciate its role. These two columns represent the same regression model run separately for women and men. This step allows for the measurement of the *relative* impact of these independent variables on the priority of social welfare issues for women and men. In looking at the column listing the results for female respondents, many of the same independent variables (orientations to the welfare state, membership in the two youngest cohorts) remain important and their impact actually increases. Furthermore, these factors are now joined by feminist values (–.294) and employment in the labour force (–.109) as relevant influences on social welfare priorities. In both cases, however, these new coefficients are negative. This suggests that employed women were less likely to view social welfare as a priority than unemployed women, a result that supports the self-interest argument. On the other hand, the negative value for feminist values indicates that instead of feminists viewing social welfare issues as a priority, it would appear that they are in fact less likely to do so. This should not be taken to mean that feminists are unsympathetic to social welfare issues. Rather, an examination of the relationship between feminism and the other priority issues reveals that women who indicated support for feminism identified jobs and unemployment as their number-one priority, ranking above anything else including social welfare issues.[3]

The results for men are in stark contrast to those of women. Only membership in the youngest cohort appeared to have any influence on men's likelihood of identifying social welfare issues as a priority. Even positive orientations towards the welfare state did not show up as statistically significant.

Conclusions

These results make it difficult to state any definite conclusions about what it is that causes women to care and leads them to place a higher priority on social welfare issues than men. The relationship between being female and support for social welfare issues remains strong even with a wide variety of controls for social and economic condition, socialization, economic evaluations, and partisanship. The fact that many of the most logical and measurable explanations, which might account for social welfare priorities do not appear to greatly reduce gender differences suggests that something about women's experiences makes them more likely than men to view social welfare issues such as health care, pensions, and education as important. These experiences clearly lie outside of the influence of self-interest, feminist attitudes, economic perception, or political allegiance.

While it is not obvious what these experiences may be, it is possible to speculate, as Brenda O'Neill has in an earlier chapter in this text, that they have something to do with women's traditional roles as society's caregivers and the different values and priorities that women possess as a result of this role. Even today women still take on the majority of child-care and elder-care responsibilities. Studies by Status of Women Canada indicate that women who are employed full-time, with young children under the age of six, and who have a spouse who is also employed full-time, do almost double the child-oriented work of men (Status of Women Canada, 1997). Other studies have indicated that a growing segment of the Canadian population is currently providing or believe that they will be called on to provide unpaid health-care services at home for aged parents.[4] Two-thirds of these current and future caregivers are women. These facts suggest that not only are women still being faced with significant responsibilities over the raising and care of children, but they are being asked to pick up the family caregiving load in other ways as governments cut back on health-care services for the ill and the aged.

Unfortunately, the 1997 Canadian Election Study, as is the case with most large-scale opinion surveys, did not include variables to allow for the testing of a 'women's culture' argument, so it is not possible at present to measure empirically whether women's priority for social welfare is linked to their caregiver roles.

While the factors examined in this study cannot answer the question posed in the title of this chapter, the results remain important nonetheless. The fact that we cannot look to explanations of self-interest, socialization, or partisanship to account for these gender gaps emphasizes the need for greater study of factors underpinning attitudes towards some of the most important political issues in election campaigns. It is important to remember that gender differences in political values can be critical in an electoral context since gender is the 'fault line of maximum potential cleavage' (Jennings, 1988: 9). Differences in support for social welfare issues are particularly noteworthy given that attitudes towards these issues are among the most significant contributors to women's vote choices (Gidengil et al., 2000). What is clear from this research is that women are more likely than men to view the state as having an important role to play in the provision of social services, and these opinions are influential in the priorities they bring to election campaigns.

Appendix

All variables employed in this analysis were coded to fall within a zero-to-one range to allow for comparisons between variables. The condition identified by the variable label is coded as 1 and the alternative is coded as 0.

Dependent Variable

Priority of Social Welfare Issues

This variable was created by recoding the responses to the question that asked 'What issue in the election is most important to you personally?' All responses indicating a social welfare issue relating to health care, day care, old-age pensions, education, or other social programs were coded as 1 and all other issues were coded as 0.

Independent Variables

Gender

Female: The variable indicating respondent's gender was recoded so that women were identified as 1 and men were identified as 0.

Measures of Self-Interest

University education: Respondents with a university education were identified as 1 and those without were identified as 0.

Marital status—married/partner: Respondents indicating they were married or living with someone were coded as 1 and all others were coded as 0.

Separated/divorced: Respondents who indicated they were separated or divorced were coded as 1 and all others were coded as 0.

Single: Respondents who indicated they were unmarried were coded as 1 and all others were coded as 0. Respondents identifying themselves as widowed were not included in the equation so as to avoid perfect multi-colinearity.

Employed: Respondents who were employed in the paid labour force were identified as 1 and all others were identified as 0.

Income: The variable for income was coded on a scale from 0 to 1. Those respondents with total household incomes under $25,000 were coded as .2, those with incomes between $26,000 and $50,000 were coded as .4, those with incomes between $51,000 and $75,000 were coded as .6, those between $76,000 and $100,000 were coded as .8 and those with incomes over $100,000 were coded as 1.

Socialization

The influence of socialization was represented by a series of birth cohorts reflecting differing levels of exposure to the women's movement as individuals 'came of age'. The *women's movement* cohort represents those respondents who were born between 1942 and 1957 who would have entered their early adulthood at the height of the women's movement. The *post-movement* cohort (1958–72) consists of those who came of age in the late 1970s and 1980s after the onset of the movement. The youngest cohort includes those born after 1973 who would have been socialized in the *third wave* of the women's movement. The cohort not included in the equation is the *feminine mystique*, which includes those respondents who came of age prior to the onset of the women's movement.

Feminism

Feminist values: Feminist values are measured by a simple additive index constructed from responses to a series of questions tapping feminist sentiments. The alpha score for the scale was .7425. The questions included:

'How much should be done for women?' (1) much less; (2) somewhat less; (3) about the same; (4) somewhat more; (5) much more.

'Do you think the government has gone too far in pushing equal rights?' (1) strongly agree; (2) agree; (4) disagree; (5) strongly disagree.

'In your opinion the feminist movement (1) just tries to get equal treatment for women or (2) puts men down.'

'In your opinion, the feminist movement encourages women (1) to be independent and speak up for themselves or (2) to be selfish and think only of themselves.'

'On a scale of one to 100 what are your feelings about feminists if 0 represents really dislike and 100 represents really like.'

'On a scale of one to seven, how much influence should feminists have if one represents very little and seven represents very influential?'

Perception of the Economy

Economic Evaluations: These evaluations are measured by a simple additive index constructed from responses to a series of questions tapping individuals sense of their personal economic situation as well as the national situation. The alpha score for the scale was .7101. The questions included:

Do you feel that you are better/worse off financially than you were a year ago? (1) better; (3) same; (5) worse.

Do you feel that you will be better/worse off financially a year from now? (1) better; (3) same; (5) worse.

Do you feel that the policies of the federal government have made you better/worse off financially? (1) better; (3) same; (5) worse.

Have unemployment levels gone up, gone down, or stayed the same since the Liberals came to power? (1) gone down; (3) stayed the same; (5) gone up.

Do you expect that in the next few years unemployment will (1) go down; (3) stay the same; (5) go up?

Do you feel that over the past year Canada's economy has (1) gotten better; (3) stayed the same; (5) gotten worse?

Do you feel that over the next 12 months Canada's economy will (1) get better; (3) stay the same; (5) get worse?

Do you feel that over the next 12 months your province's economy will (1) get better; (3) stay the same; (5) get worse?

Do you feel that the state of the economy these days in Canada is (1) very good; (2) good; (3) neither; (4) bad; (5) very bad?

Orientation to the Welfare State

Welfare state: These evaluations are measured by a simple additive index constructed from responses to a series of questions tapping individuals' beliefs about the role of the state in providing social security for its citizens. The alpha score for the scale was .4358. The questions included:

Should the government cut taxes even if it means cutting social programs or should it raise taxes in order to improve social programs? (1) cut taxes; (4) keep taxes as they are; (7) increase taxes.

Do you agree or disagree that the government can maintain social programs and eliminate the deficit? (1) strongly agree; (3) somewhat agree; (5) somewhat disagree; (7) strongly disagree.

Do you agree or disagree that the government should leave it to the private sector to create jobs? (1) strongly agree; (3) somewhat agree; (5) somewhat disagree; (7) strongly disagree.

Do you agree or disagree that the government should do more to reduce the income gap between the rich and poor in this country? (1) strongly disagree; (3) somewhat disagree; (5) somewhat agree; (7) strongly agree.

Partisanship

Liberal: Respondents who identified most closely with the Liberal Party were coded as 1 and all others were coded as 0

PC: Respondents who identified most closely with the Progressive Conservative Party were coded as 1 and all others were coded as 0

NDP: Respondents who identified most closely with the New Democratic Party were coded as 1 and all others were coded as 0

Reform: Respondents who identified most closely with the Reform Party were coded as 1 and all others were coded as 0

Respondents who identified most closely with the Bloc Québécois were not included in the equation so as to avoid perfect multi-colinearity.

Notes

1. The 1997 Canadian Election Study was conducted by the Institute for Social Research, York University. The principal investigators were André Blais, Elisabeth Gidengil, Richard Nadeau, and Neil Nevitte. Neither the ISR nor the principal investigators are responsible for the analysis or interpretations in this chapter.
2. The most appropriate procedure to use for this analysis is logistic regression since the dependent variable being examined has been recoded so that the value 1 represents those cases that viewed a social issue as the most important issue of the election campaign and 0 represents all of the cases that viewed a non-social issue as the most important. However, since logistic regression coefficients are not directly interpretable, the analysis presented here is a normal OLS regression, which produced the same pattern of results as the logistic regression.
3. These data were gathered in a nationwide survey conducted by Pollara in November and December of 1997.
4. It should be noted that for many people the jobs/unemployment issue may be defined as a social welfare issue.

References

Andrew, Caroline. 1984. 'Women and the Welfare State', *Canadian Journal of Political Science* 27, 4: 667–83.

Bashevkin, Sylvia. 1989. 'Free Trade and Canadian Feminism: The Case of the National Action Committee on the Status of Women', *Canadian Public Policy* 15, 4: 363–75.

———. 1993. *Toeing the Lines: Women and Party Politics in English Canada*, 2nd ed. Toronto: Oxford University Press.

Bolce, Louis. 1985. 'The Role of Gender in Recent Presidential Elections: Reagan and the Reverse Gender Gap', *Presidential Studies Quarterly* 15: 372–85.

Brodie, Janine, with Celia Chandler. 1991. 'Women and the Electoral Process in Canada', in Kathy Megyery, ed., *Women in Canadian Politics: Towards Equity Representation*, vol. 6 of the research studies for the Royal Commission on Electoral Reform and Party Financing. Ottawa and Toronto: RCERPF/Dundurn Press, 3–60.

Carbert, Louise. June 1995. 'Gender, Feminism, and the Welfare State', paper presented to the annual meeting of the Canadian Political Science Association, Montreal.

Carroll, Susan. 1988. 'Women's Autonomy and the Gender Gap: 1980 and 1982', in Mueller (1988: 253–67).

Conover, Pamela Johnston. 1988. 'Feminists and the Gender Gap', *Journal of Politics* 50, 4: 985–1010.

Dietch, Cynthia. 1988. 'Sex Differences in Support for Government Spending', in Mueller (1988: 192–216).

Erie, Steven P., and Martin Rein. 1988. 'Women and the Welfare State', in Mueller (1988: 173–91).

Erickson, Lynda, and Brenda O'Neill. 2000. 'The Gender Gap and the Changing Woman Voter in Canada', paper presented to the annual meeting of the Canadian Political Science Association, Quebec City.

Everitt, Joanna. 1998. 'The Gender Gap in Canada: Now You See it, Now You Don't', *Canadian Review of Sociology and Anthropology* 35, 2: 191–219.

Gidengil, Elisabeth. 1995. 'Economic Man—Social Woman? The Case of the Gender Gap in Support for the Canada-US Free Trade Agreement', *Comparative Political Studies* 28, 3: 384–408.

————, André Blais, Neil Nevitte, and Richard Nadeau. 2000. 'Women to the Left, Men to the Right? Gender and Voting in the 1997 Canadian Election', paper presented at the Congress of the International Political Science Association, Quebec City.

Goldberg, Gertrude Schaffner, and Eleanor Kremen. 1990. *The Feminization of Poverty: Only in America?* New York: Praeger.

Gurin, Patricia. 1985. 'Women's Gender Consciousness', *Public Opinion Quarterly* 49: 143–63.

Jennings, M. Kent. 1988. 'Preface', in Mueller (1988).

Klein, Ethel. 1984. *Gender Politics: From Consciousness to Mass Politics*. Cambridge, Mass.: Harvard University Press.

Lake, Celinda. 1982. 'Guns, Butter and Equality: the Women's Vote in 1980', paper presented at the Midwest Political Science Association meetings, Milwaukee, 28 Apr.–1 May.

———— and Vincent Breglio. 1992. 'Different Voices, Different Views: The Politics of Gender', in Paula Ries and Ann Stone, eds, *The American Woman 1992–93: A Status Report*. New York: W.W. Norton, 178–201.

Mueller, Carol, ed. 1988. *The Politics of the Gender Gap*. Newbury Park, Calif.: Sage.

Norris, Pippa. 1985. 'The Gender Gap in Britain and America', *Parliamentary Affairs* 28, 2: 192–201.

————. 1988. 'The Gender Gap: A Cross National Trend?', in Mueller (1988: 217–34).

O'Neill, Brenda. 1992. 'Gender Gaps in Opinion: The Canadian Situation', paper presented to the annual meeting of the Canadian Political Science Association, Charlottetown.

————. 1995. 'The Gender Gap: Re-evaluating Theory and Method', in Sandra Burt and Loraine Code, eds, *Changing Methods: Feminists Transforming Practice*. Peterborough, Ont.: Broadview Press.

Rogers, Barbara. 1983. *52%: Getting Women's Power into Politics*. London: Women's Press.

Sapiro, Virginia. 1990. 'The Women's Movement and the Creation of Gender Consciousness: Social Movements as Socialization Agents', in Orit Ichilov, ed., *Political Socialization, Citizenship, Education and Democracy*. New York: Teachers' College Press, 226–80.

Shapiro, Robert, and Harpreet Mahajan. 1986. 'Gender Differences in Policy Preferences: A Summary of Trends from the 1960's to the 1980's', *Public Opinion Quarterly* 50: 42–61.

Status of Women Canada. 1997. *Economic Gender Equality Indicators: Backgrounder*. Ottawa: Supply and Services.

Terry, John. 1984. *The Gender Gap: Women's Political Power*, current issue review 84–17E. Ottawa: Library of Parliament.

Tolleson Rinehart, Sue. 1992. *Gender Consciousness and Politics*. New York: Routledge.

Wearing, Peter, and Joseph Wearing. 1991. 'Does Gender Make a Difference in Voting Behaviour?', in J. Wearing, ed., *The Ballot and Its Message*. Toronto: Copp Clark Pitman, 341–50.

Welch, Susan, and Sue Thomas. 1988. 'Explaining the Gender Gap in British Public Opinion', *Women in Politics* 8, 3/4: 25–44.

Chapter 8

Personal Values and Environmental Attitudes

Donald E. Blake

Popular concerns regarding environmental issues have fluctuated substantially over time in Canada. For example, the first Decima quarterly survey to ask Canadians how worried they were about 'the quality of the environment in your area' reported in the summer of 1987 that 37.5 per cent of respondents were 'very concerned'. Concern peaked at 56.1 per cent during the winter of 1989 and then fell to the mid-forties in 1992. However, over the same period, the percentage reporting 'major lifestyle changes' because of concerns about the environment nearly doubled, from 16.1 per cent to 31.9 per cent.[1] Moreover, according to Nevitte and Kanji (1995), public concerns about the quality of the environment appear to be unrelated to improvements in key areas such as air and water quality and solid waste disposal.

Other researchers (McAllister, 1994; Rohrschneider, 1988) have raised questions about the focus and sources of environmental concerns. Are they primarily local, stimulated by pollution problems in the immediate neighbourhood or community, or global, sparked by phenomena such as rain forest depletion or holes in the ozone layer? Is increased concern context-driven, linked to the objective state of the environment, or is it the product of more fundamental values?

Because public concerns about the environment inevitably lead to demands for governmental action, their relevance to political scientists is readily apparent. Salience of the environment relative to other issues helps shape party platforms and public policy decisions. For example, the worldwide surge in concern in the late 1980s led to the 'Earth Summit' in Rio de Janeiro in 1992 and a concerted effort by Canadian politicians to reach agreement on endangered species legislation. In some European countries, 'Green' parties have achieved significant political support. In Germany, the Green Party entered a formal coalition with the Social Democrats after the 1998 election. In British Columbia, conflicts between environmentalists and those whose livelihood depends on logging and mining have created significant divisions within the New Democratic Party.

This chapter tries to account for differences among members of the mass public in levels of environmental concern in Canada, in particular the priority given to the environment over other issues and willingness to pay for environmental protection and improvement. As we shall see, most researchers link concern in the mass public about environmental quality to value changes that have helped transform politics in advanced industrial democracies more generally since World War II. The new set of values is usually labelled 'post-materialist', following the lead of Ronald Inglehart (Inglehart, 1977), who presented the first extended discussion of the phenomenon. The transformations attributed to post-materialism include the rise of new social movements such as feminism, campaigns for racial equality, and the crusade against nuclear weapons, as well as the environmental movement. However, if value change were the only force at work, we would not likely see the ebb and flow of concern evident in public opinion and support for Green parties and other environmentalist groups. The research reported below demonstrates that, in Canada at least, mass-level support for the strategies and goals of environmentalism reflects a combination of values and personal characteristics such as level of education and economic well-being.

The analysis relies on the data from the most recent national election studies as well as a comprehensive survey of environmental attitudes in British Columbia conducted in 1995. The national surveys contain relatively few questions dealing with the environment. On the other hand, they include measures of personal values and allow one to generalize to the country as a whole. The BC survey contains many more questions dealing specifically with environmental issues, as well as some that are similar to those asked in the national surveys. Moreover, British Columbia is a particularly good setting for the study of attitudes towards the environment. The provincial economy depends heavily on resource industries, particularly logging and pulp and paper, which necessarily have an impact on the environment. It has the highest density of environmental activist organizations in Canada. In 1994 there were 2,250 groups listed in the Canadian Environmental Network's *Green List* database, of which 529 were located in British Columbia (Stefanick, 1994: 6). At 24 per cent of the total, the number of environmental groups in BC is roughly twice the province's share of the country's population.

Environmental activists are particularly militant. Their tactics have included an invasion of the provincial legislature and massive protests over clear-cut logging. Attempts to begin logging in Clayoquot Sound in 1993 led to one of the largest acts of civil disobedience in Canadian history and the arrest of over 800 protestors, including a prominent member of Parliament. Also, BC is the birthplace of Greenpeace International, perhaps the world's best known and most aggressive environmental action group (Harrison, 1996; Hoberg, 1996; Stefanick, 1995). Moreover, public support for environmentalists appears to be strong. Over 40 per cent of British Columbians report having contributed to environmental causes through financial donations (46.6 per cent), signing petitions (44.4 per cent), or product boycotts (43.4 per cent) (Blake et al., 1997: 461).

Theoretical and Methodological Approach

The primary objective of this analysis is to compare the relative importance of personal values, political ideology, and personal economic circumstances in accounting for public opinion on environmental issues. A central focus is the explanatory power of post-materialism. According to Inglehart (1977: 3), 'the values of Western publics have been shifting from an overwhelming emphasis on material well-being and physical security toward greater emphasis on the quality of life.' He attributes the change in priorities to the fact that 'an unprecedently large portion of Western populations have been raised under conditions of exceptional economic security' (ibid.). Since the appearance of his first book on the subject, Inglehart has gone on to document the gradual increase in the proportion of national populations giving priority to post-material values. A recent analysis covering 43 countries comprising 70 per cent of the world's population, including Canada, finds that 'people with "Post-materialist" values—emphasizing self-expression and the quality of life—are much more apt to give high priority to protecting the environment' (Inglehart, 1995: 57).

However, perceived quality of the environment at the local and global levels has an impact as well. According to one study (Rohrschneider, 1988), local environmental problems, while not themselves the direct cause of demands for greater action on behalf of the environment, reinforce concerns about the environment at the national level. Demands for fundamental change, as opposed to incremental improvements in the local habitat, are more characteristic of individuals who endorse post-materialism. A study of public opinion in Australia comes to a similar conclusion. 'Cosmopolitan concerns', i.e., concerns focused at the national and international levels, are rooted in value change and lead to environmental activism and political mobilization, whereas local concerns have fewer political implications (McAllister, 1994).

Kanji and Nevitte (1997) explore 'cognitive mobilization', 'value change', and 'new left libertarian' explanations of environmental concern and action in 17 advanced industrial countries. They find that all three have explanatory power, but cognitive mobilization, reflecting substantial increases in the numbers of people with advanced educational qualifications, appears to be a more powerful determinant of concern. However, economic considerations become important when the focus shifts to environmental action. Economic circumstances have a similar impact cross-nationally. Levels of environmental concern are higher among people in the most 'ecologically degraded environments', but public support for environmental protection policies is higher in countries with the lowest levels of pollution (Nevitte, 1996: 89–90; Inglehart, 1995: 57).

Previous research confirms the importance of values such as post-materialism in explaining individual concern and activity in the area of environmental protection in Canada (Blake et al., 1996, 1997). However, it also demonstrates the importance of distinguishing among different sources of concerns about the environment and among different kinds of environmental action when trying to account for the link between concerns and behaviour. For example, there is a weaker connection between values and a belief that environmental quality has deteriorated than between values and concerns about global problems. It is difficult for people to ignore conditions that surround them, such as pollution from automobiles, as opposed to situations that are less visible or geographically remote, such as ozone depletion. On the other hand, direct action on behalf of environmental causes and willingness to pay for improvements in environmental quality are more value-driven than 'green' consumer behaviour of the 'reduce, reuse, recycle' sort. Personal economic circumstances have an impact as well. Car commuters, the unemployed, and individuals whose economic position has deteriorated are less likely to support policies that require personal sacrifices to reduce pollution than people in different circumstances who hold similar value positions (Urmetzer et al., 1999). Women are also generally more concerned than men about environmental problems and appear more willing to modify their behaviour as a result (Blake et al., 1996, 1997).

In short, the literature suggests we need to be aware of more than variations in post-materialism when trying to account for differences in levels of concern about the environment, in the likelihood of engaging in action directed at protecting the environment, and in willingness to pay for environmental protection.

In the next section, I introduce a series of models to test the power of post-materialism as well as that of other variables in explaining environmental attitudes at the national level. Following that I test similar models using public opinion in British Columbia. The models all take the following form:

An individual's position on an environmental issue (the dependent variable) is a function of personal values, level of concern about the environment, and personal economic circumstances (the independent variables).

The dependent variables are:
- priority of environmental protection over job creation
- willingness to pay for environmental protection.

The independent variables are:
- gender
- level of education
- level of environmental concern
- post-materialism
- personal financial decline.

Complete details on how each variable was measured are contained in the Appendix. As explained below, multiple regression was used to test the impact of each independent or explanatory variable on each dependent variable.

Environmental Issues in the National Electorate

As can be seen in Table 8.1, although the proportion of Canadians choosing environmental protection over job creation has declined somewhat over the past decade, nearly half chose the environment over jobs when forced to choose between the two options.[2] Indeed, although not shown in the table, nearly two-thirds of Canadian voters in 1997 thought the government should do more to protect

Table 8.1: Environment vs Jobs, Canada, 1988–1997

	1988	1993	1997
Protecting the environment is more important than creating jobs			
Strongly agree	76.7	8.0	8.4
Agree		36.1	36.1
Disagree	23.3	46.5	44.5
Strongly disagree		9.4	11.0
	N (1,782)	(1,965)	(1,616)

Note: These results are taken from the Canadian election study for the year indicated. The 1988 study offered only two response categories, 'mostly agree' and 'mostly disagree'.

the environment even if it meant higher taxes. Nevertheless, obviously not everyone endorses these two positions. What about those who hold post-material values?

Value positions in the national survey were determined by respondent rankings of four policy goals:

- maintaining order in the nation
- giving people more say in important government decisions
- fighting unemployment
- protecting freedom of speech.

People were classified as 'post-materialists' if they ranked both 'protecting freedom of speech' and 'giving people more say over government decisions' ahead of 'maintaining order in the nation' and 'fighting unemployment'. If they reversed these priorities they were classified as 'materialists'. The residual or 'mixed' category contains those who gave some other ordering.

According to Figure 8.1, post-materialists are more likely to be found in the environmentalist camp, at least as far as giving the environment higher priority over job creation is concerned. A slight majority (52.4 per cent) of post-materialists, compared to only 37.4 per cent of materialists, rank the environment ahead of jobs. Those with a mixture of materialist and post-materialist values are in the middle, with 43.6 per cent choosing the environment over jobs. However, majorities of all three groups are willing to accept tax increases if necessary in order to increase environmental protection. Post-materialists are the strongest supporters of tax increases, but there is no difference between the mixed and materialist group.

As noted in the previous section, other studies have shown that support for environmentalism is higher among post-materialists, among women than men, and among those who perceive the environment to be threatened compared to those who do not. Some scholars have also argued that post-materialism is not the real force behind environmentalism in the mass public, suggesting instead a link to the substantial increase in educational qualifications since World War II (Dalton, 1984; Luskin, 1987). In this perspective, 'cognitive mobilization' rather than post-

Figure 8.1: Personal Values and Environmental Priorities, Canada, 1997

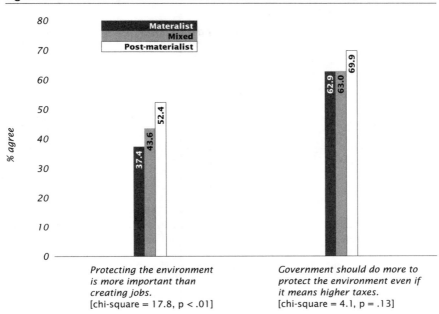

Protecting the environment
is more important than
creating jobs.
[chi-square = 17.8, p < .01]

Government should do more to
protect the environment even if
it means higher taxes.
[chi-square = 4.1, p = .13]

materialism is the most important explanatory factor. There is also some disagreement as to whether traditional ideological cleavages are relevant. Milbrath, among others, argues that 'the left-right argument between socialists and capitalists has little relevance for environmental problems' (Milbrath, 1984: 88). The problem that European socialist parties have had competing with various Green parties provides some evidence for this position. The NDP in British Columbia has also had to address divisions among its own supporters between environmentalists and organized labour in the private sector, most of whom are employed in extractive industries. Some evidence also indicates that support for environmentalism ebbs and flows with the business cycle, being higher in more prosperous times compared to periods of economic decline (Urmetzer et al., 1999).

Table 8.2 shows what happens when the independent variables described in the previous section are used to try to explain differences of opinion on two different dependent variables: priority of environmental protection over job creation and willingness to pay more taxes in order to pay for environmental protection.

The variables have been constructed so that the impact of a given independent variable is easy to assess. Variables with positive coefficients have a pro-environmental impact. Those with negative coefficients have an anti-environmental impact. Thus, in the case of the environment versus jobs, post-materialists give a higher priority to the environment whereas those whose family's financial situation has

Table 8.2: Predictors of Environmental Priority and Tax Increase Acceptance, Canada, 1997

Dependent variable	Protecting the environment more important than creating jobs		Increase taxes to pay for environmental protection	
	B	s.e.	B	s.e.
Female	−0.075**	0.014	−0.009	0.026
Post-secondary	0.026*	0.014	0.096**	0.027
Environmental concern	0.077**	0.018	0.124**	0.035
Financial decline	−0.036*	0.020	−0.100**	0.039
Post-materialism	0.060**	0.023	0.071	0.046
Constant	0.438**	0.023	0.537**	0.043
Adjusted R^2	0.04		0.02	
N	1,508		1,290	

**significant at .05 level.
*significant at .10 level.

Note: Columns labelled *B* list unstandardized regression coefficients; *s.e.* columns list associated standard errors.

deteriorated are less willing to choose the environment over jobs. Females give lower priority to the environment than males when presented with the trade-off with jobs.

The magnitude of each coefficient also has a specific interpretation. The −0.075 figure for females indicates that, other things being equal, women score 7.5 percentage points (i.e., a proportion of 0.075 times 100 = 7.5 per cent) lower than men on the environment-versus-jobs scale. Those with some post-secondary education score 2.6 points higher than people with lower levels of education. Each coefficient measures the independent effect of a given variable. Thus, for example, the significant coefficient for post-secondary education indicates that education has an effect on the priority given environmental protection even after gender, personal financial circumstances, environmental concerns, and personal values have been taken into account. Finally, the adjusted R^2 tells us what proportion of the total variation in the dependent variable is accounted for or 'explained' by the complete set of independent variables, 0.04 or 4 per cent for the environment-versus-jobs question.

It is clear from the table that post-materialism has a significant impact on the trade-off between environment and jobs. Post-materialists score 6 points higher than materialists do. However, the other independent variables also play a role in explaining differences within the mass public. This includes post-secondary education, our measure of 'cognitive mobilization'. A perception that environmental conditions have worsened, the best measure we have of the objective situation in which respondents find themselves, is also significant. In fact, it has the largest coefficient of all. While women exhibit higher levels of concern than men (47 per cent versus 39 per cent), once concern, economic situation, and values have been taken into account, they are less likely than men, on average, to give priority to the environment over jobs.

However, when respondents are asked to consider a personal financial sacrifice for environmental protection in the form of a tax increase, the second dependent variable shown in the table, the coefficient for post-materialism has the expected sign but is not significantly different from zero. Thus, post-materialists are no more likely than materialists to be willing to pay. Nor is gender statistically significant. However, people with the highest level of education are more willing to accept a tax increase.

One of the most important explanatory variables for the case of a tax increase, not surprisingly, is personal economic situation. Those whose financial situation has deteriorated are more opposed to a tax increase on behalf of the environment than are their more prosperous neighbours.[3]

Environmental Issues in the British Columbia Electorate

The analysis of public opinion on the environment in BC is based on a province-wide survey conducted in 1995.[4] Given its focus on environmental issues, the survey provides more information on these matters than do the national election studies. Unfortunately, as noted in the Appendix, not all the independent variables were measured in exactly the same way in the national and provincial surveys. However, there are enough similarities to permit a comparison of results with those discussed in the preceding section.

Table 8.3 shows the results for opinion on the trade-off between jobs and environment. As was the case at the national level, post-materialists and males give protection of the environment priority over job creation. The level of environmental concern is also linked to positions on the issue. However, two other explanatory variables exhibit a different pattern. Neither personal financial circumstances (measured by 'financial decline') nor post-secondary education has a significant effect.

With one exception, the variables significantly related to acceptance of a tax increase for environmental protection in Table 8.3 are identical to those at the national level (Table 8.2). Financial decline has the expected negative sign, but is not statistically significant. However, post-materialism, which had the expected sign but was not significant at the national level, is statistically significant in BC.[5]

To this point the analysis has provided reasonably strong support for the proposition that support for environmental policy is linked to the endorsement of post-material values. However, the combination of explanatory variables represented in Tables 8.2 and 8.3 have relatively low explanatory power. As discussed at greater length elsewhere (Blake et al., 1997; Dunlap and Van Liere, 1978), for some people pro-environment attitudes are not simply a reaction to direct experience with environmental problems. They question the placement of human beings at the top of a hierarchy of living things and advocate strong restraints on human activity in order to retain or restore a natural balance. Table 8.4 tries to capture more abstract values specifically linked to environmental issues by including an additional

Table 8.3: Predictors of Environmental Priority and Tax Increase Acceptance, British Columbia, 1995

Dependent variable	Protecting the environment more important than creating jobs		Increase taxes to pay for environmental protection	
	B	s.e.	B	s.e.
Female	−0.035**	0.014	−0.008	0.016
Post-secondary	−0.018	0.014	0.041**	0.017
Environmental concern	0.215**	0.027	0.185**	0.031
Financial decline	0.002	0.017	−0.029	0.019
Post-materialism	0.369**	0.036	0.329**	0.057
Constant	0.335**	0.028	0.321**	0.032
Adjusted R^2	0.08		0.05	
N	1,569		1,570	

**significant at .05 level.
*significant at .10 level.

Note: Columns labelled *B* list unstandardized regression coefficients; *s.e.* columns list associated standard errors.

Table 8.4: Impact of Environmentalism on Environmental Policy Attitudes, British Columbia, 1995

Dependent variable	Protecting the environment more important than creating jobs		Increase taxes to pay for environmental protection	
	B	s.e.	B	s.e.
Female	−0.056**	0.014	−0.028*	0.017
Post-secondary	−0.021	0.014	0.033*	0.017
Environmental concern	0.140**	0.028	0.135**	0.033
Financial decline	−0.003	0.017	−0.023	0.020
Post-materialism	0.173**	0.051	0.021**	0.062
Environmentalism	0.646**	0.047	0.450**	0.056
Constant	0.016	0.037	0.095**	0.044
Adjusted R^2	0.19		0.09	
N	1,326		1,372	

**significant at .05 level.
*significant at .10 level.

Note: Columns labelled *B* list unstandardized regression coefficients; *s.e.* columns list associated standard errors.

explanatory variable labelled 'environmentalism'. As described in the Appendix the measure combines responses to 10 statements that include some of the major tenets in the environmentalist creed. It has an even greater impact than post-materialism on the priority of the environment question and including it more than doubles the overall explanatory power of the variables in Table 8.3. The adjusted R^2 value rises from 0.08 in Table 8.3 to 0.19 in Table 8.4. Environmentalism has a similar, though less dramatic, effect on willingness to accept a tax increase to pay for environmental protection.[6]

More sophisticated measurement of opinion on environmental protection options also pays off. Obviously there are factors other than personal economic circumstances, materialist values, or relative lack of concern for the environment that could help account for giving jobs priority over the environment or opposition to tax increases for environmental protection. For example, some people may believe that other policy instruments, such as taxes specifically targeting pollution sources or stricter environment regulations, would be more effective. Recognizing that 'willingness to pay' for environmental protection could mean a number of things, a more complex measure combining several policy options was devised and used as the dependent variable in regression models with the same independent variables as in Table 8.4.

The dependent variable in Table 8.5—willingness to pay for environmental protection—incorporates responses to questions about five kinds of economic sacrifices in the interest of environmental protection in addition to higher taxes and job losses. As listed in the Appendix, these are limits on population growth, tougher

Table 8.5: Predictors of Willingness to Pay for Environment, British Columbia, 1995

	Model without Environmentalism Measure		Model with Environmentalism Measure	
	B	*s.e.*	*B*	*s.e.*
Female	0.012*	0.009	−0.007	0.008
Post-secondary	0.006	0.009	0.007	0.009
Environmental concern	0.170**	0.017	0.113**	0.016
Financial decline	−0.028**	0.010	−0.028**	0.010
Post-materialism	0.340**	0.031	0.203**	0.030
Environmentalism			0.500**	0.028
Constant	0.526**	0.017	0.272**	0.022
Adjusted R^2	0.16		0.32	
N	1,394		1,311	

**significant at .05 level.
*significant at .10 level.

Notes: Dependent variable: 7-item willingness-to-pay scale (see Appendix). Columns labelled *B* list unstandardized regression coefficients; *s.e.* columns list associated standard errors.

anti-pollution laws, higher costs for utilities, restrictions on industrial activity, and increased regulation of business. There is little doubt that those willing to contemplate most or all of these sacrifices place a high premium on environmental protection. With this more elaborate measure of willingness to pay, post-materialism is seen to have a strong impact. Personal economic circumstances are important as well. Once again, environmentalism makes a powerful contribution to explanation. Adding it to the model raises explained variance from 16 to 32 per cent.

Conclusion

Data from the 1997 Canadian Election Study indicate that British Columbia voters are more concerned about the environment than those in any other province— 53 per cent believe that the environment has deteriorated, compared to 44 per cent in the nation as a whole. However, they are no more willing to sacrifice jobs or pay higher taxes to protect the environment.[7] Moreover, despite differences in levels of concern nationally and in British Columbia and differences in how certain variables are measured, the models developed to explain willingness to make sacrifices in the interests of environmental protection are strikingly similar.

Post-materialism is a key determinant of the priority assigned to environmental protection versus jobs at both levels. Moreover, while in the country as a whole post-materialists are no more likely than materialists to endorse personal sacrifices in the form of higher taxation in order to increase environmental protection, this is probably an artifact of using such a crude measure of willingness to pay for environmental protection. Using a more sensitive indicator of willingness to make financial sacrifices for the environment, available in the BC survey, confirms the impact of post-materialism.[8]

Values are not the only factors at work. Concern about the quality of the local environment is linked to greater support for environmental protection policies. However, in the national models, this is counterbalanced to some extent by less support among those experiencing a deteriorating family economic situation. The situation in BC is slightly more complicated. While concern has the same effect, financial situation is statistically significant only in models using the more elaborate measure of willingness to pay.

Finally, while post-materialism is clearly linked to views on environmental policy, it is not the only set of values at work. This analysis also demonstrates the crucial importance of value positions based specifically on the weighing of the benefits of population growth and economic development against the costs in terms of environmental degradation.

Appendix: Details of Variable Construction

For both the national and British Columbia analyses, female and post-secondary education are dummy variables scored, respectively, 1 for females, 0 for males and 1 for some post-secondary education, 0 for none. The specific questions used to construct these variables are described below. In most cases questions were worded differently in the national and BC surveys or offered somewhat different response alternatives. However, all variables were rescaled to the range 0 to 1 to compensate, in part, for these differences as well as to allow comparison of the relative impact of particular variables.

1. Environment versus Jobs

In both surveys, respondents were asked to respond to the statement: 'Protecting the environment is more important than creating jobs.' National survey respondents were given four alternatives from 'strongly agree' to 'strongly disagree'. BC respondents were asked to answer with a score from 1 (strongly agree) to 7 (strongly disagree). Responses in both surveys were rescaled to run from 0 (most job-oriented) to 1 (most environment-oriented).

2. Increase Taxes to Pay for Environmental Protection

NATIONAL SURVEY

Respondents were asked to choose between two options:

- The government should do more to protect the environment even if it means higher taxes.
- The government should keep taxes from going up even if this means less protection for the environment.

Responses were rescaled to run from 0 (keep taxes from going up) to 1 (protect the environment).

BC SURVEY

Respondents were presented with the statement: 'The government should do more to protect the environment even if it means higher taxes.' Response options ranged from 1 (strongly agree) to 7 (strongly disagree). These were recoded and rescaled to run from 0 (strongly disagree) to 1 (strongly agree).

3. Willingness to Pay

Information used to construct this scale was available only in the BC survey. It is based on responses to the following items.

- The size of British Columbia's population must be limited even if it means less economic development.
- There should be tougher anti-pollution laws, even if such laws decrease our standard of living.
- We should do more to protect the environment even if it means losing jobs.
- [Government should] place higher environmental taxes on gasoline.
- Do you support or oppose sharply limiting resource companies' access to BC's wilderness lands, even though it would mean a loss of jobs in some areas?
- Do you support or oppose closing down businesses that do not meet environmental regulations after they've received a warning, regardless of job losses?
- Do you support or oppose requiring electric and gas utilities to spend a larger share of their budgets on ways to increase energy efficiency, even if it means higher rates for consumers?

Respondents were asked to answer using a scale from 1 (strongly agree) to 7 (strongly disagree). Responses were averaged and then rescaled to run from 0 (least willing to pay) to 1 (most willing to pay).

4. Environmentalism

The information used to construct this scale is available only in the BC survey. Respondents were asked to choose a score from 1 (strongly agree) to 7 (strongly disagree) in response to each of the following statements:

- When people interfere with nature it often produces disastrous consequences
- The 'ecological crisis' has been greatly exaggerated.
- People must live in harmony with nature in order to survive.
- People are severely abusing the environment.
- We are approaching the limit to the number of people that the earth can support.
- Plants and animals exist primarily to be used by people.
- To maintain a healthy economy we will have to control industrial growth.
- People have the right to modify the natural environment to suit their needs.
- People need not adapt to the environment because they can remake it to suit their needs.
- There are limits to growth beyond which our industrialized society cannot expand.

Responses were recoded so that higher scores on each question indicate a pro-environmentalist response and rescaled to run from 0 (least environmentalist) to 1 (most environmentalist).

5. Environmental Concern

NATIONAL SURVEY

In the national survey, concern was measured using responses to the question: 'Do you think that pollution in Canada has got worse, got better, or stayed about the same in the last few years?' Responses were rescaled to run from 0 (got better) to 1 (got worse).

BC SURVEY

In the BC survey, concern was measured using responses to the question: 'On a scale from 1 to 7, could you please tell me how concerned you are about the quality of the environment in your local area?' Responses were rescaled to run from 0 (not concerned at all) to 1 (very concerned).

6. Financial Decline

Both national and BC survey respondents were asked this question: 'Would you say you and your family are better off, or worse off, financially than you were a year ago?' 'Same' was also offered as a response category. Responses were rescaled to run from 0 (worse off) to 1 (better off).

7. Post-materialism

NATIONAL SURVEY

In the national survey, respondents were asked to rank the following goals:

- maintaining order in the nation
- giving people more say in important government decisions
- fighting unemployment
- protecting freedom of speech

Respondents were classified as 'post-materialists' if they ranked both 'protecting freedom of speech' and 'giving people more say over government decisions' ahead of 'maintaining order

in the nation' and 'fighting unemployment'. If they reversed these priorities they were classified as 'materialists'. The residual or 'mixed' category contains those who gave some other
ordering. Scores were rescaled from 0 (materialist) to 1 (post-materialist).

BC SURVEY

In the BC survey, respondents were asked to indicate whether they give high priority,
medium priority, low priority, or no priority to the each of following eleven goals:

Materialist Goals

- maintain a high rate of economic growth
- make sure Canada has strong defence forces
- maintain a strong economy
- fight rising prices
- maintain order in the nation
- fight against crime

Post-materialist Goals

- give people more say in important government decisions
- progress towards a less impersonal, more humane society
- see that people have more say in how things get decided at work and in their community
- protect freedom of speech
- protect nature from being spoiled and polluted
- progress toward a society where ideas are more important than money.

Each respondent was given a score of +1 for each post-materialist value assigned high priority. An additional point was added for each materialist value considered to have low priority
or no priority at all. Then, a point was subtracted for each materialist value viewed as high
priority. Finally, the scale was adjusted to produce a range of scores from 0 (materialist) to 1
(post-materialist).

Notes

1. These data were supplied by Robert Burge of the Centre for Public Opinion Research at
   Queen's University.

2. The 1988, 1993, and 1997 Canadian Election Studies were conducted by the Institute for
   Social Research, York University. The principal investigators for the 1988 study were
   Richard Johnston, André Blais, Henry Brady, and Jean Crête. The principal investigators
   for the 1993 study were Richard Johnston, André Blais, Henry Brady, Elisabeth Gidengil,
   and Neil Nevitte. The principal investigators for the 1997 study were André Blais, Elisabeth Gidengil, Richard Nadeau, and Neil Nevitte. The data for 1988 were made available
   by Richard Johnston. The data for 1993 and 1997 were supplied by the ISR at York University. Neither the ISR nor the principal investigators are responsible for the analysis or interpretations in this chapter.

3. Political ideology, as measured by support or opposition to cuts in welfare spending, is
   also significantly related to both independent variables. Those who favour welfare cuts
   give the environment a lower priority than job creation and are more opposed to tax
   increases. However, because no similar measure of ideology was available in the BC data
   it has been omitted from the table.

4. The survey was conducted by Campbell, Goodell, Traynor Consultants Limited of Vancouver under the supervision of Donald E. Blake and Neil Guppy. A total of 1652 telephone interviews was completed from the general population age 18 or over. These were supplemented by an additional 100 interviews from Mandarin- and Cantonese-speaking households, 101 from Punjabi-speaking households in the Lower Mainland, and 101 interviews from the Abbotsford area. The survey is a component of the Fraser Basin Eco-Research Study at the University of British Columbia. Funding from the Social Sciences and Humanities Research Council, the Medical Research Council, and the National Science and Engineering Research Council for the study is gratefully acknowledged. Arlene Strom and Peter Urmetzer provided invaluable assistance in developing the survey instrument.

5. As explained in the Appendix, post-materialism was measured somewhat differently in the two surveys, hence one would not expect identical results.

6. Environmentalism and post-materialism are moderately correlated (Pearson $r = 0.25$). The fact that the two variables share some explanatory power accounts for the drop in the value of the post-materialism coefficients between Tables 8.3 and 8.4.

7. On the environment-versus-jobs trade-off, 46.2 per cent of British Columbia respondents chose the environment compared to 44.5 per cent for the sample as a whole. Support for higher taxes was 63.5 per cent in BC compared to 64.5 per cent nationally.

8. Differences between left and right are also significant regardless of the topic or level of analysis. While environmentalism is often portrayed as a 'new politics' issue, most proposals for environmental protection involve increased government activity of some sort. The role and size of government has become a major political issue so it is not surprising that environmental problems have been caught up in the debate between left and right. This theme is explored in Blake et al. (1997). Unfortunately, differences in the way political ideology is measured in the national and BC surveys prevent our examining its effect in this chapter.

References

Blake, Donald E., Neil Guppy, and Peter Urmetzer. 1996. 'Being Green in BC: Public Opinion on Environmental Issues', *BC Studies* 112: 41–61.

———, ———, and ———. 1997. 'Canadian Public Opinion and Environmental Action: Evidence from British Columbia', *Canadian Journal of Political Science* 30: 452–72.

Carty, R.K., ed. 1996. *Politics, Policy and Government in British Columbia*. Vancouver: University of British Columbia Press.

Dalton, Russell. 1984. 'Cognitive Mobilization and Partisan Dealignment in Advanced Industrial Democracies', *Journal of Politics* 46: 264–84.

Dunlap, Riley, and Kent Van Liere. 1978. 'The New Environmental Paradigm', *The Journal of Environmental Education* 9: 10–19.

Harrison, Kathryn. 1996. 'Environmental Protection in British Columbia: Post-material Values, Organized Interests and Party Politics', in Carty (1996: 290–309).

Hoberg, George. 1996. 'The Politics of Sustainability: Forest Policy in British Columbia', in Carty (1996: 272–89).

Inglehart, Ronald. 1977. *The Silent Revolution: Changing Values and Political Styles among Western Publics*. Princeton, NJ: Princeton University Press.

———. 1995. 'Public Support for Environmental Protection: Objective Problems and Subjective Values in 43 Societies', *PS: Political Science and Politics* 28: 51–72.

Kanji, Mebs, and Neil Nevitte. 1997. 'Environmental Support, Concern and Action: An Exploratory Crossnational Analysis', *International Journal of Public Opinion Research* 9: 66–76.

Luskin, R. 1987. 'Measuring Political Sophistication', *American Journal of Political Science*, 31: 856–99.

McAllister, Ian. 1994. 'Dimensions of Environmentalism: Public Opinion, Political Activism and Party Support in Australia', *Environmental Politics* 3: 22–42.

Milbrath, Lester. 1984. *Environmentalists: Vanguard for a New Society*. Albany: State University of New York Press.

Nevitte, Neil. 1996. *The Decline of Deference*. Peterborough, Ont.: Broadview Press.

——— and Mebs Kanji. 1995. 'Explaining Environmental Concern and Action in Canada', *Applied Behavioral Science Review* 3: 85–102.

Rohrschneider, Robert. 1988. 'Citizens' Attitudes Toward Environmental Issues: Selfish or Selfless', *Comparative Political Studies* 21: 347–67.

Stefanick, Lorna. 1994. 'The Green Wave: Canada's Environmental Lobby', paper presented to the annual meeting of the Canadian Political Science Association, Calgary.

———. 1995. 'From Protest to Participation: A Comparison of Environmental Activism in B.C. and Ontario', paper presented to the annual meeting of the Canadian Political Science Association, Montreal.

Urmetzer, Peter, Donald E. Blake, and Neil Guppy. 1999. 'The Environment and Public Opinion: Changes Over Time in the United States, Canada, United Kingdom, and (West) Germany', unpublished manuscript.

Chapter 9

Understanding Opinion Formation on Quebec Sovereignty

PIERRE MARTIN AND RICHARD NADEAU

On 30 October 1995, Quebecers voted in a referendum that could have transformed the province into a sovereign country. The result was surprisingly close: 50.6 per cent voted 'No' and 49.4 per cent voted 'Yes'. To make sense of contemporary Canadian politics, it is essential to try to understand the formation of opinion on sovereignty in Quebec. This issue is also a fertile ground for inquiry about the nature of political choice. As we explore this case, we develop a framework for analysing political choice that integrates the existing literature and evidence into a coherent model of how Quebecers choose to support or reject sovereignty.

Our framework of analysis includes three dimensions. *Dispositions* are enduring traits, such as socio-demographic characteristics, values, and identity, that make a voter more or less receptive to sovereignty or federalism. *Incentives* are the perceived costs and benefits associated with each option in economic, cultural, or political terms. A third dimension encompasses more proximate or *contextual* factors related to the act of making a choice, including the influence of leaders and campaign dynamics. Although this model is static, it has implications for the understanding of opinion change. Quebec opinion has evolved considerably since the contemporary sovereignty movement rose to prominence in the 1960s, but this trend has not followed a straight path upward. Opinion fluctuates yearly and monthly. It can also shift in a matter of days, as it did during the 1980 and 1995 referendum campaigns. In this chapter, we explore the three dimensions of opinion formation and show how they can help us understand both long-term trends and short-term shifts in Quebec opinion.

Dimensions of Individual Political Choice

Political scientists often distinguish between sociological (or social-psychological) approaches and economic (or rational-choice) approaches to political behaviour. The former emphasize identity, values, and group ties as determinants of choice, while the latter give priority to the way individuals assess the relative attractiveness of the options at stake.

Studies of opinion formation on sovereignty show that both types of factors operate in the choices of Quebecers. Early studies emphasized sociological and socio-demographic factors, on the assumption that an individual's choice is conditioned by the interests of his or her reference group or groups (Blais and Nadeau, 1984; Pinard and Hamilton, 1984a, 1984b, 1986). Recent studies integrate insights from the economic approach (Blais et al., 1995b, 1996; Nadeau and Fleury, 1995; Martin, 1994). Some authors claim that perceptions of costs and benefits are largely determined by dispositions (Howe, 1998), while others argue that cost-benefit calculations underlie even deeply entrenched dispositions (Prager, 1996). Empirically, it may not be possible to disentangle the part that incentives play in forming and transforming identities or the extent to which cost-benefit evaluations simply reflect prior dispositions. Thus, instead of pitting sociological and economic approaches against one another, we combine dispositions and incentives in a model of individual choice where both can be interrelated yet analytically distinct (the terms 'dispositions' and 'incentives' are borrowed from Chong, 2000: 47).

To illustrate the three dimensions of our model, let us consider an analogy with another kind of big decision: buying a house. Dispositions are akin to the buyer's objective needs (interests) and tastes (values, including considerations of identity that can make a given location desirable or unacceptable), while incentives are comparable to the balance of costs and benefits (certain or uncertain; material or immaterial; short-term or long-term). If a house corresponds to the buyer's needs and tastes (if dispositions are favourable), she may be willing to pay a high purchase price and high future maintenance costs. A negatively disposed buyer, however, would need to be convinced that short-term and long-term costs were considerably lower than those of alternative choices, or she might simply reject the house at any price. Note that in this case, as in any political choice, much of the cost depends on the decision-maker's more or less informed forecast of future events.

Beyond dispositions and incentives, contextual factors may also affect the choice. In the house purchase analogy, the buyer may be influenced by advice about alternative choices from a trusted person, just as voters may be influenced by how much they trust the leaders defending contending options. Voters, like buyers, may also be uncertain, confused, or they may feel insufficiently informed to compare alternatives.

Dispositions: Identity, Social Groups, and Values

When individuals assess competing political options, they rarely do so in a vacuum, without preconceptions. Indeed, any political choice involves a priori preferences (interests or values), which tend to condition the perception of contending options or to make an individual more or less receptive to arguments for or against either option. Such dispositions may be linked to group membership or to a process of identity formation. Support for sovereignty in Quebec is shaped by a number of lasting influences, which we divide into three broad categories:

socio-demographic categories, collective identity, and values. We also discuss another kind of disposition, which we have termed 'cognitive engagement'.

Socio-demographic Categories: Who Voted for Sovereignty and Why?

The most important cleavage over sovereignty is language, because arguments for this option begin with the need for the political means that will allow Quebec to preserve and promote its distinctness as a predominantly French-speaking society. Using a survey conducted immediately before the referendum, we estimate that 57.8 per cent of Francophones voted 'Yes' while only 5.6 per cent of non-Francophones made the same choice (see Table 9.1).[1] This difference is not surprising: if most French speakers identify primarily with Quebec, nearly all non-Francophones identify with Canada and its English-speaking majority. The same survey showed that most Francophones identified primarily or exclusively with Quebec (58 per cent) while as few as 7 per cent of non-Francophones identified with Quebec first (data not shown on Table 9.1; see Blais et al., 1995a).

Early studies interpreted the growth of nationalism as a reflection of the interests of middle-class professionals, whose work was linked with the use of the French language, and public-sector employees (Breton,1964). Others have noted the predominance of intellectuals in the Parti Québécois and the independence movement (Pinard and Hamilton, 1984a). To explain mobilization among workers, sociologists have hypothesized that modernization increases the level of competition for jobs across ethnic groups, thus fuelling grievances and nationalist responses (Bélanger and Pinard, 1991). This argument was plausible in the 1960s and 1970s, when monolingual French speakers occupied the bottom of Quebec's socio-economic scale, but it is less relevant after a quarter-century of language legislation and of notable economic improvement for Francophones (Vaillancourt, 1993).

Neither education nor income had a clear-cut effect on the 1995 vote, in contrast with 1980 (Blais and Nadeau, 1984). Also, differences between occupational groups decreased over time (Blais and Nadeau, 1992; Nadeau, 1992). Among Francophones, the 'Yes' vote was highest among students and professionals. The fact that blue-collar workers, union members, and the unemployed were more likely to vote 'Yes' reflects in part the ideological tone of the campaign, enduring differences between political parties, and business resistance to sovereignty. Although recent surveys on sovereignty have not included measures of union membership, the relationship between union membership and vote for sovereigntist parties is well documented (see Nevitte et al., 1999, ch. 10).

A gender gap also has been observed in numerous sovereignty polls, as women tend to be more opposed to sovereignty than men. The leaders of the 'Yes' campaign in 1995 were aware of this and targeted much of their advertising towards women. This gap is only partly explained by the fact that women tend to live longer than men. Other factors have been proposed to explain this difference but few if any appear conclusive (Gidengil, 1996).

Table 9.1: Estimated 'Yes' Vote in the 1995 Referendum, within Categories of Voters

	All Respondents 'Yes' per cent (n)		Francophones 'Yes' per cent (n)		Non-Francophones 'Yes' per cent (n)	
Total Vote	49.4	(986)	57.8	(827)	5.6	(159)
Identification						
Quebecer only	92	(239)	92	(236)	100	(3)
Quebecer first	75	(250)	76	(243)	47	(7)
Both equally/none/n.a.	20	(322)	25	(249)	4	(73)
Canadian first	7	(97)	12	(55)	0	(43)
Canadian only	6	(78)	11	(44)	0	(34)
Age						
18–34	60	(353)	70	(292)	8	(61)
35–54	52	(364)	60	(312)	5	(53)
55 and over	32	(268)	38	(222)	2	(46)
Gender						
Women	46	(514)	54	(433)	4	(81)
Men	53	(472)	62	(394)	7	(78)
Education						
Primary	42	(102)	44	(96)	10	(7)
Secondary	52	(422)	60	(364)	4	(58)
College/some univ.	52	(277)	61	(230)	8	(47)
University degree	44	(166)	57	(124)	5	(43)
Family Income						
Less than $20,000	49	(188)	55	(164)	5	(23)
$20,000–$39,999	54	(322)	61	(278)	5	(44)
$40,000–$59,999	51	(218)	60	(180)	11	(38)
$60,000–$79,999	59	(65)	68	(57)	0	(8)
$80,000 and over	43	(75)	57	(57)	0	(18)
Employment Category						
High/middle manager	30	(55)	44	(38)	0	(17)
Professional	61	(137)	74	(114)	0	(24)
Small owner	55	(56)	63	(46)	21	(11)
White-collar worker	49	(118)	55	(100)	15	(18)
Blue-collar worker	59	(210)	65	(185)	8	(25)
At home	35	(94)	42	(77)	6	(17)
Student	62	(89)	70	(78)	0	(11)
Retired	36	(187)	42	(155)	4	(32)
Unemployed	54	(32)	64	(26)	0	(5)

Note: Among respondents who said they would vote in the referendum, 11.8 per cent did not reveal their choice. For them, voting intention was obtained from a multivariate prediction model that relies on variables known to correlate highly with the vote, including the identity variables, the cost-benefit variables, and socio-demographic characteristics. This model is used to apportion the votes of non-respondents in a way that makes the overall total correspond with the actual result of the referendum held a few days later (49.4 per cent of 'Yes'). Percentages may not add up to 100 because of rounding; case totals may not add exactly because each case was weighted.

Source: Blais et al. (1995a).

Finally, aside from language, the most critical socio-demographic factor is the differences among generations. Since collective identity in Quebec is tied to language, and because identity acquired at a young age can have lasting effects, we discuss the effect of generation in conjunction with identity.

Collective Identity: From French Canadians to Quebecers

Collective identity is the sense of primary allegiance to a political community. To understand the rise of sovereignty since the 1960s, we need to look at the foundations of collective identity and at the transformation of underlying attitudes towards Quebec and Canada. As postwar Quebec modernized, notably during the 'Quiet Revolution' of the 1960s, the focus of collective identity of French-speaking Quebecers began to shift from the traditional identification as French Canadians, largely based on religion and ethnicity, to an identification as Quebecers, based on a shared language and on the evolving institutions of a modernizing society (McRoberts, 1993; Bourque and Duchastel, 1996).

These changes took some time to register in the public psyche (see Figure 9.1). In 1970, 21 per cent (mostly the young) identified themselves as Quebecers, while 44 per cent and 34 per cent identified themselves as French Canadians and Canadians, respectively (Pinard, 1970). Less than 30 years later, identification with Quebec became dominant (63 per cent in 1997), partly due to the replacement of older generations by younger ones, who are more likely to identify with Quebec, but also due to the impact of social change and political events.

This identity shift evolved in a party system where the dominant parties, the Parti Québécois (PQ) and the Quebec Liberal Party, articulated competing nationalist visions. The PQ's sovereignty project and the Liberals' demands for autonomy within the federation were responses to this emerging collective identity, and both fuelled its consolidation. The first PQ government (1976–81) coincided with a rise in identification with Quebec. In the late 1980s the rise was associated not with the fortunes of sovereigntists but rather with the federalists' efforts to obtain Quebec's constitutional recognition as a 'distinct society'. Following the Meech Lake fiasco in 1990, identification with Quebec increased yet again, and this increased level survived the referendum defeat of 1995.

Identification with Quebec is offset for some by feelings of attachment to Canada. Between 1980 and 1995, the proportion of Francophones who agreed completely that they were 'profoundly attached to Canada' dropped from 48 per cent to 32 per cent (Pinard, 1980; SOM/SRC, 1995). Within particular generations, however, such dispositions remained stable through the 1980s and the replacement of older generations by the young explained most of the overall change (Nadeau, 1992). The stability of support within generations leads some to project that, other things being equal, demographic change alone would generate an annual increase of half a percentage point in support for sovereignty after 1995 (Nadeau et al., 1995).

Figure 9.1: Collective Identification Among French-Speaking Quebecers, 1970–1997

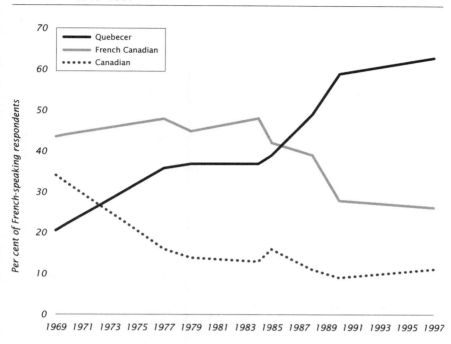

Sources: Pinard et al., 1997; Bernier et al., 1998.

Values and the New Quebec Nationalism

Social values tend to shape political behaviour and to give meaning to political movements. The new Quebec nationalism, emerging from the rapid postwar modernization of state and society, has been in many ways a reaction against the traditional values of the old French-Canadian nationalism. This traditional nationalism was conservative, rural, ethnic, centred around the Catholic Church, and wary of state intervention. The new Quebec nationalism is largely progressive, urban, secular, and interventionist, and it strives to define itself as civic.

The first and perhaps most enduring difference between the value structure of sovereigntists and that of the old nationalism is religious practice. Since the 1960s, surveys have shown that, even when controlling for age and other attributes, the degree of religious practice is negatively related with sovereignty support (Pinard and Hamilton, 1984b; Blais and Nadeau, 1984).

Second, the PQ and the sovereignty movement have been shaped by the militancy of the more progressive elements in Quebec society. Although the PQ attracts some conservative nationalists, and although leftist groups have been critical of the PQ's record in government, the sovereignty movement remains left of centre and as such enjoys the support of major labour unions. Surveys confirm that sovereigntists tend to be more on the left ideologically and closer to unions than federalists (Nevitte et al., 1999, ch. 10).

Third, Quebec nationalists emphasize collective rights. In the 1950s and 1960s, Pierre Elliott Trudeau argued that the best antidote to the backwardness of French-Canadian society was a turn to individualistic liberalism. Quebec's new nationalists, however, whether they support sovereignty or autonomy, tend to share a belief in collective rights. This clash of values is most acute over language rights. Thus, most Francophones favour the maintenance of strong collective defences for the French language in Quebec, and for many of them this is a central consideration in their support of sovereignty (Nadeau and Fleury, 1995).

Fourth, the old French-Canadian nationalism was often branded as xenophobic and intolerant, and critics of the new Quebec nationalism sometimes voice the same opinion (Breton and Breton, 1995). This conjecture, largely based on anecdotal evidence, does not stand up to close empirical scrutiny (Martin, 1998). Even analysts not known for their pro-sovereignty leanings have noted that sovereigntists are no more and no less intolerant than other Quebecers, and that fears of a weakening or disappearance of the French language should not be confused with intolerance towards non-Francophones (Dion, 1996).

Fifth, political scientists have noted a shift towards 'post-materialist' values in industrial societies (Inglehart 1990). This shift is congruent with values underpinning the new Quebec nationalism. Research shows that PQ militants are more prone to post-materialism than liberals (Pelletier and Guérin, 1996), and postmaterialist values tend to be positively associated with support for sovereignty (Martin, 1998).

The changes in dispositions identified above have benefited the sovereignty movement. These changes have been gradual, however, despite the wide variations of opinion recorded in polls over this same period.

Cognitive Obstacles to Deliberation

Although group interests, identity, and values provide a firm base to allow individuals to make a choice between sovereignty and federalism, our model emphasizes the capacity of each voter to assess the relative costs and benefits of each option, and this cognitive process may be quite complex. In short, to make a difficult choice in support of radical change, an individual must first invest some effort in acquiring information and engaging in deliberation—whether with others or within himself or herself. Other studies of referendum voting have suggested that voters who resist engaging in deliberation tend to support the status quo (Bowler and Donovan, 1998: 34–5; Butler and Kitzinger, 1976: 281).

In analyses of both the 1980 and 1995 referendum results in Quebec, we have shown that interest in politics is clearly related to support for the 'Yes' option (Martin and Nadeau, 2000). This suggests that the proponents of major change face a double challenge. Not only do they need to convince voters of the relative merits of their option, but they must first overcome political apathy and make sure that voters are tuned into the debate. By contrast, proponents of the status quo face no such prior obstacle. If people remain disengaged, they will also tend to resist change. In the run-up to the 1995 referendum, public interest on constitutional issues was at a high point, but the level of interest has since ebbed palpably.

Incentives: Weighing the Costs and Benefits of Sovereignty

Economic explanations of political choice revolve around the notion that individuals choose on the basis of the costs and benefits of contending options. This raises several questions. Which incentives matter the most? Do people make political decisions based on past experiences, present circumstances, or future expectations? Is the immediate future more important than the long term? And in assessments of the costs and benefits of various options, do individuals refer to themselves, the groups to which they belong, or society at large as the benchmark for evaluation? In this section we review the literature that has addressed these questions, but first we begin with a look at what the 'market' for the sovereignty option looks like.

The 'Market' for the Sovereignty Option

The evolution of collective identities in Quebec suggests that an increasing number of people have become favourably disposed towards Quebec sovereignty. Such disposition does not automatically translate into actual support, however. The problem is that sovereignty itself and the transition period leading to it entail a complex balance of potential costs and benefits.

In a February 1995 CROP/SRC survey, respondents were asked how they would vote under three different pairs of positive and negative scenarios related to three types of incentives: *cultural* (the status of French), *economic* (the existence of an economic association with Canada), and *political* (whether Quebec would keep its territory) (see Figure 9.2). In each case, the more optimistic scenario yielded approximately 56 per cent of 'Yes' and 36 per cent of 'No', while the scenario that emphasized costs drew about 28 per cent of 'Yes' and 64 per cent of 'No'. By combining individual answers to these questions, we can construct a scale that differentiates between solid 'Yes' voters (who support sovereignty under all scenarios, even the least favourable) and solid 'No' voters (those who always oppose it, even under optimistic scenarios).

On the whole, 20 per cent of respondents always said 'Yes' and 28 per cent always said 'No' (85 per cent of the non-Francophones). These two groups of seemingly 'immovable' voters consist largely of people with a strong sense of attachment to Quebec (among consistent 'Yes' supporters) and an attachment to Canada that at least equals their attachment to Quebec (among consistent opponents). The real market for votes is found between these extremes, primarily among the 20 per cent who reveal themselves most sensitive to variations in incentives.

Figure 9.2: Sensitivity to Cost/Benefits and Sovereignty Support, by Levels of Attachment to Quebec and Canada

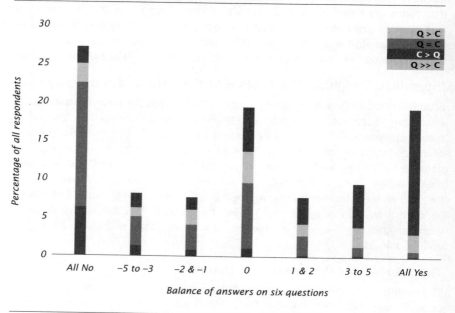

Note: Each category on the horizontal axis represents the balance of positive answers (scored +1), negative answers (−1), and 'don't know/no answer' (0) on the following six questions: How would you vote in a referendum on sovereignty under the following conditions. Would you vote for sovereignty or against sovereignty: (1) if you were fairly sure that the rest of Canada would maintain an economic association with a sovereign Quebec? (Y=57%/N=36%/DK=7%); (2) if you were fairly sure that the rest of Canada would not maintain an economic association with a sovereign Quebec? (Y=28%/N=64%/DK=8%); (3) if you were fairly sure that the situation of the French language would be better in a sovereign Quebec? (Y=56%/N=37%/DK=7%); (4) if you were fairly sure that the situation of the French language would not be better in a sovereign Quebec? (Y=28%/N=64%/ DK=8%); (5) if you were fairly sure that the rest of Canada would recognize Quebec's present territory? (Y=56%/N=36%/DK=8%); (6) if you were fairly sure that the rest of Canada would not recognize Quebec's present territory? (Y=27 per cent/N=65 per cent/DK=8 per cent). Only 3 per cent answered none of the six questions.

The bars represent the percentage of all respondents, divided into four groups defined by the level of relative attachment to Quebec and Canada: much more attached to Quebec (38%); more attached to Quebec (15%); equally attached to Quebec and Canada (36%); or more attached to Canada (10%).

Source: CROP/SRC Survey # 4369, Feb. 1995.

Which Incentives Matter?

In an October 1995 survey, we asked respondents to identify, immediately after their answer to the referendum question, the reasons why they intended to vote 'Yes' or 'No' (Blais et al., 1995a, 1998). Of all respondents, 31 per cent mentioned an economic motive (an equal proportion of 'Yes' and 'No' voters), 10 per cent mentioned the language issue (mostly 'Yes' voters), and 28 per cent referred to the constitutional status of Quebec or to self-determination (nearly all were 'Yes' voters). These responses are congruent with research showing that the choice for or against sovereignty can be explained by cultural, economic, and political incentives (Blais et al., 1995b; Pinard, 1992).

Although we concentrate on cultural and economic incentives in the following discussion, it should be noted that political incentives also matter. Retrospectively, the judgement made by voters about past failures of constitutional proposals to grant Quebec greater autonomy is a key factor in explaining support for sovereignty. Few studies have looked at the prospective dimension of political incentives, but the changing nature of the sovereignty debate, which increasingly involves issues such as territory, citizenship, international recognition, and Aboriginal rights, will make this dimension more important in the future.

Cultural Incentives: Grievances, Assurance, or Affirmation?

Sociologist Maurice Pinard traces the sources of demand for sovereignty to 'ethnic grievances'. In his view, the perception of deprivation and unfair treatment felt by the French-speaking population is the primary motivational factor in triggering mobilization for independence (Pinard and Hamilton, 1986; Pinard et al., 1997; see also Dion, 1996). Although the status of French and the relative economic status of Francophones improved following the passage of language laws in the 1970s (Vaillancourt, 1993), the perception of substantial threats to the French language in Quebec has not been greatly reduced. The sense of cultural insecurity inherent in Quebec's status as a small French-speaking island in an ocean of English leads many Francophones to consider sovereignty as a form of linguistic assurance (Nadeau and Fleury, 1995).

Beyond grievances and fear of a distant disappearance, many Francophone Quebecers tend to be attracted to sovereignty because of the more immediate gains they think it would entail in terms of cultural affirmation. In October 1995, 51 per cent of Francophones believed the situation of the French language would be better in a sovereign Quebec, while only 6 per cent believed it would be worse (Blais et al., 1995a, 1995b).

Economic Incentives: Brakes on the Sovereignty Movement

What would happen to Quebec's economy in the event of a successful referendum leading to independence? On this question, expert opinion ranges from assured cataclysmic consequences to potential modest gains. Voters share this mixed assessment. From the earliest surveys, perceptions of the economic consequences of sovereignty have remained a major determinant of support for this option (Breton et al.,1963; Pinard, 1970, 1980; Martin, 1998).

Given that voters, on balance, are more pessimistic than optimistic about economic consequences, economic incentives act as brakes for the sovereignty movement (Blais and Nadeau, 1992; Martin, 1994). As Maurice Pinard (1992) argues, however, the perception of the economic fallout from sovereignty has evolved considerably since 1970. Pinard, echoed by Dion (1996), traces this evolution to an increase in economic self-confidence linked with progress in Francophone control of the economy. It can also be argued that continental and global economic integration makes threats of economic isolation less credible (Martin, 1995).

When economic incentives are compared across time horizons, two observations stand out. First, Quebecers tend to be less pessimistic about the long-term than the short-term economic impact of sovereignty. In October 1995, 55 per cent believed the economy would worsen in the immediate aftermath of a 'Yes' vote (including 36 per cent of 'Yes' voters), while only 15 per cent expected immediate gains. By contrast, 48 per cent envisioned long-term economic gains and 27 per cent anticipated long-term losses. Second, support for sovereignty is more strongly linked to long-term than to short-term economic expectations (Blais et al., 1995a, 1995b).

In sum, among voters who can be mobilized to vote 'Yes', economic pessimism is a key restraining influence. Indeed, analysis shows that in the run-up to the 1995 referendum, the improvement of economic expectations explains the rise in support for sovereignty better than competing variables such as the rise in cultural expectations or strengthening of Quebec identity (Blais et al., 1996).

Balancing Costs and Benefits or Avoiding the Worst?

The role of incentives in political choice opens the door to many other research questions. For example, with André Blais we asked whether, and under what conditions, voters base their decision on the fear of a catastrophic outcome. Our research suggests that people who are more tolerant of risk come to their decisions on the basis of anticipated costs and benefits, while those who are reluctant to take risks also consider the probability of a catastrophe (Nadeau et al., 1999). This does not mean that scare tactics necessarily win votes. During the referendum campaign, federal Finance Minister Paul Martin claimed that one million jobs were jeopardized if the 'Yes' won, but this did not stop the 'Yes' side's progression. This suggests that catastrophic claims may, if they are perceived as vastly exaggerated, undermine the credibility of more realistic assessments of potential losses.

Contextual Influences on Political Choice

Dispositions and incentives suggest explanations for long-term and medium-term changes in Quebec opinion on sovereignty, but the 1995 referendum campaign highlighted the importance of short-term opinion shifts. Indeed, both the 1980 and 1995 referendum campaigns were marked by considerable movement of opinion. In 1995, the 'Yes' side progressed from a low of about 42 per cent in mid-September to the final result of 49.4 per cent on 30 October. In 1980, the 'No' side gained significantly in the last weeks of the campaign, from about 53 per cent in April to 59.6 per cent on 20 May.

The representation of the 'market' for sovereignty support in Figure 9.2 shows that a substantial proportion of the electorate can change its mind on this issue. For some voters, dispositions and incentives do not translate into stable opinions. Indeed, voters may be influenced by factors inherent to the context of the vote.

Among the debates encompassed in this contextual dimension is the one regarding the relative impact of leaders and issues in campaigns. Also important is a debate between those who contend either that voters may be confused on the nature of the choice or that they are voting strategically. Because of these and other factors, many voters may change their minds during a campaign, for reasons unrelated to their assessment of the options at stake.

Voting for an Idea or for a Person?

One of the most widely discussed aspects of the 1995 referendum campaign is the so-called 'Bouchard effect', or the contention that the de facto replacement of Jacques Parizeau by Lucien Bouchard as leader of the sovereigntist forces at mid-campaign was determinant in giving momentum to the 'Yes' side. A close look at polls published during the campaign shows, however, that most of the increase came before the 7 October rally when Bouchard was named 'negotiator in chief'. Maurice Pinard, relying on private polls commissioned by the 'No' Committee and on a rejection of all Léger & Léger polls, insists that there was a Bouchard effect (Pinard et al., 1997). Reviewing the evidence, Robert Young (1998: 292) notes that the 'Yes' side's progression began well before 7 October, that the 'No' Committee's polls contain a high proportion of undecided respondents, and that Pinard's reasons for rejecting all Léger & Léger polls, are unconvincing. In contrast, Young locates the sources of the 'Yes' progression in changed perceptions of the economic consequences of sovereignty (see also Blais et al., 1996).

Another method for ascertaining the impact of leadership is to add a variable measuring perceptions of the main leaders to a regression that includes a complete set of controls. Harold Clarke and Allan Kornberg (1996) use this method to show—credibly—that Lucien Bouchard's personal appeal to the Quebec electorate had a significant impact on the vote. Sovereigntist leaders do not have a monopoly on charisma, however. In 1980, the size of the 'No' victory was largely attributable to the fact that Pierre Elliott Trudeau was, at the time, more popular than his opponent, René Lévesque (Pinard and Hamilton, 1980).

Confused Voters or Smart Strategists?

Another puzzle arising from studies of opinion formation in Quebec is the fact that polls detect some degree of confusion over the meaning of sovereignty. Maurice Pinard and his colleagues have observed, from polls conducted in October 1995 for the 'No' Committee, that a sizeable proportion of the electorate (36 per cent early in the campaign and 23 per cent towards the end) believed that a 'Yes' victory meant that Quebec would remain a Canadian province, albeit with a distinct status (Pinard et al., 1997: 350).

Many of the 'Yes' voters who shared this perception also preferred renewed federalism to sovereignty. Pinard dismisses the notion that these voters might have made a strategic calculation that a 'Yes' vote could force a renewal of federalism. Rather, he stresses the persistence of confusion about the meaning of sovereignty, noting that polls show variations in support to this option depending on how the question is worded (Pinard et al., 1997: 348–53). Others have noted, however, that such variations have decreased significantly over time, suggesting a gradual decrease of confusion (Nadeau et al., 1998).

The confusion hypothesis has also been criticized on theoretical (Young, 1998: 441) and empirical grounds. For example, in a 1997 survey, 12 per cent of respondents claimed that a sovereign Quebec would still be a part of Canada. Of that number, however, 40 per cent explained their answer by stating their belief that a 'Yes' vote would bring federalist renewal, and 36 per cent envisioned a common market between a sovereign Quebec and Canada. Only 20 per cent (less than 3 per cent of all respondents) believed that sovereignty was the same as being a province (Groupe Léger & Léger, 1997).

Conclusion

This chapter has presented a general framework for analysing the different dimensions of the formation of opinion on sovereignty. Most empirical studies have shown that these dimensions matter in the decision to vote for or against sovereignty. They also matter in shaping the strategies of the main actors in the debate. Since the last referendum, for example, the federal government has sought to alter the balance of identity by maximizing the visibility of Canadian symbols in Quebec. At the same time, it has established seemingly insurmountable obstacles to negotiations for an eventual economic partnership following a 'Yes' vote, thus consolidating perceptions that the transition to sovereignty would be costly. Also, of course, the whole debate on 'clarity' is premised on interpretations of the contextual dimension of the choice.

Our model is static in nature, but some of its elements allow us to make inferences about the dynamics of opinion change. The generational makeup of the vote in the 1995 referendum, in conjunction with the steady progression of the main dispositions affecting the vote since the 1960s, suggests that, if other things remained equal, support for sovereignty would gain a distinct advantage in the next decades.

In politics, however, 'other things' seldom remain equal. The trend of change in identities and values is likely to continue, if only because of the replacement of generations, and that could assure that a substantial part of the electorate will remain receptive to the notion of sovereignty for at least a generation. There is no guarantee, however, that this large potential support will necessarily materialize and be translated into a majority vote for independence. As the evidence on the effects of incentives on the vote shows, the only way to achieve a solid majority for sovereignty or for some form of renewed federalism is to convince Quebecers that their political, cultural, and economic aspirations would be served better by that option. Moreover, the level of energy and attention that a decision of this magnitude requires may be difficult to re-create in an era when citizens seem to feel increasingly disengaged from the realm of politics.

In spite of the close result of the 1995 referendum, a great deal of uncertainty remains in the public's mind about the sovereignty option. But this uncertainty is nothing new. In the mid-1980s many commentators and journalists had announced the end of the sovereignty movement and the death of Quebec nationalism. A few years later, the mood had changed dramatically with many observers and politicians speaking of the 'inevitability' of sovereignty (Cloutier et al., 1992). When the PQ regained power in 1994, however, the political climate had changed once again and the opportunity that the post-Meech Lake context offered for radical change seemed to have slipped away (CROP, August 1994). Indeed, as late as the summer of 1995, analysts sympathetic to sovereignty argued that the 'Yes' had no chance of even approaching victory and urged the Parizeau government to postpone the referendum rather than risk another humiliating defeat (Guay et al., 1995). This conclusion was premature, but the significant surge in support that followed was not quite sufficient to achieve a majority.

After the 1995 referendum, support for sovereignty climbed to a high of about 55 per cent and remained at the majority level for several months, but it slipped back to a little more than 40 per cent at the time of the November 1998 election. The Parti Québécois hoped to win more votes than in any previous election after coming from behind following the arrival of Jean Charest as Liberal leader, but voters handed Lucien Bouchard's party a bittersweet victory. Although the PQ preserved its majority in the National Assembly, it won fewer votes (42.9 per cent) than the Liberals (43.5 per cent). During the campaign, Lucien Bouchard claimed he would wait for 'winning conditions' to call a new referendum. Quebecers seemingly agreed, but they were unwilling to give him these conditions just yet. Since the PQ's re-election, support for sovereignty has hovered around 40 per cent, without giving much evidence of a takeoff.

Predictions about politics or public opinion are always hazardous—especially when they concern the future—and support for sovereignty clearly is no exception to this rule. The evidence presented in this chapter suggests that the fortunes of sovereignty depend on a complex interaction of long-term trends and short-term factors. In spite of the difficulties faced by the Parti Québécois government after its unconvincing victory, it would seem reasonable to conjecture that long-term trends offer the sovereigntists a window of opportunity. Whether they will be able to capitalize on these favourable trends, however, remains an open question.

Note

1. Francophones are people who use French at home. According to 1996 census data, 81.9 per cent of Quebecers use French at home, 10.1 per cent English, 5.8 per cent a third language and 2.1 per cent use several languages. N.B.: Because many non-Francophones do not meet the citizenship or residency requirements for voting, Francophones constitute between 83 per cent and 85 per cent of the electorate (84 per cent in our sample).

References

Bélanger, Sarah, and Maurice Pinard. 1991. 'Ethnic Movements and the Competition Model: Some Missing Links', *American Sociological Review* 56 (Aug.): 446–57.

Bernier, Léon, James Csipak, Donald Cuccioletta, Albert Desbiens, Jeanne Kissner, Guy Lachapelle, and Frédéric Lesemann. 1998. 'L'assurance identitaire se conjugue avec l'ouverture sur le monde'. *Le Devoir*, 15 July, A7.

Blais, André, Pierre Martin, and Richard Nadeau. 1995a. 'Sondage omnibus référendaire' (computerized dataset; survey conducted by the Groupe Léger & Léger, 23–26 Oct.).

――――, ――――, and ――――. 1995b. 'Attentes économiques et linguistiques et appui à la souveraineté du Québec: Une analyse prospective et comparative', *Canadian Journal of Political Science* 28 (Dec.): 637–57.

――――, ――――, and ――――. 1996. 'Pourquoi le Oui a-t-il fait des gains pendant la campagne référendaire?', in John E. Trent, Robert Young, and Guy Lachapelle, eds, *Québec-Canada: What Is the Path Ahead?* Ottawa: University of Ottawa Press, 71–6.

――――, ――――, and ――――. 1998. 'Can People Explain Their Own Vote? Introspective Questions as Indicators of Salience in the 1995 Quebec Referendum on Sovereignty', *Quality & Quantity: International Journal of Methodology* 32 (Nov.): 355–66.

―――― and Richard Nadeau.1984. 'La clientèle du OUI', in Jean Crête, ed., *Comportement électoral au Québec*. Chicoutimi, Que.: Gaëtan Morin éditeur, 321–34.

―――― and ――――. 1992. 'To Be or Not To Be a Sovereignist? Quebeckers' Perennial Dilemma', *Canadian Public Policy* 18 (Mar.): 89–103.

Bourque, Gilles, and Jules Duchastel. 1996. *L'identité fragmentée: Nation et citoyenneté dans les débats constitutionnels canadiens, 1941–1992*. Montréal: Fides.

Bowler, Shaun, and Todd Donovan. 1998. *Demanding Choices: Opinion, Voting, and Direct Democracy*. Ann Arbor: University of Michigan Press.

Breton, Albert. 1964. 'The Economics of Nationalism', *Journal of Political Economy* 72 (Aug.): 376–86.

―――― and Margot Breton. 1995. 'Nationalism Revisited', in Breton, Gianluigi Galeotti, Pierre Salmon, and Ronald Wintrobe, eds, *Nationalism and Rationality*. Cambridge: Cambridge University Press, 98–115.

――――, Raymond Breton, and Howard Roseborough. 1963. *Separatism, July-August 1963*. Ann Arbor, Mich.: Inter-University Consortium for Political and Social Research, Study No. 9007.

Butler, David, and Uwe Kitzinger. 1976. *The 1975 Referendum*. London: Macmillan.

Chong, Dennis. 2000. *Rational Lives: Norms and Values in Politics and Society*. Chicago: University of Chicago Press.

Clarke, Harold D., and Allan Kornberg. 1996. 'Choosing Canada? The 1995 Quebec Sovereignty Referendum', *PS: Political Science and Politics* 29 (Dec.): 676–82.

Cloutier, Édouard, Jean-H. Guay, and Daniel Latouche. 1992. *Le virage: L'évolution de l'opinion publique au Québec depuis 1960*. Montréal: Québec/Amérique.

Dion, Stéphane. 1996. 'Why Is Secession Difficult in Well-Established Democracies? Lessons from Quebec', *British Journal of Political Science* 26 (July): 269–83.

Gidengil, Elisabeth. 1996. 'The Gender Gap in Support for Sovereignty', paper presented to the Canadian Political Science Association annual meeting, St Catharines, Ont., June.

Groupe Léger & Léger. 1997. *Sondage politique Léger & Léger—Le Journal de Montréal —Globe and Mail, septembre 1997*. Montréal: Groupe Léger & Léger.

Guay, Jean-H., Pierre Drouilly, Pierre-Alain Cotnoir, and Pierre Noreau. 1995. 'Référendum: Les souverainistes risquent de rencontrer une dure défaite', *La Presse*, 26 Aug., B3.

Howe, Paul. 1998. 'Rationality and Sovereignty Support in Quebec', *Canadian Journal of Political Science* 31 (Mar.): 31–59.

Inglehart, Ronald. 1990. *Culture Shift in Advanced Industrial Societies*. Princeton, NJ: Princeton University Press.

Martin, Pierre. 1994. 'Générations politiques, rationalité économique et appui à la souveraineté au Québec', *Canadian Journal of Political Science* 27 (June): 345–59.

———. 1995. 'When Nationalism Meets Continentalism: The Politics of Free Trade in Quebec', *Regional and Federal Studies* 5 (Spring): 1–27.

———. 1998. 'Identity, Reference Groups and Values: Dispositions and Choice on the Question of Sovereignty in Quebec', paper presented to the annual meeting of the American Political Science Association, Boston, Mass., 3–6 Sept.

——— and Richard Nadeau. 2000. 'Choosing a Nation: The 1995 Referendum on Sovereignty in Quebec', paper presented at the conference 'Making Big Choices: Individual Opinion Formation and Societal Choice', Harvard University, 25–6 May.

McRoberts, Kenneth. 1993. *Quebec: Social Change and Political Crisis*, 3rd edn. Toronto: McClelland & Stewart.

Nadeau, Richard. 1992. 'Le virage souverainiste des Québécois,' *Recherches sociographiques* 23 (Jan.–Apr.): 9–28.

———, André Blais, Elisabeth Gidengil, and Neil Nevitte. 1998. 'L'appui à la souveraineté varie-t-il selon la formulation de la question?', *La Presse*, 16 mars, B2.

——— and Christopher Fleury. 1995. 'Gains linguistiques anticipés et appui à la souveraineté du Québec', *Canadian Journal of Political Science* 28 (Mar.) : 35–50.

———, Pierre Martin, and André Blais. 1999. 'Attitude Toward Risk-Taking and Individual Choice in the Quebec Referendum on Sovereignty', *British Journal of Political Science* 29 (July): 523–39.

———, Norbert Robitaille, and Christine Noël. 1995. 'Si la tendance se maintient . . . Les changements démographiques favoriseront à moyen terme l'appui à la souveraineté du Québec', *La Presse*, 25 Nov., B4.

Nevitte, Neil, André Blais, Elisabeth Gidengil, and Richard Nadeau. 1999. *Unsteady State: The 1997 Canadian Federal Election*. Toronto: Oxford University Press.

Pelletier, Réjean, and Daniel Guérin. 1996. 'Postmatérialisme et clivages partisans au Québec: les partis sont-ils différents?', *Canadian Journal of Political Science* 29 (Mar.): 71–109.

Pinard, Maurice. 1970. 'Study of the Movement for the Independence of Quebec' (computerized dataset), McGill University, Department of Sociology.

———. 1980. 'Study of the May 1980 Referendum in Quebec' (computerized dataset), McGill University, Department of Sociology.

———. 1992. 'The Quebec Independence Movement: A Dramatic Reemergence', *Working Papers in Social Behaviour* (Montreal: McGill University, Department of Sociology, typescript).

———, Robert Bernier, and Vincent Lemieux. 1997. *Un combat inachevé*. Sainte-Foy, Que.: Presses de l'Université du Québec.

———— and Richard Hamilton. 1980. 'Referendum Survey' (computerized dataset), McGill University, Department of Sociology and INCI (interviews conducted 4–9 May).

———— and ————. 1984a. 'The Class Bases of the Quebec Independence Movement: Conjectures and Evidence', *Ethnic and Racial Studies* 7 (Jan.): 19–54.

———— and ————. 1984b. 'Les Québécois votent NON: le sens et la portée du vote', in Jean Crête, ed., *Comportement électoral au Québec*. Chicoutimi, Que.: Gaëtan Morin éditeur, 335–85.

———— and ————. 1986. 'Motivational Dimensions in the Quebec Independence Movement: A Test of a New Model', *Research in Social Movements, Conflicts and Change* 9: 225–80.

Prager, Joel. 1996. ' "Seek Ye First the Economic Kingdom!" In Search of a Rational Choice Interpretation of Quebec Nationalism', in Jocelyne Couture, Kai Nielson, and Michel Seymour, eds, *Rethinking Nationalism*. Calgary: University of Calgary Press, 551–78.

SOM/SRC. 1995. 'Sondage référendaire SOM/SRC, 19–25 septembre 1995' (computerized dataset). Montréal: Société Radio-Canada.

Vaillancourt, François. 1993. 'The Economic Status of the French Language and Francophones in Quebec', in Alain-G. Gagnon, ed., *Quebec: State and Society*. Scarborough, Ont.: Nelson Canada, 407–21.

Young, Robert A. 1998. *The Secession of Quebec and the Future of Canada*, 2nd edn. Montreal and Kingston: McGill-Queen's University Press.

Part IV

Voting and Elections

Chapter 10

The Theories of Voting and Their Applicability in Canada

MEBS KANJI AND KEITH ARCHER

Predicting the outcome of a legitimate, democratic election is by no means a simple and straightforward task: the process of electoral choice is inherently complex and one can never be entirely sure what voters will do once they actually go to the polls. In some ways, the challenge of calling an election is a bit like predicting the weather: the forecast may point to mild conditions and pleasant temperatures, but one can never completely rule out the possibility of an unexpected storm.

The most recent Canadian federal election makes for a useful case in point. Almost immediately after the campaign was under way, the pundits began speculating on how the different parties might fare. Some argued that the governing Liberals would be badly hurt by the mishandling of the Transitional Jobs Fund (otherwise known as the 'billion-dollar boondoggle') and various other accusations of ethical misconduct. Others claimed that the Canadian Alliance might make a significant breakthrough in central Canada, perhaps even taking as many as 40 seats in Ontario alone. And still others were doubtful that the Progressive Conservative Party would be capable of retaining official party status and whether Joe Clark, the party's leader, would win his seat in the riding of Calgary Centre. Lastly, both Gilles Duceppe, the leader of the Bloc Québécois (BQ), and Alexa McDonough, leader of the NDP, predicted that their respective parties would do better in this election than they had in 1997.

Once the votes were counted, however, it was apparent that many of these earlier predictions had been considerably off the mark. The governing Liberals, for instance, were re-elected for a third consecutive term, with an increased majority. The Canadian Alliance, despite winning an increased number of seats, failed to make a substantial breakthrough east of the Manitoba border, winning only two seats in Ontario. The Progressive Conservatives not only retained official party status but the party's leader managed to handily win his seat in Calgary Centre. And both the BQ and the NDP ended up losing a significant number of the seats they had previously held.

In spite of the complexity, the purpose of this chapter is to briefly review the core theories of voting and examine their application in the Canadian case.

Most voting research centres on two primary concerns: Why do citizens vote the way they do? And what are the key factors explaining electoral choice? The earliest studies indicated that voters were neither very interested in nor motivated by politics; they lacked access to the relevant types of information and seemed altogether too disjointed in their views to suggest that they reasoned politically. Rather, most citizens tended simply to vote in accordance with their social group affiliates or in line with their conventional partisan ties. Such long-term loyalties were considered to be primarily responsible for both stabilizing and explaining the vote.

More recently, however, it has been suggested that the impact of various structural advancements resulting from the rhythms of late industrialism has altered the calculus of electoral choice. The emergence of the knowledge-based economy, together with improvements in information technology, mass communications, and rising levels of education, is said to be contributing to making electorates more interested, better informed, highly skilled, and more efficacious. Not only do voters seem better prepared and more motivated for political decision-making, but they also appear more independent and calculating when it comes to electoral choice. Long-term loyalties, although still important, seem to have less of an immediate effect. Instead, short-term factors, such as where the competing parties stand on key issues and perceptions of political candidates, particularly party leaders, seem to be more relevant. As a result, electoral volatility appears to be on the rise and the stability of party systems less assured.

The Three Main Theories of Voting

The Sociological Model

Some of the very first studies of voting behaviour were conducted by researchers—Paul Lazarsfeld, Bernard Berelson, Hazel Gaudet, and William McPhee—at Columbia University's Bureau of Applied Social Research (see Lazarsfeld et al., 1948; Berelson et al., 1954). Now commonly referred to as the Columbia School, this particular group of scholars proposed that voters are driven largely by their *social group affiliations*; that is, 'a person thinks, politically, as he is socially' (Lazarsfeld et al., 1948: 27). Electoral decisions, according to this theory, are simply responses to various sociological 'pressures' and 'cross-pressures' resulting from differences in factors such as social class, religious affiliation, ethnicity, and/or urban versus rural residency, just to name a few.

Proponents of the sociological model argue that during elections the most attentive members within various social groups try to influence other less mobilized members (who form the majority) to vote in a manner that is consistent with the group's overall interests. When a voter's primary group memberships and/or affiliations coincide, the decision is made easier and is likely to correspond with the combined group preference. If, on the other hand, voters are faced with divergent political loyalties (for example, a working-class Protestant with ties to both the Liberals and Conservatives), they must first sort through the opposing cross-pressures and decide which of their particular group affiliations are the most important. This process is likely to make the task of voting more difficult, as well as more time-consuming.

To further complicate matters, this model poses no limit on the number of socio-demographic attachments that may affect a voter's electoral choice. However, as Figure 10.1 illustrates, a clear distinction is made between those factors deemed to be the least important and those seen as being considerably more relevant. *Secondary factors* such as sex and age, for example, were said at the time to have only a weak influence on the vote, whereas *primary factors* were thought to play a much more significant role. Differences in *socio-economic status, religious and ethnic background,* and *regional/urban-rural residency*[1] were thought to be key in 'that people of unlike characteristics are affected in different ways by a single political policy.' Moreover, these particular cleavages are also more likely to be perpetuated from one generation to the next: 'parents and children sharing the same characteristics provide a condition of continuity in which political choices can be taught, however subtly and unconsciously, by the one to the other.' Finally, fault lines such as these are further reinforced by the forces of close physical and social proximity, thereby helping to promote greater group consensus (and longevity) through increased contact (Berelson et al., 1954: 74).

The sociological model, then, sees voting as being heavily conditioned by an individual's social network. Although people may cast their ballots as individuals, they make up their minds as members of groups. This theory, therefore, argues

Figure 10.1: The Sociological Model of Voting

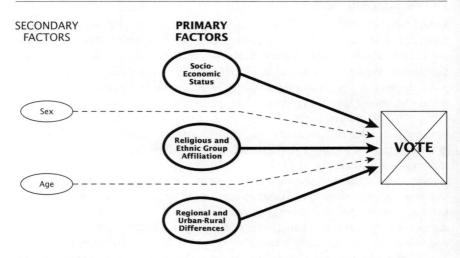

that the study of voting should be geared mostly towards uncovering an individual's primary social and community bonds.

As parsimonious as the sociological model seems, it is not without its drawbacks—it explains only a small fraction of the total variations in vote and accounts for very little, if any, change over time (Dalton and Wattenberg, 1993). Sociological differences, in other words, tell us only so much about why voters vote the way they do, and they are even less compelling when it comes to explaining vote switching. Thus, it was largely in response to these two weaknesses that another group of researchers—Angus Campbell, Philip Converse, Warren Miller, and Donald Stokes—from the University of Michigan proposed a second, more comprehensive theory of voting known as the socio-psychological approach (Campbell et al., 1960; see also Butler and Stokes, 1969; Budge et al., 1976).

The Socio-Psychological Model

Beginning with the premise that voting is inherently complex, the Michigan School contends that no single-factor theory is likely to suffice. Instead, a broader explanatory framework is required to unite a multitude of different determinants, each of which is expected in some way to influence the vote. A truly robust theory of voting must also be generalizable; that is, it should be able to accept evidence pertaining to any particular case and generate an ultimate prediction of behaviour (Campbell et al., 1960).

The socio-psychological model, as outlined by Campbell and his colleagues, is depicted in Figure 10.2. The axis of this funnel-like framework represents the dimension of time; 'events are conceived to follow each other in a converging sequence of causal chains, moving from the mouth to the stem of the funnel.' Those influences located closest to the voting decision are considered to be the most political, personal, and relevant, whereas those determinants located nearer to the mouth of the funnel are perceived as being less political, less personal (i.e., external), and in some cases even exogenous (ibid., 23, 24).

The most powerful predictors of voting behaviour, according to this theory, are those forces that are the most *proximate* and *psychological* in nature. As Campbell et al. put it,

> the effect of all factors leading to behavior is finally expressed in the direction and intensity of the forces of a psychological field. . . . most events or conditions that bear directly upon behavior are perceived in some form or other by the individual prior to the determined behavior, and . . . much of behavior consists of reactions to these perceptions. (ibid., 66, 27).

Thus unlike the sociological model, which conceives of voting decisions as being the product of one's social context, the socio-psychological approach focuses instead on voters as individuals and seeks to uncover how, psychologically, they arrive at their electoral decisions.

The core determinant within this model is *party identification*, or the affective tie that is believed to bind voters to their most preferred political parties. Attachments

Figure 10.2: The Socio-Psychological Model of Voting

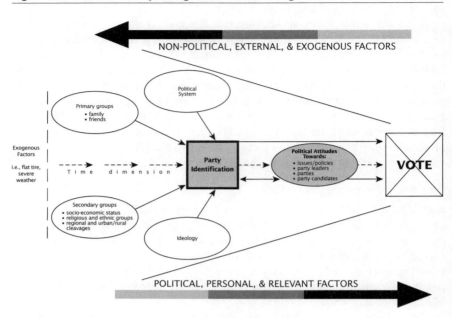

of this sort are thought to be well entrenched (that is, they are most probably transmitted and developed early on in one's life through both primary and secondary group interactions), influenced by the nature of the political system and one's personal ideologies, and can exist independently of any formal membership or active connection to the party. Loyalties to parties are expected to remain more or less stable over time, and are said to be passed on from one generation to the next.

The function of this particular variable is critical in that voters are expected to use their partisan ties to filter their *political attitudes and opinions* towards key issues and party candidates, and as a final basis of vote. 'The stronger the party bond, the more exaggerated the process of selection and perceptual distortion will be.' In those instances where one's political attitudes/opinions are inconsistent with his or her partisan affiliation, the former may exert pressure on the latter, and if 'intense enough, a stable partisan identification may actually be changed' (ibid., 133, 135). Conversely, in situations where voters may not be well versed with the relevant issues or the different party candidates, they may simply refer to their already established party ties for a quick and dependable basis for their electoral choice.

While party identification has often been found to be a strong determinant of electoral choice, the key drawback of the socio-psychological model is that it focuses primarily on explanations likely to be closely intertwined with the vote itself. The danger, therefore, is that factors such as party identification may be so closely interconnected with the behaviour being explained that they provide very little, if any, additional insight. As Campbell et al. note, 'measurement close to behavior runs the risk of including values that are determined by the event we are trying to predict—that is, the voting decision' (ibid., 35). Furthermore, evidence from the last two decades or so indicates that partisan loyalties, particularly among younger, postmodern generations (Canadians included), have been in decline (see, e.g., Inglehart, 1997; Dalton et al., 1984; Dalton, 1996; Dalton and Wattenberg, 2000; Stewart and Clarke, 1998). Newer cohorts, it is argued, are not as likely to be accepting of the 'authority of hierarchical, oligarchical organizations like the old line parties' (Inglehart, 1997: 311).

The Rational Choice Model

One reason why the sociological and socio-psychological models became as prominent as they did is because most researchers had concluded fairly early on that the majority of citizens were simply unsuited to reason politically: many voters were neither interested in, nor motivated by politics (Berelson et al., 1954: ch. 14). As such, they often tended to be 'muddle-headed or empty-headed—or both' (Sniderman, 1993: 219).[2] Moreover, the costs of acquiring political information were such that most voters rarely had access to the types of 'full' and 'perfect' information required to make calculated political choices (Converse, 1964). And even if voters did somehow manage to gain access to the necessary information, it was questionable whether they possessed the abilities and skills required to process that information (Dalton, 1996). Thus most voters, it was thought, relied heavily on their social and psychological cues when it came to electoral decision-making.

More recently, however, there has been evidence to suggest that voters are not only more interested in politics, but also more motivated to become politically involved (see Barnes and Kaase, 1979; Jennings and van Deth, 1990; Nevitte, 1996). The transition from industrialism to late industrialism and its resulting structural transformations, such as the rise of the knowledge-based economy, the technological revolution, the expansion of mass communications, and the education explosion, are shown to have greatly improved the public's access to political information and enhanced their cognitive skills (Dalton, 1984, 1988; Dalton and Wattenberg, 1993; Inglehart, 1970, 1977, 1990; Bell, 1973, 1976). Significant proportions of the mass public now possess 'the level of political skills and resources necessary to become self-sufficient in politics' (Dalton, 1988: 18), and they appear considerably more critical of political élites (Norris, 1999; Inglehart, 1990, 1997; Putnam et al., 2000; Pharr et al., 2000). While this is not to suggest that all voters are highly sophisticated,[3] it does breathe new life into the possibility that in addition to acting on their social and psychological cues, voters might also base their voting decisions on their rational evaluations of where competing parties stand on key issues and how they feel about the various candidates competing for office.

The rational choice model assumes that all 'citizens act rationally in politics.' Based on the pioneering work of a political economist, this particular theory contends that the primary reason why citizens vote for (or prefer) a particular political party is because it provides the best policies, the best candidates, and/or the best benefits overall. In other words, all voters are rationally motivated utility maximizers, and 'given several mutually exclusive alternatives, a rational [person] always takes the one which yields him the highest utility...i.e., he acts to his own greatest benefit' (Downs, 1957a: 36–37).

The calculus (or cost/benefit analysis) of rational voting can be expressed as follows:

$$\text{Voting Preferences} = (U^A t) - E(U^B t)$$

The symbols 'U^A' and 'U^B' stand for the *total maximum utility income* that voters derive (or stand to derive) from both the incumbent government (party 'A') and the next best political party (party 'B'). The variable 't' refers to the *current election period*, while 'E' is expected value. Thus, in determining how to vote, rational, economic voters simply estimate the total utility income (or benefits) they currently derive from the incumbent party and detract from that the total expected utility income (or benefits) they might have received had the next best party been in power. If the resulting *benefit differential* is 'positive', the voter will most likely choose to support the incumbent party. If the benefit differential turns out to be 'negative', the voter will probably opt instead to vote for the next best party. And if there is no difference between the two parties, the voter may abstain from voting altogether (ibid.).

The most obvious weakness of this theory is that it rests entirely on the assumption that voters behave rationally in politics. But if they do, this raises the concern that voters may conclude that it is entirely irrational to vote. The reason, Downs (1957b: 146–7) argues, is straightforward:

> Since the cost of voting is very low, hundreds, thousands, or even millions of citizens can afford to vote. Therefore, the probability that any one citizen's vote will be decisive is very small indeed. It is not zero, and it can even be significant if he thinks the election will be very close; but, under most circumstances, it is so negligible that it renders the return from voting 'correctly' infinitesimal.... As long as each person considers the behaviour of others as given, it is simply not worthwhile for him to acquire information so as to vote 'correctly' himself.[4]

How, then, do these three theories of voting apply to the Canadian case? What do the empirical findings tell us about Canadians and their voting habits?

The 'Unsociological' Canadian Voter

Attempts to test the sociological model in Canada have produced mixed results. On the one hand the model has been criticized widely for both its lack of generalizability (Elkins and Blake, 1975; Terry and Schultz, 1973) and its remarkably weak explanatory significance (Irvine, 1976; Clarke et al., 1979, 1991, 1996; LeDuc, 1985). As Laponce (1969: 181) puts it: 'if our knowledge of the relationship between politics, religion, occupation, age, and sex has increased, our probability of making correct prediction[s] in future elections has not progressed very much.'

The problem, Alford argues, is not so much the model itself, but the fact that both the Canadian electorate and the Canadian party system are immensely fragmented: there are very few 'collective social group experiences', and very few political parties consistently appeal to those who share those collective experiences. In other words, there is both an 'ambiguity of party imagery and a lack of homogeneity of political experience and socialization among various groups.' Being Catholic or part of the working class, for example, cannot be constituted as being a political predisposition 'unless the connections between group membership and its "normal" political affiliations are clearly perceived by individuals' (Alford, 1964: 233; also see Regenstreif, 1965). As a consequence, the simple pressures and cross-pressures (i.e., the expected push and pull) between different social group affiliations do not provide a very strong explanation for why Canadians vote the way they do.[5]

Of course, it might be that the weak results produced by the sociological approach are also partly a reflection of weaknesses in earlier methodologies. Most research on the sociology of Canadian voting has tended to rely on 'elementary data analysis techniques' (Elkins and Blake, 1975: 322), and the focus, more often than not, has been on examining the direct links between various socio-demographic indicators and voting preferences (Alford, 1964; Regenstreif, 1964; Van Loon and Whittington, 1971; Meisel, 1972, 1975). The earliest modelling devices, for instance, were used mainly to identify various combinations of socio-demographic factors that best described a party's core support. Such techniques were considered crude at best and rarely, if ever, identified any stable combination of predictors for any particular party (Laponce, 1972). Moreover, 'the more variables [that were] combined, the greater the power to predict, but the fewer the number of people to whom the prediction [could] apply' (Laponce, 1969: 181).

With the advent of high-powered microcomputers and state-of-the-art statistical software packages, researchers have begun to experiment more vigorously with newer, more sophisticated investigative techniques. It is now common practice, for instance, for scholars to look simultaneously at the *net independent effects* of several different socio-demographic factors on voting (Irvine, 1976; Clarke et al., 1979; LeDuc, 1985). Some studies even go so far as to compare how various combinations of socio-demographic predictors can work together to produce both powerful and significant *interactive effects* (Blake, 1972; Gidengil, 1989). And through the use of a technique known as *regression decomposition*, Gidengil and her colleagues (1999) show how differences in religion, ethnicity, and urban versus rural residency are heavily conditioned by differences in region.

Thus, it is not as though the sociological approach has produced no results. In fact, a number of key findings have been reported to stand out time and time again. Cleavages based on ethnoreligious and regional differences, for instance, have been noted as being more significant than divisions based on socio-economic status (or social class). Consider, then, how each of these three social forces are said to affect electoral choice.

The Ethnoreligious Cleavage

The basis of Canada's ethnoreligious cleavage and its effects on voting have been amply well documented (Regenstreif, 1965: ch. 6; Schwartz, 1974a; Meisel, 1975; Johnston et al., Blais, Brady, and Crête, 1992). A key distinction that is frequently drawn is between Catholics and Protestants, although the most visible expression of this cleavage is often linguistic, i.e., French versus English' (Johnston et al., 1992: 588). Most of the early evidence shows that Catholics are more inclined to support the federal Liberal Party, while Protestants, at least historically, have tended to divide their vote more or less evenly between both the Liberals and the Conservatives (Alford, 1964; Regenstreif, 1964, 1965; Meisel, 1967, 1975; McDonald, 1969; Laponce, 1969; Schwartz, 1974a; Clarke et al., 1979; Nevitte et al., 2000), a gap that seems by some accounts to have deteriorated of late. According to Richard Johnston et al., although 'the major Canadian Protestant denominations once differed politically among themselves, they no longer do so.' Evidence collected during the 1988 federal election shows that 'Protestants tended to be Conservatives and Catholics tended to be Liberals' (Johnston et al., 1992: 85–6). It is also clear that religious group differences are in no way a surrogate for deeper, more enduring French/English differences; although 'ethnicity reinforces religious voting, it is not the cause' (Meisel, 1975: 260; see also Laponce, 1969; Irvine, 1974; Irvine and Gold, 1980; Johnston, 1985, Johnston et al., 1992).

The fact that religious differences continue to be important, even in today's more secular climate (Nevitte, 1996), is in some ways quite puzzling. With possibly the exception of the abortion issue and perhaps the debate over gay rights, relatively few religiously oriented matters can be said to permeate the federal political agenda. Rarely do Canadian parties 'divide over religious questions or mobilize the electorate in these terms' (Mendelsohn and Nadeau, 1997: 130). In fact, as Meisel (1975) notes, even that which is perceived as being religious voting has relatively little, if anything, to do with religion in a narrow sense. Yet, time after time, the effect of religion on voting continues to remain robust, not easily 'washed out' by other social and political factors (Gidengil et al., 1999). What, then, explains the enduring significance of religious voting in Canada?

To date, a number of different explanations have been provided; in fact, there may be more than one definitive answer. William Irvine (1974, 1985), for example, suggests that the persistence of the religious cleavage is due mostly to the continuing forces of intergenerational change. That is, 'religious differences persist mainly through the family perpetuating old cleavages' (Irvine, 1974: 562). Conversely, Johnston (1985: 108) claims that the religious cleavage, or any other social group cleavage for that matter, is maintained primarily by forces outside the immediate family: 'a Catholic Liberal father is more likely than a non-Catholic Liberal father to pass on his Liberal loyalty because his influence on his offspring is more likely to be reinforced by influences outside the home in the larger Catholic community.' In the same way, the religious basis of the Canadian party system lies not primarily in faith and morals, but in denominationally differentiated conceptions of the nationality' (Johnston et al., 1992: 85). Most recently, Mendelsohn and Nadeau (1997: 142) suggest that regular church attendance and a limited exposure to the media are also key factors. 'The most resilient cleavages', they argue, 'are between regular churchgoers with low media exposure, while the weakest are between heavily exposed non-practisers.'

The Regional Cleavage

A second important demographic cleavage is one based on territory (Alford, 1964; Regenstreif, 1965; Schwartz, 1974a, 1974b; Clarke et al., 1979; Carty, 1996): 'fresh documentation of inter-provincial and inter-regional heterogeneity in party-support patterns is provided by each set of federal election returns', and on average, the mean range in popular support for all three conventional parties—the Liberals, the Conservatives, and the New Democrats—varies in excess of 30 per cent from one province to the next (Clarke et al., 1979: 99). Moreover, since the arrival of the Bloc Québécois (BQ) in Quebec and the Reform Party in western Canada (now known as the Canadian Alliance), the impact of region on vote is said to have become even more pronounced. 'At the beginning of the decade, the regionalization of the vote in Canada was already stronger than in other advanced democracies...and in 1997 the vote became even more regionalized' (Gidengil et al., 1999: 248).

During the late 1970s, it was found that although not all Canadians think in regional terms, a sizeable majority (59 per cent) do (Clarke et al., 1979). Moreover, divisions spurred by feelings of regional consciousness were detected to be driven largely by intergenerational change. At the time, the most powerful regional effects were said to exist in the four western provinces, whereas today, significant differences in regional voting can be found more or less across the land. 'Of all the social background characteristics, region of residence turns out to be the strongest single predictor of vote' (Gidengil et al., 1999: 248; also see Blais et al., 1998).

Probably the most consistent explanation thus far has been that regional differences 'colour the relationship between other variables and party preference' (Terry and Schultz, 1973: 272). The most recent variant of this argument, for example, suggests that citizens in different regions have different issue priorities and different economic perceptions (Gidengil et al., 1999), thereby lending further support to Mildred Schwartz's earlier contention that regional distinctions most likely include 'some consciousness on the part of residents that they have distinctive, regionally based interests' (Schwartz, 1974b: 5). It has also been argued that regional variations may reflect the distinct socio-economic characteristics of different constituencies (Blake, 1978), as well as differences in political cultures (Simeon and Elkins, 1974). However, the evidence from the 1997 federal election indicates that differences in vote are 'not simply a matter of relative proportions of the haves and have nots... [nor is it] simply that residents of different regions have different beliefs or differ in their political judgements, as important as these differences are' (Gidengil et al., 1999: 257, 271).

The Social Class Cleavage

Unlike ethnoreligious and regional differences, class cleavages have been found to have only a relatively modest impact on Canadian elections: 'working-class' Canadians, for example, are not much more likely than their middle- and upper-class counterparts to vote for parties of the left (Alford, 1964; Regenstreif, 1965; Terry and Schultz, 1973; Van Loon and Whittington, 1971; Schwartz, 1974a; Meisel, 1975; Clarke et al., 1979; Hunter, 1982). In fact, cross-nationally, Canada is purported to have significantly lower levels of class voting than several other Anglo-American democracies. And amid earlier expectations of increased class voting with corresponding increases in urbanization, industrialization, and secularization, as prescribed by the 'evolutionary' model (see Alford, 1963), most follow-up studies indicate that no such transformation has yet taken place (Blake, 1972; Clarke et al., 1979). 'Surveys conducted since the mid-1960s show that relationships typically are quite weak between indicators of social class such as education, income, and occupation, on the one hand, and voting behaviour on the other' (Clarke et al., 1996: 94).[6]

Even attempts to measure 'subjective class voting' (using semantic differential-style indicators of party class positions) have usually ended in weak results (Ogmundson, 1975a, 1975b, 1975c, 1979; Ogmundson and Ng, 1982). Lambert and Hunter (1979: 301), for example, argue that 'when voter perceptions were used as the measure of the class orientations of political parties, some small amount of class voting could be observed', but as for whether or not this constitutes a breakthrough in our current understanding of why Canadians vote the way they do, the answer, they suggest, is 'a confident "no"'. For a more recent analysis, see Lambert and Curtis, 1993.

Different explanations have been put forth to account for the lack of strong class voting in Canada (Pammett, 1987). Schwartz (1974a) and several others (Engelmann and Schwartz, 1967; Brodie and Jenson, 1980; Clarke et al., 1996), for example, suggest that the problem may be linked once again to unclear and indistinct party alternatives. In other words, although class-based voting may well exist, 'consistent class-based parties . . . are missing' (Schwartz, 1974a: 589). Likewise, another prominent explanation contends that the problem may be due to conceptual inconsistencies and low overall levels of class-consciousness. While there are, without a doubt, some clear exceptions,[7] the terms 'left' and 'right' are typically not as well understood by most North Americans as they are by intellectuals (Ogmundson, 1979: 800).[8] Moreover, Lambert et al. (1986b: 396) report that for nearly half of all Canadians (45 per cent) 'the idea of social class [either] meant nothing . . . or they were unsure of its meaning.'

In light of these findings, then, it is remarkable indeed to find that many voters still manage to use these concepts in somewhat meaningful ways (Lambert et al., 1986a, 1986b). Both ideology and subjective class (i.e., social class self-placements) have significant direct and indirect effects on voting (Lambert et al., 1987). Moreover, union membership, sometimes considered a proxy for social class, also turns out to have important effects: members of union locals, particularly those affiliated with the New Democratic Party, are more inclined to support the NDP (Alford, 1964; Laponce, 1969, 1972; Archer, 1985, 1987, 1990; Pammett, 1987). In fact, one recent analysis reports that 'a union family was about eight points more likely than a non-union one to support the NDP' (Johnston et al., 1992: 89). And regardless of the absence of any national class cleavage, within specific regions social class differences have been reported to have varying degrees of effect (Lambert et al., 1987; Gidengil, 1989). In British Columbia, for example, differences in class are found to drive the party system even 'more decisively than does religion or culture' (Johnston et al., 1992: 90).

Party Identification And Voting In Canada

Similar to the sociological model, the socio-psychological approach has also been tested extensively within the Canadian setting and it, too, has had varying success. Recall that the central premise of this theory revolves around the concept of party identification and the expectation that the affective bond or affiliation that each respective voter shares with his/her most preferred political party is likely to have a long-term stabilizing influence on voting choice, either directly or indirectly, through candidate evaluations and issue preferences. Recall, too, that although this model permits voters to deviate occasionally from their normal partisan preference—because they prefer either another party's candidates or another party's stand on the issues—the general expectation is that voters' electoral choices typically will be in line with their long-term partisan attachments. The danger in this argument, of course, is that if 'party identification travels too often with the vote, the entire theoretical edifice on which the concept rests will collapse' (Gidengil, 1992: 231).[9] Indeed, for this reason John Meisel declared party identification (and thus the socio-psychological model) to be largely inapplicable in the Canadian case. Based strictly on prima facie evidence from the 1965 and 1968 Canadian elections, party identification, Meisel (1972: 67) argued, seemed as volatile as vote itself. Others, such as Regenstreif (1965), reached the same conclusion.

However, the debate over the socio-psychological model's applicability in Canada was not to end there; it was resurrected once again in 1974 when Paul Sniderman and his colleagues revisited the topic and launched two counter-propositions that went directly against the earlier interpretation advanced by Meisel:

> We reject the view that in Canada, the absence of party loyalties leads to electoral volatility. The reasoning is sound, but both the premise and the conclusion are false. In Canada, identification with a party is the rule, not the exception, and the vote is marked by continuity, not volatility. (Sniderman et al., 1974: 286).

Working from the same survey data as Meisel, Sniderman et al. found that approximately four in every five Canadians admitted to identifying with a political party and only one in every five Canadians ever reported switching voting preference. Moreover, Sniderman and his colleagues also discovered that three in every four major party supporters never switched their party identification, and that the proportion of Canadians maintaining stable party loyalties, while changing their voting preferences, was consistently greater than in either the United States or Britain.[10] These findings, they argued, showed that party identifications in Canada reflect 'relatively enduring attachments to a party, and not simply superficial preferences related to the most recent election or the contemporary political scene' (ibid., 280).

Reactions to the arguments posed by Sniderman et al. have been mixed: not everyone disagrees (see, e.g., Jacek, 1975), but there are those who agree only in part. It is true, Jenson argues, that Canadians exhibit loyalties to political parties and that these loyalties are separate and distinct from one's actual voting preference. 'To know a voter's party identification is to know *something* about how the vote will be cast, but it is not to *know* how that individual will vote.' That said, however, the proposed stability of partisan attachments remains still very much in doubt. In other words, 'while a partisanship is acknowledged by Canadians, instability of that tie is high' (Jenson, 1975: 548, 550). Over a third of Canadians have at one point or another changed their party identification, whereas less than one-fifth of Americans have done the same.

Elkins, however, contends that even though the frequency of shifts in Canadian party loyalties may appear greater than similar shifts in the United States, 'what matters for the question of comparable phenomena in different societies is the total *pattern* of relationships between party identification (especially the differing degrees of intensity) and its potential effect on voting' (Elkins, 1978: 422). Elkins finds that despite the 'difference of incidence', the 'identity of patterns' in Canada and the United States is remarkably similar: the strongest identifiers in both countries are significantly more likely than weaker identifiers to consistently accord with their partisan affiliations. However, even Elkins agrees that absolute levels of fidelity in Canada are much lower than in the US.[11]

So why, then, do party affiliations in Canada seem so unstable? The answer, according to Johnston et al., is at least in part methodological: the conventional survey question used to tap partisan attachments is, in their view, seriously flawed. Prior to 1988, Canadians were literally forced to give what appears at face value to be a partisan commitment, even though in reality they may be entirely 'independent'. This in turn has had the effect of inflating 'the percentage appearing to identify with some party and [has] made the identifier group appear quite unstable over repeated measurements' (Johnston et al., 1992: 82). Using a measure that is more comparable to the one generally employed in the American context, Johnston et al. confirm that the Canadian electorate is not as undifferentiated as some might suggest, although they too find that more than one-third of the electorate does not identify with any particular party, thereby leaving 'ample scope for massive shifts' (ibid., 84).

In a slightly different vein, Jenson (1976) contends that instability within the party system causes instability in partisan loyalties, whereas LeDuc and others suggest that the federal system of government in Canada, with its inherent federal/provincial party differences, produces very little, if any, cross-level rein-forcement of partisan attitudes (LeDuc et al., 1983; Clarke and Stewart, 1985; Clarke et al., 1979; Clarke et al., 1991).[12] To some extent, the lack of strong (long-term) ideological and/or social group forces on party identification probably also contributes to the instability of party attachments (Lipset and Rokkan, 1967; LeDuc et al., 1983; Clarke et al., 1979; Clarke et al., 1991, 1996), as might the fact that party affiliations likely mean different things for different people. Clarke and his colleagues, for example, demonstrate that stable and unstable identifiers have differing conceptions of 'party' influences. The former conceive of party attach-ments as being long-term, general characterizations of party performance, whereas the latter see partisan ties as representing little more than perceptions of a party's current position on various salient issues. Loyalties of the latter variety are likely to be continuously updated and modified (see Johnston et al., 1992), thereby further contributing to the perception of instability. Findings such as these suggest that a more elaborate measure of partisan attachments might be needed to take into account the very real possibility that differing publics may have differing levels of partisan commitment (Clarke et al., 1979, 1991).

One such alternative, Clarke et al. argue, is to implement a composite indicator that taps a variety of different dimensions, including 'the consistency or inconsis-tency of feelings for a party across the federal and provincial levels, as well as the intensity and stability over time of these feelings at both levels' (Clarke et al., 1979: 155). *Flexible* partisans, according to this measure, are those voters who exhibit a low intensity of partisanship, shifting partisan attachments, and/or inconsistent attachments to parties at the federal and provincial levels, whereas *durable* partisans are those whose partisan orientations are strong, stable, and consistent. The latter constitute the 'loyalists who usually may be counted upon to support their parties regularly, while flexible partisans are much more likely to switch their votes between parties in successive elections' (Clarke et al., 1991: 48). Through the use of this measure, Clarke et al. have produced an image of Canadi-ans that is virtually the opposite of what others have suggested in the past. Their findings show that nearly three in every four Canadians are flexible partisans (Clarke et al., 1996).[13]

But if Clarke and his colleagues are right, then the question that inevitably arises is: Why is it that in 17 of the 24 elections contested since 1921 the same fed-eral party—the Liberals—has consistently emerged as the government of choice? The answer, according to LeDuc, has to do with a process known as 'stable dealignment' (LeDuc, 1984, 1985, 1989), which means essentially that, in Canada, shifting voter preferences rarely combine to favour any one particular opposition party because regional and subnational diversities generally preclude any such nationwide collaboration from taking place. That said, however, when dealigned partisans do converge, either nationally or regionally, the extent of electoral change can be quite striking (LeDuc, 1984: 423).[14] The 1993 election, for instance, shows how devastating the consequences can be. The Conservatives during that election went from being one of the strongest governments ever in Canadian history to not even having enough seats to merit official party status. Indeed, the effects of that election continue to haunt the Conservatives today.

The Rational Canadian Voter

What the preceding findings suggest is that voting in Canada cannot be entirely explained by long-term forces alone, thereby adding to the possibility that electoral decisions might also be influenced by the various short-term forces that form the substance of each particular election campaign. The rational choice model argues that all voters are utility maximizers and that when it comes to electoral decision-making, the voter is likely to opt for the party that he or she perceives as providing the greatest personal gain. In other words, contrary to both the Columbia and Michigan schools, the Downsian model contends that voters are independent and calculating when making their electoral choice. But is that the case? What does the Canadian evidence suggest?

One test for this proposition is to search for dynamics within election campaigns. If it were true that Canadians voted mainly in line with their long-term loyalties, then we would expect that election campaigns and the influences therein would have little or no effect on electoral decision-making. At best, campaigns might be construed as opportunities for parties to remind voters of old cleavages and to reassert and re-establish their traditional bonds. Johnston and his colleagues (1992), however, provide evidence to the contrary; their study of the 1988 Canadian election suggests that campaigns are more than just opportunities for rebuilding old coalitions. That is, campaigns really do matter (see also Nevitte et al., 2000).

By employing a novel sampling technique known as *rolling cross-section*, Johnston et al. demonstrate that 'while parties commonly work to activate interest in their own camp and thus to reinforce long-standing patterns, they also work to split other camps and they choose which interests within their own camp to activate' (ibid., 243). Their conclusion, therefore, is that voters are far from immune to change and are strikingly sensitive (and, indeed, responsive) to the information they receive during an election campaign through advertising, leadership debates, and/or the media in general.[15] Not only do voters entertain a wide range of considerations, but they also, it seems, possess the capacity to deliberate. Moreover, 'the way in which 1988 mattered suggests that at some level *all* campaigns matter, even when they do not exhibit the spectacular ups and downs of 1988' (ibid., 245).

Looking more systematically at which specific short-term influences are likely to have the most effect, Harold Clarke and his colleagues (1979, 1991, 1996) argue that the most *highly interested*, flexible partisans have the most fully developed images of the entire gamut of contesting parties and are therefore the best able to consider a variety of different alternatives (Clarke et al., 1979). These voters tend to be the most issue-oriented and are the most likely to base their electoral decisions on their most current issue opinions. Conversely, *less interested* flexible partisans, because they are not as likely to be informed about the issues of the day, tend to rely more heavily on their personal evaluations of party leaders. Whichever the case, the evidence clearly shows that the direct effects of issues and party leaders are much more significant than the effects of local candidates and that compared to durable partisans, flexible partisans are generally more likely to take longer to determine their voting preferences.[16]

Are we to conclude, then, that most Canadians are actually quite independent and calculating when it comes to electoral choice? Not entirely, as there is also compelling evidence to suggest that both social and psychological influences are still important considerations for a great many Canadians. But compared to the mid-1960s, the evidence shows that voters today are more informed, better educated, and more involved in the political process (Kanji, 1999; Kanji and Archer, 1998; also see Inglehart, 1970; Dalton, 1984, 1988, 1996; Nevitte, 1996). Improvements in information technology and mass communications have made it easier for citizens to acquire information. A growing number of Canadian households have two or more radios and cable TV. Newspaper sales have exploded by more than 50 times, and the number of Canadian households with home computers, modems, and access to the Internet continues to rise. The data also show that Canadians have become more attentive to information: compared to three decades ago, citizens today are significantly more inclined to watch television news, to read about news in the newspapers, and to listen to news on the radio.

The empowering effects of these shifts are clearly evident both in the electorate's growing sense of internal efficacy and in the increasing coherency of voter rationale (Kanji, 1999). Improvements in *human capital* (i.e., the gamut of knowledge and skills acquired during the course of one's life) work to elevate citizens' understanding of politics and make them more inclined to feel that they can significantly affect the political system. Moreover, the consistency with which Canadians' voting decisions coincide with their overall evaluations of party leaders, their personal rankings of important issues, and their perceptions of which parties are best suited to deal with salient concerns has improved remarkably. Coherent voters are much more inclined to base their voting decisions on the information they acquire and on their political know-how, as opposed to their conventional social and/or partisan cues (ibid.).

In addition, the propensity for strategic voting also appears to be on the rise. Blais and his colleagues, for example, report that in 1997 as many as 12 per cent of Canadian voters outside of Quebec cast a strategic vote. At least half of these voters 'decided to vote for a party other than the one they preferred because that party was perceived to have better chances of winning in their riding' (Blais et al., 1998: 8). The remainder 'went on to support a party that was not their first choice because that party was perceived to have better chances of unseating the Bloc Québécois as the official opposition' (ibid.). Findings such as these lead us to suggest that an increasing number of Canadians may be less dependent on their traditional long-term loyalties and more capable of reasoning politically.

The Implications For Future Research

Predicting election outcomes remains a risky business, but the three main theories of voting—the sociological, the socio-psychological, and the rational (economic) choice models—have proven quite useful, both in helping researchers to better understand why Canadians vote the way they do and in determining which influences are especially key. The more we learn, however, the more we realize how extremely intricate and complicated the so-called 'simple act of voting' really is. Thus, considerable work remains to be done. The old theories need to be revisited and updated to incorporate all that we have learned, and new research initiatives need to be set in order to ensure continuity and provide for future direction.

The sociological model, for instance, has led us to many useful findings (as well as non-findings) relating to the relationship between various primary factors (such as religion, region, social class) and vote. At the same time, evidence has suggested that in Canada the effects of various background factors on voting are heavily conditioned by variables such as region (Gidengil et al., 1999). Even secondary factors such as gender can have a significant influence on candidate choice (see Wearing and Wearing, 1991; O'Neill, this volume). Findings such as these lend further support to earlier claims suggesting that a more sustained and systematic analysis is required to determine how different intervening variables mediate the relationship between social group memberships and vote (Gidengil, 1992; Johnston, 1985). In other words, certain social group influences may occur more indirectly than others. We suggest, therefore, that future research using the sociological approach be expanded to incorporate these additional, more complicating possibilities.

In the same way, studies employing the socio-psychological model have also proved quite beneficial; to the extent that Canadians possess long-term partisan loyalties, they have been shown to have powerful effects on vote. However, differing interpretations of the stability of partisanship raise concerns about consistency and how well we truly understand this concept. It may be that there are good reasons for these discrepancies; after all, the preliminary evidence (Clarke et al., 1979) suggests that in Canada partisanship means different things to different people. More work is required, then, to flesh out the underlying dimensionality of partisan ties.

Lastly, the presence of campaign dynamics and the undeniable impact of various short-term influences on the vote raise questions about the future of electoral stability. LeDuc and others (LeDuc, 1977, 1984, 1985, 1989; LeDuc et al., 1983; Van Loon and Whittington, 1971) have consistently maintained that 'in spite of its seemingly more stable aggregate electoral patterns, Canada exhibits levels of volatility at the individual level as high or higher than those found in countries where patterns of volatility in elections are more readily apparent' (LeDuc, 1984: 60). That said, however, a key challenge for future research will be to determine whether the recently established five-party system (see Nevitte et al., 1996; Carty et al., 2000) constitutes a *realignment* of voter preferences or whether the continued impact of short-term campaign-related influences and the instability of party ties are likely to contribute to increasing electoral volatility and greater overall instability. For some preliminary interpretations, see Clarke et al., 1999; Nevitte et al., 2000.

Questions about the media's influence on voting are also likely to become increasingly important. Voters today refer more frequently to the media for their political information and it is clear that the media significantly influence the process of electoral choice (Johnston et al., 1992; Kanji, 1999; Jenkins, this volume; Mendelson, 1994, 1996). But more research is required for a better understanding of exactly how the media affect the vote. Which media in particular are the most influential? Do the content of the message and the predispositions of voters make a difference? And in what ways might improvements in information technology, in particular the Internet, affect the process of electoral choice?

Notes

1. For a more in-depth account of the origin of these differences, see Lipset and Rokkan (1967).
2. This particular sentiment persisted even despite others who claimed 'voters are not fools' (Key, 1966: 7).
3. Popkin (1994), for example, argues that, at best, the average citizen employs only a very basic 'gut reasoning' (or 'low information rationality') when dealing with issues of government and politics.
4. By voting 'correctly', Downs simply means voting for the party likely to provide the highest utility income.
5. It is interesting to note, however, that for Canadians, social group affiliations (to the extent that they exist) turn out to be more 'reinforcing' than 'cross-cutting': Canadians 'who are in the same group on one cleavage are in the same group on others' (Clarke et al., 1979: 95). In fact, reinforcing tendencies of social cleavages among the Canadian population turns out to be more predominant than similar tendencies in several other Western democracies (Clarke and Kornberg, 1971).
6. That said, however, it is important to note that the relationship between social class and vote is found on some occasions to be more powerful than others (see, e.g., Clarke et al., 1996).
7. For instance, Gibbins and Nevitte (1985; Nevitte and Gibbins, 1990), as well as Lambert et al. (1988), find that university students (and/or those who are more educated) have less conceptual difficulty with the concepts of 'left' and 'right'.
8. See also Ogmundson (1975a); Kay (1977); Lambert and Hunter (1979); Lambert (1983); Lambert et al., (1986a). Moreover, Zipp's (1978) work provides a slightly different set of reasons for why the 'left/right' dimension is not entirely appropriate for the Canadian case.
9. Elkins (1978: 427) refers to this phenomenon as the paradox of vote stability: 'The theory that party identification is a stabilizing force and the theory that it is an unimportant concomitant of the vote decision both point to the same evidence for corroboration.'
10. Note, however, that most of the findings reported by Sniderman and his colleagues are based heavily on voter recollections of past partisan preferences, and we know from MacDermid's (1989) work that many Canadians have 'feeble memories'.
11. By fidelity, Elkins means the act of voting consistently with one's party identification and maintaining that identification over time.

12. At least one study (Blake, 1982), however, has found that inconsistent partisan loyalties between government levels does not necessarily mean unstable voting within levels; in other words, patterns of fidelity for split identifiers are no more inconsistent than for cross-level consistent identifiers.
13. This conclusion, however, has been challenged as being overly inflated. Voters who do not have the same partisan options to choose from at the federal and provincial levels, for example, may be unfairly classified as being weak partisans.
14. The advent of parties such as the BQ, and the Reform Party (now the Canadian Alliance), it is argued, further simplifies the recipe of electoral change (see, e.g., Nevitte et al., 1996; Clarke and Kornberg, 1992).
15. It is interesting to note, however, that in a more recent analysis Blais et al. (1999) find that although leaders' debates and advertising might have an initial impact on voting intentions, the majority of that direct effect tends to dissipate by election day.
16. For more on the effects of various short-term factors on Canadian voting behaviour, see Clarke et al., (1982); Clarke and Stewart (1985); Archer and Johnson (1988); Clarke and Kornberg (1992); Johnston et al., (1994a, 1994b); Nevitte et al., (1996).

References

Alford, Robert. 1963. *Party and Society: The Anglo-American Democracies*. Chicago: Rand McNally & Company.

———. 1964. 'The Social Bases of Political Cleavage in 1962', in John Meisel, ed., *Papers on the 1962 Election*. Toronto: University of Toronto Press.

Archer, Keith. 1985. 'The Failure of the New Democratic Party: Unions, Unionists, and Politics in Canada', *Canadian Journal of Political Science* 18: 353–66.

———. 1987. 'A Simultaneous Equation Model of Canadian Voting Behaviour', *Canadian Journal of Political Science* 20: 553–72.

———. 1990. *Political Choices and Electoral Consequences: A Study of Organized Labour and the New Democratic Party*. Montreal and Kingston: McGill-Queen's University Press.

——— and Marquis Johnson. 1988. 'Inflation, Unemployment and Canadian Federal Voting Behaviour', *Canadian Journal of Political Science* 21: 569–84.

Barnes, Samuel, and Max Kaase. 1979. *Political Action: Mass Participation in Five Western Democracies*. Beverly Hills, Calif.: Sage.

Bell, Daniel. 1973. *The Coming of Post-Industrial Society: A Venture in Social Forecasting*. New York: Basic Books.

———. 1976. *The Cultural Contradictions of Capitalism*. New York: Basic Books.

Berelson, Bernard, Paul Lazarsfeld, and William McPhee. 1954. *Voting: A Study of Opinion Formation in a Presidential Campaign*. Chicago: University of Chicago Press.

Blais, André, Richard Nadeau, Elisabeth Gidengil, and Neil Nevitte. 1998. 'Voting Strategically Against the Winner: the 1997 Canadian Election', paper presented at the annual meeting of the Midwest Political Science Association, Chicago, 23–6 Apr.

———, ———, ———, and ———. 1999. 'Campaign Dynamics in the 1997 Canadian Election', *Canadian Public Policy* 25, 2.

Blake, Donald. 1972. 'The Measurement of Canadian Regionalism in Canadian Voting Patterns', *Canadian Journal of Political Science* 5: 55–81.

———. 1978. 'Constituency Contexts and Canadian Elections: An Exploratory Study', *Canadian Journal of Political Science* 11: 279–305.

———. 1982. 'The Consistency on Inconsistency: Party Identification in Federal and Provincial Politics', *Canadian Journal of Political Science* 15: 691–710.

Brodie, Janine, and Jane Jenson. 1980. *Crisis, Challenge, and Change: Party and Class in Canada*. Toronto: Methuen.

Budge, Ian, Ivor Crewe, and Dennis Farlie. 1976. *Party Identification and Beyond: Representations of Voting and Party Competition*. New York: Wiley.

Butler, David, and Donald Stokes. 1969. *Political Change in Britain: Forces Shaping Electoral Choice*. New York: St Martin's Press.

Campbell, Angus, Philip Converse, Warren Miller, and Donald Stokes. 1960. *The American Voter*. New York: Wiley.

Carty, R. Kenneth. 1996. 'The Electorate and the Evolution of Canadian Electoral Politics', *American Review of Canadian Studies* (Spring): 7–29.

———, William Cross, and Lisa Young. 2000. *Rebuilding Canadian Party Politics*. Vancouver: University of British Columbia Press.

Clarke, Harold, Jane Jenson, Lawrence LeDuc, and Jon Pammett. 1982. 'Voting Behaviour and the Outcome of the 1979 Federal Election: The Impact of Leaders and Issues', *Canadian Journal of Political Science* 15: 517–52.

———, ———, ———, and ———. 1991. *Absent Mandate: The Politics of Discontent in Canada*, 2nd edn. Toronto: Gage.

———, ———, ———, and ———. 1996. *Absent Mandate: The Politics of Discontent in Canada*, 3rd edn. Toronto: Gage.

——— and Allan Kornberg. 1971. 'A Note on Social Cleavages and Democratic Performance', *Comparative Political Studies* 4: 349–60.

——— and ———. 1992. 'Support for the Canadian Federal Progressive Conservative Party Since 1988: The Impact of Economic Evaluations and Economic Issues', *Canadian Journal of Political Science* 25: 29–53.

———, Lawrence LeDuc, Jane Jenson, and Jon Pammett. 1979. *Political Choice in Canada*. Toronto: McGraw-Hill Ryerson.

——— and Marianne Stewart. 1985. 'Partisan Inconsistency and Partisan Change in Federal States: The Case of Canada', *American Journal of Political Science* 31: 383–407.

———, Peter Wearing, Allan Kornberg, and Marianne Stewart. 1999. 'The Contest Nobody Won: The 1997 Canadian Federal Election and the National Party System', paper presented at Regionalism and Party Politics in Canada: A Conference in Honour of Mildred Schwartz, University of Calgary, 11–13 Mar.

Converse, Philip. 1964. 'The Nature of Belief Systems in Mass Publics', in D. Apter, ed., *Ideology and Discontent*. New York: Free Press.

Dalton, Russell. 1984. 'Cognitive Mobilization and Partisan Dealignment in Advanced Industrial Democracies', *Journal of Politics* 46: 264–84.

———. 1988. *Citizen Politics in Western Democracies*. Chatham, NJ: Chatham Publishers.

———. 1996. *Citizen Politics in Western Democracies*, 2nd edn. Chatham, NJ: Chatham Publishers.

————, Scott Flanagan, and Paul Beck.1984. *Electoral Change in Advanced Industrial Democracies: Realignment or Dealignment?* Princeton, NJ: Princeton University Press.

———— and Martin Wattenberg. 1993. 'The Not So Simple Act of Voting', in Ada W. Finifter, ed., *Political Science: The State of the Discipline.* Washington: American Political Science Association.

———— and ————, eds. 2000. *Parties Without Partisans: Political Change in Advanced Industrial Democracies.* New York: Oxford University Press.

Downs, Anthony. 1957a. *An Economic Theory of Democracy.* New York: Harper.

————. 1957b 'An Economic Theory of Political Action in a Democracy', *Journal of Political Economy* 65: 135–50.

Elkins, David. 1978. 'Party Identification: A Conceptual Analysis', *Canadian Journal of Political Science* 11: 419–35.

———— and Donald Blake. 1975. 'Voting Research in Canada: Problems and Prospects', *Canadian Journal of Political Science* 8: 313–25.

Engelmann, Frederick, and Mildred Schwartz. 1967. *Political Parties and the Canadian Social Structure.* Scarborough, Ont.: Prentice-Hall.

Gibbins, Roger, and Neil Nevitte. 1985. 'Canadian Political Ideology: A Comparative Analysis', *Canadian Journal of Political Science* 18: 577–98.

Gidengil, Elisabeth. 1989. 'Class and Region in Canadian Voting: A Dependency Interpretation', *Canadian Journal of Political Science* 22: 563–87.

————. 1992. 'Canada Votes: A Quarter Century of Canadian National Election Studies', *Canadian Journal of Political Science* 25: 219–48.

————, André Blais, Richard Nadeau, and Neil Nevitte. 1999. 'Making Sense of Regional Voting in the 1997 Canadian Federal Election: Liberal and Reform Support Outside Quebec', *Canadian Journal of Political Science* 32: 247–72.

Hunter, Alfred. 1982. 'On Class, Status, and Voting in Canada', *Canadian Journal of Sociology* 7: 19–39.

Inglehart, Ronald. 1970. 'Cognitive Mobilization and European Identity', *Comparative Politics* 3: 45–70.

————. 1977. *The Silent Revolution: Changing Values and Political Styles among Western Publics.* Princeton, NJ.: Princeton University Press.

————. 1990. *Culture Shift in Advanced Industrial Society.* Princeton, NJ: Princeton University Press.

————. 1997. *Modernization and Postmodernization: Cultural, Economic and Political Change in 43 Societies.* Princeton, NJ: Princeton University Press.

Irvine, William. 1974. 'Explaining the Religious Basis of the Canadian Partisan Identity: Success on the Third Try', *Canadian Journal of Political Science* 7: 560–3.

————. 1976. 'Testing Explanations of Voting Turnout in Canada', in Budge et al. (1976).

————. 1985. 'Comment on the Reproduction of the Religious Cleavage in Canadian Elections', *Canadian Journal of Political Science* 18: 115–17.

———— and H. Gold. 1980. 'Do Frozen Cleavages Ever Go Stale? The Bases of the Canadian and Australian Party Systems', *British Journal of Political Science* 10: 187–218.

Jacek, H. 1975. 'Party Loyalty and Electoral Volatility: a Comment on the Study of the Canadian Party System', *Canadian Journal of Political Science* 7: 144–45.

Jennings, Kent M., and Jan van Deth. 1990. *Continuities in Political Action*. New York: Walter de Gruyter.

Jenson, J. 1975. 'Party Loyalty in Canada: The Question of Party Identification', *Canadian Journal of Political Science* 8: 543–53.

———. 1976. 'Party Strategy and Party Identification: Some Patterns of Partisan Allegiance', *Canadian Journal of Political Science* 9: 27–48.

Johnston, Richard. 1985. 'The Reproduction of the Religious Cleavage in Canadian Elections', *Canadian Journal of Political Science* 18: 99–113.

———, André Blais, Henry Brady, and Jean Crête. 1992. *Letting the People Decide: Dynamics of a Canadian Election*. Montreal and Kingston: McGill-Queen's University Press.

———, André Blais, Elisabeth Gidengil, Neil Nevitte, and Henry Brady. 1994a. 'The Collapse of a Party System? The 1993 Canadian General Election', paper presented at the annual meeting of the American Political Science Association, New York.

———, Neil Nevitte, and Henry Brady. 1994b. 'Campaign Dynamics in 1993: Liberals, Conservatives, and Reform', paper presented at the annual meeting of the Canadian Political Science Association, Calgary.

Kanji, M. 1999. 'Information, Cognitive Mobilization and Representative Governance in Canada', paper presented at the Value Change and Governance Seminar, Toronto, 11 June.

——— and Keith Archer. 1998. 'When and How Canadian Voters Decide: Searching for Systematic Trends in Canadian Election Campaigns', paper presented at the annual meeting of the Canadian Political Science Association, Ottawa, May–June.

Kay, Barry. 1977. 'An Examination of Class and Left-Right Party Images in Canadian Voting', *Canadian Journal of Political Science* 19: 127–43.

Key, V. Donald. 1966. *The Responsible Electorate*. Cambridge: Belknap Press.

Lambert, Ronald. 1983. 'Question Design, Response Set and the Measurement of Left/Right Thinking in Survey Research', *Canadian Journal of Political Science* 16: 135–44.

——— and James Curtis. 1993. 'Perceived Party Choice and Class Voting', *Canadian Journal of Political Science* 26: 273–86.

———, ———, Stephen Brown, and Barry Kay. 1986a. 'In Search of Left/Right Beliefs in the Canadian Electorate', *Canadian Journal of Political Science* 19: 541–63.

———, ———, ———, and ———. 1986b. 'Canadian Beliefs about Differences between Social Classes', *Canadian Journal of Sociology* 11: 379–99.

———, ———, ———, and ———. 1987. 'Social Class, Left/Right Political Orientations, and Subjective Class Voting in Provincial and Federal Elections', *Canadian Review of Sociology and Anthropology* 24: 526–49.

———, ———, Barry Kay, and Stephen Brown. 1988. 'The Social Sources of Knowledge', *Canadian Journal of Political Science* 21: 359–74.

——— and Albert Hunter. 1979. 'Social Stratification, Voting Behaviour, and the Images of Canadian Federal Political Parties', *Canadian Review of Sociology and Anthropology* 16: 287–304.

Laponce, Jean. 1969. *People vs. Politics: A Study of Opinions, Attitudes, and Perceptions in Vancouver-Burrard*. Toronto: University of Toronto Press.

———. 1972. 'Post-dicting Electoral Cleavages in Canadian Federal Elections, 1949–68: Material for a Footnote', *Canadian Journal of Political Science* 5: 271–86.

Lazarsfeld, Paul, Bernard Berelson, and Hazel Gaudet. 1948. *The People's Choice: How the Voter Makes Up His Mind in a Presidential Campaign*. New York: Columbia University Press.

LeDuc, Lawrence. 1977. 'Political Behaviour and the Issue of Majority Government in Two Federal Elections', *Canadian Journal of Political Science* 10: 311–39.

———. 1984. 'Canada: The Politics of Stable Dealignment', in Dalton et al. (1984).

———. 1985. 'Canada', in Ivor Crewe and David Denver, eds. *Electoral Change in Western Democracies: Patterns and Sources of Electoral Volatility*. New York: St Martin's Press.

———. 1989. 'The Changeable Canadian Voter', in Alan Frizzell, Jon Pammett, and Anthony Westell, eds, *The Canadian General Election of 1988*. Ottawa: Carleton University Press.

———, Harold Clarke, Jane Jenson, and Jon Pammett. 1983. 'Partisan Instability in Canada: Evidence From a New Panel Study', *American Political Science Review* 78: 470–83.

Lipset, Seymour Martin, and Stein Rokkan. 1967. *Party Systems and Voter Alignments*. New York: Free Press.

MacDermid, R. 1989. 'The Recall of Past Partisanship: Feeble Memories or Frail Concepts?', *Canadian Journal of Political Science* 22: 363–75.

McDonald, Lynn. 1969. 'Religion and Voting: A Study of the 1968 Canadian Federal Election in Ontario', *Canadian Review of Sociology and Anthropology* 6: 129–44.

Meisel, John. 1967. 'Religious Affiliation and Electoral Behaviour: A Case Study', in J. Courtney, ed., *Voting in Canada*. Scarborough, Ont.: Prentice-Hall.

———. 1972. *Working Papers on Canadian Politics*. Montreal: McGill-Queen's University Press.

———. 1975. *Working Papers on Canadian Politics*, 2nd edn. Montreal and Kingston: McGill-Queen's University Press.

Mendelsohn, Matthew. 1994. 'The Media's Persuasive Effects: The Priming of Leadership in the 1988 Canadian Election', *Canadian Journal of Political Science* 27: 81–97.

———. 1996. 'The Media and Interpersonal Communications: The Priming of Issues, Leaders and Party Identification', *Journal of Politics* 58, 1: 112–35.

Nevitte, Neil. 1996. *The Decline of Deference*. Peterborough, Ont.: Broadview Press.

———, André Blais, Elisabeth Gidengil, and Richard Nadeau. 2000. *Unsteady State: The 1997 Canadian Federal Election*. Toronto: Oxford University Press.

——— and Roger Gibbins. 1990. *New Elites in Old States: Ideologies in the Anglo-American Democracies*. Toronto: Oxford University Press.

———, Richard Johnston, André Blais, Henry Brady, and Elisabeth Gidengil. 1996. 'Electoral Discontinuity: The 1993 Canadian Federal Election', *International Social Science Journal* 146: 583–99.

Norris, Pippa. 1999. *Critical Citizens: Global Support for Democratic Governance*. Oxford: Oxford University Press.

Ogmundson, Rick. 1975a. 'On Measurement of Party Class Position: The Case of Canadian Federal Political Parties', *Canadian Review of Sociology and Anthropology* 12: 565–76.

———. 1975b. 'On the Use of Party Image Variables to Measure the Political Distinctiveness of a Class Vote: The Canadian Case', *Canadian Journal of Sociology* 1: 169–77.

———. 1975c. 'Party Class Images and the Class Vote in Canada', *American Sociological Review* 40: 506–12.

———. 1979. 'A Note on the Ambiguous Meanings of Survey Research Measures Which Use the Words "Left" and "Right"', *Canadian Journal of Political Science* 12: 799–805.

——— and M. Ng. 1982. 'On the Inference of Voter Motivation: A Comparison of Subjective Class Vote in Canada and the United Kingdom', *Canadian Journal of Sociology* 7: 141–60.

Pammett, Jon. 1987. 'Class Voting and Class Consciousness in Canada', *Canadian Review of Sociology and Anthropology* 24: 269–89.

Pharr, Susan, Robert Putnam, and Russell Dalton. 2000. 'Trouble in the Advanced Democracies? A Quarter-Century of Declining Confidence', in *Journal of Democracy* 11, 2.

Popkin, Samuel. 1994. *The Reasoning Voter*. Chicago: University of Chicago Press.

Putnam, Robert, Susan Pharr, and Russell Dalton. 2000. 'Introduction: What's Troubling the Trilateral Democracies', in Pharr and Putnam, eds, *Disaffected Democracies: What's Troubling the Trilateral Countries?* Princeton, NJ: Princeton University Press.

Regenstreif, Peter. 1964. 'Group Perceptions and the Vote: Some Avenues of Opinion Formation in the 1962 Campaign', in John Meisel, ed., *Papers on the 1962 Election*. Toronto: University of Toronto Press.

———. 1965. *The Diefenbaker Interlude: Parties and Voting in Canada*. Toronto: Longmans Canada.

Schwartz, Mildred. 1974a. 'Canadian Voting Behaviour', in R. Rose, ed., *Electoral Behavior: A Comparative Handbook*. New York: Free Press.

———. 1974b. *Politics and Territory: The Sociology of Regional Persistence in Canada*. Montreal and Kingston: McGill-Queen's University Press.

Simeon, Richard, and David Elkins. 1974. 'Regional Political Cultures in Canada', *Canadian Journal of Political Science* 7: 397–437.

Sniderman, Paul. 1993. 'The New Look in Public Opinion Research', in Ada W. Finifter, ed., *Political Science: The State of the Discipline*. Washington: American Political Science Association.

———, H.D. Forbes, and Ian Melzer. 1974. 'Party Loyalty and Electoral Volatility: A Study of the Canadian Party System', *Canadian Journal of Political Science* 8: 268–88.

Stewart, Marianne, and Harold Clarke. 1998. 'The Dynamics of Party Identification in Federal Systems: The Canadian Case', *American Journal of Political Science* 42: 197–216.

Terry, J., and R. Schultz. 1973. 'Canadian Electoral Behaviour: A Propositional Inventory', in Orest Kruhlak et al., eds, *The Canadian Political Process*, rev. edn. Toronto: Holt, Rinehart and Winston of Canada.

Van Loon, Richard, and Michael Whittington. 1971. *The Canadian Political System*. Toronto: McGraw-Hill.

Wearing, Peter, and Joseph Wearing. 1991. 'Does Gender Make a Difference in Voting Behaviour?', in J. Wearing, ed., *The Ballot and Its Message: Voting in Canada*. Toronto: Copp Clark Pitman.

Zipp, J. 1978. 'Left-Right Dimensions of Canadian Federal Party Identification: A Discriminant Analysis', *Canadian Journal of Political Science* 11: 251–77.

Chapter 11

Do Party Supporters Differ?

André Blais, Elisabeth Gidengil,
Richard Nadeau, and Neil Nevitte

There is a debate, in Canada as elsewhere, about whether political parties really make a difference. Much of the literature on this question looks at whether policies and spending differ according to the partisan composition of governments (see Blais et al., 1993). The approach adopted here is different. Using survey data from the 1997 Canadian Election Study,[1] we examine the extent to which each party's voters differ in their views on the major issues of the day.

In theory, parties are supposed to present alternative perspectives on what governments should and should not do and electoral democracies give citizens the opportunity to vote for the party that best represents their own viewpoints. If both conditions are fulfilled, that is, if parties present real alternatives and if voters vote on the basis of party positions, then we should be able to observe real differences among supporters of the various parties.

Some analysts express skepticism about these assumptions. Canadian parties have been characterized as brokerage-style parties, taking middle-of-the-road and often fuzzy positions on most issues, while voters have been portrayed as making up their minds about which party to support on the basis not of party positions as such, but of leader evaluations and/or the performance of the economy (Clarke et al., 1984, 1991, 1996).[2] This picture of Canada's electoral politics is complemented by evidence that many voters are unfamiliar with the left-right terminology conventionally used to differentiate party positions in Western democracies (Lambert et al., 1986).

This is not the picture that would emerge, though, from a reading of news reports and media commentary on the so-called 'fight for the right' and the prospects for a consolidation of the political parties of the right (the Canadian Alliance and the Progressive Conservative Party). Two assumptions are implicit in this commentary: that the electorate can be characterized in left-right terms and that Canada does have ideologically distinct parties.

The two pictures are not necessarily entirely at odds with one another. Voters do not have to be familar with ideological terminology to take ideologically distinctive positions on the issues of the day. Nor do issues have to be highly salient in voters' choice of party in a given election for issue positions to differentiate each party's voters.[3] The question of whether supporters of the various parties do indeed differ on the issues is thus very much an empirical one. And so is the question of whether those differences are consistent with a left-right ordering of the parties.

To answer these two questions, we compare the views on a wide array of issues of those who voted Liberal, Reform (the predecessor of the Canadian Alliance),[4] Conservative, NDP, and Bloc Québécois in the 1997 federal election. In particular, we want to determine whether it is possible to locate party supporters on a left-right continuum anchored by NDP voters on the left and those who voted Reform on the right, with Liberal voters in the centre, Conservative voters at centre-right, between Liberal and Reform voters, and Bloc voters at centre-left, between Liberal and NDP voters.

The terms 'left' and 'right' have proved quite flexible, accommodating new issues while retaining their older meanings (Mair and Smith, 1990). At the core of the distinction are opposing beliefs about the free enterprise system and about the appropriate balance between government and the market. This is the so-called 'old' left-right cleavage. In contrast to the right, the left tends to be skeptical of the workings of the capitalist system. This skepticism is reflected in support for collective action to protect the interests of labour and a greater willingness to rely on the state to provide a social safety net. In the Canadian context, this cluster of beliefs has also made for a long-standing opposition to closer ties with the United States, seen as the bastion of free enterprise. This opposition was galvanized by the negotiation of the Canada-US Free Trade Agreement which was perceived to be a threat both to Canadian jobs and to Canada's social programs (Johnston et al., 1992).

To this fundamental division over the free enterprise system has been added a series of issues that together make up the 'new' left-right distinction. These issues can be grouped under four broad headings: traditionalism, gender, law and order, and accommodating diversity. The 'new' right is more traditional when it comes to a variety of issues that relate to so-called 'family values', such as marriage, children, and alternative lifestyles. This traditionalism is also reflected in a reluctance to accord women an equal role and a lack of sympathy for feminism and its goals. The right is also more concerned about law and order and readier to take a tough line with those who commit crimes. Finally, the 'new' right is associated with an unwillingness to accommodate racial and ethnic diversity, an unwillingness often manifested in more negative views about immigration and immigrants.

We have selected survey items to represent each of these dimensions that together make up the left-right cleavage. In doing so, we have been guided by an in-depth analysis of issue positions and ideological orientations in the 1997 federal election, which is reported elsewhere (Nevitte et al., 1999; see also Johnston et al., 1996). This analysis predictably also indicated the importance of attitudes towards accommodating Quebec. At first blush, this might appear to be an issue that

simply cannot be encompassed within even the most flexible of left-right definitions. It is worth noting, however, that the parties of the 'new' right in Western
Europe have often served as a lightning rod for resentment of regions that are seen
as a drain on the country's resources (Betz, 1993; Betz and Immerfall, 1998;
Kitschelt, 1995; Nevitte et al., 1998).

Different items used different response categories. Feelings about various
groups, for example, were measured on a 0 to 100 scale, while other items
employed an agree/disagree format or offered fixed response alternatives (such as
'do more', 'do less', or 'about the same as now'). To facilitate comparison of the
items, we have transformed all our measures so that they are on an identical scale.
The scale ranges from –1 to +1, with zero indicating a neutral or standpat position
on the item in question. The numbers should not be interpreted in absolute terms.
What matters are how party supporters are ordered and whether they are far apart
or close together. Details of the questions and response categories can be found in
the Appendix. In discussing the results we refer back to these response categories
rather than using the rescaled values. All the numbers reported in this chapter
exclude don't knows and refusals.

Table 11.1 shows the mean position of each party's voters for each item on our
–1 to +1 scale, as well as the mean value for the whole sample. The more positive
(negative) the value, the more right (left) wing the mean position. The overall
range on each item is also shown. The overall range is the difference between the
two polar parties. The significance level indicates the likelihood of obtaining differences like the ones observed in our sample if there were really no differences
between each party's supporters in the electorate at large. For each issue domain,
we begin by describing the overall distribution of opinion for the electorate at large
and then look at the ordering of party supporters.

Business

Overall, Canadians appear to be fairly well disposed towards business. On the
question of how much should be done for business, as many as 46 per cent say
'more' and only 19 per cent opt for 'less', and the mean rating given to big business on a 0 to 100 scale (59) is clearly favourable. At the same time, though, Canadians do not unequivocally endorse business practices. An overwhelming majority
of respondents (85 per cent) agreed with the assertion that the profits of Canadian
banks are a scandal. But perhaps the most telling indicator of Canadians' ambivalence towards business and the capitalist system in general comes from the finding
that 61 per cent disagree with the view that 'when businesses make a lot of money,
everyone benefits, including the poor.'

This last item best captures respondents' general orientations towards free
enterprise, and it is on this question (see Table 11.1) that the predicted left-right
distribution of party supporters most clearly emerges (though Reform and Conservative voters are indistinguishable). The situation is more ambiguous with respect
to the other three questions, which relate to opinions on business as such rather
than general orientations towards the system. Now it is only the left that appears

Table 11.1: Comparing the Views of Party Supporters

Business						Mean	Range
How much should be done for business?	NDP (−0.09)	Reform (+0.17)	Liberal (+0.19)	PC (+0.23)	Bloc (+0.25)	+0.19	0.34
How do you feel about big business?	NDP (−0.06)	Reform (+0.17)	Bloc (+0.21)	Liberal (+0.21)	PC (+0.26)	+0.17	0.32
Profits Canadian banks make are a scandal.	NDP (−0.72)	Bloc (−0.69)	Reform (−0.58)	PC (−0.54)	Liberal (−0.49)	−0.57	0.23
When businesses make money, everyone benefits.	NDP (−0.57)	Bloc (−0.30)	Liberal (−0.14)	PC (−0.05)	Reform (−0.05)	−0.19	0.52

Unions						Mean	Range
Unions should have more power.	NDP (−0.06)	Bloc (+0.15)	Liberal (+0.33)	Reform (+0.38)	PC (+0.41)	+0.27	0.47
How do you feel about unions?	NDP (−0.17)	Bloc (−0.02)	Liberal (+0.13)	Reform (+0.16)	PC (+0.22)	+0.10	0.39

Social Programs						Mean	Range
Importance: protecting social programs.	NDP (−0.80)	Liberal (−0.59)	PC (−0.51)	Bloc (−0.51)	Reform (−0.34)	−0.54	0.46
No cuts: welfare.	NDP (−0.44)	Bloc (−0.37)	Liberal (−0.15)	PC (−0.12)	Reform (−0.02)	−0.16	0.42
No cuts: health care.	NDP (−0.91)	Bloc (−0.81)	Liberal (−0.80)	PC (−0.76)	Reform (−0.73)	−0.79	0.18
No cuts: unemployment insurance.	NDP (−0.63)	Bloc (−0.56)	Liberal (−0.36)	PC (−0.34)	Reform (−0.30)	−0.41	0.33
No cuts: education.	NDP (−0.90)	Liberal (−0.77)	Bloc (−0.77)	PC (−0.75)	Reform (−0.70)	−0.77	0.20
How do you feel about people on welfare?	NDP (−0.09)	Bloc (+0.05)	PC (+0.07)	Liberal (+0.10)	Reform (+0.14)	+0.09	0.23

US and International Trade						Mean	Range
Canadian ties with US.	NDP (−0.09)	Bloc (+0.04)	Liberal (+0.09)	Reform (+0.10)	PC (+0.11)	+0.08	0.20
How do you feel about US?	Bloc (+0.06)	NDP (+0.06)	Reform (+0.19)	Liberal (+0.20)	PC (+0.20)	+0.15	0.14

Table 11.1. *(continued)*

US and International Trade						Mean	Range
International trade creates more jobs.	NDP (–0.07)	Bloc (–0.02)	PC (+0.17)	Liberal (+0.22)	Reform (+0.25)	+0.14	0.32
Free trade with US is good.	NDP (–0.26)	Liberal (+0.16)	Reform (+0.19)	Bloc (+0.21)	PC (+0.29)	+0.13	0.55

Traditionalism						Mean	Range
Only married people should have children.	Bloc (–0.66)	NDP (–0.42)	PC (–0.23)	Liberal (–0.19)	Reform (+0.12)	–0.22	0.78
Men are less patient when caring for children.	NDP (–0.21)	Bloc (–0.19)	Liberal (–0.12)	PC (–0.11)	Reform (–0.01)	–0.10	0.20
Fewer problems if more emphasis on traditional family values.	NDP (+0.18)	Bloc (+0.28)	Liberal (+0.39)	PC (+0.41)	Reform (+0.58)	+0.39	0.40
Newer lifestyles contribute to breakdown in society.	NDP (–0.19)	Liberal (–0.00)	Bloc (+0.01)	PC (+0.06)	Reform (+0.39)	+0.09	0.58
How do you feel about gays and lesbians?	NDP (–0.24)	PC (–0.00)	Bloc (+0.01)	Liberal (+0.02)	Reform (+0.21)	+0.04	0.45
Homosexual couples allowed to legally marry.	NDP (–0.14)	Bloc (–0.02)	PC (+0.24)	Liberal (+0.25)	Reform (+0.50)	+0.23	0.64
Abortion: choice.	Bloc (–0.71)	NDP (–0.70)	PC (–0.57)	Liberal (–0.47)	Reform (–0.39)	–0.50	0.32

Women						Mean	Range
Women should stay at home with children.	Bloc (–0.30)	NDP (–0.24)	Liberal (–0.14)	PC (–0.14)	Reform (+0.19)	–0.10	0.49
How much should be done for women?	Bloc (–0.61)	NDP (–0.52)	PC (–0.43)	Liberal (–0.39)	Reform (–0.18)	–0.39	0.43
How do you feel about feminists?	NDP (–0.12)	Bloc (–0.02)	Liberal (+0.09)	PC (+0.15)	Reform (+0.24)	+0.12	0.36
Should lay off women whose husbands have jobs.	NDP (–0.69)	Bloc (–0.65)	PC (–0.65)	Liberal (–0.64)	Reform (–0.50)	–0.62	0.19
Difficult for women to get jobs when equal abilities.	NDP (–0.28)	Bloc (–0.16)	PC (–0.15)	Liberal (–0.12)	Reform (+0.08)	–0.13	0.36
More women in Parliament to protect women's interests.	NDP (–0.25)	Bloc (–0.16)	PC (–0.13)	Liberal (–0.12)	Reform (+0.07)	–0.09	0.32

Table 11.1. *(continued)*

Crime						Mean	Range
Importance: fighting crime.	NDP (+0.47)	Bloc (+0.48)	PC (+0.62)	Liberal (+0.64)	Reform (+0.68)	+0.63	0.21
Deal with young offenders of violent crime.	NDP (−0.17)	Bloc (−0.12)	PC (+0.17)	Liberal (+0.31)	Reform (+0.58)	+0.25	0.75
Capital punishment is never justified.	NDP (−0.08)	Bloc (+0.02)	Liberal (+0.15)	PC (+0.25)	Reform (+0.50)	+0.20	0.58
Feel about the police.	Bloc (+0.17)	NDP (+0.33)	Liberal (+0.42)	PC (+0.42)	Reform (+0.45)	+0.37	0.28
Only the military and the police allowed to have guns.	Liberal (−0.31)	Bloc (−0.24)	NDP (−0.20)	PC (−0.08)	Reform (+0.21)	−0.12	0.50

Immigrants						Mean	Range
Canada should admit more immigrants.	NDP (+0.20)	Liberal (+0.33)	PC (+0.35)	Bloc (+0.40)	Reform (+0.49)	+0.39	0.29
Should look after Canadians born here first.	NDP (−0.19)	Liberal (−0.02)	PC (+0.05)	Bloc (+0.17)	Reform (+0.18)	+0.05	0.37
Too many recent immigrants do not want to fit.	NDP (−0.10)	Liberal (+0.14)	PC (+0.24)	Bloc (+0.34)	Reform (+0.39)	+0.23	0.49
Immigrants make an important contribution.	NDP (−0.50)	Liberal (−0.34)	PC (−0.34)	Reform (−0.26)	Bloc (−0.11)	−0.30	0.39

Quebec (outside Quebec only)					Mean	Range
Quebec be recognized as distinct society.	NDP (−0.21)	Liberal (−0.07)	PC (−0.07)	Reform (+0.42)	+0.08	0.63
How do you feel about Quebec?	NDP (−0.23)	Liberal (−0.19)	PC (−0.17)	Reform (+0.04)	−0.09	0.27
Gone too far pushing bilingualism.	NDP (−0.06)	Liberal (+0.21)	PC (+0.32)	Reform (+0.69)	+0.33	0.75
Quebec has the right to separate.	NDP (+0.52)	Reform (+0.62)	Liberal (+0.62)	PC (+0.66)	+0.59	0.14

Notes: Variables have been coded on a scale from −1 to +1, where −1 corresponds to a leftist orientation and +1 indicates a rightist perspective. See Appendix for complete questions and scales. All mean differences are significant at the .01 level or higher, except for the final Quebec issue (Quebec has the right to separate).

to be set apart, while supporters of the other parties all take more or less the same position. On the first two questions, only NDPers differ from the rest and even they are not particularly ill-disposed towards business. With respect to bank profits, on which opinion is generally unfavourable, there is a small cleavage between NDP and Bloc voters and the rest.

The degree of divergence among parties, then, is relatively modest. It is strongest with respect to general orientations towards the working of the system, with a range of 0.52 on our −1 to +1 scale. Fully 81 per cent of NDPers reject the idea that everyone benefits when business makes money, but the percentage drops to 53 per cent among Reformers and Conservatives.

Unions

The data indicate that unions have a more negative image than business. When it came to how respondents felt about unions and whether unions should have more power or less, the average response was relatively negative. Unions received a mean rating of slightly below 50 (45) on a 0 to 100 scale, and only 13 per cent of our respondents said that unions should have more power, while nearly half (49 per cent) argued that they should have less.

Not surprisingly, NDP voters are most favourable to unions. The anti-union pole, however, is occupied not by people who voted Reform but by Conservatives. Liberal voters are faithful to their image of being centrist, and Bloc voters come up between Liberal and NDP supporters, as befits a left-of-centre party. The overall ranking of the parties is thus close to the standard assumption, except for the fact that those who voted Reform are outflanked on the right by Conservatives. The overall range of opinions about unions could be characterized as relatively wide. For instance, the percentage of respondents who believe that unions should have less power goes from 21 per cent among NDPers to 62 per cent among Conservatives.

Social Programs

Most Canadians (60 per cent) say that protecting social programs is a very important issue. This is why an overwhelming majority opposes cuts in health care (81 per cent) and education (79 per cent). Resistance to cuts in unemployment insurance is also fairly strong (47 per cent). More people (66 per cent) are willing to consider cuts in welfare payments, though perhaps because Canadians have mixed feelings about people on welfare (average rating of 45).

Predictably, the two most extreme positions are held by NDPers and people who voted Reform. The Liberals and the Conservatives are more or less indistinct. As for BQ supporters, they are not too distant from the NDP in their opposition to cuts, even though they do not express such overwhelming support for the general idea of protecting social programs.

Generally, the standard hypothesis about the distribution of party supporters tends to be confirmed. The exception is that the Conservatives are as centrist as the Liberals. Differences between the parties are relatively small with respect to education and health but they are more substantial in the case of welfare. Cuts in welfare were approved by as many as 76 per cent of Reformers but by only 47 per cent of NDPers.

The United States and International Trade

General feelings towards the United States are positive, with Canadians giving our southern neighbour a mean rating of 57. The dominant view (56 per cent) is that ties with the United States should remain about as they are now. Few (17 per cent) think that these ties should be weakened. A clear majority (63 per cent) believes that free trade with the US has been good for the Canadian economy. Consistent with these views, assessment of the overall impact of international trade is relatively sanguine: 63 per cent think it creates more jobs than it destroys.

On these questions, the main cleavage is between ndp and Bloc voters, on the one hand, who tend to be less pro-American, and the Liberals, Conservatives, and people who voted Reform, on the other hand. There is one small exception. The Conservatives come out as the most supportive of the Free Trade Agreement. This is not surprising since the deal was struck by the former Conservative government of Brian Mulroney. Bloc voters are also particularly supportive of free trade with the United States, perhaps because it is perceived to facilitate the road to sovereignty.

The standard classification tends not to be supported in this case. There is the predictable cleavage between the left and the right but no cleavage between the centre and the right. Differences between the parties are also somewhat muted. For instance, the percentage who believe that Canada should have more distant ties with the US goes from 13 per cent among Conservatives to 30 per cent among NDPers.

Traditionalism

On most of the questions tapping so-called family values, Canadians could be characterized as moderately traditional. There is strong support (75 per cent) for the general view that we would have fewer problems if traditional family values were given more emphasis. This could well explain why 59 per cent of the sample are opposed to allowing homosexual couples to get legally married. A small majority also agrees that new lifestyles contribute to the breakdown of society (55 per cent). Nonetheless, 63 per cent disagree with the statement that only married people should have children, 59 per cent believe that abortion should be a matter of personal choice (only 9 per cent think it should be never permitted), and 57 per cent disagree with the notion that men are less patient and giving than women when it comes to caring for babies and small children.

The pattern of responses to these questions is a familiar one. NDPers are the least traditional, followed by Bloc voters (the latter are least traditional with respect to marriage), while people who voted Reform are the most traditional. Liberals and Conservatives are in the middle, usually very close to each other. As with social programs, the usual classification of party supporters appears to be adequate, except for the fact that the Conservatives are in the centre and not on the right.

Differences between party supporters turn out to be particularly large. For instance, while 55 per cent of Reform voters shared the view that only married people should have children, only 12 per cent among Bloc supporters ascribed to this view.

Women

Many voters are inclined to accept the claim that women's concerns need to be given special attention. A majority (59 per cent) agrees that there is discrimination against women in the job market and 57 per cent think that we need more women in Parliament to protect women's interests. Fifty-four per cent of Canadians disagree with the view that society would be better off if more women stayed home with their children. Most Canadians (60 per cent) support the idea that more should be done for women in general and there is strong rejection (86 per cent) of the suggestion that having a job could be less important for women whose husbands are already employed. Nonetheless, there is ambivalence about feminist groups, whose average rating is only 44, about the same as for unions.

On all of these questions, NDPers and Bloc supporters come out as more favourable to women's issues and Reform voters as the most opposed, with the Liberals and the Conservatives systematically in the middle. On this issue dimension, the standard left-right classification is mostly borne out. The exceptions turn out to be the Conservatives, who are as centrist as the Liberals, and the BQ voters, who are as leftist as the NDPers.

Differences of opinions among the parties are substantial. The percentage who said that more should be done for women, for instance, was only 38 per cent among Reform voters but as high as 84 per cent among the Bloc voters.

Crime

Canadians are concerned about crime. Most respondents (69 per cent) told us crime was a very important issue for them. Perhaps because of this concern, they tend to give the police high ratings (68). When it comes to choosing between tough and soft approaches to dealing with crime, Canadians lean towards the former. More opt for tougher sentences (60 per cent) than for rehabilitation (35 per cent) to deal with young offenders, and a majority (62 per cent) supports capital punishment. But Canadians are also tough with gun owners: a majority (56 per cent) supports the strong position that nobody except police officers and the military should be allowed to have guns.

On the first four questions, those who voted Reform stand out as most concerned with crime and more willing to be tough, while NDPers and Bloc supporters are softest. The Liberal and the Conservative voters again occupy the middle ground. On the question of guns, the Reform Party was the only party among which a majority (63 per cent) opposed a ban on guns. People who voted Reform are tough with criminals but soft on gun owners and the reverse is true of NDPers and Bloc voters. On the issue of guns, however, the toughest of all are the Liberals: 65 per cent favour a complete ban on guns (except for the police and the military).

With respect to guns, the distribution of party supporters does not fit the standard left-right continuum. On the other questions, however, the hypothesis is supported, though there is not much difference between Bloc and NDP voters and the Conservatives are as centrist as the Liberals. Differences of opinion are important. Only 40 per cent of NDPers opted for tougher sentences for young offenders, compared with 76 per cent of Reformers.

Immigrants

Four questions probed Canadians' sentiments towards immigrants: Should we admit more or fewer immigrants? Do immigrants make sufficient efforts to integrate into Canadian society? Do they make an important contribution to the country? Should we look after people born in Canada first?

Views about immigrants can be characterized as ambivalent but tilted towards the negative side. Half the respondents (48 per cent) think we should admit fewer immigrants (only 9 per cent would like more) and agree with the assertion that immigrants should be treated, in effect, as second-class citizens. As many as 64 per cent believe that immigrants do not really try to integrate. But a strong majority (75 per cent) thinks that immigrants make an important contribution to Canadian society.

In all cases, NDPers emerge as the most pro-immigrant and in three cases out of four Reformers were the least supportive. Liberal and Conservative voters are systematically in the centre and are hardly distinguishable. Finally, and contrary to expectations, Bloc supporters tend to side with people who voted Reform. This might reflect a perception that Quebec immigrants are inclined to integrate into the Anglophone community and to oppose sovereignty.

The findings tend to support the hypothesized ordering for Reform, the NDP, and the Liberals, but not for the Bloc, whose supporters are close to the position of Reform voters on this issue, nor for the Conservatives, who turn out to be as centrist as the Liberals. As for the amount of divergence, it is best described as moderate. For instance, the percentage wanting fewer immigrants ranged from 35 per cent among NDPers to 56 per cent among Reformers.

Quebec

The last domain to be considered is the 'Quebec' issue. How do Canadians *outside* Quebec react to issues dealing with Quebec? General feelings towards Quebec are slightly positive: the average rating is 55. There is resistance, however, to the idea of giving Quebec any special rights. Only one voter out of three thinks Quebec should be recognized as a distinct society (though one out of three among those opposed would change his/her mind if this keeps Quebec in Canada). There is the feeling, shared by 69 per cent of the sample, that we have gone too far in pushing bilingualism in Canada, and an overwhelming majority (83 per cent) disagrees that Quebec has the right to separate unilaterally.

It might be argued that the Quebec issue is qualitatively different from the others that have been considered and that there is no reason to expect a similar rank ordering of the parties. Yet, Table 11.1 indicates that, as on most issues, NDPers and those who voted Reform occupy the polar positions, and that Conservative and Liberal voters occupy the centre. The only exception is with respect to Quebec's right to secession, where supporters of all the parties share similar views.

Differences of opinion among the parties are substantial. For instance, willingness to recognize Quebec as a distinct society ranged from 18 per cent among Reformers to 48 per cent among NDPers.

Conclusions

We began by posing two basic questions. First, do party supporters differ in their views about various issues? Second, are these differences consistent with a left-right ordering of the parties, with the NDP occupying the left, the Bloc Québécois the centre-left, the Liberals the centre, the Conservatives the centre-right, and Reform the right?

It turns out that differences among parties vary from one domain to another. They are particularly substantial with respect to traditionalism: five of the seven questions yielded a range greater than .40 on the –1 to +1 scale. The differences tend to be smaller, though, with respect to business, unions, and the United States. The median range on the 42 questions listed in Table 11.1 is .39 on the –1 to +1 scale. We can illustrate what this means in terms of the original response categories by looking at the actual distribution of responses to an item on which the range corresponds to the median, namely, the question about whether immigrants make an important contribution. The two polar parties on this question are the Bloc and the NDP. Fully 86 per cent of NDPers agree with the statement, compared to only 61 per cent of BQ voters, a difference of 25 percentage points. The difference between Liberal and Conservative voters on this question is almost nil: the percentages agreeing are 77 per cent and 79 per cent, respectively. Perhaps the most telling indicator is that the average difference between pairs of supporters on this question is 11 percentage points. We may thus surmise that on a typical issue, the typical difference (in the level of agreement with a given position) between supporters of pairs of parties is about 10 percentage points. All in all, party differences are not huge, but neither are they inconsequential. To return to the assumptions about electoral democracy with which this chapter began, these findings suggest that people with different views about the issues do vote for different parties and that the party system does reflect differing viewpoints. The range of differences expressed, however, is relatively modest.

Our second question was concerned with the order of party supporters on the various issues. The conclusion is that the standard depiction of each party's supporters on a left-right scale, from NDPers on the left to Blocists, to Liberals, then Conservatives, and finally people who voted Reform on the right, generally makes sense. The exception is the Conservatives.

On all nine dimensions considered here, NDPers occupied the left pole, and on six of them Reformers occupied the opposite pole.[5] Intriguingly, Reformers were *not* the most 'rightist' on several of the issues that define the 'old' left-right cleavage, such as the role of unions and business and our links with the United States. The ideological distinctiveness of people who voted Reform is much more evident when it comes to issues associated with the 'new' right than with the 'old' right.

The hypothesis that Bloc supporters occupy the centre-left of the political spectrum is generally confirmed. There is one important exception—immigration—and in this instance Bloc voters sided with Reformers. The most plausible reason for this finding is the historical pattern of immigration in Quebec and the place of immigrants in the nationalist debate.

The view that Liberal voters are centrist is also generally supported in the sense that Liberals are very seldom to be found at one of the poles. But clearly the Liberals do not have the monopoly of the centre. On most issues, there is hardly any difference between Liberal and Conservative voters (see Table 11.2). Perhaps the best illustration of this is the percentage in favour of cuts to social programs, which is almost the same among the two groups (differences are between two and five percentage points). There is one exception and this concerns views about unions, where Conservative voters come out as the most 'rightist'. On all of the other issues, there is little to support the characterization of Conservative voters as clearly to the right of Liberals. And on the majority of dimensions, Conservative voters are much closer to Liberal voters than they are to people who voted Reform. This is especially true of issue domains that relate to the 'new' left-right distinction, such as traditionalism, gender, law and order, and accommodating diversity.

When it comes to ideology, then, there is very little difference between Conservative and Liberal voters. In this sense, the portrait of the two parties as brokerage parties, competing for the median Canadian voter, remains intact. This is only a very partial picture of Canada's electoral politics in the 1990s, however. Despite a brief flirtation with brokerage politics in the 1988 federal election (Johnston et

Table 11.2. Conservative-Liberal and Conservative-Reform Differences Compared

	Conservative-Liberal Difference	Conservative-Reform Difference
Business	+0.03	+0.05
Unions	+0.08	+0.04
Social Programs	+0.03	−0.08
US and International Trade	+0.02	+0.01
Traditionalism	−0.01	−0.23
Women	−0.01	−0.21
Crime	+0.03	−0.21
Immigrants	+0.05	−0.12
Quebec (outside Quebec only)	+0.04	−0.26

Note: The column entries are the average differences in the mean scores of the respective parties on each dimension. Positive differences indicate that Conservative supporters were to the right of the other party's supporters on average, while negative differences indicate that they were to the left.

al., 1992), the NDP remains a party clearly to the left of the Canadian centre in its appeal. And both the Reform Party and the Bloc broke through in the 1993 federal election by refusing to play by the rules of brokerage politics. In the 1997 election, the two parties' voters continued to occupy distinct positions on many of the issues that define the left-right cleavage.

It remains to be seen whether Reform's successor, the Canadian Alliance, will be successful in attracting erstwhile Conservative voters. As we have seen, Conservative supporters are typically closer to their Liberal counterparts in the centre than they are to partisans of the right. Should some sort of 'united alternative' emerge to challenge the Liberals' current dominance, it will likely say more about the compelling logic of brokerage politics than about any reunification of the right.

Appendix: Description of Variables

Variables have been coded on a scale from –1 to +1, where –1 corresponds to a leftist orientation and +1 indicates a rightist perspective. The numbers in parentheses indicate the value given to categories (unless otherwise specified). The codes in square brackets correspond to the variable names in the original data file.

Business

How much do you think should be done for business: much more (1), somewhat more (0.5), about the same as now (0), somewhat less (–0.5), or much less (–1)? [pese2]

How do you feel about big business? On a scale from 0 to 100, where 0 means you really dislike them and 100 means you really like them. [pesf1] The scale was transformed to –1 to 1, where 1 indicates the respondent really likes big business and –1 indicates she really dislikes them.

For each statement below, please indicate if you strongly agree (–1), agree (–0.5), disagree (0.5), or strongly disagree (1): The profits Canadian banks are making these days are a scandal. [mbsd9]

Do you strongly agree (1), somewhat agree (0.5), somewhat disagree (–0.5), or strongly disagree (–1) with the following statement: When businesses make a lot of money, everyone benefits, including the poor. [pese20]

Unions

How much power do you think unions should have: much more (–1), somewhat more (–0.5), about the same as now (0), somewhat less (0.5), or much less (1)? [pese3]

How do you feel about unions? On a scale from 0 to 100, where 0 means you really dislike them and 100 means you really like them. [pesf12] The scale was transformed to –1 to 1, where –1 indicates the respondent really likes unions and 1 indicates she really dislikes them.

Social Programs

How important are the following issues to you personally in this election: very important (–1), somewhat important (0), not very important (1)? Protecting social programs [cpsa2f].

If you had to make cuts, would you cut spending in the following areas a lot (1), some (0), or not at all (–1)? Welfare? [pese6b]

If you had to make cuts, would you cut spending in the following areas a lot (1), some (0), or not at all (–1)? Health care? [pese6d]

If you had to make cuts, would you cut spending in the following areas a lot (1), some (0), or not at all (–1)? Unemployment insurance? [pese6e]

If you had to make cuts, would you cut spending in the following areas a lot (1), some (0), or not at all (–1)? Education? [pese6f]

How do you feel about people on welfare? On a scale from 0 to 100, where 0 means you really dislike them and 100 means you really like them. [pesf5] The scale was transformed to –1 to 1, where –1 indicates the respondent really likes people on welfare and 1 indicates she really dislikes them.

The United States and International Trade

Do you think Canada's ties with the United States should be much closer (1), somewhat closer (0.5), about the same as now (0), more distant (–0.5), or much more distant (–1)? [pese4]

How do you feel about the United States? On a scale from 0 to 100, where 0 means you really dislike the US and 100 means you really like the US. [pesf13] The scale was transformed to –1 to 1, where 1 indicates the respondent really likes the US and –1 indicates she really dislikes the US.

For each statement below, please indicate if you strongly agree (1), agree (0.5), disagree (–0.5), or strongly disagree (–1): International trade creates more jobs in Canada than it destroys. [mbsd11]

For each statement below, please indicate if you strongly agree (1), agree (0.5), disagree (–0.5), or strongly disagree (–1): Overall, free trade with the US has been good for the Canadian economy. [mbsg10]

Traditionalism

Do you strongly agree (1), somewhat agree (0.5), somewhat disagree (–0.5), or strongly disagree (–1) with the following statement: Only people who are married should be having children. [cpsf2]

Do you strongly agree (1), somewhat agree (0.5), somewhat disagree (–0.5), or strongly disagree (–1) with the following statement: Society would be better off if more women stayed home with their children. [cpsf3]

For each statement below, please indicate if you strongly agree (1), agree (0.5), disagree (–0.5), or strongly disagree (–1): When it comes to caring for babies and small children, men by nature are less patient and giving than women. [mbsg5]

For each statement below, please indicate if you strongly agree (1), agree (0.5), disagree (–0.5), or strongly disagree (–1): This country would have many fewer problems if there were more emphasis on traditional family values. [mbsa9]

For each statement below, please indicate if you strongly agree (1), agree (0.5), disagree (−0.5), or strongly disagree (−1): Newer lifestyles are contributing to the breakdown of our society. [mbsa7]

How do you feel about gays and lesbians? On a scale from 0 to 100, where 0 means you really dislike them and 100 means you really like them. [pesf10] The scale was transformed to −1 to 1, where −1 indicates the respondent really likes gays and lesbians and 1 indicates she really dislikes them.

For each statement below, please indicate if you strongly agree (−1), agree (−0.5), disagree (0.5), or strongly disagree (1): Homosexual couples should be allowed to be legally married. [mbsg3]

Now we would like to get your views on abortion. Of the following three positions, which is closest to your own opinion: abortion should never be permitted (1), should be permitted only after need has been established by a doctor (0), should be a matter of the woman's personal choice (−1)? [pese5a]

Women

Do you strongly agree (1), somewhat agree (0.5), somewhat disagree (−0.5), or strongly disagree (−1) with the following statement: Society would be better off if more women stayed home with their children. [cpsf3]

How much do you think should be done for women: much more (−1), somewhat more (−0.5), about the same as now (0), somewhat less (0.5) or much less (1)? [pese1]

How do you feel about feminists? On a scale from 0 to 100, where 0 means you really dislike them and 100 means you really like them. [pesf3] The scale was transformed to −1 to 1, where −1 indicates the respondent really likes feminists and 1 indicates she really dislikes them.

For each statement below, please indicate if you strongly agree (1), agree (0.5), disagree (−0.5), or strongly disagree (−1): If a company has to lay off some of its employees, the first workers to be laid off should be women whose husbands have jobs. [mbsa3]

For each statement below, please indicate if you strongly agree (−1), agree (−0.5), disagree (0.5), or strongly disagree (1): Discrimination makes it extremely difficult for women to get jobs equal to their abilities. [mbsa5]

For each statement below, please indicate if you strongly agree (−1), agree (−0.5), disagree (0.5), or strongly disagree (1): The best way to protect women's interests is to have more women in Parliament. [mbsd8]

Crime

How important are the following issues to you personally in this election: very important (1), somewhat important (0), or not very important (−1)? Fighting crime. [cpsa2g]

Which is the best way to deal with young offenders who commit violent crime: give them tougher sentences (1), spend more on rehabilitating them (−1), both (0), depends (0), or corporal punishment (1)? [cpsj21]

Do you strongly agree (–1), somewhat agree (–0.5), somewhat disagree (0.5), or strongly disagree (1) with the following statement: Capital punishment is never justified, no matter what the crime? [pese13]

How do you feel about the police? On a scale from 0 to 100, where 0 means you really dislike them and 100 means you really like them. [pesf7] The scale was transformed to –1 to 1, where 1 indicates the respondent really likes the police and –1 indicates she really dislikes them.

Do you strongly agree (–1), somewhat agree (–0.5), somewhat disagree (0.5), or strongly disagree (1) with the following statement: Only police officers and the military should be allowed to have guns? [pese12]

Immigrants
Do you think Canada should admit more immigrants (–1), fewer immigrants (1) or about the same as now (0)? [cpsj18]

For each statement below, please indicate if you strongly agree (1), agree (0.5), disagree (–0.5), or strongly disagree (–1): We should look after Canadians born in this country first and others second. [mbsa11]

For each statement below, please indicate if you strongly agree (1), agree (0.5), disagree (–0.5), or strongly disagree (–1): Too many recent immigrants just don't want to fit into Canadian society. [mbsg4]

For each statement below, please indicate if you strongly agree (–1), agree (–0.5), disagree (0.5), or strongly disagree (1): Immigrants make an important contribution to this country. [mbsd12]

Quebec (outside Quebec only)
Should Quebec be recognized as a distinct society? Yes, no, or depends? [cpsj3] Would you change your mind if this keeps Quebec in Canada? Yes, no, or depends? [cpsj3c] If the respondent said 'yes' to the first question, the variable equals –1. If the respondent said 'depends' to the first question or said 'no' to the first question and 'yes' or 'depends' to the second, the variable equals 0. If the respondent said 'no' to both questions, the variable equals 1.

How do you feel about Quebec? On a scale from 0 to 100, where 0 means you really dislike Quebec and 100 means you really like Quebec. [pesf12] The scale was transformed to –1 to 1, where –1 indicates the respondent really likes Quebec and 1 indicates she really dislikes Quebec.

For each statement below, please indicate if you strongly agree (1), agree (0.5), disagree (–0.5), or strongly disagree (–1): We have gone too far in pushing bilingualism in Canada. [mbsd7]

For each statement below, please indicate if you strongly agree (–1), agree (–0.5), disagree (0.5), or strongly disagree (1): Quebec has the right to separate no matter what the rest of Canada says. [mbsg7]

Notes

1. The Canadian Election Study consists of a three-wave survey conducted by the Institute for Social Research at York University under our direction. The study was funded by the Social Sciences and Humanities Research Council of Canada. The data may be obtained from: < www.isr.yorku.ca/ISR >. During the campaign, 3,949 eligible voters were interviewed, of whom 3,170 were re–interviewed after the election and 1,727 returned a mail-back questionnaire. The campaign response rate was 59 per cent. For further information on the study, see Northrup (1998).
2. For the counter–thesis that Canada's political parties are ideologically distinct, see, for example, Horowitz (1966) and Campbell and Christian (1996).
3. For a discussion of the distinction between compositional differences and differences in the effects of issues and other factors on vote choice, see Gidengil et al., (1999).
4. The Reform Party membership voted on 25 March 2000 to reconstitute as the Canadian Reform Conservative Alliance.
5. For an analysis of the relationship between the NDP and the old and new left in Canada, see Butovsky (1999).

References

Betz, Hans-George. 1993. 'The New Politics of Resentment: Radical Right-Wing Populist Parties in Western Europe', *Comparative Politics* 25: 413–27.

——— and Stefan Immerfall. 1998. *The New Politics of the Right: Neo-Populist Parties and Movements in Established Democracies*. New York: St Martin's Press.

Blais, André, Donald Blake, and Stéphane Dion. 1993. 'Do Parties Make a Difference? Parties and the Size of Government in Liberal Democracies', *American Journal of Political Science* 37: 40–62.

Butovsky, Jonah. 1999. 'The Old and New Left in Canada: Conflict or Compatibility?', paper presented at the annual meeting of the Canadian Political Science Association, Sherbrooke, Que.

Campbell, Colin M., and William Christian. 1996. *Parties, Leaders and Ideologies in Canada*. Toronto: McGraw-Hill Ryerson.

Clarke, Harold D., Jane Jenson, Lawrence LeDuc, and Jon Pammett. 1984. *Absent Mandate: The Politics of Discontent in Canada*. Toronto: Gage.

———, ———, ———, and ———. 1991. *Absent Mandate: Interpreting Change in Canadian Elections*. Agincourt, Ont.: Gage.

———, ———, ———, and ———. 1996. *Absent Mandate: Canadian Electoral Politics in an Era of Restructuring*. Vancouver: Gage.

Gidengil, Elisabeth, André Blais, Richard Nadeau, and Neil Nevitte. 1999. 'Making Sense of Regional Voting in the 1997 Canadian Federal Election: Liberal and Reform Support Outside Quebec', *Canadian Journal of Political Science* 32: 247–72.

Horowitz, Gad. 1966. 'Conservatism, Liberalism and Socialism in Canada: An Interpretation', *Canadian Journal of Economics and Political Science* 32: 143–71.

Johnston, Richard, André Blais, Henry E. Brady, and Jean Crête. 1992. *Letting the People Decide: Dynamics of a Canadian Election*. Montreal and Kingston: McGill-Queen's University Press.

————, ————, ————, Elisabeth Gidengil, and Neil Nevitte. 1996. 'The 1993 Canadian Election: Realignment, Dealignment, or Something Else?', paper presented at the annual meeting of the American Political Science Association, Washington, DC.

Kitschelt, Herbert. 1995. *The Radical Right in Western Europe: A Comparative Analysis.* Ann Arbor: University of Michigan Press.

Lambert, Ronald D., James E. Curtis, Steven D. Brown, and Barry J. Kay. 1986. 'In Search of Left/Right Beliefs in the Canadian Electorate', *Canadian Journal of Political Science* 19: 541–63.

Mair, Peter, and Gordon Smith. 1990. *Understanding Party System Change in Western Europe.* London: Frank Cass.

Nevitte, Neil, André Blais, Henry Brady, Elisabeth Gidengil, and Richard Johnston. 1998. 'The Populist Right in Canada: The Rise of the Reform Party of Canada', in Betz and Immerfall (1998).

————, ————, Elisabeth Gidengil, and Richard Nadeau. 1999. *Unsteady State: The 1997 Canadian Federal Election.*Toronto: Oxford University Press.

Northrup, David A. 1998. *The 1997 Canadian Election Study: Technical Documentation.* North York, Ont.: Institute for Social Research.

Chapter 12

Ecological Factors and Voting

MUNROE EAGLES

> *While the individual man is an unsolvable puzzle, in the*
> *aggregate he becomes a mathematical certainty.*
> Sir Arthur Conan Doyle

While scholars may debate the significance of elections for liberal democracy, the simple act of voting provides political scientists with an important opportunity to study the political behaviour of citizens and groups. Since voting is the single participatory act engaged in regularly by majorities of citizens, there are few alternatives to electoral analyses for students of mass political behaviour. Reflecting their importance, elections have been analysed from a wide variety of perspectives. Early electoral studies in most countries were often impressionistic and historical/journalistic, concerned primarily with such aspects of elections as leaders, dominant issues, campaign platforms, and descriptive analyses of modal party supporters. However, since votes are easily counted and are cast in large numbers, electoral analysis was one of the first enterprises to attract the attention of pioneers in statistical analysis in political science.

The earliest quantitative studies of elections in states with single-member plurality electoral systems involved a search for empirical patterns in turnout and party support across electoral districts or constituencies. Typically, election results would be explained by relating the share of the vote going to a party to underlying socio-economic, ethnocultural, and other geographically differentiated factors associated with these settings. The central unit of observation in such analyses, then, is the electoral district. Data for these analyses typically were drawn from election returns, election maps, and census tabulations. In some cases, these analyses were limited to commentaries on electoral maps (e.g., Krehbiel, 1916; Wright, 1932), while in other cases cartographic and geographic interpretations were either replaced with or complemented by statistical analysis (Siegfried, 1913; Tingsten, 1967).

Popular as these studies were in the first half of this century, at least two factors accounted for a sharp decline in ecological, or geographically limited, analyses. First of all, a problem arising from attempts to draw inferences about the behaviour of individuals from analyses of aggregate or ecological data (the ecological inference problem) was first recognized in 1919 when efforts were made to anticipate how newly enfranchised American women would cast their ballots nationwide. While some voting statistics were available from prior state elections in which women were participants, the ecological inference problem prevented scholars from distinguishing men's and women's votes within the same electoral precinct. Subsequently, W.S. Robinson's (1950) identification of the 'ecological fallacy', in which aggregate-level correlations between race and literacy were not replicated in individual-level (survey) research, definitely had a chilling effect on aggregate data researchers. Robinson's critique was published precisely at the time when information on the attitudes and behaviour of individuals, collected by public opinion surveys, were becoming generally available (the first American national election survey, for example, was conducted in 1952). Since that time, survey-based analyses have been preferred by students of political behaviour. For many years, then, ecological factors have been devalued in electoral analyses.

There are a number of indications that this unfortunate and premature truncation of the research agenda of ecological research has ended. Recent advances in statistical methods (spatial econometrics) and computer software (specifically, the emergence of geographic information systems, or GIS, software) have combined with a number of other factors to revitalize this research tradition. Today, the ecological analysis of elections represents an important complement to other approaches to the understanding of electoral politics and political behaviour discussed in this book. I contend that the quantitative analysis of constituency-level patterns in voting and elections offers at least four advantages over other methodologies. First, constituency-level political and demographic data are cheaply available and are as reliable as the data from election agencies and census bureaus (Eagles et al., 1991, 1995). Second, these data are often available over long periods of time, therefore enabling quantitative historical explorations of early elections. Third, these data are geographically exhaustive, offering coverage of the entire country (something that cluster sampling frames and the small sample sizes employed in many surveys precludes). Finally, such data are frequently superior to other possible sources of data for the answering of an important subset of questions in electoral analysis (e.g., for estimating the incumbency advantage or campaign and/or local party organization effects, to mention but two examples).

In this chapter I will outline a political ecological perspective on voting and elections. I will first differentiate the broad types of factors that figure prominently in such an ecological approach. I will then discuss some methodological challenges confronting this perspective. Finally, I will briefly review the contributions that some applications of ecological analysis have made to the study of Canadian elections. While hardly exhaustive, this overview will demonstrate that ecological factors are important determinants of election outcomes. Because of this importance, the ecological analysis of elections will continue to make significant contributions to our understanding of the not-so-simple act of voting in Canadian elections.

Types of Ecological Influences on Elections

The perspective of political ecology seeks to explain patterns in political life by relating them to aspects of the geographic setting such as the social characteristics of an area's residents, its local economy, and the stability of its social structure (see Berglund and Thompsen, 1990; Eagles, 1990; Ersson et al., 1990). Basic to this approach, then, is an assumption that political behaviour is a product *both* of the characteristics, attitudes, orientations, and beliefs of individuals and of extra-individual forces that are features of, or structured by, the geographic context. In other words, the ecological perspective focuses on the spatial patterning of political behaviour and seeks to draw insights about the nature of political behaviour from the study of spatial variations in such things as party support, voter turnout, and so on. Ecological models of constituency politics differ from the customary survey-based studies of voting behaviour in a number of ways. Most importantly, while surveys measure the correlates of political behaviour across individuals, ecological analysis attempts to identify and explain patterns of variation in the behaviour of constituency electorates. Normally, variation in citizen interest (e.g., voter turnout, party support, campaign funding, etc.) is explained by a combination of social, geographic, and political variables.

Three general aspects of the local setting-social, political, and locational factors-can be expected to influence political behaviour. First, local areas vary widely in terms of the characteristics of their residents. Some areas are home to concentrations of immigrants, for example, while others may be disproportionately populated by the affluent or the poor. Some areas are religiously homogeneous, others are home to a variety of religions. Some areas have highly transient populations; others do not. In many different ways, then, *geographic space is subject to different patterns of social organization.* As a result, the nature and intensity of community formation differs radically from locale to locale. Similarly, the social content of routine and more intimate social interactions in Canadian communities will vary systematically in terms of the characteristics of their resident populations. Because politics is part of the broader social life of the community, these differences will be associated with variations in electoral behaviour. Paul Lazarsfeld and his colleagues recognized that even personal decisions such as voting have a collective dimension: 'Voting is essentially a group experience. People who work or live or play together are likely to vote for the same candidates' (Lazarsfeld et al., 1968: 137).

Second, local variations in political behaviour may well result from the activities of political organizations and local political leaders who seek to mobilize support from particular segments of their community (and demobilize opposition from competing segments of the community). In countries with single-member plurality electoral systems, political campaigns have both national and local dimensions. With respect to the latter, in some fundamental respects a Canadian federal election is actually a collection of 301 local elections held simultaneously. Each of these local contests is played out on a particular geographic terrain. Campaigns seek to mobilize particular neighbourhoods where their supporters are concentrated, or where residents possess social or other characteristics that are presumed to dispose them to support a candidate or party. Over time, the activities of parties and candidates will foster and perpetuate distinctive local political cultures. Related to this, party organizations will grow stronger over time in their more favoured locales, and thus will be able to mount more vigorous campaigns in some areas than others. Patterns of party competition will vary across geographic space as a result of the accumulation of these political practices. Some areas may be characterized by relatively close competition while others may remain strongholds of a party for some time. Some races will feature strong candidates (so-called 'star candidates' or 'local heroes/heroines') and/or well-known incumbents seeking re-election while others may attract only novices. For all these reasons, the political stimuli acting on a voter, and the character of the political choices she/he confronts, will vary according to where the person lives because of the differences in what can be called the *political organization of space*.

Finally, the political outlook and behaviour of voters may be affected by their geographic location, that is, by the nature of the socio-geographic relationship between their home and other communities in Canada. Remote communities, cut off from the mainstream of Canadian political currents, may well develop a distinctive political outlook and pattern of electoral behaviour. Jeremy Wilson's analysis of electoral patterns in British Columbia, for example, demonstrates that the province's uneven geographic topography (operating along with social marginalization) insulates remote communities from electoral forces operating elsewhere in the province (Wilson, 1980). Here the locational influence is 'remoteness' or geographic isolation. In addition, residents of a 'periphery', such as the Maritimes or western Canada, may develop attitudes of alienation from and resentment to the domination of a distant 'centre'. Both of these regions have historically given rise to regionally based protest movements or parties-between 1919 and 1927 in the Maritimes, and at various times in the West (see Forbes, 1979; Bercuson, 1986). Here the locational influence at work is the outcome of the spatial dimension of demographic, economic, and/or political inequality.

Clearly, this threefold classification of ecological factors is not exhaustive, but it indicates something of the range of features of the local setting that can influence an election outcome. Therefore, two individuals with similar personal characteristics may well vote differently depending on where they live. Much of this spatial variation will not be captured by random sample survey research (which plucks individuals out of such local contexts and aggregates them in a 'sample' in which no two members are likely to have any social interaction) (Barton, 1968). Something of a debate has emerged in the study of Canadian elections as to the supposed superiority of one or another of these approaches (see Wiseman, 1986, 1989; Archer, 1989). It is more fruitful, however, to regard survey and ecological analyses as complementary, in that each is based on different assumptions about what causes voting behaviour and each is suited to answer different kinds of questions. Each approach has a role to play in our understanding election outcomes.

The Challenges of Quantitative Ecological Analysis

The primary objective of ecological analysis is to explain constituency electoral patterns and outcomes. Measures used in this research can be further differentiated as falling into one of two classes, compositional or contextual. Constituency scores on *compositional measures* are determined by aggregating the characteristics and qualities of individual residents of the constituency. Such measures give 'aggregate data' its name, in that constituency totals reflect the densities of aggregated individual characteristics. *Contextual measures*, on the other hand, refer to attributes of the constituency settings themselves that are not derived from the characteristics of their residents. Such contextual factors may reflect aspects of the geographical setting, such as the location or size of the riding. Alternately, they may represent aspects of the competitive or strategic setting of political competition, such as the presence (or not) of an incumbent, the strength of local party organizations, the intensity of campaigning and the level of campaign spending in the constituency, and so on. As such, these data stand as proxies for other social or political processes hypothesized to have political consequences.

For this purpose, aggregate data are not an inferior substitute for survey information based on individuals, as is often believed. Rather, when the objective is to provide an understanding of the determinants of constituency-level outcomes or the influence of constituency-level processes, such data may be more appropriate than information derived from randomly sampled survey respondents. Critics of ecological analysis may object to an analysis of Canadian politics that focuses on constituencies, since the dependent political behavioural variables that are often the focus of interest in electoral studies, such as turning out to vote and supporting a political party, are ultimately performed by individuals and not constituencies or groups. Following Robinson's critique, cross-level inferences were considered problematic: 'The relation between ecological and individual correlations . . . provides a definitive answer as to whether ecological correlations can be used as substitutes for individual correlations. They cannot.' (Robinson, 1950: 357). This conclusion, however, is almost certainly overstated (Hanushek et al., 1974) and recent advances in ecological methods have offered solutions that reduce, if not completely resolve, the problems associated with the ecological fallacy (King, 1996).

There are certainly situations in which the measures of relationships estimated using individual and grouped data are likely to diverge, making cross-level inferences in either direction (from ecological to individual level or vice versa) unreliable (Wellhofer, 1991). Such instances may result from the peculiarities of ecological or aggregate data. Alternatively, however, they may signal the existence of a process of importance for a complete understanding of political behaviour. In either instance, divergent results from individual and ecological analyses are not something to be swept under a methodological rug. Rather, they call for closer inspection and further research.

At least three identifiable processes can be responsible for producing divergent results from parallel analyses at individual and group levels: aggregation bias, contextual effects, and 'spatial dependence'. *Aggregation bias* refers to the distortion that may be introduced into ecological analysis from the process of grouping individuals together into aggregate units. There are virtually an infinite number of *possible* aggregate units that might be created from a group of individuals, depending on the size, number, and disparity in the aggregate districts that are produced. For the purposes of ecological analysis of elections, the aggregating is done by those responsible for drawing electoral boundaries (in the Canadian case, the 10 federal boundaries commissions, one for each province). As practitioners of gerrymandering (the partisan manipulation of electoral boundaries) have long appreciated, tinkering with electoral boundaries can have important electoral consequences. More generally, however, it may be that analytic results taken from one set of boundaries may not exactly conform to results based on a differently designed set of aggregate units (even though the underlying configuration of individuals would remain the same). Geographers refer to this as the 'modifiable areal unit problem' or MAUP. Research shows, for example, that aggregating the same individuals into different geographic groups and performing the same analysis on these data greatly influences the results of analyses, changing both the magnitude of coefficients and occasionally even their signs (see Fotheringham and Wong, 1991). While this problem may loom large in many aggregate analyses based on arbitrarily or randomly defined geographic units, in a country such as Canada where electoral boundaries reflect, among other things, communities of interest, it is less likely to be a serious threat to analysis. As such, constituency boundaries may be modifiable over time, but they also are meaningful in the sense that they define coherent sociological and political environments, within which processes of interest to students of elections (e.g., campaigning and political organization) take place.

Second, the results of ecological analysis may differ from those of individual-level analyses whenever individuals' behaviour not only reflects their own characteristics and dispositions but also is affected by some aspect of their social or political environment. Differences in environments, then, may cause similar individuals to manifest different political orientations or behaviours. An example of this might be when a poor person who lives in a well-to-do area begins to adopt the attitudes and behaviours of her or his neighbours. Known as *contextual effects*, these situations can only be fully understood by using data from both individuals and their group contexts simultaneously. However, in situations where contextual effects are found or can be anticipated, ecological analyses on their own yield a reasonable representation of the foundations of political behaviour, and are probably as or more reliable than conventional survey analysis. This is because data for groups incorporate the characteristics of individuals comprising them, but they also serve as proxies for the kinds of group-level processes responsible for producing the observed contextual effects. While unique advantages accrue from analyses that simultaneously combine individual survey and aggregate data in a single analysis, a discussion of such multi-level or 'contextual analyses', as they have come to be known, is beyond the scope of this chapter (see Eagles, 1995; for Canadian applications, see Blake, 1978; Laponce, 1969; Pammett, 1991).

Finally, for our purposes, it is important to note that data derived from geographic units of analysis provide observations that are not statistically independent of one another. This reflects the operation of Waldo Tobler's 'first law of geography', which states that 'everything is related to everything else, but near things are more related than distant ones.' For example, because of the regionalized nature of economic conditions, the rate of unemployment in one constituency is likely to be similar to the rate of unemployment in neighbouring ridings. The presence of 'spatial dependence' in aggregate data structures violates the statistical assumptions of most multivariate analyses, which are premised on the assumption of the statistical independence of all observations (something, of course, that is assured by the random sampling process in opinion survey research). This problem, known technically as 'spatial autocorrelation', is not particularly acute in analyses based on relatively large aggregate units such as parliamentary constituencies. However, when the aggregate units of analysis are smaller, it frequently becomes necessary to measure the extent and nature of spatial dependence. In these cases, of course, the spatial patterning of measures on different variables can themselves be of substantive interest to the analyst (the clustering of high levels of partisan support in a subset of neighbouring districts, for example), and not simply represent a nuisance for statistical estimations. In any case, geographers and spatial econometricians have developed (and are continuing to develop) variations of familiar regression models used in the multivariate analysis of aggregate data that, to greater or lesser degrees, will correct for underlying spatial dependence problems.

What Have Ecological Analyses Contributed to Our Understanding of Canadian Elections?

The challenges confronting the statistical analysis of ecological measures are becoming more widely understood. As a result, today scholars are more cautious about drawing simple inferences concerning the behaviour of individuals from ecological analysis, and they are more careful to employ suitable diagnostic measures to check for the incidence of spatial autocorrelation or aggregation effects. Further research into the nature and impact of these issues promises to improve the quality of inferences drawn from aggregate data. In the meantime, however, ecological analysts have made, and continue to make, important contributions to our understanding of Canadian elections. A brief survey of existing studies of Canadian elections reveals that the contributions of ecological analyses of elections are found with respect to each of the types of ecological factors discussed earlier (social, political, and locational).

A fundamentally important set of questions concerning elections and parties investigates the impact on elections of the social organization of constituencies. Here, ecological analysis has demonstrated that people in wealthy, well-educated, residentially stable communities are likely to be disproportionately active in the election process, both in terms of voting and in making financial contributions to constituency campaigns. A regression analysis of patterns of voter turnout at the constituency level in the 1988 election, after controlling for a variety of factors (such as region and various political factors), found that for every 1 per cent increase in the proportion of lower-income families in a riding, the level of voter turnout decreased by over a fifth of a per cent. Similarly, for every percentage increase in the proportion of those moving residences in the previous five years, other things being equal, turnout declined by almost a fifth of a per cent (see Eagles, 1991: 18, Table 1.6). A similar pattern has been found in the analysis of the fund-raising activities of political parties across Canadian federal constituencies in 1988. For example, total fund-raising by all parties was over $2,700 higher for every percentage increase in the proportion of university graduates, but was almost $1,000 lower for every percentage increase in the proportion of low-income families (see Eagles, 1992: 552, Table 5).

An important aspect of electoral analysis concerns the determinants of the partisan choices of voters. Some of the earliest systematic studies of this important question adopted an ecological perspective. Escott Reid's analysis of the 1930 election result, for example, identified and assessed the strength of the traditional Francophone/Liberal and the Anglophone/Conservative alignment characteristic of so much of the politics of the twentieth century (Reid, 1967: 74). Indeed, any systematic or quantitative account of elections prior to the 1960s in Canada must necessarily rely on ecological methods and data since survey evidence from earlier periods is simply not available (see Brodie and Jenson, 1988; Graesser, 1993; Wiseman and Taylor, 1974).

More recent elections have also been analysed from an ecological perspective. Some ecological studies, for example, uncover a relationship between the social class composition of constituencies and patterns of party support (Gerber, 1986). Others note the importance of ethno-religious differences in voting behaviour (Eagles, 1999). In other respects, however, these studies reinforce the image of the traditionally dominant Canadian parties (prior to 1993, the Liberals and Tories) having only relatively weak ties to social groups. Support for the smaller parties in the Canadian party system, such as the New Democrats, Reform (now the Canadian Alliance) and the Bloc Québécois, tends to be more strongly related to the underlying features of a constituency's social structure (Blake and Erickson, 1998).

Ecological analysis is well suited to explore these longer-term relationships between aspects of social structure and party choice. For example, such analyses repeatedly document that the strongest determinant of a party's support at any given election is likely to be the level of its support at the previous election (Eagles, 1999). Particularly remarkable in this respect is the constituency-level and regional continuity in party support between the 1988 and 1993 elections, an election characterized by unprecedented individual-level and system-level discontinuity (resulting in the election of 203 rookie MPs) (Eagles et al., 1995; Swayze, 1996; Blake and Erickson, 1998). The coefficient measuring the impact in 1993 of the Conservative Party's 1988 vote suggests that even in the midst of an electoral debacle of extraordinary magnitude, all else being equal, for every 1 per cent won by the party in a riding in 1988, its 1993 vote increased by half a per cent (a coefficient of .50 in the ecological regression). For the Liberals in that election, the coefficient for inter-election continuity in party support is even higher (0.88), while the NDP's is the same (0.50) (see Eagles, 1999: Tables 2–4). By contrast, much of the survey-based analysis of Canadian voting behaviour emphasizes the high levels of partisan instability in the Canadian electorate. The difference in emphasis arising from the two methodologies is interesting.[1] Even in elections when large proportions of Canadian voters shift their partisan allegiances and large numbers of seats change partisan hands, there is a relatively high level of constituency-level continuity in the levels of party support. The ecological perspective on party support, then, suggests that Canada's local party organizations, and the campaigns they wage, may be especially influential in harnessing and directing the movements of Canada's especially dealigned electorate.

Ecological analyses of the effects associated with the political organization of space have also made contributions to our understanding of Canadian elections. Studies of campaign expenditures, for example, have demonstrated that, in general and with some important caveats, the more that local candidates and parties can spend in a political campaign, the better they do at the polls. As Table 12.1 illustrates, however, the fortunes of any one party are in part also likely to be a function of the campaign spending of their competitors. For example, after controlling for a wide range of political, socio-economic, and regional factors, the proportion voting Conservative in 1988 went up 4.34 per cent for every additional dollar the party spent per elector. However, PC voting went down almost 4 per cent for each dollar per elector spent in constituencies by the Liberals, down about 4% for every dollar per elector spent by the NDP, and down 5.24% for every dollar per elector spent by minor/independent candidates.

Table 12.1: Campaign Spending and Party Support, 1988 (unstandardized OLS regression coefficients/[t-statistics])

	% Progressive Conservative	% Liberal	% NDP
$ per elector, Conservative spending	4.34 (1.99)	–4.44 (–1.85)	2.48 (1.25; n.s.)
$ per elector, Liberal spending	–3.90 (–2.11)	10.40 (4.94)	–7.21 (–4.25)
$ per elector, NDP spending	–4.12 (–2.78)	–10.15 (–6.11)	16.51 (11.27)
$ per elector, minor party/ independent spending	–5.24 (–2.67)	–5.67 (–4.97)	(–2.58) (–2.70)

Note: Partial results from multivariate models presented in full in Eagles (1993: 440, Table 2). Dependent variable in each model was the percentage of the popular vote won by the party.

Other aspects of the local campaign, such as the availability of local volunteers for door-to-door canvassing, also contribute to the vote shares a party wins. For example, in the 1988 federal election, a regression analysis demonstrates that adding 10 volunteers to a local party's campaign organization returned an additional 0.09 per cent in terms of extra popular vote for Progressive Conservatives, 0.13% for Liberal candidates, and 0.12 per cent for New Democrats (see Carty and Eagles, 1999: 81, Table 2). Such studies also demonstrate that despite the high turnover of Canadian MPs, incumbents running for re-election generally still enjoy electoral advantages over their non-incumbent counterparts. The advantage varies by party and over time, but it is generally worth between a couple and upwards of 10 percentage points in terms of the popular vote (Krashinsky and Milne, 1985; Eagles, 1993).

Finally, locational influences also figure prominently in ecological research on Canadian elections. For example, one of the strongest and most enduring determinants of Canadian voting behaviour is region. Survey analysts have long appreciated the importance of geography for understanding Canadian voting patterns and their research has contributed greatly to our understanding of this phenomenon. However, ecological analysis is attractive for studying regional patterns because of its ability to include all areas of the country. Analysis of regional variations in electoral behaviour, then, has long been one of the mainstays of the ecological perspective (Blake, 1972; Campbell and Knight, 1976; Lemieux, 1988). The more comprehensive and nuanced geographical coverage offered by an ecological perspective can be useful, for example, in refining the identification of regions and facilitating the identification of sub-provincial regions (e.g., Weller, 1977).

Conclusion

The ecological analysis of Canadian elections develops a distinctive and important perspective on our electoral process and its outcomes. It uses data aggregated at the constituency level to explore and explain the impact of social, political, and locational characteristics of constituency settings on the outcome of elections. The challenges that confront the statistical analysis of ecological data are increasingly being understood, and applications of the perspective have made important contributions to our knowledge about the determinants of election outcomes. Important as existing contributions have been, however, there is reason to believe that the promise of ecological analysis is greater still. Advances in geographic information systems and statistical software have made the analysis and cartographic display of ecological data easier and more powerful than ever before. Readily available data for constituencies for contemporary and historical analysis make the approach increasingly attractive in an era of diminished research budgets. Finally, there is a growing awareness in political science that various aspects of geographic space and the sense of place matter (Agnew, 1986). For all these reasons, the ecological analysis of elections in Canada offers students of Canadian politics a powerful set of tools, theories, and interpretations.

Note

1. The analysis of the 1997 Canadian Election Survey by Blais et al. (1998: 19) acknowledges, however, that the strongest determinant of voter choice in Canada remains 'traditional loyalties'.

References

Agnew, John. 1986. *Place and Politics: On the Geographical Mediation of State and Society*. Boston: George Allen & Unwin.

Archer, Keith. 1989. 'The Meaning and Demeaning of the National Election Studies', *Journal of Canadian Studies* 24, 4 (Winter): 353–66.

Barton, A.H. 1968. 'Bringing Society Back In: Survey Research and Macro-Methodology', *American Behavioral Scientist* 12, 2 (Nov.–Dec.): 1–9.

Bercuson, David Jay. 1986. *Canada and the Burden of Unity*. Toronto: Macmillan of Canada.

Berglund, Sten, and Søren Risbjerg Thomsen, eds. 1990. *Modern Political Ecological Analysis*. Åbo, Finland: Åbo Akademis Frlag.

Blais, André, Elizabeth Gidengil, Richard Nadeau, and Neil Nevitte. 1998. 'Accounting for the Vote in the 1997 Election', paper presented at the annual meeting of the Canadian Political Science Association, Ottawa.

Blake, Donald E. 1972. 'The Measurement of Regionalism in Canadian Voting Patterns', *Canadian Journal of Political Science* 5, 1 (Mar.): 55–81.

———. 1978. 'Constituency Contexts and Canadian Elections: An Exploratory Study', *Canadian Journal of Political Science* 11, 2 (June): 279–305

——— and Lynda Erickson. 1998. 'Electoral Volatility and Realignment in 1993', paper presented at the annual meeting of the Canadian Political Science Association, Ottawa.

Brodie, Janine, and Jane Jenson. 1988. *Crisis, Challenge, and Change: Party and Class in Canada, Revisited*. Ottawa: Carleton University Press.

Campbell, Rosemary Vasco, and David B. Knight. 1976. 'Political Territoriality in Canada: A Choropleth and Isopleth Analysis', *The Canadian Cartographer* 13, 1 (June): 1–10.

Carty, R.K., and Munroe Eagles. 1999. 'Do Local Campaigns Matter? Campaign Spending, the Local Canvass, and Party Support in Canada', *Electoral Studies* 18 (Mar.): 69–87.

Eagles, Munroe. 1990. 'Political Ecology: Local Influences on the Political Behaviour of Canadians', in Alain-G. Gagnon and James P. Bickerton, eds, *Canadian Politics: An Introduction to the Discipline*. Peterborough, Ont.: Broadview Press, 285–307.

———. 1991. 'Voting and Non-Voting in Canadian Federal Elections: An Ecological Analysis', in Herman Bakvis, ed., *Voter Turnout in Canada*, vol. 15 of the Research Studies for the Royal Commission on Electoral Reform and Party Financing. Toronto and Ottawa: Dundurn Press and Minister of Supply, 3–32.

———. 1992. 'The Political Ecology of Campaign Contributions in Canada: A Constituency-Level Analysis', *Canadian Journal of Political Science* 25, 3 (Sept.): 535–55.

———. 1993. 'Money and Votes in Canada: Campaign Spending and Parliamentary Election Outcomes, 1984 & 1988', *Canadian Public Policy* 19, 4 (Dec.): 432–49.

———, ed. 1995. *Spatial and Contextual Models in Political Research*. London: Taylor & Francis.

————. 1999. 'Continuity and Change in a Brokerage Party System: The Political Ecology of Party Support in Canada, 1988–1997', paper presented at the Association of American Geographers annual conference, Honolulu, Mar.

————, James P. Bickerton, Alain-G. Gagnon, and Patrick J. Smith. 1991. *The Almanac of Canadian Politics*. Peterborough, Ont.: Broadview Press.

————, ————, ————, and ————. 1995. *The Almanac of Canadian Politics*, 2nd edn. Toronto: Oxford University Press.

Ersson, Svante, Kenneth Janda, and Jan-Erik Lane. 1990. 'The Logic of Political Ecology Analysis', in Dag Anckar, Erik Damgaard, and Henry Valen, eds, *Partier, Ideologier, Valjare: En Antologi*. Åbo, Finland: Åbo Akademi Frlag.

Forbes, Ernest R. 1979. *The Maritime Rights Movement, 1919–1927: A Study in Canadian Regionalism*. Montreal and Kingston: McGill-Queen's University Press.

Fotheringham, A.S., and D.W.S. Wong. 1991. 'The Modifiable Areal Unit Problem in Multivariate Statistical Analysis', *Environment and Planning A* 23, 7 (July): 1025–44.

Gerber, L.M. 1986. 'The Federal Election of 1968: Social Class Composition and Party Support in the Electoral Districts of Ontario', *Canadian Review of Sociology and Anthropology* 23, 1: 118–35.

Graesser, Mark W. 1993. 'Religion and Voting in Newfoundland: Party Alignment and Realignment, 1889–1949', paper presented at the annual meeting of the Canadian Political Science Association, Ottawa, 8 June.

Hanushek, Eric A., John E. Jackson, and John F. Kain. 1974. 'Model Specification, the Use of Aggregate Data, and the Ecological Correlation Fallacy', *Political Methodology* 1, 1 (Winter): 89–107.

King, Gary. 1996. *A Solution to the Ecological Inference Problem*. Princeton, NJ: Princeton University Press.

Krashinsky, M., and W.J. Milne. 1985. 'Additional Evidence on the Effect of Incumbency in Canadian Elections—Research Note', *Canadian Journal of Political Science* 18, 1 (Mar.): 155–65.

Krehbiel, E. 1916. 'Geographical Influences in British Elections', *Geographical Review* 2: 419–32.

Laponce, Jean. 1969. 'Ethnicity, Religion, and Politics in Canada: A Comparative Analysis of Survey and Census Data', in Mattei Dogan and Stein Rokkan, eds, *Quantitative Ecological Analysis in the Social Sciences*. Cambridge, Mass: MIT Press, 187–216.

Lazarsfeld, Paul, Bernard Berelson, and Hazel Gaudet. 1968. *The People's Choice*, 3rd edn. New York: Columbia University Press.

Lemieux, Vincent. 1988. 'Les régions et le vote libéral des années 1980', *Recherches Sociographiques* 29, 1: 45–59.

Pammett, Jon. 1991. 'The Effects of Individual and Contextual Variables on Partisanship in Canada', *European Journal of Political Research* 19, 4 (June): 399–412.

Reid, Escott M. 1967 [1933]. 'Canadian Political Parties: A Study of the Economic and Racial Bases of Conservatism and Liberalism in 1930', in John C. Courtney, ed., *Voting in Canada*. Scarborough, Ont.: Prentice-Hall Canada, 72–81.

Robinson, W.S. 1950. 'Ecological Correlations and the Behaviour of Individuals', *American Sociological Review* 15: 357.

Siegfried, André. 1913. *Tableau Politique de la France de L'ouest*. Paris: Armand Colin.

Swayze, Mikael Antony. 1996. 'Continuity and Change in the 1993 Canadian General Election; Research Note', *Canadian Journal of Political Science* 29, 3 (Sept.): 555–66.

Tingsten, Herbert. 1967 [1937]. *Political Behavior: Studies in Election Statistics*. Totawa, NJ: Bedminster Press.

Weller, G.R. 1977. 'Hinterland Politics: The Case of Northwestern Ontario', *Canadian Journal of Political Science* 10, 4: 727–54.

Wellhofer, E. Spencer. 1991. 'Confounding Sources of Variance in the Macro-Analysis of Electoral Data', *European Journal of Political Research* 19, 4 (June): 425–39.

Wilson, Jeremy. 1980. 'Geography, Politics, and Culture: Electoral Insularity in British Columbia', *Canadian Journal of Political Science* 13, 4: 751–83.

Wiseman, Nelson. 1986. 'The Use, Misuse, and Abuse of the Canadian National Election Studies', *Journal of Canadian Studies* 21, 1 (Spring): 21–35.

———. 1989. 'The National Election Studies Revisited', *Journal of Canadian Studies* 24, 4 (Winter): 141–7.

——— and K.W. Taylor. 1974. 'Ethnic vs. Class Voting: The Case of Winnipeg, 1945, Research Note', *Canadian Journal of Political Science* 7, 2 (June): 314–28.

Wright, J.K. 1932. 'Voting Habits in the United States: A Note on Two Maps', *Geographical Review* 22: 666–72.

Chapter 13

The Media, Voters, and Election Campaigns: The Reform Party and the 1993 Election

RICHARD W. JENKINS

The 1993 Canadian election vaulted the Reform Party from a minor party to the third largest party in Parliament. Since the news media are the principal channels of political communication between parties and voters in a modern campaign, the news should play a key role in producing campaign effects. The analysis in this chapter demonstrates how the campaign, especially the news coverage, changed both voters' evaluations of Reform and Reform's share of vote intentions.

In the past, the party organization and the party press provided the key means of communication with potential supporters (Carty, 1988). Today, we should expect that most of the information voters learn during the campaign will come from the mass media—either newspapers, television and radio news and commentary, and/or political advertising. Obviously, the news media cannot report everything that candidates do and say, so there is potential for the audience to be exposed to different information depending on what stories reporters tell and how they tell them.

Despite their key role in distributing information, the news media are not all-powerful. The power of the media to influence public opinion is limited by the public's attention to the news and the ability of people to resist persuasion. Although Reform became more visible in the media as the campaign went on, not all voters responded to this increased visibility. Only those voters predisposed to like the Reform Party platform and those likely to be aware of the news coverage recognized Reform's position on a key policy issue in 1993—the deficit—and became more likely to support the Reform Party.

Media Coverage

Given the reach of the mass media it seems counterintuitive to suggest that the media have little influence on the attitudes and behaviour of the mass public. Yet, for many years, this was the standard claim about the political impact of media coverage (Klapper, 1960; McGuire, 1986). Research into the effects of the media in campaigns and on electoral results found that the media had little influence, and what influence existed tended to be in the direction of strengthening previously held beliefs. As a result, research efforts generally did not focus on media effects. The hold of the minimal effects claim is much weaker now, and researchers are demonstrating significant if not substantial media effects in recent elections.

Even as the 'minimal effects thesis' was accepted as conventional wisdom, empirical analyses were demonstrating the potential influence of news coverage on public opinion. Considerable research demonstrated that even if the media are unable to change opinions, they are certainly able to change the importance that people attach to some social problems rather than others (Iyengar and Kinder, 1987; Jenkins, 1996). Researchers examined the extent to which media coverage could change the considerations the public used in coming to judgements about political leaders. For example, analysis revealed that exposure to stories about the economy increases the importance of economic perceptions on leader evaluations (Iyengar et al., 1984).

Two examples of the refocused scholarly attention on the news media are the systematic studies of the media's role in the 1992 American presidential elections (Just et al., 1996) and in the British general election of 1997 (Norris et al., 1999). Using a multi-method approach that relied extensively on content analysis and focus groups, as well as traditional public opinion surveys, the authors of the American study showed that campaigns are dynamic interactions among candidates, the media, and voters. Voters bring their own agendas to the interpretation of the news, which itself is the product of news decisions and the strategic efforts of politicians. The British researchers also made use of a multi-method approach to study media effects on the relationships between candidates, the media, and the public. Content analysis, campaign panel surveys, and experimental studies were combined. For example, one of the important findings that emerged from the experimental component of the study was that the public is influenced more by positive than negative news about a party. While there are a number of differences in the two works, both approaches share a willingness to take media coverage and its effect on the election seriously.

The study of media and elections is underdeveloped in Canada. A number of studies identify the broad nature of election coverage, including the tendency for coverage to focus on the horse race instead of substantive issues (Fletcher, 1987, 1988; Wagenberg et al., 1988). Horse-race coverage emphasizes who is winning the election campaign and the strategic actions of the parties. While these stories can be entertaining, they do not provide information upon which voters can base their decision. While these studies help understand media practices, they do not evaluate the effect of the coverage on the audience. Thus, while a recent discussion of the media's role in elections takes the media seriously, its conclusions are largely speculative because the effects of the coverage must be inferred from very general evidence (Taras, 1990: ch.6).

Recent efforts to identify effects of news coverage on voters in the 1988 federal election have, however, identified significant effects. Mendelsohn found that those people who report high media exposure are more likely to base their decision on leadership rather than issues and to reach a decision about who to vote for earlier (Mendelsohn, 1994, 1996). Effects of coverage on attitudes and vote intentions have also been identified. Respondents to the Canadian Election Study in 1988 were more likely to think positively about John Turner, the Liberal Party leader, if they were interviewed when the balance of positive versus negative coverage of Turner during the previous days was positive (Johnston, 1992). The same study found that support for free trade was higher when arguments in the news favoured the agreement.

Measuring Media Effects

There are two general methodological approaches to the study of media effects. The first is to use an experimental design, in which the researcher compares a group that was exposed to a persuasive message to a control group that did not see the message. While this approach allows for a clear conclusion about the effect of the message, it sacrifices realism by removing the test subjects from their natural setting. The second approach is to compare the attitudes or behaviour of survey respondents who report high exposure to the mass media with those who report low exposure. The assumption is that people who are exposed to more news will be more likely to be affected by the coverage. Since most surveys are based on a sample collected over only a few days, the traditional survey does not enable one to observe the direct effects of changes in the media on individuals because there is no variation in the exposure.

The survey approach can be improved by complementing the survey in two ways. The first is to add data on the content of the news. The second is either to survey respondents at two different times or to spread the interviews across a period when the coverage is expected to change. The result is that attitudinal changes can be compared with changes in the content of the news. The analysis that follows adopts both of these modifications by adding data about daily television news coverage to the campaign wave of the 1993 Canadian Election Study.[1] The media data are discussed more fully below, but it is necessary to introduce more fully the unique character of the election study data. Rather than interviewing all of the random sample at the same time (or within a couple days), recent Canadian Election Studies have made use of a rolling, cross-section design. Approximately 90 Canadians were interviewed each of the 45 days of the election campaign, which effectively means 45 separate random samples of a combined total of about 4,000 respondents.

The survey data also allow for the testing of the most realistic model of media effects and attitude change. Since the effect of media messages will depend in part on two broad characteristics of the individual: the person's likelihood of receiving a persuasive message and his or her likelihood of accepting it (McGuire, 1968, 1986; Zaller, 1992, 1996), the analysis undertaken here uses a two-mediator model of media effects: exposure and ideological commitment.

Despite the fact that elections tend to dominate the news for the campaign period, not everyone is interested enough to pay much attention to the news on a nightly basis or to read carefully the campaign stories in the daily newspaper. As a result, not everyone will be affected by the content of the news. Empirical evidence indicates that some people are more likely than others to consume and remember information they received from the mass media (Price and Zaller, 1993; Rhee and Cappella, 1997; Brians and Wattenberg, 1996). In examining for potential media effects, it is therefore important to have a measure of exposure to or reception of the news. Exposure is therefore the first mediator or step in the effects process. A measure of awareness or political knowledge, derived from a series of questions in the survey, is used to distinguish those who are more likely to receive and understand news from those who are unlikely to receive the news about Reform.[2] While a measure of self-reported news attention is often used to distinguish reception, it has been persuasively argued that a measure of knowledge is better because it accurately distinguishes people who have received previous information from those who did not (Price and Zaller, 1993). Self-reports are prone to error because people do not generally monitor their media use.

In addition to expecting different levels of exposure to the news, one would expect to find that citizens are differently affected by the exposure to the same news. Citizens are not simply ciphers responding to the content of the mass media. Some messages are accepted and acted on, others are rejected or discounted. People tend to reject information that conflicts with previously held beliefs, which has been labelled 'cognitive dissonance' (Festinger, 1957). Research has found that people often avoid information that challenges their beliefs and will reinterpret or counter-argue belief-challenging information. As a result, we would expect that the effects of the media will be stronger among people who are predisposed to accept the message (Joslyn and Ceccoli, 1996). People's previously held ideological commitments thus serve as the second mediator or step.

Since the growth in Reform support has been linked to the mobilization of fiscally conservative voters, an anti-welfare state index is used as an indicator of underlying predispositions.[3] The anti-welfare state index captures the respondent's general attitudes about government spending and the priority of the deficit. Those people who express anti-welfare state attitudes should be more likely to accept and act on new information about Reform because this information is consistent with their predispositions.

The 1993 Campaign and Reform Party Success

The 1993 election campaign offered dramatic evidence of the potential volatility of electorates. While the campaign began with the Progressive Conservatives apparently in a close race with the Liberals (Johnston et al., 1994), the Conservative Party faltered significantly and two new parties—the Reform Party in the West and the Bloc Québécois in Quebec—emerged on the scene. Reform's 18.7 percent of the vote and 53 seats clearly represented a success for the party given that this was the first election in which the party contested all of the seats in English Canada. This raises the question of how the Reform Party managed to convince voters to abandon the traditional parties. While others have focused on the ideological and populist appeal of the party (Flanagan, 1995; Harrison, 1995), the analysis here focuses on the role of media coverage in providing the stimulus for the campaign movement towards Reform.

The Reform Party, which combined a fiscally conservative agenda and a resistance to a substantive accommodation with Quebec, offered a clear right-wing alternative to the Conservative Party, but despite its positioning, Reform entered the campaign with only a small share of electoral support. After winning the leadership convention in the spring of 1993, Kim Campbell orchestrated a significant rise in Conservative support in the polls, leaving it as the main player on the right. The party began the campaign in a close race with the Liberal Party. Of course, the campaign would reveal that support for the Conservatives was fairly soft, so that by election day the party received only 16 per cent of the national vote and two seats in the House of Commons.

While Conservative support declined during the campaign, Reform support underwent a significant increase. According to the vote intention data in the election study, the growth of Reform vote intentions began around 22 September, two weeks after the campaign began. From that point, Reform's share of vote intentions increased fairly gradually until it peaked about 10 days before election day. In the last week, intentions then fell back several points.

A number of researchers have provided us with an understanding of Reform Party activists and voters in the 1993 election. Three things stand out about the ideological appeal of the party. First, the party managed to capitalize on feelings of alienation or populism in the electorate (Clarke and Kornberg, 1996; Harrison et al., 1996; Johnston et al., 1996). Reform voters were more likely to think that special interests had too much influence and that the political system was not responsive to the average voter. Second, people who were opposed to doing more for Quebec or for ethnic minorities were more likely to vote Reform (Johnston et al., 1996). This is not surprising given Reform's opposition to the Charlottetown Accord in 1992 and its general antipathy towards equality rights in the Charter (Arseneau, 1994). Finally, those opposed to the welfare state were more likely to vote for Reform (Johnston et al., 1996). Importantly, attitudes towards such things as spending on health care and unemployment insurance, rather than more general conservative economic attitudes, distinguished Reform from the other parties.

Of these three ideological factors related to Reform voting, the campaign mattered most because it allowed voters to find out where the Reform Party stood on the welfare state (Johnston et al., 1994). One way to demonstrate the importance of attitudes about the welfare state to Reform's success is to examine how voters perceived the party's position on the welfare state at different times during the campaign. Since a commitment to deficit reduction means a low priority for social programs and public sector spending generally, public perceptions of Reform's credibility on deficit reduction can be used to identify public perceptions of its ideological orientation. Credibility was measured for each of the large parties competing in the 1993 election by the following question:

Suppose the ____ Party wins the election, what do you think will happen to the deficit? Would a ____ government make the deficit: much bigger, somewhat bigger, about the same as now, somewhat smaller, or much smaller?

To ease the interpretation of the results, Figure 13.1 presents the daily mean, averaged over seven days, for the three major parties' perceived credibility on the deficit.[4] Respondents can thus be placed on a five-point scale with the *same as now* category assigned zero. Since a *somewhat smaller* or *much smaller* response reflects a belief that the party is credible, these responses were assigned values of 1 and 2 respectively. Conversely, those who responded with *somewhat bigger* or *much bigger* were assigned –1 and –2.[5] For each day the values were averaged so that a positive value indicates that respondents on average believed that the party in question would produce a smaller deficit if it won the election. Since the daily samples are small, the figure shows the average of the daily means for three days prior and three days after every day.

At the start of the campaign, the Reform Party was perceived to be as credible as the Conservative Party on deficit reduction. By the second week of the campaign, however, the Conservative Party had lost much of its early credibility on the deficit while Reform's credibility surged. The Liberal Party was never considered a credible party on the deficit and the public's perception of its position never underwent a re-evaluation. Early in the campaign, the question remained whether or not voters would have the combination of information and motivation to re-evaluate Reform on this dimension. Such a re-evaluation took place. Importantly,

Figure 13.1: Credibility of Parties on Deficit by Day of Campaign

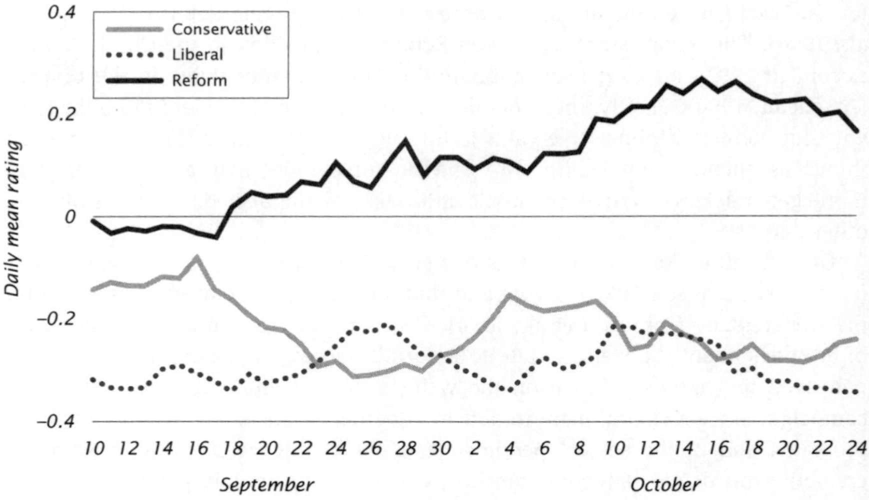

Note: Lines represent seven-day moving average.

the re-evaluation took place at the same time in the campaign as Reform's share of vote intentions changed. We can conclude, therefore, that the campaign provided voters with information about Reform's stand on the deficit, and on public spending more generally, and voters used that information to identify more accurately Reform's position as the campaign progressed.

The most likely source of information about the Reform Party's positions, including on the deficit, was the news media. Fortunately, data on how CTV and CBC national news covered the election campaign are available.[6] The content analysis of the election news involved several steps. The first step was to select all those stories pertaining to the election. The second step was to break down each story into smaller elements to capture a particular idea or reference. Finally, the content of each element was identified, including the speaker of the coded phrase, the party being discussed in the phrase, the issue or campaign theme most prominent in the phrase, and the tone. The focus in this paper is on a simple but effective indicator of the availability of information about the Reform Party—the amount of coverage Reform received on each day of the campaign.

Figure 13.2 represents the Reform's share of television news coverage[7] and share of vote intentions in the non-Quebec sample of the electorate. During the first two weeks of the campaign Reform received a small proportion of coverage and was generally treated as a minor player in the campaign drama. Before there were tangible indications that the Conservative vote share had collapsed or that Reform had become more popular, Reform began to receive more media attention.

Figure 13.2: News Coverage of and Public Support for Reform

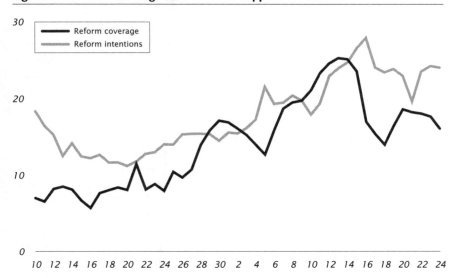

Note: Lines represent five-day moving average.

In fact, with 12 days remaining in the campaign 25 per cent of the political party coverage was associated with Reform.

Given that the media data contain more information than just the party being talked about, it could be objected that the variable for media coverage is a poor indicator of Reform coverage. The variable does not capture changes in either the tone of the coverage (positive, negative, or mixed) or the issue content of the coverage (welfare state, jobs, national unity, leadership, etc.). There are two reasons why the measure is in fact a reasonable one. The first is that other analyses (not shown) demonstrate that coverage of the Reform Party focused on social programs and the deficit, especially after the coverage increased.[8] Information in the news media was relevant to a re-evaluation of Reform's deficit position and of a person's intention to vote Reform. The second reason is that given the lack of information that most voters had about Reform prior to the 1993 campaign, both positive and negative information about the party's positions should have been informative. Partisan attacks of Reform's position on social programs by other parties should have given voters unsure about Reform's actual position a good idea of the party's stance relative to the parties they were more informed about.

The three variables—vote intentions, credibility on the deficit, and Reform's share of the coverage—all follow the same path through the campaign, which is early evidence that the three variables are related. The general pattern of Figure 13.2 suggests that media coverage of Reform changed before vote intentions changed. More sophisticated analysis of this relationship reported elsewhere establishes this causal order (Jenkins, 1999a).

Individual Receptivity to Media Coverage

The close temporal relationship between the three variables in the aggregate is good preliminary evidence of an important media effect, but the goal was to establish whether or not individuals responded to the news coverage in ways predicted by the two-mediator model discussed above. Our hypothesis is that voters who are both habitually aware of news events and politics and predisposed to accept Reform's message will be more likely to respond to the news coverage. The approach here is to represent graphically the changes in credibility and vote intentions for voters with different characteristics.

The expectation is that those predisposed to accept anti-welfare state messages will be more likely to re-evaluate Reform on this dimension. Since awareness of messages is a necessary but insufficient condition for learning or persuasion, awareness should magnify the effect of the respondent's welfare state predisposition. Those respondents with a pro-welfare state orientation are unlikely to be persuaded even if they are sufficiently aware to get the message. We are interested, then, in comparing four types of respondents: those aware and predisposed; those aware but not predisposed; those unaware but predisposed; and those unaware and not predisposed. These four groups are created by dividing both of the scales—awareness and attitudes about the welfare state—at their mean. This produces four approximately equal groups.

Figure 13.3 shows the movement in perceptions of Reform credibility within each of the groups. True to expectations, almost all of the re-evaluation of Reform takes place among the politically aware, anti-welfare state respondents. The weekly mean values for the low-awareness respondents, regardless of their ideological position, are stable across the campaign. This suggests that these two groups did not even receive information. The hypothesis is that high awareness, pro-welfare state respondents will get the message but will be unaffected by it. While these respondents rate Reform's credibility to be higher on average than the low-awareness ones, the trend is not particularly interesting. To the extent that national television news provided the audience with information about Reform's ideological commitment to a lower deficit, those people more likely to be exposed to the news reacted in predictable ways. Those predisposed to like the message were persuaded by it, while those predisposed to dislike the message were not.

The next step is to repeat the analysis for vote intentions. As before, the analysis begins with a picture of the evolution of Reform intentions within the four groups identified earlier. Paralleling the earlier findings with respect to the evolution of credibility, almost all of the change in Reform's share of vote intentions takes place among those respondents who are in both the high-awareness and anti-welfare state groups. The rise in this group is dramatic. For the first three weeks of the campaign there is no change, but between the week of 27 September

Figure 13.3: Perceptions of Reform Credibility within Ideological and Awareness Groups

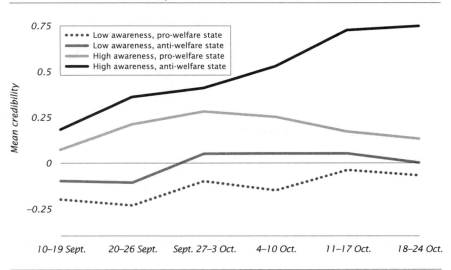

Note: The sample was divided into four groups by dividing the awareness and welfare state scales at the mean. The resulting four groups are approximately the same size.

and the week of 11 October the percentage intending to vote Reform increases by 25 points. The low-awareness, anti-welfare state respondents became more likely to vote Reform as election day neared, but the magnitude of this increase is small. On election day, it appears that awareness only slightly differentiated the anti-welfare state respondents. The lines representing both pro-welfare state groups are fairly flat across the campaign reflecting the lack of effects of media coverage for these groups (Figure 13.4).

The graphical analysis illustrates the responsiveness of particular kinds of individuals to campaign information. The two anti-welfare state groups underwent different changes during the campaign. The high awareness group became both more likely to vote Reform and more likely to think that Reform was credible on deficit reduction at the same time as news coverage, and therefore information, about the party increased. Surprisingly, this group underwent a significant trend away from the Reform Party in the last week. Given that this group was most likely to receive new information from the media it seems reasonable to suggest that this change was also induced by media coverage.

The movement away from Reform among the high-awareness, anti-welfare state group can be linked to the kind of information that was available about Reform at the end of the campaign. While, in general, news coverage of Reform actually declined somewhat in the last two weeks—suggesting that the media were backing off from covering Reform—the nature of that coverage also changed. In the last

Figure 13.4: Vote Intentions for Reform among Ideological and Awareness Groups

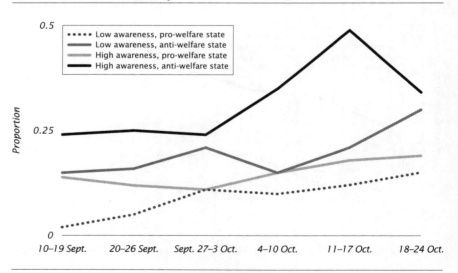

Note: The sample was divided into four groups by dividing the awareness and welfare state scales at the mean. The resulting four groups are approximately the same size.

two weeks the Reform Party was hurt by revelations of racism in the party[9] and, more generally, the party was the target of attacks from other parties on issues such as national unity, multiculturalism, and immigration.[10] These issues reminded voters that the Reform Party stood for more than a lower deficit and reduced role for the state in economic maters (Jenkins, 1999b). It is clear that the decline was not motivated by questions of fiscal policy. As Figure 13.3 demonstrates, Reform remained credible on the deficit even as the likelihood of voting for the party decreased.

The low-awareness group gradually became more likely to vote Reform, but did so without any change in their perception of Reform's deficit position. This indicates that low-awareness voters came to their decision to support Reform in a different manner from the high-awareness voters. Information about Reform took longer to reach these people and it only affected their evaluation of the Reform Party, not their understanding of the party's issue positions. More importantly, the information that drove the high-awareness group away from Reform never reached the low-awareness groups.

Conclusion

During the 1993 election campaign, the Reform Party was transformed from a minor party to a more serious contender for political power. The analysis undertaken here emphasizes the role that the media played in assisting this process. Media attention to the Reform Party increased two weeks into the campaign and this increase corresponded with critical changes in voter perceptions of the party's stance on deficit reduction and, more importantly, in the size of the party's share of vote intentions. One can be confident that news coverage contributed to the change because a change in both credibility and vote intentions occurred within the group most likely to be exposed to and learn from the news media.

The persuasive power of the news media should not, however, be overstated. News coverage of Reform did not produce an irrational movement towards the Reform Party. In fact, it is comforting that those who were opposed to the Reform position on the welfare state basically ignored the amount of media coverage the party received on television. It appears that news coverage cannot help a party that has little potential electoral support.

While it is also comforting to know that low-awareness and high-awareness respondents appeared to come to the same conclusion about Reform on election day, the manner in which this convergence occurs raises real concerns about the democratic process. Two things stand out about the anti-welfare state voters. The first is that low-awareness respondents took a long time to change their vote intentions to Reform and they did so without changing their perception of where the party stood on the deficit. This suggests that even though they intended to vote for a party that shared their ideological position on the welfare state, they did not make this link themselves. The second is that the low-awareness group did not respond to the information at the end of the campaign that drove the high awareness respondents away from Reform. If the election had been held on 17 October rather than 25 October, the gap between the low-awareness and high-awareness respondents would have been very large. This raises the possibility that the unaware reach their decision differently and under certain circumstances may vote for the 'wrong' party, in the sense of it being different from the choice of voters with similar ideological positions but more knowledge of party positions.

While media coverage appears to have played an important role in Reform's success in 1993, one needs to be careful in attributing too much importance to the media in other situations. The news is not just the product of journalists' decisions about what is news. Candidate strategies are relevant, as are each journalist's understanding of the information people want and each citizen's own interpretation of that information. More research is necessary to determine how much the coverage and its influence were the product of news decisions as opposed to the result of these other factors.

Afterword

The media facilitated Reform's rise in 1993, and the party's significant success in terms of seats should have positioned it well for fighting future elections. As the second largest party in English Canada, Reform should have benefited from news coverage of its parliamentary performance, especially in comparison with the Conservative Party—its main opposition on the right—which was in disarray.

The inter-election period was not, however, an overwhelmingly positive experience for Reform as it struggled to meet the demands of the news media and the tensions between its approach to politics and the reality of parliamentary government. The party soon felt itself the brunt of negative news coverage about its performance and its ideological extremism. Some viewed the negative coverage as emanating from an anti-Reform bias: 'Reform's failings are revealed and magnified but its achievements are generally ignored' (Coren, 1997). The most compelling explanation is that the negative coverage flowed from the norms of newsworthiness (Jenkins, 2002), but what is important is that the coverage was not sympathetic to Reform.

The 1997 election is generally viewed as a failure for Reform. It achieved Official Opposition status but failed to make a breakthrough in Ontario despite its targeting of the province and its attempts to moderate its image to attract Ontario voters. For some, the failure to completely displace the Conservative Party was caused by the image that voters, especially those in Ontario, had of Reform's policies and character. The 'unite the right' movement and the subsequent creation of the Canadian Alliance out of the Reform Party was motivated in part as a means to shed Reform's image as an intolerant and western party.

It seems likely that the coverage of Reform before and during the 1997 election reinforced the previous understandings of Reform and worked against its effort to appear as a 'government in waiting'. Reform's continued failure to broaden significantly its electoral base suggests that we need to do more research on how voters respond to political information during and outside of election campaigns.

Notes

Note: This chapter is based on the author's doctoral research. Parts of this paper were presented at the annual meeting of the Canadian Political Science Association, June 1998. This research was made possible by the financial support of the Social Science and Humanities Research Council of Canada. The author would like to thank Patrick Fournier and the editors for their helpful advice on the manuscript. All errors or omissions remain those of the author.

1. The source for all public opinion data reported in this chapter is the 1992–3 Canadian Referendum and Election Study, for which Richard Johnston, André Blais, Elisabeth Gidengil, Neil Nevitte, and Henry Brady were co-investigators. The investigators are not responsible for the analysis reported here.

2. The awareness scale is an additive scale that varies between 0 and 1 and is based on: the interviewer's subjective assessment of the respondent's knowledge; two questions about the economy (inflation and unemployment rate); and four questions asked in the post-election survey about which party took particular policy positions (increase public works spending; reduce deficit in three years; reduce deficit in five years; withdraw from NAFTA).

3. The index, which varies between 0 and 1, was originally constructed by Johnston et al., (1996). A score of 1 on the index indicates antipathy towards the welfare state and the costs associated with government spending. The index is based on the responses to the following five questions asked in the campaign wave of the survey. The answers to each question vary between 0 and 1 so the respondent's score on the index is created by summing the scores on the individual questions and dividing by 5.

   1. On the deficit, which comes closest to your own view?

      a. We must reduce the deficit even if it means cutting programs.

      b. Governments must maintain programs even if it means continuing to run a deficit.

   2. Which comes closer to your own view:

      a. If people had to pay a fee each time they go to [a doctor/ a hospital] there would be less waste in the health care system.

      b. If people had to pay a fee, [low income/some] people would not be able to get the health care they need.

   3-5. If you had to, would you cut spending in the following areas a lot, some, or not at all.

      Welfare?

      Health care?

      Unemployment Insurance?

4. The Bloc Québécois is not represented on Figure 13.1 because the respondents outside of Quebec were not asked to evaluate this party's credibility. While respondents were asked about the New Democratic Party's position, including the NDP in the figure contributes little to understanding the dynamics of the campaign. The NDP was viewed as the least credible by the public and its credibility did not change during the campaign.

5. Those who lacked the information necessary to guess Reform's position—those who said 'Don't know'—were coded as zero.

6. Data on news coverage were provided by the National Media Archive (Fraser Institute, Vancouver. Each of the CBC and CTV national evening news programs was transcribed and coded.

7. The share is the number of times Reform was being spoken about divided by the total number of elements for each day (excluding all of those cases in which no party was being discussed).

8. Approximately 70 per cent of issue coverage associated with Reform pertained to the deficit and social programs.

9. The media reported that a Reform candidate, John Beck, had made racist statements, and although Reform leader Preston Manning acted quickly in removing the candidate and distancing the party, the incident may have driven away pro-minority voters attracted to Reform's fiscal agenda.

10. More than one-quarter of Reform issue coverage in the last two weeks of the campaign was about these kinds of issues compared with about 5 per cent in the previous four weeks.

References

Arseneau, Therese. 1994. 'The Reform Party of Canada; Past, Present and Future', in Douglas M. Brown and Janet Hiebert, eds, *Canada: The State of the Federation*. Kingston, Ont.: Institute of Intergovernmental Relations, 37–59.

Brians, Craig L., and Martin P. Wattenberg. 1996. 'Campaign Issue Knowledge and Salience: Comparing Reception From TV Commercials, TV News, and Newspapers', *American Journal of Political Science* 40, 1: 172–93.

Carty, R.K. 1988. 'Three Canadian Party Systems', in George C. Perlin, ed., *Party Democracy in Canada*. Toronto: Prentice-Hall, 15–31.

Clarke, Harold D., and Allan Kornberg. 1996. 'Partisan Dealignment, Electoral Choice and Party-System Change in Canada', *Party Politics* 2, 4: 455–78.

Coren, Michael. 1997. 'As Election News, Reform Again Falls Victim to the Media's Bias', *Financial Post*, 30 Apr., 17.

Festinger, Leon. 1957. *A Theory of Cognitive Dissonance*. Stanford, Calif.: Stanford University Press.

Flanagan, Tom. 1995. *Waiting for the Wave: The Reform Party and Preston Manning*. Toronto: Stoddart.

Fletcher, Frederick. 1987. 'Mass Media and Parliamentary Elections in Canada', *Legislative Studies Quarterly* 12, 3: 341–72.

———. 1988. 'The Media and the 1984 Landslide', in Howard Penniman, ed., *Canada at the Polls, 1984*. Durham, NC: Duke University Press, 161–89.

———. 1994. 'Media, Elections, and Democracy', *Canadian Journal of Communication* 19: 131–50.

Harrison, Trevor. 1995. *Of Passionate Intensity: Right-Wing Populism and the Reform Party of Canada*. Toronto: University of Toronto Press.

———, Bill Johnston, and Harvey J. Krahn. 1996. 'Special Interests and/or New Right Economics? The Ideological Bases of Reform Party Support in Alberta in the 1993 Federal Election', *Canadian Review of Sociology and Anthropology* 33, 2: 159–79.

Iyengar, Shanto, and Donald R. Kinder. 1987. *News That Matters: Television and American Opinion*. Chicago: University of Chicago Press.

——, ——, Mark D. Peters, and Jon A. Krosnick. 1984. 'The Evening News and Presidential Evaluations', *Journal of Personality and Social Psychology* 46: 778–87.

Jenkins, Richard W. 1996. 'Public Opinion, the Media and the Political Agenda', in James Guy, ed., *Expanding Our Political Horizons*. Toronto: Harcourt Brace, 261–8.

——.1999a. 'How Much Is Too Much? Media Attention and Popular Support for an Insurgent Party', *Political Communication* 16, 4: 429–45.

——. 1999b. 'The Media and Insurgent Success: The Reform Party and the 1993 Election', PhD thesis, University of British Columbia.

——. 2002. 'More Bad News: The Uneasy Relationship Between the Reform Party and the Media', in Gianpietro Mazzoleni, Bruce Horsfield, and Julianne Stewart, eds, *The Media and Neo-Populist Movements: Processes of Media Construction of Political Reality*. Westport, Conn.: Praeger.

Johnston, Richard. 1992. 'Party Identification Measures in the Anglo-American Democracies: A National Survey Experiment', *American Journal of Political Science* 36, 2: 542–59.

——, André Blais, Henry E. Brady, Elisabeth Gidengil, and Neil Nevitte. 1996. 'The 1993 Canadian Election Campaign: Realignment, Dealignment, or Something Else?', paper presented at the annual meeting of the American Political Science Association, San Francisco.

——, ——, Elisabeth Gidengil, Neil Nevitte, and Henry E. Brady. 1994. 'The Collapse of a Party System? The 1993 Canadian General Election', paper presented at the annual meeting of the American Political Science Association, New York.

Joslyn, Mark R., and Steve Ceccoli. 1996. 'Attentiveness to Television News and Opinion Change in the Fall 1992 Presidential Campaign', *Political Behavior* 18, 2: 141–70.

Just, Marion R., Ann N. Crigler, Dean E. Alger, Timothy E. Cook, Montague Kern, and Darrell M. West. 1996. *Crosstalk: Citizens, Candidates, and the Media in a Presidential Campaign*. Chicago: University of Chicago Press.

Klapper, Joseph. 1960. *The Effects of Mass Communication*. New York: Free Press.

McGuire, William J. 1968. 'Personality and Susceptibility to Social Influence', in E.F. Borgatta and W. W. Lambert, eds, *Handbook of Personality Theory and Research*. Chicago: Rand-McNally.

——. 1986. 'The Myth of Mass Media Impact: Savagings and Salvagings', *Public Communication and Behavior* 1: 173–257.

Mendelsohn, Matthew. 1994. 'The Media's Persuasive Effects: The Priming of Leadership in the 1988 Canadian Election', *Canadian Journal of Political Science* 27, 1: 81–97.

——. 1996. 'The Media and Interpersonal Communications: The Priming of Issues, Leaders, and Party Identification', *Journal of Politics* 58, 1: 112–35.

Norris, Pippa, John Curtice, David Sanders, Maggie Scammell, and Holli A. Semetko. 1999. *On Message: Communicating the Campaign*. London: Sage.

Price, Vincent, and John Zaller. 1993. 'Measuring Individual Differences in Likelihood of News Reception', *Public Opinion Quarterly* 57: 133–64.

Rhee, June W., and Joseph N. Cappella. 1997. 'The Role of Political Sophistication in Learning From News', *Communication Research* 24, 3: 197–233.

Taras, David. 1990. *Newsmakers: The Media's Influence on Canadian Politics*. Scarborough, Ont.: Nelson.

Wagenberg, Ronald H., Walter C. Soderland, Walter I. Romanow, and E.D. Briggs. 1988. 'Campaigns, Images, and Polls: Mass Media Coverage of the 1984 Canadian Election', *Canadian Journal of Political Science* 21, 1: 117–29.

Zaller, John. 1992. *The Nature and Origins of Mass Opinion*. New York: Cambridge University Press.

———. 1996. 'The Myth of Mass Media Impact Revived: New Support for a Discredited Idea', in Diane C. Mutz, Paul M. Sniderman, and Richard Brody, eds, *Political Persuasion and Attitude Change*. Ann Arbor: University of Michigan Press, 17–78.

Part V

Political Participation

Chapter 14

The Concept of Political Participation

SANDRA BURT

Political participation is a broad concept that includes a wide range of activities and attitudes. It has been the subject of democratic theorists for centuries and continues to preoccupy political scientists and philosophers in the twenty-first century. Its significance is due to its centrality in democratic theory and in understandings of citizenship, or 'membership of a community (itself an increasingly contested concept), the rights and obligations that flow from that membership, and equality'. Consequently, the notion of participation allows us to differentiate among types of political regimes (Lister, 1997: 14–15).

Most commonly, the concept of political participation is used in Western liberal democratic societies to include citizens' attempt to take part in the formulation and/or implementation of public policy. Léon Dion defines political participation as direct personal involvement in the political process (Dion, 1968: 433). Similarly, Sidney Verba calls the *participant* one who takes part in political decisions (Verba, 1962: 22). In general, political theorists who use the term refer to activities or actions intended to have either a direct or indirect impact on public policy and/or the policy-making process. In one sense, this definition is fairly straightforward. It implies action taken in the interest of affecting policy outcomes, and can include a wide range of activities: giving money to a political party, lobbying government as a member of an interest group, voting, or becoming an activist in social movements. Some of these activities will be directed towards the election of democratic representatives. Others will focus on influencing or overturning those representatives or other public officials. Political participation can range from successful attempts to convince a government to adopt a policy to unsuccessful protests against policies already in place. It can also include both direct involvement in decision-making and indirect involvement through representatives.

In another sense, however, the concept of 'taking part' is imprecise. When we explore the attitudes that citizens hold about participation, we learn that even the same actions mean different things to different people. Or the same actions may mean different things in a variety of contexts. Furthermore, even within the construct of liberal democracy, some argue for participation rights within the context of a negative concept of liberty, while others propose a positive form of freedom. For the former, 'there is a preoccupation with the formal political, legal and social rights which underpin that participation' (i.e., with the *right* to participate). For the latter, 'the focus shifts to the attitudes and actions that constitute the identity of a citizen in the active rather than the passive sense' (Lister, 1997: 15).

In this chapter I review political scientists' use of 'political participation' since the early 1950s, when Western states began the project of rebuilding civil societies following World War II. I explore some of the reasons for the dramatic narrowing in the meaning of 'participation' that emerged in the early 1950s, particularly in the United States, to include only those activities associated with the election of public officials. I discuss as well the state of research on political participation in Canada. Given the theoretical significance of participation to democracy, studies of who participates, and with what effect, should be of great interest to students of Canadian politics. However, a review of the literature reveals that while there was some early interest in rates of participation (or the instrumental dimension), research on the expressive dimension has been more recent. Such a review reveals that early Canadian participation research was heavily influenced by American patterns of study. Behavioural studies of political participation began in the United States shortly after the end of World War II when aggregate data analysis and social surveys were moving on to the research agendas of political scientists and sociologists. Canadian researchers moved into the field somewhat later and borrowed the tools and conceptual frameworks from their American colleagues.

Early Understandings of Participation

The earliest participation studies were grounded in a narrow definition of the political as pertaining to the formal political process, and there was a widespread agreement on a clear division between the public (men's sphere) and the private (women's sphere), a division explored in the chapters by Yasmeen Abu-Laban and Brenda O'Neill in this volume. And while the following observation by Robert Lane (1959: 213) now appears incongruous, it informed much of early participation research:

> A major feature of our culture's typing of the two sexes is the assignment of the ascendant, power-possessing role to the man and the dependant, receptive role to the woman. . . . Politics is precisely such an area of power, and a woman enters politics only at the risk of tarnishing, to some extent, her femininity.

By the late 1970s, feminists and theorists of participatory democracy were arguing that the division between the public and the private is indistinct. Feminists proposed that the personal is political and that a political sphere exists 'whenever citizens gather together to make political decisions' (Pateman, 1989: 110). Participatory democratic theorists suggested that democracy is not confined to politics and economics but is needed as well in the organization and relations of social and cultural life (Gould, 1988: 255).

These complexities of meaning are significant, for participation is linked to the larger concept of democracy and is a crucial variable for differentiating among democratic regimes. Both democratic theorists and researchers concerned with measuring participation rates acknowledge the relationship, for 'if democracy is interpreted as rule by the people, then the question of who participates in political decisions becomes the question of the nature of democracy in a society' (Verba and Nie, 1972: 1). C.B. Macpherson develops the connection between participation and democracy, and proposes four models or forms of liberal democracy (protective, developmental, equilibrium, and participatory), differentiated in part by the nature of the interactions between citizens and their government (Macpherson, 1977).

Macpherson's four models offer a wide range of possibilities for citizen participation in a liberal democracy. At one end of his democratic continuum is the *protective model*, where participation occurs primarily through voting and is primarily a means of both protecting citizens from arbitrary rule and ensuring the election of responsible trustees. In a protective democracy, electoral participation is 'crucial to the democratic method for it is primarily through elections that the majority can exercise control over their leaders' (Pateman, 1970: 14). At the next stage on the continuum lies *developmental democracy*, fashioned on John Stuart Mill's vision of a society where citizens have a direct interest in government. Participation in elections is a means to self-improvement and provides citizens with an essential connection to their government. From there, Macpherson argues, democracy advances to an *equilibrium model*, which best resembles the nature of liberal democratic society in the mid-twentieth century. It is a pluralist model, where élites compete for votes at election time and elected representatives balance competing claims of interest groups. Finally, there is the most developed form, the participatory model of democracy, where the ideal is a policy-making process in which decisions are made and evaluated by the people most likely to be affected by their outcome. In participatory democracy, freedom *for* political action is a priority, and the political decision-making process is 'continuous, direct rather than through representatives, and organized around issues rather than personalities' (Benello and Roussopoulos, 1971: 5–6).

In their search for ways to differentiate among different forms of participation, some writers have proposed that the concept is two-dimensional. Geraint Parry identifies these two dimensions as the *instrumental* and the *expressive* (Parry, 1972: 19–26). 'Instrumental' refers to the impact of an activity on public policy, and 'expressive' to one's sense of involvement in the decision-making process. Researchers concerned about the instrumental dimension focus on quantifying citizens' rates of involvement in the various options available (such as voting, working for a political party, and interest group activity) and try to evaluate the policy impact of that participation. Those interested in the expressive dimension measure participants' sense of involvement. This concept of two-dimensionality is helpful, for it improves our capacity to differentiate among democratic regimes. In protective democracy, for example, citizens will have a weak sense of involvement and low to moderate levels of primarily electoral activity. In a participatory democracy, citizens will hold intense views on political issues and have expectations of clear and effective input on policy choices both during and between elections. A guiding principle of participatory democracy is that the citizens most seriously affected by a proposed policy will be the ones most heavily involved in setting it.

Conceptualizing participation as two-dimensional leads to questions about the democratic process and issues of citizenship. For example, in terms of the instrumental dimension of participation—or doing something in the anticipation of affecting policy outcomes or implementation—a researcher would ask what options are available, who uses them, and with what effect. These are system-level issues. How do elected officials respond to participants' activities, ranging from exercising the vote to participating in a protest? Which strategies work, and why? What are the various factors that determine success?

In terms of the expressive dimension—or having a sense of involvement in one's political system—a researcher would try to measure the subjective emotional state accompanying an action. In this way, one could more meaningfully differentiate, for example, between political silence as lack of interest, on the one hand, or political support, on the other. In order to measure the expressive dimension of political participation, it is important to know how citizens perceive their political worlds. What do they consider to be political? How connected are they to their political system? One's sense of involvement, after all, is an individual feeling, but the source may be the political system. The expressive dimension may be related to one's sense, either real or imaginary, of the potential impact of an action on public policy. It helps researchers to differentiate among citizens engaged in the same political activity, as well as to evaluate the significance of different forms of participation for any one individual.

Yet in spite of this rich array of questions that need to be asked when political participation is broadly constructed, early researchers restricted their focus almost completely to the electoral process and generally ignored the expressive dimension of participation. This was due to their narrow construction of participation within a protective/equilibrium view of democracy.

The American Influence

Early research on political participation took place primarily in the United States, and it coincided with the beginnings of survey research in the social sciences. This coincidence of interests had a profound impact on the development of research on the topic. It meant that, for the most part, research was carried out with the use of random sample surveys with closed questions that force respondents to choose from a listed set of answers. And it meant that researchers tended to focus on events that could be measured fairly easily with such surveys—in particular, national elections. The mould for future studies was set as early as 1950, when Julian Woodward and Elmo Roper published their report on the political activity of Americans and developed a participation scale with four items—support for pressure groups;

personal communications with legislators; participation in a political party; and habitual political discussion. From the outset, researchers were concerned with the issues of questionnaire reliability and validity. For example, Woodward and Roper (1950: 873–84) offered two criteria for evaluating their questionnaire:

> (1) that it seems to have a good deal of 'face validity' as a measure of citizen political activity, and (2) that it works well in a public opinion interview in the sense that the questions are comprehended and answered with apparently little exaggeration by people of all educational levels and political persuasions.

Although both validity and reliability are considered to be important concepts by behavioural researchers, they are not without problems. In the interest of valid operationalization, researchers will opt for apparently straightforward questions such as voting turnout, and avoid more complex questions about one's sense of involvement. In addition, value-laden concepts such as satisfaction may be used, but with little regard for nuances of meaning attached to the same word by different groups within the populations. And finally (and most significantly for participation research), in the interest of replication, researchers will often opt for questions that have been used in earlier studies without taking the time to discover whether these questions still 'work'. In the case of participation research, the early studies set the pattern for later work and were often transported into Canada without much apparent concern for suitability. Thus, although these and other early researchers omitted discussion of how they applied these criteria to their questions, their published lists of acceptable measures of political participation became part of 'accepted wisdom' in the discipline.

In their 1950 report, Woodward and Roper set another pattern for later studies when they argued that citizens are differentiated in their political activities. They proposed five channels of participation (voting; interest group activity; personal communications with legislators; party activity; habitual political discussion) and concluded that 'all the questions were positively correlated with each other' in each channel, 'indicating that some common factor (or factors) was measured to some degree by all of them' (ibid., 873–4). Somewhat later, Verba, Nie, and Kim dropped interest group activity from the list, and renamed the channels 'participation modes' (Verba et al., 1971). These early studies had several things in common. They focused almost exclusively on electoral behaviour and concentrated on the instrumental rather than the expressive dimension of participation. And the researchers carrying out these studies saw it as part of their function to make value judgements about the civic-mindedness of citizens engaged in different levels of activity. Each level of activity was assigned a weight, and respondents were assigned participation scores (low, medium, or high) according to the number of times they engaged in these different forms of activity.

Subsequent studies began with unchallenged assumptions that arose from Woodward and Roper's report. Researchers examining political participation throughout the 1960s and 1970s largely restricted their investigations of political participation to electoral activities, and were preoccupied with instrumental measures, especially the frequency and direction of voting. This selection of the vote for particular study had a practical basis, for the national funding agencies were prepared to provide research money for election studies. This availability of funds coincided with the developing preoccupation with prediction and causality in political behaviour research. It coincided as well with the developing postwar theoretical preoccupation with the vote as the most appropriate vehicle for mass citizen involvement in liberal democratic societies. In the context of postwar concerns for political stability, the vote offered a straightforward and peaceful option for exercising political influence. There was fairly widespread agreement that to participate in politics was to do something related to elections. As a result, most of the early conclusions reached by American researchers of participation were really conclusions about electoral involvement. This equation of political activity with elections coincided with the growing preoccupation of American political scientists in the 1960s with issues of political stability (Easton, 1965).

Nevertheless, the questions developed for these earliest American studies were often better than those used in later years. Early researchers were interested in attitudinal as well as socio-economic correlates of political participation. Some researchers tried to discover respondents' degree of affection for their political system (Bronfenbrenner, 1960; Milbrath, 1960). Others focused on the personality traits of participants (Milbrath and Klein, 1962; Allardt and Pesonen, 1960). Stein Rokkan (1962) went even further, examining situational factors—such as a person's role in the household—that might affect participation. In other words, the list of independent variables used by American participation researchers from the 1950s to the mid-1970s included socio-economic status, association memberships, personality traits (in particular, sociability and self-esteem), and civic attitudes (political interest, political efficacy, and attention to politics).

It was generally agreed, on the basis of the studies that explored correlations between these independent (or, it was sometimes argued, intervening) variables and participation, that high socio-economic status, in particular a high education level, was a good predictor of a high level of political participation. The link was explained by the development of 'appropriate' civic attitudes, combined with a heightened sense of political and personal efficacy. Researchers who noted this link developed what became known as the 'socio-economic model of participation'. It was generally agreed that participation input is weighted in favour of people with higher socio-economic standing because 'the higher-status individual has a greater stake in politics, he has greater skills, more resources, greater awareness of political matters, he is exposed to more communications about politics, he interacts with others who participate' (Verba and Nie, 1972: 126).

The socio-economic model of participation, however, could not provide all of the answers to the questions of who participates, and why. These early researchers noted that the motivations could be quite different for different kinds of activity, and that the impact of socio-economic status was greater on some forms of participation than on others. Lester Milbrath and M. Goel, for example, concluded that voting requires little initiative and is not very dependent on skills, information, and psychological involvement (Milbrath and Goel, 1977: 12, 46). In addition, some people are mobilized to vote by political parties or interest groups. There were other problems as well. In Verba and Nie's 1972 report on participation in America, 14 per cent of the most active group had low socio-economic status. An additional 29 per cent were from the middle class. In other words, 43 per cent of participants did not fit the model.

In addition, it was difficult to know which of several intervening variables (such as political knowledge, political interest, political satisfaction, or sense of efficacy) were most useful for explaining why only some higher-status persons take part in politics fairly actively. This was due in part to problems with measuring these intervening variables. For example, Angus Campbell proposed that low involvement was synonymous with political satisfaction (Campbell, 1962: 15–16). E.E. Schattschneider had a rather different view. He argued that citizens stay away from political involvement when politicians reduce the scope of the conflict—primarily by limiting the possibilities for involvement. 'A conclusive way of checking the rise of conflict is simply to provide no arena for it or to create no public agency with power to do anything about it' (Schattschneider, 1960: 71). When viewed in this light, low levels of participation could reflect frustration rather than satisfaction with the existing political system.

These early participation studies suffered, then, from considerable conceptual fuzziness. For example, researchers liked to use participation scales to simplify the presentation of their findings. The use of scales led to the conclusion that there is a hierarchy of participation, where the most active are candidates for elected office and the least active are voters. The scale developed by Lester Milbrath in 1965 became the benchmark for future research. Milbrath saw political participation as both hierarchical and élitist, and distinguished among three types of participants, whom he labelled apathetics, spectators, and gladiators. While this hierarchy was widely used by participation researchers in both the United States and Canada until the early 1980s, it was problematic for several reasons. First, the hierarchy was restricted to electoral activities despite political participation spanning a much broader range of activities than merely elections. Second, it resulted in a gender bias in research, since more men than women historically were involved in partisan activities beyond the level of voting. And finally, the Milbrath hierarchy was based exclusively on the instrumental dimension of participation.

The Milbrath conceptualization of participation was constructed within an understanding of politics as a 'rough and tumble' gladiatorial arena. 'The political arena', Milbrath wrote, 'is not a hospitable place for insecure, timid and withdrawn people who do not have great faith in their ability to deal with their environment' (Milbrath, 1965: 89). Political participation, in this context, is 'natural' only for those people who are aggressive and self-assured. The implication here is that this is an empirical observation. In fact, it was nothing more than Milbrath's own construction of the social-psychological makeup of participants.

One of the problems with this work—as well as with later studies that followed the Milbrath model—was that it was based on a taken-for-granted understanding of the expressive dimension of participation. Margrit Eichler and Aisla Thompson (1979: 14) propose that this is particularly problematic for women, for the Milbrath hierarchical model

> rests on three basic, although implicit assumptions: that political involvement rests on personal choice rather than on the political opportunity structure, that access to all types of political involvement is similar for all participants, and that the only relevant type of political involvement is some form of participation in the electoral process. We submit that all three assumptions are inappropriate for women.

But Milbrath's impact on participation research was substantial. In addition to reinforcing the focus on electoral participation, he established the tradition of assigning weights to different kinds of activities on the basis of the researcher's evaluation of their 'worth' rather than the participants' own assessment of meaning or value. Qualitative surveys make it clear that the same activity (for example, voting) can mean different things for different people (Burt, 1986). A voter with disabilities who needs assistance to travel to the voting booth may see the vote as a significant act of protest or support. Another voter who regularly interacts with cabinet ministers in social settings may see the vote as a formal and generally quite insignificant part of the political process. If one is evaluating participation from the perspective of its impact on short-term political outcomes (in this case, the winners of the election), each of these two votes has equal weight and both are relatively insignificant in the overall count. But if one is evaluating longer-term political support and citizens' attachment to and involvement in their political system (in other words, participation viewed from the perspective of the citizens), these two votes should be assigned different weights. Yet, these early participation studies were embedded in the construct of protective democracy, and those considerations measuring the expressive dimension of participation were ignored. 'The institutions of democracy were seen primarily as mechanisms for choosing between different sets of decision-makers, and thereby affecting the direction which decisions would take' (Richardson, 1983: 120).

In 1971 this belief that participation is exclusively electoral was challenged by Sidney Verba, Norman Nie, and Jae-on Kim with their publication of a new comparative work in which they explored the relationship between organizational involvement and participation. While they continued to restrict their research to instrumental participation, they did broaden the range of activities under study. Verba et al. proposed that participation clusters into four modes—voting, campaigning, contacting others, and communal activity. In later work they also distinguished between individual and group-based motivations for political activity, and contributed to the growing recognition that participation is a complex phenomenon (Verba and Nie, 1972). This was an important step forward in participation research.

By the late 1970s, participation researchers in the United States were generally agreed on several points. They accepted the position that there are several participation modes and that instrumental participation is weighted in favour of persons of higher socio-economic status. These researchers concluded that they could offer a predictive model of participation. They proposed that white middle-class or upper-class men with higher than average levels of education were most likely to be the most active participants. And they explained this correlation in terms of their well-developed sense of personal and political efficacy.

American participation research also confirmed that the United States was not a nation of political activists, at least in terms of the Milbrath hierarchy of participation. In a book that continues to have an impact on the discipline generally, and participation research in particular, Gabriel Almond and Sidney Verba (1963) presented an argument for what they called the civic culture—a society in which only a small group of well-educated citizens participates actively in politics and where most citizens are content to leave politics to these experts. They argued that the majority of citizens have only a weak commitment to democratic norms and that their active involvement in politics could be a destabilizing influence that would lead to the emergence of authoritarian politics. Support for the civic culture (or what some political analysts have termed élitist politics) permeated early American participation research.

But this research could not explain why socio-economic status was such an important predictor of instrumental participation. Nor could it explain the emergence of social movements in the 1970s populated primarily by people who did not fit the socio-economic model of participation. These problems were due primarily to the fact that there were some serious methodological and conceptual problems with most of these early American studies. While they did provide information about some aspects of the instrumental dimension of participation (i.e., they focused on a numerical counting of citizens who took part in predominantly electoral activities—notably, the vote), they were grounded in a set of assumptions that excluded most women, people with low socio-economic status, minority groups, Aboriginal peoples, and people of colour. Yasmeen Abu-Laban discusses some of the reasons for and consequences of these exclusions in her chapter in this volume.

The exclusion problem was both explicit and implicit in the research designs. Most of the findings were based on information obtained in random-sample surveys using closed questions. Respondents were asked to report their levels of activity and then to rate themselves, using assigned labels, on questions about political interest, political knowledge, and political satisfaction. This technique had some methodological flaws. A non-response was viewed as an indication of political apathy. Later studies have demonstrated that no response to questions could be an indication that the respondent does not understand the question, may be uncomfortable in the interview situation, or is unhappy with the set of available responses (Harding, 1987).

In addition, participation researchers assigned weights to various kinds of political activity. But the costs and rewards of these activities are not fixed, and may vary significantly in different parts of the country, even within the same time period. Finally, these studies were framed within a concern for the state and for the ongoing preservation of stable democratic societies. Researchers therefore focused on how citizen involvement affected stability, ignoring the impact of state policies and actions on the individual. When we think of participation as two-dimensional, the need to think about citizens' engagement with their state becomes apparent. And this in turn suggests the need for researching participation from the perspective of individual citizens (i.e., what have they learned or gained from participating?) as well as from the perspective of the state (i.e., does participation contribute to the maintenance of a stable political order?). Participation research should be approached from the perspective of citizen dissatisfaction as well as satisfaction, and researchers need to focus on the reasons why people do not participate as well as the reasons why they do. Also, they cannot assume that similar levels of participation mean the same things in different parts of the country or in different political systems—or even for different groups of people within the same political system.

These and related critiques of the early participation studies were articulated first by feminist scholars (Bourque and Grossholtz, 1974; Reinharz, 1992; McCormack, 1975) who argued that participation research was grounded in the positivist tradition, where 'understanding is viewed as being akin to measuring' (Smith, 1999: 42). Early feminist scholars took issue with the notion that American women (who generally had lower scores than American men on the early participation scales) were poor citizens. They argued that situational factors, such as the need to provide care for young children, often kept women from some of the standard electoral activities. They argued as well that political party officials often acted as gatekeepers, restricting women's access to some of the more powerful positions on the participation hierarchy. Susan Welch led the way in her 1977 study of women's participation, where she argued that 'women as a whole participate as much as men once structural and situational factors are considered' (Welch, 1977: 726).

In spite of these emerging critiques, the American research model was popular among those few Canadian researchers engaged in participation research in the late 1960s and early 1970s. In general, participation was not a popular topic among Canadian scholars. This was at least partly due to the emerging preoccupation with issues of federalism, heightened by the emergence of a revolutionary separatist movement in Quebec in the 1960s. Nevertheless, by the mid-1970s a few political scientists and sociologists were beginning to take a look at citizen participation.

Early Canadian Studies

In Canada, participation research was much less prominent than in the United States, at least until the early 1980s. The earliest researchers either applied or adapted the Milbrath model. For example, in his study of voters in British Columbia, Jean Laponce used the hierarchy, but labelled voters as barbarians rather than as apathetics (Laponce, 1969). Richard Van Loon, another early participation researcher, constructed a Canadian hierarchy of participation and concluded that Canadians are spectator-participants. He based this conclusion on reported frequencies of electoral participation (Van Loon, 1970). When William Mishler published his 1979 overview of political participation in Canada, he concluded that, up to that point, most early studies were based on the assumption 'that political participation is all of a type, or that all forms of participation require the same resources, or evoke identical results' (1979: 19). As Mishler noted, this is an untenable position.

Mishler argued that there are at least six interrelated types of political participation: voting; campaign activity; holding political office; contacting public officials for individual goals; communal activity; and political protest (ibid., 21). He concluded that participation in Canada at that time looked like a sharply tapered pyramid —even when all of these forms of activity are considered. According to his data, fewer than one-third of Canadian citizens had ever participated in any activity other than voting, and 'fewer than ten per cent—and probably closer to one per cent—have ever participated in the most demanding activities, such as running for office or taking part in certain forms of political protest'(ibid., 1979: 36). But unlike his American colleagues, Mishler paid some attention to the factors inhibiting the involvement of some groups in the population, and warned against a facile dismissal of Canadians as undemocratic. He proposed that:

> far from being products of man's intrinsic apathy, as elitist theories frequently imply, the relatively low levels of citizen participation in Canada appear to be consequences of complex sets of individual motivations or attitudes whose origins can be traced to a series of individual social and economic experiences associated with the nature of the times in which the individual was reared and the individual's current position in society. (Ibid., 157)

This important observation coincided with the views of a group of democratic theorists and political activists who were arguing for the adoption of some form of participatory democracy in Canada in the early 1970s. They proposed that political decisions should be made by the people most directly affected by their outcome and conceptualized a radical restructuring of the Canadian political system. The leading theorists included social activists who were part of the new social movements emerging on the political left in Canada in the late 1960s and early 1970s (Woodcock, 1971; Wilson, 1974). They were unified in their critique of existing avenues of electoral participation, and a popular slogan of the day was 'don't vote—you'll only encourage them.' In Quebec, these activists rallied around the call for the political separation of Quebec from the rest of Canada, in part as a protest against the limits of electoral democracy. The most radical factions were part of the Front de libération du Québec (FLQ), a Marxist revolutionary movement formed in the 1960s that developed a manifesto calling for, among other things, direct citizen involvement in political decision-making (Vallières, 1969). The more moderate groups within the separatist movement were also committed in their early years to some form of participatory democracy, and when the Parti Québécois formed in 1968 it included participatory democracy in its list of desired reforms. Following its election as the Quebec government in 1976, the PQ moderated its stance and conformed generally to the principles of indirect participation through elections. But for almost 10 years at its annual conventions the party annually reaffirmed its commitment to increased citizen participation in decision-making.

Also in the 1970s, Canadian feminists were developing critiques of existing avenues of participation in Canada as well as of participation research. Sylvia Bashevkin's review of the Canadian and American literature on participation made it clear that Canadian researchers generally had ignored women because they did not appear to fit the model of the ideal participant. Bashevkin concluded that most researchers simply were not interested in women's participation in politics. And even in those instances where women were the subject of study, researchers failed to distinguish among them in terms of 'age, place of residence, occupational and family status, education, and other potentially relevant factors' (Bashevkin, 1979: 27). Even more significant was her finding that researchers up to that point had failed to investigate the opportunity structures available to women.

Thelma McCormack's analysis of social change also developed out of a literature review, in this case one focused on theories of social change. McCormack noted three biases in the literature: 'first, the notion that women are for social reasons impaired politically; second, that women are rooted in family roles; and third, a tendency to judge the political performances of women by male norms' (McCormack, 1975: 12). She suggested that the data showing that women have lower scores than men on participation scales are flawed—that they in fact reflect women's recognition that politics, as it has been constructed, is a man's preserve. 'Kept out of power, they [women] bring other criteria to bear on public issues and persons in public life' (ibid., 25).

These and related studies proved to be the starting point for a more general critique of the gender, race, and class perspectives that have informed political science research until recently, and have largely excluded the values and behaviours of people who do not 'fit' the traditional norm of the white, able-bodied, Anglo-Saxon, male participant. In the 1980s, new Canadian research shifted to a more textured understanding of participation. A team of researchers who had conducted some of the national election studies turned their attention to the people who were disenchanted with governments in power (Clarke et al., 1991). They tried to use those election data to predict the response of disenchanted voters to the policies of federal governments. They concluded that 'the future will emerge from much less democratic political forms [than elections], including the sequestered world of the senior bureaucracy, royal commissions, and federal-provincial First Ministers' conferences. It will also arise from the non-partisan activities of social movements and interest groups' (ibid., 156). In other words, they were arguing that electoral participation will have little to do with political outcomes.

In the face of these critiques—of positivist assumptions historically built into participation research agendas; of research grounded in white, Western, and privileged men's ways of knowing; and of the significance of electoral participation for public policy—interest in participation research per se declined dramatically. By the early 1990s, research with the specific label of 'political participation' had almost disappeared, to be replaced by more specific investigations of interest groups, social movements, referenda, and citizen participation in electoral politics (discussed at length by the contributors to this volume). A review of Canadian politics textbooks illustrates this transition. In 1995, for example, Glen Williams and Michael Whittington included a chapter on political participation in their fourth edition of *Canadian Politics*. For this chapter, William Mishler and Harold Clarke report on data from the Canadian national election studies carried out between 1965 and 1993. Working within a traditional understanding of citizen participation, they note that 'there are few activities other than voting in which as many as half of the adult population participates even on an occasional basis' (Mishler and Clarke, 1995: 135).

Conclusion

As long as researchers conceptualize participation as an instrumental activity directed towards the election of political élites, the study of this phenomenon will be incomplete. But such piecemeal investigation of this topic was rejected by serious researchers in the early 1980s, and, beginning in the 1990s, political participation as a particular area of research was replaced by studies of citizenship, representation, and social movements. Early participation studies in the United States and in Canada have been criticized methodologically for focusing on men and for proposing a Western-centred view of liberal democracy. Later studies emphasized the importance of gender, situation, and space. But it is important to note that the Milbrath hierarchy of political participation has been put to rest. We have moved on to discussions of ethnicity, gender, and age that will, hopefully, make the next generation of political scientists more sensitive to the issues that have been ignored for so long by leading members of the discipline. Participation research has benefited from this transition.

References

Allardt, Erik, and Pertti Pesonen. 1960. 'Citizen Participation in Political Life in Finland', *International Social Science Journal* 12, 1: 27–39.

Almond, Gabriel, and Sidney Verba. 1963. *The Civic Culture*. Princeton, NJ: Princeton University Press.

Bashevkin, Sylvia. 1979. 'Women and Politics: Perspectives on the Past, Present and Future', paper presented at the annual meeting of the Canadian Political Science Association.

Benello, C. George, and Dimitrios Roussopoulos, eds. 1971. *The Case for Participatory Democracy*. New York: Grossman.

Bourque, Susan C., and Jean Grossholtz. 1974. 'Politics an Unnatural Practice: Political Science Looks at Female Participation', *Politics and Society* 4, 2 (Winter): 225–66.

Bronfenbrenner, Urie. 1960. 'Personality and Participation: The Case of the Vanishing Variables', *Journal of Social Issues* 16, 4: 54–63.

Burt, Sandra. 1986. 'Different Democracies? A Preliminary Examination of the Political Worlds of Men and Women', *Women and Politics* 6, 4 (Winter): 57–79.

Campbell, Angus. 1962. 'The Passive Citizen', *Acta Sociologica* 6: 9–21.

Clarke, Harold D., Jane Jenson, Lawrence LeDuc, and Jon H. Pammett. 1991. *Absent Mandate*, 2nd edn. Toronto: Gage.

Easton, David. 1965. *A Framework for Political Analysis*. Englewood Cliffs, NJ: Prentice-Hall.

Eichler, Margrit, and Aisla Thompson. 1979. 'Women's Political Participation: A Critique', Participation of Women in Canada Report no. 3. Toronto: Ontario Institute for Studies in Education.

Dion, Léon. 1968. 'Participating in the Political Process', *Queen's Quarterly* 75, 3: 432–47.

Gould, Carol. 1988. *Rethinking Democracy*. Cambridge: Cambridge University Press.

Harding, Sandra. 1987. *Feminism and Methodology*. Bloomington: Indiana University Press.

Lane, Robert. 1959. *Political Life*. New York: Free Press.

Laponce, Jean. 1969. *People vs Politics*. Toronto: University of Toronto Press.

Lister, Ruth. 1997. *Citizenship: Feminist Perspectives*. New York: New York University Press.

McCormack, Thelma. 1975. 'Toward a Nonsexist Perspective on Social and Political Change', in Marcia Millman and Rosabeth Moss Kanter, eds, *Another Voice: Feminist Perspectives on Social Life and Social Science*. Garden City, NY: Anchor Press/Doubleday, 1–33.

Macpherson, C.B. 1977. *The Life and Times of Liberal Democracy*. Oxford: Oxford University Press.

Milbrath, Lester. 1960. 'Predispositions Toward Political Contention', *Western Political Quarterly* 13: 5–18.

———. 1965. *Political Participation*. Chicago: Rand McNally.

——— and M.L. Goel. 1977. *Political Participation*, 2nd edn. Chicago: Rand McNally.

——— and Walter Klein. 1962. 'Personality Correlates of Political Participation', *Acta Sociologica* 6: 53–66.

Mishler, William. 1979. *Participation in Canada*. Toronto: Macmillan of Canada.

——— and Harold D. Clarke. 1995. 'Political Participation in Canada', in Williams and Whittington (1995: 129–51).

Parry, Geraint. 1972. 'The Idea of Political Participation', in Parry, ed., *Participation in Politics*. Manchester: Manchester University Press.

Pateman, Carole. 1970. *Participation and Democratic Theory*. Cambridge: Cambridge University Press.

———. 1989. *The Disorder of Women*. Cambridge: Polity Press.

Reinharz, Shulamit. 1992. *Feminist Methods in Social Research*. New York: Oxford University Press.

Richardson, Ann. 1983. *Participation*. London: Routledge & Kegan Paul.

Rokkan, Stein. 1962. 'Approaches to the Study of Political Participation', *Acta Sociologica* 6: 1–8.

Schattschneider, E.E. 1960. *The Semi-Sovereign People*. New York: Holt, Rinehart and Winston.

Smith, Linda Tuhiwai. 1999. *Decolonizing Methodologies*. London: Zed Books.

Vallières, Pierre. 1969. *Nègres blancs d'Amérique*. Montréal: Editions parti pris.

Van Loon, Richard. 1970. 'Political Participation in Canada: The 1965 Election', *Canadian Journal of Political Science* 3, 3 (Sept.): 376–99.

Verba, Sidney. 1962. 'Political Participation and Strategies of Influence: A Comparative Study', *Acta Sociologica* 6: 22–42.

—— and Norman Nie. 1972. *Participation in America*. New York: Harper and Row.

——, ——, and Jae-On Kim. 1971. *The Modes of Democratic Participation: A Cross-National Comparison*. Beverly Hills, Calif.: Sage.

Welch, Susan. 1977. 'Women as Political Animals? A Test of Some Explanations for Male-Female Political Participation Differences', *American Journal of Political Science* 21, 4: 711–30.

Williams, Glen, and Michael Whittington, eds. 1995. *Canadian Politics in the 1990s*. Scarborough, Ont.: Nelson.

Wilson, Harold B. 1974. *Democracy and the Work Place*. Montreal: Black Rose Books.

Woodcock, George. 1971. 'Democracy: Heretical and Radical', in Benello and Roussopoulos, (1971).

Woodward, Julian, and Elmo Roper. 1950. 'Political Activity of American Citizens', *American Political Science Review* 44, 4: 872–85.

Chapter 15

Consulting the People: The Canadian Experience with Referendums

Lawrence LeDuc

Although less common in polities whose institutions derive from British parliamentary traditions, referendums have now taken place in a number of countries where they had not previously been widely used. In Britain, referendums were employed to approve the plans to establish Welsh and Scottish assemblies, and several other European nations have held referendums on EU membership and/or on acceptance of the Maastricht Treaty on European Union. In newly democratizing nations also, the referendum has been employed as a means of establishing or legitimizing new political institutions. Referendums, in the view of many modern political theorists, enhance the quality of democracy through citizen participation in the political process in a way that elections alone cannot (Budge, 1996). Patrick Boyer (1992a: 21), a long-time advocate, argues the case for referendums: 'Canada's democratic process, under increasing criticism for not providing sufficient voice to the public at large, can be broadened and strengthened through greater use of referendums as an effective means of helping Canadians achieve an energizing degree of self government.'

Yet in Canada, our experience with referendums, particularly at the federal level, is both modest and controversial. The three federal referendums that have taken place over our history singularly failed to resolve the particular political problem that each was intended to address.[1] At the provincial level, referendums or plebiscites have occurred more often but are still far from commonplace events.[2] The two Quebec sovereignty referendums, of course, were events of major national significance. Newfoundland employed the referendum in 1948 in its decision to enter Confederation, and votes in the Northwest Territories in 1982 and 1992 prepared the way for the creation of the new territory of Nunavut. Referendums on the construction of a fixed-link bridge in Prince Edward Island, daylight savings time in several western provinces, and education reform in Newfoundland provide some additional modern-day examples of the use of the referendum at the provincial level (see Table 15.1).³ Ontario, one of only two provinces currently without legal provisions for province-wide referendums, recently drafted new legislation that would allow both citizen-initiated and government-sponsored votes, and would *require* a referendum on tax increases or constitutional proposals.⁴

Of course, in a few countries, primarily mature democracies, the referendum is a long-established and more frequently used device for obtaining popular consent on public policy questions. Switzerland uses the referendum as an integral part of its process of government, and Australia does so as the sole legal means of approving constitutional amendments. Instruments of direct democracy are widely employed in a number of American states, notably California, although there has never been a nationwide referendum in the United States.⁵ In a few other instances, such as Italy and Ireland, the referendum is a more frequently used, but far from routine, part of the political process. Irish referendums on divorce (1986, 1995) and abortion (1983, 1992), for example, and the 1993 Italian referendum on decriminalizing drug use illustrate both the possibilities and limitations of the

Table 15.1: Federal and Provincial Referendums in Canada, 1970–1999

	Date	Subject	% 'Yes'	% Turnout^a
Canada	26 October 1992	Charlottetown Accord	45	75 [70]
British	30 August 1972^b	Daylight savings time	64	69 [*]
Columbia	17 October 1991	Initiative	83	75 [*]
	17 October 1991	Recall	81	75 [*]
Alberta	30 August 1971	Daylight savings time	62	72 [*]
Saskatchewan	21 October 1991	Balanced budget legislation	86	83 [*]
	21 October 1991	Constitutional referendums	87	83 [*]
	21 October 1991	Abortion funding	40	83 [*]
Quebec	20 May 1980	Sovereignty-association	40	86 [83]
	26 October 1992	Charlottetown Accord	44	83 [82]
	30 October 1995	Sovereignty	49	94 [82]
Prince Edward Island	18 January 1988	Fixed-link crossing	59	65 [81]
Newfoundland	12 September 1995	Education reform	54	52 [74]
Northwest	14 April 1982	Division of territory	56	53 [70]
Territories	5 May 1992	Boundary line	54	54 [76]
	3–5 Nov. 1992^c	Creation of Nunavut	69	80 [76]

^a Figure in brackets provides a turnout comparison for the nearest federal or provincial election. [*] denotes that the referendum was held concurrently with a provincial election.
^b Held in five electoral districts only.
^c Held in eastern Arctic only.

referendum as a device for dealing with complex and contentious issues of public policy (Gallagher and Uleri, 1996).

Considering the extent to which the referendum has been employed in modern democratic politics and the steadily growing advocacy of its use by both practitioners and theorists, the referendum remains much understudied by political scientists.[6] In North America particularly, there is a tendency to idealize the referendum as a democratic device while knowing relatively little about the behaviour of voters in the instances where referendums have occurred. While referendums can appear on one level to be the ultimate democratic expression, they can also be subject to manipulation by élites, imperfect levels of information, or low voter turnout. Referendums often provide an electoral environment of greater volatility than that found in elections (LeDuc, 2000). Such was the case in the 1992 referendum on the Charlottetown Accord, as vote intention shifted dramatically during the campaign.[7] However, this aspect of voting behaviour in referendums might be expected to vary considerably from one case to another because referendums are unique political events in which the political context can vary widely. One would not expect the same degree of volatility in the two Quebec cases, where the referendum question was rooted in long-standing divisions on the sovereignty issue, which in turn is reflected in the structure of the party system itself. Likewise, in Ireland, one might expect that the votes on moral questions like divorce and abortion would reflect relatively strong and stable religious feelings. By contrast, the several European votes on the Maastricht Treaty may have involved a range of different attitudes, some of which could shift rapidly, others more slowly. Examining the two Danish referendums on this issue, Franklin et al. (1994, 1995) argue that attitudes towards domestic political actors can sometimes provide a more plausible explanation of shifts in voter sentiment than feelings about the referendum issue itself (see also Siune et al., 1993).

The argument for referendums as a superior device for democratic citizen participation depends heavily on the creation of institutions and rules that can guarantee high levels of participation. But the evidence shows that voting turnout can vary widely in referendums. In Switzerland, where referendums are commonplace events, turnout is often well below 50 per cent, although it can rise to higher levels when a particular issue engages wider voter interest. In US state referendums, turnout is notoriously low and can be subject to even more extreme fluctuations. In their worldwide survey of referendums, Butler and Ranney (1994: 14–17) found that referendum turnout averaged 15 per cent lower than that for national elections. However, it is not necessarily the case that turnout in referendums is lower than that found in elections; in fact, it may vary much more widely from case to case. Turnout is also low in elections in both the US and Switzerland, but turnout in some of the more important European referendums has generally been comparable to that found in national elections. Canadian examples show a similar pattern. Turnout was higher in the 1992 Charlottetown Accord referendum (75 per cent) than in the federal election a year later, a pattern similar to that found in both the 1948 Newfoundland Confederation referendum and the 1980 Quebec vote on sovereignty-association.[8] Turnout in the 1995 Quebec sovereignty referendum registered an astonishing 94 per cent, higher than in any provincial or federal election. In some instances, notably in the western provinces, referendums have sometimes been held in conjunction with provincial elections, thereby ensuring participation at comparable rates.

In a few instances where a separate referendum was held on a particular issue, some distinction in rates of participation can be observed. The two Northwest Territories plebiscites on territorial division drew rates of participation just above 50 per cent, as did the 1995 Newfoundland vote on merging public and separate schools. These participation rates are substantially lower than those found in the most nearly comparable election. Clearly, a referendum held separately on a less salient issue runs the risk of lower voter participation. Because of this concern, some countries have adopted minimum participation requirements or specific thresholds for a referendum to be considered valid.[9] Double majorities are sometimes also required, such as in Australia, which requires that, to be adopted, constitutional amendments must gain a majority in *both* the nation as a whole and in at least four of the six states. It is interesting to speculate on what might have happened had the Charlottetown Accord gained a majority of the national electorate but failed in some provinces. Or if it had produced a different result in Quebec alone, as the conscription plebiscite did in 1942. Or if it had passed, but with an unacceptably low rate of voter participation. These types of counterfactuals can serve to focus our attention on some of the major issues concerning the theory and practice of direct democracy. But more information can be gained from a careful examination of actual cases of referendum voting. The three examples to be considered here in more detail—the 1992 federal constitutional referendum and the two Quebec sovereignty referendums—provide a good test of some of these arguments, in part because of the availability of survey data that offers more detailed evidence on the behaviour and attitudes of voters. Taken together, they can provide us with a more empirically based understanding of both the possibilities and limits of direct democracy in the Canadian setting.

The 1992 Referendum on the Charlottetown Accord

The constitutional impasse after the failure of the Meech Lake Accord in June 1990 made more compelling the idea of involving the people directly in any new constitutional initiatives that might be undertaken. However, as the negotiations that led to the signing of the Charlottetown Accord in August 1992 approached a conclusion, it was not obvious that the country was headed towards a referendum. Like the Meech Lake Accord, the agreement might have been put to Parliament and the provincial legislatures for debate and ratification.[10] But Quebec was already committed by law to hold its own referendum, either on 'sovereignty' or on a federal constitutional proposal, no later than 26 October 1992. Alberta and British Columbia had likewise made commitments to hold referendums on any new constitutional agreements. Under these circumstances, a quick federal vote, held on the same day as the already scheduled Quebec referendum (which was then only two months away), became the only plausible strategy.

Given this unusual context, it is perhaps not surprising that the public was somewhat ambivalent towards this new political development. The Canadian people were not to be asked to choose among competing visions of federalism or even whether they wanted to embark on a journey of constitutional reform. Rather, their role was only to approve the document in its entirety now that other stages in the process had all been completed. Nevertheless, public attitudes towards the idea of a referendum were cautiously positive (Figure 15.1). Nearly two-thirds of a national sample agreed with the proposition that the referendum would give 'ordinary people a chance to help decide Canada's future'.[11] But many also believed that such matters were better decided by governments than in a referendum. Similarly, a substantial number felt that, like the infamous conscription plebiscite, the referendum might actually do more to divide the country than to unite it. Respondents in Quebec were somewhat more likely than those in other provinces to see the event as potentially divisive. Large majorities of the survey respondents agreed that the referendum would not 'settle any of the important issues facing the country' and that it would be preferable to concentrate 'on solving the country's economic problems' instead. While Canadians were interested in the vote and took it seriously, many feared that most people 'don't understand what the referendum was all about.' Regardless of the outcome, few believed that it would finally and

Figure 15.1: Attitude towards the Referendum, 1992

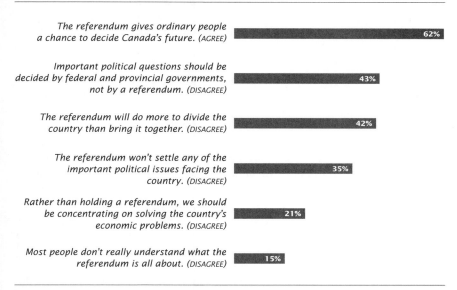

The referendum gives ordinary people a chance to decide Canada's future. (AGREE)	62%
Important political questions should be decided by federal and provincial governments, not by a referendum. (DISAGREE)	43%
The referendum will do more to divide the country than bring it together. (DISAGREE)	42%
The referendum won't settle any of the important political issues facing the country. (DISAGREE)	35%
Rather than holding a referendum, we should be concentrating on solving the country's economic problems. (DISAGREE)	21%
Most people don't really understand what the referendum is all about. (DISAGREE)	15%

Source: 1992 Carleton Referendum Study (N = 1,115).

decisively resolve the long standing constitutional impasse (Clarke et al., 1996: 148–50). Quebecers in particular were more likely to feel this way. To them and to many other Canadians, the referendum seemed more like just another move in the continuing constitutional chess game rather than the logical conclusion of a truly democratic process.

There were few differences in these attitudes between various subgroups of the Canadian population. Aside from the more skeptical views of Quebecers noted above, the only notable differences between regions of the country regarding attitudes towards the referendum were found among westerners, who were significantly more likely to disagree with the statement that 'important political questions should be decided by . . . governments' rather than in a referendum. Younger voters were also more likely to disagree with this view, while older respondents tended to prefer the more traditional political processes. But aside from these relatively minor variations, there were remarkably few differences among groups of the population categorized by place of residence, age, education, or gender. Most Canadians appeared to combine a generally positive view of their opportunity to participate in the referendum with a measure of skepticism regarding its potential consequences.

The referendum ballot provided only for a simple 'Yes' or 'No' on 'the agreement of August 28th'. Because the decision to hold a referendum was taken so quickly, little thought had been given to matters of organization, strategy, or even the wording of the question. At the outset of the campaign, it seemed that a real contest might take place only in Quebec, where an organized opposition was already in place. The Parti Québécois almost immediately announced its intention to campaign for a 'No' vote, but there was little initial opposition elsewhere. All 10 provincial premiers representing three different political parties supported the agreement. The leaders of the three main federal parties each announced that they would campaign actively for a 'Yes' vote. Leaders of the Aboriginal groups involved in various phases of the constitutional negotiations indicated that they would also support it. But gradually, opposition outside of Quebec began to surface. Preston Manning announced that the Reform Party would oppose the agreement and campaign against it nationally. At about the same time, several prominent Quebec Liberals came out against the proposals, revealing the split in Premier Robert Bourassa's own party and indicating that the agreement was in more serious trouble in Quebec than initially thought. Judy Rebick, president of the National Action Committee on the Status of Women, announced her organization's opposition. Momentum suddenly seemed to be shifting away from the poorly organized and overconfident architects of the agreement. This gradual forming of opposition lines set the stage for a dramatic intervention by former Prime Minister Pierre Trudeau about three weeks into the campaign. While it was perhaps not surprising that Trudeau, also a critic of Meech Lake, would oppose the agreement, his views commanded wide attention. The various groups and individuals supporting the 'No' had little in common, ranging widely across the political spectrum and often holding contradictory views on other issues. But arrayed against them were the pillars of the Canadian establishment: business, government, academia, and seemingly much of the press and media.

Because there was really no long-term basis of opinion on many of the specific issues arising from the agreement, the referendum campaign held the potential for even greater volatility and uncertainty about the outcome than would typically be found in an election. Some voters, of course, would have been able to make up their minds quickly on the basis of partisan cues or familiarity with one or more of the long-standing issues in the constitutional debates, such as the recognition of Quebec as a 'distinct society' or the provision for reform of the Senate. Strong supporters of either the Parti Québécois or the Reform Party would hardly have needed a campaign to make up their minds. In addition, there were the cues provided by such political leaders as Trudeau, Prime Minister Brian Mulroney, Bourassa, and Manning—personalities about whom many voters had strong opinions.

Levels of voter interest were high, with over 80 per cent of survey respondents reporting that they were 'very interested' or 'somewhat interested' in the referendum. Turnout, at 75 per cent, was comparable to the average in federal elections, and 5 per cent higher than that of the 1993 federal election only a year later. Turnout in Quebec, at 83 per cent, was even higher, and also comparable to that found in elections.[12] The pattern of voter decision-making was similar to that which occurs in an election campaign (Clarke et al., 1996). There were no significant differences in voting participation among demographic groups within the population categorized according to gender, education, or socio-economic status. Younger respondents (under age 30) were almost as likely to report having participated in the referendum as those in the higher age groups. Among the reasons given by non-voters in our survey for *not* participating, relatively few related to the referendum question itself. Only about 10 per cent of these respondents cited the difficulty of the voting decision or the complexity of the issues as reasons for their non-participation. Neither did feelings about the referendum itself predict non-participation. The majority of non-voters cited personal reasons such as health, work schedules, family commitments, etc. Thirty-eight per cent of those surveyed indicated that they made up their minds early—at the time that the agreement was announced or even before. About a third of the respondents in our sample decided on their vote during the early or middle part of the campaign, and a nearly equal number (29 per cent) reserved their decision until the final two weeks (Figure 15.2). The 'No' side pulled ahead in the polls during the first week of October and stayed there throughout the remainder of the campaign. With nearly three weeks to go, the contest was effectively over even though public opinion polls continued to show large numbers of undecided voters right up until the very end of the campaign.

While there were partisan divisions in the vote, it is clear that the contest was not fundamentally a partisan one. Partisan feelings were only a modest correlate of participation in the referendum, as respondents with no party leanings or weak levels of partisan commitment were almost as likely to report voting in the referendum as were those with stronger feelings about the parties. Since the leaders of all

Figure 15.2: Reported Time of Vote Decision, 1992 Referendum and 1993 Federal Election

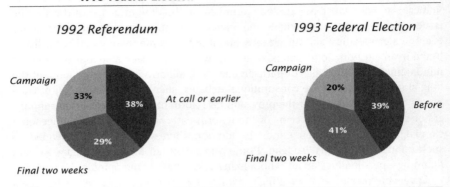

Source: 1992 Carleton Referendum Study (N = 739); 1993 CNES (N = 2,710).

three of the main federal parties had actively campaigned for a 'Yes' vote, many of the normal partisan cues that voters might be expected to respond to were completely absent from the referendum campaign. This is reflected in the distribution of Liberal, Conservative, and NDP voters, who are found in substantial numbers in *both* the 'Yes' and 'No' camps (Figure 15.3). BQ and Reform identifiers, on the other hand, voted overwhelmingly 'No'. For these voters, there was no ambiguity in the messages emanating from the campaign, the parties, or their leaders. For other voters, leaders mattered more. Had those whose task it was to sell this agreement to the Canadian people been more popular, the outcome conceivably might

Figure 15.3: Party Composition of Voting Groups in the 1992 Referendum

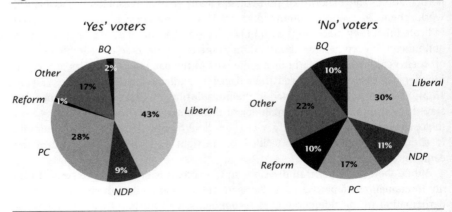

* Includes non-identifiers.
Source: 1992 Carleton Referendum Study (N = 778).

have been different. At the time of the referendum, Brian Mulroney's popularity with the public was close to its nadir (Figure 15.4), and he would subsequently indicate his intention to resign from office only four months after the referendum. Feelings about some of the provincial leaders also mattered. But in the final analysis, the agreement failed because of both the message and the messengers.

Figure 15.4: Feelings about Political Leaders at the Time of the 1992 Referendum

Mean thermometer scores

Source: 1992 Carleton Referendum Study (N = 1,115).

Because the 1992 referendum was such an unusual event in Canadian electoral politics, it is difficult to generalize from it. Once begun, any electoral campaign, including a referendum, takes on a life of its own and can only be managed in limited ways by those who set it in motion. The 1992 referendum unexpectedly provided Canadian voters with a rare opportunity to pass judgement on the nation's entire political establishment, together with one of that establishment's most cherished projects. For many, the referendum seemed to become a battle of the people against the establishment. Seen in this light, it is perhaps more surprising that 45 per cent of Canadians ultimately voted *for* the Charlottetown agreement than that it went down to defeat.

The Quebec Sovereignty Referendums

The two Quebec cases differ significantly from the Charlottetown referendum in the relative importance of long-term and short-term factors in explaining the vote.[13] The difference in outcome between the two Quebec referendums is partly attributable to the growth in sovereigntist sentiment over the 15-year period, as well as to gradual demographic changes in the Quebec electorate (Cloutier et al., 1992; LeDuc, 1997). The PQ's electoral strategy in the 1976 election that first brought it to power had been to 'decouple' the sovereignty question from other issues in the election by promising to hold a separate referendum on sovereignty, thereby avoiding the type of polarization of the electorate that had caused the party's massive defeat in 1973 (Pinard and Hamilton, 1977, 1978). But the 41 per cent of the popular vote that the PQ obtained in 1976, while sufficient to produce a majority government, was clearly not enough to carry a referendum on the sovereignty issue. During its first term in office, much attention was given by the PQ government to developing a strategy for the referendum to follow.

At the time that the text of the 1980 referendum question was released to the public, its wording (see box) was widely considered a winning formula. It provided the reassurance of a continued economic association and a common currency and asked only for a 'mandate to negotiate' an agreement, not for sovereignty itself. Further, it provided an additional margin of safety in that any agreement that might be achieved would have to be approved in another referendum. Polls commissioned by the government suggested that this strategy was capable of attracting the support of well over 50 per cent of the electorate (Cloutier et al., 1979). Yet this proposal ultimately went down to a rather decisive 60–40 defeat.

In part, this was because the federalist side was able to shift the terms of the debate over the course of the campaign. Its concept of 'renewed federalism' was a potentially appealing alternative to the vision of 'sovereignty-association'

Wording of the Ballot Question:
1980 and 1995 Quebec Referendums

1980
'The Government of Quebec has made public its proposal to negotiate a new agreement with the rest of Canada, based on the equality of nations;

This agreement would enable Quebec to acquire the exclusive power to make its laws, levy its taxes, and establish relations abroad—in other words, sovereignty—and at the same time to maintain with Canada an economic association including a common currency;

No change in political status resulting from these negotiations will be effected without approval by the people through another referendum;

On these terms, do you agree to give the Government of Quebec the mandate to negotiate the proposed agreement between Quebec and Canada?'

1995
'Do you agree that Quebec should become sovereign, after having made a formal offer to Canada for a new economic and political partnership, within the scope of the bill respecting the future of Quebec and of the agreement signed on June 12, 1995?'

contained in the referendum question. Like 'sovereignty-association' itself, 'renewed federalism' softened the harder edges of the federalist position and made it sound less like a defence of the status quo. Public opinion polls at the time suggested that both of these softer versions of the federalist and sovereigntist messages were more appealing to the public than the harder options (Figure 15.5). On this ground, however, the federalists held a distinct edge in 1980. The same polls that suggested substantial electoral support for 'sovereignty-association' also showed that in a straight fight between these two concepts, 'renewed federalism' would win. And indeed, the actual outcome of the 1980 referendum came very close to reflecting the then existing public preferences between these two alternative visions of Quebec's constitutional future.[14] While 'renewed federalism' as such was not on the ballot, the campaign ultimately persuaded voters to view the choice in these terms.

Opinion shifted steadily away from the 'Yes' side over the course of the 1980 campaign, reflecting in part the struggle between the two sides to redefine the referendum question in their own competing terms (Pammett et al., 1983; Pinard and Hamilton, 1984). The relative newness of these issues at that time, the complexity of the ballot question, and the nature of the campaign discourse itself meant that the decision would not be a clear-cut or easy one for many voters. Nevertheless, compared to the 1992 Charlottetown referendum, a larger proportion of Quebec voters had made up their minds even before the referendum was actually called. Many also came to a decision fairly early in the campaign, leaving only 5 per cent still undecided by the final week according to the Canadian National Election Study (CNES) survey conducted at the time of the 1980 referendum (Figure 15.6).[15]

By 1995, the picture had changed dramatically with respect to perceptions of the various constitutional options.[16] Support for a 'sovereignty-association' type of alternative remained high, but favourable attitudes even towards the 'hardest'

Figure 15.5: Attitudes towards Constitutional Options for Quebec, 1980 and 1995

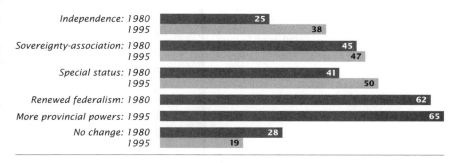

Per cent 'very favourable' or 'somewhat favourable'

Source: 1980 CNES, Quebec Referendum wave (N = 325); 1995 Carleton ISSP survey, Quebec respondents only (N = 519).

Figure 15.6: Reported Time of Vote Decision in the Quebec Referendums

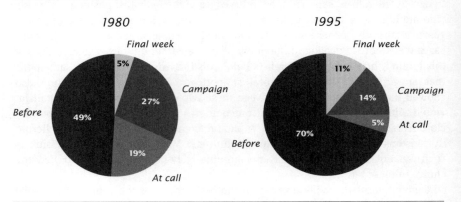

1980

Final week
5%
Campaign
27%
Before
49%
19%
At call

1995

Final week
11%
Campaign
14%
5% At call
70%
Before

Source: 1980 CNES, Quebec Referendum wave (N = 271); 1995 Carleton ISSP survey, Quebec respondents only (N = 458).

option of independence had risen sharply (Figure 15.5). The 1995 referendum question was shorter and still proposed a negotiated agreement with the rest of Canada. But it put a one-year time limit on these talks, after which time Quebec would become sovereign regardless of their outcome. There was no promise, as in 1980, of a second referendum. In the wake of the failure of both the Meech Lake and Charlottetown initiatives, a concept like 'renewed federalism' had little remaining credibility.

Many older voters, having previously participated in the 1980 referendum, would have recognized immediately many of the themes and arguments being put forward in 1995. Even for those who had not voted in 1980, or who may have entered the electorate subsequent to those events, 15 years of ongoing debate on sovereignty provided considerable familiarity with the basic issues and positions of the leading actors.[17] Further, the parties in Quebec, long polarized around the sovereignty issue, provided ample cues to voters on the 1995 referendum question. One might therefore expect that voters in the second referendum would have been able to come to a decision much more quickly on the issue and that the process of coming to a voting decision might have been a fairly straightforward and simple one for 1995 Quebec voters. To some degree this was true. As is seen in Figure 15.6, the number of respondents who knew how they would vote even before the referendum was called was much higher in 1995 than in 1980. Yet the percentage of voters reserving judgement until the final week, approximately double the comparable figure from the 1980 contest, was also important. The actual call of the referendum seemed an unimportant part of the dynamic in 1995, perhaps because it had been so widely anticipated. But the campaign itself was important, a fact substantiated by the shift towards the 'Yes' that took place in the final weeks of the campaign, producing an extremely close outcome.

In referendums, as in elections, the messengers often matter as much as the message. Although no candidates' names or party affiliations appear on the ballot, the arguments over the course of the campaign are interpreted and delivered by participants who are familiar to the voters—the political parties and their leaders. In the case of the 1992 Charlottetown referendum, there is no doubt that Brian Mulroney's personal unpopularity with the electorate contributed to the defeat of the agreement (LeDuc and Pammett, 1995; Johnston et al., 1996). While the question and its interpretation were new to the political scene, the parties and leaders who conveyed information to the voters in the 1992 referendum campaign were all too familiar.

The role of the parties and their leaders was also crucial in the case of the two Quebec referendums. In both instances, the two major political parties themselves formed the core of the umbrella committees that carried on the campaign. With the party system in Quebec firmly polarized around the sovereignty issue, the prominent role played by the parties would have come as no surprise to the voter. As is shown in Figure 15.7, the fit between partisanship and the vote in both of the Quebec referendums was very strong. Yet, one of the important differences between the 1980 and 1995 contests was the extent to which partisanship itself had weakened within the electorate over this period. By 1995, nearly a quarter of the Quebec electorate did not identify with *either* of the two main provincial parties, thus introducing a greater element of uncertainty into the referendum outcome.[18] Appeals to partisanship alone, however strongly felt, were even less likely to carry the day in 1995 than in 1980.

At the time of the 1980 referendum, the two main provincial parties stood about equal in overall popularity as measured in surveys conducted at that time (Figure 15.8). René Lévesque was a popular Premier and party leader, scoring well above his party. The provincial Liberal leader of the time, Claude Ryan, lagged far behind Lévesque in personal popularity. However, the leadership deficit on the federalist side in 1980 was more than compensated for by the presence of Pierre Trudeau. Although not at the peak of his national popularity at the beginning of his final term as Prime Minister, Trudeau was still well regarded by Quebec voters at the time of the 1980 referendum (Figure 15.8).[19] His rating in the 1980 CNES was a full 10 points higher than that for Lévesque and more than 20 points higher than Ryan. Trudeau was equally well liked by both Francophone and Anglophone respondents in the 1980 survey, an achievement recorded by very few politicians in Quebec.[20] The message of 'renewed federalism' which ultimately swung the 1980 referendum result to the 'No' side was thus delivered to a relatively receptive electorate by a highly credible and popular federal Prime Minister, who more than counter-balanced the provincial popularity enjoyed by Premier Lévesque. Although both sides held certain advantages, the playing field on which the 1980 referendum campaign was fought was tilted towards the federalist side from the beginning.

The position of the political parties and their leaders at the time of the 1995 referendum was very different. The provincial Liberal Party received a rating of 46 among Quebec respondents in the 1995 ISSP survey, compared with a solidly

Figure 15.7: Party Composition of Voting Groups in the Quebec Referendums

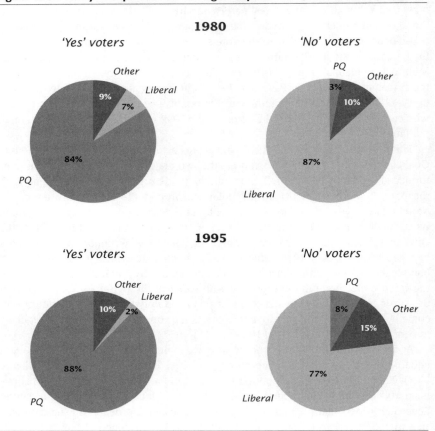

* Includes non-identifiers.

Source: 1980 CNES, Quebec Referendum wave (N = 271); 1995 Carleton ISSP survey, Quebec respondents (N = 458).

positive mean score of 57 for the PQ (Figure 15.8). There was thus an 11-point spread in voter esteem of the two parties in 1995, rather than the nearly equal positions that had existed in 1980. Substantially fewer Quebec voters identified themselves as Liberals than was the case in 1980, the percentage of Liberal identi- fiers having dropped by 13 per cent from the 1980 to the 1993 Canadian Election Study (CES). Premier Jacques Parizeau received a mean rating at the neutral mark among 1995 ISSP respondents, but this was caused largely by his strongly negative perception among Anglophones. Among Francophone respondents, Parizeau at the time obtained a respectable rating of 53. His ally in the 1995 referendum campaign, Mario Dumont, received a nearly comparable rating. But Liberal leader Daniel Johnson was by far the most unpopular of the Quebec party leaders, receiving a

Figure 15.8: Thermometer Scale Ratings of Parties and Leaders in Quebec

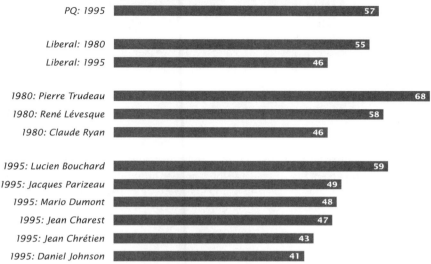

Source: 1980 CNES, Quebec Referendum wave (N = 325); 1995 ISSP survey, Quebec respondents only (N = 519); 1980 CNES, post-election wave, Quebec respondents only (N = 441)— rating for Trudeau only.

score of 40 among 1995 ISSP respondents (Figure 15.8), including a highly negative 38 among Francophones. His federalist ally, Jean Chrétien, was nearly as unpopular, particularly among Francophone respondents.

If the tilt, then, was slightly to the 'Yes' side among the parties and leaders going into the 1995 campaign, the balance shifted even more sharply in that direction when Lucien Bouchard was added to the equation. In some respects, Bouchard played a role in the 1995 referendum comparable to that of Pierre Trudeau in 1980. His personal popularity, particularly among Francophone voters, was nearly as high as that of Trudeau at the time of the 1980 referendum.[21] Perhaps even more important than his high personal standing was the fact that Bouchard was regarded by many voters as a politician who was 'trustworthy'. As the potential 'chief negotiator' following a 'Yes' vote in the referendum, Bouchard projected an image of strength and of a man who could be trusted in such a role. Jean Chrétien, by contrast, was hugely unpopular among Francophones and carried with him a reputation as the man who had 'betrayed Quebec' in the 1982 constitutional scenario. Such a combination tilted the campaign advantage in 1995 strongly towards the sovereigntist side. An electorate that on balance was less partisan than that of 15 years earlier was prepared to listen to the arguments put forward by Bouchard during the course of the campaign. A plausible post-referendum scenario coming from a 'trusted' source was all the more potent.

The extraordinarily high turnout in the 1995 referendum is indicative of the extent to which the issue at stake was capable of engaging and mobilizing the electorate. The call of the referendum itself had little effect in motivating voters because partisan attitudes were already well entrenched. As the campaign progressed, however, small groups of voters with weaker leanings for or against sovereignty were gradually pulled into the respective camps. The 'No' side appeared initially to do better among these uncertain voters, as some sovereigntist leaners became wary of the possible implications of a 'Yes' result. But by the final week a different pattern had begun to take hold. The 'Yes' side was quite successful in gaining and holding the support of 'soft sovereigntist' voters as the campaign drew to a close (Pammett and LeDuc, 1998). The 1995 referendum thus featured a real campaign much like an election, in which the struggle for the eventual support of wavering voters was decisive. While smaller in numbers, those voters who made their decision late in the 1995 campaign were more likely to end up voting 'Yes'. It is hard to escape the conclusion that ineffective leadership of the federalist side was partly responsible, and that the campaign mattered a great deal in producing the extremely close result.

Conclusion

A referendum presents a somewhat different set of choices to the voter than does an election. Clearly, it provides an opportunity for citizens to participate directly in the political process in a way that an election does not. But in a referendum, unlike an election, voters must decide among alternatives that are often unfamiliar and perhaps lacking in partisan cues. One might therefore expect greater volatility and uncertainty in referendum voting. But at least some of the factors we are accustomed to considering in studies of elections—parties and partisanship; the images of political leaders; the issues underlying the question on the ballot; the dynamics of campaign strategies; the media—are important to the outcome of a referendum in much the same way as in elections. However, the relative balance of these factors can vary considerably. In the 1992 constitutional referendum, party positions were not as readily distinguishable because Liberals, Conservatives, and New Democrats all campaigned on the same side, urging voters to support the package of constitutional changes negotiated by the Progressive Conservative federal government and the provinces. Thus, although the Charlottetown Accord was closely associated with Prime Minister Mulroney, and was defeated in part because of his unpopularity, that campaign was not the scene of an intensely partisan battle. In both Quebec referendums, however, partisan forces lined up predictably on the different sides of the question, and the relative popularity of such well entrenched opposing forces could readily be expected to have significant effects on voting. Feelings about an issue like sovereignty may well change less readily than attitudes towards individual politicians or even political parties. For some voters, opinions on Quebec sovereignty reflect their fundamental beliefs about the country or the province as a political community. For others, such attitudes may be less the product of deeply held beliefs than a shorter-term decision based on the persuasive arguments of an advertising campaign, apprehensions about the economic conse- quences of the vote, or judgements about the relative credibility of those delivering the message.

Campaigns are important in determining referendum outcomes. All three of the cases considered here have seen very high levels of participation by voters, in part because of the salience of the issues and the novelty of the event. The short-term understanding of the issue and the images of parties and leaders that drive the campaigns motivate both the decision to participate and a substantial amount of voting behaviour. It follows, therefore, that the results of referendums, even on such a long-standing question as Quebec sovereignty, are not easily predictable in advance. On a matter such as the Charlottetown Accord, they may not be pre- dictable at all. The dynamics of a referendum campaign can be hard to anticipate, and the breadth of participation of the electorate cannot always be assured. In all three cases examined here, public opinion polls taken in advance of each of the campaigns suggested different results from those that actually occurred. While longer-term factors may be important, the short-term impact of opposing campaign strategies and tactics can easily make the critical difference in determining both the outcome of a referendum and its relative success as an exercise in democracy.

Notes

1. The three cases are: the Prohibition plebiscite of 29 September 1898, which was con- ducted by the Laurier government; the Conscription plebiscite of 27 April 1942 initiated by Mackenzie King; and the referendum on the Charlottetown constitutional agreement that took place on 26 October 1992. See Boyer (1992b) for a discussion of the particular political circumstances surrounding each of these federal votes.
2. I use the terms 'referendum' and 'plebiscite' interchangeably here, reflecting the confu- sion that has crept into Canadian discourse on the subject. Strictly speaking, the term 'plebiscite' is more applicable, since none of the Canadian cases discussed here could truly be considered legally binding on their respective governments. But the term 'refer- endum' is nevertheless more commonly encountered in contemporary Canadian usage and in the political science literature. See Boyer (1992b), Butler and Ranney (1994), and Gallagher and Uleri (1996).
3. Omitted here are several provincial cases in which referendums were held simultaneously in a number of municipalities in conjunction with municipal elections. Examples of this practice include a 1983 vote in Manitoba on French-language services and the 1998 refer- endum held in 30 Alberta municipalities on video lottery terminals.
4. See the Ontario government discussion papers, 'Your Ontario, Your Choice' (1996) and 'Provincial Referendums: A Proposed Legislative Framework' (1997).
5. The devices used in the American states are often 'initiatives' rather than 'referendums', the key difference being when the ballot question originates from citizen petitions rather than from government bodies. The specific rules for initiating ballot proposals vary widely from state to state. See Magleby (1984) and Cronin (1989).

6. For a synthesis and discussion of many of the theoretical and practical arguments concerning the use of referendum devices, see especially Budge (1996). Butler and Ranney (1994) provide a worldwide overview of the use of referendums in national politics, including a comprehensive listing of referendums conducted in 98 countries. For a broadly comparative discussion of the legal frameworks of referendums, see Suksi (1993) and Setälä (1999). A comprehensive review of research on European referendums, organized by country, may be found in Gallagher and Uleri (1996). On Switzerland, see particularly Kobach (1993) and Kriesi (1993). In Canada, Patrick Boyer (1992a, 1992b) has written several books advocating the use of referendums and assembling information on their historical usage and characteristics.

7. An Angus Reid poll on 2 September, less than a week after the signing of the Accord, found 67 per cent in favour. On 15 October, Environics published a poll showing that the potential 'Yes' vote had declined to 44 per cent, very close to the actual result two weeks later (45 per cent). See LeDuc and Pammett (1995: 13).

8. Turnout in the second Newfoundland Confederation referendum (22 July 1948) was 85 per cent, compared to 76 per cent in the subsequent provincial election (27 May 1949). For turnout comparisons between other provincial referendums and elections, see Table 15.1.

9. In Britain, for example, the 1979 referendum on the devolution of powers to Scotland specified 40 per cent of the total electorate as a minimum threshold. Thus, although the proposition gained a 'Yes' vote of 52 per cent, this combined with a 64 per cent turnout was insufficient to proceed with the legislation. In the case of the 1992 vote on Nunavut held in the eastern Arctic, the voting rules specified that abstentions were in effect counted as 'No' votes. But the turnout of 80 per cent of the electorate and a 69 per cent vote in favour of the proposal yielded a winning combination.

10. On the constitutional negotiations leading up to the Charlottetown Accord, see Russell (1993) or Pal and Seidle (1993). On the referendum itself, see Johnston et al. (1996).

11. Data reported in this section are from a national survey organized by Harold D. Clarke, Lawrence LeDuc, Jon H. Pammett, Allan Kornberg, and Allan Frizzell and carried out by the Carleton University Survey Centre at the time of the 1992 referendum. This study involved 1,115 respondents. More detailed analyses of these data may be found in LeDuc and Pammett (1995) and Clarke et al. (1996). We also use data from the 1992 wave of the Canadian Election Study (CES). This study was conducted by the York University Institute for Social Research and was directed by Richard Johnston, André Blais, Henry Brady, Elisabeth Gidengil, and Neil Nevitte. There were 2,530 respondents in the 1992 referendum wave of the CES. For a more detailed analysis of data from this study, see Johnston et al. (1996).

12. Legally speaking, the referendum in Quebec was separate from the one conducted under federal jurisdiction in the rest of the country. This had various implications regarding the conduct of the campaign, particularly with respect to advertising, campaign organization, and finance. See Côté et al. (1992).

13. Much of the discussion of the two Quebec referendums reported here is based on a more detailed analysis in Pammett and LeDuc (1998). See also Clarke and Kornberg (1996).

14. The CROP poll cited above showed 51 per cent for renewed federalism, 32 per cent for sovereignty-association, and 17 per cent undecided (Cloutier et al., 1979).

15. The 1980 CNES and Quebec referendum studies were conducted by Harold D. Clarke, Jane Jenson, Lawrence LeDuc, and Jon H. Pammett. This series of studies incorporated a panel of respondents who were first interviewed in 1979 and subsequently re-interviewed at the time of the 1980 federal election and again at the time of the 1980 Quebec referendum. Supplementary samples of new voters were added in each wave. These studies were funded by the Social Sciences and Humanities Research Council of Canada, whose support for this research is gratefully acknowledged. Neither the other principal investigators nor the SSHRC is responsible for the analyses and interpretations presented here.

16. The 1995 data used here are from the Carleton ISSP survey, which was conducted coincidentally at the time of the referendum. The International Social Survey Program is a yearly comparative survey, which in 1995 included 25 countries. The Canadian survey is administered by the Carleton University Survey Centre, under the direction of Alan Frizzell. The 1995 survey, on the topic of 'national identity', had a weighted national N of 1,544, including an oversample of 524 cases in Quebec. Several of the questions used in the analysis here were added to the ISSP core questionnaire in Quebec only.

17. At least a third of the electorate would have been composed of different individuals in 1995 than in 1980, as a result of aging, population replacement, migration, etc. (LeDuc, 1997). On the linkages between voting in the referendums and in federal and provincial elections, see Saint-Germain and Grenier (1994).

18. In the 1993 CNES, 38 per cent of Quebec respondents identified themselves as Liberals, 36 per cent as PQ, and 26 per cent reported no party identification. This compares with 1980 figures of 51 per cent Liberal, 39 per cent PQ, and 9 per cent non-identifiers (Pammett and LeDuc, 1998).

19. For Trudeau's ratings over the length of his career in federal politics, see Clarke et al. (1991).

20. In the 1980 CNES, Trudeau's mean score among Francophone respondents was 69, compared with 66 among Anglophone respondents.

21. Bouchard's mean rating among Francophone respondents in the 1995 ISSP survey was 64. It is also interesting to note the extent to which Trudeau's reputation had declined in Quebec following his retirement from politics. Trudeau registered a rating of only 42 among Quebec respondents to the 1993 CES and a dismal 38 among Francophones in that survey.

References

Boyer, Patrick. 1992a. *The People's Mandate: Referendums and a More Democratic Canada*. Toronto: Dundurn Press.

———. 1992b. *Direct Democracy in Canada: The History and Future of Referendums*. Toronto: Dundurn Press.

Budge, Ian. 1996. *The New Challenge of Direct Democracy*. Cambridge: Polity Press.

Butler, David, and Austin Ranney. 1994. *Referendums Around the World: The Growing Use of Direct Democracy*. London: Macmillan.

Clarke, Harold D., Jane Jenson, Lawrence LeDuc, and Jon H. Pammett, 1991. *Absent Mandate: Interpreting Change in Canadian Elections*, 2nd edn. Toronto: Gage.

——, ——, ——, and ——. 1996. *Absent Mandate: Canadian Electoral Politics in an Era of Restructuring*, 3rd edn. Toronto: Gage.

—— and Allan Kornberg. 1996. 'Choosing Canada?: The 1995 Quebec Sovereignty Referendum', *PS* (Dec.): 676–82.

Cloutier, Edouard, et le Centre de recherches sur l'opinion publique. 1979. *Sondage sur la perception des problemes constitutionnels Québec-Canada par la population du Québec*. Gouvernment du Québec, Ministère des Affaires intergouvernmentales.

——, Jean H. Guay, and Daniel Latouche. 1992. *Le Virage: l'évolution de l'opinion publique au Québec depuis 1960*. Montréal: Québec/Amérique.

Côté, Pierre F., et al. 1992. *Démocratie et référendum: la procédure référendaire*. Montréal: Québec/Amérique.

Cronin, Thomas. 1989. *Direct Democracy: the Politics of Initiative, Referendum and Recall*. Cambridge, Mass.: Harvard University Press.

Franklin, Mark, Cees van der Eijk, and Michael Marsh. 1995. 'Referendum Outcomes and Trust in Government: Public Support for Europe in the Wake of Maastricht', *West European Politics* 18: 101–17.

——, Michael Marsh, and Christopher Wlezien. 1994. 'Attitudes Toward Europe and Referendum Votes: A Response to Siune and Svensson', *Electoral Studies* 13.

Gallagher, Michael, and Pier Vincenzo Uleri. 1996. *The Referendum Experience in Europe*. London: Macmillan.

Government of Ontario. 1996. 'Your Ontario, Your Choice', discussion paper.

Government of Ontario. 1997. 'Provincial Referendums: A Proposed Legislative Framework'.

Johnston, Richard, André Blais, Elisabeth Gidengil, and Neil Nevitte. 1996. *The Challenge of Direct Democracy: The 1992 Canadian Referendum*. Montreal and Kingston: McGill-Queen's University Press.

Kobach, Kris. 1993. *The Referendum: Direct Democracy in Switzerland*. Aldershot: Dartmouth.

Kriesi, Hanspeter. *Citoyenneté et démocratie directe*. Zürich: Seismo.

LeDuc, Lawrence. 1997. 'The Sovereignty Generation: A Cohort Analysis of the Quebec Electorate', paper presented at the annual meeting of the Canadian Political Science Association, St John's.

——. 2000. 'Referendums and Elections: How Do Campaigns Differ?', paper presented at the European Consortium for Political Research Joint Sessions Workshops, University of Copenhagen.

—— and Jon H. Pammett. 1995. 'Referendum Voting: Attitudes and Behaviour in the 1992 Constitutional Referendum', *Canadian Journal of Political Science* 28: 3–33.

Magleby, David. 1984. *Direct Legislation: Voting on Ballot Propositions in the United States*. Baltimore: Johns Hopkins University Press.

Monière, Denis, and Jean H. Guay. 1996. *La bataille du Québec*. Québec: Fides.

Pal, Leslie, and F. Leslie Seidle. 1993. 'Constitutional Politics: 1990–92: The Paradox of Participation', in Susan Phillips, ed., *How Ottawa Spends, 1993–94: A More Democratic Canada?* Ottawa: Carleton University Press.

Pammett, Jon H., Harold D. Clarke, Jane Jenson, and Lawrence LeDuc. 1983. 'Political Support and Voting Behaviour in the Quebec Referendum', in Allan Kornberg and Harold Clarke, eds, *Political Support in Canada: The Crisis Years*. Durham, NC: Duke University Press, 323–52.

———— and Lawrence LeDuc. 1998. 'Attitudes Toward Sovereignty and the Vote Decision in the 1995 Quebec Refrendum', paper presented at the annual meeting of the Canadian Political Science Association, Ottawa.

Pinard, Maurice, Robert Bernier, and Vincent Lemieux. 1997. *Un combat inachevé*. Sainte-Foy: Presses de l'Université du Québec.

———— and Richard Hamilton. 1977. 'The Independence Issue and the Polarization of the Electorate: The 1973 Quebec Election', *Canadian Journal of Political Science* 10, 2: 215–59.

———— and ————. 1978. 'The Parti Québécois Comes to Power: An Analysis of the 1976 Quebec Election', *Canadian Journal of Political Science* 11, 4: 739–75.

———— and ————. 1984. 'Les québécois votent 'NON: le sens et la portée du vote', in Jean Crête, ed. *Le comportement électoral au Québec*. Chicoutimi, Que.: Gaetan Morin.

Russell, Peter. 1993. *Constitutional Odyssey*, 2nd edn. Toronto: University of Toronto Press.

Saint-Germain, Maurice, and Gilles Grenier. 1994. 'Le parti québécois, le "NON" à Charlottetown et le bloc québécois: est-ce le même électorat?', *Revue québécoise de science politique* 26: 161–78.

Setälä, Maija. 1999. *Referendums and Democratic Government*. New York: St Martin's Press.

Siune, Karen, Palle Svensson, and Ole Tonsgaard. 1993. 'The European Union: Why the Danes said 'No' in 1992 but 'Yes' in 1993', *Electoral Studies* 13: 107–16.

Suksi, Markku. 1993. *Bringing in the People: A Comparison of Constitutional Forms and Practices of the Referendum*. Dordrecht, Netherlands: Nijhoff.

Chapter 16

Challenging the Gendered Vertical Mosaic: Immigrants, Ethnic Minorities, Gender, and Political Participation

YASMEEN ABU-LABAN

In Canada, historical processes and practices, including European settler colonization, the expropriation of lands from indigenous peoples, and selective immigration and citizenship policies geared towards assimilation, seem to stand in stark
contrast with the federal government's official policy of multiculturalism, enacted
in 1971. However, as a result of this multiculturalism policy, in recent years the
metaphor of the 'mosaic' has enjoyed a popular resonance within Canada as a
depiction of ethnic relations. The mosaic image signifies separate pieces, that,
when combined, form a distinguishable entity but never lose their individual distinctiveness. Today, Canadians often contrast the 'mosaic' metaphor with that of
the 'melting pot' used to symbolize American ethnic relations, and in this exercise
the 'melting pot' is typically presented as a vessel of assimilation that is intolerant
of diversity (Reitz and Breton, 1994; Abu-Laban and Lamont, 1997: 38). From the
vantage point of political behaviour, the Canadian mosaic metaphor suggests that
political participation is not set on the terms of historically dominant groups (the
British and, to a lesser extent, the French) but on the basis of a variety of distinctive identities. If Canada is truly a mosaic, diversity would be a key representational fact in Canadian political life.

The purpose of this chapter is to examine the nature of the Canadian mosaic by
combining two social categories of relevance to understanding Canadian politics:
gender and ethnicity. Traditionally, gender and ethnicity have not been central
areas of concern for political scientists. Moreover, when gender and ethnicity have
been addressed, with few notable exceptions (Trimble, 1998; Ship, 1998), they
have typically been approached as separate and discrete areas of study. This is
problematic because the experiences of ethnic minorities and majorities may differ
depending on their gender, and the experiences of men as a group and women as a
group may differ depending on their ethnicity. A more complete understanding of
both ethnicity and gender may be facilitated by beginning to consider how these

social cateogories intersect. Accordingly, the purpose of this chapter is to examine the political participation of ethnic minorities (non-British, non-French, and non-Aboriginal immigrants and their descendants) with attention to possible differences between minority men and women.

When it comes to formal political power in Canada, the mosaic metaphor might be aptly qualified by calling it a *gendered vertical mosaic*. The mosaic is vertical because majority groups hold more power than minority groups, and the mosaic is gendered because within majority groups and minority groups men hold more power than women. Nonetheless, the range of activities that both male and female immigrants and ethnic minorities engage in suggests that they are not politically passive. Coming to grips with the political agency of minority ethnic groups, and with the ongoing challenges to the gendered vertical mosaic, requires broadening traditional understandings of political participation and using both quantitative and qualitative methods.

In demonstrating this argument, this chapter takes a threefold approach. First, it addresses the question of how gender and ethnicity relate to issues of power. Second, it examines the question of whether the under-representation of minorities in the House of Commons is explained by level of political participation in electoral and party politics. The chapter concludes by addressing how political scientists might better study the political participation of Canadian men and women of minority ethnic backgrounds.

The Gendered Vertical Mosaic and Power

In the Canadian context, gender and ethnicity are worth exploring in relation to politics because, historically, women as a group were excluded from voting and running for office, and so were certain minorities (for example, between the 1870s and 1950s laws excluded the participation of Chinese, Japanese, and South Asians from Canadian political life). Yet, neither gender nor race/ethnicity was a major area of research focus within the discipline of political science as it evolved in the first three decades following World War II (Burt, 1995; Taylor, 1996).

Since the 1980s, gender has emerged as a substantive research area within Canadian political science, through work that took as its starting point the presence of women in legislatures (Burt, 1995: 359; Trimble, 1998: 257). Since the 1990s, Canadian political scientists have increasingly registered concern with the need to study race and ethnicity beyond the long-standing focus on 'French-English' relations (Cairns, 1989; Whitaker, 1997; Abu-Laban, 1997; Ship, 1998). The actual creation of a section on race, ethnicity, and politics within the American Political Science Association in 1995, and its stunning growth, is also a significant development. Since some 75–80 per cent of the world's political scientists are located in the United States (Taylor, 1996: 885), the creation of this section will likely propel Canadian political scientists to attend more to questions of race and ethnicity. Indeed, the complex relationship between numerical representation in legislatures (e.g., of women and/or minorities) and the substantive representation of interests of specific groups (Stasiulis and Abu-Laban, 1991; Stasiulis, 1997a;

Trimble, 1998; Tremblay, 1998) forms one component of a broader agenda concerned with identity and politics that promises to continue to engage political scientists well into the twenty-first century.

Nonetheless, some definitional difficulties are inherent with ethnicity that make it somewhat more unwieldy than gender, and therefore necessary to employ careful and multiple methods for assessing the presence of ethnic minorities in legislatures or other institutions (for a discussion, see Black in this volume). Specifically, ethnicity is difficult to define and interpret because it has *both* subjective and objective components (Isajiw, 1983: 108). Thus, the notion of ethnicity depends on 'subjective' self-definition and serves as an 'objective' analytical concept for research.

Ideally, in classifying specific individuals or enumerating the presence (or absence) of specific groups in Canada or in Canadian institutions, researchers should incorporate how people define their own ethnic background (or backgrounds). Yet, this can be a complicated process, as the national census, taken every five years, reveals. In the most recent 1996 census, respondents were asked which ethnic or cultural group(s) their ancestors belonged to and were given four blank spaces to write their origins. In addition, 24 examples of possible origins (including, for the first time, that of 'Canadian') were listed, although respondents could, as applicable, self-define outside of those origins listed. The results of the 1996 census reveal that about 17 per cent of the population report a British Isles-only ancestry, 9 per cent a French-only ancestry, and 28 per cent report other single origins (Statistics Canada, 1998: 3). The 1996 census also shows that 11.2 per cent of the population self-define as being a member of a group considered a 'visible minority' (ibid., 9). For the Canadian government, visible minorities are defined as 'persons, other than Aboriginal peoples, who are non-Caucasian in race or non-white in colour', and include Chinese, South Asians, blacks, Arabs and West Asians, Filipinos, Southeast Asians, Latin Americans, Japanese, Koreans, and Pacific Islanders (ibid., 8). Overall, 36 per cent of Canadian respondents in the 1996 census claimed multiple (two or more) origins (ibid., 3).

Further confounding the picture that emerges from the 1996 census is the fact that a dramatic high of 19 per cent of respondents chose 'Canadian' as their only origin; in contrast, when this was not listed as a possible origin, in the 1991 census, less than 3 per cent of respondents did so (ibid., 1–2). The popularity of the term 'Canadian' may stem from how the term 'ethnic' (and by extension ethnic group) often carries with it a pejorative or negative meaning, which means that many people may not see themselves (or wish to see themselves) as belonging to an ethnic group. Indeed, Manoly Lupul (Isajiw, 1983: 111–12) contends that part of the failure of the federal policy of multiculturalism revolves around the fact that neither the French nor the Anglo-Celts in Canada consider themselves to be 'ethnic' because this term is perceived to apply to those groups outside of 'mainstream' Canadian society. Notably, a comparison with the 1991 census suggests that those most likely to identify only with the category of 'Canadian' in 1996 were people who previously reported British-only or French-only origins (Statistics Canada, 1998: 2–3).

Setting aside the possibly negative connotations of ethnicity and the difficulties of interpreting self-identification in instances when individuals claim labels like 'Canadian' or claim multiple origins, ethnicity does serve as an important analytic concept for political science. In particular, as with gender, it is critical to employ race and ethnicity in the context of historical and contemporary power relations. In this way, the feature of diversity in and of itself does not reflect on power. Even prior to settler colonization by the French and British in the seventeenth century, Aboriginal societies were diverse in cultural, linguistic, social, and political terms (Dickason, 1997: 43–62). However, the historically shifting processes by which people are categorized into groups and given (or denied) privileges as a result of group membership do relate to power and, therefore, command the attention of political scientists.

In Canada, following the conquest of New France in 1760, the British-origin group became ascendant in asserting economic, political, cultural, and linguistic control over other groups and over newcomers entering and residing in Canada. Indeed, for much of Canada's history, the state's immigration policy was explicitly discriminatory and favoured the entry of white, British-origin Protestants, who were viewed as the 'model' settlers and citizens (Abu-Laban, 1998). Reflecting on this history, in 1965, Canadian sociologist John Porter wrote a widely acclaimed book entitled *The Vertical Mosaic*. The book's title derived from its thesis that in Canada status and power in the economic, political, and social spheres were connected to ethnicity. According to Porter's data, those of British and to a much lesser extent French origin had greater power, and incoming non-British/non-French immigrants assumed an 'entrance status' at the bottom of the occupational and status hierarchy (1965: 73).

The idea that all immigrants to Canada assume an 'entrance status' at the bottom of the occupational hierarchy, along with the idea of an ethnic division of labour, has been challenged in the years since Porter wrote his book (Lautard and Guppy, 1999). Since 1967, Canada's immigration policy has become officially non-discriminatory in terms of race and ethnicity, as potential immigrants are mainly assessed on how their educational and professional skills may contribute to Canada's labour market.[1] In this context, more recent immigrants to Canada have come from countries outside of Europe, and some have entered Canada with considerable educational and professional training and even capital (Abu-Laban, 1998). Immigrants now constitute 17.4 per cent of the population (Statistics Canada, 1997: 1) and fill a range of occupational positions (Stasiulis, 1997b: 153–8). While Porter's work did not systematically address power and status in relation to gender, it is important to recognize that about half of all people who immigrate to Canada each year are female, and this percentage has remained relatively stable over the past three decades (Statistics Canada, 1995: 117).[2]

If the variety of occupations filled by immigrants and minorities today suggests that labour market stratification is somewhat more complex than at the time Porter wrote in 1965, what about the numerical representation of minorities in the federal legislature? Historically, the composition of the House of Commons has reinforced the idea that direct access to political power is determined by ethnic origin (Dahlie and Fernando, 1981: 1). For example, between Confederation in 1867 and 1964, a total of only 97 individuals of non-British/non-French origin were members of the House of Commons (Royal Commission on Bilingualism and Biculturalism, 1970: 272).

Data collected for the period 1965 to 1988 suggest that non-British, non-French, non-Aboriginal minorities continued to be under-represented relative to their numbers in the general population, although the number of minorities in the House of Commons increased continuously from 9.4 per cent in 1965 to 16.3 per cent in 1988 (Pelletier, 1991: 129–30). However, the increase for visible minorities was smaller. Between 1965 and 1988 the number of visible minorities in the House of Commons ranged from 0.8 to 2 per cent (ibid.). Confirming the gendered nature of the vertical mosaic, in the period between 1965 and 1988, as a group women were under-represented compared to their numbers in the general population, and only 5 per cent of those MPs of minority background were women (or six out of a total of 120) (ibid., 130).

In Canada, the 1990s witnessed some increased minority representation, including representation of visible minorities in the federal government. As well, the numbers of women and of female minorities in the House of Commons have increased. Following the 1993 federal election, the number of female MPs reached 18 per cent and the number of non-British, non-French, and non-Aboriginal minority MPs reached 24 per cent, 16 per cent of whom were women (11 out of 71) (Black, 1997a: 19–20). Nonetheless, visible minorities in particular remained under-represented in the House of Commons, standing at about 4.4 per cent of MPs (or 11, of which two were women) (Black and Lakhani, 1997: 7). Thus, women of non-dominant ethnicities—especially visible minorities—are particularly under-represented in the federal House of Commons. The under-representation of visible minorities as MPs is also reflected in the results of the 1997 election (see Black in this volume), as is the under-representation of women as a group (standing at only 21.5 per cent).

The persistent under-representation in the House of Commons of women as a group, visible minorities as a group, and female visible minorities in particular underscores how the Canadian 'mosaic' is not one in which diversity is a representational fact, but rather is gendered and vertical. This raises the question of whether and how political participation or other factors account for the gendered vertical mosaic. Political participation has been and remains central to what political scientists study. The conventional notion of political participation as established in the work of American political scientists Sidney Verba and Norman H. Nie defined it as 'those actions of private citizens by which they seek to influence the selection and/or action of government officials' (Lien, 1994: 245). Political scientists studying gender have demonstrated that the under-representation of women as a group in élite levels of politics (in elected assemblies) cannot be explained by differences in the rate or type of political participation in mass or citizen politics (e.g., voting or attending public meetings) (Brodie, 1985: 1–15). Instead, the historical legacy of women's exclusion from electoral politics, sexist attitudes, and the structure of parties themselves help to explain this (ibid.; Ship, 1998).

In considering immigration and ethnicity historically and today, the exploration of political participation may be approached in two distinct though overlapping ways. One approach is to view ethnic politics in terms of a group's internal dynamics. The second approach perceives ethnic politics in terms of the external behaviour of an ethnic group in such areas as voting patterns, lobbying, and participation in party politics. Clearly, these two dynamics can be interrelated. For example, the laws excluding the participation of the Chinese, Japanese, and South Asians from voting in Canada led these groups to focus on building their own internal community structures (Burnet and Palmer, 1988: 160). Thus, for example, denied the franchise, the Chinese in Canada developed a variety of internal political organizations representing different ideological factions of 'homeland' (i.e., Chinese) politics (ibid., 151).

With respect to external ethnic politics, in addition to possible differences among majority, indigenous, and minority groups, a variety of factors might effect specific ethnic groups. As Burnet and Palmer (ibid.) note:

> the behaviour of members of an ethnic group is related not only to their cultural and educational background and their previous experience, but also their status in Canadian society, their degree of geographical concentration, their economic circumstances, and the degree of discrimination or acceptance they experience.

Keeping in mind these issues, the role of ethnic minorities and immigrants in mass/citizen politics will be examined.

The Official Political Arena: Elections and Parties

The question of whether minorities and immigrants participate in mass politics, while seemingly simple, has provoked some very different responses. As a result, the question has been answered in contradictory ways in the literature and over time, and the answer varies depending on the questions asked and methods used.

In the 1960s and 1970s most political scientists either did not think the study of ethnic minorities was 'politically relevant' or tended to treat ethnic minorities and immigrants as a homogeneous bloc that did not participate in the same way as the native-born and majority groups. One way in which the specificity of 'specific' minority groups was erased was through the study of political cleavages, which was tied to the question of partisan support, as revealed in election studies. Cleavages can be defined as 'the criteria which divide the members of a community or subcommunity into groups, and the relevant cleavages are those which divide members at specific times and places' (Rae and Taylor, 1971: 1). Cleavages can refer to ascriptive characteristics (for example, race or gender), attitudes (for example, ideology or political preference), or behaviour (for example, membership in a union or party) (ibid.). As well, cleavages can be cross-cutting or reinforcing. In other words, cross-cutting cleavages imply that persons divided by one cleavage are brought together by another, whereas reinforcing cleavages ensure that those divided by one cleavage are also divided by another.

The Canadian literature on cleavages, as well as party and electoral support, traditionally approached ethnicity in narrow terms. The national election survey of

1968, one of the first of its kind, did ask questions relating to respondents' self-defined ethnicity (Laponce, 1994: 183–8). However, writing in 1974, John Meisel, using data drawn from the 1968 national sample, argued that Canada has eight enduring cleavages. Among these is an 'ethnic cleavage', which he defined as the French versus English. It is noteworthy that nowhere in his analysis of the 1968 election study did he discuss the divisions between other language/ethnic groups (Meisel, 1974).

For those analysts who have attempted specifically to deal with the category of ethnicity beyond the French-English dichotomy, the all-inclusive category of 'other' has often been employed to deal with all non-French/non-British minorities. This sometimes led to generalizations that pathologize minorities and immigrants in relation to majorities and the native-born. Peter Regenstreif (1965: 91), in dealing with the elections of 1958, 1962, and 1963, placed all non-French non-Anglo-Celtic groups together and confidently asserted that they were less politically astute:

> Probably because of their special position in the country, minority-ethnic groups have a remarkably low threshold of awareness with regard to the performance of the political and economic system. They also appear more disposed than other groups to lay the blame or praise for failure or success at the door of politicians. In contrast, voters of English background have tradition and party identification, which act as stabilizers of political affiliation. Such factors are obviously missing among those who have recently immigrated to Canada.

Other studies have attempted to unpack the category of 'minority' more systematically and to account for specific groups. It is notable that in Canada, the research conducted in the 1970s contrasts with the work done in the 1980s and 1990s (Stasiulis, 1997a). This may be due to differences in research procedures and study designs (Chui et al., 1991: 377). For example, in the 1970s Anthony Richmond and John Goldlust argued that on measures of activity in political organizations, the political participation of immigrants (specifically Jewish, Greek, Portuguese, Asian, and black) was lower than non-immigrants (Stasiulis, 1997a: 1). Jeffrey Reitz proposed that strong loyalty to one's country of origin led to weaker participation in relation to voting and knowledge of public affairs in Canada (ibid., 2).

In contrast, during the 1980s Jerome Black's path-breaking work using the 1974 election study found that the political participation of immigrants (including British, South and East European, and West Indian immigrants) was not significantly different from Canadian-born levels as measured in terms of voting, campaign activity, communal activity (i.e., working with others to solve local problems), and contacting politicians. Black (1982) concludes that, contrary to the assumption that non-British, foreign-born immigrants are politically inactive, they show little or no difference with respect to efficacy and strength of partisan attachment from British-born immigrants and the Canadian-born. In a study of Toronto, Black (1987) demonstrated that immigrants were able to transfer past political experiences into current Canadian politics and, again, that they resembled the

Canadian-born in terms of activities. Black and Leithner (1988) also demonstrated that consumption of the ethnic media, presumably an indicator of interest in one's origins, actually increased political participation and understanding of mainstream Canadian issues. Simard (1991) used qualitative interviews to reveal considerable interest and knowledge of Canadian political issues among immigrant and visible minority community leaders of Arab, South and East Asian, and Caribbean descent residing in Montreal.

Given these more recent studies, the reduction of numerous minority ethnic groups to the single category of 'other' (whether defined by ethnicity or language) is of limited utility in understanding the relationship of ethnicity to party politics and voting patterns. Indeed, Laponce (1994: 195) concludes that both political scientists and political sociologists:

> have given little attention to not only what is written small but also to what is written very large on the ethnic map of the country. In their studies of electoral participation and party preference they have too often ignored the smaller minorities and too often bypassed those who, ethnically, define themselves simply as 'Canadians',

Moreover, there might be variations both within and between minority ethnic groups on such factors as country of origin (be it Canada or abroad), length of time and location in Canada, socio-economic status, gender, and official-language acquisition (Stasiulis and Abu-Laban, 1991; Ship, 1998).

The work of Chui, Curtis, and Lambert (1991), employing the 1984 Canadian Election Study, confirms the problems of lumping 'other ethnic groups' into a single homogeneous category. This study uniquely addressed not only the length of residence of the foreign-born, but the birthplace and generational patterns of immigrant cohorts (i.e., the children, grandchildren, great-grandchildren, and so on of immigrants from different ethnic groups). Chui et al. suggest that in terms of campaign involvement, voting, membership in political organizations, and interest in elections there was no significant difference between Canadian-born and immigrant respondents, except for the greater likelihood of the Canadian-born to contact politicians. Their work also stressed that political involvement tends to peak in the second generation and go down in the third, fourth, and fifth generations (ibid., 375–96). They suggest the need for qualitative interviews with first-generation immigrants and their second-generation offspring to understand fully this striking feature (ibid., 393). Thus, this study not only showed that the foreign-born were not less active than the native-born, but challenged the idea that Canadians with deep roots are the most participatory, as well as the belief that there is a progressive increase in participation with generations in Canada.

One particularly useful way of examining the behaviour of specific minority groups is to focus on specific urban settings. For example, John Wood (1981) uses survey data to demonstrate the interest of South Asians in Vancouver South in the BC provincial and federal elections of 1979. More recently, Miriam Lapp has examined the Jewish, Italian, Greek, Portuguese, and Chinese communities in Montreal during the 1993 Canadian federal election and the 1994 Montreal municipal and

Quebec provincial elections. Lapp's findings suggest that mobilization tactics by ethnic community leaders have little impact on voter turnout (Lapp, 1999a: 179–80). On the other hand, Lapp also reveals significant differences in voter turnout among the five ethnic groups under examination as compared to the general Canadian population. In particular, voter turnout in the Jewish and Chinese communities was lower than the general population, the Italian and Portuguese communities were the same, and the Greek community was actually higher (Lapp, 1999b: 22–4). She suggests the difference in voter turnout may be attributable to the political culture of each ethnic community, since citizenship status and time of immigration appeared to have little impact (ibid., 35).

Overall, most recent survey data suggest that while there may be some variation between specific ethnic groups, immigrants and ethnic minorities are not politically passive and are engaged in mass politics in Canada. Indeed, evidence suggests that the second-generation offspring of immigrants are among the most politically engaged in the country. Thus, the under-representation of minorities in élite politics (e.g., the House of Commons) cannot be adequately explained by saying that they do not participate in mass politics. As with the literature on women in politics, the explanation for under-representation seems to lie elsewhere.

A focus on specific urban settings and constituencies may provide some useful clues not only for the behaviour of specific minority groups, as mentioned, but also for the political under-representation of minorities. In the post-World War II era immigration has been predominantly urban, with a significant concentration of immigrant settlements in the cities of Montreal, Vancouver, and Toronto. Starting in the mid-1980s, in large and medium-size cities attracting immigrants there were numerous attempts by ethnic minorities to run as candidates in federal elections, particularly, though not exclusively, for the Liberal Party. Qualitative interviews with minority candidates and party activists reveal that minorities perceived a number of barriers to their participation in party politics, including the incumbency factor (an unwritten rule across parties that there should not be challenges to those in power); that ethnic minorities were not understood and often perceived negatively and stereotypically by the establishment within their parties; and feelings of exclusion stemming from the informal culture of parties (Stasiulis and Abu-Laban, 1991). This suggests that there are barriers to the participation of minorities in élite-level politics.

As noted, few existing studies have systematically linked gender and ethnicity. The small gains made by minorities and women in terms of formal representation in the House of Commons during the 1990s have provided one opportunity for addressing this under-examined combination. Biographical data collected about female MPs from visible minority and immigrant backgrounds suggest that such women who do make it into public office are 'exceptional,' with unusually strong credentials and advanced degrees compared to other female or male MPs (Black, 1997b). The exceptionality of visible minority women in public life is a striking finding, which, paradoxically, suggests that to capture fully the activities of ordinary immigrant and minority women we must look beyond legislative politics per se.

Indeed, given that the bulk of the literature on women and politics does not fully consider ethnicity and that most literature on ethnicity and politics does not fully consider gender, a better understanding of the intersection between ethnicity and gender may be gleaned by considering political participation not just in relation to official electoral and party politics but in what has been termed 'unofficial politics'.

The Unofficial Political Arena and the Intersections of Ethnicity, Race, and Gender

In Canada, as Jill Vickers has pointed out, a disciplinary problem within political science makes it difficult to account in general for women and their political activities. Specifically, political science as a discipline has been biased towards looking at the 'official politics' of the state and parties, as opposed to the 'unofficial politics' of unions, churches, the women's and other social movements, and local government and communal organizations (Vickers, 1997: 48). This, Vickers argues, has marginalized the impact and insight into women as political actors because most activist women are to be found in the arena of 'unofficial politics'. This insight has implications for the study of the intersection of gender and ethnicity and raises a broad issue concerning how researchers think about political participation and what is studied to address political participation.

The traditional definition of political participation concerned the activities of citizens directed at influencing the selection and/or action of government officials, and one shortcoming of this definition relates to the focus on citizens only. In the Canadian context, while incoming immigrants are usually accorded Canadian citizenship after three years, there are ways in which non-citizens may become politically involved. For example, it is possible to become involved in party politics even if one is not a citizen and cannot vote, and there is evidence that some non-citizens do this (Stasiulis and Abu-Laban, 1991). More graphically, in the 1980s and 1990s, foreign domestic workers, principally from developing countries, and primarily women, have consistently demanded through protests and through organizations like Intercede that the Canadian government end the 'live-in' requirements that make domestic workers extremely vulnerable to a wide range of abuses in employers' homes (Ramirez, 1982; Villasin and Philips, 1994). Thus, despite their vulnerability, the case of foreign domestic workers reveals how non-citizens may engage in activities aimed at influencing government officials.

Also, the tendency to ignore the local level in addressing political participation has tended to make women as actors invisible. The same may be said for ethnic minorities. Race, ethnicity, and immigration may play out in a distinct way at the local level, and may involve distinct responses. For example, Vancouver is a city with a long-established Chinese-origin population, which has also had many recent immigrants arriving from Asia since the 1980s, including business-class immigrants with capital. Over the 1990s, extensive debate and disagreement over proposed zoning bylaws have taken place on city council around the problem of so-called 'monster houses'. For much of this period, Vancouver has been characterized by a booming real estate market (Li, 1994: 18–19). In the context of escalating prices, expanded profits, and efforts to maximize the use of land, many older British Victorian-style and Tudor-style homes in the affluent west side of the city were torn down and replaced by larger new homes (ibid., 19). Critics charged that these new homes destroy the architectural beauty and landscaping in Vancouver's wealthier districts. This discourse on 'monster houses' is very much racialized, as the large houses are perceived to be owned by wealthy Chinese immigrants who are stereotyped as lacking good taste. The expansive houses are further argued to exist at the expense of trees, which are deemed in need of protection from immigrant homeowners. Interestingly, local Chinese business people have moved to counter these stereotypes by introducing a well-publicized annual local tree-planting campaign (Abu-Laban, 1997). Given the Vancouver context, this action, although not directly aimed at government officials, should be viewed as a political act.

Recent developments in Toronto are also relevant. Siemiatycki and Isin's analysis of contemporary Toronto reveals that both immigrants and diverse ethnocultural groups, though residing in dispersed residential areas, are politically active in a variety of ways:

> they have established their own organizations to influence the direction of local government and policy; they are actively pursuing electoral office and the extension of voting rights for non-naturalized immigrants, and they are busily laying claim to public space, the streets and civic squares of their new urban home. Immigrant and diverse ethno-cultural groups are staking out new rights in the city of Toronto. (Siemiatycki and Isin, 1997: 99)

Given that both women and many minority groups were historically excluded from voting, understanding non-electoral and party forms of politics is critical to understanding Canadian social and political history, and how the categories of gender and ethnicity may intersect. Canadian research may be informed by American work suggesting that the bias in the American voting and electoral literature— towards behavioural measures of politics that are either dominated by men or defined by political scientists as politics—results in the erasure of immigrant and minority women as political actors (Hardy-Fanta, 1993: 22).

For example, work on Latino women in the United States suggests that women's own definition of politics often engages with the private sphere (e.g., ending abusive relationships) (ibid.). This observation has pertinence for Canada, too, where issues such as dealing in a culturally sensitive way with wife abuse have been important for women in African, Asian, and Caribbean immigrant communities in the late 1980s and 1990s (Agnew, 1996). Hardy-Fanta's American work also suggests that women play a central role in generating Latino political participation through their work in the community and extensive interpersonal relationships (1993: 25). Nonetheless, such activities of women in some ethnic minority groups can be hidden from the overt electoral and party focus that dominates most of the research done in the name of examining political participation, and would not be captured by a focus on women as a generic category. Indeed, as Vijay

Agnew (1996: 134) points out, the activities of immigrant women from Asia, Africa, and the Caribbean in Canada have included forming immigrant and ethno-cultural women's associations since the 1970s, a response both to how the main-stream women's movement did not represent the concerns of minority women and to how minority organizations subordinated the specific interests of women to the collective rights of the ethnic group.

Agnew's work suggests that immigrant and minority women as actors are to be found in community groups—because they are the primary users of the services offered by these groups and they are the main service providers, especially in ser-vices relating to community participation. In fact, some immigrant women in Canada have been able to use their connections in the community to form a base to propel themselves into local and federal political arenas (ibid., 153, 162). This underscores again the need to look at the local associational level in considering male and female immigrants and their non-electoral, and even electoral, political activities. It also suggests that a fruitful avenue to pursue would be to begin to incorporate women's, men's, and minorities' *own definitions of their political engagement*, rather than working from pre-established definitions. This requires qualitative work, not just quantitative work, and thinking and rethinking through the assumptions behind traditional definitions of political participation and where we look to see the expression of participation.

Conclusion

This chapter has addressed the question of gender, ethnicity, and political partici-pation in Canada. Although political participation has been central to what politi-cal scientists study, attention to the intersection of gender and the activities of minorities in this country has been limited. The available evidence shows that women, ethnic minorities, and particularly visible minorities are under-repre-sented in positions of formal power in Canada. The evidence also suggests that minorities—both male and female—are not politically passive and engage in a range of activities from voting and electoral politics to community activities. Seri-ously attending to questions of immigration, ethnicity, gender, and political activism requires rethinking and redefining political participation and making use of both quantitative methods (e.g., survey research) and qualitative methods (e.g., open-ended unstructured interviews). These are the tasks of a political science geared to address politics in the twenty-first century in a globalizing, immigrant-receiving, ethnically diverse country like Canada, where, undoubtedly, the gen-dered vertical mosaic will be further challenged.

Notes

For helpful and constructive comments on earlier versions of this chapter, I would like to thank Linda Trimble, and the editors of this volume, Joanna Everitt and Brenda O'Neill. The financial support of a research grant from the Prairie Centre for Excellence for Research on Immigration and Integration is also gratefully acknowledged.

1. The emphasis on skills applies most explicitly to those applying as independent immigrants. Refugees are not explicitly assessed on this criteria, nor are immigrants applying as part of the family class intake.
2. Notably, women who enter Canada typically come in under the family class, as the 'dependent spouses' of male independent applicants. For an overview of the gendered nature of Canadian immigration policy criteria, see Abu Laban (1998).

References

Abu-Laban, Yasmeen. 1997. 'Ethnic Politics in a Globalizing Metropolis: The Case of Vancouver', in Tim Thomas, ed., *The Politics of the City: A Canadian Perspective*. Scarborough, Ont.: ITP Nelson, 77–95.

———. 1998. 'Keeping 'em Out: Gender, Race and Class Biases in Canadian Immigration Policy', in Joan Anderson, Avigail Eisenberg, Sherrill Grace, and Veronica Strong-Boag, eds, *Painting the Maple: Essays on Race, Gender and the Construction of Canada*. Vancouver: University of British Columbia Press.

——— and Victoria Lamont. 1997. 'Crossing Borders: Interdisciplinarity, Immigration and the Melting Pot in the American Cultural Imaginary', *Canadian Review of American Studies* 27, 2: 23–43.

Agnew, Vijay. 1996. *Resisting Discrimination: Women from Asia, Africa and the Caribbean and the Women's Movement in Canada*. Toronto: University of Toronto Press.

Black, Jerome H. 1982. 'Immigrant Political Adaptation in Canada: Some Tentative Findings', *Canadian Journal of Political Science* 15, 1 (Mar.): 9–27.

———. 1987. 'The Practice of Politics in Two Settings: Political Transferability Among Recent Immigrants to Canada', *Canadian Journal of Political Science* 20, 4 (Dec.): 731–53.

———. 1997a. 'Minority Women in the 35th Parliament', *Canadian Parliamentary Review* (Spring): 17–22.

———. 1997b 'Minority Women as Parliamentary Candidates: The Case of the 1993 Canadian Election', paper presented at the annual meeting of the Canadian Political Science Association, St John's.

——— and Aleem S. Lakhani. 1997 'Ethnoracial Diversity in the House of Commons: An Analysis of Numerical Representation in the 35th Parliament', *Canadian Ethnic Studies* (Nov.): 13–33.

——— and Christian Leithner. 1988. 'Immigrants and Political Involvement in Canada: The Role of the Ethnic Media,' *Canadian Ethnic Studies* 21, 1: 1–20.

Brodie, Janine. 1985. *Women and Politics in Canada*. Toronto: McGraw-Hill Ryerson.

Burnet, Jean R., and Howard Palmer. 1988 *"Coming Canadians": An Introduction to the History of Canada's Peoples*. Toronto: McClelland & Stewart.

Burt, Sandra. 1995. 'The Several Worlds of Policy Analysis: Traditional Approaches and Feminist Critiques', in Sandra Burt and Lorraine Code, eds, *Changing Methods: Feminists Transforming Practice*. Peterborough, Ont.: Broadview Press.

Cairns, Alan C. 1989. 'Political Science, Ethnicity and the Canadian Constitution', in David P. Shugarman and Reg Whitaker, eds, *Federalism and Political Community: Essays in Honour of Donald Smiley*. Peterborough, Ont.: Broadview Press, 113–40.

Chui, Tina W.L., James E. Curtis, and Ronald D. Lambert. 1991 'Immigrant Background and Political Participation: Examining Generational Patterns', *Canadian Journal of Sociology* 16, 4 (Fall): 375–96.

Dahlie, Jorgen, and Tissa Fernando. 1981. 'Reflections on Ethnicity and the Exercise of Power: An Introductory Note', in Dahlie and Fernando, eds, *Ethnicity, Power and Politics in Canada*. Toronto: Methuen.

Dickason, Olive Patricia. 1997. *Canada's First Nations: A History of Founding Peoples from Earliest Times*, 2nd edn. Toronto: Oxford University Press.

Hardy-Fanta, Carol. 1993. *Latina Politics, Latino Politics: Gender, Culture and Political Participation in Boston*. Philadelphia: Temple University Press.

Isajiw, Wsevolod W. 1983. 'Multiculturalism and the Integration of the Canadian Community', *Canadian Ethnic Studies* 15, 2: 107–17.

Laponce, J.A. 1994. 'Ethnicity and Voting Studies in Canada: Primary and Secondary Sources 1970–1991', in J.W. Berry and Laponce, eds, *Ethnicity and Culture in Canada: The Research Landscape*. Toronto: University of Toronto Press.

Lapp, Miriam. 1999a. 'Incorporating Groups into Rational Choice Explanations of Turnout: An Empirical Test', *Public Choice* 98: 171–85.

———. 1999b. 'Ethnic Group Leaders and the Mobilization of Voter Turnout: Evidence from Five Montreal Communities', *Canadian Ethnic Studies* 31, 2: 17–42.

Lautard, Hugh, and Neil Guppy. 1999. 'Revisiting the Vertical Mosaic: Occupational Stratification Among Canadian Ethnic Groups', in Peter S. Li, ed., *Race and Ethnic Relations in Canada*, 2nd edn. Toronto: Oxford University Press.

Li, Peter S. 1994 'Unneighbourly Houses or Unwelcome Chinese: The Social Construction of Race in the Battle over "Monster Homes" in Vancouver, Canada', *International Journal of Comparative Race and Ethnic Studies* 1, 1: 14–33.

Lien, Pei-te. 1994. 'Ethnicity and Political Participation: A Comparison between Asian and Mexican Americans', *Political Behavior* 16, 2: 237–64.

Megyery, Kathy, ed. 1991. *Ethnocultural Groups and Visible Minorities in Canadian Politics: The Question of Access*, vol. 7 of the Research Studies for the Royal Commission on Electoral Reform and Party Financing. Toronto: Dundurn Press.

Meisel, John. 1974. *Cleavages, Parties and Values in Canada*. London: Sage.

Pelletier, Alain. 1991. 'Politics and Ethnicity: Representation of Ethnic and Visible-Minority Groups in the House of Commons', in Megyery (1991: 101–59).

Porter, John. 1965. *The Vertical Mosaic: An Analysis of Class and Power in Canada*. Toronto: University of Toronto Press.

Rae, Douglas W., and Michael Taylor. 1971. *The Analysis of Political Cleavages*. New Haven: Yale University Press.

Ramirez, Judith. 1982. 'Domestic Workers Organize', *Canadian Woman Studies* 4, 2 (Winter): 87–91.

Regenstreif, Peter. 1965. *The Diefenbaker Interlude: Parties and Voting in Canada*. Toronto: Longmans.

Reitz, Jeffrey G., and Raymond Breton. 1994. *The Illusion of Difference: Realities of Ethnicity in Canada and the United States*. Toronto: C.D. Howe Institute.

Royal Commission on Bilingualism and Biculturalism. 1970. *Report*, vol. 4. Ottawa.

Ship, Susan. 1998. 'Problematizing Ethnicity and "Race" in Feminist Scholarship on Women and Politics', in Manon Tremblay and Caroline Andrew, eds, *Women and Political Representation in Canada*. Ottawa: University of Ottawa Press, 311–39.

Siemiatycki, Myer, and Engin Isin. 1997. 'Immigration, Diversity and Urban Citizenship in Toronto', *Canadian Journal of Regional Science* 20, 1–2 (Spring): 73–102.

Simard, Carole. 1991. 'Visible Minorities and the Canadian Political System', in Megyery (1991: 161–261).

Stasiulis, Daiva K. 1997a. 'Participation by Immigrants, Ethnocultural/Visible Minorities in the Canadian Political Process', paper prepared for the Department of Canadian Heritage, 23 Nov.

———. 1997b. 'The Political Economy of Race, Ethnicity and Migration', in Wallace Clement, ed., *Understanding Canada: Building on the New Canadian Political Economy*. Montreal and Kingston: McGill-Queen's University Press, 139–71.

——— and Yasmeen Abu-Laban. 1991. 'The House the Parties Built: Reconstructing Ethnic Representation in Canadian Politics', in Megyery (1991: 3–99).

Statistics Canada, 1995. *Women in Canada*. Ottawa.

———. 1997. '1996 Census: Immigration and Citizenship', *The Daily*, 4 Nov. 1997. Available at http://www.StatCan.ca/Daily/English/971102/d971104.htm

———. 1998. '1996 Census: Ethnic Origin, Visible Minorities', *The Daily*, 17 Feb. 1998. Available at http://www.StatCan.ca/Daily/English/980217/d980217.htm

Taylor, Rupert. 1996. 'Political Science encounters "race" and "ethnicity"', *Ethnic and Racial Studies* 19, 4 (Oct.): 884–94.

Tremblay, Manon. 1998. 'Do Female MPs Substantively Represent Women? A Study of Legislative Behaviour in Canada's 35th Parliament', *Canadian Journal of Political Science* 31, 3 (Sept.): 435–65.

Trimble, Linda. 1998. 'Who's Represented? Gender and Diversity in the Alberta Legislature', in Manon Tremblay and Caroline Andrew, eds, *Women and Political Representation in Canada*. Ottawa: University of Ottawa Press, 257–89.

Vickers, Jill. 1997. *Reinventing Political Science: A Feminist Approach*. Halifax: Fernwood.

Villasin, Felicita O., and M. Ann Philips. 1994. 'Falling Through the Cracks: Domestic Workers and Progressive Movements', *Canadian Woman Studies* 14, 2 (Spring): 87–90.

Whitaker, Reg. 1997. 'Canadian Politics at the End of the Millennium: Old Dreams, New Nightmares', in David Taras and Beverly Rasporich, eds, *A Passion for Identity: An Introduction to Canadian Studies*, 3rd edn. Toronto: ITP Nelson, 119–37.

Wood, John R. 1981. 'A Visible Minority Votes: East Indian Electoral Behaviour in the Vancouver South Provincial and Federal Elections of 1979', in Jorgen Dahlie and Tissa Fernando, eds, *Ethnicity, Power and Politics in Canada*. Toronto: Methuen.

Chapter 17

Building Social Capital: Civic Engagement in Farm Communities

LOUISE CARBERT

A long tradition in democratic theory, associated principally with Alexis de Toc-queville, holds that membership in secondary organizations is critical to the quality of citizenship: 'In democratic countries knowledge of how to combine is the mother of all other forms of knowledge. . . . If men are to remain civilized or to become civilized, the art of association must develop and improve at the same speed as equality of conditions spreads' (Tocqueville, 1969: 517). The associations of civil society occupy a middle ground between government and private households; they draw people out from the intimacy of families to find common ground with their neighbours and teach them to appreciate the close connection between private profit and general interest. Even associations that do not directly address government policy contribute to the maintenance of a 'public space' where people can build solidarity among themselves and resist external pressures to conform. Civic associations thus defend the autonomy of diverse communities against the potentially despotic power of public opinion and government (ibid., 690–701). Needless to say, it does not follow that all these associations occupy a moral high ground; civil society includes a diversity of groups ranging from the noble (food banks), to the nefarious (white supremacist groups), to the innocuous (bowling leagues) (Fierlbeck 1998).

In spite of, or perhaps in part as a result of, their inclusiveness, political scientists have begun to acquire a new appreciation for civic associations as essential building blocks in the construction and maintenance of prosperous and legitimate democratic regimes. There is a growing acknowledgement that civic engagement not only leads to traditional political participation in parties and elections, but may well constitute an important form of political participation on its own. One stream of research has been devoted to documenting the functions performed by civil society for the benefit of the political system at large. Another has focused on the motives that lead individual people to participate in civic associations. Both perspectives play an important role in addressing recent suspicions that civic engagement is in precipitous decline. However, they are usually considered independently of each other. Systemic functions depend only on people's actions, not on their motives. It is often difficult, though, for individuals to trace the net effects of their participation. This chapter examines a case study of an exceptional group —Ontario farm women—for whom the systemic functions of civic engagement are relatively transparent. We will see that their unusual circumstances present an opportunity to bridge the gap between the two perspectives and may help to shed light on what factors might influence future trends in civic engagement in more complex urban settings.

Theories of Civic Engagement

In recent years a good deal of talk and action from a variety of ideological perspectives and methodological approaches has converged on civil society. From the communitarian left, Michael Walzer (1995: 148) restated Tocqueville's defence in a contemporary vein: 'Dominated and deprived individuals are likely to be disorganized as well as impoverished, whereas poor people with strong families, churches, unions, political parties, and ethnic alliances are not likely to be dominated or deprived for long.' Voluntary associations cannot, of course, prevent ecological disasters or crises of globalization; Walzer's more limited claim is that associations may enable people to cope better with those crises and hence to resist the deterioration of their communities.

Even the corporate world of business and finance has acquired an appreciation for civil society. No less than the chair of the Ontario Securities Commission, Charles Waitzer (1996), defended it as essential to the operation of capitalism itself: 'At some point, successful companies should expand beyond family and friends to raise capital and recruit senior managers. In "high trust" societies, this process has proven relatively easy; people are used to forming associations beyond the family. Hence the modern business corporation was pioneered in places like the United States.' By this logic, even formal institutions, such as the Toronto Stock Exchange, rest on little else than reified networks of interpersonal trust.

Waitzer's comments draw from the work of Robert Putnam, Francis Fukuyama (1995), and James Coleman, among others, on the relationship between economic development and civic engagement under the conceptual rubric of 'social capital'. The original concept of capital refers to economic wealth that reproduces itself in a continual process of growth. Its utility has led to the introduction of a variety of related concepts. For example, just as equipment and other productive assets increase the stock of traditional capital, education and training increase the stock of 'human capital'. Similarly, and of particular interest here, the ties of community among people, and the attendant norms and trust, increase the stock of social capital and thus contribute to economic productivity.[1]

Whether one has come to bury or to praise capitalism, there is a perceived crisis in the health and vigour of civil society in Anglo-American democracies, where it has long been taken for granted as a defining cultural characteristic. Putnam has assembled substantial empirical evidence for the United States showing that membership numbers in all sorts of organizations have decreased, as have subjective measures of interpersonal trust on public opinion surveys.[2] Opposing research has countered that the rise of newer, identity-centred social movements and self-help groups without formal organizational structures and membership lists compensates for declining involvement in the traditional groups measured by Putnam (Tarrow, 1994; Wuthnow, 1994). The debate over the health of civil society has also become entangled in contentious questions about the historical role that government has played and what role it should continue to play in financing and administering voluntary organizations (Smith and Lipsky, 1993).

Ultimately, our understanding of the health and vigour of civil society comes down to the question of what motivates people to engage with each other in voluntary associations and thus produce social capital. According to the classical developmental argument for political participation, people participate because it is good for them. Participation in the voluntary associations of civil society improves people in three ways: it exercises their capacity for critical reflection and argument; it contributes to their moral sensitivity and sense of justice; and it contributes to self-understanding in that people come to know their true character only in conflict and consensus with others (Pyrcz, 1991, 57–9). The developmental argument does not draw a strict distinction between political and civic engagement so long as collective will, as opposed to the inconsequential bantering of opinion, is at stake. Nonetheless, the development rewards of participation do not seem to be drawing many citizens out of their armchairs. According to economic-based theories of collective action, people stay at home because they are self-interested rational actors seeking to maximize 'utility'. As rational actors, moreover, it is to their advantage to be 'free riders', that is, to let everyone else do the work of increasing the stock of social capital while they, as solitary individuals, enjoy the associated benefits without incurring the costs of participating (Verba et al., 1995, 99–105).

Despite its apparent logic, the rational choice model is left with what is known as 'the puzzle of participation': although being in nobody's self-interest, a fair (but possibly decreasing) number of people do, in fact, participate. In their study of the general US population, Sidney Verba, Kay Lehman Schlozman, and Henry Brady found that economic self-interest pertains chiefly to partisan politics at election time and to 'particularized contacting' of politicians, whereas non-partisan community activity is motivated chiefly by civic benefits (rhetoric of good citizenship) and social gratifications (ibid., 111–20). Their civic voluntarism model of participation accounts for civic and social benefits along with economic benefits, as well as the costs to the individual, all of which vary greatly according to the individual's socio-economic status (SES). This model emphasizes that people are not inter changeable rational actors; in particular, people with high income, greater education, and high occupational status participate more and hence influence the substantial content of policy outputs to their own advantage. This SES bias is self-perpetuating because recruitment to civic engagement occurs through networks of personal ties.

Furthermore, if people are asked directly to do a given task, they usually say yes. Thus, it matters a good deal with whom one has networks of personal ties. Nevertheless, Verba et al. identified specific mechanisms by which less privileged people are mobilized to speak and act on their own behalf: community associations and particularly churches recruit and train people to act in wider and more formally institutionalized political arenas. Unlike work-based or partisan organizations, churches are one arena where people, and women in particular, acquire civic skills, such as knowing how to run a meeting or contact an elected official, that compensate for their lack of conventional SES resources.[3] Voluntary associations of civil society thus have some capacity to offset the 'iron law of oligarchy' at the heart of contemporary liberal democracies.

Farm communities present an interesting contrast to the predominantly urban population studied by Verba et al. This subpopulation is uniformly involved in household-based enterprises in regions of low population density dominated by a single industry. These distinctions lend a relatively transparent economic dimension to the entire range of political behaviour in farm communities. This is obviously the case for sporadic episodes of farm protest that capture public attention and the national media from time to time. For example, in July 1999 the combination of a local crisis—heavy rainfall on the Prairies—and global pressures—the collapse of grain prices—prompted prairie farmers to block parts of the Trans-Canada Highway in Saskatchewan and Manitoba with field equipment to draw attention to their demands for government action (Branch, 1999). At the level of local participation, an entire rural community can often sensibly be viewed as a sort of professional association, comprising farmers, suppliers, and service providers. Joint community projects contribute to professional ties, business relations, and the long-term sustainability of the local economy; in short, they create social capital in an immediate and obvious fashion. Moreover, the small size of the communities makes it easier for individuals to perceive the resulting benefits flowing to themselves, their households, and associates. The present study was motivated by the question of whether these economic circumstances are related to historically high rates of involvement in rural areas (Verba et al., 1978: 269–85). Considering that Verba et al. (1995) found that economic self-interest plays a minor role in non-partisan engagement in the general population, one wonders whether the distinct economic circumstances in farm communities are reflected in individual motives for civic engagement or whether they enter on a different level. The discussion that follows examines the extent, nature, and individual motivations for civic engagement among a sample of Ontario farm women and attempts to frame these results in terms of the economic structure of farming.

A Study of Farm Women

This study involved face-to-face structured interviews of between one and two hours in length with 117 farm women in Huron and Grey Counties of Ontario in 1989.[4] The sample comprised 67 members of the Women's Institutes (WI) and

50 non-member neighbours. The WI is the dominant rural women's organization in Canada, as well as in the region in question. It was founded in Ontario in 1897 and quickly spread to every province in Canada and to countries throughout the world (predominantly former British colonies) as a worldwide rural women's organization, the Associated Country Women of the World (ACWW), founded in 1929. This study offers an opportunity to look at a group of actively involved Canadians whose employment, sexuality, kinship, and net worth are unified in a single economic enterprise. As a case study, its detailed results cannot be directly extrapolated to the Canadian population at large or even to the Canadian farming population.

Being interested in politics, talking about politics, and following public affairs are standard measures of subjective or psychological political involvement that are presumed to provide a foundation for specific concrete acts of political participation and increased civic engagement. Table 17.1 shows reported levels of interest in politics among these farm women as well as among Canadian women and Canadians overall, as reported in the nearly contemporaneous 1990 World Values Survey (WVS).[5] Over half (53 per cent) of the farm women reported being interested 'to some extent,' and very few (5 per cent) said 'not at all'. In contrast, the general population of Canadian women was more polarized, with fewer people reporting 'to some extent' (38 per cent) and more who were interested 'a great deal' or 'not at all'. Part of the moderation by the farm women may be related to differences in interpretation. For instance, one woman said that although she was 'very interested in politics', she felt that she did not qualify for that answer, which she reserved for party activists and politicians, and so changed her response to 'to some extent'. Modesty and self-deprecation may have something to do with differences in reported levels of political interest.

A similar pattern is revealed in regard to discussing politics (Table 17.2). The standard question posed by the WVS to all Canadians asked about 'discussing politics' with friends. This is equivalent to the question asked of farm women as reported in the first column, except that four possible responses were allowed instead of three. Again, fewer farm women chose the extreme responses, more choosing the middle options than did Canadian women and men in the 1990 WVS. When Ontario farm women were asked to distinguish between discussing politics with friends/neighbours and husbands, marked differences emerged. A full 30 per

Table 17.1: Interest in Politics

	Farm women %	Canada women %	All Canada %
A great deal	12	16	20
To some extent	53	38	38
Not much	29	29	27
Not at all	5	17	15
(N)	(117)	(887)	(1,729)

Sources: Carbert (1995); World Values Survey (1990).

Table 17.2: Discussing Politics (and Social Issues)

Farm Wife with Neighbour %		Farm Wife with Husband %	Farm Husband with Neighbour %	Canada Women %	All Canada %
Often	13 (17)	30	22	18	19
Occasionally	45 (48)	40	48	—	—
At times	—	—	—	55	56
Rarely	24 (21)	16	18	—	—
Almost never	18 (14)	14	9	27	25
Can't say	—	—	3	—	—
(N)	(117)	(116)	(116)	(887)	(1,729)

*As estimated by farm wife.
Sources: Carbert (1995); World Values Survey (1990).

cent reported regular political discussions with their husbands and 40 per cent reported occasional discussions. Farm women were substantially more willing to discuss politics with husbands than with neighbours because, some said, circumspection was advisable with friends and neighbours: 'Politics is too contentious for discussion' and 'Politics is too private to discuss with neighbours.'[6] Apparently, farm men need not be so circumspect; 70 per cent of wives credited their husbands with discussing politics often or occasionally with their friends and neighbours. It might be thought that women do not talk about 'politics' so much because they take 'politics' to refer to conventional, partisan politics in legislatures. Since politics encompasses much more than partisan legislatures, farm women were asked if they discussed social problems such as human rights, poverty, or the Third World with friends or neighbours. The parenthetic numbers in the first column of Table 17.2 show that this distinction is relatively minor among the farm wives, who discussed social issues only slightly more often than politics with friends and neighbours.[7]

Table 17.3 compares the political activities of the Ontario farm women to those of Canadian women as a whole. When it came to voting, the simplest political act, only four of the farm women did not participate because 'it's too hard to decide' or because 'it doesn't matter which party is in power'. Moreover, farm women were twice as likely as Canadians in general to have contacted an elected official. This suggests that the relative surplus of politicians in 'over-represented' rural ridings has participatory advantages because politicians are more accessible and known personally to constituents.[8] Farm women were also much more likely (91 per cent to 64 per cent) to watch news on television, which might reflect preferences for the local radio and television stations whose news broadcasts cover rural and agricultural issues at length. Two women spontaneously credited farming for their interest in politics, although the question was not asked; one said: 'I've gotten interested lately in farm policies. Farming has opened up doors for me because we're touched by so many policies which relate so directly to my responsibilities for our family and children now.' Farming seems to enable some women to draw

Table 17.3: Occasional and Regular Political Activities

	Farm women %	Canada women %	All Canada %
Vote in elections	95	—	—
Give money to a political party	12	12	13
Work on an election campaign	10	13	12
Get in touch with an elected official	40	18	20
Listen to news on the radio	93	—	—
Watch news/political shows on TV	91	64	69
(N)	(117)	(1,723)	(3,370)

Sources: Canadian National Election Study (1984); Carbert (1995).

connections between public policy debates and the private situation of their individual households, for instance, about the future of agricultural trade under World Trade Organization negotiations. Their ability to draw connections between the personal and political might be further assisted by the fact that farming is geographically segregated. Farmers' grievances receive a sympathetic hearing at local churches, fairs, and family get-togethers. Daily routines and informal patterns of social interaction among farm families reinforce common identities and grievances. As a result, the daily fabric of life appears to weave farm women into at least a modest level of political involvement.

Farm women have long been known as great 'joiners'.[9] The present study is consistent with this reputation. Table 17.4 lists civic engagement among the surveyed farm women, as well as Canadian women in general. Doing volunteer work in each of the listed categories indicates active, as opposed to passive, involvement. Farm women's membership in professional organizations was especially passive; although 40 per cent were members of professional organizations, only 9 per cent were volunteers or officers. In contrast, there were more volunteers than members in women's groups and community organizations. Table 17.4 includes a separate column for the non-WI portion of the sample, to reflect the fact that the farm women in the sample were selected to achieve a comparable balance of WI members and non-members.[10] The biggest WI/non-WI distinction in Table 17.4 is, of course, in women's organizations; this is a near tautology, since WI is the dominant women's group in the region, and all the members did volunteer work for WI. The two groups volunteered in similarly large proportions in the other major categories—churches, youth groups, and community organizations. Non-WI members were more likely to do volunteer work for sports clubs, education/arts groups, and unions/professional societies. These preferences can reasonably be related to the younger average age of the non-WI group. As expected, WI members were somewhat more active overall: they did unpaid volunteer work for 2.9 organizations on average, compared to 2.3 for non-members; the sample average was 2.7.

Far more farm women—WI and non-WI alike—volunteered for churches, youth groups, and community organizations than did Canadian women and men overall.

Table 17.4: Volunteer Work for Organizations

	Farm women %	Non-WI Farm women %	Canada women %	All Canada %
Churches/religious organizations	77	72	20	16
Women's organizations	63	14	8	5
Youth groups	44	42	8	7
Community or service groups	40	42	11	9
Sports clubs	13	22	9	12
Education/arts groups	10	14	10	9
Unions/professional societies	9	14	6	8
Political movements or parties	3	—	3	4
Animal welfare, environment	2	2	5	5
Other	8	8	9	9
Third World development	—	—	2	3
Peace	—	—	2	2
Health groups	—	—	8	7
No volunteer work	2	4	51	53
Average number of organizations	2.7	2.3	1.0	0.9
(N)	(117)	(50)	(887)	(1,729)

Sources: Carbert (1995); World Values Survey (1990).

Even the non-WI farm women managed to volunteer for women's organizations more than Canadian women in general, despite the fact that this group is defined by not belonging to the dominant women's organization in the region. The average numbers of organizations in 1990 for Canadian women and all Canadians were far lower than for the farm women studied here: 1.0 and 0.9, respectively. Furthermore, 51 per cent of Canadian women and 53 per cent of all Canadians did no volunteer work for any organization, whereas all but two of 117 farm women interviewed did some volunteer work for at least one organization. And fully 97 of 117 farm women (60 WI members and 37 non-WI) served as officers in at least one organization. This remarkably even distribution of volunteer work among the farm women in the region is further supported by the fact that only two women volunteered more than 10 hours per week, compared to the average of 3.3 hours. A picture emerges of pervasive community service, in which virtually every woman contributes her 'fair share', and few make a career or obsession of it. What is it about the circumstances of farming that leads so many ordinary people to engage in civic affairs?

For many of the farm women, the motives for civic engagement were associated with qualities other than the instrumental achievement of public policy goals for private profit. While one woman claimed that the government heeded WI policy resolutions, no respondent said that she joined the WI (or didn't join) to achieve specific legislative or policy changes. Instead, some articulated gratifications that hark back to the developmental claims of classical democratic theory.

> WI led to me being poll clerk, enumeration. It helped me to get up nerve to do things. I used to get in a sweat about doing things. You just have to go do it!

> Doing the babysitting course was a big accomplishment for me. I had three helpers, but it was me who got the speakers and handed out awards at the graduation ceremony, which was very tense for me. I was forced to do it, but it was good for me.

> I didn't think I could do it, but being [WI] president gave me more confidence in myself.

Other women spoke proudly of their acquisition of specific skills:

> WI gave me my start in Fair Board. The WI structure, which includes parliamentary procedure, teaches you to belong to other organizations. The provincial executive of the Fair Board uses it, and I was ready. You can pick out WI women by their skilled use of parliamentary procedure at meetings.

The practical and transferable skills that many of these women acquired through their community involvement provide an opportunity to make the transition to traditional political participation. Indeed, my sample accidentally included four politicians, each of whom was the first woman in her area to be elected to township or county government. Each had been responsible, at one time, for most of the farm work on a marginal enterprise; none had a university education. Three of the four explicitly credited the Women's Institutes for their political careers; two of these are quoted below:

> WI led to other groups. WI taught me to stand up and talk, how to organize for a meeting, how to deal with strangers and not be shy. The old women at WI meetings are a little deaf, so this taught me good speaking skills, to speak loud and clear. I practised my campaign speech on my local WI branch. When I was younger, WI was the closest and easiest group for me to attend because my husband was away and I could bring babies and children to WI meetings. The women in my local branch called me up to run. And I topped the polls.

> I've had the experience of being able to develop leadership. I credit my ability to do what I'm doing today to WI and to their short courses and officers' conferences I've attended over the years. Getting involved in politics makes women more worldly. It gets them out of their kitchens and out of their homes and they are able to talk about political issues. Still they are wives and mothers and caregivers, and they still find time to make a contribution to issues facing the community.[11]

I had stumbled upon a pool of decidedly non-élite politicians.

These women could have acquired these transferable skills only through experience in an organization like the WI, whose organizational complexity and formality mirrors that of traditional political bodies. The WI's elaborate and top-heavy structure comprises neighbourhood branches organized into districts, areas, and provinces. A national co-ordinating body, the Federated Women's Institutes of Canada (FWIC), belongs to the international body (ACWW). This structure, with an abundance of officers and adherence to parliamentary procedure, is typical of long-established service organizations. It ensures that a large number of members keep busy maintaining the infrastructure, and in so doing they acquire the relevant skills. Rather than excluding members from executive positions, there are so many offices to be filled that everyone is pressured to hold almost every position, at the branch and district level, at one time or another.

In enabling the development of civic skills among people who are otherwise low in standard SES resources, the Women's Institutes and other Canadian rural community organizations seem to play a similar mobilizing role to that attributed by Verba et al. (1995) to evangelical churches in the United States. Two significant features set WI members apart in this study: they were older, and they were less educated (even after controlling for age). In a twist on the conventional urban SES model of participation, the socio-economic resources of wealth and education may have actually restricted some farm women from being as active as others. For example, one woman interviewed had married into perhaps the most prosperous and respected family in the township. She had met her husband at university while they were both doing professional graduate degrees some five years earlier. She had not joined the local junior chapter of WI, even though its members were all her own age and she admitted to having been lonely; she said that she would have been too embarrassed if anyone at university—her former classmates or professors—ever found out. She worked for a major farm publication and justified her career in terms of the family enterprise: 'Even though I'm away working, it's for the farm really instead of my career. It's not just the money; it's the contacts and the information that I bring to help out the farm.' Although her primary commitment was to the family enterprise, her participatory options were restricted because her father-in-law and brothers-in-law monopolized enterprise-related activities. In fact, in the overall sample no relationship was found between socio-economic status and civic engagement among the farm women interviewed; for example, hours of volunteer work were not significantly predicted by education level, capital value of the farm enterprise, farm acreage, employees hired, or husband's employment (Carbert, 1995: 96).

The young, educated woman cited above was not alone in admitting to being lonely. Sociability was the most frequently given reason for belonging to a Women's Institute. As one woman recalled: 'Moving from [an urban centre] to here was hard. Joining WI was a way of belonging to the community. There was nothing for women to do in the area.' The affection that some farm women felt, not only for their individual friends in the Institute but for the WI as a collectivity whose history went back almost a century, encompassing all their married life and their mothers' before them, was striking. More than one woman said: 'I was born, grew up in WI.' Another woman said that 'WI friendships are special—closer and more enthusiastic compared to women's auxiliaries in the Church.' Affection is ritualized in WI memorial services upon a member's death and in ceremonies held to commemorate disbanding Institutes whose collective property, notably Tweedsmuir histories,[12] is transferred to neighbouring branches.

Nineteen WI members articulated simple altruism as the motivation for their involvement, citing community service or helping others as a goal in itself. As one reeve encouraged her audience, 'The secret to happiness is J-O-Y: put Jesus first, others second, and yourself last.' This discourse seizes the moral high ground and justifies participation in traditional terms acceptable to family and neighbours; but it also articulates a sincerely held conviction that their efforts can indeed improve public life.

That said, the women interviewed made it abundantly clear that the universe of public life to be improved here is very limited. Some women explained that they preferred traditional community activity as opposed to lobbying for public policy at a national or international level because local activities produce immediate, concrete results:

> I like the local focus on community service. I prefer Women's Institutes to other 'distant' groups. It's a good balance between yourself and the community.

> It's for our own kids and seniors. The money that we raise stays right here in the community rather than being sent off.

> WI is for 'home and country' [official motto]—right here. Last year, someone on the line had their barn burn down. We helped them immediately. The money didn't go away through administrative channels. We're made aware of other people's problems, which is difficult because farm people don't talk. But WI members will confide problems to each other and still respect each other's privacy.

This local emphasis is substantiated by a review of WI projects across Ontario (ibid., 164). A particularly telling incident arose at an Institute meeting that I attended, at which a Mennonite woman (associated with the now-defunct group Concerned Farm Women) gave a slide show on her Oxfam-sponsored farm women's tour of Nicaragua; she spoke with conviction about how she had been deeply and personally moved by the experience, and attempted to enlist broader support for ongoing co-operative projects with Nicaragua. In response, a member of the audience replied that charity begins at home, and another articulated a distrust of Oxfam. An immediate consensus arose against the international linkage, and the topic was dropped like a lead balloon. The aplomb and lack of hesitation on the part of the responding audience members showed that not only did they feel strongly about what they were saying, but also that they knew the rest of the audience felt the same way. This remarkable consensus indicates that their substantial civic engagement not only results in, but is premised on, material benefit to the local community. The result is a transparent process whereby these women can see benefits flowing from their volunteer efforts.

Social Capital in Farm Communities

Until recently, all production in developed economies was expected eventually to be incorporated into large-scale corporate units that hire waged labour. Nonetheless, major sectors of agriculture have resisted corporate concentration of ownership and production for reasons that are based in the very nature of plant and animal life. Large-scale corporate investment prefers a continuous cycle of production and exchange, a cycle in which products are manufactured and marketed and profits reinvested all at the same time. But agriculture is characterized by a prolonged production cycle during which animals and crops take time to grow. For example, grain farmers wait all summer for crops to grow, harvest once a year in a single intense burst of labour, and then live off the proceeds during the winter. Another barrier to investment is the vast amount of land required relative to the volume and value of commodity produced; because the day-to-day work of farming is dispersed over a large area, it would be difficult to supervise relatively unskilled and low-paid employees. When the production cycle is shorter in time and requires less land (as with eggs and poultry), it becomes more profitable and hence more attractive to outside investment. In the end, aspects of the industry amenable to continuous cycles of factory production have been taken up by large-scale corporate investment, leaving farmers with the rump of whatever cannot be produced at a steady and predictable rate of profit. Family farming thus fills a necessary, continuing niche within capitalism (Freshwater, 1989; Ghorayshi, 1987; Goodman and Redclift, 1986; Mann and Dickinson, 1978).

Farmers manage tò keep a tenacious grip on their production niche, in part because they are embedded in communities that are supportive in functionally substantive ways.[13] In general, farm enterprises operate in areas of low population density that do not support extensive commercial or industrial facilities except where adjacent to larger urban areas. Hence, rural municipalities can scarcely tax themselves to provide the same level of services that urban centres enjoy. As a result, rural people are forced to make do and provide services for themselves. Examples of local services provided through the WI by the women interviewed in this study include scholarships, libraries, hospital fund-raising, day cares during harvest season, recycling, layettes to single mothers, and aid to women's shelters. The rural tax base has always been low, but the situation has been exacerbated in recent years as provincial governments have cut payments and devolved responsibilities to municipalities.

Despite cutbacks, however, government continues to play an important role in the agricultural industry. Agriculture and Agri-Food Canada, provincial ministries of agriculture, and universities provide massive research, educational, financial, administrative, and trade infrastructure without which small-scale independent enterprises could not operate. Where cutbacks have been perceived as excessive or arbitrary, protest has ensued. For example, following New Brunswick's merging of its departments of fisheries and agriculture in spring 2000, a mass protest (complete with farm machinery) successfully convinced Premier Bernard Lord's fiscally pressed government to back down on privatization of agricultural services, such as veterinarians, to postpone financial cutbacks, and to make no further changes without first consulting with the industry (*Moncton Times and Transcript*, 2000).

In addition to support for the agricultural industry itself, government historically has also provided organizational support for groups not directly related to commodity production, such as leadership and skills training through the networks of 4-H Clubs and Women's Institutes. This support has contributed a good deal to high levels of civic engagement in organizations that deliver, fund, or facilitate projects that governments do not want to implement single-handedly. In recent years, however, ministries of agriculture increasingly see the security of access to export markets and income stabilization as their chief responsibility, at the expense of quality-of-life services and infrastructure at the local level (Wiebe, 1995: 140–2).

As well as providing much needed local services, civic engagement in farm communities contributes to maintaining levels of trust in long-term relationships. Farmers are, as a class, defined by fixed private property. Unlike waged workers, they cannot transport their assets in pursuit of economic opportunity, and thus their individual financial livelihood is tied to the collective prosperity of their neighbourhood. Even when farms produce commodities for global export markets, enterprises depend on the local provision of business services such as seed suppliers, equipment dealers, accountants, and café operators. The result is a long-term commitment to being satisfied with a particular network of ongoing business relations. Hence, the need for building a substantial pool of social capital is far more transparent than in urban settings.

Even the social gratifications of civic engagement cannot be separated from economic considerations. Farming is lonely, isolated work, and sociability does not happen as easily as it does from waged work. Instead of meeting for scheduled coffee breaks, farm households deliberately plan for sociability by scheduling events such as sports days, fairs, or suppers that have little financial cost. Much of this activity is organized through traditional women's groups. On another level, this sociability can in some cases represent an alternative to divorce in unhappy marriages. As one woman said, 'People talk about "farm widows". Women do community work because there's nothing else to do.' This function can have major economic implications. Matrimonial property law entitles a divorcing spouse to claim equal share of the farming enterprise, which usually means liquidating major assets, if not the entire farm, for a one-time cash settlement. By selling the means of production, both spouses—and often adult children as well—would in effect lose their jobs. In this sense, both spouses in a farm marriage may 'hold each other hostage' in a way that is rarer in urban marriages, which are more often characterized by wage labour and one-way economic dependence.[14]

Conclusion

The commitment to community service by the farm women is thus an individual strategy for personal happiness and a collective strategy for satisfying the systemic needs of rural economies. On an individual level, their stated motivations for community involvement are not altogether distinct from those found by Verba et al. among predominantly urban American church and community volunteers; they cited sociability, networks of personal ties, and good citizenship as reasons for being involved. On a collective level, their notable intensity of involvement appears to be related to economic factors. For over a century now, the agricultural industry has struggled to balance rapid and expensive technological advances such as farm machinery, fertilizer, genetically altered seed, artificial insemination, and embryo products against long-term declines in commodity prices associated with the innovations and short-term price volatility due to global economic forces, all the while coping with rural depopulation. Nevertheless, agriculture remains one of Canada's leading industries. Part of its success is arguably attributable to vigorous and pervasive civic engagement. We have seen how the particular economic structure contributes to a blurring of the distinctions among civic and social gratifications and collective and individual material self-interest associated with the community service. This convergence appears to be a powerful motivator for the production of social capital by the farm women studied here.

Although the detailed results of this case study cannot be directly extrapolated to the population at large, one wonders if other subpopulations sharing similar relevant characteristics might also feature high civic engagement. For example, family farming is a durable and successful model of self-employed, flexible, and skilled household-based production for capitalist markets. Are urban self-employed people more sociable, trusting, and participatory than those employed in wage labour? Such questions can be addressed directly via survey research. Recent trends point to future increases in self-employment. If so, the present findings might suggest the possibility of important consequences for the stock of social capital. At minimum, they advise careful attention to economic circumstances as context for civic engagement and its motivations.

Notes

1. Putnam (1995a: n4) gives principal credit to James Coleman (1988, 1990) for developing the 'social capital' theoretical framework.
2. Putnam's evidence situates long-term declines in civic engagement in terms of individual-level changes in the socio-demographic composition of the population and system-level changes that affected the entire society at the same time. For example, civic engagement is positively associated with education and employment. Over the past few decades, Americans became more educated and a large number of housewives entered the workforce. In spite of these positive influences, civic engagement still managed to decline (Putnam, 1995b: 667–74), implying a strong negative influence of one or more independent factors. After reviewing an array of possible causes, Putnam proposed that the arrival of television in about 1960 is the single main 'culprit' responsible for reducing civic engagement. Other research indicates that the role of television is nuanced in terms of the type of programming being viewed (Norris, 1996).

3. Verba et al. (1995: 520–1) note that church-based participation provides for the acquisition of civic skills among less well-off Americans, but American churches are not neutral vehicles for the voices of the disadvantaged. So long as these institutions have their own theological and social policy concerns, most notably on abortion, church-based participation does not generate direct egalitarian outcomes.

4. Interviews of married women living on commercial agricultural enterprises were conducted in selected townships of Huron and Grey Counties in a corridor along Lake Huron. The area was chosen to take advantage of a remarkable diversity of landscape and commodities in a manageable geographic area. The area's commodity structure thus profiles, in microcosm, Ontario's prosperous and diversified agricultural industry. With the approval of the provincial executive of the Federated Women's Institutes of Ontario, local leaders introduced me at WI meetings and provided names of women to be interviewed (Carbert, 1995).

5. In 1981 and 1990, the WVS asked nearly the same set of questions to a representative sample of people in 50 countries. Unlike election studies, the WVS focused primarily on fundamental value orientations towards wealth, competition, religion, family life, and national identity. These questions are meaningful to people from all cultures and have been extensively tested and refined through two decades of use on the Euro-Barometer series of surveys. For further details, see Nevitte (1996: 35–8) and Inglehart (1997: App.1).

6. Quotations not otherwise cited are from women interviewed, who remain anonymous.

7. A much stronger distinction appeared in a parallel study of Quebec and French farm women, both of whom very much preferred to discuss social problems over politics (Brandt and Black, 1999).

8. My survey accidentally caught a number of women who had worked in various elections over the years. Ten women had been poll clerks, two had been scrutineers, and three had been deputy returning officers. Only two women held their own party membership, which suggests that their involvement was connected with their husbands' partisanship.

9. Rachel Rosenfeld's national survey (1985) found that 74 per cent of American farm women belonged to at least one organization; the largest block (61 per cent) belonged to a community organization such as a church group, PTA, or League of Women Voters (1985). Seena Kohl (1976: 40–1) found similar activity among Saskatchewan farm/ranch women during the 1960s and 1970s.

10. It is unclear whether the sample of 67 members and 50 non-members over-represents or under-represents WI membership among the farm women in the region; nobody compiles WI membership ratios. Discussions with local women revealed that in some townships nearly all farm women were members. Furthermore, the survey was very extensive in certain townships. In either case, the differences between WI members and non-members appear to be smaller than their distinction from Canadians in general.

11. Pat Salter, Reeve of Peel Township (Roelens-Grant, 1991: 7–9).

12. A Tweedsmuir history is an ongoing documentation of the history of the township in which a WI branch is located. These collections were begun in 1936 at the encouragement of Lady Tweedsmuir, wife of Canada's Governor-General (Federated Women's Institutes of Ontario, n.d.: 60–2).

13. This discussion draws from Piore and Sabel (1984) and Putnam (1993).
14. This might help to explain why middle-aged farm women on extended-family operations were more likely to forgive infidelity than young women on small operations, despite being more conservative on other sexual matters (Carbert, 1995: 113).

References

Branch, Julian. 1999. 'Protesting farmers hit the highway', *Globe and Mail*, 17 July, A7.

Brandt, Gail, and Naomi Black. 1999. *Feminist Politics on the Farm*. Montreal and Kingston: McGill-Queen's University Press.

Carbert, Louise. 1995. *Agrarian Feminism: The Politics of Ontario Farm Women*. Toronto: University of Toronto Press.

Coleman, James. 1988. 'Social capital in the creation of human capital', *American Journal of Sociology* (Supp.) 94: S95–S120.

———. 1990. *Foundations of Social Theory*. Cambridge, Mass.: Harvard University Press.

Federated Women's Institutes of Ontario. n.d. *Ontario Women's Institute Story*. Toronto: Federated Women's Institutes of Ontario.

Fierlbeck, Katherine. 1998. *Globalizing Democracy: Power, Legitimacy, and the Interpretation of Democratic Ideas*. Manchester: Manchester University Press.

Freshwater, David. 1989. 'Canadian Agricultural Finance in the 1980s and 1990s', *Canadian Journal of Agricultural Economics* 37: 1–27.

Fukuyama, Francis. 1995. *Trust: The Social Virtues and the Creation of Prosperity*. New York: Free Press.

Ghorayshi, Parvin. 1987. 'Canadian Agriculture: Capitalist or Petit Bourgeois?', *Canadian Review of Sociology and Anthropology* 24, 3: 358–73.

Goodman, David, and Michael Redclift. 1986. 'Capitalism, Petty Commodity Production, and the Farm Enterprise', in Graham Cox, Philip Lowe, and Michael Winter, eds, *Agriculture: People and Politics*. London: Allen & Unwin, 20–40.

Inglehart, Ronald. 1997. *Modernization and Postmodernization: Cultural, Economic and Political Change in 43 Societies*. Princeton, NJ: Princeton University Press.

Kohl, Seena. 1976. *Working Together: Women and Family in Southwestern Saskatchewan*. Toronto: Holt, Rinehart, and Winston.

Lambert, Ronald D., Steven D. Brown, James E. Curtis, Barry J. Kay, and John M. Wilson. 1984. *Canadian National Election Study*. Available from ISR, University of Michigan, Ann Arbor.

Mann, Susan, and James Dickinson. 1978. 'Obstacles to the Development of a Capitalist Agriculture', *Journal of Peasant Studies* 5, 4: 466–81.

Moncton Times and Transcript. 2000. 'Lord halts farm cuts', 8 Apr., A1.

Nevitte, Neil. 1996. *The Decline of Deference*. Peterborough, Ont.: Broadview Press.

Norris, Pippa. 1996. 'Does Television Erode Social Capital? A Reply to Putnam', *PS* 29, 3: 4754–79.

Piore, Michael, and Charles Sabel. 1984. *The Second Industrial Divide: Possibilities for Prosperity*. New York: Basic Books.

Putnam, Robert. 1993. *Making Democracy Work: Civic Traditions in Modern Italy*. Princeton, NJ: Princeton University Press.

————. 1995a. 'Bowling Alone', *Journal of Democracy* 6, 1: 65–78.

————. 1995b. 'Tuning In, Tuning Out: The Strange Disappearance of Social Capital in America', *PS* 28, 4: 664–83.

Pyrcz, Greg. 1991. 'Democracy and Political Participation', in D.J.C. Carmichael, T.C. Pocklington, and G. Pyrcz, eds, *Democracy and Human Rights in Canada*. Toronto: Harcourt Brace Jovanovich.

Roelens-Grant, Janine. 1991. 'Salter Encourages Women to get Involved in Local Politics', *Home & Country* 57, 2: 7–9.

Rosenfeld, Rachel. 1985. *Farm Women: Work, Farm, and Family in the United States*. Chapel Hill: University of North Carolina Press.

Smith, S.R., and M. Lipsky. 1993. *Nonprofits for Hire: The Welfare State in the Age of Contracting*. Cambridge, Mass.: Harvard University Press.

Tarrow, Sidney. 1994. *Power in Movements: Social Movements, Collective Action, and Politics*. New York: Cambridge University Press.

Tocqueville, Alexis de. 1969 [1848]. *Democracy in America*, trans. George Lawrence, ed. J.P. Mayer. New York: Doubleday.

Verba, Sidney, Norman Nie, and Jae-on Kim. 1978. *Participation and Political Equality: A Seven-Nation Comparison*. Cambridge: Cambridge University Press.

————, Kay Lehman Schlozman, and Henry Brady. 1995. *Voice and Equality: Civic Voluntarism in American Politics*. Cambridge, Mass.: Harvard University Press.

Waitzer, Edward J. 1996. 'Presentation to the 1995 annual meeting of the Canadian Association of Gift Planners, Toronto, Ontario', available at: www.charityvillage.com/charityvillage/research/rphl4.html

Walzer, Michael. 1995. 'The Idea of Civil Society', in Thomas Bateman, Manuel Mertin, and David Thomas, eds, *Braving the New World*. Toronto: Nelson Canada, 142–53.

Wiebe, Nettie. 1995. 'Farm Women: Cultivating Hope and Sowing Change', in Sandra Burt and Lorraine Code, eds, *Changing Methods: Feminists Transforming Practice*. Peterborough, Ont.: Broadview Press, 137–62.

World Values Survey. 1990. Available from ISR, University of Michigan, Ann Arbor.

Wuthnow, Robert. 1994. *Sharing the Journey: Support Groups and America's New Quest for Community*. New York: Free Press.

Part VI

Leaders and Activists

Chapter 18

The Study of Political Leaders and Activists

Anthony M. Sayers

Political leadership is crucial to the governance of all societies and is most often associated with discussion of political élites, authority, and power. Two aspects of political leadership attract the greatest attention: the vision or set of ideas concerning the future development of a society offered by leaders, and their capacity to marshal the necessary political support and organizational resources to achieve a set of policy objectives (Heifetz and Sinder, 1990: 181). We are mainly interested in the second of these—how leaders, in particular, leaders of Canadian political parties, gather together organizational support to win control of the parties and, if electorally successful, to direct the legislative agenda.

Most efforts at shaping public policy in Canada are directed at those invested with formal decision-making authority via their leadership of public institutions, especially legislatures, executives, the judiciary, and public services. These may be divided into national and provincial jurisdictions and elected and appointed offices (Mancuso et al., 1994: 2–3). This chapter focuses on elected national leaders.

Elections legitimate the power of these leaders to make decisions that shape the lives of all Canadians. Just as importantly, elections ensure a smooth succession from one government and leader to the next. Because the nomination of candidates from among whom citizens select leaders and representatives is crucial to political outcomes, representative democracy has spurred the development of specialized non-state organizations, political parties, that co-ordinate these activities. A party provides voters with candidates who are committed to a set of agreed policies and selects a leader who, if the party is successful, becomes the head of government. The head of government may change as a result of a change in the governing party (usually at elections) or because a party selects a new leader.

Because political parties are central to the task of selecting elected representatives and leaders, they remain the focus of much political activism. The study of party activists has a relatively short history that dovetails with the arrival of representative democracy, the widening of the franchise, and the subsequent development of the modern mass party in the late nineteenth and early twentieth century. Popular involvement in politics via political parties marked a profound shift in the institutions and structures of state and society and now attracts close study (for Canadian examples, see Perlin, 1988; Archer and Whitehorn, 1997; Cross, 1996; Stewart, 1997). Over the last 30 years activists have shifted some of their efforts to non-party mechanisms such as interest groups in an attempt to influence government policy (Dalton, 1994). Less has been written about activists than leaders, a balance reflected in this chapter.

Studying Political Leadership

There have been several major approaches to the study of political leaders in representative democracies. Each theory of power posits a different understanding of whose interests are served by state institutions. One approach has been to consider whether leaders are drawn from a particular class or group of people, an élite, with identifiable characteristics. With certain limitations aimed at ensuring order, the ruling élite is seen to pursue the interests of their own segment of society (Mosca, 1939). This approach emphasizes social structures that give some individuals privileged access to power and seeks to understand how such groups maintain themselves and ensure their control of the state to further their interests (Pareto, 1966).

Political parties have been a major focus of this research. In particular, they allowed for the replacement of aristocratic élites in Europe with new élites that had their roots in democratic politics and the middle class and working classes (Duverger, 1954: 160). In the New World, they undercut the development of aristocratic élites. Michels argues that all mass organizations, including political parties, exhibit an 'iron law of oligarchy'. That is, a few gifted individuals always rise to positions of power and control the direction of the organization and the behaviour of its members. Élites circulate—i.e., change via the addition of new members— but do so in a constrained fashion, with new members socialized into the ways of the existing group, preventing the state from radically altering its priorities (Michels, 1962; Pareto, 1968).

Extending this line of analysis, C. Wright Mills (1956) argues that political leaders in America are drawn from an identifiable élite with extensive social linkages resulting from intermarriage and shared experiences. Porter (1965) applies an élite view of political leadership to Canada, arguing that the focus on institutional arrangements in much political science literature obscures the reality of power in Canada, which resides with a relatively narrow group of office-holders and business leaders. The debate between this view of society and that proposed by pluralists such as Robert A. Dahl (1961) has been central to the study of industrial democracies over the last half-century. Pluralists argue that a wide, and somewhat unpredictable, set of groups and individuals have access to political leadership and power. No group or set of groups can monopolize state power, and, thus, state priorities can and do change as different groups gain influence.

Neo-pluralism modifies the pluralist position by suggesting that while there are no identifiable élites who constantly control access to state power, business has a privileged position with respect to government policy-making because its behaviour helps determine rates of economic growth. To sustain economic growth, and hence to remain electorally popular, political leaders listen to and act in favour of business interests (Lindblom, 1977).

Corporatists argue that political leadership in modern industrial states takes the form of élite accommodation among leaders of business, government, and trade unions (Schmitter and Lehmbruch, 1979; Lehmbruch and Schmitter, 1982). The application of this theory has been problematic in Canada because of the complexities associated with federalism and the limited role for unions in policy-making (McRae, 1979; Panitch, 1979). Marxists consider political leadership subservient to the bourgeoisie or ruling class. Since the 1960s, neo-Marxists have argued that the political leaders have some independence from capital, leading them to explore social and structural linkages among the bourgeoisie and between it and those in charge of the state apparatus (Miliband, 1969; Poulantzas, 1973; Nordlinger, 1981; Wright, 1985, 1997; Block, 1987; Panitch, 1977; Clement and Williams, 1989). Neo-Marxists have also sought to integrate aspects of Marxist analysis with other approaches to explain policy outcomes (Mahon, 1984; Clement, 1988: chs 7, 8).

The limited number of women and minorities in leadership positions in most Western countries has led to research into how gender and ethnicity affect the selection of leaders. In Canada and elsewhere, the under-representation of women in particular has been the subject of much study (see Erickson, 1991, 1993; Megyery, 1991; Lovenduski and Norris, 1993; Tremblay and Andrew, 1997). While some feminists argue that traditional patterns of political activity exclude women, others have suggested ways in which women can gain access to power through existing structures (for a discussion, see Young, 2000, 4–10). The exclusion of a wide range of minorities from positions of political power is similarly judged to reflect structural biases (see Carroll, 1997; Kymlicka, 1995). As is the case for women, there is evidence that change is occurring with respect to minority representation, a matter Black and Abu-Laban address in this volume.

Two additional approaches to understanding political decisions and, indirectly, leadership are worth mentioning. Rational choice theory suggests that political decisions are best understood as the result of bargaining between rational individuals. To a degree, discussions of power are subsumed in the rules of bargaining, which assign those involved various levels of influence (Flanagan, 1998). This approach is largely congruent with pluralist models of power. Neo-institutionalism, a state-centred view of politics, investigates the logic of state institutions as a means of understanding political power. It is an attempt to refocus attention on the institutions of governance, which some researchers argued were too readily overlooked when behaviouralism overtook the traditional institutional approach of political science. This theory suggests that the nature of state institutions shapes political outcomes (March and Olsen, 1989). While constrained by institutions, individuals and groups still play a key role in the political process. As such, neo-institutionalism can be wedded with accounts of power that focus on individuals and groups.

Pluralist and institutionalist conceptions of power have dominated the study of leadership in Canada, with political parties and elections, federalism, Parliament and cabinet government used as lenses to focus analysis (Franks, 1987; Smiley, 1987; Pal and Taras, 1988; Mancuso et al., 1994; Bakvis, 1991; Savoie, 1999a). Behaviouralist accounts of the roots of power in political culture are also strongly shaped by institutional considerations (Elkins and Simeon, 1980; Johnston et al., 1992, 1996a).

Most recently, the process of globalization has led some analysts to question the notion of national political leadership. If the international economy is taken to be independent of any one nation, that is, beyond the power of any nation to control, and is seen to have the power to change the living conditions of many of the world's citizens, then traditional political leadership may be redundant[1]. Such a view places the power to shape what traditionally have been considered political decisions in the boardrooms of large transnational companies. Their decisions—about investments, the types of goods and services they provide, and how they will be provided—directly influence our lives and, just as importantly, constrain the decisions of political leaders.

As well, international organizations increasingly shape the policy environment on everything from investments to human rights, leading some to accept the inevitability of global governance (Falk, 1995). Decisions about what we eat and drink, what we read and see, and the jobs available to us are made beyond the realm of domestic politics. Domestic political leaders still shape many areas of government policy and can petition international capital and influence international organizations, but it can be argued that their domain is shrinking (Horsman and Marshall, 1994).

Leaders, Activists, and Political Parties

Leaders of some interest groups, such as the National Action Committee on the Status of Women, the Canadian Medical Association, and the Business Council on National Issues, are important players in the policy-making process. These groups aim to promote the interests of a section of society, usually with respect to a limited number of issues, by influencing governments (Key, 1958: 23).

Despite the growth in the number of such groups over the last 40 years, political parties remain central to the political process primarily because their control of the selection of candidates and leaders makes them the gatekeepers of access to the formal powers of government. To be a political leader, one must lead a political party. Political parties can be thought of as consisting of three parts—the leader's office, the Parliamentary wing made up of members of Parliament, and the extra-Parliamentary organization run by party activists. Although connected, each operates somewhat independently of the others. The exact nature of each component varies across parties and regions and is further shaped by whether or not a party is in government.

As in many European and Commonwealth countries, but unlike in the American system, Canadian political élites have responded to the institutional incentives offered by Parliament by developing parties with strong levels of Parliamentary discipline, thereby ensuring that members of Parliament vote along party lines. Leaders dominate the Parliamentary arena via powerful, well-organized central offices. Activists at the grassroots level of Canadian politics mimic their American cousins to some degree in the manner in which they have access to the process of selecting political leaders. Either by way of conventions or direct votes, party members elect party leaders. In addition, and unlike US parties, party members control the nomination of local candidates and oversee relatively autonomous constituency election campaigns (Sayers, 1999). This combination of powerful leaders, autonomous local activists, and disciplined Parliamentary parties sets Canadian politics apart from all others.

Leadership Selection: From Caucus to Convention to Direct Member Voting

Leaders of modern political parties are important because they preside over the organizations that control the central institutions of democracy—the legislature and the executive. Canadian parties have long been considered leader-dominated (Siegfried, 1966: 136). The leader of the governing party enjoys relatively uncontested control of the legislative process and access to cabinet positions and other sinecures (Savoie, 1999a) with which to dominate the Parliamentary party. Because of this, governing parties have come to rely on leaders to co-ordinate their critical brokerage role.[2] The move to conventions and then direct election to select leaders has further strengthened their position.

Given that voters indirectly elect first ministers from among the leaders selected by their parties, this selection process has been a key concern of the study of leadership in Canada. For the most part, until the late nineteenth century, leaders were selected in the manner still used today in most English-derived Parliamentary systems—the caucus or members of Parliament from a particular party met privately to select one of their number to lead the party.[3]

Because it was a private process, very little was known about the machinations of caucus leadership selection and leadership generally. Senior members had more say than their junior counterparts, while the power of the Prime Minister was measured by his capacity for independent action. Prime ministers whose control of cabinet rested on the support of powerful ministers were seen as less dominant than those who successfully intimidated their cabinets (Courtney, 1973; Carty et al., 1992: 20). The power of particular members of cabinet was held to be indicated by their success in achieving control of important ministerial positions, such as finance, which shaped their capacity to deliver political goods to their regions. Leaders were beholden to their fellow caucus members who selected them and, arguably, were less powerful in relation to their Parliamentary colleagues than more recent leaders selected by convention or party-wide ballot (Courtney, 1973: 1995).

Following the Liberals' fracturing as a result of the conscription crisis during World War I, Sir Wilfrid Laurier chose to rebuild the party by calling a convention to determine party policy. Laurier died before the 1919 convention, which became a de facto leadership selection convention, despite the fact that caucus had already selected a Parliamentary leader.[4] The convention included Parliamentary and extra-Parliamentary members, allowing the party to involve representatives from all regions of the country in the selection of a leader. In the end, the selection of Mackenzie King ushered in a period of electoral success for the Liberals. The Tories continued to use the caucus selection for leaders until 1927, when they selected R.B. Bennett as leader at a party convention. Bennett won the next election. This electoral success, coming on the heels of the Liberals' experience with Mackenzie King, cemented the appeal of leadership conventions, which came to be seen as both a natural development and the democratic face of Canadian parties (Carty, 1992a: 236; Courtney, 1973: chs 2, 4).

The arrival of conventions altered the dynamics of leadership selection and marked a new phase in the development of the Canadian party system and political leadership (Smiley, 1968: 390; Carty, 1988: 22). Whereas caucus selection favoured candidates with Parliamentary experience who had built reputations and alliances within cabinet, successful candidates now had less Parliamentary experience than their predecessors. Between 1919 and 1958 five of the nine leaders selected in this first period were not even MPs, although all but two of them were serving provincial premiers at the time (Courtney, 1995: 16–17). Tory Brian Mulroney (1983) had no Parliamentary experience.[5]

Conventions allowed leaders to claim an independent mandate—party-wide support—to justify their control of party policy and the Parliamentary party. Caucuses now felt constrained in removing leaders, and did so only sporadically, further bolstering the power of party leaders (Blake et al., 1995: 226). Conventions increased the number of leadership candidates in comparison with caucus selection and, it is claimed, encouraged a democratic openness by providing marginal candidates equal time to address delegates (Smiley, 1968: 376). More ballots were required to choose a winner, and more candidates reduced winning margins (Courtney, 1995: 214). Because delegates were a heterogeneous group drawn relatively evenly from across the country, leadership contenders conducted nationwide, relatively inclusive campaigns, offsetting to some degree the regionalization of politics encouraged by the electoral system. This openness restricted the capacity of party élites to control who would be nominated and who would be successful.

Analysing who wins has involved various approaches to understanding candidates and how they build support. Building and funding a team of supporters is crucial in attracting delegate support at the constituency level and at the convention, as well as for convincing failed candidates to support a particular candidate on subsequent ballots. It is also important for maintaining good relations with influential news media (Fletcher, 1988, 1991). Despite the advantages of good organization, a candidate's appeal and capacity for coalition-building are structured by his or her personal background and beliefs and links to existing networks among members based on religious, ethnic, or geographic factors (Stewart, 1991). Understanding how beliefs are structured in the party and how candidates either tap into these beliefs or somehow reflect them is crucial to understanding success (Blake, 1988; Johnston, 1988a).

Conventions spurred the development of extra-Parliamentary organizations to help run parties between elections, and these organizations came to compete with caucus for control of the party. The formalization of periodic party-wide leadership reviews in the 1960s displaced the almost moribund role of caucus in dismissing leaders. Most MPs are now absorbed into the organizations of the various leadership contenders rather than acting as power-brokers in their own right. That leaders could claim an independent power base and legitimacy in speaking for the party has been celebrated as evidence of the democratizing impact of conventions (Mallory, 1971: 205; Blake et al., 1995). However, leadership reviews have been criticized for encouraging infighting and instability within parties and producing leaders immune to criticism from those most qualified to act as judges, their Parliamentary colleagues (Courtney, 1995: 41–7, ch. 3).[6] Moreover, it has also been argued that having been elected to Parliament, MPs have greater democratic legitimacy and are more representative of the will of the people than convention delegates, who are not representative of the wider population (ibid., 37).

Conventions strengthened the personalization of politics and policy-making around party leaders. Despite regular leadership reviews and the existence of biennial policy conventions in most parties, the leader remains free to interpret policy as developed by members at these conventions (Wearing, 1989). Moreover, the traditional tendency for leaders to rely on a group of hand-picked advisers and trusted assistants has been strengthened by leadership conventions. Party members involved in the winning campaign often staff the leader's office, and party notables that supported the winner are likely to figure in any informal advisory group.[7]

Conventions are well suited to media coverage. In particular, they provide a visual tableau on which television can tell its story of Canadian politics.[8] The media attention directed at leaders and the language used to describe leadership contests have played a role in strengthening the personalization of politics and the dominance of party leaders.[9] By the late 1960s, coverage was extensive and media outlets sponsored public opinion and delegate polls for opinion on candidates for the leadership. As well, media coverage introduced 'horse-race' analogies to help describe the process, entrenching the idea that politics was about contests between leaders (Fletcher, 1988). Polling, direct marketing, consulting, and mass media campaigns have all contributed to the strengthening of the role of party leaders in relation to other elements of the party (Gagnon and Tanguay, 1989: 7–11). To make use of these technologies, parties have developed sophisticated central offices dominated by paid professionals hired directly by the leader and his or her supporters, who are loyal to the leader and inclined to see the world through the eyes of the leader. The central office staff organize the party conventions, oversee policy development, organize election campaigns, and manage relations between various elements of the party and the media and other organizations. All this is particularly true of first ministers, who have the extensive resources of cabinet or the Privy Council Office at their command.

The growing personalization of politics is also suggested by the impact of newly elected leaders on the Parliamentary and electoral fortunes of their party. Liberal leaders St Laurent, Trudeau, and Turner and Progressive Conservative leader Campbell all called elections soon after being selected as party leader. In many of these cases, the opposition party had also recently elected a new leader and the elections were purposefully constructed by the government as contests between party leaders. Of course, it may also be that leaders hope to gain a new electoral mandate on the back of their recent leadership success. However, at the provincial level selecting a new leader does not provide a boost to the party's performance at the next election (Stewart and Carty, 1993).

Conventions remained the dominant form for selecting party leaders until the 1980s, when they were challenged at the provincial level by the use of various forms of direct member voting. Although most direct elections have occurred at the provincial level, Joe Clark was elected leader of the national Progressive Conservative Party by this method in 1998 and Stockwell Day won the leadership of the Canadian Alliance (previously the Reform Party) in 2000. When the time comes, the Liberal Party is committed to selecting a replacement for Jean Chrétien in a similar manner, but the NDP retains the traditional convention process as its preferred method of leadership selection with some minor modifications, most notably the use of primaries (Archer and Whitehorn, 1997).

Contemporary researchers share many of the same concerns with respect to the introduction of direct member voting as did those who studied conventions. Just as the earlier move to conventions was rooted in an attempt to revitalize party organizations and electoral support, and was justified in terms of democracy and representation, so, too, has been the move to direct election of leaders (Cross, 1996: 296). There is evidence that direct election produces a more representative voting population than conventions (see David Stewart in this volume). However, direct election does have its problems. Conventions cease to be media events that attract public attention, and perhaps members and eventually votes. There is evidence of the distorting effect of 'instant members' who join and cast a vote, but have no past and perhaps no future in the party (Stewart, 1997). And the 2000 Canadian Alliance vote was marred by a range of irregularities and difficulties with membership lists, vote counting, and the use of different voting methods across the country.

The Parliamentary Party

Methods for selecting leaders contribute to their domination of parties, but this dominance reflects deeper institutional biases. Using Lijphart's (1984) analysis of the logic of political institutions, Canadian political institutions can be seen as heavily majoritarian in nature. That is, once a party has a *majority* of the seats in legislature (the House of Commons, federally), it has control of nearly all the executive powers of Parliament. Effective executive power is exercised by the leader of the majority party (Prime Minister or Premier). The use of first-past-the-post electoral systems, which tend to produce majority governments by rewarding the largest party with a greater proportion of the seats than it receives of the votes, strengthens the majoritarian nature of Canadian Parliaments.[10] The lack of an elected Senate nationally and second chambers at the provincial level ensures that the legislative programs of Canadian governments are rarely challenged.

The first minister dominates the Parliament and its members, both government and opposition. Within his or her party, the first minister has the capacity to reward supporters with benefits such as cabinet portfolios and to punish opponents by limiting their career advancement or access to the advantages of office. The Prime Minister also has control over appointments to the unelected Senate, as well as oversight of judicial appointments. By extension, leaders of non-governing parties (and in particular, the opposition) also exercise considerable power, although less than that of first ministers. The growth of executive power has underpinned a debate over whether the Prime Minister's position has become 'presidentialized', diminishing the role of Parliament. First ministers spend less time in Parliament answering opposition questions and defending the government than was previously the case.

High rates of turnover among MPs contribute to the power of party leaders over their Parliamentary colleagues and reduce Parliament's capacity to question the executive. In general, more MPs lose their seats at Canadian elections than in any other Western democracy, resulting in larger numbers of amateur Parliamentarians (see Docherty in this volume; Blake, 1991; Johnston et al., 1996b). On the government side, this means backbenchers have less experience in questioning their own leader and members of cabinet in Parliament or the party room. Among opposition members, this means relatively few with the skills necessary to embarrass the government or check executive excesses (Franks, 1987: 75–9).

In the last century and a half power has increasingly been concentrated in the hands of the executive, first understood to include the cabinet, and most recently, the Prime Minister and his or her advisers. Ordinary Parliamentarians on both sides of the House and now even some cabinet ministers play only a limited role in the making of government policy (Savoie, 1999a). It is not surprising that, given the limited number of influential offices available to Parliamentarians, most find their greatest satisfaction in assisting their constituents and only hope to influence policy outcomes through discussion in caucus meetings (Docherty, 1997: 251–64). Opposition leaders still have the advantage of press coverage and the capacity to question the government in Parliament, but the odds remain stacked very much against them.

Cabinet Government and Prime Ministerial Power

The style of cabinet government has varied since 1867. Between then and 1937, a period of élite accommodation saw cabinets with strong regional ministers and independent power bases who controlled autonomous departments, usually chosen for a connection or value to their region (for example, Fisheries would be given to a Maritimer) (Simeon, 1990: 22). Within the party they oversaw fund-raising, election and leadership campaigns, and the flow of information about voters in their region to the Prime Minister and cabinet. They shaped government policies that had a direct impact on their region, and implemented cabinet decisions and distributed government patronage in their part of the country.

The 'Mandarin' period, from 1938 to 1959, saw the growth of central bureaucratic agencies and a growing role for bureaucrats in line departments such as Agriculture, Health, and Transportation in developing and implementing government policy. This was followed by what has been called the rational planning period, lasting from 1960 to 1978, dominated by faith in the tools of management and the belief that government should be run much like a business. Bureaucrats played a key role in providing technical advice but the explicit aim of changes made during this period was to reassert ministerial control over policy-making. From 1979 to the 1990s the so-called envelope system was largely aimed at developing a decision-making process that could be used to control the growth and scope of government (Simeon, 1990: 27–30). Policy was indirectly shaped by strict new budgeting requirements, with cabinet committees establishing priorities. As the new century begins, this process has been increasingly centralized around a few senior ministers and bureaucrats (Savoie, 1999a).

A central debate about the nature of modern cabinets concerns the degree to which the role of regional ministers has declined over the last half century. Some argue that changes to the nature of cabinet have reduced the autonomy of individual ministers. The growth of the administrative state, where bureaucrats have a greater say in the development and implementation of government policies and programs (Dupré, 1987: 238–9; Pross, 1982: 107–29), leaves even senior ministers with relatively little discretionary power except with respect to obtaining assistance for their regions (Cairns, 1979: 6; Smiley, 1980: 134; Bakvis, 1991: 3). In addition, central institutions such as the Privy Council Office and the Prime Minister's Office increasingly serve the objectives of the Prime Minister and act as conduits for bureaucratic policy advice on the full range of policy issues facing the government, thereby diminishing the role of cabinet ministers in policy development (Savoie, 1999a).

Bakvis counters that the strength of regional ministers has always waxed and waned, and while it declined during the 1960s and 1970s, it has since grown. In particular, ministers have taken advantage of changes in the modes of cabinet behaviour, such as how funding for major projects is organized, and linkages with provincial governments to play key roles in directing resources (Bakvis, 1991: 287–9). The key change that seems to be agreed upon is that ministerial portfolios and the growing assertiveness of provincial governments, rather than regional party organizations, are the bases of this power.

In an era of globalization, the nearly unfettered power of the Prime Minister to make international agreements places him or her at the centre of an increasingly important policy-making process from which other domestic actors are or can be excluded. This is also true of the Prime Minister's role with respect to federal-provincial relations. The Canadian constitution is such that both levels of government share responsibilities over a wide range of matters, requiring extensive intergovernmental negotiations to develop policies in these areas. Just as Prime Ministers dominate the federal Parliament, so, too, do premiers dominate their legislatures. Meetings of first ministers, who negotiate largely without fear of legislative oversight, are perhaps the central decision-making forum in Canadian politics. Executive federalism, as it is known, has created a powerful political élite. The result is that, just as the Prime Minister and cabinet bypassed Parliament for much of the last 150 years, now the Prime Minister often bypasses cabinet in developing and executing government policy. Court government, as Savoie (1999b: 635) calls this development, means that:

> in the late 1990s, effective power rests with the Prime Minister and a small group of carefully selected courtiers. These include key advisors in his office, two or three senior cabinet ministers (notably the minister of finance), carefully selected lobbyists, pollsters and other friends of the court, and a handful of public servants.

The dominance of the executive and party leaders may have its advantages, largely in terms of the leaders' capacity to act as brokers. Unencumbered by detailed party platforms, clear ideologies, or the need to explain themselves at length to party members or the Parliament, party leaders, and at times powerful ministers, have been able to pursue pragmatic deal-making and respond to the varying demands that flow from ethnolinguistic and regional differences in Canada. As well, because a Prime Minister chooses the cabinet, he or she can attempt to ensure representation from the regions and of important interests. This principle, adopted by Sir John A. Macdonald in 1867, has since guided the selection of ministers. This allows the cabinet to fill a 'dual role, for in addition to exercising the usual functions of executive leadership, the cabinet has provided an arena in which the élites may counter the dysfunctional and unstabilizing effects of cultural, regional and religious fragmentation' (Matheson, 1976: ix).

The regional representation principle is one of the few checks on the power of a Prime Minister, who must be cautious in appointing or dismissing ministers so as not to offend an important segment of Canadian society. The other is elections, at which voters may always choose another party and leader. So powerful are Prime Ministers, however, that their dismissal is very rare and only a few cases can be culled from Canadian history. Macdonald can be said to have been dismissed by the House of Commons in 1873, Mackenzie Bowell was replaced in 1896 as a result of cabinet discontent, and King was effectively forced out of office by the Governor General in 1926 (ibid., 233).

The judiciary is also an important element of élite politics in Canada, and despite growing diversity among judges the judiciary is still overwhelmingly middle-class, male, and white (Porter, 1965; McCormick and Greene, 1990). The appointment of senior judges gives the Prime Minister indirect power to influence how the constitution is interpreted. Judicial decisions shape criminal and civil law, the interpretation of crucial government functions such as taxation, and the balance of power between the federal and provincial governments. The addition of the Charter of Rights and Freedoms to the constitution in 1982 has extended the role of the courts in setting the balance of power between governments and citizens. Not only has this enhanced the power of the judiciary, it has made it an object of political activism.

Political Activists

The extension of the franchise, beginning in the late nineteenth century and continuing for much of the twentieth century, was accompanied by profound shifts in the institutions and structures of the state and society. In Europe, political parties, particularly of the left, responded to the widening of the franchise by developing permanent extra-Parliamentary organizations to allow the previously excluded working class to engage in political activity. Activists in these *mass* parties, so named because their organization was based on mass membership, were involved in organizing elections as well as setting policy for the Parliamentary branch of the party.

In contrast to their European and Commonwealth cousins, Canadian parties retained an older, cadre-style of organization. Traditionally, members in *cadre* parties help to organize elections but do little else (see Carty, 1991). In Canada, the introduction of leadership conventions spurred the development of extra-Parliamentary organizations and heightened the influence of ordinary party members acting as delegates, in comparison with both leadership candidates, who were wooing them, and local MPs. Initially, local MPs influenced the selection of constituency delegates and thus retained a role in selection (Powers, 1992: 241). This power waned over time, as the process of delegate selection became more formalized and the number of ex officio delegates and representatives of various non-constituency groups grew.

Unlike in most other liberal democratic countries, local members of Canadian parties control the nomination of candidates and the organization of local campaigns, two key party functions. This allows them more influence over the electoral and Parliamentary character of their party. However, compared with European parties, the role of members with respect to policy development is limited. With the exception of the New Democratic Party, and more recently the Canadian Alliance, which adopted a mass party form for ideological reasons, Canadian parties were nearly entirely electoral rather than policy-making organizations.[11] This produced a cyclical pattern of activity, with party membership and activist involvement peaking around elections and leadership contests and declining thereafter (Carty, 1991: Table 5.3).

The arrival of leadership conventions allowed for direct assessment of intra-party coalitions and surveys of delegates, providing new means for studying political parties. Researchers discovered that the majority of delegates to conventions have been middle-class, middle-aged, white men (Perlin, 1988). This, as well as their failure to adopt detailed, strictly enforced platforms, was seen as evidence that Canadian political parties were non-ideological, brokerage parties (Winn and

McMenemy, 1976). Rather than strict ideological differences, factors such as religion, region, and whether activists were involved in the federal or provincial party were important in determining activists' beliefs (Stewart and Stewart, 1997). Yet there is still evidence that members of different parties exhibit distinctive political belief systems (Blake, 1988; Johnston, 1988a, 1988b; Archer and Whitehorn, 1997).

The 1960s saw attempts by parties to expand the representation of activists at conventions. In 1967, the Tories made the first effort to broaden both the image and appeal of the party by stipulating that women and young people gain a proportion of delegate positions in each constituency. Other parties soon followed suit (Courtney, 1995: 129). This approach has been adopted by all parties and has been formalized in the existence of internal party organizations to represent the interests of women, youth, Aboriginals, ethnic minorities, and, in some cases, seniors. These groups elected representatives to leadership conventions, guaranteeing them higher levels of representation. The recent move to direct election of leaders in most parties limits opportunities for special representation of this form.

Evidence of the broadening membership and appeal of parties can be seen in the recent election of the first Indo-Canadian leader of a Canadian party (and Premier), Ujjal Dosanjh, who won the leadership of the New Democratic Party in British Columbia in February 2000. Yet while this is a noteworthy success, women and minorities are still relatively rare in the leadership contests of most parties, and have tended to do better when parties have been in electoral decline. Moreover, as Black notes in Chapter 21, parliamentary representation of minorities remains limited. And while some have pointed to the value of more diversity (Bashevkin, 1985; Brodie, 1988; Megyery, 1991), others have suggested that although reforms have generated diversity with respect to gender, age, and ethnicity, they have also resulted in less diversity in other characteristics, such as income and education (Courtney, 1995: 138–43).

Despite these changes, the realignment of the party system in the 1993 Canadian election is evidence of discontent with Canadian parties. In part, the turmoil of 1993 can be explained by the incapacity of existing parties to represent and express adequately the diversity of demands thrown up by Canadian society. This, in turn, reflects the relatively limited policy-making function of Canadian parties, an understudied aspect of Canadian parties (Meisel, 1996: 231, 237). Combined with the Liberal dominance of the national Parliament during much of the past century, which reduces the openness and responsiveness of the legislative process, voters and activists have little incentive to use the party system to influence policy outcomes. This encourages them to seek alternative means of influencing government policy.

The shift to forms of policy engagement other than those provided by parties began in the 1960s, with activists turning their attention to forming interest groups to lobby governments.[12] A number of factors spurred these changes. The growth of social movements—various waves of new thinking about many aspects of society, including the role of women in society, the nature of human sexuality and ethnicity, humankind's impact on the environment, and so on—shifted popular thinking on many issues (Carroll, 1997). Growing affluence, higher levels of education, disillusionment with political parties and the role allowed for activists in them, as well as the growing complexity of government and the issues facing it reinforced this trend to new forms of political involvement (Inglehart, 1977; Nevitte, 1996). Federalism provides many access points for interest groups in Canada (Pross, 1986), and some groups have become adept at building relations with the powerful provincial and national executives that dominate the legislative process (Pal, 1993). The Charter of Rights and Freedoms allows groups to pursue political objectives through the courts (Knopff and Morton, 1992), while globalization provides new international opportunities for political activism (Held and Archibugi, 1995: 4). In many ways these new forms of political activity may have supplanted the parties with respect to many policy issues, yet parties retain a crucial role in deciding who sets the overall direction of government policy, and therefore will continue to attract activists.

Conclusion

The study of political leadership in Canada has been dominated by pluralist and institutionalist views of politics. Pluralism gives full weight to the role of leaders and activists in shaping policy outcomes via political party and interest group activity. Institutionalism allows analysts to focus on features of Canadian politics, such as federalism, Parliament, cabinet government, the party system, and the policy process, in studying both leadership and activism.

Party leaders and first ministers have been the main focus of leadership research. The move from caucus selection to conventions and more recently to direct member voting has increased the power of party leaders. At the federal level, and one suspects at the provincial level as well, there is ample evidence that the Prime Minister now dominates cabinet as cabinet once dominated Parliament. Together, the method for selecting party leaders and the majoritarian logic of the House of Commons ensure that Canada has one of the most powerful government leaders in the democratic world.

Despite their growing importance, researchers have paid much less attention to the leadership of interest groups. Most interest group analysis follows the familiar pattern of considering their position in the institutional firmament. In this regard, the last 40 years have seen a remarkable increase in the numbers of interest groups and much greater diversity in the issues they pursue. This reflects a combination of disillusionment with existing mechanisms for political engagement, such as parties, changes in the issues facing Canadians, the emergence of more sophisticated citizens, and, most recently, the impact of globalization.

The growing role for party activists in selecting leaders has become a defining characteristic of Canadian politics. Despite this, there is a sharp disjunction between their capacity to select leaders and the opportunities available to them for discussing party policy. To the degree that this allows leaders greater leeway in brokering competing interests, this arrangement may be desirable. However, it may still be dysfunctional for parties in terms of their capacity to play a role in addressing important policy concerns and in legitimating the political process. Activists to some degree can choose alternative routes of engagement, such as interest groups that may help legitimate the political process, but events since 1993 suggest that only political parties may be in a position to address some critical matters.

Notes

Thanks to Charlie Gray and Tracey Raney for their research assistance.

1. A caveat is necessary here. It would seem that even with globalization the leaders of some countries, most notably the US, continue to have a disproportionate capacity to influence domestic and international political outcomes.

2. By extension, this is also true, though in reduced degree, for the leaders of non-governing parties.

3. There are many exceptions to this simple description, including the capacity for the caucus to select a leader from outside the party or even from outside Parliament.

4. Conventions involve bringing together representatives of local associations and other elements of the party at a single place and having them vote in successive ballots until one of the leadership contenders receives a majority of votes cast. The exact rules governing leadership contests differ between parties and have changed over time, but in general follow this pattern:
   - the ballot is secret and individual;
   - the winner must have a clear majority of the valid votes cast;
   - the low candidate(s) is eliminated if there is no winner on a ballot and any candidate may withdraw from the race between ballots;
   - no new nominations are permitted between ballots;
   - the candidates are not permitted to address the delegates once the balloting gets under way, but announcements declaring their elimination or withdrawal are read from the podium; and
   - there is continuous voting with non-preferential ballots until a winner is declared. (Courtney, 1995: 212)

5. See, for example, the comparisons of legislative experience of leaders, their religious affiliations, and other characteristics in Courtney (1995: 345–51, Tables 8–6 to 8–12).

6. A good example of this from the provincial arena is the continuation in office of the NDP Premier of British Columbia, Glenn Clarke, in 1999 despite the clear preference of many ministers that he be replaced. Public acknowledgement of a police investigation into his involvement in decisions affecting the business of an acquaintance finally led Clarke to resign.

7. The NDP has offered members some opportunity to be involved in policy development, as did the Reform Party. Whether the Canadian Alliance will do so is yet to be seen.

8. One of the best examples is the 1976 Tory leadership campaign in which Flora MacDonald walked over to the Joe Clark group, delivering him her supporters and the leadership.

9. This personalization process, which has occurred at both the national and provincial levels, has been encouraged by a range of developments including the centralization and professionalization of campaign organizations, the power of leaders to veto candidates chosen by local associations, and the growing stature of first ministers' conferences.

10. In 1997, the largest party, the Liberals, received about 38 per cent of votes cast, but won about 51 per cent (a majority) of the seats in the House of Commons.
11. See Duverger (1954) for a more detailed description of the differences between mass and cadre parties. The Reform Party adopted many of the policy-making mechanisms (involving members in such discussions) associated with mass parties. Whether its successor, the Canadian Alliance, continues in this vein depends on how such structures fit with its strategy of becoming a national, electorally successful party.
12. These groups joined existing groups—mainly business and occupational associations—that have a much longer history of trying to influence government policy. The explosion in the number of groups, and the range of issues they champion, sets the last 40 years apart from earlier periods in Canadian history.

References

Archer, Keith, and Alan Whitehorn. 1997. *Political Activists: The NDP in Convention*. Toronto: Oxford University Press.

Bakvis, Herman. 1991. *Regional Ministers: Power and Influence in the Canadian Cabinet*. Toronto: University of Toronto Press.

Bashevkin, Sylvia B. 1985. 'Women's Participation in Ontario Political Parties', in Sylvia B. Bashevkin, ed., *Canadian Political Behaviour: Introductory Readings*. Toronto: Methuen.

Blake, Donald E. 1988. 'Division and Cohesion: The Major Parties', in Perlin (1988: 32–53).

———. 1991. 'Party Competition and Electoral Volatility: Canada in Comparative Perspective', in *Representation, Integration and Political Parties in Canada*, vol. 14 of the research studies for the Royal Commission on Electoral Reform and Party Financing. Ottawa and Toronto: RCERPF/Dundurn Press.

———, R.K. Carty, and Lynda Erickson. 1995. 'Coming and Going: Leadership Selection and Removal in Canada', in Alain G. Gagnon and A. Brian Tanguay, eds, *Canadian Parties in Transition*, 2nd edn. Toronto: Nelson Canada.

Block, Fred. 1987. *Revising State Theory: Essays in Politics and Postindustrialism*. Philadelphia: Temple University Press.

Blondel, J. 1987. *Political Leadership: Towards a General Analysis*. London: Sage.

Brodie, Janine. 1988. 'The Gender Factor and National Leadership Conventions in Canada', in Perlin (1988: 172–87).

Cairns, Alan C. 1979. *From Interstate to Intrastate Federalism in Canada*. Kingston: Institute for Intergovernmental Relations.

Carroll, William H. 1997. *Organizing Dissent: Contemporary Social Movements in Theory and Practice*. Toronto: Garamond Press.

Carty, R.K. 1988. 'Three Canadian Party Systems: An Interpretation of the Development of National Politics', in Perlin (1988).

———. 1991. *Canadian Political Parties in the Constituencies*, vol. 23 of the research studies for the Royal Commission on Electoral Reform and Party Financing. Ottawa and Toronto: RCERPF/Dundurn Press.

———, ed. 1992a. *Canadian Political Party Sytems: A Reader*. Peterborough, Ont.: Broadview Press.

———. 1992b. 'The Coming of Leadership Conventions', in Carty (1992a).

———, Lynda Erickson, and Donald E. Blake. 1992. *Leaders and Parties in Canadian Politics: Experiences of the Provinces*. Toronto: Harcourt Brace Jovanovich.

Clement, Wallace. 1988. *The Challenge of Class Analysis*. Ottawa: Carleton University Press.

——— and Glen Williams, eds. 1989. *The New Canadian Political Economy*. Montreal and Kingston: McGill-Queen's University Press.

Courtney, John. 1973. *The Selection of National Party Leaders in Canada*. Toronto: Macmillan of Canada.

———. 1995. *Do Conventions Matter? Choosing National Party Leaders in Canada*. Montreal and Kingston: McGill-Queen's University Press.

Cross, William. 1996. 'Direct Election of Provincial Party Leaders in Canada, 1985–1995: The End of the Leadership Convention?', *Canadian Journal of Political Science* 29, 2: 295–315.

Dahl, Robert A. 1961. *Who Governs? Democracy and Power in an American City*. New Haven: Yale University Press.

Dalton, Russell. 1994. *The Green Rainbow: Environmental Groups in Western Europe*. New Haven: Yale University Press.

Docherty, David C. 1997. *Mr. Smith Goes to Ottawa: Life in the House of Commons*. Vancouver: University of British Columbia Press.

Dupré, J.S. 1987. 'The Workability of Executive Federalism in Canada', in H. Bakvis and W. Chandler, eds, *Federalism and the Role of the State*. Toronto: University of Toronto Press.

Duverger, Maurice. 1954. *Political Parties*. New York: Wiley.

Elkins, David, and Richard Simeon, eds. 1980. *Small Worlds*. Toronto: Methuen.

Erickson, Lynda. 1991. 'Women and Candidacies for the House of Commons', in Megyery (1991: 101–24).

———. 1993. 'Making Her Way In: Women, Parties and Candidacies in Canada', in Lovenduski and Norris (1993: 60–85).

Falk, Richard A. 1995. *On Human Governance: Toward a New Global Politics*. Cambridge: Polity Press.

Flanagan, Thomas. 1998. *Game Theory and Canadian Politics*. Toronto: University of Toronto Press.

Fletcher, Frederick J. 1988. 'The Mass Media and the Selection of National Party Leaders: Some Explorations', in Perlin (1988: 97–122).

———, ed. 1991. *Media, Elections and Democracy*. Ottawa and Toronto: RCERPF/Dundurn Press.

Franks, C.E.S. 1987. *The Parliament of Canada*. Toronto: University of Toronto Press.

Gagnon, Alain, and Brian Tanguay, eds. 1989. *Canadian Parties in Transition: Discourse, Organization and Representation*. Scarborough, Ont.: Nelson Canada.

Heifetz, R., and R. Sinder. 1990. 'Political Leadership: Managing the Public Problem Solving', in R. Reich, ed., *The Power of Public Ideas*. Cambridge, Mass.: Harvard University Press.

Held, David, and Daniele Archibugi, eds. 1995. *Cosmopolitan Democracy: An Agenda for a New World Order*. Cambridge: Polity Press.

Horsman, Mathew, and Andrew Marshall. 1994. *After the Nation-State—Citizens, Tribalism and the New World Disorder*. London: Harper Collins.

Inglehart, Ronald. 1977. *The Silent Revolution: Changing Values and Political Styles Among Western Publics*. Princeton, NJ: Princeton University Press.

Johnston, Richard. 1988. 'The Ideological Structure of Opinion on Policy', in Perlin (1988: 54–71).

——. 1988a. 'The Final Choice: Its Social, Organizational, and Ideological Bases', in Perlin (1988: 204–42).

——, André Blais, Henry Brady, and Jean Crête. 1992. *Letting the People Decide: Dynamics of a Canadian Election*. Montreal and Kingston: McGill-Queen's University Press.

——, ——, Elisabeth Gidengil, and Neil Nevitte. 1996. *The Challenge of Direct Democracy: The 1992 Canadian Referendum*. Montreal and Kingston: McGill-Queen's University Press.

——, ——, Henry E. Brady, Elisabeth Gidengil, and Neil Nevitte. 1996b. 'The 1993 Canadian General Election: Realignment, Dealignment or Something Else', paper presented at the annual meeting of the American Political Science Association.

Key, V.O. 1958. *Politics, Parties and Pressure Groups*, 4th edn. New York: Crowell.

Knopff, Rainer, and F.L. Morton. 1992. *Charter Politics*. Scarborough, Ont.: Nelson Canada.

Kymlicka, Will. 1995. *Multicultural Citizenship*. Toronto: Oxford University Press.

Lehmbruch, Gerhard, and Philippe C. Schmitter, eds. 1982. *Patterns of Corporatist Policy Making*. London: Sage.

Lijphart, Arend. 1984. *Democracies: Patterns of Majoritarian and Consensus Government in Twenty-One Countries*. New Haven: Yale University Press.

Lindblom, Charles. 1977. *Politics and Markets: The World's Political Economic Systems*. New York: Basic Books.

Lovenduski, Joni, and Pippa Norris, eds. 1993. *Gender in Party Politics*. London: Sage.

McCormick, Peter, and Ian Greene. 1990. *Judges and Judging: Inside the Canadian Judicial System*. Toronto: James Lorimer.

McRae, Kenneth D. 1979. 'Comment: Federation, Consociation, Corporatism—An Addendum to Arend Lijphart', *Canadian Journal of Political Science* 12, 2: 517–22.

Mahon, Rianne. 1984. *The Politics of Industrial Restructuring: Canadian Textiles*. Toronto: University of Toronto Press.

Mallory, J.R. 1971. *The Structure of Canadian Government*. Toronto: Macmillan of Canada.

Mancuso, Maureen, Richard G. Price, and Ronald Wagenberg, eds. 1994. *Leaders and Leadership in Canada*. Toronto: Oxford University Press.

March, James G., and Johan P. Olsen. 1989. *Rediscovering Institutions: The Organizational Basis of Politics*. New York: Free Press.

Matheson, W.A. 1976. *The Prime Minister and the Cabinet*. Toronto: Methuen.

Meisel, John. 1996. 'The Dysfunctions of Canadian Parties: An Exploratory Mapping', in Hugh G. Thorburn, ed., *Party Politics in Canada*. Scarborough, Ont.: Prentice-Hall.

Megyery, Kathy, ed. 1991. *Women in Canadian Politics: Toward Equity in Representation*. Toronto: Dundurn Press.

Michels, Robert O. 1962 [1915]. *Political Parties: A Sociological Study of the Oligarchical Tendencies of Modern Democracy*. New York: Crowell-Collier.

Miliband, Ralph. 1969. *The State in Capitalist Society*. London: Wiedenfeld and Nicolson.

Mills, C. Wright. 1956. *The Power Elite*. New York: Oxford University Press.

Mosca, Gaetano. 1939. *The Ruling Class: elementi di scienza politica*, trans. by Hannah D. Kahn. New York: McGraw-Hill.

Nevitte, Neil. 1996. *The Decline of Deference: Canadian Value Change in Cross-National Perspective*. Peterborough, Ont.: Broadview Press.

Nordlinger, Eric. 1981. *On the Autonomy of the Democratic State*. Cambridge, Mass.: Harvard University Press.

Pal, Leslie. 1993. *Interests of State: The Politics of Language, Multiculturalism and Feminism in Canada*. Montreal and Kingston: McGill-Queen's University Press.

_____ and David Taras. 1988. *Prime Ministers and Premiers: Political Leadership and Public Policy in Canada*. Scarborough, Ont.: Prentice-Hall.

Panitch, Leo, ed. 1977. *The Canadian State: Political Economy and Political Power*. Toronto: University of Toronto Press.

_____. 1979. 'Corporatism in Canada', in R. Schultz, O.M. Kruhlak, and J.C. Terry, eds, *The Canadian Political Process*, 3rd edn. Toronto: Holt, Rinehart and Winston, 53–72.

Pareto, Vilfredo. 1966. *Sociological Writings*. New York: Praeger.

_____. 1968. *The Rise and Fall of the Elites: An Application of Theoretical Sociology*. Totowa, NJ: Bedminster Press.

Perlin, George, ed. 1988. *Party Democracy in Canada: The Politics of National Party Conventions*. Scarborough, Ont.: Prentice-Hall.

Porter, John A. 1965. *The Vertical Mosaic: An Analysis of Social Class and Power in Canada*. Toronto: University of Toronto Press.

Poulantzas, Nicos. 1973. *Political Power and Social Class*. London: NLB and Sheed and Ward.

Powers, C.G. 1992 [1966]. 'Two Liberal Leadership Conventions', in Carty (1992a).

Pross, Paul A. 1982. 'Space, Function, and Interest: The Problem of Legitimacy in the Canadian State', in O.P. Dwivedi, ed., *The Administrative State in Canada: Essays for J.E. Hodgetts*. Toronto: University of Toronto Press.

———. 1986. *Group Politics and Public Policy*. Toronto: Oxford University Press.

Savoie, Donald J. 1999a. *Governing from the Centre: The Concentration of Power in Canadian Politics*. Toronto: University of Toronto Press.

_____. 1999b. 'The Rise of Court Government in Canada', *Canadian Journal of Political Science* 32, 4: 635–64.

Sayers, Anthony M. 1999. *Candidates, Parties and Constituency Campaigns in Canadian Elections*. Vancouver: University of British Columbia Press.

Schmitter, Philippe C., and Gerhard Lehmbruch. 1979. *Trends Towards Corporatist Intermediation*. London: Sage.

Siegfried, André. 1966 [1906]. *The Race Question in Canada*. Toronto: McClelland & Stewart.

Simeon, James C. 1990. 'The Central Decision-Making Process in the Federal Government: Past, Present and Future', *Optimum* 21, 1: 18–33.

Smiley, Donald. 1968. 'The National Party Leadership Convention in Canada: A Preliminary Analysis', *Canadian Journal of Political Science* 1, 4: 373–97.

———. 1980. *Canada in Question: Federalism in the Eighties*. Toronto: McGraw-Hill Ryerson.

———. 1987. *The Federal Condition in Canada*. Toronto: McGraw-Hill Ryerson.

Stewart, David K. 1992. 'Friends and Neighbours Politics at Maritime Conventions', in Carty et al. (1992).

————. 1997. 'The Changing Leadership Electorate: An Examination of Participants in the 1992 Alberta Conservative Leadership Election', *Canadian Journal of Political Science* 30, 1: 107–28.

———— and R.K. Carty. 1993. 'Does Changing the Party Leader Provide an Electoral Boost? A Study of Canadian Provincial Parties: 1960–1992', *Canadian Journal of Political Science* 26, 2: 313–30.

———— and Ian Stewart. 1997. 'Fission and Federalism: The Disaggregation of Canadian Activists', *Publius* 27, 3: 97–112.

Tremblay, Manon, and Caroline Andrew. 1997. *Women and Political Representation in Canada*. Ottawa: University of Ottawa Press.

Wearing, Joseph. 1989. 'Can an Old Dog Teach Itself New Tricks? The Liberal Party Attempts Reform', in Gagnon and Tanguay (1989).

Winn, C., and J. McMenemy. 1976. *Political Parties in Canada*. Toronto: McGraw-Hill Ryerson.

Wright, Erik Olin. 1985. *Classes*. London: Verso.

————. 1997. *Class Counts: Comparative Studies in Class Analysis*. New York: Cambridge University Press.

Young, Lisa. 2000. *Feminists and Party Politics*. Vancouver: University of British Columbia Press.

Chapter 19

Electing a Premier:
An Examination of the 1992
Alberta PC Universal Ballot

DAVID K. STEWART

For most of the twentieth century Canadian party leaders were elected at conventions dominated by delegates chosen by local constituency associations but leavened by the presence of the party's legislative and organizational élites. Since 1985 these conventions have been gradually replaced by universal ballots in which everyone who holds a party membership is entitled to vote directly for the leader. As a result most Canadians are currently governed at the provincial level by someone chosen through a universal ballot and each of the parties represented in the federal House of Commons has adopted mechanisms through which their members will have a direct voice in leadership selection.[1]

The selection of Canadian party leaders has attracted much scholarly attention. This attention is warranted by the importance of leaders in Canadian politics since, as Perlin (1988: 2) writes, 'The choice of the leader sets the course of the major Canadian parties in virtually everything they do.' Indeed, as Jeffrey Simpson (1999) pointed out in a recent book review, 'the prime minister is the political equivalent of the Sun King, more powerful by far within the Canadian system than the U.S. president within the American.' The decisions parties make in selecting leaders indirectly (and at times directly) determine the country's 'first ministers' by providing voters with the short list from which these ministers will be drawn. Thus, a full appreciation of Canadian democracy requires an understanding of the dynamics of leadership selection.

Past analysis of leadership selection has explored two basic themes. The first is an institutional examination of the rules and processes used. In a seminal book, Courtney (1973) demonstrated how the emergence of convention-based selections affected the characteristics of leaders by limiting the value of extensive parliamentary careers. As he put it, 'Not only has the convention system made it easier for men with little in the way of parliamentary and ministerial experience to be elected as party leaders, it has made it more difficult for those politicians with considerable experience in federal politics to be chosen by the convention delegates as leaders of their party' (Courtney, 1973: 145). Not surprisingly, broadening the electorate beyond the parliamentary caucus provided candidates lacking extensive parliamentary careers with a more sympathetic audience. Other scholars have noted additional institutional effects. For instance, Smiley (1968: 378) argued that the requirement of successive ballots 'held at short intervals until one candidate has a majority of all votes cast' discouraged rationality by forcing delegates to make decisions in the heat of the moment and with imperfect information. In a similar vein, Levesque (1983: 783) showed that rules requiring that the candidate with the lowest vote total be dropped after each ballot could result in a party choosing as leader someone who was not 'the first choice of a majority of the convention'. More recently, Courtney (1995) and Perlin (1991b) have warned that universal ballots will ensure that future leaders are chosen by a relatively uninformed electorate that is not well-versed in party history.

The second theme pursues a more behavioural focus. It has used survey data to profile those who participate in leadership selection and to assess how these participants behave with respect to candidate support. These examinations of candidate support provide an important and rare window into the activities of political parties. The ability to examine what divides parties internally when they make their most important decision contributes to a better understanding of intra-party cleavages. The weight of scholarship on this subject suggests that conventions are mini-elections and that the cleavages relevant in the wider polity are also important at conventions (see Krause and LeDuc, 1979). Examining what goes on at a convention can provide insight, not only directly into the relevant political party, but indirectly into the broader nature of politics. This is particularly valuable for students of provincial politics since few systematic studies of provincial politics (let alone provincial political parties) exist.

This chapter builds on previous research by examining the participants in the most 'universal' ballot ever held in Canada: the 1992 Alberta Progressive Conservative leadership election. It shows how the participants in that election differ from traditional delegates to leadership conventions and looks at differences in the support patterns of the two leading candidates. The key questions addressed concern the degree to which different rules of selection enfranchise a different sort of electorate and the nature of voting divisions among the universal ballot electorate.

The 1992 Alberta leadership election was unique in its accessibility (Carty and Blake, 1999). All Canadian citizens who were 16 or older and who had lived in Alberta for six months were eligible to vote, provided they paid the party's five-dollar membership fee. These memberships could be purchased at any time before the close of balloting and were on sale at each polling station. Nine candidates sought the party's leadership but none was able to secure a majority on the first ballot. Health minister Nancy Betkowski held a slim one-vote lead over Environment Minister Ralph Klein, with the remaining candidates trailing far behind. A second run-off election between these candidates[2] was held a week later and Klein triumphed with the support of almost 60 per cent of the 78,251 voters. The data on the 1992 Alberta PC leadership election presented here are taken from a survey administered to a sample of these second-ballot voters. Questionnaires were sent to 2,728 voters, 943 of whom responded, producing a sample representative of the total population in terms of region and reported vote (see Stewart,1997).

The Convention Electorate

An evaluation of the degree to which universal ballots differ from conventions in terms of the composition of the electorate requires a description of both electorates. The premise underlying universal ballots is that every member of the party is entitled to vote directly for the party leader. In contrast, participation in leadership conventions is restricted to those holding some sort of party or public office and those who were elected to serve as delegates by their constituencies. Participation in a convention is thus both restricted and mediated. As a result, leadership conventions in Canada's Liberal and Conservative parties enfranchised a particular sort of electorate. One of the most important features of this electorate was its regional representativeness. In Courtney's words, 'It is an incontestable fact that members and active supporters of any party are more concentrated in some regions...than others. Those differentials have been discounted by Canada's two oldest parties since the outset of conventions by their insistence that each constituency send the same number of delegates to a convention as every other constituency, regardless of the size or complexity of its local membership' (1995: 286). This conscious decision constructed a delegate body representative of the geographic nature of the country or province.

Conventions were also used by the Liberal and Conservative parties 'to manipulate the composition of the electorate in order to achieve particular representational goals: gender parity, inclusion of younger people, integration of aboriginal people into the party system' (MacIvor, 1994: 20). In practice then, parties were unwilling to let their constituency associations choose delegates without regard to considerations such as age or gender. In 1983 and 1984, when both national parties chose leaders, these efforts ensured that women accounted for almost 40 per cent of the delegate total (Brodie, 1988: 176) and that delegates under 30 years of age 'constitute[d] the largest age grouping attending conventions' (Perlin et al., 1988: 189). The 1990 and 1993 federal Liberal and Conservative leadership conventions represented women and youth in similar proportions (Courtney, 1995: 336). The parties wished to inoculate themselves from charges that women did not have a strong voice in party decisions and undoubtedly hoped that the substantial over-representation of youth would provide them with a cadre of young volunteers who would remain active for years to come.

Another consideration affecting the composition of the electorate was the expense involved in attending conventions. Delegates were required to travel to a central location and pay a registration fee, in addition to the accommodation costs needed to subsist in that location for a few days. This effectively disqualified most

Canadians and ensured that the vast majority of delegates came 'from the wealthiest, best-educated and highest status occupational groups in Canadian society' (Perlin, 1991a: 61). Most of these delegates were also veterans in terms of past involvement in the party.

Finally, conventions were designed to preserve a strong voice for the party's élite by enfranchising many of these people as ex officio delegates. As Courtney (1995: 128) notes, the Liberal and Conservative parties decided to provide automatic delegate status to '[e]lected or appointed party notables, such as MPs and senators, provincial leaders and legislative members, and executive officers of the various national and provincial branches of a party's organization'. Since universal ballots allow each member to vote directly for the leader, the representational guarantees provided by conventions are lost.

The Universal Ballot Electorate

An examination of the 1992 Alberta PC electorate illustrates the dramatic changes in the composition of the electorate that can accompany a universal ballot (see Table 19.1). Perhaps the most significant change is the increase in the proportion of women who participated. At the 1985 Alberta PC convention, women held only 30 per cent of the delegate spaces, and eight years later at the federal PC convention the proportion of women was still only 34 per cent.[3] In contrast, women achieved virtual parity in the universal ballot of 1992, accounting for 47 per cent of the electorate. Women obviously found it easier to participate in the universal ballot, despite the absence of guarantees associated with conventions. Not only did more

Table 19.1: Universal Ballot Voters compared to Provincial and Federal PC Delegates

	1992 Alberta PC Voters	1985 Alberta PC Delegates	1993 Federal PC Delegates
% women	47	30	34
% under 25 years	5	16	21
% 65 years or older	14	6	12 (over 60 years)
% from Edmonton or Calgary	57	54	na
% with university degree	35	46	52
% blue collar	13	na	4
% held party office	5	59	66
% joined just to vote	55	na	na
% member of federal PCs	21	75	na
% member for less than one year	55	14	7
% worked previously for party	18	79	84
(N)	(943)	(325)	(1,455)

Sources: Data on the 1985 Alberta PC delegates from Hunziker (1986). Data on the 1993 Federal PC delegates from Courtney (1995).

women participate, but the women who did participate (unlike female convention delegates) differed from the male voters with respect to previous party involvement and occupational background (see Brodie, 1988). The women voters' previous party involvement had been less substantial than that of the men, and women were much more likely to be employed part-time or not at all outside the home. The more open universal ballot, with its self-selection and low participation costs, enhanced the opportunity for women with this sort of background to become involved.

The universal ballot electorate can also be distinguished from the convention electorate with respect to age. Simply put, the universal ballot enfranchised a much greater proportion of older voters. At the 1985 provincial convention almost one delegate in six (16 per cent) was under the age of 25 and only one delegate in 17 (6 per cent) was 65 or older. The 1993 federal PC convention enfranchised a similarly youthful electorate, with 21 per cent of the delegates under 25 and only 12 per cent over the age of 60. The universal ballot virtually reversed these proportions: 14 per cent of the voters had reached the age of 65 (almost a quarter were 60 or older) and a mere 5 per cent were under 25. Young voters had a much smaller role to play in the universal ballot.

Social status differences are also apparent between universal ballot voters and convention delegates. This was particularly obvious in terms of education. With the universal ballot the proportion of voters without university degrees increased from just over half to almost two-thirds and the percentage of voters who 'had not finished high school more than doubled. Nonetheless, the voters remained relatively affluent and those from business and professional backgrounds continued to be over-represented. Still, it is worth noting that while less than 5 per cent of the delegates to the 1990 and 1993 federal conventions held occupations classified as blue collar, trade, or labour, almost 13 per cent of the 1992 universal ballot voters described their jobs as clerical, blue collar, trade, or labour.

Some critics of universal ballots have pointed out that the 'potential exists for one or more regions to dominate the selection of the leader' (Courtney, 1995: 245). This fear of geographic distortion was not borne out by the 1992 experience. The absence of guaranteed equal constituency representation had virtually no impact on the regional distribution of the voters. Those areas of the province where the Conservative Party was weak, notably Edmonton, continued to possess a proportionate say in the party's choice and the regional origins of 1992 voters closely parallel those of 1985 delegates.

Dramatic differences between voters and delegates were apparent, however, with respect to previous involvement in the party. Typically, party or former party office-holders make up a majority of convention delegates. This was certainly the case at the 1985 Alberta convention, where former office-holders constituted almost three-fifths of the delegate total. Three-quarters of these delegates were also members of the federal PC Party, and four-fifths of them had previously worked on a provincial election campaign. Similarly, more than four-fifths of the 1993 federal PC delegates had worked previously for the party and two-thirds of them were veterans of party office.

The universal ballot voters reported a much lower degree of past party involvement. Indeed, a majority of the voters claimed that they had joined the party just to vote for the leader—and almost one in five took out membership on the day of the second ballot. Only about one-fifth (21 per cent) were members of the federal party, less than one-fifth (18 per cent) worked for the party in the previous election campaign, and barely one in 20 (5 per cent) had previously held office in the party.

Unquestionably, the universal ballot electorate differs from that enfranchised at conventions. Those who voted in the 1992 leadership election reflected the general population more accurately with respect to sex, age, and socio-economic status. However, these voters were not long-term Tory partisans and possessed only limited backgrounds in party affairs. The selection of a leader by this new sort of electorate is likely to affect the nature of leadership politics and, since elections are fought by the leaders chosen by this process, these changes are of more than academic interest.

Candidate Support Coalitions

A full understanding of the implications of a new electorate must address the factors which influence leadership voters as they make their selections. Many of the factors discussed above affected to some degree the nature of candidate support coalitions in 1992. That factors such as region and age should affect leadership choice is no surprise. As Krause and LeDuc (1979: 116) argued, 'the division of a party by factors such as East and West, French and English, left and right, old and young is an important part of the fabric of Canadian party politics and cannot be neglected in any analysis of convention behaviour.' Similarly, Johnston (1988: 208) suggested that 'ideological affinity, social group, and geographic identification come readily to mind as criteria that might govern individual's choices.'

Added to these perspectives must be the choices made by the party élite. Previous studies of convention voting indicate that the so-called ex officio delegates often have different preferences and behave differently from other delegates. As Ian Stewart (1988a: 156–7) concluded in his analysis of the 1983 and 1984 federal conventions, 'there was a discernible difference in the voting behaviour of the party establishment and rank and file delegates.'

The Alberta PC universal ballot was marked by voting divisions based on region, socio-economic factors, partisan background, and issue positions. Stark differences on these dimensions between those who supported Klein and those who backed Betkowski are readily apparent.

One of the most obvious differences is regional (see Table 19.2). Betkowski's candidacy was very strong in her hometown of Edmonton, where she topped the polls. Klein was also popular in his hometown of Calgary, but he was also successful in attracting majorities in the northern, central, and southern parts of the province. The Conservative stronghold of southern Alberta was especially supportive of Klein, rewarding him with 79 per cent of their votes. Essentially, Betkowski was able to beat Klein only in the capital region. The Conservative Party, like the province more generally, is marked by the unique political preferences of Edmontonians.

Table 19.2: Geographic Voting Divisions

Region*	Edmonton Area	Calgary Area	North	Central	South	(N)
Betkowski	58%	34%	36%	35%	21%	(345)
Klein	42%	66%	64%	65%	79%	(532)

Community Size*	<1,000	1,000 to 9,999	10,000 to 49,999	50,000 to 499,999	>500,000	(N)
Betkowski	27%	27%	46%	45%	45%	(337)
Klein	73%	73%	54%	55%	55%	(520)

*Relationship is statistically significant at .05 or better.

This was not the only geographic effect. The levels of support for Klein were particularly high in Alberta's small towns and villages. In these areas Klein drew even more support than he had in Calgary, as his share of the vote approached three-quarters. Since the Conservative Party also draws disproportionate electoral support from these rural areas, Klein's support is indicative of his ability to hold the party's core areas of strength.

Research on public opinion in Alberta has revealed a gender gap in support for the Conservative Party, with women less likely to support the Conservatives than men (Archer and Gibbins, 1997). A similar gap could be seen in 1992 (see Table 19.3). Klein's support among men was more than 10 percentage points higher than his support among women. The gender gap was actually stronger on the first ballot, where Betkowski secured plurality support from women and Klein was the preferred choice of men. Like the province at large, the Conservative Party is marked by differences between the genders.[4]

Conservative leadership voters were also split on the basis of socio-economic status. Support for Klein was inversely related to income. That is, the higher the level of family income, the lower the support for Klein. Betkowski did best among Albertans reporting family incomes of more than $75,000. Almost half (49 per cent) of these people supported her. In contrast, her support among those with family incomes below $20,000 dropped to 30 per cent.

Further evidence of a division based on socio-economic status is gleaned from an examination of occupation. Betkowski equalled or surpassed Klein in terms of support from those who claimed higher status occupations such as professionals, health-care providers, and educators. She also had greater support among students. Klein received an overwhelming endorsement from those employed in trades and others paid by the hour. He also drew disproportionate strength from farmers and clerical workers.

The final socio-economic variable, education, reveals the strongest gap in leadership choice. Among those leadership voters with no post-secondary education,

Table 19.3: Socio-Economic Voting Divisions

	Betkowski (%)	Klein (%)	(N)
*Sex**			
Men	34	66	(496)
Women	46	55	(432)
*Family Income**			
Income less than $20,000	30	70	(60)
Income between $20,000 and $34,999	30	70	(114)
Income between $35,000 and $49,999	33	67	(173)
Income between $50,000 and $74,999	39	61	(234)
Income of $75,000 or greater	49	51	(269)
*Occupation**			
Health-care worker	59	41	(59)
Professional	57	43	(44)
Educator	56	44	(66)
Student	50	50	(18)
Administrator	47	53	(51)
Homemaker	46	54	(52)
Business	39	61	(205)
Sales	35	65	(52)
Clerical	28	72	(46)
Farmer/rancher	26	74	(76)
Blue collar	13	87	(60)
Other occupation	39	61	(89)
*Education Level**			
Elementary school education	42	58	(26)
Some high school	14	86	(80)
High school graduates	25	75	(158)
Some post-secondary	35	65	(298)
University degree	55	45	(189)
Post-graduate education	63	37	(123)

*Relationship is statistically significant at .05 or better.

Klein secured huge majorities and his support from those with some post-secondary education equalled his overall levels of support. However, university graduates were much less willing to support Klein; 55 per cent of those with university degrees voted for Betkowski, and almost two-thirds (63 per cent) of those with post-graduate education backed her candidacy.

Our examination of socio-economic variables reveals an unambiguous portrait of the candidates' support patterns. The higher the income, occupational status, or education, the greater the likelihood of a vote for Betkowski. This suggests that socio-economic divisions may play a more important role with universal ballots. Divisions based on socio-economic status were apparent at some leadership conventions (see Stewart,1988b), but the relatively small proportion of delegates with lower-status jobs, low salaries, and without university degrees limited its importance. The universal ballot, with its lower costs and limited barriers to participation, seems likely to produce more significant divisions on this dimension. Certainly if those with university degrees, students, and professionals had formed the same proportion of the electorate in the universal ballot that they do at federal conventions, Betkowski's chances for victory would have been substantially enhanced. Klein's campaign, which portrayed him as an ordinary Albertan and Betkowski as part of the Tory 'establishment', undoubtedly contributed to these voting cleavages. But this strategy cannot be separated from the universal ballot since it might have proved less successful in attracting the votes of the long-time and well-educated Tories who traditionally were convention delegates.

The relatively small proportion of students voting reveals an interesting difference from conventions. In the 1992 universal ballot, age was not significantly associated with voting—as those under 25 were as likely as those over 65 to vote for Klein. Students, however, were equally divided between Klein and Betkowski. The age divisions that have been significant in a number of federal conventions are usually treated as intergenerational differences of opinion. However, the evidence from the Alberta universal ballot suggests the possibility that the differences observed were based on the fact that the vast majority of young delegates were students. At the very least, the divergent behaviour of the young voters in 1992 who were not students suggests that discussions of generational differences should determine whether the younger voters are students or not.

The support coalitions of the two candidates could also be distinguished on the basis of attitude (see Table 19.4). While scales attempting to measure views towards welfare, continentalism, and individual responsibility revealed no significant differences between those who backed Klein and those who preferred Betkowski, favourable attitudes towards government in general and on issues of special concern to women were associated to some degree with support for the leaders (see Appendix 1 for a description of scale construction). That is, the more favourable a voter was towards a positive role for government or the more supportive of 'feminist' positions, the more likely one was to cast a ballot for Betkowski.

Nonetheless, the socio-demographic variables were more useful in distinguishing support for the two candidates than for discerning attitudes on these issues. Table 19.5 uses Cramer's V[5] to report the measure of association with voting of various socio-demographic and attitudinal variables. Positive attitudes towards government or support for a feminist agenda were less strongly associated with voting than almost all of the socio-demographic variables discussed earlier.

One set of opinions, however, was more strongly associated with voting than any of the socio-demographic variables: populism. This scale was composed of variables that attempted to determine whether people thought there was too much

Table 19.4: Mean Scores of Candidates' Supporters on Attitudinal Scales

	Betkowski Voters	Klein Voters	Range
Individualism	1.5	1.5	0–4
Continentalism	1.2	1.3	0–3
Pro-welfare	.86	.82	0–3
Pro-government*	1.0	.88	0–3
Concern for women's issues*	1.2	1.0	0–2
Populism*	2.1	3.0	0–4
(N)	(348)	(534)	

*Difference of means is statistically significant at .05 or better. Higher scores indicate greater support for each scale's label.

Table 19.5: Strength of Association between Set of Variables and Leadership Vote

Variable	Cramer's V
Region	.24
Community size	.17
Sex	.12
Income	.16
Occupation	.25
Education	.31
Age	—
Individualism	—
Continentalism	—
Pro-welfare	—
Pro-government	.09
Issues of special concern to women	.12
Populism	.36
Held party office	—
Worked for party in '89 election	—
Joined just to vote	.09
When joined the party	.25
Late joiner	.19
Vote in 1989 election	.12
Intended federal vote	.11

Note: Cramer's V reported only when differences are statistically significant at .05.

red tape, there should be referendums for all constitutional amendments, problems could be solved if they were brought back to the grassroots, and the thinking of ordinary people was to be trusted over that of experts. In general, the Alberta PC voters were a relatively populist lot, with 88 per cent believing there was too much red tape, 67 per cent thinking the grassroots could solve problems, 61 per cent trusting ordinary people over experts, and 48 per cent desiring a referendum for each constitutional amendment. The strength of populist sentiment is not overly surprising since, as Carty and Blake (1999: 216) note, 'Alberta has long been the heartland of populist politics in Canada.'

The populist scale summed opinions from these issues so that someone who responded in a populist fashion to each variable would be scored '4' and someone with no populist responses scored a '0'. The results are striking. Betkowski was supported by almost four-fifths of those who scored '0' while Klein was supported by almost four-fifths of those who scored '4'. Fortunately for Klein, three-fifths of the voters gave at least three populist responses and populist attitudes played an important role in the vote for the Conservative leader. Previous studies of populism indicate that these attitudes are related to the socio-economic variables discussed earlier. That is, people who are better educated or have higher-status occupations are generally less populist. Since the Conservative universal ballot enfranchised an electorate with fewer educational attainments and fewer high-status occupations, populism was likely to be more influential to the outcome. This may have helped the Conservatives choose a leader who could better connect with the province's populist impulses.

The final set of variables analysed in this examination of leadership voting focuses on party background. As noted earlier, conventions were the almost exclusive purview of party veterans. For instance, two-thirds of the delegates to the 1993 PC federal convention had previously held a position on a riding executive, as had 58 per cent of the 1990 federal Liberal delegates (Courtney, 1995: 338). We saw earlier that this kind of role was experienced by barely 5 per cent of the universal ballot participants. This raises questions as to the importance of these factors in candidate support. Did voters who previously held party office or who worked for the party in an earlier election differ in their choice of candidate from those without such experience?

The short answer to this question is no (see Table 19.6). There were no significant differences in the voting choices made by those with or without these characteristics. This does not mean, however, that the relatively open rules used by the Conservatives did not affect candidate choice.

It appears that Betkowski was the disproportionate choice of party 'tourists'.[6] She was supported by 44 per cent of those who joined the party just to vote in the leadership election but by only 34 per cent of those who claimed a deeper commitment. Her support from 'tourists' becomes more obvious when we examine the respondents' reported voting behaviour in the 1989 Alberta election. Betkowski received majority support from former Liberal and New Democratic voters and disproportionate support from those who had not voted, while Klein was the clear choice of past Conservative voters. Contrary to the fears of many critics of universal ballots, the choice of the party leader was not determined by an influx of voters who supported other parties—even the vast majority of those who voted for Betkowski were past Tory voters. However, voters who did not support the Conservative Party in 1989 accounted for 19 per cent of the electorate.

Table 19.6: Vote by Party Involvement

	Betkowski (%)	Klein (%)	(N)
Previously held PC Party Office			
Yes	33	67	(42)
No	40	60	(840)
Party Member at Time of First Ballot*			
Yes	44	56	(705)
No	21	79	(173)
Joined PC Party in 1992 Only to Vote*			
Yes	44	57	(487)
No	34	66	(390)
Timing of Initial PC Party Membership*			
Joined on day of 2nd ballot	19	81	(108)
Joined between 1st and 2nd ballots	23	77	(65)
Joined on day of 1st ballot	53	47	(76)
Joined during leadership campaign	56	44	(195)
Joined earlier in 1992	40	60	(45)
Joined 1985–1991	36	64	(135)
Joined 1971–1984	37	63	(175)
Joined before 1971	46	54	(79)
Worked for Party in 1989 Election			
Yes	36	64	(149)
No	40	60	(729)
1989 Provincial Voting Behaviour*			
Voted PC in 1989	37	63	(687)
Voted Liberal in 1989	54	46	(68)
Voted NDP in 1989	54	46	(37)
Voted for other party in 1989	31	69	(16)
Did not vote in 1989	45	55	(64)

*Relationship is statistically significant at .05 or better.

Their votes were not sufficient to lead her to victory and the Conservative Party was in no danger of 'capture'.[7]

Further insight into the nature of the Conservative leadership vote is revealed by an examination of when voters first joined the party. The voters can be sorted into three categories: those whose first Tory membership occurred before the vote was announced, those who joined during the first stage of the campaign or on the day of the first ballot, and those who joined after the first ballot. The differences in voting choice are interesting.

Klein was the clear choice of veteran Conservatives. He received the support of 62 per cent of those whose first Tory membership dated before the commencement of the 1992 election. Betkowski, however, clearly won the first stage of the election, with support from 53 per cent of those who joined after the announcement or on the day of the first ballot. If, as in every other universal ballot in Canada, second-ballot voting had been restricted to these voters, she would have had a much stronger showing on the final ballot. However, unlike the previous universal ballots, the voters list remained open throughout the entire process. People could purchase memberships in the week between the ballots (7 per cent of the second-ballot voters did so) or on the day of the second ballot (another 12 per cent of second-ballot voters.) These latecomers were relatively hostile to Betkowski, as almost four-fifths of them supported Klein.

The relative hostility motivating second-ballot voters can be seen in answers to an open-ended question asking voters for the single most important factor influencing their vote. Only 0.2 per cent of the voters offered the response of 'anybody but' as an explanation for their first-ballot vote.[8] However, this response was given by 13 per cent for their second-ballot choice, and most of these people voted for Klein.

Conclusion

This analysis of the 1992 Alberta leadership election reveals that an open universal ballot enfranchises an electorate very different from that enfranchised at leadership conventions. The universal ballot allowed a much higher proportion of women, the elderly, and those with less education to participate. It also ensured that the final choice was made by those without an extensive background of service to the Conservative Party. Although some may lament the loss of a major voice for youth within the party, it is difficult to condemn a process that produces an electorate more reflective of its society. It is easier to be critical if one focuses on the diminished party ties possessed by these voters. Debates on these issues must consider whether the demographic advances outweigh the loss of political experience. They must also address the fact that in 1992 former party office-holders and workers voted no differently from those without such experience.

The examination of candidate support coalitions indicates that the universal ballot resembles conventions in that the cleavages dividing leadership voters mirror those dividing citizens in elections. The choice of Klein over Betkowski reflected divisions based on region, gender, and socio-economic status, divisions that influence the wider world of Alberta politics as well (see Archer and Gibbins, 1997). These differences are of particular interest given that in April 1998, Betkowski (now known as Nancy MacBeth) became the leader of the Alberta Liberal Party. The next election will provide a rematch of the Klein-Betkowski battle of 1992.

The impact of populist attitudes on the 1992 results suggest that Klein is well positioned to defeat Betkowski again. Populism is one of the major elements in Alberta's political culture and Klein's support from voters with more populist attitudes played a major role in both his 1992 leadership victory and his 1993 triumph in a general election (Tupper, 1996).

The 1992 universal ballot reveals that parties using such a leadership mechanism risk some vulnerability to 'tourism'. Almost one-fifth of the electorate had not voted for the Conservative Party in the 1989 provincial election and these voters possessed candidate preferences that diverged from those of traditional PC voters. Nonetheless, this group was not sizeable enough to affect the final outcome. As in the 1998 federal PC universal ballot, 'tourists' affected the race but could not change the outcome. The involvement of 'tourists' in a party's most important decision will undoubtedly concern many observers. It should be noted that we have little data on the degree to which 'tourists' participated in delegate selection meetings for conventions. Since many candidates attempted to influence the outcome of these selection meetings it would be naïve to assume they did not avail themselves of 'tourist' resources.

Holding the decisive vote a week after the first vote changed the dynamics of the election considerably. As was the case in the 1998 federal PC election, many of those who voted on the first ballot did not return to the polls for the second. If the Alberta Tories had used the rules of their federal cousins, the number of people voting on the second ballot might have declined. However, the first-ballot voters who sat out the second were instead replaced by a massive influx of new voters. Many of these new voters actually purchased their memberships after the first ballot was completed and many of them were motivated by an antipathy to one of the finalists. The behaviour of these latecomers ensured an overwhelming majority for Klein.

The profile of the 1992 voters and the role of 'tourists' and latecomers confirm the importance of the rules governing leadership elections. Election rules affect the composition of the electorate and thus the election outcome. We have seen how gender and socio-economic status were associated with voting in 1992. The universal ballot clearly enfranchised a distinctive electorate. Moreover, deciding when to close the membership list can influence the outcome. Citizens whose attention is not engaged until voting day can be prevented from voting by early cut-off dates for registration. As well, decisions to hold ballots separated by a period of days and to allow people to join after the first ballot practically ensure that the second-ballot electorate will differ from that of the first. And with a different electorate, a different outcome is by no means impossible. Reflective consideration of these issues is crucial for those interested in the way democracy manifests itself in Canada.

Appendix: Attitudinal Scales

The attitudinal scales were constructed from responses to the following statements. The responses noted were scored as 1, all other responses were scored as 0, and all of the responses were then summed to produce the scale.

Individualism

1. The government ought to make sure that everyone has a decent standard of living. (Agree)
2. Let's face it, most unemployed people could find a job if they really wanted to. (Agree)

3. Why should the government spend my tax money on sick people; my family always put something aside for a rainy day. (Agree)
4. After a person has worked until 65, it is proper for the community to support him or her. (Disagree).

Continentalism

1. We must ensure an independent Canada even if that were to mean a lower standard of living for Canadians. (Disagree)
2. The Canada/US Free Trade Agreement has been good for Alberta. (Agree)
3. Canada's independence is threatened by the large scale ownership in key sectors of the economy. (Disagree)

Issues of Special Concern to Women

1. Abortion is a matter that should be decided solely between a woman and her doctor. (Agree)
2. Governments should make a strong effort to improve the social and economic position of women. (Selected this item over) Women should help themselves and should not expect governments to make special efforts on their behalf.

Pro-Government

1. A lot of welfare and social security programs we have now are unnecessary. (Disagree)
2. Without government regulations, some people just take advantage of the rest of us. (Selected this item over) Government regulation stifles personal initiative.
3. If I do my best, it is only right that the government should help me when I get some bad breaks. (Selected this item over) Each individual should accept the consequences of his/her own actions.

Pro-Welfare

1. A lot of welfare and social security programs we have now are unnecessary. (Disagree)
2. The size of government in Alberta should be reduced even if this means a lower level of public services. (Disagree)
3. Social programs should remain universal. (Agree)

Populism

1. In the long run, I'll put my trust in the simple down-to-earth thinking of ordinary people rather than the theories of experts and intellectuals. (Agree)
2. We would probably solve most of our big national problems if government could actually be brought back to the people at the grassroots. (Agree)
3. What we need is a government that gets the job done without all this red tape. (Agree).
4. There should be a referendum on all amendments to the constitution. (Agree)

Notes

1. The NDP in 1995 used a series of regional mail-in, all-member votes to determine the eligibility of candidates to contest the leadership at the convention. To be on the ballot a candidate had to win one of the regional votes or attract at least 15 per cent of the votes cast by all members.

2. The party's rules also required the inclusion of the third-place candidate's name on the second ballot. This candidate did not campaign and, indeed, formally endorsed Betkowski.
3. Data on the 1985 PC delegates were derived from a delegate survey conducted by Margaret Hunziker. Data on the 1993 federal PC delegates (and the 1990 federal Liberal delegates) were derived from survey results presented in Courtney (1995).
4. Media coverage of the election suggested two explanations for this gap. One was that women from outside the party were joining in order to elect Alberta's first woman Premier (*Edmonton Journal*, 1 Dec. 1992, A7). The other explanation is based on oblique hints from some Klein supporters that Betkowski's sex would effect her ability to govern. As one MLA put it, 'You know women, they get moody' (*Edmonton Journal*, 4 Dec. 1992, A7). Public expressions of such sentiments by a prominent Klein supporter may have discouraged some women from voting for Klein.
5. Cramer's V is a measure of association used when at least one of the variables is coded at the nominal level. Its range is from 0 to 1 with higher numbers indicating a stronger association between the variables.
6. This phrase was used by Joe Clark in the 1998 federal PC universal ballot to describe supporters of David Orchard. Clark believed that these people (and Orchard himself) had not previously supported the party, possessed no long-term interest in its future, and hence, were simply 'visiting'.
7. Some 'tourists' preferred Klein. Seven per cent of the 1992 voters reported voting for an unnamed other party in the 1989 provincial election and Klein was supported by 69 per cent of these voters.
8. The term 'anybody but' is used to describe voting motivations focused on ensuring that a particular candidate is unsuccessful. Voters driven by this motive wish to prevent someone from winning and are willing to support the candidate best placed to assure such an outcome.

References

Archer, Keith, and Roger Gibbins. 1997. 'What Do Albertans Think?', in Christopher J. Bruce et al., eds, *A Government Reinvented*. Toronto: Oxford University Press.

Brodie, Janine. 1988. 'The Gender Factor and National Leadership in Canada', in Perlin (1988).

Carty, R.K., and Donald E. Blake. 1999. 'The Adoption of Membership Votes for Choosing Party Leaders', *Party Politics* 5, 2: 211–24.

Courtney, John C. 1973. *The Selection of National Party Leaders*. Toronto: Macmillan.

———. 1995. *Do Conventions Matter*. Montreal and Kingston: McGill-Queen's University Press.

Hunziker, Margaret. 1986. 'Leadership Selection: The 1985 Alberta Progressive Conservative Leadership Convention', MA thesis, University of Calgary.

Johnston, Richard. 1988. 'The Final Choice', in Perlin (1988).

Krause, Robert, and Lawrence LeDuc. 1979. 'Voting Behaviour and Electoral Strategies in the Progressive Conservative Leadership Convention of 1976', *Canadian Journal of Political Science* 12, 1: 97–135.

Levesque, Terrence J. 1983. 'On the Outcome of the 1983 Conservative Leadership Convention: How They Shot Themselves in the Other Foot', *Canadian Journal of Political Science* 16, 4: 779–84.

MacIvor, Heather. 1994. 'The Leadership Convention: An Institution under Stress', in Maureen Mancuso, Richard G. Price, and Ronald Wagenberg, eds, *Leaders and Leadership in Canada*. Toronto: Oxford University Press.

Perlin, George, ed. 1988. *Party Democracy in Canada*. Scarborough, Ont.: Prentice-Hall.

———. 1991a. 'Attitudes of Liberal Convention Delegates Toward Proposals for Reform of the Process of Leadership Selection', in Herman Bakvis, ed., *Canadian Political Parties: Leaders, Candidates and Organization*. Toronto: Dundurn Press.

———. 1991b. 'Leadership Selection in the PC and Liberal Parties: Assessing the Need for Reform', in Hugh Thorburn, ed., *Party Politics in Canada*, 6th edn. Scarborough, Ont.: Prentice-Hall.

———, Allan Sutherland, and Marc Desjardins. 1988. 'The Impact of Age Cleavage on Convention Politics', in Perlin (1988).

Simpson, Jeffrey. 1999. 'All Hail the Supreme Prime Minister', *Globe and Mail*, 8 May, D10.

Smiley, Donald V. 1968. 'The National Party Leadership Convention in Canada: A Preliminary Analysis', *Canadian Journal of Political Science* 1, 4: 373–97.

Stewart, David K. 1997. The Changing Leadership Electorate', *Canadian Journal of Political Science* 30, 1: 107–28.

Stewart, Ian. 1988a. 'The Brass Versus the Grass: Party Insiders and Outsiders at Canadian Leadership Conventions', in Perlin (1988).

———. 1988b. 'Class Politics at Canadian Leadership Conventions', in Perlin (1988).

Tupper, Allan. 1996. 'Debt, Populism and Cutbacks: Alberta Politics in the 1990s', in Hugh Thorburn, ed., *Party Politics in Canada*, 7th edn. Scarborough, Ont.: Prentice-Hall.

Chapter 20

Political Careers in Canada

DAVID C. DOCHERTY

Political behaviour is more than simply the study of activities, attitudes, and beliefs of political participants. It is also concerned with understanding both the micro- and macro-demographic characteristics of citizens and voters to determine if and how political activities and decisions are related not just to what people think, but also to who people are. Thus, the study of the careers of politicians should be concerned with two things. First, the demographics of political careers. This means addressing several questions. What do political careers look like? Who is most likely to be in cabinet? And what regional, gender, and other such variations do we find in political careers in Canada?

The second area of concern should be the relationship between the portrait of political careers and the decisions politicians make. The questions here derive from the results of the demographic profile. How do differences in the first set of questions (if in fact there are differences) influence the type of legislature that these men and women serve in? One method of understanding a legislature is to understand the people who sit inside the building. This has important representational ramifications. For example, a legislature that holds and attracts only successful business*men*, is likely to produce laws that might not be in the best interests of women and non-business people (or unsuccessful business*men*, for that matter).

Legislatures are really a product of people and rules. Certain institutional rules, legislative salaries, and opportunities for promotion inside the legislative arena, for example, are likely to attract different types of people to office (see Squire, 1988). In the parlance of legislative scholars, the combination of these rules is known as the opportunity structure of office (Schlesinger, 1966). The rules and people of an elected assembly are all part of the political puzzle. To understand why people act in certain ways and believe in certain things, we must understand the norms of their organization (in our case the Canadian House of Commons) and how these impact on a legislator's ability to perform his or her desired tasks. This study of

Parliament reveals that it is now more representative of Canadian society than it was 25 years ago in terms of demographic characteristics. However, many of the amateur qualities that characterized House of Commons members in the late sixties and early seventies can still be found today. The result, it is argued, is a positive reinforcement of the rules and roles of members of Parliament.

The Study of Political Careers in Canada

Parliament is one of the least studied branches of Canadian government and politics. Perhaps taking their signal from Pierre Trudeau's comment that 15 minutes from Parliament Hill, MPs are nobodies, academics have not paid great attention to federal legislators. Studies of Parliament have followed the traditional evolution of the discipline. Early studies, which focused on questions of process and procedure (see Ward, 1950; Dawson, 1947), were eventually replaced with studies of people and Parliamentary behaviour (Atkinson and Thomas, 1993).

One of the defining characteristics of these behavioural studies was their empirical bent. In the case of the Canadian Parliament the concern centred on influence of members, such as Allan Kornberg's classic study (1967) of legislative behaviour in the 25th Parliament of Canada. Other similar works attempted to measure if and how some backbench members of Parliament held more influence than others (Kornberg and Mishler, 1976). Robert Jackson and Michael Atkinson's study (1980) of the Canadian Parliamentary system was not as concerned with measures and models, but did examine the ties between the member's ideological dispositions and his or her political actions inside the legislative environment. Other studies of Parliament looked at the electability of its members, suggesting that both getting elected and remaining in office in Canada were difficult tasks (Lovink, 1973; Irvine, 1982). The primary culprits were a lack of safe electoral seats and electoral and Parliamentary systems that both formally and informally emphasized leader and party attributes and minimized the role of most members of Parliament. Barrie and Gibbins (1989) found that parliamentary careers in Canada were rather static. Few members take a natural career path from local to provincial to federal office.

The late 1970s and early 1980s saw a return to more institutionally based treatments of Parliament. John Stewart (1977) concentrated almost entirely on questions of procedure and House organization. In the most comprehensive book on Parliament since Norman Ward's treatment, C.E.S. Franks (1987) took an traditional approach to his discussion. He argued that the strong party discipline stifled some independence of members but did produce national policies that might not have been possible with a weaker party system. Franks also warned against wholesale reform of an institution without fully thinking through the ramifications of such reform.

The lack of study of Parliament is unfortunate. Studying careers sheds light both on questions of legislative behaviour and on the types of policy legislators produce. In addition, knowing who are attracted to certain offices and who are turned off by the same offices tells us something about the office itself (Squire, 1988). We may disagree with the oft-heard comment that there are not enough talented men and women in the Canadian House of Commons. But there is something to be taken seriously from this concern. Perhaps it is not the men and women running for office who are at fault, but the office itself. None of us apply for jobs we do not want and Parliament is no different. If we understand who runs for the Commons and why, it may help us understand what it looks like and the type of tasks it is best suited to performing.

We now turn our attention to political careers in the 1980s and 1990s. After examining the characteristics of the men and women who served during this period the chapter discusses some of the implications of the career structure in the House of Commons. Specifically, despite the dramatic personnel changes that occur with each election, the profile of the House of Commons remains remarkably resistant to change. The individuals may be different, but from a distance the pictures look remarkably similar. Such a profile helps to maintain power in the hands of party leaders and front-bench parliamentarians. In many ways, this simply serves to reinforce high levels of amateurism and an unattractive career path for would-be federal politicians.

Political Careers in the 1980s and 1990s

If one thing defines elections in Canada it is high turnover. Going into every election, members of Parliament face a job evaluation where anywhere from 30,000 to 100,000 people have a say in their work performance. Unfortunately for most members, this same job evaluation process includes an evaluation of their leader and party. In fact, as numerous election studies have demonstrated (e.g., Clarke et al., 1979, 1984, 1991, 1996), members are usually ranked last on the list of leader, party, and local candidate in importance for the voting decisions of Canadians.

The result in Canada is a surprisingly high level of defeats. Coupled with normal retirement (members deciding not to run for re-election) this adds up to substantial turnover of legislators at each election. In typical US congressional elections, re-election rates are over 90 per cent (Cooper and West, 1981; Hibbing, 1991). In Canada, they rarely exceed 60 per cent. Even when majority governments are re-elected, as were Brian Mulroney's Conservatives in 1988 and Jean Chrétien's Liberals in 1997, the turnover rate is over 40 per cent.

Taken at face value, a steady turnover rate might not be a bad thing. After all, no one can accuse the Canadian House of Commons of becoming stale. Such a regular influx of 'new blood' keeps veteran members on their toes and invigorates the organization of the legislature. As an added bonus, we can justifiably brag when we compare ourselves to the United States. Our closest neighbour faces great difficulty in turfing out incumbent members of Congress. In fact, many in the US have begun to look at term limits as a solution to such high re-election rates. Although the notion of making it illegal to serve for over a certain time in office would probably not stand up to constitutional scrutiny, this has not stopped over 22 states from adopting term limits at the subnational level (Carey, 1998: 12; Benjamin and Malbin, 1992). It is something Canadians never have to contemplate. If we do not like a member of Parliament, we simply vote against that person at election time. It is something we do quite regularly.

But a closer look at defeat rates suggests that we should not be so smug, at least not about the question of new blood versus institutional stability. It is all well and good to look at large turnover rates as a sign of an active electorate. But the question we should ask ourselves is, who loses elections? The answer, unfortunately, is those with the least power, namely, opposition and government private members (or backbenchers, as they are often called). While it is true that backbenchers make up a disproportionate cohort of members (only 10–13 per cent of all MPs are in cabinet at any one time), they are still more likely to be defeated than are individuals who have served in some form of leadership position.

Table 20.1 examines the defeat rates of private members versus those who have served in some form of leadership position.[1] It compares the percentage of each cohort (leader versus private member) defeated in the previous four elections. The table only includes incumbents who are seeking re-election, not those retiring from elected life. Private members, both as a group and per capita, are much more electorally vulnerable than their colleagues who have had some experience in a front-bench or caucus leadership position. In 1984, for example, over one-third of all private members who had served in the last Trudeau Parliament were defeated at the polls, compared to just over one-fifth of those who had leadership experience. In 1993, nearly one-half of all private members in the final Mulroney Parliament lost in the vote that saw Jean Chrétien come to power, compared to a mere 37 per cent of former leaders. When governments fall, those who were in cabinet setting policy and legislation are unlikely to pay the ultimate penalty. Rather, sanctions are more likely to hit those who had the least power to influence policy decisions— men and women on the backbenches, removed from the executive and other leadership posts (see Docherty and White, 1999).

Not surprisingly, the 1988 and 1997 elections, re-elections for the Conservatives and Liberals respectively, saw lower overall defeat rates. But these elections were particularly kind to those in leadership (or who had previously served in leadership) positions. Less than 10 per cent of these individuals lost in these elections. So even when governments are dealt reduced majorities, those furthest removed from power are most vulnerable to electoral defeat. This is important, for beyond the partisan makeup of legislatures, perhaps the largest distinction is between those in front-bench positions and those on the backbenches.[2]

Table 20.1: Defeat Rates of Private Members vs MPs with Leadership Experience

Election Year	Private Members	Front-Bench Leaders
1984	36.1% (75)	22.2% (16)
1988	28.9% (59)	8.1% (6)
1993	47.1% (104)	37.0% (27)
1997	13.3% (32)	7.5% (4)

Note: The percentages represent the percentage of each cohort who were defeated; figures in parentheses are the total number who were defeated.

Sources: Canadian Parliamentary Guides and Election Canada Official Results.

What this means is that members who have had the opportunity to serve in some form of leadership position are more likely to retire from politics voluntarily than to lose at election time. Not only do members of cabinet and other 'leaders' have increased electoral security, but, by definition, they also have a greater say in when and how they leave political life. In this sense at least, these 'leading' members of Parliament experience a much more enjoyable political career. Not only do they have the privilege of influencing public policy more so than their private member colleagues, but they also have the ability to decide when to vacate their careers.

Table 20.2 lists other telling differences between private members and those with leadership experience. The top half of the table compares all leaders with all private members. The variations between these groups are quite revealing. First, members who eventually wind up in a position of leadership tend to enter Parliament at an earlier age. The four-year difference between these two groups represents almost the life of one Parliament. This could mean that these leaders are more ambitious and inclined to view Parliament as a potential career, as opposed to non-leaders who wait until a slightly later stage of life to take the political plunge.[3] In addition, and supporting this assertion, these leaders also serve for longer periods of time in office, on average over five years longer.

The bottom half of Table 20.2 looks at a subset of the first half—those members who retired by choice. This group is used to paint a more accurate picture of the career desires or satisfaction in these two groups. That is, many individuals in the first group, including private members and leaders, left politics via defeat. We have no accurate way of knowing just how long they would have wanted their careers to last if it were up to them. By examining only those individuals who voluntarily left office we have a more reliable picture of what careers would look like if members alone were to determine their length.

Once again, members who eventually work their way into a leadership post begin their national careers at an earlier age. But the more telling difference is in career length. It is apparent from the latter half of the table that given a chance, both private members and front-bench leaders would prefer a slightly longer political

Table 20.2: Differences in Careers between Private Members and 'Leaders',
1984–1997

	Private Members	Front-Bench Leaders
All MPs, 1984–97		
Age entering Parliament	43.6 (850)	39.9 (269)
Years served in Parliament	7.4 (872)	12.6 (271)
Voluntary Retirees Only		
Age entering Parliament	45.5 (130)	42.2 (79)
Years served in Parliament	10.6 (136)	15.4 (80)

Note: Figures in parentheses are the total number in the cohort.
Source: Canadian Parliamentary Guides.

career. For front-bench leaders, this career would be just over 15 years. Perhaps not surprisingly, 15 years is the point at which members of Parliament are eligible for their maximum pension. Given that pension entitlements are based on the average of an MP's best three years of salary, and that cabinet ministers and other leaders are entitled to 'top-up' salaries, the timing of retirements for this cohort makes economic sense. Why run for re-election if you are already hitting the best pension eligibility possible?

While the distinction between front and back bench is significant, it is not the only one that we can examine to understand better the role of Parliament in determining what type of member is attracted to serve in national office. The issue of gender representation in political life is nowhere more apparent than in the House of Commons. Women enter Parliament at an average age of just over 45 while their male counterparts enter three years earlier (Table 20.3). The age differences, while statistically significant, are not far enough apart to draw any strong conclusions. Among all MPs, women also have much shorter careers. The three-year difference is slightly less than one full term in office. In other words, males serve, on average, two terms in office while women serve one and a half.

What is perhaps more interesting is the subset of MPs who become voluntary retirees. Once again, males serve longer, in this case by over five years. But the seven and a half years served by females suggests that shorter female careers are not simply the result of electoral defeat. Nor is it a matter of age. Among voluntary vacators, the average ages of both males and females was just over 57.

This leaves three possible choices. First, it may be that most members of Parliament decide to leave when they are in their mid- to late fifties. The real determining factor in stepping down from office is timing. Most members who retire do so at a time when they can move into a new career, or step back into their old one, and work for 8–10 years before retiring altogether. The fact that members who retire do not begin to receive pension benefits until they are 55 lends some credibility to this

Table 20.3: Differences in Careers between Men and Women, 1984–1997

	Male MPs	Female MPs
All MPs, 1984–97		
Age entering Parliament	42.4	45.3
Years served in Parliament	9.0	6.0
Total number of MPs	1,012	135
Voluntary Retirees Only		
Age entering Parliament	43.9	49.1
Years served in Parliament	12.8	7.4
Total number of MPs	199	21

Note: All calculations are based on Parliaments. Therefore, the high totals represent the double counting of some members.

Source: Canadian Parliamentary Guides.

hypothesis. However, the starting age of 55 is a relatively recent part of pension reform (Fleming and Glenn, 1997). This change does not affect members of the 32nd through 34th Parliaments (1980 through to 1993), and therefore was probably not a large factor in the minds of many of the retirees reported here.

Alternatively, it could be evidence of a real gender difference; that is, it may be that females are less inclined to see Parliament as a place they wish to stay for 15 years or more. After two terms in office, many women decide to pursue different career paths, while men are more likely to stick out their careers for at least one more term. The reason for this could be an unwelcoming environment inside the legislative world or the greater problems women face in re-entering previous careers after a long absence.

Finally, there could be gender differences in the opportunity structure of office. Perhaps women are less likely to be in positions of influence and authority within the Parliamentary world and therefore more likely to exit office early. A quick analysis, however, suggests that, on average, women are just as likely as men to be promoted. Between 1980 and 1997, 21 per cent of all male MPs served either in cabinet or as a party leader. During that same time, 21.6 per cent of all women served in a similar capacity. While women are certainly under-represented at the highest levels of political life, the chances of those women who do make it to Ottawa are no less than those of men. Unfortunately, therefore, the data above do not allow us to understand fully why women leave by choice after a briefer career in Parliament.

Shorter stays in Parliament by women do mean one thing. Among retirees, women are far less likely to be classified as political careerists, at least in the Parliamentary sense. They are not amateurs, having successfully survived their first term in office and returned for a second run. In leaving prior to their third term, however, they are leaving after becoming effective legislators and debaters. Franks (1987) and others have argued with some conviction that it takes a full term to become well acquainted and familiar with Parliamentary norms and both its written and unwritten rules (Lovink, 1973). After a few terms in office members become wily lawmakers, knowing when and how best to obtain all kinds of 'goodies', from national press coverage to federal funding for local projects. Knowing who the career politicians are and who the amateurs (or rookies) are is also a telling indicator of who has more power and influence within the Parliamentary arena and about what type of politician the Canadian House of Commons attracts. Many women stay in Parliament long enough to be very capable legislators. They do not stick around to take as much advantage of their knowledge as many male lawmakers. For Parliament, this may help reinforce gender imbalance.

Classifying politicians by experience is a useful measure beyond questions of gender. Following on recent work, this study measures career status using a threefold classification. Members in their first term are classified as rookies, those serving two and three terms (more accurately, 5–12 years) are identified as seasoned, and those who stay beyond 12 years of service are considered to be careerists (Docherty, 1997; Docherty and Oakes, 1997). Using this measure we can compare the composition of Parliaments.

Broken down in this fashion, the data in Table 20.4 provide insights into the composition of the House. First, and not unexpectedly, when governments change there is an associated substantial increase in the number of rookies. When Brian Mulroney and the Progressive Conservatives won their first majority government in 1984, they brought with them a whole new group of rookie MPs. Just about half of the House was made up of rookie members feeling their way around their new work environment. Similarly, when Jean Chretién became Prime Minister in 1993, there was a huge influx of rookie members.

There are much smaller cohorts of rookies when governments are re-elected. The 5 per cent of rookies that arrived with the 34th Parliament are primarily opposition MPs that caused Mulroney to have a decreased majority government. The re-election of a large number of rookie Tories in 1988 helped boost the size of the Seasoned cohort in the 34th Parliament.

But if changes of government signal an increasing rookie influx, why did the Trudeau victory in 1980 only bring with it a less than significant number (20 per cent) of rookies? The answer to this riddle lies in the short duration of the Joe Clark government. Many Liberals, first elected in the 1974 majority government of Pierre Trudeau, lost their seats in the 1979 vote. When Joe Clark went to the polls just eight months later, some of these defeated MPs returned from their sabbatical to become seasoned members. This also helps to explain the significant percentage of seasoned members in the 32nd Parliament.

Perhaps the most startling figure in Table 20.4 is the minimal number of career members in the 35th Parliament of Canada. Fewer than one in 10 members entering the House of Commons after the 1993 election had served more than 12 years in federal elected office. The amount of institutional memory of the Commons was at its lowest point in decades. In order to be a careerist in 1993 an MP's first election would have had to have been in 1980 or earlier. Further, the MP could not have suffered electoral defeat in four successive elections. It is not surprising that there were few of these individuals around for the Chrétien era of governance in Canada. Those who were sat through four interesting Parliaments, with five different Prime Ministers, and voted on a myriad of important national issues, including the repatriation of the Canadian constitution, the Meech Lake Accord, free trade

Table 20.4: Career Stages in Five Parliaments

	32nd Parl. 1980–4	33rd Parl. 1984–8	34th Parl. 1988–93	35th Parl. 1993–7
Rookies	19.7 %	49.6 %	5.0 %	68.6 %
Seasoned	58.8 %	29.5 %	68.2 %	21.6 %
Careerists	21.5 %	27.8 %	24.8 %	9.8 %
Number	279	282	295	295

with the United States, the North American Free Trade Agreement, gun control (twice), and abortion rights (several times).

An important measure of institutional renewal is the question of who is rewarded by an institution. Earlier we examined the age of entry and political success of private members versus those in leadership positions. In a similar vein, it is worthwhile exploring who is likely to find success climbing the career ladder within the legislative environment. In the United States, for example, important congressional positions were historically decided on the basis of seniority. For most of the twentieth century, careerists were the most important legislators. When reforms of Congress changed the seniority system, the makeup of Congress changed also (Hibbing, 1991). Suddenly members of Congress with less than 10 years of service were becoming influential players. This changed the profile of key legislative personnel.

Of course, the seniority system, as a formal or even informal method of promotion, is not a readily obvious feature of the Canadian parliamentary career ladder. Members of Parliament are appointed to cabinet (the highest rung on the ladder short of Prime Minister) based on various factors. The positive causes of promotion include wisdom, experience, and expertise (Smith, 1995). Considerations such as region, gender, and ethnic balance can also be viewed as positive. Given that cabinet makes decisions that affect all Canadians, it would be helpful to have many different views represented at the cabinet table. When these demographic variables overlap with talent, then the cabinet is doubly blessed. There are, of course, other, less noble reasons for cabinet appointments. Loyalty to the Prime Minister, according to many members of Parliament, is a central consideration that often takes precedence over skill and talent (Docherty, 1997). Sometimes a cabinet spot is used to entice high-profile Canadians to seek federal office, including, in recent years, Lucien Bouchard, Stéphane Dion, Pierre Pettigrew, and, most recently, Brian Tobin.

The coveted leadership roles in the House of Commons tend to be reserved for those MPs who manage to survive not just their initial tour of duty but also make it through the seasoned stage. Table 20.5 shows the differences between leaders and non-leaders (maintaining the distinction used in the earlier tables) for the three career stages. Despite the few positions available to all members of Parliament, the greatest opportunity for gaining a position of power is reserved for those in the more senior stages of a political career. Just slightly more than 10 per cent of all MPs achieve a leadership position in their rookie term. While that number doubles for those in their second or third term, the odds for seasoned members of getting a leadership post are hardly greater than one in five. For those who have the ability (or desire) to make federal elected life a career calling, the odds increase to almost even. While Table 20.5 treats all four Parliaments inclusively, a separate analysis found little difference from one to another. Even when Brian Mulroney and Jean Chrétien formed their first respective governments, positions of influence and leadership disproportionately fell on Parliamentary veterans rather than rookies. In this sense at least the Lucien Bouchards of the Canadian parliamentary world are the exceptions rather than the rule.

Table 20.5: Career Stage and Position of Authority in Four Parliaments, 1980–1997

	Rookies	Seasoned	Careerists
Private member	355	399	118
	(89%)	(77.6%)	(51.5%)
Leadership position	44	115	111
	(11%)	(22.4%)	(48.5%)

Source: Canadian Parliamentary Guides.

The extensive reliance on old hands at the parliamentary game is a bit of a double-edged sword. On one side, keeping rookies out of cabinet makes sense. After all, if it takes up to a full term to become familiar with the formal and informal nuances of Parliament, parachuting a neophyte into cabinet can hold the potential for trouble. In 1993, Toronto lawyer and highly touted Alan Rock ran for public office for the first time in his life. He was widely expected to be in a Chrétien cabinet. However, his appointment as Justice Minister was a mixed blessing. Without any legislative experience, Rock's natural talents and wisdom helped him stay afloat, but not to steer the boat in the desired direction. It is difficult to be an effective member of Parliament in the House and in one's own riding if one is also in charge of a large government department. It is often helpful, therefore, to give new members a term or two to learn the ropes. Theoretically, this means giving some rookies junior positions, as committee chairs or parliamentary secretaries (MPs who assist ministers in their departmental roles), to demonstrate their talent, loyalty, and other assets to the Prime Minister. At the same time, these new members have a chance to become comfortable with Parliament so that when they eventually assume leadership roles, they are well ensconced in the legislative culture.

Alternatively, the reliance of successive Prime Ministers on parliamentary veterans for leadership positions, especially cabinet posts, means that the accountability function of Parliament suffers. Specifically, if most ministers are veterans and most opposition members rookies, the cabinet holds an unfair advantage in terms of experience and parliamentary know-how. A comparison of the first two years of both the 35th and 36th Parliaments of Canada provides a perfect illustration of how the advantage of experience on the government front bench can compromise the accountability function of government.

At the start of the 35th Parliament (1993) the cabinet had an average of eight years' experience, or two full terms in office. By contrast, opposition members, those who are supposed to raise questions in Question Period, propose amendments to legislation, and provide the public with alternative public policies, had, on average, a mere 1.2 years of legislative experience. In fact, if we discount the experience of the PC leader Jean Charest and the NDP caucus, none of whom could fully participate in House proceedings since they lacked official party status, the average experience in opposition drops to less than six months. No wonder the opposition was seen as clumsy and the government had its way on most issues. Even on issues where the government might have seemed vulnerable, such as cutting taxes on cigarettes, the opposition was ineffective in exploiting such vulnerability to its fullest advantage (Docherty, 1999: 43–5).

At the start of the 36th Parliament (1997), the experience gap was just as large. However, while the cabinet had an average of just over 11 years' experience, the opposition had almost three years of know-how to fall back on. That additional two years' experience allowed the opposition parties to take full advantage of government stumbles. These stumbles included a failure to compensate all Hepatitis C victims, the unruly handling of protesters at the APEC summit in Vancouver, and the perceived influence of the Prime Minister's Office in security decisions surrounding the APEC summit. With a term under the belts of most opposition MPs and the return to official party status of the NDP, the opposition was performing its accountability functions admirably (or too well for the government, perhaps).[4]

Of course, another way to deal with the accountability question is to enter a legislature with relatively sophisticated law-making skills already in place. Or, to put it differently, if rookies enter federal office having already spent some time in a provincial legislature, then their learning curve will be less steep. While every legislative assembly is different, with distinct informal rules and norms, the apprenticeship period of these individuals will be much shorter. The problem is that very few MPs come to Ottawa from provincial office. In fact, of all members of Parliament since 1980, just over 5 per cent have had provincial legislative experience (Docherty, 1997; also Barrie and Gibbins, 1989). About one-quarter of all members during this same time had spent some time in local elected office (either school board or local council).

These rather low numbers suggest that there is little in the way of a natural career progression from local to provincial to federal office. This runs counter to experience in the United States, where most members of Congress build up a base of support (and money) at the local and state level before making the leap to the national stage. Why do so few Canadian politicians experience an upwardly mobile career path? The brief answers suggest a combination of institutional rules and personal experience. For a start, the separation of provincial and federal party structures has meant that the ties between political parties at various levels are more tenuous now than they ever were in the past (Dyck, 1996). This is particularly true of the two historically successful federal parties, the Liberals and Progressive Conservatives. Furthermore, the increasing importance of provinces in national affairs and the increased political importance of executive federalism have meant that provincial cabinet ministers can often find themselves building a national profile without making the move to federal politics. A career in the provinces is not necessarily a career without national recognition, and this may serve to keep some ambitious provincial lawmakers' hats out of the federal ring.

But beyond these institutional differences, there are also very personal or ratio-nal reasons for not trying to move from one level to another. First, provincial offices differ greatly not just vis-à-vis the federal legislature but also among them-selves. The workload of a legislator from PEI is very different from that of an Ontario or British Columbia provincial lawmaker, for example.[5] These differences translate into different career choices. Some politicians in Ontario, for example, can have a full-time career provincially that would not be possible (particularly outside of cabinet) in some Atlantic provinces. One would expect, therefore, that more provincial members from smaller assemblies would seek a career in Ottawa than would politicians from central or western Canada.

As it turns out, there is empirical support for this argument. With four members chosen at each election, Prince Edward Island holds less than 2 per cent of seats in the Commons. Yet of all members in the 1980s and 1990s with subnational experi-ence, 11 per cent have come from Canada's smallest province. By contrast, roughly one-third of all MPs represent Ontario. Yet only 20 per cent of all MPs with provin-cial legislature experience come from Canada's most populous province (Canadian Parliamentary Guides, 1980–98).

It does not appear as if provincial experience gives ambitious members of Par-liament any large advantage in seeking a promotion to the front benches. Over 70 per cent of former provincial legislators who go to Ottawa remain on the back benches. This compares favourably to those with municipal experience, 82 per cent of whom stay on the backbenches, and is just slightly better than MPs who arrive with neither local nor provincial experience. Just under three-quarters of these individuals (74.7 per cent) stay on the back benches. None of these differ-ences are statistically significant, leading us to conclude that Prime Ministers and party leaders are not likely to confer extra value in having a caucus member who was successful in a previous political career.

Canada's unique party system and the varying success rates of different parties in different regions of the country make a step down from national to subnational office seem like a progressive career move for some ambitious individuals. The New Democratic Party has been far more successful provincially than it has nationally. It should not be surprising, therefore, that—depending on the region they represent—some federal New Democrats leave federal office to run provin-cially, where they have a much greater opportunity of becoming a cabinet minister. Federal Liberals and Conservatives also make the move to the provinces, but usu-ally to lead parties that are already in power. The point is, there is not a natural sequence of stepping stones for high office. Like most other things in Canadian politics, the answer to questions about politicians' personal motives is always, 'it depends'.

Finally, it is worth briefly exploring the question of how regionally or provin-cially representative the Canadian cabinet truly is. This chapter began by suggest-ing that a government may do a better job of representing interests if those interests can be expressed around the cabinet table. This notion goes to the spirit of representative democracy. We do not expect mirror representation (where the cabinet or Parliament is seen to mirror the demographic, economic, and social profile of the population). However, we recognize that any deliberative, representative body can do a better job representing interests if those interests can be articulated while decisions are being taken.

Table 20.6 compares the number of seats in each region, as a percentage of total seats in the House of Commons, to the number of cabinet ministers in the region as a percentage of all elected cabinet ministers. For example, in 1980–4, the West had 29.6 per cent of all seats in the House of Commons. However, westerners made up only 3.4 per cent of the cabinet.[6] The West therefore had a representation deficit of 26.2 per cent. During this same administration, Ontario held 34.6 per cent of all seats and had 41.4 per cent of all federal cabinet seats for a representation surplus of 6.8 per cent. The final Trudeau government was not very effective at regional representation in cabinet.

By contrast, the Mulroney cabinets, in particular the cabinet in his first term, were relatively close reflections of the regional seat distribution. In fact, only in Ontario during the second Mulroney majority did any significant aberration exist. Of course, it would be hard to imagine Ontario gaining sympathy from other regions over the issue of under-representation! Nonetheless, Table 20.6 does help to emphasize the importance of having a truly national majority if the goal is to have equitable cabinet representation. Among other things, the collapse of the Mulroney-led coalition of the West and Quebec in 1993 meant a return to a representation deficit for the West and a surplus for Quebec.

For members and prospective members of Parliament this type of detailed analysis probably does not figure into decisions about career paths. However, it does establish questions about likelihood of career success. Individuals with cabinet ambitions who live in the West must realize that the odds of getting elected as a Liberal are slim. If elected, though, the odds of being chosen to serve in cabinet increase dramatically. By contrast, there is always a greater chance of a Liberal being elected in Ontario (in 1997, 101 of 103 Ontario seats were won by Liberal candidates). But with such a plethora of regional talent to choose from, the Prime Minister can afford to bypass many dedicated men and women. These calculations might spur some MPs to seek a provincial career.

Table 20.6: Percentage of Elected Representatives in Cabinet by Regional Seat Share

	1980–4	1984–8	1988–93	1993–7
Western	−26.2	−1.5	2.8	−7.8
Ontario	6.8	−.4	−9.3	4.8
Quebec	13.3	0	3.4	.8
Atlantic Canada	6.1	2.1	3.0	2.7

Source: Canadian Parliamentary Guides.

Conclusions

This admittedly exploratory chapter has suggested the importance of a 'behavioural' approach to the study of political careers. It has argued that the benefits to such an undertaking are twofold. First, and perhaps most obviously, an empirical and behavioural study of Parliament does a good job of describing the demographics of a representative assembly. This allows us to judge whether or not legislatures are representative of the populations they seek to serve. Although this chapter did not undertake the next step—offering and testing explanations about the failure of modern legislatures to be more representative—the approach certainly allows us to move to this logical next stage. In fact, chapters in this text (see O'Neill, Everitt, Black, Abu-Laban) suggest that groups traditionally under-represented in Canada's legislatures have interests and concerns differing from those who have been more successful in getting elected.

Second, and perhaps more interesting, a behavioural approach allows us to investigate more fully the relationship between an institution and the men and women who work within the walls and rules of that body. The Canadian Parliament has often been described as an 'executive-centred' legislature. As the term suggests, this means a legislature dominated by a Prime Minister and his or her executive and an opposition held in check by strong party leaders. The high level of party discipline in Ottawa does nothing to detract from the image of domineering party leaders in front rows and 'trained seals' on the backbenches. But many men and women run successfully for federal office eschewing this type of role for members. Why does it persist?

The analysis outlined in the preceding pages suggests a relatively simple explanation for how these roles are maintained. Specifically, most members of Parliament are too electorally vulnerable to enjoy lengthy careers. While there are no seniority rules in the Canadian House of Commons, the analysis above demonstrates how most positions of authority are held by more senior (in terms of years served) members of Parliament. This is no doubt disheartening for many ambitious office-holders. They seek a position in the executive, but many are not in office long enough to see themselves at the cabinet table. Understanding this helps us understand what is meant by an 'unwelcoming opportunity structure' of office. Not only is there little opportunity for advancement, but it requires an ability to survive changes of government and large seat swings across the nation.

Making this opportunity structure even more unwelcoming is the electoral fate of backbenchers compared to those in positions of authority. Cabinet ministers and other leaders are more likely to win re-election than private members. This is, of course, strongly correlated with years served. It only makes sense that members who serve in office longer win more re-elections. But it does not diminish the fact that backbenchers face a rougher fight for their electoral lives and serve without the rewards of office (larger pension, more input into policy, car and driver, national recognition and media exposure, to name but a few) provided for those who manage to make it to the top of the career ladder.

Few would argue with the idea that we should be trying to attract the best minds and most experienced citizens to run for federal office. Yet we also often hear a slightly different argument: that we should be trying to attract better people to run for office than currently sit in Parliament. This chapter has not tried to evaluate the level of talent and wisdom in the present or past Parliaments of Canada.[7] It has, however, done a cursory empirical analysis of career in the House of Commons that allows us to put forth a rival explanation. It may be that many members of Parliament are simply not in office long enough or are not given the opportunities necessary to demonstrate just how capable they truly are.

Notes

1. By leadership position I am referring to cabinet member, party leader, party House leader, whip, or caucus chair, or Speaker of the House. Assistant whips and House leaders, parliamentary secretaries, committee chairs, and members of shadow cabinets are all considered private members.

2. In fact, the larger distinction is between members of the executive who have the power to introduce money bills and really set the legislative agenda for the House of Commons and private members. As discussed earlier (see note 1), this chapter uses a slightly different and expanded dichotomy between 'front-bench leaders' and private members.

3. Among these MPs who have had some electoral defeats prior to becoming MPs, the percentage that become cabinet ministers is lower than among those whose first electoral contest was successful.

4. The Progressive Conservatives also returned to official party status in the 36th Parliament. However, the early resignation of Jean Charest to head the Quebec Liberal Party left the 20-member caucus with only one MP, Elsie Wayne of Saint John, with any Commons experience. The new leader, Joe Clark, has a wealth of legislative knowledge, but only returned to the House in the fall of 2000, shortly before yet another election.

5. These differences are largely ones of size. MPPs in Ontario, for example, have much larger ridings (with approximately 16 times as many constituents) than MLAs from Prince Edward Island. This results in a larger workload both in constituency service and in research and legislative work in the provincial capital.

6. The number of seats as a percentage of all seats includes by-elections. In this sense, some seats (where a member retires mid-term and a new member is elected) are counted twice. However, the number of by-elections per term are not enough to skew the data. In addition, the introduction of a new member should be reflected in the calculations of cabinet opportunities, even if the member is not a part of the governing party.

7. The author is on record elsewhere as stating his personal view about members of Parliament. He is not afraid to pronounce publicly his support for members and the difficult and thankless jobs they do, and is more sanguine than most about the level of talent in the Canadian House of Commons.

References

Atkinson, M.M., and P. Thomas. 1993. 'Studying the Canadian Parliament', *Legislative Studies Quarterly* 18, 3: 423–52.

Barrie, D., and R. Gibbins. 1989. 'Parliamentary careers in the Canadian federal state', *Journal of Canadian Political Science* 22, 1: 137–45.

Benjamin, Gerald, and Michael J. Malbin, eds. 1992. *Limiting Legislative Terms*. Washington: Congressional Quarterly.

Carey, John M. 1998. *Term Limits and Legislative Representation*. Cambridge: Cambridge University Press.

Clarke, Harold D., Jane Jenson, Lawrence LeDuc, and Jon Pammett. 1979. *Political Choice in Canada*. Toronto: McGraw-Hill Ryerson.

———, ———, ———, and ———. 1984. *Absent Mandate: The Politics of Discontent in Canada*. Toronto: Gage.

———, ———, ———, and ———. 1991. *Absent Mandate: Interpreting Change in Canadian Elections*, 2nd edn. Toronto: Gage.

———, ———, ———, and ———. 1996. *Absent Mandate: Canadian Electoral Politics in an Era of Restructuring*, 3rd edn. Toronto: Gage.

Cooper, J., and J. West. 1981. 'Voluntary Retirement, Incumbency and the Modern House', *Political Science Quarterly* 96, 2: 279–300.

Dawson, R. MacGregor. 1947. *The Government of Canada*, 5th edn. Toronto: University of Toronto Press.

Docherty, David C. 1997. *Mr. Smith Goes to Ottawa*. Vancouver: University of British Columbia Press.

———. 1999. 'Parliamentarians and Government Accountability', in Martin Westmacott and Hugh Mellon, eds, *Public Administration and Policy: Governing in Challenging Times*. Scarborough, Ont.: Prentice-Hall Allyn and Bacon Canada, 38–52.

——— and Judith McKenzie Oakes. 1997. 'Incumbency and Retirement in the 1993 Federal Election', in Fleming and Glenn (1997: 36–47).

——— and Graham White. 1999. 'Throwing the Rascals Out: The Electoral Accountability of Ministers and Backbenchers in Westminster Systems', paper presented at the Midwest Political Science Association, Chicago.

Dyck, Rand. 1996. 'Relations Between Federal and Provincial Parties', in A. Brian Tanguay and Alain-G. Gagnon, eds, *Canadian Parties in Transition*. Toronto: Nelson Canada, 160–89.

Fleming, Robert J., and J.E. Glenn, eds. 1997. *Fleming's Canadian Legislatures 1997*, 11th edn. Toronto: University of Toronto Press.

Franks, C.E.S. 1987. *The Parliament of Canada*. Toronto: University of Toronto Press.

Hibbing, J. 1991. *Congressional Careers: Contours of Life in the U.S. House of Representatives*. Chapel Hill: University of North Carolina Press.

Irvine, W. 1982. 'Does the Candidate Make a Difference? The Macro-politics and Micro-politics of Getting Elected', *Canadian Journal of Political Science* 15, 4: 755–85.

Jackson, Robert, and Michael M. Atkinson. 1980. *The Canadian Legislative System*, rev. edn. Toronto: Macmillan of Canada.

Kornberg, Allan. 1967. *Canadian Legislative Behavior*. Toronto: Holt, Rinehart and Winston.

——— and William Mishler. 1976. *Legislatures and Societal Change: The Case of Canada*. Beverly Hills, Calif.: Sage.

Lovink, J.A.A. 1973. 'Is Canadian Politics Too Competitive?', *Canadian Journal of Political Science* 6, 2: 341–79.

Schlesinger, J. 1966. *Ambition and Politics: Political Careers in the United States*. Chicago: Rand McNally.

Smith, David. 1995. 'The Federal Cabinet in Canadian Politics', in Michael S. Whittington and Glen Williams, eds, *Canadian Politics in the 1990s*, 4th edn. Toronto: Nelson Canada, 382–401.

Squire, P. 1988. 'Member Career Opportunities and the Internal Organization of Legislatures', *Journal of Politics* 50, 3: 726–44.

Stewart, J. 1977. *The Canadian House of Commons: Procedures and Reform*. Montreal and Kingston: McGill-Queen's University Press.

Ward, Norman. 1950. *The Canadian House of Commons: Representation*. Toronto: University of Toronto Press.

Chapter 21

Representation in the Parliament of Canada: The Case of Ethnoracial Minorities

Jerome H. Black

Democratic governance is first and foremost an ideal that citizens should be able to assert themselves and express their political preferences in order to provoke appropriate responses from government. In polities such as the Canadian, widely understood to be essentially representative in form, the forces of citizen expression and governmental response play out largely through the actions and interactions of parties, electorates, and interest groups, and depend to a significant degree on the composition and activity of legislative (and associated executive) bodies. While not every political claim focuses on legislatures and the processes that determine their makeup and ongoing policy priorities,[1] these continue to be instrumental in the exercise of political power and provide important opportunities for influencing the nature and direction of public policy.

This reality is readily understood not only by well-established social groups that have long been major forces in Canadian politics, but also by non-traditional or non-dominant groups, such as women and ethnic and racial minorities, that have customarily wielded less political clout and have sought to alter this situation. In the past, the recognition of the significance of legislatures by non-traditional groups typically was translated into lobbying efforts to sway legislators to respond to group concerns, and, at the electoral level, working for parties and candidates judged to be sympathetic to the group's policy priorities. More recently, however, increasingly strong currents of opinion within such groups have emerged, arguing that these methods are insufficient and declaring instead the need for a more 'authentic' form of representation that can only be guaranteed by getting group members elected. Driving this political strategy is the conviction that only individuals who share the defining characteristic(s) of the group can understand its true experiences—not least the hardships and biases it may have long faced—and therefore have the empathy and insight necessary to promote effectively the group's interests. From this perspective, then, the group can only be assured of obtaining concrete responses to its claims by having a significant presence among legislators. Furthermore, apart from whatever benefits might result from such *sub-stantive* representation, group legislators can also provide representation in important *symbolic* ways.[2] Merely by having some of their own in the legislature, members of the group may derive psychological satisfaction from feeling that they are represented. In this way, the presence of such legislators may affirm the group's sense of belonging in Canadian society and politics.[3] This, in turn, is likely to evoke more positive sentiments towards those institutions that do include them.

This chapter considers these substantive and symbolic facets of group representation in the Canadian Parliament for ethnic and racial minority groups, that is, individuals whose ancestral origins lie outside of the two dominant or 'majority' British and French communities.[4] This entails first actually evaluating the numerical presence of minorities in Parliament, which is accomplished by combining a variety of methods for determining the origins of MPs. This is followed by an analysis aimed at exploring whether or not minorities have distinctive political views, which is considered to be an important precondition for substantive representation. A survey of candidates in the 1993 general election (described below) provides the database for this part of the investigation.

The focus on ethnoracial minorities is itself easy to justify. First of all, understanding of their role in Canadian politics remains quite limited and thus whatever can be learned about the dimensions of their political representation almost automatically constitutes new knowledge.[5] The sizeable numerical presence of minorities in Canada's multicultural and multiracial population magnifies the seriousness of this traditional neglect and by itself justifies the specific consideration of minorities and representational politics in Canada.[6] Such a focus is also supported by the reality of political activism among minorities. The little research that has been done in this area is sufficient to dismiss the idea that minorities are somehow less important to study because they are politically passive. Particularly with regard to mass-level activities, the literature points unequivocally to minorities (and indeed immigrants) as being rather substantially involved participants in Canadian politics (e.g., Black, 1991; Chui et al., 1991). Such engagement may, indeed, be connected to emerging evidence of greater involvement by minorities in élite-level politics, including running for and winning legislative office. Certainly, there are concrete signs, discussed below, that more minorities have won their way into Parliament in the last few elections. This trend adds greater meaning to the exploration of the kinds of representation that can be said to occur as a result of more minorities entering the legislature, but it also calls attention to the consequences of under-representation for particular minority groups, such as visible minorities, that have achieved only a limited toehold in Parliament. Other reasons for studying minority representation include the benefits of comparative analysis that might accrue from the consideration of their circumstances and experiences relative to other non-traditional groups such as women, and, as well, the possibility of exploring diversity within different groups, such as majority versus minority distinctions among women (Black, 2000b).

Some Preliminary Considerations

The first step to be taken in the study of ethnoracial minorities and representational politics in Parliament is an assessment of 'numerical representation'. The term embraces consideration not only of the group's absolute numbers in the House of Commons but comparative or benchmark perspectives as well. An obvious benchmark is the proportion of seats held relative to that by parliamentarians of majority background. Another is the minority group's degree of 'electoral representation',[7] that is, the ratio of its seat share to its population proportion. Given how frequently such population-anchored evaluations are invoked in both formal analysis and informal commentary, electoral representation would appear to play a particularly significant role in judgements about 'how well' social groups are represented in various élite settings. Shortfalls in electoral representation are especially likely to be discussed in symbolic terms and to be seized upon by group activists and commentators as evidence of unfairness, bias, and exclusion. Numerical representation also has a direct bearing on the premise that only legislators who are members of a group can ensure adequate responsiveness to its political agenda. If that assumption is valid, then substantive representation is indeed dependent on the voice and actions of legislators who share the group's characteristics. Put simply, without a presence, there is neglect.[8]

Not only does standard procedure deem that evaluations of symbolic and substantive representation be rooted in and preceded by numerical assessments for minorities, but it also requires that minorities must first be 'counted' on the basis of an objective determination of membership. This is not to say that subjective-oriented perspectives, which register individuals as group members based on their sense and degree of felt attachment to the collectivity, are unimportant for the analysis of group representation. Indeed, they constitute important sources of variability with regard to group sentiments. Thus, just as women parliamentarians differ in their self-images as feminists—some do not at all identify themselves as such—minority politicians also have alternative outlooks about their origins, some regarding their ancestral roots as being central to their sense of self-definition, others giving their ancestry little, if any, regard. More to the point, subjective categorizations ought to be helpful in establishing who among minority politicians are more or less inclined to promote minority causes.[9]

For its part, an objective vantage point emphasizes group membership classifications that are external to the individuals involved, that is, independent of any self-labelling. Thus, women legislators are understood to be 'members' of their social category by virtue of their sex. Similarly, minority legislators can be identified as having origins outside those associated with the majority communities. The value of the objective approach stems, in part, from its necessary precedence vis-à-vis the subjective approach, since sentiments of belonging can only be conceptualized and measured properly with reference to categories of potential attachment. Furthermore, objective-based appraisals by themselves can communicate a great deal about the nature of representation in its symbolic guise, even in the face of evidence of weak subjective sentiments. As Black and Lakhani (1997: 4) point out, 'even if MPs fail to identify with or, indeed, disavow their ancestry, this does not necessarily dissuade others, inside and outside the community of origin, from regarding and remarking upon the symbolic aspects of their presence.'

While it is a straightforward ideal that minorities must first be counted on the basis of their ancestral origins, achieving this goal in practice through the use of specific measurement procedures is another matter entirely. Two methods, last-name analysis and the use of biographical material, have dominated research into the measurement of the origins of élites in Canada and have even been (varyingly) applied to classify the origins of MPs in different Parliaments over the 1965–88 period.[10] Both procedures are valuable as methods of classification provided there is sensitivity to their respective limitations. With the biographical approach, the concerns are that origins are only infrequently set out in the published record and that the more prevalent markers, such as birthplace and religion, are only imperfectly associated with origins.[11] For their part, surnames often can be linked to ancestry (a task aided by the availability of last-name dictionaries), but classification errors arise when, as often happens, last names are altered. In some cases individuals (but more likely their ancestors) may have had their names changed by others (including immigration officials), while in other instances people may have modified their surnames, perhaps anglicizing them in order to ease their integration into mainstream society. More routinely, women have taken the last names of their marriage partners, which contributes to the broader problem that maternal lineages tend to be undercounted in last-name analysis.

Fortunately, it is possible to employ more enhanced versions of these methods, especially in the case of last-name analysis, to lessen the amount of classification error. This was true of a study (Black and Lakhani, 1997) undertaken to classify the ethnoracial origins of MPs elected in 1993 to the 35th Parliament, the main results of which are reproduced below. It consulted a wider variety of last-name dictionaries, tried to take into account the last names of parents for married women, and sought to capture mixed ancestry. Moreover, the overall measurement process was improved by the concurrent consideration of biographical material. The study also employed a survey based on a census-like question on ancestral origins, which was faxed to MPs. Since such directly solicited responses probably produce the best data on origins, they were used to classify those who responded. However, since response rates tend to be low in surveys of parliamentarians, in some cases very low, the two traditional methods were used for those who did not reply.[12]

The survey results were also the principal source of findings of mixed ancestry, which characterizes the background of many MPs. While such responses somewhat complicate the classification of origins, they are not unexpected in light of increasing reports of multiple origins among the Canadian population at large.[13] Another classification issue centres on the level of origin specificity. While it would be preferable to identify and comment at the more specific level (e.g., Greek, Lebanese), there is also a concern to avoid too few cases in some instances and to allow for a more reliable sense of general patterns. A pragmatic response is to use more summary categories that can still be meaningfully distinguished as separate groupings. Visible minorities were grouped into a single category (based on the classifications used by Statistics Canada[14]) because they have the most distinctive experience as minorities, much of it stemming from discrimination. Minority European origins were collected together under three areal headings, i.e., Northern and Western, Eastern, and Southern European, in recognition of the differences in the contexts of their historical integration and how early and how well they have been accepted by majority Canadians. In fact, it can be easily argued that the three European categories in the order listed reflect a pattern of increasing group distinctiveness and outgroup status flowing from their differential incorporation. Indeed, some might object—perhaps fairly—that it may be a bit of a stretch to regard as true minorities groups such as the Dutch, Germans, and Scandinavians that have long established themselves in Canadian society. At the same time, this would also be an argument to consider the Europeans in separate categories.

The Numerical Representation of Minorities in Recent Parliaments

Table 21.1 reports results from a systematic analysis carried out on the numerical representation of minorities in the House of Commons for the 35th Parliament, associated with the 1993 general election. Shown are estimates of the distribution of the origins of MPs in that Parliament, in both raw numbers and percentage terms. In general, the data indicate a substantial presence on the part of minorities but with decided unevenness in certain categories, including significant under-representation in some. As expected, most MPs had origins rooted in the two majority communities. Altogether, 193 of the 295 parliamentarians (65.4 per cent) were found to have either British (107) or French (78) ancestry, or both (8). Four parliamentarians were judged to have Aboriginal roots. Among the remaining 98 legislators, 27 had mixed ancestry involving both majority and minority dimensions. The remaining 71 MPs (24.1 per cent of the House) had backgrounds exclusively associated with either single or multiple minority categories. Among them, Europeans clearly dominate. Altogether, 53 of the 71 minority MPs (18 per cent of the House) were determined to have European origins, distributed in the following way: 16 Northern and Western Europeans, 12 Eastern Europeans, 21 Southern Europeans (including 15 Italians), and four with origins in multiple areas of Europe. A further four MPs were judged to have Jewish backgrounds and one other was classified as Chilean.

In turn, 13 MPs were reckoned to have origins associated with the visible minority category. Three of them had Lebanese backgrounds and one had an Armenian heritage. Also elected were three South Asians, as well as one individual with Chinese origins, one with Filipino ancestry, and two with black/Caribbean roots. A further two individuals were determined to have multiple backgrounds. This figure of 13 can be situated in several different ways. Relative to earlier Parliaments, it represents a noticeable increase. According to Pelletier (1991), only 10 visible minority individuals in total had won their way into Parliament during the previous

Table 21.1: Estimates of the Ethnoracial Origins of MPs Elected in 1993

Ethnoracial Origins	Number	%
British[a]	107	36.3
French	78	26.4
British-French	8	2.7
British and/or French *and* European	27	9.2
European	53	18.0
Northern and Western European	16	
Eastern European	12	
Southern European	21	
Multiple regions	4	
Jewish	4	1.4
Visible minorities[b]	13	4.4
Aboriginal[c]	4	1.4
Other[d]	1	0.3
	(295)	(100%)

[a] Includes single British and British-only multiples.
[b] Visible minority categories follow Statistics Canada classifications.
[c] Includes one multiple, Aboriginal-Eastern European.
[d] Chilean.
Source: Adapted from Black and Lakhani (1997: Table 1).

eight general elections (over the 1965–88 period). Of these, the author reports that six won seats in the 1988 election. Viewed longitudinally, then, the election of 13 visible minorities in 1993 stands out as a notable development. At the same time, even at such an historically high level, visible minorities remained dramatically under-represented in Parliament when their relative share of seats—4.4 per cent —is contrasted with their population proportion. Based on several questions posed in the 1991 Canadian census, Statistics Canada (1993) has estimated that visible minorities comprised 9.4 per cent of the Canadian population. According to this benchmark, it would have taken the election of 28 visible minority MPs to bring their representation in line with their population. Instead, the 35th Parliament saw visible minorities being only 47 per cent of the way towards the achievement of proportionality.[15] Of course, some specific origin groups were more under-represented than others. For example, the single MP of Chinese origin stands in sharp contrast to a Chinese population of over half a million.

By contrast, the Europeans as a group had already established a significant presence in Parliament before the 1993 election. Pelletier, for example, estimated that for the 1965–88 period 94 different individuals of European origin (along with 13 of Jewish background) entered Parliament. Indeed, even by the 1980s, Europeans had already come close to achieving complete electoral representation, so that the effect of the 1993 election was really to close most of the small remaining gap. All this said, it is important to bear in mind important disparities in numerical representation that are unmistakable at the level of specific origin. For example, no MP of Portuguese origin was elected in 1993, while 15 of Italian ancestry were.

Still, the most important feature of minority representation in the 35th Parliament is the under-representation of visible minorities. An analysis of the 1997 election results suggests that their situation has improved, but only in a marginal way (Black, 2000a). It would appear that 19 visible minority individuals won election to the 36th Parliament, an increase of six over the earlier tally. The new number translates into 6.3 per cent of the 301 seats in the House (expanded from 295). While this increase represents an improvement over the previous Parliament and suggests that visible minorities continue to press for access to the legislature, it hardly constitutes a dramatic shift. That change has been incremental at best is also evident when these results are viewed from the perspective of electoral representation, by considering an updated assessment of the demographic weight of visible minorities available from the 1996 census. Based on the results of a question that, for the first time, directly inquired about race, Statistics Canada (1998) reported that visible minority communities comprised 11.2 per cent of the population. This suggests that full electoral representation would require the presence of 34 MPs. Alternatively put, visible minorities were still only 56.3 per cent of the way towards achieving full electoral representation.

To reiterate, these snapshots reveal that significant numbers of minorities have been successful in joining the parliamentary élite but that key origin categories nevertheless remain under-represented in the legislature. This pattern of both change and persistence would appear to sustain two alternative assessments about the symbolic nature of minority representation. On the one hand, the increasing presence of minorities sends important signals that institutional change and inclusion are possible, encouraging those who believe that Parliament in principle ought to mirror the social diversity of Canadians. As well, the specific minority communities themselves are likely to attach great symbolic importance to the election of group members to such a high-profile institution. The symbolism of having a presence is probably greatest when the community elects its first member of Parliament. On the other hand, more critical evaluations may develop if the group's numerical representation remains in a token range, especially if it lags behind what the community regards as fair given its demographic weight. Negative sentiments may also be expressed by spokespeople for communities that have yet to establish any parliamentary presence.

The Substantive Representation of Minorities

Evidence that the Canadian Parliament is more reflective of the country's ethnoracial diversity than ever before but does not yet fully mirror it also gives impetus to a consideration of the substantive aspects of representation. The relative presence or absence of minorities in Parliament would surely matter more if it turned out that minority MPs bring and communicate alternative political perspectives that might otherwise not be expressed and debated in their absence. The consequences of there being fewer or more MPs would be especially significant if such orientations included an emphasis on highlighting and promoting the concerns of their particular minority communities or of minorities in general.

As already noted, expectations that minority politicians have different perspectives are rooted in claims about the overriding importance and particularity of their experiences as minorities. At the same time, it has also been stressed that not all minority individuals, objectively classified, have such a predisposition. Furthermore, some minority legislators who do have a sense of self-identification as a member of a particular community of origin might still regard their attachments as entirely private in nature, without any relevance to the political arena.[16] But even those who are inclined to give a public face to minority concerns still confront external constraints that limit their ability and perhaps even their determination to articulate and/or act on behalf of minority priorities. The most significant inhibitor of independent action—one that exists for all legislators—is party discipline, the requirement that backbenchers acquiesce to the dictates of the party leadership. With political parties being the uncontested organizers of Parliament and its deliberations, Canadian legislators fully understand that they are first and foremost members of party teams and consequently develop a compliance orientation that is constantly reinforced by the rewards and sanctions that the party leadership has at its disposal. Insofar as minority concerns do not rank high on the party's agenda, minority MPs confront significant challenges in providing effective representation of minority interests.

The fact that politicians with minority origins tend to be relative newcomers to Parliament may also limit their effectiveness. Entering a political context not of their making, they can face pressures to conform to established norms and procedures, thus constraining their ability to act in distinctive ways. Those who are extremely ambitious to ascend the parliamentary hierarchy might find it especially hard to twin the promotion of minority concerns with actions and behaviour deemed appropriate by the traditions of the institution and the established majority groups. They might feel that they have to, as Norris (1996: 93) puts it in the case of women entering legislatures, 'go along to get along'. More generally, minorities run the risk of being pigeonholed if they are perceived as speaking out too often or too stridently on behalf of minority matters, a constraint that flows from the lesser salience attached to such concerns by majority politicians. Indeed, it may well be that only by significantly increasing their numbers will minorities be able partially to redefine prevailing norms and practices, and thus diminish such 'marginalizing' pressures.

In the absence of appropriate empirical studies, it is only possible to speculate on how well, if at all, *minority-conscious* MPs are able to surmount these obstacles and act on the basis of their predispositions. Some preliminary insights are possible, however, from a survey of candidates who ran for the main parties in the 1993 election (Erickson, 1997). This data set provides a means to assess one of the preconditions of minority representation, namely, the holding of distinctive political views. Presumably, if the views of minority politicians are no different from those of majority politicians, then their absence would matter less. The available data set is not, however, without its weaknesses, particularly its lack of coverage of policy areas normally understood to be of specific interest to many minorities (e.g., immigration and refugee matters, cultural diversity concerns, anti-discrimination policy, employment equity).[17] Another problem stems from the fact that in some origin categories only small numbers of office-seekers were sampled—to be sure, a reflection of their under-representation within the candidate pool—which limits the reliability of inferences in some instances.[18] This difficulty is compounded by the need to control for party affiliation since candidates are expected to reflect their party's general viewpoints. Thus, sample size problems dictated that the party variable could only be worked in an imperfect way, by grouping the parties into broader categories. Because 'ideology' does correlate with many of the attitudes examined, it made sense to use it as the basis of the party categorization; thus, the NDP and Liberals were bracketed together as a leftist and centrist category, and the Conservative and Reform parties were grouped together within a right-wing category.[19]

Even though it is expected that party affiliation will strongly influence the patterns of response, initially the attitudes of candidates are examined without its consideration. This provides a useful baseline against which both to judge the impact of partisan divisions and to view their effects relative to those of ethnoracial origin. In fact, Table 21.2 anticipates the relevance of party alignment. Candidates with a majority background and those with Northern or Western European origins were distributed almost evenly between the two party groupings, while Eastern European and visible minority candidates were strongly associated with the left/centre parties (at about 70 per cent levels), and Southern Europeans more modestly so (57 per cent). These distributions overlap with results shown for an ideology item, which asked candidates to place themselves along a one-to-seven (left-right) ideology scale. Visible minorities and Eastern Europeans, with the lowest mean scores (3.75 and 3.82, respectively), leaned mildly to the left compared to the other groups (overall mean: 4.01).

These are modest results, as are those based on a question about political representation that queried candidates about the desirability of more women in Parliament. Visible minorities and Southern Europeans were slightly more inclined to support the idea of 'many more' women in Parliament (62 per cent and 65 per cent, respectively) compared to 55 per cent for office-seekers of majority background. On a parallel item asking about racial minorities, however, the pattern is much more dramatic. Only 35 per cent of majority candidates endorsed the notion of having many more such individuals in Parliament while an even lower percentage of Northern and Western Europeans felt this way. These comparatively lower levels of support for racial minorities on the part of the established groups are noteworthy in and of themselves and suggest that race-connected barriers may be more formidable than those associated with gender. In contrast, an overwhelming 70 per cent of visible minority candidates supported a marked increase in the presence of racial minorities. While this may not be surprising, it is interesting to

Table 21.2: Party, Ideology, and Political Attitudes by Ethnoracial Origins

	Majority	Northern/ Western Europeans	Eastern Europeans	Southern Europeans	Visible Minorities	All
Party and Ideology						
NDP/Liberal (vs Conservative/Reform)[a]	49	47	72	57	70	51
Left-right ideological self-placement (1 = left, 7 = right)[b]	4.01	4.00	3.75	4.45	3.82	4.01
Representation						
Many more women in Parliament	55	46	56	62	65	55
Many more racial minorities in Parliament**	35	29	50	62	70	37
Environmentalism						
More protection even if higher taxes[c]	70	75	83	70	88	72
Protection more important than job creation	25	20	24	23	11	24
Social Traditionalism						
Welfare state makes people less willing to look after selves***	69	69	67	55	50	68
Must crack down on crime regardless of criminals' rights*	55	50	40	77	53	55
Not enough respect for traditional values	64	68	52	64	67	64
Gone too far in pushing equal rights	38	55	28	45	20	38
Moral Traditionalism						
Abortion not woman's personal choice[c]	38	45	25	52	26	38
Banning pornography necessary for moral standards	41	51	33	64	63	43
Economic Traditionalism						
People who can should pay for government services[c]	52	42	42	41	45	50
Government should leave people to get ahead on their own[c]	41	47	27	33	24	40
Government should not reduce income gap	26	25	16	23	15	25
Government should control inflation even if less jobs[c]	37	34	25	23	21	35
N	(363–426)	(30–6)	(22–4)	(18–22)	(17–20)	(450–527)

Note: Unless otherwise noted, entries show percentages of candidates who agree or agree strongly with statement. [a] Percentage NDP/Liberal. [b] Mean scores. [c] Entries show percentages choosing indicated option.

Significance level: * = .10, ** = .05, *** = .01

observe that many Eastern (50 per cent) and Southern (62 per cent) European candidates also embraced the idea, suggesting a certain empathy with visible minority under-representation.

Visible minorities also tended to provide the most distinctive response on two questions posed about the environment, but in directionally opposite ways. When asked about a trade-off between higher taxes and environmental protection, they were most likely to choose protection (88 per cent vs 72 per cent for candidates as a whole), but in a trade-off involving jobs they were least likely to give the nod to protection over job creation (11 per cent vs 24 per cent for all candidates). Taking these data at face value, it would appear that visible minority candidates carefully differentiate among the particular economic considerations that should override environmental concerns. It can be noted that Eastern Europeans were also more prepared to give a priority to the environment.

Next considered are attitude items in separate categories of social, moral, and economic concerns, which were coded in such a way that larger percentages signify more 'traditionalist' or conservative responses.[20] Patterns of both similarity and dissimilarity appear to characterize answers to four questions tapping 'social traditionalism'. For those that probed views about the welfare state creating dependency and the need to crack down on crime, the differences are even statistically significant. Visible minorities (50 per cent) and Southern Europeans (55 per cent) were least likely to believe that welfare has such an effect, while on the crime question, Southern Europeans (77 per cent) were the most prepared to take a tough stance. Although visible minorities did not differ from the norm on the crime issue, Eastern European candidates were least predisposed (40 per cent) to adopt a strict approach. This group also emerged as the least conservative with regard to 'moral traditionalism'. On a question about abortion, only a quarter of the Eastern Europeans responded that abortion was not a women's personal choice (compared to 38 per cent of candidates as a whole) and 33 per cent wanted pornography banned (compared to 43 per cent for all candidates). Interestingly, visible minorities differed across the two questions, matching the Eastern Europeans' liberalism on the abortion issue but ranking at the top of moral traditionalism on the pornography item. For their part, Southern Europeans came across as highly traditionalist on both questions, perhaps as a result of their (mostly Catholic) religious backgrounds. The lesser conservatism of visible minority and Eastern European candidates was also true for three of the four questions related to the economy. For example, while 41 per cent of majority candidates and even more Northern or Western Europeans (47 per cent) agreed that people should 'get ahead on their own' (without government help), only 27 per cent of Eastern Europeans and 24 per cent of visible minorities supported this notion. On two of these questions, Southern Europeans also were less traditionalist.

In summary, the main message in Table 21.2 (bearing in mind the generally statistically insignificant results) is that candidates in the different origin categories are far from alike in terms of their political perspectives and attitudes. Visible minority office-seekers most often differ from the other candidates and, with a

couple of exceptions, they diverge by being more leftist or liberal in their orientations, especially compared to candidates from the majority communities and those
of Western and Northern European background (who are often the most conservative of all). The viewpoints of Southern and Eastern European candidates are also
somewhat distinctive. The former tend to be 'progressive' in their attitudes about
political representation and some economic priorities, but are generally conservative on social and moral matters. The latter stand out as being consistently leftist or
liberal in their views, but this is largely a reflection of their partisan affiliation. This
conclusion is drawn from Table 21.3, which re-examines the responses to most of
the attitude and orientation items while taking into account party groupings.

The impact of party affiliation is evident in the larger differences occurring
between party groupings rather than across origin categories. Only in secondary
fashion do ethnicity and race leave an imprint on the data, and even this must be
viewed cautiously because of the now smaller number of cases involved and the
virtually complete lack of statistical significance. The muted effects of origins relative to party are especially apparent with regard to ideological self-placement. The
mean positions of Liberal and NDP candidates in the various ancestry categories
clustered around the 3-point mark, with Northern and Western Europeans being a
bit more to the left (2.41) and Southern Europeans a bit more to the right (3.58).
For their part, Conservative and Reform candidates in the different origin categories clustered more uniformly at the 5-point (right-of-centre) mark. Origin effects
are more pronounced, however, for the item about more racial minorities in Parliament. While Liberal and NDP candidates were in general the most sympathetic to
such a development, the ancestry-based relationship seen earlier still basically
holds. Thus, while 52 per cent of majority candidates were supportive, 71 per cent
of Eastern Europeans endorsed the notion and even larger proportions of Southern
Europeans (83 per cent) and visible minorities (86 per cent) did so. Interestingly,
ancestry also has some modest effects among Conservative and Reform candidates; here, too, the most supportive were Southern Europeans (25 per cent) and
visible minorities (33 per cent).

On the remaining items, the effects of ethnicity and race are far less systematic.
As alluded to, the association of Eastern European candidates with more progressive orientations diminishes considerably once party is taken into account. Only
among Conservative and Reform candidates in connection with one of the environmental items did Eastern Europeans appear to differ (by being more liberal). At
the same time, some of the earlier results seen in connection with Southern Europeans and visible minorities continue to persist even with party taken into
account. In both party categories, Southern Europeans remain traditionalist on
crime but not necessarily on economic issues.[21] For their part, visible minority candidates continue to have strong anti-pornography views, but in general their lesser
traditionalism seen earlier is more apparent within the Conservative and Reform
parties than within the Liberals and the NDP. Among the latter two parties, visible
minorities only differ noticeably with regard to being decidedly more pro-environment. However, within the two more right-wing parties (apart from the pornogra-

Table 21.3: Ideology and Selected Political Attitudes by Ethnoracial Origins and by Party Grouping

		Environmentalism			Social Traditionalism		Moral Traditionalism		Economic Traditionalism		
	Left-right ideological self-placement (1 = left, 7 = right)[a]	Many more racial minorities in Parliament	More protection even if higher taxes[b]	Protection more important than job creation	Welfare state makes people less willing to look after selves	Must crack down on crime regardless of criminals' rights	Abortion not woman's personal choice[b]	Banning pornography necessary for moral standards	Government should not reduce income gap	Government should control inflation even if less jobs[b]	(N)
NDP/Liberal											
Majority	3.06	52	81	34	46	37	25	38	13	4	(184–92)
Northern/Western Europeans	2.41	59	100	44	31	12	23	38	6	—	(16–17)
Eastern Europeans	3.00	71	88	28	53	28	17	29	11	—	(17–18)
Southern Europeans	3.58	83	83	25	25	67	27	58	8	—	(11–12)
Visible minorities	3.25	86	92	8	36	39	21	54	7	14	(12–14)
All	3.02	58	83	33	44	36	25	39	12	4	(241–89)
Conservative/Reform											
Majority	5.06	17	56	18	91	74	56	47	52	77	(163–99)
Northern/Western Europeans	5.50	—	42	—	100	84	69	63	47	67	(12–19)
Eastern Europeans	5.57	—	71	14	100	71	50	43	43	86	(6–7)
Southern Europeans	5.78	25	43	22	89	89	78	67	44	63	(7–9)
Visible minorities	5.20	33	75	17	83	83	40	83	33	40	(4–6)
All	5.16	16	55	17	92	75	57	50	51	75	(193–274)

Note: Unless otherwise noted, entries show percentages of candidates who agree or agree strongly with statement.
[a] Mean scores. [b] Entries show percentages choosing indicated option.

phy item) visible minorities appear to be much less conservative on the abortion issue, the two economic traditionalism items, and on one of the environmental questions. In other words, it would seem that one of the consequences of visible minority recruitment into parties of the right is to add voices that, compared to the parties' general orientations, are more moderate in tone.

Finally, some data analysis addresses the subjective dimension of attachment; it makes use of a question that asked candidates whether they thought that their ethnic background was very, somewhat, not very, or not at all important to them.[22] As might be expected, the degree of attachment varied across the origin categories. Among majority office-seekers, 62 per cent replied that their origins were very or somewhat important,[23] while a lesser proportion of Western and Northern Europeans did so (52 per cent). In contrast, 82 per cent of Eastern Europeans, 83 per cent of Southern Europeans, and 85 per cent of the visible minorities responded that this was the case. Moreover, fully half of the visible minority candidates signalled that their backgrounds were very important to them.[24] The consequences of stronger attachment for the political attitudes already seen are evident largely for the Southern European and visible minority candidates (specific data not shown). Where there were strong correlations between the importance of background and attitude stance, they overwhelmingly occurred for these two origin categories and consistently indicated that the impact of greater attachment is to amplify their more progressive leanings. Thus, for Southern Europeans the greater the importance they attached to their origins, the more likely that they both supported having many more racial minorities in Parliament and placed themselves on the left side of the ideology continuum. Strong attachments also meant less agreement with traditionalist economic positions and, somewhat unexpectedly, even with social traditionalist stances. For visible minorities, deeper attachments had the same effect in these areas, though less frequently with regard to economic items. Interestingly, not only do these results generally confirm the wisdom of paying attention to the subjective dimension of ethnicity and race, but they also specifically suggest that conscious membership works to enhance leftist and centrist positions. Such a conclusion perhaps contradicts some conventional perspectives that hold ethnicity and race to be conservative forces, tending to detract from a politics of change.

Conclusion

It bears repeating that these glimpses of patterns of substantive representation in the candidate survey make reference not to actual behaviour but to expressed attitudes and orientations. For reasons already discussed, minorities who do win their way into the House of Commons—and particularly those who might be inclined to champion minority concerns—may find it difficult to offset the constraints they face in order to act in ways that correspond to their policy predispositions. Still, in the absence of research that directly focuses on and chronicles what they can and cannot accomplish, it would be premature to dismiss the possibility that their presence matters. Indeed, as more minorities enter Parliament, their increased numerical weight may very well precipitate changes in how their colleagues and the institution itself respond to both their presence and the issues and priorities they bring with them. In the meantime, the best available evidence suggests that there is greater potential for substantive representation with more minorities being inside Parliament rather than outside of it. This stems from what is surely the key finding in this analysis, namely, that important categories of minorities—those who are the most distinctive as minorities—do have particular predispositions and attitudes. The balance of opinion in Parliament would appear to depend on the number of minority MPs elected there.

In turn, the idea that having more minorities in Parliament probably matters in substantive terms reinforces the importance of analysis aimed at documenting the number of minorities in Parliament and the alterations that occur over time. It also has implications for judging the particular significance of the numerical under-representation of minorities. To the extent that some origin categories have and continue to have less of a presence in Parliament than might be expected in accordance with their relative population share, then the consequences are not just confined to the realm of symbolism and the lack of recognition that such absence implies. Minorities also run the risk of being on the losing end in terms of the attention given to their policy concerns. If further research sustains the sense gained in this preliminary work that having group representation is an important condition for effective representation, then the numerical under-representation of key groups, such as visible minorities, suggests that the real costs of exclusion may be considerable.

Notes

Thanks are owed to Lynda Erickson for making her 1993 candidate data set available and to Chris Anderson for his research assistance.

1. Some demands, particularly those associated with social movement agitation, are often expressed in the 'unofficial' political sites of civil society. See, for example, Vickers's (1997) discussion of the alternative arenas of political activity used by women and the women's movement.

2. Pitkin (1967) provides a comprehensive treatment of the different ways in which representation has been conceptualized over the years in *The Concept of Representation*. In this chapter, 'symbolic representation' most closely approximates the 'descriptive approach' that she discusses, which emphasizes the importance of legislators 'resembling' those they represent. 'Substantive representation', on the other hand, parallels her discussion of the 'acting for' approach, which focuses on what legislators actually do to 'respond' to those they are supposed to represent.

3. The importance of social groups being able to 'see themselves' in the institutions of society is persuasively argued by Breton (1985).

4. Racial minorities may be distinguished from ethnic minorities, typically of European origin, by phenotypical characteristics, though this distinction is not meant to imply that race has any inherent biological significance; rather, race is recognized as having importance only as a social construct and in light of the sharply different social life experiences

of racial minorities. In the Canadian context, racial minorities are frequently referred to as visible minorities, who for the purposes of the Employment Equity Act are defined as 'persons other than Aboriginal Peoples, who are non-Caucasian in race or non-white in colour.' Here the two terms, 'racial minorities' and 'visible minorities', are used interchangeably. As for the term 'majority'—used to characterize the British and French communities—it is more properly thought of in the context of the two groups' dominance (at the very least, numerically speaking) in their respective domains, outside and inside Quebec. Finally, another important minority, the Aboriginal peoples, is not considered as part of this focus on ethnoracial minorities. They are, in any event, more properly thought of as 'national minorities', as are the Québécois from a pan-Canadian perspective. In this regard, see Kymlicka (1995).

5. The limited amount of research carried out on the place of minorities within Canadian politics is arguably the chief feature of the literature. Characterizations of the literature in this regard (as well as complaints about this situation) have been made most recently by Black (1997) and Stasiulus (1997).

6. In the 1991 census, those of non-British, non-French ancestry ranged from about 25 per cent of the population, when tabulating only single-origin responses, up to 40 per cent, when taking into account mixed ancestry, including majority-minority patterns.

7. 'Electoral representation' and 'percentage of electoral representation' are terms specifically used by the Royal Commission on Electoral Reform and Party Financing (the Lortie Commission) to gauge the under-representation of women and visible minorities in the House of Commons. See Royal Commission (1991: vol. 1, ch. 3).

8. Presence would imply more than token numbers. Questions about how many group members have to be in the legislature before their numbers might make a difference have typically not been raised in connection with minorities, but have been considered with regard to women legislators. See, for example, Norris (1996) and Gotell and Brodie (1991).

9. On the other hand, minority identity is not a *necessary* condition for the championing of the group's interests since some non-group legislators, including those of majority background, may truly empathize with the group; others who personally may be less inclined might nevertheless find that they face pressures, such as a large presence of the minority in their constituency, to respond to the group.

10. Pelletier (1991) analysed the composition of each of the eight Parliaments covering this period using a biographical approach and an informal analysis of last names. Ogmundson and McLaughlin (1992) analysed the Parliaments associated with the elections of 1965, 1974, and 1984 exclusively on the basis of a surname analysis. For some critical commentary on these two studies, see Black and Lakhani (1997).

11. Birthplace, of course, would be of little help in the classification of the origins of the Canadian-born.

12. The response rate for the survey was, in fact, a respectable 49 per cent.

13. In the 1991 census, for instance, about 29 per cent of Canadians indicated that they have multiple origins.

14. Ten visible minority groups have been specifically designated: black, Indo-Pakistani, Chinese, Korean, Japanese, Southeast Asian, Filipino, other Pacific Islander, Arab and West Asian, and Latin American (except Chileans and Argentinians).

15. Since this ratio does not take into account the growth in the visible minority population from 1991 to 1993, their actual degree of electoral representation would be less than this.

16. This would appear to be the case, for example, of the visible minorities who were elected in 1997 under the banner of the Reform Party (see Simpson, 1997).

17. Note that the focus here on the attitudes of candidates and not legislators is not a serious problem for the analysis. The question becomes simply how might Parliament differ if more minorities were elected.

18. The distribution of candidates among the origin categories in the effective sample of 567 is as follows: Majority, 75.8 per cent (N = 430), Northern and Western Europeans, 6.3 per cent (N = 36), Eastern Europeans, 4.4 per cent (N = 25), Southern Europeans, 3.9 per cent (N = 22), and visible minorities, 3.5 per cent (N = 20). A further 1.8 per cent of candidates had mixed majority-minority origins, 3.4 per cent other European (including mixed and Jewish) origins, and .9 per cent Aboriginal background. It should be noted that a large number of candidates in the survey either refused to respond to the question about origins or asserted that they were 'Canadian'. The nature of these problems and how they were largely solved are discussed in Black (2000b).

19. The Bloc Québécois was not included in the analysis as only one of the party's 36 candidates who participated in the survey was classified as a minority (Southern European). The twofold categorization of the four parties is partially justified by the self-described ideological positions of the candidates themselves. On a one-to-seven left-right scale (see below), NDP candidates placed themselves well to the left (mean: 2.37), the Liberals near the centre (3.83), and Conservative and Reform candidates distinctly to the right and at about the same position (5.14 and 5.18, respectively).

20. The grouping of the specific items under the three 'traditionalist' categories parallels, in part, what Erickson (1997) did in her analysis of women candidates and political attitudes.

21. On the abortion issue, Southern Europeans remain more traditionalist only within the right-wing parties.

22. Those who refused to respond to the survey question on origin and those who replied that they were 'Canadian' (see note 18) were excluded from this part of the analysis.

23. As would be expected, those of French origin were much more likely to indicate that their background was important to them (92 per cent) than were those of British origin (45 per cent).

24. For the other candidates, the percentages who indicated 'very important' are as follows: majority (29 per cent), Western and Northern European (19 per cent), Eastern European (36 per cent), Southern European (28 per cent).

References

Black, Jerome H. 1991. 'Ethnic Minorities and Mass Politics in Canada: Some Observations in the Toronto Setting', *International Journal of Canadian Studies* 3: 129–51.

―――. 1997. 'Citizenship, Immigration, and Politics', paper presented at the biennial meeting of the Canadian Ethnic Studies Association, Montreal.

―――. 2000a. 'Ethnoracial Minorities in the Canadian House of Commons: The Case of the 36th Parliament', *Canadian Ethnic Studies* 32: 105–14.

———. 2000b. 'Entering the Political Elite in Canada: The Case of Minority Women as Parliamentary Candidates and MPs', *Canadian Review of Sociology and Anthropology* 37: 143–66.

——— and Aleem S. Lakhani. 1997. 'Ethnoracial Diversity in the House of Commons: An Analysis of Numerical Representation in the 35th Parliament', *Canadian Ethnic Studies* 29: 1–21.

Breton, Raymond. 1985. 'Multiculturalism and Canadian Nation-Building', in Alan Cairns and Cynthia Williams, eds, *The Politics of Gender, Ethnicity and Language*. Toronto: University of Toronto Press, 27–66.

Chui, Tina W., et al. 1991. 'Immigrant Background and Political Participation: Examining Generational Patterns', *Canadian Journal of Sociology* 16: 375–96.

Erickson, Lynda. 1997. 'Might More Women Make a Difference? Gender, Party and Ideology among Canada's Parliamentary Candidates', *Canadian Journal of Political Science* 30: 663–88.

Gotell, Lise, and Janine Brodie. 1991. 'Women and Parties: More than an Issue of Numbers', in Hugh G. Thorburn, ed., *Party Politics in Canada*, 6th edn. Scarborough, Ont.: Prentice-Hall Canada, 53–67.

Kymlicka, Will. 1995. *Multicultural Citizenship: A Liberal Theory of Minority Rights*. New York: Oxford University Press.

Norris, Pippa. 1996. 'Women Politicians: Transforming Westminster?', *Parliamentary Affairs* 49: 89–102.

Ogmundson, R., and J. McLaughlin. 1992. 'Trends in the Ethnic Origins of Canadian Elites: The Decline of the BRITS?', *Canadian Review of Sociology and Anthropology* 29: 227–41.

Pelletier, Alain. 1991. 'Politics and Ethnicity: Representation of Ethnic and Visible Minority Groups in the House of Commons', in Kathy Megyery, ed., *Ethno-cultural Groups and Visible Minorities in Canadian Politics*. Toronto: Dundurn Press, 101–59.

Pitkin, Hanna. 1967. *The Concept of Representation*. Berkeley: University of California Press.

Royal Commission on Electoral Reform and Party Financing. 1991. *Reforming Electoral Democracy*, vol. 1. Ottawa: Supply and Services Canada.

Simpson, Jeffrey. 1997. 'Reform's Visible-Minority Members Support its Line on Equality', *Globe and Mail*, 2 Oct., A22.

Stasiulus, Daiva. 1997. 'Participation by Immigrants, Ethnocultural/Visible Minorities in the Canadian Political Process', paper presented at the Metropolis Research Domain Seminar on Immigrants and Civic Participation, Montreal.

Statistics Canada, Interdepartmental Working Group on Employment Equity Data. 1993. *Employment Equity Data Highlights*. Ottawa, Dec.

———. 1998. *The Daily*. Available at: http:/www.statcan.ca:80/Daily/English/980217/d980217.htm

Vickers, Jill. 1997. *Reinventing Political Science: A Feminist Approach*. Halifax: Fernwood.

Chapter 22

Grassroots Participation in Candidate Nominations

WILLIAM CROSS

The vast majority of party activists associate with their party only through their participation in a local constituency association. Most will never attend a national political convention or rise to high party office. Instead, they will participate in party politics at the riding level—nominating candidates, voting for party leaders, and volunteering in election campaigns. It is thus essential to examine each of these party activities in some detail, and the role of the local members in them, in any assessment of grassroots participation in our political parties. In contributing to this discussion, this chapter examines grassroots participation in candidate nominations.

Candidate nominations are a central feature of party democracy. Prior to each general election campaign, Canadians of all political stripes organize in each of the country's 301 constituencies to choose their local candidates. The selection of these candidates is important, for from among the men and women nominated by the five major federal parties the voters choose their member of Parliament. Canadian electoral politics is dominated by the major parties, and those not nominated by one of them have little opportunity for electoral success. This is evident in the results of the 1997 election—300 of the 301 successful candidates were nominees of one of these five parties.[1]

Students of Canadian politics have long argued that candidate nomination is one of the events in which grassroots voters have the most influence. The process appears to be locally controlled and easily permeated by interested activists. This chapter examines these assumptions, first considering the balance of power between local associations and the national party, then examining the patterns of grassroots participation, and finally evaluating the effectiveness of voter participation in candidate nominations.

Local versus Central Control over Candidate Nominations

One of the principal determinants of whether grassroots participation in candidate nominations is meaningful is whether control over nominations lies with the central or local party association. In the Canadian parties the normal method of candidate selection is the constituency convention at which local partisans gather to select the standard-bearer of their choice. Thus, local autonomy appears to be the norm. This conclusion is supported by the literature, as most observers have described the nominating process as being essentially within the purview of local constituency associations. This observation has been made by students of Canadian politics dating back nearly 100 years. In 1906, André Siegfried observed that: 'Five or six weeks before the voting-day the candidates are nominated by a local convention held in each constituency' (1966: 119). Some 40 years later, R. MacGregor Dawson (1947: 446) concurred with Siegfried, observing that nomination 'conventions are extremely jealous of their own powers and independence, and they will not tolerate interference from any quarter, particularly from the higher party circles.' Similar conclusions have been reported more recently by Scarrow (1964: 55), Perlin (1975: 114), Williams (1981: 91), and Erickson and Carty (1991: 332), who suggest that 'Conventional wisdom has it that candidate selection is a highly localized phenomenon, primarily an activity of local partisans who choose their own nominees and who make the rules and practices with respect to that choice with virtually no legal encumbrances and few requirements imposed by their national parties.' Carty, Cross, and Young describe this local autonomy as part of a basic organizational trade-off: local autonomy for national discipline. The essence of this bargain is that in return for being given great discretion in the running of their own affairs, including the choosing of candidates, 'national party leaders are deferred to in setting policy directions and enforcing the parliamentary discipline required by the system' (Carty et al., 2000: 155).

Local authority over candidate nomination, however, is not absolute. The literature on parties in Canada includes several examples of central party interference with the nomination process. In his study of the federal Liberal Party from 1930 to 1958, Reginald Whitaker (1977: 143) observes that candidate nomination meetings were often orchestrated events with regional ministers having significant influence over who the local candidates would be. In a study of Newfoundland politics, S.J.R. Noel (1971: 282) observes that from 1949 to 1968 Premier Joey Smallwood had absolute authority over federal Liberal Party nominations in that province. Similarly, in Social Credit Alberta in the 1930s, Premier William Aberhart selected candidates from lists of three or four names submitted by each constituency association (Williams, 1981: 92). Recent evidence suggests that national party involvement in the process continues and may be more intrusive and pervasive than widely believed. Support for this contention is found in survey data collected after the 1993 federal election indicating that 34 per cent of Liberal associations reported outside interference by their national party in their selection of a candidate.[2]

One of the structural characteristics of Canadian politics that facilitates greater central party involvement is a 1970 amendment to the Canada Elections Act that effectively gives party leaders a veto over the selection of candidates. Support for the amendment was driven by a desire to display party affiliation beside the candidate's name on the election ballot.[3] To effect this provision, party leaders are now required to endorse their party's candidate in each constituency. The denial of candidacy to a duly nominated individual, or the threat of denial of candidacy to dissuade undesirable candidates, is now a regular part of every election campaign. The first time this provision was used to deny a nominated candidate party endorsement was in the case of Leonard Jones, who was mayor of Moncton, New Brunswick, and a vociferous critic of French-language rights. Robert Stanfield, then Conservative Party leader, refused to accept Jones's nomination by the local party association for the 1974 election and demanded that they nominate someone else.[4]

Party leaders have relied on this authority to deny candidates the privilege of seeking office under their party label on many occasions since. Leaders have often denied candidacy to individuals who were under an ethical cloud. For example, Brian Mulroney refused to authorize Sinclair Stevens's renomination for the 1988 election. Stevens, a former cabinet member, had been found by a judicial inquiry to have breached conflict-of-interest guidelines on 14 occasions. Similarly, in the 1993 campaign, Kim Campbell refused to certify the nominations of three incumbent MPs who had been renominated by their constituency associations. All three of these MPs (Gilles Bernier, Carole Jacques, and Gabriel Fontaine) were facing criminal charges related to their service in elected office.

It is not always publicly apparent when this authority is used. For example, Jean Chrétien used it in both 1993 and 1997 to prevent would-be candidates from even seeking nominations in the Liberal Party. Chrétien told reporters: 'I denied some people the right to run. I said: if you run, I will not sign your papers. It did not go in the press, but I did it in a couple of cases where characters were questionable' (*Globe and Mail*, 1993). David Smith, who oversaw the party's nomination process in Ontario for both 1993 and 1997, informed several individuals who were interested in seeking nominations that their candidacy papers would not be signed by the leader should they be successful. These cases usually involved questionable conduct by the potential candidates, such as pending criminal charges.[5]

This authority can also be used by the central party to prevent the nomination of extremist candidates. The Reform Party was concerned about the potential nomination of candidates from the ideological far right. The party effectively removed the veto power over nominations from its leader and vested it in the party's executive council.[6] In 1993, the council refused the candidacy of former Conservative MP and leadership candidate John Gamble, who had been nominated by the Reform association in the riding of Don Valley West (Ontario), on the grounds that his politics were too far right for the party. Reform's Calgary office also required nomination candidates to sign an 'Affirmation Form' signalling their support for Reform's positions 'on such basic issues as a Triple-E Senate, Canada being a federation of equal provinces, the equality of all Canadians, the Party's position on moral issues and its language policy'. In addition, potential candidates must complete a background information form and 'obtain [a] Certificate of Conduct (police report)'. This background information is used by the central office 'to perform background and/or credit checks' at the request of a riding association (Reform Party, 1996). Would-be candidates who fail to provide such information or to pledge agreement with the party's positions on these 'basic issues' are denied candidacy.

The national parties also involve themselves in candidate nomination by setting the framework of party rules that must be followed by local associations. For the most part, these rules are rather benign attempts to ensure conformity in the process across the country and fairness at the local level and to make the timing of nominations consistent with the party's electoral strategy. These provisions typically include rules dictating the timing of nomination meetings, membership cut-off dates for participation, a standard membership fee, a minimum voting age, and rules governing the participation of voters from outside a constituency. In recent elections, however, this rule-making authority has been used by the central party to influence the choice of a nominee. An example of this occurred in the Ontario riding of Renfrew-Nipissing-Pembroke in the 1993 election. Incumbent Liberal MP Len Hopkins was facing a tough challenge for renomination from a candidate favoured by the local party executive. To ensure the renomination of Hopkins, an outcome favoured by Liberal leader Jean Chrétien, who wanted all incumbent MPs renominated, the party's Ontario campaign chair, David Smith, opened and closed nominations for the riding on the same day. Smith did this from his Toronto office without giving notification to the local association until 30 minutes after nominations closed. Hopkins was the only candidate made aware that nominations were being accepted and thus was acclaimed. Despite local protests over this type of manipulation, the Liberals repeated this exercise in 1997 in several ridings, including that of Toronto's St Paul's to ensure the renomination of MP Carolyn Bennett.

The national parties have also moved recently to set nomination rules that favour female and minority candidates. All of the parties, with the exception of Reform (now the Canadian Alliance), have publicly committed themselves to attracting more female and minority candidates. For the 1997 election, Chrétien set a target of 25 per cent of Liberal nominations going to women. Liberal field workers felt substantial pressure from their national headquarters to see to it that the ridings within their region were in compliance with this national target. In turn, field staff applied pressure on riding associations to encourage them to nominate female candidates.[7]

The New Democrats have been at the forefront of efforts to set national candidate nomination rules that will have the effect of encouraging female and minority candidacies. The party has adopted a *Nomination and Affirmative Action Policy* that includes the following objectives: 'A minimum of 60 per cent of ridings where the NDP has a reasonable chance of winning shall have women running as NDP candidates for election', and, 'A minimum of 15 per cent of ridings where the NDP has a reasonable chance of winning shall have NDP candidates for election who reflect the diversity of Canada and include representation of affirmative action groups.' To give effect to these objectives, local associations are required to establish that 'a candidate search committee has been established reflecting the diversity of the riding' and that 'there is one or more candidate for the nomination from affirmative action groups.' Riding associations are not permitted to hold a nomination meeting until these conditions are met or, 'in extraordinary cases', they are granted an exemption. The New Democrats further encourage female and minority candidates by reimbursing these candidates up to $500 for costs incurred in seeking the nomination in ridings where the NDP incumbent is retiring, offering them up to $500 for child-care expenses incurred in seeking the nomination, reimbursing them an additional $500 for costs incurred in seeking nomination in large ridings, and permitting them to receipt up to $1,500 in contributions for income tax purposes (NDP, 1997). While these sorts of provisions do not take the nominating decision out of the hands of the local activists, they do potentially influence the composition of the field that the local party members will have to choose from.

The Liberal Party interfered the most directly in local constituency autonomy in both 1993 and 1997 when its leader, Chrétien, appointed the party's candidate in a total of 20 ridings. The party amended its constitution in 1992 to give the National Campaign Committee, whose members are appointed by the party leader, complete authority over the rules and processes of candidate nomination.[8] Newfoundland MP Brian Tobin, later that province's Premier and most recently once again on the national scene as Industry Minister, was correct in observing that the new rules amounted to 'a massive shift of power from riding associations and provincial organizations to the national leader and the national campaign committee' (*Globe and Mail*, 1992). When Chrétien's 20 appointments are scrutinized there appear to be four discrete, though sometimes overlapping, motivating factors. The first has been the party's concern to increase the number of women and minority candidates—12 of the 20 have been women. The second is the protection of incumbent MPs caught in difficult renomination battles. An example of this was the appointment of Sarkis Assourian, whose previous riding had been broken up in the most recent redistribution, to renomination in the riding of Brampton Centre in 1997. The third involves the appointment of star candidates, such as former Toronto Mayor Art Eggleton in the riding of York-Centre and senior civil servant Marcel Masse in Hull-Aylmer. Chrétien wanted both of these men for his cabinet and used a guaranteed nomination as an inducement to convince them to offer as candidates. Finally, appointments have been made to prevent the takeover of a nomination contest by activists concerned with a single policy issue. An example of this is the appointment of Jean Augustine in the Toronto riding of Etobicoke-Lakeshore in 1993. While Augustine, then chair of the Metro Toronto Housing Authority, met other apparent criteria for candidate appointment—being of high profile, a woman, and a minority—the choice of riding for her nomination was likely related to Dan McCash's campaign for the nomination in Etobicoke-Lakeshore. McCash was at the time national co-ordinator of Liberals for Life, an anti-abortion group, and was mounting a vigorous challenge for the nomination (*Montreal Gazette*, 1993). Preventing this type of single-issue candidacy was one of the announced reasons for the leadership's efforts to amend the party's constitution to give the leader absolute authority over the nomination process (*Montreal Gazette*, 1992).

The evidence reviewed above illustrates that while candidate nomination in Canadian parties generally remains a constituency-based process, there is an increasing willingness on the part of the national parties to interfere with this local process. It remains to be seen whether this trend will continue with the national offices assuming greater control over nominations or whether the local associations will reassert themselves in defence of their traditional autonomy in this regard.

Voter Participation in Candidate Nominations

Evaluations of voter participation in candidate nominations depend on whether the observer chooses to see a glass that is half-full or half-empty. On the positive side, more voters participate in nominations than in any other party activity. Party membership rates decline dramatically between elections. Carty et al. (2000: 158) have noted that: 'Between elections these local associations are quiescent, perhaps meeting once or twice a year but otherwise leaving the routine tasks of maintaining membership lists and raising money to a small coterie of dedicated activists.' Riding associations spring to life and membership numbers increase dramatically as an election nears and candidate nomination battles heat up at the constituency level. Party supporters routinely renew memberships that have lapsed since the prior election in order to participate and hundreds of new members are routinely mobilized by the nomination candidates. This phenomenon is illustrated in Figure 22.1, which examines membership patterns in the Progressive Conservative Party in 1992, 1993, and 1994. Party membership doubled from 1992 to 1993 and then decreased by two-thirds in the year after the election campaign.[9] The membership numbers for associations with contested nominations illustrate that this increase is largely driven by voter desire to participate in nomination contests. Riding associations with contested nominations saw their membership totals increase by almost 350 per cent in the run-up to the election.

While nomination contests substantially drive up membership totals, a small percentage of voters choose to participate. The average attendance at 1993 nomination meetings in the Liberal, Conservative, and Reform parties was only 413, and this number is greatly increased by a few ridings that had very large meetings (3 per cent over 2,000). The median attendance was just 201 and one-third of associations had 100 or fewer members participate.[10] Most ridings had four major parties contest the 1993 election; thus, it is likely that in most constituencies fewer than 1,000 voters participated in all of the local candidate nomination meetings combined. On average, this represents less than 2 per cent of general election voters.

The number of party members participating in nominations appears to have decreased over time. More than a half-century ago, Dawson (1947: 444) observed that 'A normal attendance is four or five hundred.' This figure is two times the current median and represents an even greater decrease in participation for two reasons: (1) there were fewer voters in each riding over 50 years ago; and (2) those attending early nomination meetings were often delegates chosen from subdivisions

Figure 22.1: Progressive Conservative Constituency Association Membership by Type of Nomination Contest for the 1993 Election

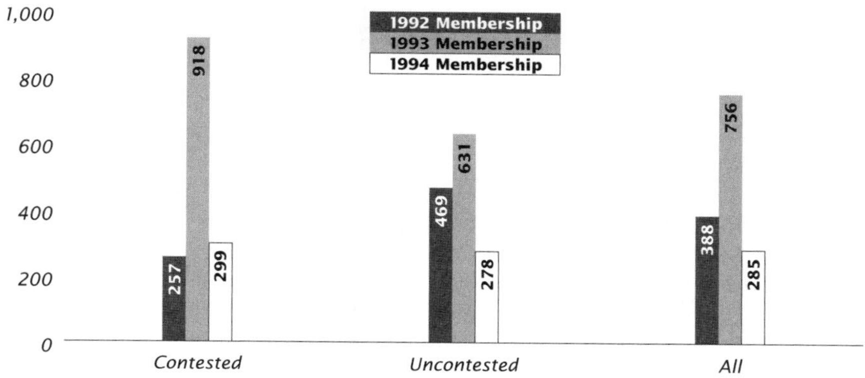

Source: Data derived from survey of constituency association presidents following 1993 election.

within the riding, meaning that many more party members participated in the selection of these nomination meeting delegates.

Not only do nomination meetings attract a very small percentage of voters, they also attract only a minority of party members. The 1993 election data indicate that less than half of party members participated in the nomination meeting. This is consistent with the 1988 election findings of Carty and Erickson (1991: 114), who reported that 'On average, only about a third of a riding's membership attends.' The remainder of this chapter examines why so few Canadians choose to participate in nomination campaigns.

For the most part the parties' rules governing candidate nomination encourage voter participation. Voters who have never belonged to the party until a month before the nomination contest, past members whose memberships have lapsed, those too young to vote in general elections,[11] and even those without Canadian citizenship are often permitted to participate. In many ways the process is remarkably open, and as Carty et al. (2000: 160) have observed: 'Individuals who want to be candidates can easily recruit new party members and urge them to come to the nomination meeting.' Voter recruitment by candidates is key to participation in nomination campaigns. It appears that a large percentage of nomination voters are recruited by individual candidates while few Canadians are attracted to these contests on their own. A result of this phenomenon is that the number of voters participating in individual nomination contests reflects the number of candidates seeking the nomination. Table 22.1 illustrates that the number of voters participating increases with the entry of each additional candidate into the contest.

In recent elections half or more of the major parties' nominations have been uncontested. Contested nominations draw many times more voters than do the

Table 22.1: Constituency Voter Participation in 1993 Liberal, Reform, and Progressive Conservative Nominations by Number of Candidates Seeking Nomination

Number of Candidates	Mean Number of Voters Participating	N
1	183	(149)
2	422	(81)
3	434	(61)
4	763	(36)
5	834	(18)
6 (or more)	1,023	(21)
	415 (average)	Total: (366)

Source: Data derived from survey of constituency association presidents following 1993 election.

uncontested.[12] For example, Erickson and Carty (1991: 349) found that contested 1988 nomination meetings 'drew, on average, almost six times as many people as uncontested ones'. Of the associations participating in the 1993 study, those with uncontested meetings had a mean membership turnout of 183 and a median of 100. The mean attendance at a contested meeting was 574 and the median 300. One-third of contested nominations had more than 500 members present.

One of the significant factors determining whether a nomination is contested is whether there is an incumbent MP seeking renomination. Incumbent MPs are rarely challenged for renomination. The 1993 data show that nine out of 10 incumbents seeking renomination were unopposed. This illustrates the effectiveness of central party activities, like those recounted above in the Liberal Party, that seek to assure the renomination of incumbents.

While there has been little systematic study of the participants in candidate nomination meetings in Canada, some general patterns are observable. Voter participation is largely driven by group mobilization. Candidates find it difficult to recruit the needed several hundred members one at a time and thus concentrate their efforts on recruiting groups of supporters, often from ethnic groups. These tightly knit communities, which often have organized communication structures through churches, associations, and the ethnic press, can quickly mobilize scores of supporters for a preferred candidate. An example of this occurred in the battle for the 1997 Liberal nomination in the British Columbia riding of Surrey Centre. The contest was between two individuals representing competing interests in local Sikh temple politics. Both candidates recruited heavily from the Sikh community, and what had been a typically quiescent riding association suddenly saw its membership rise to over 5,000. On voting day, as party members voted at a local hotel under police presence to prevent the outbreak of violence, it appeared that at least four out of every five voters were members of the Sikh community. There is nothing new about this scenario. For at least the past few decades, each nomination season has included a number of highly publicized contests that have included mobilization of large numbers from various ethnic communities. This voter mobilization gives the process the appearance of accessibility and permeability. However, the nomination process is easily accessed only by highly organized groups—like the Sikh community in Surrey Centre—that decide to support a nomination candidate and mobilize their members in that effort. Voters face several very real obstacles to participation. These include a membership fee, generally $10 to $20. This fee effectively serves as a poll tax for most would-be voters, while members who are recruited by a particular candidate often have their membership fees paid by the candidate's campaign. Unlike a general election, when polling places are located in every neighbourhood, nomination voters are required to travel to a single location to vote. Candidates will often rent buses to transport their supporters to the voting location while other would-be voters are left to find their own transportation. Other obstacles to participation include the difficulties that many may find in freeing themselves from family and work responsibilities in order to be able to spend three hours or so listening to candidate speeches and voting in a nomination contest. Candidates' supporters will often arrange services such as child care to ensure the participation of their voters.

Voters may also choose not to participate in nomination contests because they very rarely have anything to do with matters of public policy. Carty and Erickson (1991: 122) concluded of the 1988 nominations, 'this is largely a portrait of a process typically neither disciplined nor driven by issues or distinctive social groups.' The data collected after the 1993 election support this conclusion. Only one in four associations reported important policy differences among the candidates for their nomination, and there was no significant difference among the parties in this regard. Overall, contested nominations in which there were 'substantive policy differences' that were 'significant in the nomination campaign' had considerably more voters than was the case in contests without policy contestation. The mean attendance at contested nominations with policy disagreements was 670 and the median 400, while for those without policy differences the mean was 545 and the median 300. This may indicate that voters are substantially more interested in contests revolving around policy ideas than personality.

Respondents were also asked if a public debate was held among nomination candidates. Overall, just over half of all associations with contested nominations reported holding such an event. This number is greatly inflated by the frequent occurrence of debates in the Reform Party—four-fifths of contested Reform nominations had a debate compared with half that number for both the Liberals and Conservatives. As shown in Table 22.2, when controlling for party affiliation, substantially more voters participated in contested nominations that included a candidate debate than in those without. This reinforces the conclusion of greater voter interest in contests centring on policy discussion rather than personality.

The timing of nomination campaigns further obscures the role of policy issues. Nomination meetings are usually held before the election is called. For example, Carty and Erickson (ibid., 112) found in 1988 that 'fully 80 per cent of the party nominations had been completed by the time the election was called.' This means that nomination campaigns often take place well before the campaign's key policy

Table 22.2: Constituency Voter Participation in Contested 1993 Nomination Contests by whether a Public Debate Was Held

Type of contest		Mean attendance	Median attendance	Cases
Conservative	with a debate	801	700	19
	without a debate	512	450	27
Liberal	with a debate	1,042	450	29
	without a debate	534	350	45
Reform	with a debate	499	300	78
	without a debate	127	150	19
Overall	with a debate	669	360	126
	without a debate	443	300	91

Source: Data derived from survey of constituency association presidents following 1993 election.

issues are decided. Similarly, voter interest in the campaign has yet to peak at the time of most nominations. The requirement by local associations that voters belong to the party for a period of up to a month prior to the nomination contest to be eligible to participate also discourages participation. Potential voters whose interest is captivated during the nomination contest are ineligible to vote unless they joined the party at least a month earlier—often before the public phase of nomination campaigns begins.

Conclusion

General election voters are presented with a candidate for each major party, and if they prefer the leader or policies of a particular party, their only rational option is to vote for that party's local candidate regardless of that individual's qualifications or personal policy positions. It cannot be said with any degree of general accuracy that voters deliberately use their franchise to select particular individuals to represent their interests in Parliament. The only genuine opportunity for voters to cast judgement on the individuals wishing to represent them in the House of Commons is at the time of nomination. Yet these opportunities are deficient in several respects. The cost of participation in nomination contests is substantial for most voters, participation is not particularly meaningful as nominations are often uncontested and rarely have anything to do with public policy, and the central parties are displaying an increasing willingness to meddle in what has traditionally been an area of local discretion.

That relatively few voters participate in candidate nomination meetings is not surprising, considering the process most associations use to nominate their candidates. The process offers neither the widespread opportunity of US-style primary elections nor the deliberative possibilities of British-style candidate nominations dominated by local party élites. Instead, Canadian parties impose substantial barriers to participation for average voters and at the same time encourage candidates to recruit their friends and neighbours to join in the nomination contest. The result is a process not dominated by the informed views of long-serving party members or by the general desire of voters in the riding. Instead, a premium is placed on candidates' organizational strengths. The ability to mobilize hundreds of partisans and bring them to a nomination meeting is valued over party service or mastery of policy issues.

This outcome may well be favoured by the traditional brokerage parties. Candidates nominated by these processes cannot legitimately claim to have a mandate from their constituents on any particular policy question. The national parties, desiring strict party discipline in their parliamentary caucuses, may well prefer such a system devoid of widespread participation and policy debate. However, if voters should demand more direct representation of their interests in Parliament, and there is some evidence of voter opinion moving in this direction (Blais and Gidengil, 1991), they would be wise to focus their attention on the manner in which the parties select their candidates.

Notes

The author wishes to thank R. Kenneth Carty, S.J.R. Noel, and Lisa Young for helpful comments on an earlier draft of this essay. Valuable research assistance was provided by Anamitra Deb.

1. The only exception was John Nunziata, who was elected as a Liberal in 1988 and 1993 and re-elected as an independent in 1997.

2. Twenty-four per cent of Progressive Conservative and 12 per cent of Reform associations also reported outside interference. The data were collected by a mail survey administered in January 1995. Constituency association presidents in the Liberal, Progressive Conservative, and Reform parties were surveyed. Four hundred completed surveys were received for a response rate of 52 per cent. Respondent associations are representative in terms of their performance in the 1993 election and responses for all three parties were received from all provinces. For more details on this survey, see Cross (1998).

3. The relevant provisions are currently found in *Canada Elections Act*, section 81(1)(h) and 82(1).

4. Jones went on to win election as an independent. For a discussion of this, see Perlin (1975: 114–15).

5. Interview with David Smith, 1997 Liberal Party campaign chair, Toronto, 14 July 1998.

6. Reform Party of Canada Constitution, section 4: Candidate Recruitment, Nomination and Development, subsections (c) and (e).

7. Interview with Steve Kukucha, 1997 campaign director, Liberal Party of Canada (BC), Vancouver, 3 Apr. 1997.

8. The Liberal Party of Canada Constitution, as amended by the 1994 Biennial Convention, 'National Campaign Committee', s. 14(6), p. 50.

9. This membership pattern is similar to that found in the Liberal and Reform parties. The New Democrats do a better job of maintaining their members between elections and

realize a much smaller increase at election time. This is consistent with their characterization as a mass-membership party while the Conservatives and Liberals are normally thought of as cadre-style parties. For a full explanation of this distinction, see Duverger (1964).

10. These numbers reflect those associations participating in the 1993 election constituency survey.

11. A common minimum age for participation in nomination contests is 14 years.

12. Carty and Erickson (1991: 120) report that 65 per cent of 1988 nominations resulted in acclamations. The 1993 data indicate substantial differences among the three participating parties: 60 per cent of Conservative nominations, 50 per cent of Liberal nominations, and only 20 per cent of Reform nominations in 1993 ended with an acclamation. The lower number of Reform acclamations resulted from their having only one incumbent seeking renomination. The increase in competitiveness in the Liberal ranks from 1988 reflects the increased likelihood that they would win the election and form the next government— making their nominations more desirable.

References

Blais, André, and Elisabeth Gidengil. 1991, *Making Representative Democracy Work: The Views of Canadians*. Toronto: Dundurn Press.

Carty, R. Kenneth, William Cross, and Lisa Young. 2000. *Rebuilding Canadian Party Politics*. Vancouver: University of British Columbia Press.

———— and Lynda Erickson. 1991. 'Candidate Nomination', in Herman Bakvis, ed., *Canadian Political Parties: Leaders, Candidates and Organizations*. Toronto: Dundurn Press, 97–189.

Cross, William. 1998. 'The Conflict Between Participatory and Accommodative Politics: The Case for Stronger Parties', *International Journal of Canadian Studies* 17 (Spring): 37–55.

Dawson, R. MacGregor. 1947. *The Government of Canada*, 5th edn. London: Oxford University Press.

Duverger, Maurice. 1964. *Political Parties: Their Organization and Activity in the Modern State*. London: Methuen.

Erickson, Lynda, and R. Kenneth Carty. 1991. 'Parties and Candidate Selection in the 1988 Canadian General Election', *Canadian Journal of Political Science* 24, 2: 331–50.

Globe and Mail. 1992. 'Liberals clean up nomination process: Recruitment of instant members and ethnic groups to end', 21 Feb., A1, A6.

————. 1993. 'Bad apples can't run', 29 July, A4.

Montreal Gazette. 1992. 'Chrétien thwarts hijack by pro-lifers', 21 Feb., B11.

————. 1993. 'Chrétien names five women candidates', 20 Mar., A11.

New Democratic Party (NDP). 1997. *Nomination and Affirmative Action Policy*.

Noel, S.J.R. 1971. *Politics in Newfoundland*. Toronto: University of Toronto Press.

Perlin, George. 1975. 'The Progressive Conservative Party in the Election of 1974', in Howard R. Penniman, ed., *Canada at the Polls: The General Election of 1974*. Washington: American Enterprise Institute for Public Policy Research, 97–120.

Reform Party of Canada. 1996. *Candidate Recruitment and Selection Manual*.

Scarrow, Harold A. 1964. 'Nomination and Local Party Organization in Canada: A Case Study', *Western Political Quarterly* 17: 55–62.

Siegfried, André. 1966 [1906]. *The Race Question in Canada*. Toronto: McClelland & Stewart.

Whitaker, Reginald. 1977. *The Government Party: Organizing and Financing the Liberal Party of Canada, 1930–1958*. Toronto: University of Toronto Press.

Williams, Robert J. 1981. 'Candidate Selection', in Howard R. Penniman, ed., *Canada at the Polls, 1979 and 1980: A Study of the General Elections*. Washington: American Enterprise Institute for Public Policy Research, 86–120.

Part VII

Interest Groups and Social Movements

Chapter 23

Crashing the Party:
The Politics of Interest Groups
and Social Movements

JACQUETTA NEWMAN AND A. BRIAN TANGUAY

In recent years, politicians, pundits, and scholars in Canada and other developed democracies have blamed interest groups and social movements for all manner of contemporary ills. Gridlock and overload in legislatures—what Rauch (1994) calls 'demosclerosis', the silent killer of democratic government—are traced to the post-war explosion of needy, self-interested groups armed with new techniques of political persuasion. The increasing ineffectiveness of mainstream political parties, along with the growing hostility among voters towards politicians and a perceived decline in civility, is also ascribed to the pernicious influence of organized interests. So, too, is the triumph of the politics of identity and the consequent tribalization of society.

There is another view of interest groups and social movements in the political science literature, even though it might not be the dominant one. Some theorists (the authors of this chapter among them) consider these organizations—especially social movements, since they offer well-developed critiques of the status quo and 'politics as usual'—to be more than just 'party crashers' that undermine the effectiveness of the traditional political parties. Because interest groups and social movements articulate demands and ideas often ignored by the political parties, whose primary preoccupation seems increasingly to win elections at all costs, they are essential elements of a healthy and vibrant democracy. It would therefore be best in the long run for the political parties and policy-makers in Canada and elsewhere to extend an invitation to organized interests and try to work with them.

Theoretical understandings of organized interests, as the following review of the literature will show, are crucially important for shedding light on the nature of democratic representation, the changing dimensions of political debate and conflict in late modern society, and the behaviour of the contemporary state. They are important for another, somewhat esoteric reason: theories of interest groups and social movements may serve to overcome the state-society dualism that has bedevilled the discipline of political science for much of this century. By this we mean the tendency among political scientists to study the state and society in isolation from one another and for the discipline as a whole to oscillate between state-centred perspectives (the constitutional-legal approach at the turn of the century or neo-institutionalism more recently) and sociological ones (pluralism, systems theory, and structural-functionalism, for example, which were dominant in the 1950s and 1960s). Migdal (1997: 208–12) has recently criticized the 'analytic isolation of the state' and called for the elaboration of theoretical frameworks that situate states in 'the web of relationships between them and their societies'. He points to theories of nationalism as one promising avenue for bridging the state-society divide. In our view, theories of interest groups and social movements are equally well-suited to this task.

In this chapter we provide an overview of the principal theoretical approaches used to study interest groups and social movements, the key questions that have informed research in this subfield, the various methodologies employed by researchers, and the specific contributions made by Canadian social scientists to our understanding of group behaviour. As well, we highlight some of the most obvious gaps that remain in our knowledge of interest groups and social movements and suggest research topics that might be pursued in order to fill these lacunae.

It's Not Just a Matter of Semantics: Labels Matter

Scholars, politicians, and media observers alike use a bewildering variety of terms to describe organized interests in contemporary societies: interest group, pressure group, lobby, single-issue group, citizens' group, public interest group, and so on. These labels are frequently normative as well as descriptive. 'Special interest', for instance, has entered the political lexicon as a handy term of abuse applied by populist politicians to the many groups or social categories—women, ethnic minorities, trade unions, ecologists, and so on—they claim have hijacked the governmental agenda and sapped the economic strength of democratic nations with their endless demands. In order to clear up some of this terminological confusion, we make the following observations.

(1) The terms 'pressure group' and 'lobby'—each freighted with a number of unsavoury associations and pejorative connotations—appear to have been eclipsed in the scientific literature by the more value-neutral 'interest group'. 'Pressure group' is a perfectly acceptable label to designate an organized interest, and in the formative years of group theory it was probably the most common term used (see Finer, 1958: 3–4). It does carry with it, however, more than a hint of disapproval for the tactics employed to influence public decision-makers (Truman, 1951: 38–39). 'Lobby' and 'lobbyist' are even more obviously loaded: each, in contemporary parlance, evokes images of influence-peddling and corruption, whether this is warranted or not (Brooks, 1996: 464–5). It seems prudent, therefore, to limit the use of this label to describe professionals who, for payment, contact public

office-holders in an effort to influence policy, legislation, or the awarding of government contracts.[1]

(2) By process of elimination, then, 'interest group' is the least biased generic term available to social scientists to designate organizations or associations that seek to influence public policy without actually fielding candidates for office. This definition is intentionally expansive: it includes not only membership organizations such as the Canadian Federation of Independent Business or Mothers Against Drunk Driving (MADD), for example, but individual institutions like hospitals, corporations, and municipalities. The latter do not accept members in the normal sense of the word, and yet they frequently seek, either singly or in association with similar institutions, to influence public decision-makers in a variety of policy sectors. The category of interest group includes both sectional interests—those based on a specific socio-economic category of the population (trade unions and business associations, for example)—and organizations promoting a cause, such as the Audubon Society or Parents for a Quality Education.

Defining the term 'interest group' as broadly as possible ensures that potentially interesting and relevant avenues of research are not closed off prematurely. It does, however, have its drawbacks, since researchers may be tempted to extrapolate their findings to situations that are not strictly comparable (Baumgartner and Leech, 1998: 43).

(3) Interest groups and social movements are separate analytical entities, even if in the real worlds of politics the distinctions between them can be less than watertight. The term 'social movement', and specifically '*new* social movement' (NSM), is used to cover a variety of political and social collective actions focused on issues such as gender equality, sexual freedom, health, civil rights, anti-racism, international development, the environment, and peace. To paraphrase Melucci (1996), the term 'social movement' refers to a form of collective action where the collective actor: (1) invokes and is defined by a sense of solidarity and shared meaning; (2) makes manifest a social, political, and cultural conflict; and (3) within that conflict presents a vision that contains an inherent or immanent critique of society. These movements focus on issues of a moral and social nature; emphasize participatory, inclusionary, and democratic organization; make greater use of non-institutional forms of political expression such as protest and public education; and often hold critical attitudes towards bureaucratic and state agendas and solutions. Unlike interest groups, their goals and forms of action are not negotiable within the existing arrangement of social power, as with, for example, the vision of the women's movement of an end to patriarchy and the peace movement's critique of conceptions of security predicated on militarism. In addition, social movements are less dependent on formal organization for their emergence and maintenance than are traditional interest groups, since they often represent new forms of social or political identity, and they define success not simply in terms of influencing public policy but more generally as the popularization of unorthodox understandings of politics.

Interest Groups: Crashing the Party from Inside

The Comparative Literature

The origins of interest group theory can be traced to the publication in 1908 of Arthur Fisher Bentley's *The Process of Government*. This book was informed by a hard-nosed empiricism: to Bentley, ideas and feelings were 'spooks' and therefore of no explanatory value to social scientists. 'It is impossible to attain scientific treatment of material that will not submit itself to measurement in some form', Bentley wrote. 'Measure conquers chaos' (Bentley, 1967: 200). The fundamental building blocks of social scientific analysis, he argued, were 'groups of men, each group cutting across many others, each individual man a component part of very many groups' (ibid., 204). Every group in society has a specific and identifiable interest, in Bentley's view, and the objective of the social scientist is to classify and analyse these various groups. 'When the groups are adequately stated, everything is stated. When I say everything I mean everything. The complete description will mean the complete science' (ibid., 208–9). For Bentley, the process of government consisted in the balancing and adjustment of group pressures. Later critics of Bentley would attack his conviction that there is a tendency in democratic polities towards an equilibrium of competing interests. In Bernard Crick's view (1959: 130), Bentley assumed 'a harmony and a single calculable natural order of society, the lack of which . . . is the very reason for the existence of government and politics.'

Bentley's book languished in obscurity for over 30 years, until it was rediscovered in the 1940s and 1950s.[2] Bentley's positivism—his belief that the philosophy of the natural sciences must be extended into the study of society—his anti-Marxism, and his desire to use social science as a tool of progressive reform dovetailed perfectly with the scientism,[3] optimism, and activism that characterized mainstream American political science during this later era. Some of the fundamental assumptions undergirding Bentley's book were eventually incorporated into the theory of pluralism, elaborated in the works of Truman (1951), Dahl (1961), and Almond and Powell (1966), among others.

Group theory and pluralism, which came close to constituting the dominant paradigm in American political science in the 1950s, made the following assertions about the role of groups in liberal democracies, the United States being considered by many advocates of the approach as simply the most highly developed polity in the Western world:[4]

- A vast number of voluntary associations exist in democratic societies to represent the interests of various groups. These organizations emerge more or less spontaneously (they are not created by the state) in response to perceived threats or disturbances in the political and economic environments.
- To advance their interests, these groups bring a variety of pressure tactics to bear on government. Government outputs, in the form of policies, regulations, and laws, can be taken to be a crude barometer of the balance of group interests at any one moment.

- Interest groups compete in a political market, or arena, which no one of them can dominate for any length of time. There is a rough equality, and equilibrium, in this market; government decisions will not routinely and systematically favour one group over time. All legitimate interests can in principle be mobilized and organized.
- Multiple overlapping memberships—the fact that one individual can belong simultaneously to many different groups—foster moderation and democratic stability. Moreover, according to Truman (1951: 165), '[t]he evidence regarding individual differences stemming from multiple group memberships . . . challenges the Marxist assumption that class interests are primary and the more common assumption that occupational group interests are always dominant.'
- The most highly developed democratic polities are characterized by a specialized division of political labour. A profusion of interest groups articulates the numerous demands in society, which are then aggregated into competing political programs by a limited number of pragmatic, non-ideological political parties. In some societies, such as Italy and France, where the political division of labour is not as specialized or fully developed as it is in the Anglo-American democracies, political parties and interest groups interpenetrate each other, and the result is a highly ideological political culture, instability, and governmental paralysis.

Pluralism and group theory were subjected to a forceful multi-pronged attack in the late 1950s and early 1960s. Some critics, like Macridis (1977: 322–3), dismissed the approach as a crude form of determinism that downplayed the role of ideology and non-rational motives in political behaviour and was utterly unconcerned with the histories of different political systems.

Probably the most common criticism levelled against pluralism was that the approach was prescriptive and normative, not merely descriptive or analytical. Pluralists and group theorists were accused of constructing an idealized view of the American political system, one that overlooked the obvious disparities in power among social groups. Business, most notably, was 'more equal' than any other group, and there was an obvious class bias to the entire pressure group system. As a number of scholars observed, it was the highly educated and relatively affluent who participated disproportionately in lobbying activity. This view was best summed up in E.E. Schattschneider's well-known epigram: 'the flaw in the pluralist heaven is that the heavenly chorus sings with a strong upper-class accent' (1960: 35).

Another fundamental defect in pluralist analysis was a methodological one: by focusing on issues that actually made it to the governmental arena, theorists like Robert Dahl (in *Who Governs?*) erroneously concluded that the struggle of organized group interests was the paramount feature of democratic politics and that no single group dominated the process over time and across all issues. What Dahl and others ignored, according to Schattschneider and Bachrach and Baratz (1967), was the 'mobilization of bias' inherent in the system. By this they meant the tendency for certain issues or proposals—those that touched on the existing structure of authority in liberal democracies, on property rights and so on—to be organized out of politics, to be excluded beforehand as Utopian, illegitimate, or impractical (Garson, 1978: 127). Bachrach and Baratz (1967: 150) coined the term 'nondecision-making' to describe this process, and claimed that pluralists overlooked the possibility that 'some person or association could limit decision-making to relatively uncontroversial matters, by influencing community values and political procedures and rituals, notwithstanding that there are in the community serious but latent power conflicts.'[5]

By the time Mancur Olson's monumental work, *The Logic of Collective Action*, was published in 1965, pluralism was a 'research agenda on the road to oblivion' (Baumgartner and Leech, 1998: 50). Olson's elegant and sophisticated deductive model of group behaviour, derived from microeconomics generally and the theory of public goods in particular, simply hastened the demise of the pluralist paradigm. According to Olson (1965: 126), orthodox theorists of pressure groups—Bentley and Truman, for instance—held an unrealistically benign view of the results of interest group activity, 'not from any assumption that individuals always deal altruistically with one another, but rather because they think that the different groups will tend to keep each other in check because of the balance of power among them.' This view was based on a logical fallacy, he argued. If one examines the interests of rational individuals (which Bentley and Truman failed to do, so concerned were they with *group* interest and identity), one would have to conclude that pressure groups do not emerge automatically or spontaneously in response to some disturbance in the political or economic environment. Any group seeking a public good like a tariff or some other government regulation—which by its nature is indivisible, and supplied to any member of a group no matter how much or how little he or she contributes to its activities—faces enormous obstacles to collective action, since rational individuals will prefer to enjoy the good while expending a minimum of energy to obtain it. Rational individuals are naturally 'free riders'. The larger the potential group (tenants seeking rent controls, for example, or women lobbying for the Equal Rights Amendment), the greater the barriers to mobilization. Groups with small potential memberships, such as an association of oligopolistic corporations from a single sector of the economy, enjoy a systematic advantage over others in mobilizing to achieve their objectives, since each member of a small group will receive a relatively large portion of the collective good and will therefore not be as likely to play the free rider as would a member of a large group.

Olson concluded that 'the outcome of the political struggle among the various groups in society will not be symmetrical. Practical politicians and journalists have long understood that small "special interest" groups, the "vested interests," have disproportionate power. ... The small oligopolistic industry seeking a tariff or a tax loophole will sometimes attain its objective even if the vast majority of the population loses as a result' (ibid., 127–8). Large groups do, of course, manage to get organized—the American Federation of Labor (AFL-CIO), the American Medical Association (AMA), and the American Farm Bureau Federation are all cited by Olson as examples of 'large and powerful economic lobbies' (ibid., 132–67). However, these large groups are 'by-products of organizations that have the capacity to "mobilize" a latent group with "selective incentives"' (ibid., 133). Large economic lobbies are able to attract members either through 'subtle forms of coercion'—laws and regulations mandating compulsory membership in some professional organizations, for example—or through the provision of services and goods that are exclusive to their membership, in the way that some trade unions once offered special life insurance packages to their members. Despite the existence of these large economic lobbies, Olson concludes that '[t]he multitude of workers, white-collar workers, farmers, and so on are organized *only in special circumstances*, but business interests are organized as a general rule' (ibid., 143; emphasis added).

It would be difficult to overestimate the influence of Olson's work, not just on interest group theory itself but on the discipline of political science as a whole. The study of the dilemmas of collective action remains at the core of interest group theory today (and it is of key importance to theories of social movements as well). A number of important studies (e.g., Salisbury, 1969; Moe, 1980) have examined the motivations that drive people to join groups. These investigations have expanded on Olson's notion that selective material benefits allow large groups to overcome the free-rider problem; other incentives—solidarity (friendship, prestige, or status) and purposiveness (satisfaction from contributing to a good cause), for example—can also play a crucial role in the formation of interest groups. As well, Salisbury and others have drawn attention to the key role played by political entrepreneurs in the creation and maintenance of interest groups.

Although Olson did much to revitalize the empirical study of interest groups, he has been criticized on a number of grounds, in particular for overestimating the barriers to group mobilization. As Baumgartner and Leech (1998: 78–9) point out: 'The 1960s and 1970s were simultaneously the period of ascendancy of the Olsonian perspective and the setting for massive marches on Washington by exactly those types of groups that Olson argued faced such powerful hurdles to collective mobilization.' Moreover, in a curious reversal of the situation of the 1950s, contemporary interest group theorists who focus narrowly on the dilemmas of collective action have seemingly lost sight of the 'big picture'—the distribution of power in liberal democracies and the role played by organized interests in the political process.

Since the mid-1960s two other noteworthy developments have occurred in the field of interest group theory. First, social scientists in Western Europe (and Canada as well), reacting against the overwhelmingly *American* nature of pluralism, attempted to rehabilitate a much older theory, corporatism, to explain the configuration of group interests and the balance of power in their societies. Prior to the 1960s, corporatism, both as a theory and as a political practice, had been associated with the brutal authoritarian regimes that proliferated in Europe in the interwar period (fascist Italy, Franco's Spain, Nazi Germany, Vichy France). By the early

1960s, however, such scholars as S.H. Beer (1965) and Andrew Shonfield (1965) were arguing that attempts by some Western European governments to manage their modern capitalist economies had engendered a form of *liberal corporatism* in which the principal social partners—business, labour, and the state—were brought together in a variety of planning and consultative bodies (the Social and Economic Council in the Netherlands, the Labour Market Board in Sweden, and the National Economic Development Council in Great Britain, for example). An implicit bargain was reached by the social partners in liberal corporatist systems: in exchange for a voice in economic planning and a fiscal policy oriented more towards full employment than price stability, the organizations of labour and business committed themselves to maintaining industrial peace (keeping strikes to a minimum). In effect, the peak associations of business and labour became instruments of public policy, providing the state with advice, acquiescence, and approval.

With the publication of Philippe Schmitter's seminal article, 'Still the Century of Corporatism?', in 1974, an extremely fruitful research program was launched in the comparative study of interest groups. There were drawbacks to this rapid growth in corporatist research, however, evident in the sloppy application of the concept to cases that clearly did not fit the framework (the United States and Canada, notably). By the early 1980s, the Canadian political scientist Leo Panitch, himself one of the key contributors to the international study of corporatism, was dismissing the approach as an academic 'growth industry' and an intellectual fashion (Panitch, 1980).

The second noteworthy development in the field of interest group research since the mid-1960s has been the continued pursuit of large-scale collaborative studies of the influence of organized interests on policy-making, especially in the United States (see Heinz et al., 1993, for a particularly good example). Despite the fact that much of this research has provided valuable insights into policy networks and policy communities, Baumgartner and Leech (1998: 83) argue that 'few strong conclusions emerge from this literature, partly because scholars cannot agree on a shared point of reference.'

The Canadian Literature

The first major study of interest groups undertaken in Canada was S.D. Clark's monograph, *The Canadian Manufacturers' Association: A Study in Collective Bargaining and Political Pressure*, published in 1939. At the time, Clark (1939: xi) observed that 'the pressure group', which had been subjected to intense scrutiny in the United States for a number of years, had 'escaped . . . serious investigation in [Canada]', largely because of the institutional differences between the two countries. In the US, as Clark pointed out, the weakness of the political parties, combined with the presidential system of government, '[has] resulted in a considerable shift of legislative leadership to voluntary associations.' In Canada, by contrast, the institutional weight of cabinet, along with the highly centralized nature of the party organizations, has strengthened the hand of party leaders in directing activity in the capital and in wag-ing elections in the country. As a result, interest groups have had to play a more restricted role. They have had to work through, rather than outside, party organiza-tions. The lobbyist has not been able to break down the party loyalties of the elec-torate, nor has the propagandist been able to break down the party loyalties of the electorate.

Clark's institutional explanation of the comparative lack of attention given to inter-est groups in Canada in the early part of this century is still relevant today, even if Canada's political parties have declined in strength over the course of the last 60 years. One could add to Clark's explanation that interest group research became the dominant paradigm in American political science in the 1950s in large part because of the scientific optimism generated by the behavioural revolution. As Smiley (1974: 34–7) and Cairns (1974: 209–11, 218–21) have pointed out, however, there was always considerably more skepticism towards behaviouralism in Canada than in the United States, and one of the consequences was the reduced impor-tance assigned to the measurement of interest group influence.

This is not to say that interest group research has been of no consequence in Canadian political science; in fact, this subfield has been and still is an important (though not central) part of the discipline. We can single out a number of key con-tributions made by researchers based in Canada:

- Presthus (1973) and Thompson and Stanbury (1979) have examined the different tactics employed by interest groups in Canada and the US to influ-ence legislation or policy, along with the different pressure points targeted in each country (primarily individual legislators in the US and the bureaucracy or cabinet in Canada).

- One of the most important contributions by Canadian researchers, not sur-prisingly, has been in the area of federalism and its impact on interest group activity. The work of Armstrong and Nelles (1973), though not specifically concerned with interest groups as such, illustrated how competing groups of capitalists—bankers and small manufacturers, for instance—have relied on judicial review in the pursuit of their organizational and economic interests, provoking intense federal-provincial conflict in the process. Bucovetsky's classic study (1975) of the mining industry in Canada similarly demon-strated that our federal system increases the number of access or pressure points that can be targeted by interest groups to defeat or hamstring threat-ening legislation or policies. Kwavnick (1972), in a series of case studies of organized labour in Canada, also argued that federal-provincial conflict can be the by-product of interest group leaders' pursuit of their own organiza-tional objectives. Coleman's study of interest group organization concluded that there is no 'simple one-to-one relationship' between the type of political system (federal vs unitary) and association type: federated interest group structures exist in unitary systems, as do unitary associations in certain sec-tors of federal political systems. Nor is there a straightforward relationship between interest group effectiveness and the type of political system, contrary to the 'dominant opinion that federalism generally weakens the cohesion of interest associations and in doing so ultimately harms their effectiveness' (Coleman, 1987a: 171, 183–4).

- John Porter's classic study, *The Vertical Mosaic* (1965), was both a rich source of data on various organized interests in Canadian society and an important contribution to the debate between pluralists and élite theorists on the nature of power in liberal democracies. As mentioned earlier, Canadian researchers have also made key contributions to the corporatist literature; a number of case studies have examined the reasons for the failure of corporatist structures to take root in this country (Panitch, 1979) and the corporatist tendencies in Quebec society (Tanguay, 1984). Langille (1987) and Coleman (1988) have undertaken detailed case studies of business organization in Canada, and Yates (1990) has attempted to situate Canadian trade unionism in the context of the postwar international political economy.
- More recently, researchers in Canada have investigated the growing use of the Charter of Rights and Freedoms by interest groups and social movement organizations to advance their causes (Seidle, 1993), the controversial issue of interest group spending in elections (Hiebert, 1998; Tanguay and Kay, 1998), and government financing of interest groups (Pal, 1993).
- Canadian researchers have made key contributions to the literature on policy communities, the constellations of groups and governmental agencies involved in policy-making (Coleman, 1987b; Coleman and Skogstad, 1990; Pross, 1992). One of the greatest strengths of this approach is its ability to bridge the state-society divide, along with its tendency to examine the *reciprocal* relationship between groups and the state. From this perspective, interest groups do not merely make demands on the state or provide the government with much-needed information. In some cases, the state seeks either to create groups to achieve its overriding objectives—national unity, for example—or to co-opt existing organizations in an attempt to legitimate its own policies (see Baetz and Tanguay, 1998). Pal's important book on the politics of language, multiculturalism, and feminism in Canada, for example, underscores the diverse ways in which the federal Department of Secretary of State sought to mobilize citizens and create 'core constituencies of support for government action' (Pal, 1993: 257).

Probably the best-known Canadian work on interest groups is that of Paul Pross (1992). Pross classifies interest groups according to their organizational capacity and degree of institutionalization. He argues that most groups pass through an organizational life cycle, starting out as underdeveloped single-issue groups and eventually evolving into mature interest groups, *if they successfully adapt to the political system*. While Pross's framework is certainly useful for understanding the nature and activities of traditional interest groups—those that opt to work *within* the existing system—it is unable to explain adequately the behaviour of groups that operate outside the conventions of traditional pressure politics. In short, it cannot account for the success of social movements and social movement organizations whose objectives are qualitatively different from those of interest groups.

Social Movements: Crashing the Party from the Margins

Compared to interest groups, social movements are quite different political and social animals. While, along with interest groups, they are seen as alternative expressions of political identities and interests, and provide opportunity for political participation outside of political parties, they characterize themselves as the foremost 'party crashers' because they present a form of 'new politics', an alternative to what many participants perceive as the corrupt politics of both parties and interest groups. Social movement politics, it is argued, is a form of small-p politics focused on the building of consensual participatory communities, while the pluralist politics of interest and the politics of the national state associated with parties and interest groups are rejected as large-P politics (Bellah et al., 1985). Much of this has to do with perceptions of power involved in party and government politics. Social movement activists see themselves practising a form of politics not from a corrupting desire for power, but for justice, fellowship, and the common good. For example, in discussing social movement participation with Canadian peace activists, a participant of the student protests of the late 1960s and the peace protests of the 1980s described her approach to power as follows: 'we fought the conventional concept of power, [we felt] that any one of us could have power. . . . I would like to see political parties having vision in terms of reflecting social change, but I think because it's such a power-hungry structure you're not going to get that' (interview with Jennifer Mains in Newman, 1998).

The idea that social movement activities are truly antithetical to party politics is open to question, however. The political practice of social movements bears similarities to the conception of participatory civic republicanism, whereby knowledgeable citizens engage in a participatory politics that emphasizes self-government in everyday life, and is also directed at the institutions of community, state, and the world. In keeping with a conception of civic republicanism, there is an associated participatory culture of political action, implicit in which is an understanding of having a responsibility to engage in the national politics open to citizens, i.e., voting, participating in elections, and, on certain issues, working with parties. Consequently, social movement activity can be seen as complementing political party and interest group activity.

The focus on small-p politics and the rejection of large-P politics reflects the efforts of social movements to create a politics of civil society. 'They imply a "democratization dynamic" of everyday life and the expansion of civil versus political dimensions in society' (Larana et al., 1994: 7). The common thread that binds social movements together, although their concerns are diverse, is a belief that the way to bring about change is through the creation and transformation of community and society, starting with the self. They adopt slogans such as 'the personal is political' and 'think globally, act locally', and the building of individual and collective identities around shared visions of a just world becomes as important as the political pursuit of a particular issue. Hence, their politics are seen to be concerned as much with social and cultural change as with political change.

The emergence of new social movements is often traced to the political and social protests of 1968, which occurred around the world (Berger, 1979). These protests, which emphasized spontaneity and imagination in political action and an anti-bureaucratic and anti-institutional nature in organizing, were seen as a youthful rejection of traditional political agents and ideologies. Characterized as being motivated by post-materialist values, the movements associated with these protests were not based on class cleavages and interests, but were defined by age cleavages and demands that emphasized cultural and social self-actualization (Inglehart, 1977). It was the unruly politics of the generation socialized during the period of economic affluence following World War II—a 'new middle class' of educated and affluent cultural and social service professionals (ibid.; Parkin, 1968). This represented a new form of politics and the development of a new political paradigm in Western industrial democracies, a politics based not on material issues or standard-of-living grievances but on state-of-living grievances (Habermas, 1981; Offe, 1987).

Again, this needs to be qualified. We must be careful how enthusiastically we accept these social movements as new and representative of a new political paradigm. As Weir (1993: 98) points out, the term 'new social movements' is 'pervasively ideological'. It carries the baggage of a dispute between the old and new left over the privileging of class and labour struggle as the site of revolutionary potential. In response to Marxism's privileging of class, the NSM literature privileges non-class struggle. The result of creating this dualism of new versus old social movements, on the one hand, underestimates the significance of social movements outside organized labour and socialist parties during the nineteenth and twentieth centuries (e.g., the women's and peace movements), and, on the other, undervalues the diversity of practices and visions, both political and cultural, within socialism.

It is not evident that contemporary social movements truly represent a distinct break with previous political forms and styles. Historically, social movements, such as the labour movement and European social democracy, have served as a source of new collective identities within society and engaged in community-building and education. Also, a common theme of democratic participation and inclusion runs through all of the movements of the last two centuries. In addition, there are difficulties with attributing causality to the concept of post-materialism. It does not explain why self-actualization is translated into a new form of *politics* rather than private consumption-based 'lifestyles of the affluent and post-materialist'. Nor does it account for the participation of those not considered post-materialist, or for the continuation of such politics in periods of declining economic affluence and by the generation following the post-materialist baby boomers (Offe, 1987). Consequently, it seems more appropriate to refer to today's movements as contemporary social movements rather than as new ones.

The Comparative Literature

The literature on contemporary social movements can be divided into two general approaches or paradigms: resource mobilization approaches associated with work done in the United States and new social movement approaches associated with the European literature. However, in the last 10 years there has been an effort to combine these two approaches and to focus on the study of the identity practices of movements.

Resource Mobilization Theory

Resource Mobilization Theory (RMT) reflects its roots in the pluralist framework of political action and organization associated with interest groups. While social movements are conceived as distinct from parties and interest groups because of the more nebulous and transitory nature of their organization, they are organized political groups nonetheless. ' "Social movement" means "organization", and that means creating and maintaining an organization, and lots of work' (Oberschall, 1993: 22). The concern, then, is with the organizational capacity for collective action: the availability of resources to a collectivity, the position of individuals in social networks, and, related to this, the rationality of participation in social movements (Gamson, 1975; McCarthy and Zald, 1977). RMT concentrates on the availability and employment of resources, such as leaders' organizational and entrepreneurial skills, political opportunities for action, influence, and protest, and the ability to provide motivations for participation and commitment through incentives that range from the selective (personal) to the collective (purposive).

Criticism can be levelled at RMT because the focus on organization, resources, and incentives limits what can be said about the content and context of social movements. RMT is generally indifferent to explanations that focus on ideological and cultural resources (outside the narrow focus of solidarity resources) and social transformation. For example, RMT rejects the idea of 'grievances' as a reason for social movement formation because they are seen to be ubiquitous in every society. Consequently, it obscures the socio-cultural basis of social movements and the causes of solidarity, which are preconditions for collective activity.

New Social Movements

While encompassing a diverse literature with a number of ongoing debates within it, the new social movement approach concentrates on macro-structural and subjective processes as the roots of social movement emergence (whether those processes are worked out in discursive or material realms). It sees contemporary social movements (which most of this literature categorizes as 'new') as reactions to conditions prevalent in late capitalism or post-industrial society (Touraine, 1981; Habermas, 1981; Laclau and Mouffe, 1985; Offe, 1987). Within this approach a number of common interrelated characteristics of new social movements are identified and examined. (1) Movements are new social-cultural forms focused on creating new identities (or re-establishing traditional ones) and on empowerment through the assertion of self-autonomy and control in resistance to the perceived commodification, bureaucratization, and homogenization of society. They attempt to express new relationships with society. (2) Consequently, new social movements typically incorporate new political action forms antagonistic to conventional political expression and favour protest mobilization, cultural expression (theatrical forms, clothing, music, etc.), decentralized, anti-hierarchical organizations, and participatory democracy. (3) The people predominantly predisposed to participate in these movements are those most affected by or aware of the structural changes in society, such as marginalized segments of society, e.g., the unemployed, housewives, students, retired persons, youth, and those in society who through education or professional contact are particularly sensitive to the problems caused by structural change.

The primary criticism directed at the New Social Movement literature is the obverse of that directed at RMT; the emphasis on the socio-cultural aspects of the movements neglects the political and organizational preconditions and processing of social movements. At its extreme this focus detaches the movements and their participants from any institutional constraints and from specific political contexts.

A more appropriate understanding of social movements can be had by attempting to combine or reconcile these two approaches (Klandermans and Tarrow, 1988; Melucci, 1989). Both are useful because social movements cannot be understood without examining both their organizational and socio-cultural aspects. Social and political networks bring individuals and groups together around common goals, provide political opportunities and outlets for collective action, and result in the construction of new meanings out of which new collective actors emerge. Consequently, movements combine both an identity and a network structure, and organization follows this in that the more extensive the group's common identity and internal networks the stronger and more cohesive the group will be.

Solidarity and Collective Identity

The construction of new meanings out of which new collective actors emerge is ultimately at the root of social movement practice. Social movements are dynamic structures that build communities and solidarities; consequently they are intimately associated with the emergence of 'identity politics':

> the collective search for identity is a central aspect of movement formation. . . . New social movements are said to arise in defense of identity. They grow around relationships that are voluntarily conceived to empower members to 'name themselves.' What individuals are claiming collectively is the right to realize their own identity: the possibility of disposing their personal creativity, their affective life, and their biological and interpersonal existence. (Melucci, 1980: 21)

Within the NSM and RMT approaches, Melucci and Snow and Benford, respectively, have infused the development of identity with a corresponding development of organization. Melucci (1989, 1996) focuses on the question of collective identity formation through political, symbolic, and interpersonal interactions, the establishment and mobilization of networks arising out of these interactions, and the resulting emotional investments that confirm and support new identities. This entails a continuous negotiation and renegotiation of the movement understandings of goals, means, and the environment of action, the maintenance and creation of networks of communication and decision-making between participants, and the development of emotional bonds that allow for the recognition of shared values and beliefs. Consequently, the construction of collective identity, and thus the movement, is a combination of identity, organizational, and external imperatives. Snow and Benford (1988) point to the importance of ideological or identity factors (values, beliefs, meanings) as a resource for social movement activity. Like Melucci, they argue movements are more than carriers and transmitters of beliefs and ideas; they also create meanings and identities for participants, antagonists, and observers. Movements engage in 'framing' activities when they 'assign meaning to and interpret relevant events and conditions in ways that are intended to mobilize potential adherents and constituents, to garner bystander support, and to demobilize antagonists' (Snow and Benford, 1988: 198).

Organization

Unlike more institutionalized interest groups and political parties, the emphasis on network organizations and socio-cultural activities, rather than more straightforward political campaigns, results in a perception of the new social movements as fragile and vulnerable phenomena. Continuity depends on their ability to sustain a critical challenge to the forces at work in society and to keep their constituency mobilized, but they are also vulnerable to the gradual professionalization and bureaucratization and to the displacement of their goals, which leads to institutionalization (Piven and Cloward, 1979; Offe, 1987, 1990). To be permanent, these movements have to establish routine structures, formalize administrative forms, and constitute their structures on a stable everyday organizational basis. Eventually, however, this can blunt the militancy and grassroots action that is the fundamental source of a movement's influence.[6] The result is that the differences between them and traditional interest groups become more rhetorical than real.

Melucci (1989, 1996) makes a call for observers not to focus on movements as structurally specific and unified entities, but rather to view social movements as expressions of collective action made up of plural and heterogeneous socio-cultural networks engaged in a continual process of redefinition and adaptation of movement and participant identities. Similarly, Gerlach and Hine (1970) object to the tendency to describe the loose organization of a movement as a sign of significant deficiencies and evidence of its coming demise. They argue that while organizational unity may be functional in steady-state social institutions intent on maintaining the status quo, the characteristics of social movements are functional for social institutions designed for rapid growth and the implementation of social change.

Organizationally, the loose, heterogeneous, non-hierarchical networked character of social movements is *naturally* innovative and adaptable. Movement networks are decentralized, segmented, and reticulated structures. They are decentralized in the sense that there is no identifiable specific centre of power and leadership. There is no single leader, little distinction between leaders and followers, and membership is open.[7] Movements are segmented in that they are composed of a variety of localized groups that are essentially independent and autonomous but combine to form larger configurations—or divide to form still smaller units— and reticulated in that the network of loosely connected local units is linked by organizational and personal ties and informal connections such as ritual activities, ideology, and so on. This allows for continual innovation because, although some segments are content to take more conventional forms, this does not preclude other groups and segments in the movement from experimenting with new forms of activities and types of social organizations (Gerlach and Hine, 1970: 73). This helps to minimize failure, as the failure of one group has little effect on others in the movement; groups and members can disband, reform, or be reabsorbed into other groups, and the movement continues to learn from the experience.

This process is aided by the characteristic moral discourse of social movements, which allows them to be multi-dimensional and flexible. Although it is often argued to be the case, social movements are not naturally concerned with single issues and single goals: 'When moralism, and not pragmatism, is the name of the game, there are few intellectually feasible justifications for dealing with only one particular social issue' (Hermann, 1993: 191). The focus of participants' commitments to the movement may not be directly connected to specific movement goals so much as motivated by the movement's challenge to the state or the socio-political order. Consequently, movements develop flexibility as well as stability through redefining and broadening movement goals as well as organization. This appears to be essential to the preservation of the movement's momentum and to its ability to respond to various challenges.

As organizations, movements are not as vulnerable as often described, but are dynamic phenomena capable of adaptation and transformation. This requires three key values: participation, community, and empowerment. Collective identity can be seen as 'three embedded layers: organization, movement and solidarity' where the sense of agency and empowerment that results from participation in the movement community links the three layers together (Gamson, 1991: 4). Consequently, social movement organizations are sites of experimentation, connecting individual, organization, and movement together through the development of a collective identity and agency.

Insertion into Political Process
Conceiving of movements as networks of social 'process' rather than specific phenomena can seem, not surprisingly, nebulous and vague, particularly when one attempts to examine the dynamics of social movements as political actors. Such a position does not really account for the fact that movements can be unified *political* actors, thanks to the fact that participants see themselves as being part of a social and political movement—a feeling as simple as participants identifying themselves, for example, as 'a peacenik' or 'a feminist'. And, as Tarrow (1994: 25) reminds us, 'although movements almost always conceive of themselves outside of

and opposed to institutions, collective action inserts them into complex policy networks, and, thus, within the reach of the state.' Hence, there is a tendency to treat social movements in much the same manner as purely political interest groups, which can be somewhat misleading.

Generally, because of the diffuse organizational nature of social movements it is argued that they insert themselves into the political process only when conditions are ripe, that is, when political opportunity structures allow for a fair expectation of success. The term 'political opportunity structure' is used to refer to the political context that either encourages or discourages protest activity. This includes specific configurations of resources, institutional arrangements, and historical precedents that facilitate the development of movements and their activities (Kitschelt, 1986; Tarrow, 1994). As they would for most political actors, these structures further or limit the ability of social movements to insert themselves into the political process through: (1) determining the informational, financial, and ideological (in the form of grievances and issues) resources available to a movement; (2) setting the institutional rules of access, 'such as those reinforcing patterns of interaction between government and interest groups, and electoral laws' (Kitschelt, 1986: 61), and (3) the success of other social movements, the influence of political parties, and the availability of influential allies. The political opportunity structures available at a given time determine a movement's decision to mobilize, the outcomes of collective action, and its institutional effects.

State structures create stable opportunities, but changing opportunities within states provide the openings that resource-poor actors can use to create new movements (Tarrow, 1994: 18). Consequently, the political presence of social movements tends to be cyclical, occurring in cycles of protest and disappearance. A cycle of activism occurs when political opportunities allow a movement to make claims that resonate with others, provide incentives for new movement organizations to form, invite others to seek similar outcomes, and generally illustrate the susceptibility of the political system to challenge. In such situations collective action grows from the mobilized to the less mobilized segments of society, and 'even conventional interest groups are tempted by unconventional collective action' (ibid., 24). As the cycle widens, opportunities are created for élites and opposition groups and alliances are created. The cycle comes to an end as the political initiative shifts to élites and parties. The state then responds with either repression or reform (or both), and movements adopt a more political logic to engage in implicit bargaining with members of the polity to maintain alliances with conventional political groups. The movements disappear as they are either repressed and their opportunities closed off or their issues and concerns become part of the accepted political landscape and leaders and leading organizations are absorbed into parties or allied to public agencies.

Here we see a need for a middle ground between looking at social movements as purely social phenomena of identity and network formation or as purely political phenomena like institutionalized interest groups. Unfortunately, the tendency here is to measure movement activity and strength by their most overt political manifestations—their ability to maintain a political presence through protest politics, getting people on the streets, political lobbying, etc.—and their success in achieving specific policy changes. In so doing, *social* movements are treated solely as *political* movements very akin to 'interest groups'. Little attention is paid to their social processes and practices, the formation and sustenance of identity and commitment networks. In addition, the impact or success these movements have in changing social values and attitudes within the movement and in society is neglected.

While a characteristic feature of social movements is their tendency to appear as intense and boisterous political mobilizations for only limited periods, to read this as a chronic tendency to decline is pessimistic and does not understand that a great deal of activity takes place during latent phases. A useful metaphor is to envisage movements as whales, surfacing for periods and submerged in others. This is a side of movement activity that has rarely been explored.

Latency does not necessarily mean movement decline or inactivity; it constitutes a period when the socio-cultural processes of personal and movement production continue. 'Collective action is nourished by the daily production of alternative frameworks of meaning, on which the networks themselves are founded and live from day to day' (Melucci, 1989: 70–1). While mobilizations, and sometimes movements, do disappear, the strength and continuity of the movement thus are seen to rest in the submerged networks that are still active when the movement is invisible. 'The submerged networks are laboratories of experience . . . [where] [n]ew answers are invented and tested, and reality is perceived and named in different ways' (ibid., 208), and changes in social and cultural attitudes are effected for both participants and society in general.

Research on Canadian Social Movements

Compared to work in the US and Europe, a social movement focus has been somewhat under-represented in Canadian research, where the tendency has been to focus on topic areas of regional, labour, or feminist protest, rather than viewing such protest from the perspective of social movement practice, the formation of collective identity and action, and the praxis of movement mobilization. While early sociological works focused on the frontier religious and secular movements that helped to create Canada, and the work of Seymour Lipset examined the emergence of a prairie protest movement (Clark, 1968; Lipset, 1950), as Carroll (1992: 1) has argued, despite the academic interest in contemporary movements and their tangible impact on day-to-day life, there has been a 'dearth of available texts that probe the meaning of movements in a distinctively Canadian context'.

Throughout the 1990s more research on Canadian social movements has appeared; this work has generally reflected the division of the literature between new social movement and resource mobilization approaches (although these approaches are not exclusive and there is overlap). Research based on the NSM approach, combining socialist, feminist, environmental, and sometimes nationalist concerns, has worked to examine the mobilization of a politics of counter-hegemony—a politics of transformation of both society and the self, 'challeng[ing] not

only the dominant interests of society but also our own practices and belief systems' (Cunningham et al., 1988; see also Laclau and Mouffe, 1985; Melucci, 1989,
1996; Carroll, 1992). These works generally examine the possibility of creating this
politics of transformation (as opposed to revolution) within civil society and how
this relates to the practical realities of those working within Canadian social movements (e.g., Magnussen and Walker, 1988; Cunningham, 1988; Leys and Mendell,
1992; Carroll, 1992).

The bulk of Canadian research appears to fall within the resource mobilization
paradigm and is best represented by the work on the insertion of social movement
organizations into and participation in Canadian policy communities. While social
movements may lack the concrete organizations and institutionalization of interest
groups and other political actors, they are nonetheless inserted into policy communities, albeit in many cases on their margins. This requires organization and the
mobilization of participants and resources on the part of groups within social
movements (e,g., Burt, 1990; Dobrowolsky, 1998[8]). Lorna Stefanick's discussion
(this volume) of the environmental movement's participation in the southwestern
Alberta conservation policy-making process is a good example of research examining the difficulties and potential faced by social movements in Canadian policy-
making communities.

However, the danger with this approach, as Dobrowolsky (1998: 709) points
out, is that in some cases little or no distinction is made between social movements and interest groups. The work of social movement organizations is
regarded, and often disregarded (if not disparaged), as just one element of any
number of 'special' and limited interests.[9] Interest-oriented approaches alone cannot capture the complexity and broadness of the representation provided by social
movements, which, as discussed earlier, is predicated on collective identity,
empowerment and agency, and a fundamental critique of socio-political structures.

However, it is the special characteristics of Canadian social movements that are
significant for and make interesting contributions to the literature on social movements. As Stefanick's chapter suggests, while the process might have serious drawbacks, the fact that organizations associated with social movements have a degree
of inclusion, even if marginal, in Canadian policy communities illustrates relationships between movements and the state not necessarily experienced in other Western democracies. This is an important feature of Canadian democratic practice.
Particularly in the women's and international development movements, state funding has been provided to non-governmental organizations associated with these
movements. This relationship should not be overestimated, however; in the 1990s
this funding has become scarce,[10] and social movement organizations directly
involved in political lobbying have generally not been the recipients of government
largesse and have not been allowed charitable status for tax purposes.

Another interesting feature of the Canadian social movement community,
explored by Lisa Young (Chapter 24) in her discussion of the partisan orientations
of the women's movements in Canada and the US, is the relationship between
movements and parties. In Canada there has been a tendency for social movements

to act as a complement rather than competitor to the party system. There has been no concerted effort to create social movement organizations to contest elections and involvement in election campaigns has tended to take a non-partisan and educational focus (Phillips, 1994, 1996).[11] Interestingly, Canada boasts a number of social movement organizations that have not conformed to the argument that social movements are, by nature, short-lived.[12] It would appear that geographic necessity has required Canadian social movements to adopt structures that are segmented, reticulate, and decentralized. The resulting coalition-style organizations may well be models for the development of flexible and long-term political and social institutions by social movements.

Conclusion: Avenues for Future Research

This chapter has underscored the great diversity of the comparative and Canadian literatures on interest groups and social movements. The case study is by far the pre-eminent method employed to study organized interests, although survey research, experiments, and more rigorous deductive theoretical models are common in the research inspired by Olson's work and the rational choice approach. In the latter case, however, it appears that greater scientific rigour has been purchased at the cost of a narrowing of the kinds of theoretical and political questions considered by the researcher.

Theoretical eclecticism abounds in the literature on interest groups and social movements, and though this is naturally disappointing to those enamoured of the idea of a single, unified science of politics, we prefer to find virtue in diversity. In our view, the greatest strength of group theories is their capacity to situate the state in the web of its societal relationships. This field of inquiry, therefore, takes state capacities and autonomy seriously, without treating the state as an all-powerful demiurgic force.

A number of important and interesting avenues for research remain to be explored. We would identify four as particularly pressing. First, individual motivations and the question of identity still need to be examined, in spite of all of the important work inspired by Olson's *Logic of Collective Action*. If identity is multiple and subjectivity often fragmented, how are political commitments held as a coherent whole or in a way that makes sense to the individual? If multiple commitments are held by individuals, how are they put into action and how does that affect the organization of a group or movement?

Second, as we have stressed above, social movements and interest groups play an important role in connecting civil society to the state and its institutions. How exactly do they tie them together? Further research should give a better understanding of the dynamics of social movements, interest groups, and parties, the grey areas between them, and possible alliances among them.

Third, researchers need to investigate the life cycle of social movements, along with the patterns of organizational convergence that may occur between social movement organizations and interest groups as a result of the 'interactive dance' (McAdam et al., 1988) between movements and the state, on the one hand, and between movements and their counter-movements (the National Action Committee on the Status of Women and REAL Women, for example), on the other.

Fourth, there is an international dimension to organized interests. In 1995 the Report of the Commission on Global Governance, *Our Global Neighbourhood*, recognized the emergence of a vast and very active global civil society, which includes a multitude of institutions, voluntary associations, and networks (both social movement organizations and interest groups) that work and focus their energies on international issues and global well-being. Studies of interest groups and social movements have to be taken to an international level in addition to the domestic state orientation. This becomes more and more important as national governments become less the focus of decision-making and less influential over the everyday lives of their citizens, and interest groups and social movements respond by turning their attention to supranational policy-making.

Some observers have lamented the 'flattening out' of political discourse in the era of globalization, as the traditional political parties all converge around a very narrow band of policy alternatives (Furet, 1995). Increasingly, no matter what the ideological stripe of the party in power, government policy seems to vary within quite restricted parameters. In such an environment, organized interests (and especially social movements) can be extremely important as sources of innovative ideas and as critics of the conventional wisdom. These groups can also, on occasion, affect corporate behaviour in ways that traditional political parties cannot, as when European environmentalists in 1997 organized a boycott of Shell gasoline to protest the company's plans to scuttle its Brent Spar oil storage platform in the North Sea (Shell's gasoline sales in Germany plummeted by 30 per cent). In this important sense, then, organized interests are essential elements of a healthy democratic political system.

Notes

1. This is essentially the legal definition of lobbyist included in The Lobbyists Registration Act (Bill C-82), passed by the Conservative government of Brian Mulroney in 1988.
2. *The Process of Government* was reissued in 1949 and immediately hailed as one of 'the most important books on government ever written in any country' (Bertram Gross, cited in Garson, 1978: 77).
3. See Crick (1959: ch. 7) for a forceful critique of Bentley's scientism, which can be defined as the view that the sciences are more important than the arts for an understanding of the world in which we live, combined with an exaggerated faith in science's ability to resolve social problems.
4. These features of pluralist theory are drawn from Garson (1978: ch. 3), Berger (1981), and Baumgartner and Leech (1998), among others.
5. This critique resembled one formulated earlier by the élite theorist C. Wright Mills in *The Power Elite* (1956: ch. 11).
6. In other words, Michels's Iron Law of Oligarchy comes into play (Michels, 1962).
7. Although various groups may have membership structures in which rights and duties are set out to some degree, the general tendency is towards open and loose membership ties

whereby membership is determined by simple activities such as giving a donation or turning up at a meeting and, in return, receiving mailings from a group.

8. Actually, Dobrowolsky's excellent article overlaps both approaches, demonstrating, in the case of the Canadian women's movement, how identity politics was mobilized to engage in the constitutional policy-making community and process.

9. For example, Dobrowolsky points to a number of texts, including Pal (1993) and Pross (1992), which she argues equate women's movement organizations with pressure or interest groups (notwithstanding the heterogeneous nature of women's groups in Canada and the fact that, rather than a minority interest, they make up more than 50 per cent of the population).

10. At the time of writing, the National Action Committee on the Status of Women, because of funding cuts and reorganization by the federal government, had been forced to lay off all staff except for one. Other social movement organizations, such as those working on peace issues, were not as fortunate in receiving government funding (for example, Project Ploughshares had government project funding cut off in the mid-1980s) and were run predominantly through direct donations.

11. A good example of this was the Elections Priorities Project, an education program on disarmament and development issues, which through a riding-by-riding survey of candidate positions attempted to raise these issues in federal election campaigns during the 1980s (see Newman, 1998).

12. For example, Greenpeace (which has gone beyond Canada to an international presence), the peace organization Project Ploughshares, the National Action Committee on the Status of Women (notwithstanding its current financial difficulties), and the feminist peace organization The Voice of Women.

References

Almond, Gabriel, and G. Bingham Powell. 1966. *Comparative Politics: A Developmental Approach*. Boston: Little, Brown.

Armstrong, Christopher, and H.V. Nelles. 1973. 'Private Property in Peril: Ontario Businessmen and the Federal System, 1898–1911', in Glenn Porter and Robert Cuff, eds, *Enterprise and National Development*. Toronto: Hakkert, 20–38.

Bachrach, Peter, and Morton S. Baratz. 1967 [1962]. 'Two Faces of Power', in Charles A. McCoy and John Playford, eds, *Apolitical Politics: A Critique of Behavioralism*. New York: Thomas Y. Crowell, 146–57.

Baetz, Mark C., and A. Brian Tanguay. 1998. '"Damned If You Do, Damned If You Don't": Government and the Conundrum of Consultation in the Environmental Sector', *Canadian Public Administration* 41, 3 (Fall): 395–418.

Baumgartner, Frank R., and Beth L. Leech. 1998. *Basic Interests: The Importance of Groups in Politics and in Political Science*. Princeton, NJ: Princeton University Press.

Beer, Samuel H. 1965. *British Politics in the Collectivist Age*. New York: Knopf.

Bellah, Robert N., Richard Madsen, William M. Sullivan, Ann Swidler, and Steven M. Tipton. 1985. *Habits of the Heart: Individualism and Commitment in American Life*. New York: Harper & Row.

Bentley, Arthur F. 1967 [1908]. *The Process of Government*, ed. Peter H. Odegard. Cambridge, Mass.: The Belknap Press of Harvard University Press.

Berger, Suzanne D. 1979. 'Politics and Antipolitics in Western Europe in the Seventies', *Daedalus* 108, 1: 27–50.

———. 1981. 'Introduction', in Berger, ed., *Organizing Interests in Western Europe*. Cambridge: Cambridge University Press, 1–23.

Brooks, Stephen. 1996. 'Too Close for Comfort? Lobbying and Political Parties', in A. Brian Tanguay and Alain-G. Gagnon, eds, *Canadian Parties in Transition*, 2nd edn. Scarborough, Ont.: Nelson Canada, 463–78.

Bucovetsky, M.W. 1975. 'The Mining Industry and the Great Tax Reform Debate', in A. Paul Pross, ed., *Pressure Group Behaviour in Canadian Politics*. Toronto: McGraw-Hill Ryerson, 89–114.

Burt, Sandra. 1990. 'Organized Women's Groups and the State', in Coleman and Skogstad (1990: 191–211).

Cairns, Alan C. 1974. 'Political Science in Canada and the Americanization Issue', *Canadian Journal of Political Science* 8, 2 (June): 191–234.

Carroll, William K. 1992. *Organizing Dissent: Contemporary Social Movements in Theory and Practice*. Toronto: Garamond Press.

Clark, S.D. 1939. *The Canadian Manufacturers' Association: A Study in Collective Bargaining and Political Pressure*. Toronto: University of Toronto Press.

———. 1968. *Canadian Society in Historical Perspective*. Toronto: McGraw-Hill Ryerson.

Coleman, William D. 1987a. 'Federalism and Interest Group Organization', in Herman Bakvis and William M. Chandler, eds, *Federalism and the Role of the State*. Toronto: University of Toronto Press, 171–87.

———. 1987b. 'Review Article: Interest Groups and Democracy in Canada', *Canadian Public Administration* 30, 4 (Winter): 610–22.

———. *Business and Politics in Canada: A Study of Collective Action*. Montreal and Kingston: McGill-Queen's University Press.

——— and Grace Skogstad, eds. 1990. *Policy Communities and Public Policy in Canada: A Structural Approach*. Toronto: Copp Clark Pitman.

Commission on Global Governance. 1995. *Our Global Neighbourhood: The Report of the Commission on Global Governance*. Oxford: Oxford University Press.

Crick, Bernard. 1959. *The American Science of Politics*. Berkeley and Los Angeles: University of California Press.

Cunningham, Frank, Sue Findlay, Marlene Kadar, Alan Lennon, and Ed Silva. 1988. *Social Movements/Social Change*. Toronto: Between the Lines.

Dahl, Robert A. 1961. *Who Governs?* New Haven: Yale University Press.

Dobrowolsky, Alexandra. 1998. 'Of "Special Interest": Interest, Identity and Feminist Constitutional Activism in Canada', *Canadian Journal of Political Science* 31, 4 (Dec.): 707–42.

Finer, S.E. 1958. *Anonymous Empire*. London: Pall Mall Press.

Furet, François. 1995. 'Europe After Utopianism', *Journal of Democracy* 6, 1 (Jan.): 79–89.

Gamson, William. 1975. *The Strategy of Social Protest*. Homewood, Ill.: Dorsey Press.

———. 1991. 'Commitment and Agency in Social Movements', *Sociological Forum* 6, 1: 27–50.

Garson, G. David. 1978. *Group Theories of Politics*. Beverly Hills, Calif.: Sage.

Gerlach, Luther P., and Virginia Hine. 1970. *People, Power, Change: Movements of Social Transformation*. Indianapolis: Bobbs-Merrill.

Habermas, Jurgen. 1981. ' New Social Movements', *Telos* 49 (Fall): 33–8.

Hiebert, Janet. 1998. 'Money and Elections: Can Citizens Participate on Fair Terms Amidst Unrestricted Spending?', *Canadian Journal of Political Science* 31, 1 (Mar.): 91–111.

Heinz, John P., Edward O. Laumann, Robert L. Nelson, and Robert H. Salisbury. 1993. *The Hollow Core: Private Interests in National Policymaking*. Cambridge, Mass.: Harvard University Press.

Hermann, Tamar. 1993. 'From Unidimensionality to Multidimensionality: Some Observations on the Dynamics of Social Movements', *Research in Social Movements, Conflicts and Change* 15: 181–202.

Inglehart, Ronald. 1977. *The Silent Revolution: Changing Values and Political Styles among Western Publics*. Princeton, NJ: Princeton University Press.

Kitschelt, Herbert. 1986. 'Political Opportunity Structures and Political Protest: Anti-Nuclear Movements in Four Democracies', *British Journal of Political Science* 16: 57–85.

Klandermans, Bert, and Sidney Tarrow. 1988. 'Mobilization into Social Movements: Synthesizing European and American Approaches', *International Social Movement Research* 1: 1–38.

Kwavnick, David. 1972. *Organized Labour and Pressure Politics: The Canadian Labour Congress 1956–1968*. Montreal and Kingston: McGill-Queen's University Press.

Laclau, Ernesto, and Chantal Mouffe. 1985. *Hegemony and Socialist Strategy: Towards a Radical Democratic Politics*. London: Verso.

Langille, David. 1987. 'The Business Council on National Issues and the Canadian State', *Studies in Political Economy* 24 (Autumn): 41–85.

Larana, Enrique, Hank Johnston, and Joseph R. Gusfield. 1994. 'Identities, Grievances, and New Social Movements', in Larana et al., eds, *New Social Movements: From Ideology to Identity*. Philadelphia: Temple University Press.

Leys, Colin, and Marguerite Mendell. 1992. *Culture and Social Change: Social Movements in Quebec and Ontario*. Montreal: Black Rose Books.

Lipset, Seymour Martin. 1950. *Agrarian Socialism*. Toronto: Oxford University Press.

Macridis, Roy C. 1977 [1961]. 'Groups and Group Theory', in Macridis and Bernard E. Brown, eds, *Comparative Politics: Notes and Readings*, 5th edn. Homewood, Ill: Dorsey Press, 322–7.

Magnusson, Warren, and Rob Walker. 1988. 'De-centering the State: Political Theory and Canadian Political Economy', *Studies in Political Economy* 26 (Summer): 37–71.

McAdam, Doug, John D. McCarthy, and Mayer Zald. 1988. 'Social Movements', in Neil J. Smelser, ed., *Handbook of Sociology*. Beverly Hills, Calif.: Sage, 695–737.

McCarthy, John D., and Mayer Zald. 1977. 'Resource Mobilization and Social Movements: A Partial Theory', *American Journal of Sociology* 82, 6 (May): 1212–41.

Melucci, Alberto. 1980. 'The New Social Movements: A Theoretical Approach', *Social Science Information* 2: 199–226.

———. 1989. *Nomads of the Present*. Philadelphia: Temple University Press.

———. 1996. *Challenging Codes: Collective Action in the Information Age*. Cambridge: Cambridge University Press.

Michels, Robert. 1962. *Political Parties: A Sociological Study of the Oligarchical Tendencies of Modern Democracies*, trans. Eden and Cedar Paul. New York: Free Press.

Migdal, Joel S. 1997. 'Studying the State', in Mark I. Lichbach and Alan S. Zuckerman, eds., *Comparative Politics: Rationality, Culture and Structure*. Cambridge: Cambridge University Press, 208–35.

Mills, C. Wright. 1956. *The Power Elite*. New York: Oxford University Press.

Moe, Terry M. 1980. *The Organization of Interests: Incentives and the Internal Dynamics of Political Interest Groups*. Chicago: University of Chicago Press.

Newman, Jacquetta. 1998. 'Continuing Commitment: The Durability of Social Movements. Project Ploughshares in the 1990s', PhD thesis, Queen's University.

Oberschall, Anthony. 1993. *Social Movements: Ideologies, Interests and Identities*. New Brunswick, NJ: Transaction.

Offe, Claus. 1987. 'Challenging the Boundaries of Institutional Politics: Social Movements Since the 1960s', in Charles S. Maier, ed., *Changing Boundaries of the Political: Essays on the Evolving Balance Between the State and Society, Public and Private in Europe*. Cambridge: Cambridge University Press, 63–105.

–––––––. 1990. 'Reflections on the Institutional Self-transformation of Movement Politics: A Tentative Stage Model', in Russell J. Dalton and Manfred Kuechler, eds., *Challenging the Political Order: New Social and Political Movements in Western Democracies*. London: Polity Press, 232–50.

Olson, Mancur. 1965. *The Logic of Collective Action*. Cambridge, Mass.: Harvard University Press.

Pal, Leslie A. 1993. *Interests of State*. Montreal and Kingston: McGill-Queen's University Press.

Panitch, Leo V. 1979. 'Corporatism in Canada?', *Studies in Political Economy* 1 (Spring): 43–92.

–––––––. 1980. 'Recent Theorizations of Corporatism: Reflections on a Growth Industry', *British Journal of Sociology* 31: 161–87.

Parkin, Frank. 1968. *Middle Class Radicalism*. Manchester: Manchester University Press.

Phillips, Susan D. 1994. 'New Social Movements in Canadian Politics: On Fighting and Starting Fires', in James P. Bickerton and Alain-G. Gagnon, eds, *Canadian Politics*, 2nd edn. Peterborough, Ont.: Broadview Press, 188–206.

–––––––. 1996. 'Competing, Connecting, and Complementing: Parties, Interest Groups, and New Social Movements', in A. Brian Tanguay and Alain-G. Gagnon, eds, *Canadian Parties in Transition*, 2nd edn. Scarborough, Ont.: Nelson Canada, 440–62.

Piven, Frances Fox, and Richard Cloward. 1979. *Poor People's Movements: Why They Succeed, How They Fail*. New York: Vintage Books.

Porter, John. 1965. *The Vertical Mosaic*. Toronto: University of Toronto Press.

Presthus, Robert. 1973. *Elite Accommodation in Canadian Politics*. Toronto: Macmillan of Canada.

Pross, A. Paul. 1992. *Group Politics and Public Policy*, 2nd edn. Toronto: Oxford University Press.

Rauch, Jonathan. 1994. *Demosclerosis: The Silent Killer of American Government*. New York: Times Books.

Salisbury, Robert H. 1969. 'An Exchange Theory of Interest Groups', *Midwest Journal of Political Science* 13, 1 (Feb.): 1–32.

Schattschneider, E.E. 1960. *The Semi-Sovereign People*. New York: Holt, Rinehart and Winston.

Schmitter, Philippe C. 1974. 'Still the Century of Corporatism?', *Review of Politics* 36, 1 (Jan.): 85–131.

Seidle, F. Leslie, ed. 1993. *Equity and Community: The Charter, Interest Advocacy and Representation*. Montreal: Institute for Research on Public Policy.

Shonfield, Andrew. 1965. *Modern Capitalism: The Changing Balance of Public and Private Power*. London: Oxford University Press.

Smiley, Donald V. 1974. 'Canadian Political Science: A Miniature Replica', *Journal of Canadian Studies* 9, 1 (Feb.): 31–42.

Snow, David A., and Robert D. Benford. 1988. 'Ideology, Frame Resonance, and Participant Mobilization', *International Social Movement Research* 1: 197–217.

Tanguay, A. Brian. 1984. 'Concerted Action in Quebec, 1976–1983: Dialogue of the Deaf', in Alain-G. Gagnon, ed., *Quebec: State and Society*. Toronto: Methuen, 365–85.

———— and Barry J. Kay. 1998. 'Third-Party Advertising and the Threat to Electoral Democracy: The Mouse that Roared', *International Journal of Canadian Studies* 17 (Spring): 57–79.

Tarrow, Sidney. 1994. *Power in Movement: Social Movements, Collective Action and Politics*. Cambridge: Cambridge University Press.

Thompson, Fred, and W.T. Stanbury. 1979. *The Political Economy of Interest Groups in the Legislative Process in Canada*. Montreal: Institute for Research on Public Policy, Occasional Paper no. 9 (May).

Touraine, Alain. 1981. *The Voice and The Eye: An Analysis of Social Movements*. Cambridge: Cambridge University Press.

Truman, David. 1951. *The Governmental Process*. New York: Knopf.

Weir, Lorna. 1993. 'Limitations of New Social Movement Analysis', *Studies in Political Economy* 40 (Spring): 73–102.

Yates, Charlotte. 1990. 'Labour and Lobbying: A Political Economy Perspective', in Coleman and Skogstad (1990: 266–90).

Chapter 24

Going Mainstream? The Women's Movement and Political Parties in Canada and the US

Lisa Young

Social movements emerge periodically to shake up political systems. They reflect, and amplify, changes in values and attitudes. By asserting and fostering these changing social values they create a significant challenge to the political and social status quo. From the French Revolution to the contemporary environmental movement, social movements have used a variety of tactics to force a rethinking not only of the content of public policy, but also of the way politics is done.

Of course, some social movements present more fundamental challenges than others do. Revolutionary movements call for—and sometimes achieve—overthrow of the existing political regime. The activists who sought to overthrow the French monarchy or the Chinese students who challenged the Communist leadership in Tiananmen Square were seeking a more fundamental political change than are activists in the environmental or women's movement in contemporary Canada. These activists might advocate a rethinking of how politics is done in the Canadian political system and would certainly advocate different policy choices, but they are not likely to be in favour of overthrowing the political system as a whole.

Even though their challenge is not revolutionary, movements like the women's movement and the environmental movement do have the potential to affect both political processes and policy outcomes through a variety of mechanisms. They can lobby governments for legislative change, and they can pursue political change through the courts, challenging the constitutionality of statutes. The gay rights movement in Canada has used both of these techniques in its campaign to have same-sex relationships recognized on an equal footing to heterosexual relationships in laws governing pensions, adoptions, and other matters. As is often the case, gay rights activists started by lobbying government and turned to the courts after they failed to make progress through the legislative route. Alternatively, movements can concentrate their efforts away from the state, focusing instead on social change. An example of this would be anti-racism groups that devote their energies to public education rather than to lobbying for legislative change. Quite often, movements pursue a number of strategies simultaneously. For example, one group within the environmental movement might concentrate its energies on encouraging people to walk, bike, or take public transit instead of driving, while another would be lobbying government to impose a tax on gasoline. Both would be pursuing the same objective—a reduction in automobile emissions—but through different means.

The focus of this chapter is on the interaction between social movements and one specific part of the political process: political parties. By examining how social movements relate to political parties, we are able to gain some understanding of the reasons why social movements involve themselves in—or avoid—the formal political process. Political parties are the organizations that animate electoral politics in democratic nations; in the words of E.E. Schattschneider (1942), 'modern democracy is unthinkable except in terms of parties.' Parties, then, are the logical focus of social movement involvement in the political sphere. Two different theoretical accounts of social movement behaviour—movement-centred and strategic—can be used to explore this relationship. This chapter examines the utility of these approaches in accounting for the orientations of the Canadian and American women's movements to political parties since the 1970s. The comparative case study approach demonstrates that institutional and political differences between the two countries have affected the strategies movements adopt.

Social Movements' Orientation towards Parties

When we look at the relationships between social movement organizations and political parties in North America and Western Europe, we see a range of relationships. At one end of the spectrum are radical environmental or peace groups that see political parties, with their need to engage in electoral competition and thus a politics of compromise and accommodation, as antithetical to the movement's core beliefs. At the other end of the spectrum are groups like environmentalists in the former West Germany and feminists in Iceland who decided to form their own political parties. Between these two ends of the spectrum are a variety of social movement organizations that have formed alliances of some sort with one or more political parties.

This leads us to the broad question of how social movements interact with parties and why they choose the strategies that they do. Do they see political parties as potential allies, or as organizations likely to hinder the movement's ability to achieve its objectives? If they choose to seek allies in the formal partisan arena, do they ally themselves with one party or with more than one? If not all social movements adopt the same strategy towards parties, what factors might affect their decisions?

Different theoretical accounts of social movement behaviour predict very different patterns of movement engagement with, or disengagement from, the partisan arena. We can divide the theoretical accounts of movement behaviour into two basic groupings: movement-centred approaches and strategic approaches.

In movement-centred accounts, movements' orientations towards parties are endogenously determined; that is, a movement's characteristics determine its partisan orientation. Several studies of 'new' social movements—such as the peace and environmental movements that emerged in the late 1960s—argue that these movements' ideological character causes them to reject a strategy of engaging with established political parties (see Melucci, 1989; Offe, 1990). According to this argument, these movements' ideologies involve a rejection of old-style politics in favour of non-hierarchical participatory practices, so involvement with established political parties would be inconsistent with the movement's ideological outlook.

In contrast to the movement-centred theory, strategic approaches contend that movements' orientations towards political parties are shaped by exogenous variables; that is, factors external to the movement will shape its orientation. These external factors comprise what Sidney Tarrow (1989: 32) has termed the 'opportunity structure'—the set of constraints and opportunities that discourage or encourage movement behaviours and lead movements to certain forms of collective action over others. While movement-centred accounts conceptualize movements as driven primarily by ideological concerns, strategic accounts conceptualize movements—or, more precisely, movement leaders—as rational actors, seeking to maximize strategic advantage. Within this conceptualization, one would expect that movement organizations would engage with political parties only if the potential benefits of such engagement were perceived to outweigh potential costs. This calculation will take into account the relevant elements of the opportunity structure. When we are looking at a movement organization's orientation towards political parties, the elements of the opportunity structure that are likely to affect the decision to become engaged or not are the basic political institutions in the system (i.e., parliamentary versus congressional government), the structure of the party system (i.e., a two-party versus a multi-party system), and the specific characteristics of the parties within the system.

These two approaches predict very different behaviours for movements. The movement-centred approach suggests that any new, or progressive, social movement would reject engaging with established parties. The strategic approach suggests that a movement's actions would reflect an evaluation of the costs and benefits of engaging with parties, which would depend on the elements of the opportunity structure. Before going on to consider which of these two theoretical accounts offers a better explanation for the behaviour of the Canadian and American women's movements, we first need to develop a categorization of movement behaviours to facilitate comparison.

Categorizing Movement Orientations

The first dimension of a movement's partisan orientation is its emphasis on partisan and electoral politics relative to other movement activities. When such strategies are a regular element of movement activity over an extended period and consume a significant portion of the resources available to movement organizations, they can be considered a *core* activity of the movement. If movement organizations devote only minimal and sporadic effort and resources to these activities, they can be termed *peripheral*. As will be discussed below, engagement with the partisan arena has been a core activity of the American women's movement, but only a peripheral activity of the Canadian women's movement in recent years.

The second dimension of a movement's orientation involves its stance towards the party system. A movement adopting a *partisan* stance enters into some form of an exclusive relationship with one established political party. In its most regularized form this would entail a formal relationship between one or more major movement organizations and a party. An example of a partisan stance would be the formalized relationship between elements of the Canadian labour movement and the New Democratic Party.

A movement with a *multi-partisan* orientation engages with more than one party. Movement organizations avoid endorsing one party and movement leaders have meaningful contact with the leaderships of more than one party. From the early 1970s until the mid-1980s, the Canadian women's movement maintained a multi-partisan stance, never endorsing a party and being careful to maintain linkages of some sort with all of the parties, particularly the Liberals and the NDP.

A movement whose constituent organizations are not engaged with parties in any way can be termed *apartisan*. A distinction must be made between movements that are apartisan because they are not focused in any way on political change and politicized groups that have chosen not to engage with political parties. An example of a social movement organization that is focused more on social than legislative change is Mothers Against Drunk Driving. This group for the most part seeks to change personal behaviours and consequently would have little reason to involve itself in the partisan political arena. In contrast to this, a group like Greenpeace is focused on both social and political change, often in the international arena, and in this sense is overtly political. Greenpeace engages in protest actions meant to halt or draw attention to public policies, yet it does not ally itself with political parties in the countries in which it is active. A variation on an apartisan stance would be those movements, like the German environmentalists, whose adherents choose to form and support a political party of their own.

The Canadian and American Women's Movements

The women's movements of Canada and the United States offer an interesting case study of how social movements develop their orientations towards established political parties.[1] They provide a particularly useful comparison because they are ideologically similar, although by no means identical, movements operating in very different political systems. The dominant ideological tendency in both movements was liberal feminism touched by radical feminism. This changed somewhat in the mid-1980s, when social feminism became the dominant tendency in the Canadian movement (see Vickers et al., 1993: 31–51).

Because they operate in very different political systems, these movements face different opportunity structures. The American women's movement has sought political and legal change within the context of a congressional system with separation of powers, a powerful legislative branch, a fixed two-party system with relatively weak and permeable political parties, and candidate-centred electoral competition. The Canadian movement has worked to achieve similar reforms in a parliamentary system complete with fusion of powers, a constrained parliament, a party system with more than two parties, highly disciplined parties that are relatively closed to outside groups, and party-centred electoral competition.

The Canadian and American political systems have one thing in common: they make it virtually impossible for a new political party without a geographic basis of support to become viable. The two parties that have emerged in Canada in the past decade—the Bloc Québécois and Reform (now Canadian Alliance)—both started with a discrete geographic basis of support. The single-member district electoral systems used in both the US and Canada make the idea of a women's party, which might be able to win 10 or 20 per cent of the vote spread across the country, politically unworkable. Consequently, the option of forming a party has never really been available to either movement.[2]

When the contemporary Canadian women's movement first mobilized in the early 1970s, a substantial portion of the activists involved saw electoral or partisan activity as an important part of the movement's overall strategy. Delegates to the founding conference of the National Action Committee (NAC) on the Status of Women devoted considerable attention to political parties and envisioned women participating in the parties on their own terms, thereby transforming them (NAC, 1972). In 1972, a group called Women for Political Action (WPA) was formed with the intention of mounting independent candidacies by women and trying to enhance the status of women by working within the established parties. The initial enthusiasm for electoral activity soon waned as it became clear that this strategy would not produce immediate results. The WPA became defunct in 1979, and the NAC was only intermittently involved in partisan or electoral politics. The NAC's most extensive involvement in electoral politics came during the 1984 federal election, when it sponsored and organized a high-profile, nationally televised debate on women's issues among the three major party leaders. In subsequent elections, the NAC produced a voter's guide and sponsored lower-profile debates, but had little to do with parties between elections.

After 1984, some activists remained committed to working through electoral politics, but the NAC increasingly devoted its resources to pursuing alternative strategies for social and political change. Liberal feminists' continuing interest in electoral politics was signalled by the formation in 1984 of the Committee for '94. This group's purpose was to pressure the parties to remedy women's numerical under-representation. Even though many liberal feminists continued to focus on electoral politics, the mainstream of the Canadian movement, as represented by the NAC, has become less engaged in this area. The NAC has maintained a rhetorical commitment to the project of electing women, but has devoted few resources to this and is no longer as supportive of the promotion of women in the parties as it was during the 1970s.

In contrast to the Canadian experience, electoral politics went from a peripheral to a core activity of the American women's movement over the same period. When the contemporary American movement first mobilized in the mid-1960s, activists displayed little interest in parties or elections. Radical and grassroots activists saw parties not as a vehicle for social change, but rather as a barrier. They consequently focused on protest actions, while more moderate institutionalist feminists concentrated on lobbying the executive branch (Costain and Costain, 1987: 198). By 1971, however, activists were increasingly looking to the partisan arena. In 1971, women working inside the parties joined with activists from outside to form the National Women's Political Caucus. The formation of this group reflected a growing belief that the movement must become more explicitly politicized if it was to become effective, as well as a desire among some Democratic Party activists to use the emerging movement to establish a power base within the party. Events through the 1980s and early 1990s only amplified American feminists' focus on the partisan political arena. The unsuccessful campaign to achieve ratification of the Equal Rights Amendment in state legislatures left activists believing that having women elected to legislatures was essential to achieving the movement's policy objectives. Election of the overtly anti-feminist Reagan administration in 1980 also contributed to the movement's growing involvement in electoral politics. As Reagan and his successor, George Bush, appointed conservatives to the federal courts, the judicial route became ever less viable for feminists, forcing them to redouble their efforts in the electoral arena. The increasing focus on electoral activity is best observed in the proliferation and growth of women's Political Action Committees, organizations that exist to solicit and pass on campaign contributions for like-minded candidates. As Figure 24.1 shows, the total disbursements of women's PACs has increased steadily over time, peaking in 1991–2, fuelled by outrage over the spectacle of the all-male Senate Judiciary Committee grilling lawyer Anita Hill over her allegations that Supreme Court nominee Clarence Thomas sexually harassed her.

Just as they differ in the intensity of their activity related to electoral politics, the Canadian and the American women's movements have adopted different partisan orientations. Since the mobilization of the Canadian women's movement, apartisan and multi-partisan orientations have coexisted. Multi-partisanship was dominant in the early years, but as grassroots and socialist feminism has become more prevalent within the NAC, the movement's partisan orientation has tended towards apartisanship.

Almost all the women who led the NAC in its first decade had strong personal ties to one of the three major Canadian parties at the time. Within the organization, NDP women outnumbered other partisans, but Liberal and Conservative women were active in the NAC during its first decade. One former NAC president called these ties 'highly significant. . . . It was very important to have people from all parties and we actively sought them out' (confidential interview).

The left-of-centre New Democratic Party was a natural ally for the women's movement. Of the three major Canadian parties, its policies have always come closest to those of the movement. In addition, feminists and other social movement activists form a significant force within the party. Although the NAC has frequently co-operated with the party on certain policy issues, the alliance has never

Figure 24.1: Total American PAC Contributions (1996 $)

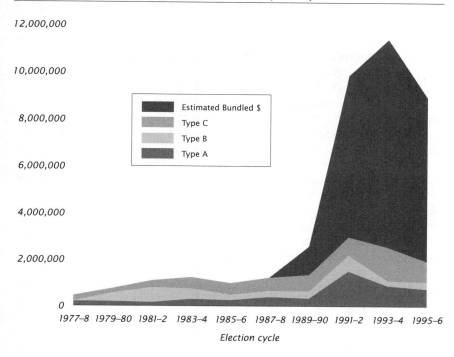

12,000,000

10,000,000

8,000,000

6,000,000

4,000,000

2,000,000

0

Legend:
- Estimated Bundled $
- Type C
- Type B
- Type A

1977–8 1979–80 1981–2 1983–4 1985–6 1987–8 1989–90 1991–2 1993–4 1995–6

Election cycle

Type A: PACs that contribute only to female candidates.
Type B: PACs that contribute to feminist candidates of either gender.
Type C: PACs that solicit contributions mainly from women and contribute to candidates of either gender on issues that are not necessarily feminist issues.
Source: Calculated from Federal Election Commission data.

been formalized. Although many Canadian feminists support the party, they doubt its commitment to the movement's agenda and are consequently reluctant to enter into any formal alliance (confidential interview). Even if the NAC's leadership did desire a formalized alliance with the party, such a move would have jeopardized the organization's government funding.[3]

After 1984, the mounting influence of socialist and radical feminists within the NAC gradually eroded its multi-partisanship, replacing it with an apartisan orientation more in keeping with radical feminists' critiques of political parties in general. This change was manifested through the weakening of interpersonal ties between the NAC leadership and parties and in the organization's rhetoric surrounding party politics. NAC leaders grew increasingly critical of parties, arguing that they privilege political advantage over the public interest.[4] For a time, just after the failure of the Charlottetown Accord in 1992, NAC leaders started to talk about the organization as an alternative to political parties. In the words of former NAC president Judy Rebick, 'people see us as one of the only progressive voices that has any power. And they want us to do everything, not just focus on women's issues. They want us to act like a political party' (quoted in Gottleib, 1993: 384). Although the NAC has not displaced political parties as an intermediary between society and the state, it is noteworthy that its leaders thought of the organization as playing the role usually assigned to parties in a liberal democracy.

Like its Canadian counterpart, the American movement adopted a multi-partisan orientation when it first began to engage with parties. Over time, however, the American women's movement became increasingly partisan in its orientation, developing close and sometimes formalized ties with the Democratic Party. The National Organization of Women (NOW) developed an exclusive relationship with the Democratic Party, endorsing its presidential nominees and contributing to its candidates. Although American feminists experienced moments of disenchantment with the Democrats, the staunch anti-feminist policy position of the Republican Party left them with few alternatives. As a result, American feminists in the late 1990s found themselves in the curious position of rallying to President Bill Clinton's aid when Republicans tried to force him from office for sexual indiscretions.

When we compare the stances of the Canadian and American women's movements towards political parties, we find some similarities. Certainly, both movements have been drawn towards engaging with political parties because such involvement offers the possibility of influencing public policy and facilitating the entry of women into political élites. Despite this attraction, feminists in both countries have found that political parties are not ideal coalition partners. Political parties exist to fight and win elections, and require that their allies share that objective. Because of their electoral orientation, parties' policy stances tend to be more moderate than those of social movements and try to balance competing interests. For the most part, feminist leaders have been unwilling to subordinate their agenda for social change to the parties' electoral agendas.

This ambivalent relationship to electoral politics is not what the movement-centred theories of social movement behaviour suggested. The movement-centred theory contended that the ideological predisposition of new social movements, like the women's movement, would prevent them from being involved in electoral politics. Clearly, this was not the case for either the Canadian or the American movement. The movement-centred approach is accurate in its identification of their predisposition away from the pragmatic deal-making and vote-chasing that characterize brokerage parties. What this theoretical account fails to capture, however, is the equally powerful lure of partisan politics that draws movements into this sphere. If social movement organizations remain outside the partisan political arena, they are less equipped to influence public policy. As a result, movement organizations can find themselves drawn into the partisan political arena in the hope of furthering their policy agendas.

Aside from their shared ambivalence towards parties, the Canadian and American women's movements have taken divergent paths. The American movement has been far more involved with party politics than its Canadian counterpart and has tended to accept a partisan relationship with the Democrats. The Canadian women's movement is much less involved in electoral politics and has largely adopted an apartisan orientation. How can we account for the very different stances that the American and Canadian women's movements have taken?

The strategic approach to studying social movements offers a helpful explanation for the differences between the two movements. Quite simply, both movements have responded to the opportunity structures embedded in the institutions and arrangements of their respective political systems. Three elements of the political opportunity structure have been particularly important in shaping the two movements' diverging paths: legislative institutions, the shape of the party system, and the structural characteristics of parties.

The American legislative branch is very powerful and individual legislators are unconstrained by party discipline. As a result, election of women has a highly visible impact on public policy. In contrast to this, the Canadian Parliament is weak relative to the cabinet, and party discipline limits the ability of individual members of Parliament to affect public policy. Even if the election of female MPs does have an impact on policy, it is most likely to take place behind closed doors in a confidential caucus meeting. If activists are unaware of the efforts of female MPs to work on issues of importance to women, they are less likely to think of female MPs as important allies for the women's movement. It is not surprising, then, that the American women's movement has focused such a substantial portion of its resources on electoral politics writ large and on the project of electing women more specifically.

The Canadian and American party systems have offered very different alternatives to movement organizations. American electoral laws have produced a highly stable two-party system. Since 1980, the American party system has been polarized around social issues, with the Democrats espousing liberal or progressive policies and the Republicans adopting socially conservative positions on such issues as abortion and gay rights. Throughout the 1980s and 1990s, Republicans have tried to reverse policies supported by the women's movement; most notably, they have introduced numerous legislative initiatives to restrict women's access to abortion. In this context, American feminists had little alternative but to ally themselves closely with the Democrats. The Canadian party system during the period from 1970 to 1993 was comprised of three parties, the Progressive Conservatives, the Liberals, and the New Democrats. Although there were certainly differences in the three parties' openness to feminism, they did not polarize around social issues in the way their American counterparts did (Young, 1995). This three-party system offered the Canadian movement a broader partisan choice. Because significant numbers of movement adherents were allied with either the Liberals or the NDP, movement organizations could not enter into a closer relationship with one of the parties without alienating a significant internal constituency. As a consequence, a partisan orientation was never an option for the movement. In the period from 1993 to the present, the Canadian party system has included five parties—the three old parties plus Reform/Canadian Alliance and the Bloc Québécois. Although the NDP and the BQ are sympathetic to the women's movement's agenda, the other parties are considerably less open to feminism. This can be attributed at least in part to the effect of the Reform Party, which essentially pulled the party system's centre of gravity to the right (see Young, 2000).

Finally, the structure and organization of political parties are very different in the two countries. At the national level, American political parties are essentially diffuse networks of activists and organizations with a fairly limited degree of cohesion. For the most part, American parties are extremely loose coalitions, held together more by bonds of convenience or necessity than loyalty or shared ideological purpose. Because American parties have no formal membership, party officials cannot control entry into party activity, nor can they revoke activists' membership. The regional, ethnic, religious, and political diversity of the American electorate, when combined with a two-party system, has forced American parties to build diverse coalitions that encompass cross-sections of society. This means that American parties tend not to be homogeneous ideological entities, but rather coalitions of various ideological factions. This has made it possible for feminists to become a constituency within the Democratic Party. In addition, American party organizations play only a limited role in election campaigns, leaving it up to candidates to develop networks of campaign workers and solicit financial contributions from other sources. Groups able to supply labour or financial resources are extremely important to candidates, who can expect only limited support from their party (see Katz and Kolodny, 1994; McSweeney and Zvesper, 1991; Rae, 1989, 1994). This has opened the door for feminist PACs to exercise influence within the party.

In contrast to this, Canadian parties have tended to be cohesive, disciplined organizations that are generally resistant to incursion from outside groups. They are membership-based, and only party members can participate in decisions concerning the party organization. Although the thresholds for such participation are low, there is little evidence to suggest that interest groups have successfully captured party organizations in Canada. Moreover, national party organizations are able to exercise a considerable degree of control over local party activities (see Carty et al., 2000).

As a result of these differences, American political parties are structurally more open to engagement with social movement organizations. There were few structural barriers to prevent NOW from becoming an important constituent group within the Democratic Party. In contrast to this, Canadian parties have been relatively closed to feminist mobilizations. Women have become a significant constituency within the Canadian parties, particularly the NDP, but feminist organizations have not. Canadian parties resist vehemently any effort from outside groups to 'capture' the party. Ironically, parties that are highly cohesive and disciplined, like the Canadian parties, would be ideal vehicles for a movement *if* they could be captured. The very cohesion that would make these parties useful vehicles, however, precludes this strategy. Conversely, the weakness of American parties invites movement intervention.

The Question of Success

Given this understanding of the very different orientations the Canadian and American women's movements adopted towards political parties, one might ask which strategy led to greater success. Unfortunately, there is no simple answer to this question. Both movements adapted their strategies in response to a range of factors, including how open political parties were to their agenda. In this sense, the parties' responses affected the movement organizations' strategies. Because the two movements pursued strategies appropriate to the institutional and political contexts in which they were operating, and because movement strategy is only one of many factors determining policy and other outcomes, we cannot judge the relative success of movement strategies based only on this analysis of the factors shaping movement orientations. For example, the Canadian movement places far less emphasis on electing women than does the American movement. Despite this, the different structural features of the two electoral and candidate selection systems have meant that the proportion of women in the Canadian House of Commons outstrips that of women in the US House of Representatives by a margin of almost two to one.

What we can draw from this analysis are the implications of movement strategies for political parties. Because movement organizations are drawn towards engaging with parties in the hope of influencing policy outcomes but also highly critical of the parties as unprincipled, they are not likely to be absorbed into one or more of the parties. The two movements' different patterns of partisan orientation have implications for the treatment of policy issues raised in the formal political arena. The American movement's closer relationship with one party has, arguably, contributed to the polarization of the US party system around gender issues (Freeman, 1987). American feminists could hope to make significant policy gains when the Democrats held office, but they also had to expect substantial setbacks when the Republicans were in power. The Canadian movement's multi-partisan approach in the 1970s and early 1980s prevented a similar polarization around such issues in the Canadian party system (Young, 2000). At least until 1993, the Canadian women's movement had no enemy among the major parties and had no reason to expect the kinds of policy setbacks that the American movement experienced at the hands of the Republicans. By the same token, neither of the parties that formed governments (the Liberals and the Conservatives) were close allies of the women's movement, so activists could not expect significant progress on policy issues when power changed hands.

Conclusion

There is no one orientation that social movement organizations are likely to adopt relative to political parties. Depending on the character of the political opportunity structure—including such factors as basic institutions, the shape of the party system, and the characteristics of specific parties within the system—some social movement organizations will determine that it is in their best interests to involve themselves in electoral politics. Faced with a different opportunity structure, other movement organizations will make different choices. Movement strategies are likely to be complex, and often highly changeable, as political circumstances change. Although movement-centred accounts can explain one element of social movement behaviour—why movement organizations are sometimes reluctant to engage with political parties—they cannot explain the full range of movement behaviour. For this fuller understanding, strategic accounts are more helpful.

Notes

1. This account is based on interviews with activists in both movements, as well as archival research. For a more detailed version, see Young (1995, 1998).
2. Despite this, both movements have at least considered the idea fairly seriously. In 1979, a group of Toronto feminists formed the Feminist Party of Canada, which neither ran candidates nor became a registered political party in either Ontario or at the federal level. In 1989, a group of American feminists tried to launch a new political party that was to be a coalition of feminists and other progressive social movement activists. Like the Feminist Party of Canada, this initiative was short-lived and had virtually no impact on the established partisan arena. For a more detailed discussion, see Young (1995).
3. From its formation until the mid-1990s, the NAC relied on the federal government for a significant portion of its operating funds. For a discussion of the Canadian government's practice of funding groups, see Pal (1993).
4. In a 1993 interview, former NAC president Judy Rebick argued that the movement had to take a stand opposing the Charlottetown Accord even if the decision would hurt the movement. To 'make a decision based on saving NAC rather than on what is in the best interests of women', she argued, would be 'doing the same thing we criticize political parties of' (Rebick, 1993).

References

Carty, R.K., William Cross, and Lisa Young. 2000. *Canadian Party Politics for the 21st Century*. Vancouver: University of British Columbia Press.

Costain, Anne, and Douglas Costain. 1987. 'Strategy and Tactics of the Women's Movement in the United States: The Role of Political Parties', in Mary Fainsod Katzenstein and Carol McClurg Mueller, eds, *The Women's Movements of the United States and Western Europe: Consciousness, Political Opportunity and Public Policy*. Philadelphia: Temple University Press, 196–213.

Freeman, Jo. 1987. 'Whom You Know versus Whom You Represent: Feminist Influence in the Democrat and Republican Parties', in Mary Fainsod Katzenstein and Carol McClurg Mueller, eds, *The Women's Movements of the United States and Western Europe: Consciousness, Political Opportunity and Public Policy*. Philadelphia: Temple University Press, 215–46.

Gottlieb, Amy, ed. 1993. 'What About Us? Organizing Inclusively in the National Action Committee on the Status of Women', in Linda Carty, ed., *And Still We Rise: Feminist Political Mobilizing in Contemporary Canada*. Toronto: Women's Press, 368–85.

Katz, Richard, and Robin Kolodny. 1994. 'Party Organizations as an Empty Vessel: Parties in American Politics', in Katz and Peter Mair, eds, *How Parties Organize: Change and Adaptation in Party Organizations in Western Democracies*. London: Sage.

McSweeney, Dean, and John Zvesper. 1991. *American Political Parties*. London: Routledge.

Melucci, Alberto. 1989. *Nomads of the Present: Social Movements and Industrial Needs in Contemporary Society*. Philadelphia: Temple University Press.

National Action Committee on the Status of Women (NAC). 1972. 'Report of the Strategy for Change Convention of Women in Canada', Canadian Women's Movement Archives, File: the NAC—Formation 1972.

Offe, Claus. 1990. 'Reflections on the Institutional Self-Transformation of Movement Politics: A Tentative Stage Model', in Russell Dalton and Manfred Kuechler, eds, *Challenging the Political Order: New Social and Political Movements in Western Democracies*. Oxford: Oxford University Press, 232–50.

Pal, Leslie A. 1993. *Interests of State: The Politics of Language, Multiculturalism and Feminism in Canada*. Montreal and Kingston: McGill-Queen's University Press.

Rae, Nicol C. 1989. *The Decline and Fall of the Liberal Republicans from 1952 to the Present*. Oxford: Oxford University Press.

———. 1994. *Southern Democrats*. Oxford: Oxford University Press.

Rebick, Judy. 1993. 'Interview with Judy Rebick' by Agnes Huang and Fatima Jaffer, in *Kinesis* 3: 10–11.

Schattschneider, E.E. 1942. *Party Government*. New York: Farrar and Rinehart.

Tarrow, Sidney. 1989. *Struggle, Politics, and Reform: Collective Action, Social Movements and Cycles of Protest*. Ithaca, NY: Cornell University Western Societies Papers.

Vickers, Jill, Pauline Rankin, and Christine Appelle. 1993. *Politics as if Women Mattered: A Political Analysis of the National Action Committee on the Status of Women*. Toronto: University of Toronto Press.

Young, Lisa. 1995. 'Women's Movements and Political Parties: A Canadian-American Comparison', *Party Politics* 2: 229–50.

———. 1998. 'The Canadian Women's Movement and Political Parties, 1970–1993', in Manon Tremblay and Caroline Andrew, eds, *Women and Political Representation in Canada*. Ottawa: University of Ottawa Press, 195–218.

———. 2000. *Feminists and Party Politics*. Vancouver: University of British Columbia Press.

Chapter 25

New Social Movements and the Environmental Policy Process: The Case of Alberta's Castle Wilderness Area

Lorna Stefanick

Studies of political participation have traditionally looked at political parties, elections, and other state-sanctioned institutions through which citizens can participate in their own governance. Participation outside these fora was often characterized in a negative light. That is, while it was recognized that groups promoting a specialized interest supplement the system of geographical representation, they 'almost inevitably promote particularistic causes and partial interests which includes at times the most indefensible advancement of human greed' (Key, 1964: 150). And while participation in interest groups was seen as potentially problematic, participation in mass movements was cast in an even more negative light. It was assumed that citizens protesting on the street did so because they had no other means through which to express their political objectives. These alienated citizens (typically those on the economic or social margins of society) were forced to operate outside traditional channels for their voices to be heard. Given the legacy of the populist movements that arose in Italy and Germany prior to World War II, mass citizen participation was viewed with suspicion.

By the 1990s, mass movements had proliferated and academic interest in them grew. The social movements of the postwar decades, however, have been conceptualized as categorically different from earlier mass movements. Scholars found that activists within the new movements are not marginalized by the political system because of poverty or systemic discrimination. Indeed, studies show that most new social movement activists (NSM) are middle class, well educated, and interested in issues of a non-economic nature (Chandler and Siaroff, 1985–6; Müller-Rommel, 1985; Rüdig, 1988). In addition, they are not exclusively focused on political change. Susan Phillips defines a social movement as '(a) an informal network of organizations and individuals who (b) on the basis of a collective identity and shared values (c) engage in political and/or cultural struggle intended to expand the boundaries of the existing system and (d) undertake collective action designed to affect both state and society' (Phillips, 1994: 189). In other words, NSM activists not only concern themselves with changing the output of the political policy process, they focus on changing the attitudes and beliefs of those who live in civil society.

The reasons behind the emergence of new social movements are complex, relating to both demographic changes and changing values. These changes are said to be difficult for parties and government institutions to accommodate because activists often prefer to rely on confrontational, protest tactics rather than more traditional strategies such as lobbying the influential. Canada is not immune to the mobilization of NSM groups or their protest-oriented activities. Indeed, the summer of 1993 saw the largest act of civil disobedience in Canadian history; over 800 people were arrested for protesting the logging of an old-growth forest in Clayoquot Sound, BC. This kind of activity puts enormous strain on Canadian institutions, as evidenced by the judicial system's difficulties in processing the Clayoquot arrestees due to the sheer magnitude of their numbers.

For political scientists, mass movements present interesting research questions with respect to the ability of institutions to accommodate diverse interests. Specifically, can our political institutions successfully integrate the interests of newly mobilized political actors, and if not, how can institutions and/or processes be altered so that interests can be expressed through state structures rather than from outside? While this question has received little systematic attention, devising new policy processes is of particular salience to Canadian decision-makers, especially in those policy arenas where NSM actors are most visible.

This chapter analyses one innovative institutional response to the challenges posed by new social movements: the round table. This process was employed in southwestern Alberta to resolve a conservation dispute and provides an illustrative case study of one attempt to integrate NSM actors into the policy-making process. Because the case in question was part of a larger province-wide process, further comparative case studies will allow future research to draw more generalized conclusions about the possibilities of integrating social movement actors into government-sponsored round table processes. For the present study, the author conducted interviews with the chairperson of the round table process, the president of the Castle-Crown Coalition, and the Alberta director of the World Wildlife Fund in the spring of 1997. Government documents, press releases, and literature for environmental groups were also examined.

The chapter begins with a discussion of the NSM phenomenon and environmentalism in Canada. It then analyses the organizational logic of the round table, explaining how this forum differs from more traditional policy-making processes. Next, it highlights the difficulties associated with the round table as a tool for integrating environmental actors into policy-making, using the southwestern Alberta conservation process as an example. If insufficient attention is paid to process, however, institutional reform has the potential to alienate rather than integrate NSM actors into government-sponsored policy-making. The danger for government officials of flirting with poorly designed processes is that actors who perceive that their energy has been wasted in previous fora may feel that their only choice to affect social and political change is to work outside of traditional channels. Moderate groups that have previously had a low profile may come to believe that their only hope for success is to engage in confrontational behaviour.

New Social Movements: Ideas and Institutions

As Nevitte and others argue, a new belief system is appearing in Western industrialized democracies (Nevitte, 1996; Inglehart, 1977). Briefly, this outlook values quality-of-life issues over economic issues; it promotes rights-based equality, as well as the democratization of, and enhanced participation in, decision-making processes. Social change is seen to be the precursor for political change. Thus, effecting change with respect to attitudes and perspectives is considered to be as important as, and often more important than, issue-specific political change. European NSM studies indicate that increasing numbers of people are participating in non-traditional political activity (Lawson and Merkl, 1988; Offe, 1985; Poguntke, 1987); these activists tend to be urbanites born after 1945 who share similar backgrounds, occupations, education, and values (Chandler and Siaroff, 1985–6; Müller-Rommel, 1985; Rüdig, 1988). Members of this generation are described as being post-materialist in orientation, that is, they are not typically marginalized either politically or economically and as a result are sufficiently secure to focus on quality-of-life issues rather than purely economic concerns (Inglehart, 1977). As noted in the chapters by Blake and Nevitte and Kanji in this volume, this same trend is apparent in Canada. In the context of environmentalism, the non-traditional ideas of post-materialists regarding economic growth and consumption are best described as being anti-industrial and anti-consumption (Cotgrove and Duff, 1980, 1981). By definition, the world view of NSM activists includes an emphasis on personal empowerment and participatory democratic principles. It is thus not surprising that the groups to which activists belong cannot easily adopt hierarchical organizational forms grounded in authority based on position, deference, and organizational secrecy (Offe, 1985).

The ultimate goal of NSM activists is to change societal values and ideas, not simply to succeed in achieving a particular policy goal. As such, activists, and the groups they work within, do not rely on the traditional lobbying tactics of other interest groups. Instead, they engage in activities designed to attract the attention of the media in order to generate public interest in their particular world view. More traditional groups lobbying for a particular policy outcome may use media-focused tactics to gain attention, but typically drop them for more effective behind-the-scenes strategies once they have gained the ear of the influential (Pross, 1992). In contrast, NSM actors continue to use these tactics even after they have succeeded in drawing the attention of both the public and the politicians to their cause. Even after they have attained a solid resource base and political connections, they do not adopt a hierarchical organizational structure, nor do they merely use the quiet but highly effective lobbying tactics employed by traditional interest groups. No matter how rich and sophisticated they become, groups that espouse ideas sharply at odds with entrenched economic and political interests will not be well received within political inner circles. And after succeeding in establishing themselves as important members of the policy community, these interest groups are reluctant to walk through the doors of political power that the public has demanded be opened for them.

In the last three decades in Canada, environmental issues have increasingly appeared on the political agenda, undoubtedly due in part to the activities of environmental organizations that have brought attention to these issues (Blake, this volume). The increasing profile of environmentalists and the issues they concern themselves with can be explained in part at the level of ideas. That is, these trends reflect the changing view of the relationship between resource exploitation and the well-being of Canadian society. For most of its history, the Canadian environmental policy arena was dictated by corporate interests perceived to be synonymous with the public interest. As Woodrow observes, Canada's resources were abundant, and little regard was paid to the consequences of their extraction on the environment (Woodrow, 1980: 24). Resource extraction was so critical to the nation's development that the state often provided subsidies and rebates to industry as incentives for them to exploit new frontiers. Policy-making thus remained within the purview of the state and the relevant resource industries. As a consequence, other interests did not have access to policy-makers, nor did they have any input into decision-making (Schrecker, 1984: 7).

Things began to change in the 1960s, however. The emergence of pollution concerns in that decade, the energy shortage of the 1970s, and the environmental disasters of the 1980s forced a re-evaluation of the commitment to resource exploitation and economic growth. Specifically, environmentalists began to challenge the notion that the public interest equalled wholesale economic development based on resource extraction, given the negative impact this development might have on the environment. These concerns resonate with post-materialists, as they place a priority on quality-of-life issues rather than economic security. Moreover, environmentalists argue that the public interest should take into account the needs of future generations and wildlife (Paehlke, 1989: 143–76). As the debate over what exactly constituted the public's interest became increasingly contentious, the tight relationship that existed between the regulator (the state) and the industry being regulated began to erode public confidence in the decision-making process. A closed process that prevents the interested public from having input will result in policy choices that are skewed in favour of interests on the inside. Needless to say, the legitimacy of this process has been repeatedly called into question by those who fear that environmental concerns are being given insufficient attention in a process that is not open to scrutiny (Paehlke, 1987: 44).

The 1990s, however, saw unprecedented shifts in the making of resource management decisions. Three major factors brought this about. First, there is no longer a consensus over what the public's best interest is. Specifically, many citizens define societal interests very broadly, including the rights of future generations and other species. Moreover, some question whether economic values should have precedence over more intangible values such as aesthetics. Second, the concept of sustainable development was popularized worldwide by the UN's Brundtland Report and adopted as a global goal (UN, 1987). While this concept is highly fluid and means different things to different people, at the very least the ensuing discussion encouraged many countries to rethink whether the world's present rate of resource extraction and consumption was sustainable in the long run (Stefanick and Wells, 1998: 246–8). Third, and partially as a result of the first two factors, there is increased public skepticism about decisions made behind closed doors. Years ago governments could credibly claim that society was united behind economic development as a key societal goal. For most citizens (particularly in Canada), the activities of government were not a concern, so long as the economy was strong and the general standard of living was high. This is no longer the case, and the desire for public participation can be seen in all sectors in Canada, from constitutional issues to health care.

As a result of the sustained critique of environmental policy-making in the late 1980s, the federal government turned to a specialist in negotiation, the Niagara Institute. The Niagara Institute developed a round table environmental consultation process under the auspices of Environment Canada. The so-called 'round table concept' brings together representatives of various core interests such as business, environmental groups, labour, and government to discuss policy problems openly. This is in stark contrast to previous processes, whereby decisions were made by politicians on the advice of public servants. As Hoberg (1992: 308) notes, '[e]nvironmental policy decisions were made in closed, quiet meetings between the affected industry and government officials.' When consultation with affected stakeholders was deemed useful, it was undertaken on an informal and ad hoc basis. Ultimately, state actors made the decisions, usually after consultation with key economic interests.

By 1991, every province and territory in Canada had set up its own environmental round table to develop the concept of sustainable development, and by the end of the decade round tables were being used to discuss all manner of environmental issues. These fora have distinct mandates and activities; some are set up to be consultative in nature, while decisions are binding in others. In some round table processes, state actors appoint participants to represent the views of relevant stakeholders. In others, a neutral facilitator chooses who will participate in the process. In either scenario, state actors have equal status to other participants once the round table begins deliberations. In the original conception, round table decisions are made collectively by consensus, ensuring that even minority voices are heard. This process has given NSM actors a voice by acknowledging them as stakeholders (Stefanick, 1998).

The round table consultative mechanism has generated great interest among both state actors and scholars. In contrast to previous processes, the round table is a formal, open process in that both the process and the participants are visible to the public. In theory, round tables are procedurally neutral and democratic, characteristics that articulate well with the values of NSM activists. In particular, the NSM aspiration that empowered individuals should control issues directly affecting them is embodied by the small-scale local round table process. In this forum the public interest is not a given but a contested concept, a goal to be defined by the actors involved in a policy dispute. Given their emphasis on inclusiveness, openness, and bottom-up decision-making, round tables represent a significant institutional shift towards the expressed values of NSM activists. Of more importance to students of political behaviour, however, is that round tables mark a turning point with respect to the participation of environmental actors in policy discussions. Previously, environmentalists were not considered important stakeholders. Now they are not only being recognized as important, but their participation in a formal, transparent process is considered integral in legitimizing policy decisions.

Although the round table concept has generated great enthusiasm, its biggest drawback is the time required to reach a decision. The underlying assumption is that ongoing discussion will reveal common values that can be built upon, producing a result at least minimally agreeable to all. Clearly, this can be both complicated and time-consuming, particularly when stakeholders are polarized. Politicians, however, are often expected to find quick fixes to complex policy problems, and those who do not achieve results by the next election will suffer at the polls. And in the end, there is always the possibility that the perspectives of the various stakeholders may not be reconcilable (Toner, 1993: 4).

The selection of participants is a second, but equally important problem for advocates of the round table forum. Which interests should be represented and how should these representatives be chosen? Critics point out that the selection method frequently remains hierarchical and closed, and thus the process will still be antithetical to NSM values (Howlett, 1990: 110–11). Moreover, if all important societal stakeholders are not represented (or if there is a perception that they are not represented) in the round table forum, the final outcome (regardless of its prescriptions) will be considered illegitimate.

These problems aside, the round table forum is by far the most popular method of integrating the viewpoints of environmental actors and obtaining resolution to environmental controversies; it has been used with varying success at both the federal and provincial levels of government. One such attempt in the Castle-Crown region of southern Alberta is a particularly interesting example of a round table process that attempted to resolve an environmental controversy. It was successful in coming to a consensus decision, yet failed to resolve the conservation dispute that was the impetus for its formation.

Alberta's Special Places 2000: The Castle-Crown Process

The Castle-Crown round table process was part of Alberta's Special Places 2000 conservation initiative. In 1992, all provinces in Canada committed to conserving representative samples of Canada's ecosystems; Special Places 2000 was Alberta's provincial campaign. As outlined in the original draft document, the objective of Special Places 2000 was to complete a conservation system that would 'represent the environmental diversity of the province's six Natural Regions (20 subregions) by the end of 1998' (Alberta, 1992: 2). The document states that the province would provide the public, local communities, industrial sectors, and environmental groups with the opportunity to participate in the site selection process, and promised a systematic and scientific approach to evaluating sites.

Special Places was a progressive six-step process that involved: (1) the nomination of a site by any Albertan as a 'special place'; (2) the submission of this nomination to a provincial co-ordinating committee (PCC) comprised of various stakeholders and an intergovernmental committee (IC) composed of affected departments; (3) the setting up of a local committee to analyse the nomination and make recommendations; (4) the return of the nomination and recommendations to the provincial co-ordinating committee for review; (5) the submission of the nomination and recommendations for ministerial and cabinet approval; and (6) site establishment and management (Alberta, 1995: 8).

In April 1995, a local environmental group, the Castle-Crown Coalition, nominated the Castle Wilderness area as a special place. This wilderness area in southwestern Alberta is part of the 'Crown of the Continent Ecosystem', which extends from the Crowsnest Pass in Alberta and BC to the Bob Marshall Wilderness south of Glacier National Park in Montana. Because of its unique climatic conditions, the Crown is home to many species of rare plants (Castle-Crown Wilderness Coalition, n.d.). In addition, the Castle Wilderness has been identified as a key wildlife corridor linking Yellowstone National Park in Wyoming to Yukon Territory in the North. This wilderness area, however, is home to a downhill ski resort and is also a favourite recreational area for snowmobile and all-terrain vehicle enthusiasts. Of even more concern to environmentalists is that the Castle contains natural resources that have generated increasing interest from forestry, oil, and gas companies; there are presently over 140 gas wells located in this area and large stands of old-growth timber have been clear-cut. While the Castle Wilderness was only recently nominated for conservation as a Special Place, the opposition to economic development in the area is decades old. The legacy of this opposition is much animosity and distrust between groups that are for and against development.

The Castle nomination was reviewed and approved by both the PCC and IC; it then proceeded to step three of the Special Places process, which saw the establishment of a local committee. In 1996, the PCC recommended that the Municipal District of Pincher Creek establish a 'local committee to develop management principles for the creation of a protected area to preserve the unique and significant features of the Castle Area for designation under the Special Places program' (Alberta PCC, n.d.: 4). The PCC's terms of reference for the Castle nomination identified 28 groups whose interests should be represented on the local committee, but given the unwieldy size of a 28-member committee, it suggested the 'interests should be lumped into sectors' and that between 12 and 15 participants should represent these sectors. It also recommended that the local committee use an outside facilitator to monitor the selection process and that the process 'function by consensus' (ibid., 3–4).

Because of the long history of conflict over local land management issues, the Municipal District of Pincher Creek was initially reluctant to accept the PCC's request for leadership. Nonetheless, it eventually did so and created a local committee that submitted detailed terms of reference for the minister's approval. These terms of reference stated that Pincher Creek 'will appoint two councillors to the local committee, one of which will chair the local committee and the other as a member of the local committee and alternate chair. There will be no more than seven members from the greater Southern Alberta community' (ibid., 3). The terms also directed the chair to obtain decisions by consensus where possible, but allowed the chair to call for simple majority votes on issues that could not be decided by consensus. These terms of reference were approved in early 1997, and six months later the local committee for the Castle candidate area completed its work, making public its conservation recommendations. While this process successfully reached consensus on what should be done with respect to the conservation of the Castle Wilderness area, its activities and final report did nothing to decrease animosity among local stakeholders. Indeed, the process resulted in increased polarization of local citizens over conservation issues, and is used by other environmentalists as an example of why activists should avoid participating in government-sponsored participatory fora.

The structure of the Castle round table consultative forum was seriously flawed from the outset, and as a consequence, the decisions it came to lack legitimacy. The most contentious issue was the terms of reference created by the Municipal District of Pincher Creek, which were subsequently approved by the minister. While the PCC identified 28 key stakeholders and recommended that 12 to 15 of these participate in the round table process, the local committee's terms of reference stated that only nine representatives would be appointed by the municipal district. In the end, participants were chosen more by luck than by design. Area residents who wished to participate in the process were invited to submit their names to the municipal district for consideration. As per the committee's terms of reference, two participants were appointed to represent Pincher Creek and Crowsnest Pass. Another participant was appointed to represent an 'outside' perspective (that is, someone who did not live or work in the local area). The names of all area residents who had indicated an interest in serving on the committee were then written down on slips of paper and put in a jar; the remaining participants were selected by the random drawing of nine names from the slips in the jar. According to the chairperson of the local committee, this decision was taken to 'get the politics out' of the decision-making process.[1] No one representing an environmental group, including the original nominator of the Castle site, the Castle-Crown Wilderness Coalition, was invited to participate.

The municipal district's rationale for changing the terms of reference was past experience with public consultation in the area, and was inspired by the 'citizens' jury' approach to decision-making. Given the entrenched positions that many locals held and the resulting 'burnout' from disputes over land management issues, it was felt that a smaller committee would function more effectively and that the chair needed the discretion to call a vote to break a deadlock on any particular issue. According to the chair, however, the committee ultimately achieved all its decisions by consensus, and thus this power was never exercised. The decision to draw participants by lot was to promote the idea that individuals came to the table as randomly selected concerned citizens, rather than as representatives of a particular sector. It was hoped that participants thus would be perceived as interested individuals making decisions based on submissions from other concerned citizens and organized interests.[2] While the remaining steps of the Special Places 2000 were completed and the committee was successful in coming to a consensus, many citizens did not view the process as fair and impartial because key area stakeholders did not have representation on the committee.

Incensed at the exclusion of organized environmental interests, the Castle-Crown Wilderness Coalition dramatically demonstrated its displeasure in March 1997. At simultaneous press conferences held in Lethbridge, Calgary, and Edmonton, it announced that it was withdrawing its nomination of the Castle as a Special Place. According to Coalition president Klaus Jericho, '[t]he government has given Albertans one process for protecting land, but it is so flawed that environmental groups like ours have decided that we can't be part of it. The local procedures of Special Places 2000 are such that we think it might actually harm our efforts to protect the Castle Wilderness, not help them' (Castle-Crown Wilderness Coalition, 1997). Environmentalists throughout Alberta were equally enraged; many threatened to withdraw their participation from other ongoing Special Places 2000 processes and began to talk of using more confrontational tactics to advance their cause. Despite this opposition, the Castle Special Places consultation proceeded and produced a final report with land-use recommendations. With no participation or support from environmental interests, however, this particular process (and ultimately, the group's recommendations) lacked legitimacy and credibility.

The Castle Special Places process exhibited three major flaws. First, participants were appointed by local government in a process that was not open to public scrutiny. This contradicts the notion of procedural neutrality because the selection task was performed by a participant (the Municipal District of Pincher Creek), which arguably had a vested interest in the process. Clearly, this participant was not 'equal' to the others. Second, important stakeholders were excluded, most notably the environmental group that nominated the Castle for protection. While it may seem expedient to remove the 'politics' from the process, the round table concept is premised on the notion that policy decisions are inherently political and that all affected stakeholders must have a voice in the policy process. Third, the consensual decision-making rule was diluted, which instantly disadvantages minority interests. Any one of these flaws on its own had the potential to jeopardize the legitimacy of the process; taken together, they proved fatal.

If the intentions of the municipality were indeed genuine with respect to arriving at a solution that would be at least minimally acceptable to all concerned parties, then it is apparent that it did not understand the fundamental premises of a round table process. The particularly bitter history of the Castle-Crown region may have swayed the minister and the PCC to accept modified terms of reference for the Castle committee. Special Places 2000, however, is meant to be a consultative process; the purpose of the local committees is to represent area stakeholders and to come to a decision at least minimally accepted by all those affected. Since the local committee in this case did not represent all stakeholders, it could not complete its mandate as originally outlined by the PCC. In any event, the local committee's mandated task of making land-use recommendations within six months was virtually impossible within a consensual-based, round table process. This suggests that even provincial officials did not understand the basic premises and constraints of the process.

The local committee argued that the land-use recommendations in its final report were a compromise that attempted to balance conservation with economic and recreational uses. The process itself, however, left many environmental actors in Alberta convinced that participating in government-sanctioned decision-making processes was a waste of time and that more confrontational tactics aimed at gaining public sympathy (such as those used by their counterparts in British Columbia) would ultimately be more effective. The change in mood was demonstrated at an international conservation conference held in nearby Waterton Park a few months after the local committee submitted its recommendation. This conference was set up to promote the idea of a wilderness corridor that would extend from Yukon Territory to Yellowstone National Park. Alberta delegates spoke repeatedly of the futility of trying to deal with provincial politicians in a co-operative manner, dubbing them 'conservation dinosaurs'. The frustration with Special Places was obvious, as were the attempts to generate international interest in the Castle-Crown Wilderness by emphasizing it as the 'weak link' in the larger trans-border conservation project.[3]

New Social Movements, Institutions, and Public Policy

The difficulties of integrating NSMs into decision-making processes using the round table forum are clearly demonstrated by the Castle-Crown process. The Special Places program was the result of a sustained critique by environmental groups that economic growth and development are always in the best interests of the public. Environmental groups articulate the new perspective that some areas need to be preserved based on non-economic values. Governments, however, have had a difficult time integrating into decision-making processes those interests whose values are substantially different from their own and from those of other important stakeholders such as local chambers of commerce and industry. The round table forum is one institutional response to NSMs; it attempts to integrate new actors into the policy process and thereby to legitimize the process as a true expression of the public interest.

Meaningful public input, however, will only be attained if the decision-making process has a degree of autonomy from the government, particularly if the government is seen to share the hegemonic world view of dominant societal actors. Autonomy necessitates a system of checks and balances so that the local process is both accountable to the public and compatible with larger societal objectives. NSM theorists posit that decentralized decision-making and local empowerment are desirable, particularly with respect to the environmental movement. But as both the Canadian Parks and Wilderness Association and the World Wildlife Fund Canada point out, local communities may not 'fully appreciate' the importance of areas that may be of national or international significance.[4] Moreover, at the local level the power differential between competing stakeholders may in fact be much greater than at the regional or national level, and thus some actors may be greatly disadvantaged.

Local-level round table processes also have serious shortcomings with respect to integrating NSM activists into the policy process. First, it may be difficult to wrest the process away from entrenched interests who may have considerably more sway at the local level than their counterparts at higher levels. Second, choosing appropriate stakeholders is problematic with respect to environmental actors. Who exactly can be chosen to represent environmentalists? Moreover, who is responsible for choosing the representatives who will sit at the table and for the selection method employed? Perception of impartiality is critical; a facilitator who has no 'history' in the local community will enhance the legitimacy of the process in the eyes of local stakeholders, as well as the larger public. And finally, consensus decision-making is critical to a stakeholder process, particularly one attempting to solve a contentious issue. A consensus requirement where impasse does not mean the status quo, but rather passes the decision-making on to another body, forces stakeholders to strive for common ground. In contrast, a straight majority vote, or, as in the case of the Castle process, the possibility of having one, gives the advantage to the status quo over the minority viewpoint. This is crucially important in a policy area where the minority viewpoint (as expressed by NSMs) challenges the dominant, entrenched economic interests within society. To promote broader provincial and national interests, there must be a provision for a higher authority to overrule local committees unable to achieve consensus. This is critical in the event that the local processes become mired down in irresolvable issues.

In the case of the Castle nomination, the modification of the terms of reference by the local committee and the subsequent acceptance of these terms by the provincial government irreparably damaged the credibility of its final report and called into question the legitimacy of the round table process. Not only was a portion of the local public alienated by this particular process, environmentalists province-wide used this case as an example of the futility of participating in government-sponsored decision-making fora. Round tables will only be effective if participation is perceived to be balanced between majority and minority interests in a process that levels the playing field. Anything less, and the process will be seen as simply a thinly disguised method used by mainstream interests to manipulate the public agenda to achieve their own goals. Whether or not the outcome of the policy process is sound is not the critical issue here; the point is that in a round table process, participants are supposed to be stakeholders representing particular sectoral interests. If critical stakeholders are excluded, if some stakeholders are allowed to act as both participant and facilitator, and if there is the possibility that the consensual decision-making model can be abandoned at the discretion of a stakeholder, the outcome (in this case, the local committee's final report) will be perceived to be biased (and therefore illegitimate) even if its recommendations are balanced and well thought out. With respect to political behaviour, a very real danger exists that a process perceived to be biased will result in polarizing positions and radicalizing actors.

In any event, difficult decisions must be made regarding the environment, and processes that favour the status quo will do nothing to help resolve complex problems. Like any new decision-making process, the round table forum will experience growing pains. It may also prove to be true, however, that the very nature of NSMs (specifically, their non-hierarchical structure and their alternative world view) will make their incorporation through such mechanisms extremely difficult, and perhaps impossible. While some serious problems surround round tables as an integrative process, the status quo will do little to integrate NSMs generally, and environmental groups specifically, into the political process. Until the wrinkles are ironed out of this process, the groups and activists within NSMs will continue to eschew traditional political participation, preferring to rely on protest and confrontation to promote their political goals.

Notes

1. Conversation with the chairperson of the Castle local committee, summer 1997.
2. Ibid.
3. These observations were made by the author through attendance at the Waterton Yellowstone-to-Yukon conference in the autumn of 1997.
4. Interview with World Wildlife Fund Alberta Special Places co-ordinator, July 1997.

References

Alberta, Environmental Protection. 1992. *Special Places 2000: Alberta's Natural Heritage*. Edmonton, Nov.

————. 1995. *Special Places 2000: Alberta's Natural Heritage* 8.

Alberta, Provincial Co-ordinating Committee. n.d. 'Rocky Mountains Recommendation'.

Castle-Crown Wilderness Coalition. 1997. News release, 20 Mar.

————. n.d. 'The Castle Wilderness'.

Chandler, William, and Alan Siaroff. 1985–6. 'Postindustrial Politics in Germany and the Origins of the Greens', *Comparative Politics* 18: 303–25.

Cotgrove, Stephen, and Andrew Duff. 1980. 'Environmentalism, Middle-class Radicalism and Politics', *Sociological Review* 28, 2: 333–51.

———— and ————. 1981. 'Environmentalism, Values, and Social Change,' *British Journal of Sociology* 32, 1 (Mar.): 92–110.

Hoberg, George. 1992. 'Environmental Policy: Alternative Styles', in Michael M. Atkinson, *Governing Canada: Institutions and Public Policy*. Toronto: Harcourt Brace Jovanovich, 307–42.

Howlett, Michael. 1990. 'The Round Table Experience: Representation and Legitimacy in Canadian Environmental Policy-Making', *Queen's Quarterly* 97: 580–601.

Inglehart, Ronald. 1977. *The Silent Revolution*. Princeton, NJ: Princeton University Press.

Key, V.O. 1964. *Politics, Parties, and Pressure Groups*. New York: Thomas Y. Crowell.

Lawson, Kay, and Peter H. Merkl. 1988. *When Parties Fail: Emerging Alternative Organizations*. Princeton, NJ: Princeton University Press.

Müller-Rommel, Ferdinand. 1985. 'New Social Movements and Smaller Parties: A Comparative Perspective', *West European Politics* 8, 1: 41–54.

Nevitte, Neil. 1996. *The Decline of Deference*. Peterborough, Ont.: Broadview Press.

Offe, Claus. 1985. 'New Social Movements: Challenging the Boundaries of Institutional Politics', *Social Research* 52, 4: 817–68.

Paehlke, Robert. 1987. 'Participation in Environmental Administration: Closing the Open Door?', *Alternatives* 14, 2: 43–8.

———. 1989. *Environmentalism and the Future of Progressive Politics*. New Haven: Yale University Press.

Phillips, Susan D. 1994. 'New Social Movements in Canadian Politics: On Fighting and Starting Fires', in James P. Bickerton and Alain-G. Gagnon, eds, *Canadian Politics*. Peterborough, Ont.: Broadview Press, 188–206.

Poguntke, Thomas. 1987. 'New Politics and Party Systems: The Emergence of a New Type of Party?', *West European Politics* 10: 76–89.

Pross, A. Paul. 1992. *Group Politics and Public Policy*. Toronto: Oxford University Press.

Rüdig, Wolfgang. 1988. 'Peace and Ecology Movements in Western Europe', *West European Politics* 11, 1: 26–39.

Schrecker, Ted. 1984. *Political Economy of Environmental Hazards*. Ottawa: Law Reform Commission of Canada.

Stefanick, Lorna. 1998. 'Organization, Administration and the Environment: Will a Facelift Suffice, or Does the Patient Need Radical Surgery?', *Canadian Public Administration* 41, 1: 99–119.

——— and Kathleen Wells. 1998. 'Staying the Course or Saving Face? Federal Environmental Policy Post-Rio', in Leslie Pal, ed., *How Ottawa Spends 1998–1999*. Toronto: Oxford University Press.

Toner, Glen. 1993. 'ENGOS and the Policy Process', *National Round Table Review* 4.

United Nations (UN), World Commission on Environment and Development, Gro Harlem Brundtland, chair. 1987. *Our Common Future*. New York: Oxford University Press.

Woodrow, R. Brian. 1980. 'Resources and Environmental Policy-Making at the National Level: The Search for Focus', in O.P. Dwivedi, ed., *Resources and the Environment: Policy Perspectives for Canada*. Toronto: McClelland & Stewart.

Part VIII

Conclusion

Chapter 26

Canadian Political Behaviour, Past and Present

Joanna Everitt and Brenda O'Neill

The study of political behaviour in Canada has seen many important developments in the decade and a half since the publication of the last edited collection to explore the field (Bashevkin, 1985). Despite the relative lack of texts available to introduce students to the various topics considered to fall within this branch of the discipline, researchers have been hard at work and have made significant theoretical and methodological advances. Many of the most recent Canadian contributions have been highlighted in this volume. Some of these authors may not openly identify their research as 'political behaviour' since it principally addresses political institutions and processes that constrain or shape political decision-making and activity. Their work nevertheless employs the empirical methods and/or adopts the focus of political behaviour research and thus the label is appropriate.

Yet, how much progress has actually been made in our understanding of the political behaviour of Canadians? Is there a need for more research and attention? This concluding chapter attempts to answer these questions by exploring how adequately scholars have dealt with concerns identified in earlier assessments of this area of research. The three most serious of these criticisms related to the positivist approach to the study of politics, the need to address methodological weaknesses, and the fear that the field represented an Americanization of the study of Canadian politics. Although Canadian scholars should remain aware of these earlier criticisms (many of which continue to present significant challenges to the discipline), they are becoming less of a concern as we move into a new century. While issues of political relevance and instrument validity remain, self-reflection on the part of researchers, a greater awareness of the difficulties of objective analysis, the development of more sophisticated research tools and methodologies, and the diversity of issues now being examined have helped to mute some of the most critical objections to behavioural research.

Criticisms of the Positivist Nature of Political Behaviour

The most common criticism levelled at behaviouralist research relates to its positivist attitude to the study of politics. As an approach it has tended to stress the empirical questions of *what is* rather than the normative questions of *what ought to be*. This is the result of its goal of producing 'scientific', 'objective', and 'unbiased' assessments of political activity. Because of this focus, studies of political behaviour have been attacked for their 'obsession with the quantifiable, and cult of methodology which result in a sterile, status quo oriented political science capable of accumulating mountains of trivia, and incapable of attacking problems of moment' (Cairns, 1975: 209).

Critics claim that by trying to make a science out of politics the field lacks social relevance by focusing on details at the expense of offering solutions to real social problems. This, it has been argued, leads to research that serves no public purpose and lacks significance. As Christian Bay (1965: 41) has written, 'problems of human welfare (including justice, liberty, security, etc.), the objects of political research and of politics, can be adequately studied, and dealt with, only if their *ought*-side is investigated as carefully as their *is*-side.'

We would argue, however, that empirical work can be politically and socially relevant. As Robert Dahl (1961: 772) warned in an article supporting the field of political behaviour, 'unless the study of politics generates and is guided by broad, bold, even if vulnerable general theories, it is headed for the ultimate disaster of triviality.' While the development of general theories is difficult in any social science, quality empirical work is driven by the need to test models, theories, and explanations. As a result, behavioural research has helped to broaden our understanding of the external and internal factors affecting, and often limiting, citizens' involvement with their political system. Evidence of relevant empirical studies is easy to find. The work of Johnston et al. (1996) on the impact of information on voting decisions in the 1992 Charlottetown referendum, Bashevkin's (1993) work on the barriers to the representation of women in Canadian political parties, and the examination by Mancuso et al. (1998) of the ethical standards that Canadian voters set for their politicians exemplify scholarship employing behavioural methods to rethink the key concepts of democracy, representation, participation, and political values.

A related criticism focuses on political behaviour's positivist claim to objectivity. Much of the early literature assumed that it was possible for researchers to determine the 'facts' in a neutral and value-free manner. Limited recognition of the inherent value biases among researchers existed. A further criticism was levelled at researchers who approached their data with the belief that Western liberal democracies represented the 'ideal' political system. This assumption resulted in a discipline that affirmed the status quo and typically offered few critical perspectives on Canadian political life. The tacit conservatism of such research was frequently anti-political because it implied that little in the existing political system was in need of improvement (Bay, 1965: 44).

Over the years, some of the strongest critiques of the field's objectivity have come from feminist and postmodern researchers who challenge the capacity of researchers to adopt a neutral and disinterested approach to the subject matter. These scholars argue that the social, cultural, and gendered backgrounds of researchers shape the decisions made in the conduct of research and its interpretation. Moreover, they have demonstrated the many ways in which these biases have influenced seemingly 'objective' interpretations of political behaviour (Bourque and Grossholtz, 1974). For example, the androcentricity of this scholarship, frequently attributing the white, educated, propertied, and heterosexual male experience as the norm, ignores the concerns and experiences of women and other disadvantaged groups and underestimates their political participation.

These criticisms have not fallen on deaf ears and the result is a greater awareness of presuppositions inherent in the questions explored in the field and the research instruments used. Researchers are now more conscious of potential value biases in their work and attempt as much as possible to acknowledge and deal with them. New methodologies have been developed and new survey instruments added to studies such as the Canadian Election Studies (CES) to allow researchers to explore previously ignored relationships. Feminist and other researchers are increasingly drawing attention to women's and minorities' participation in political parties (Bashevkin, 1993; Megyery, 1991), their involvement in election campaigns (Erickson, 1997), their different legislative priorities (Tremblay, 1998; Arscott and Trimble, 1997; Tremblay and Andrew, 1998; Black, this volume), and their varying political attitudes (Everitt, 1998, 1999; Gidengil, 1995; O'Neill, 1998). Such changes, however, have not led to an end to critiques of the field. A noticeable lack of attention continues in the behavioural literature to the issues of race, sexuality, and physical abilities and how these affect citizens' political opportunities and orientations. The result is a continuing gulf between the priorities, approaches, and goals of behaviouralists and those of critical researchers, and at least in the short term this gulf appears unlikely to be eliminated.

Another argument raised by opponents of the positivist approach relates to its reliance on the categorization and quantification of political data and to its search for universal laws governing the behaviour of independently thinking and freely acting individuals. Critics contend that people are simply too diverse and political life is too complex to allow for codification and quantification, and that attempts at generalizations are inevitably too simplistic to be of any real use.

While there is bound to be far more variability in the results of political research than in the study of chemistry or physics, this does not completely discredit the research that is conducted. Behaviouralists are aware of the limitations of their results and have moved away from sweeping generalizations of human behaviour and towards probabilities of behaviour and attitudes. It can also be argued that the information gained from examining large numbers of cases is anything but simplistic in that it leads to an understanding of broad patterns of behaviour. The ability to generalize and make predictions beyond individual cases is necessary if we wish to explore, for example, why groups of people vote the way they do or respond to stimuli differently from others.

But not all topics easily lend themselves to measurement and quantification. Research on voting, public opinion, and political participation is easily conducted with surveys and, as a result, these topics dominate the field. Other methodologies, including content analysis, experimental design, interviews, observation, and case studies, are also employed in behavioural research to broaden the focus of study and provide nuance and elaboration to some of the more sterile quantitative results. At the same time, the development of more sophisticated analytical techniques has enabled researchers to move beyond descriptions of general characteristics or simple discussions of the correlation between two events. Now, multivariate analysis makes it possible to provide greater context and assessment of the conditions under which different behaviours might occur or attitudes might develop.

Methodological Criticisms

Political behaviour researchers have been most successful in addressing methodological critiques of the field. Elkins and Blake (1975: 313) highlighted the need for a number of methodological improvements, including 'greater sophistication in data collection, measurement, and analytical techniques, such as greater use of multivariate statistical techniques, multilevel sampling, validity studies of measuring instruments, measurements of variables usually ignored (such as psychological traits) and the study of electoral change', arguing that such improvements would lead to 'better theories and cumulation of knowledge'.

Behavioural researchers adopt numerous methodologies in the gathering of data. However, many Canadian studies have relied on social surveys, especially the major surveys conducted at the time of each national election. The Canadian National Election Study (CNES) was first conducted in 1965 and the survey has been conducted in every subsequent election, with the exception of 1972. In addition, the investigators of the 1993 election included a panel element in their study, allowing them to examine attitudes and behaviours during the 1992 Charlottetown referendum.[1] While other important public opinion data sets exist[2] and many researchers have designed and conducted surveys based on their own research projects, the election studies continue to provide a valuable and primary opinion data resource for Canadian behavioural researchers.

The methodology adopted in early surveys of Canadian elections largely mirrored that employed by American researchers. In more recent surveys, however, two noteworthy differences have distinguished Canadian election studies. The first relates to the manner in which the studies are conducted and administered. Between 1952 and 1976, the American National Election Studies (NES) were designed and administered by a single group of political scientists located at the University of Michigan.[3] These studies are accessible to the larger academic community through the archival and data dissemination facilities of the Inter-University Consortium for Political and Social Research (ICPSR). The continuity provided by a single research team led to a consistency in questions across surveys, as well as a unique time-series (measurement of basic political attitudes and behaviours repeated regularly over time) aspect to the studies. Since 1977, however, responsibility for the surveys has been distributed among a wider range of researchers.[4] The result is an improvement in measurement for some of the core concepts first developed by the Michigan team and the development of instruments and designs allowing for the testing of new theories of voting and public opinion. Strong pressure nevertheless exists to maintain a relatively rigid survey design in order to maintain the time-series component of the surveys. As a result, the primary component of the American NES remains a standard set of questions administered in a pre-election wave (beginning the day after Labour Day and ending the day before the November general election) and post-election wave (re-interviewing respondents from the first wave, beginning the day after the election and continuing until approximately mid-January) panel design.

In Canada, funding for the surveys is administered by the Social Science and Humanities Research Council (SSHRC), and before that the former Canada Council, resulting in less continuity across surveys.[5] In the years leading up to an election, different teams of academics compete for the resources to conduct the studies and the result has been that responsibility for these studies has changed hands a number of times over the past three decades. As success in the competition results from an innovative research design and the relevance of the data for Canadian academics, every shift in responsibility results in significant modification in questions asked and in the measurement properties of the survey instruments. Although this rotating responsibility for the studies has seriously limited the time-series component of the data, it has allowed for significant methodological and theoretical improvement in study design (see Gidengil, this volume).

A second distinction in the Canadian election studies exists in the greater willingness of Canadian researchers to experiment with new survey methodologies. The driving force behind this innovation comes from the institutions that structure Canadian elections. Unlike in the US, Canadian governments enjoy the flexibility of setting election dates constrained only by the requirement that a government sit no longer than five years. The result for academics interested in studying elections with polling data is a limited ability to predict election timing and a concomitant inability to conduct pre-election surveys akin to those in the US. Short notice makes it impossible to get interviewers into the field in the country's many different ridings and complete the study before the end of the election campaign. As a result, the early Canadian studies, conducted as face-to-face in-home interviews, were necessarily undertaken after the election had taken place. The fact that some surveys were conducted as late as three months after the date of the election resulted in criticism of the reliability of data based on respondents' recall of their voting choice that took place weeks, if not months, earlier (Wiseman, 1986). The introduction of telephone interviewing (first employed in the 1980 CNES due to the financial constraints of conducting another study so quickly after the 1979 election) and later the adoption of new computer-assisted telephone interviewing (CATI) technologies (first used in the 1988 study) significantly reduced the time required to conduct surveys and hence increased the reliability of the data.

The American NES first experimented with telephone interviewing and a rolling cross-sectional design (which consists of a series of samples drawn each week of the election campaign) in a pilot study in 1982. Unlike Canadian election teams, however, the Americans have never fully adopted telephone interviewing in the time-series component. While CATI and rolling cross-sectional designs are used for experimental or pilot studies, the main component of the NES continues to consist of face-to-face in-home interviews in the pre- and post-election manner. In an added twist, the last three Canadian election studies have adopted a tri-panel design consisting of a rolling cross-sectional pre-election survey conducted over the course of the campaign, a traditional post-election telephone study reinterviewing the original respondents, and a self-administered mail-back survey. This unique sampling strategy has allowed Canadian scholars to be among the first to explore the dynamic element of election campaigns (Johnston et al., 1992).

More sophisticated data collection and improved sampling techniques resulting from the adoption of CATI systems have also muted the methodological criticisms directed at earlier studies. To reflect accurately the diversity of the Canadian population, the sample size of Canadian election surveys has always been quite large compared to those employed in other countries (LeDuc et al., 1974). This larger sample necessarily increases the cost of the project given Canada's land mass and the geographic dispersion of its population. Early opinion studies balanced the tension between larger sample size and manageable costs by employing a multi-staged, stratified, clustered sample in which the sample was randomized first at the level of the constituency, second at the level of the polling district, and finally among the eligible voters in these chosen polls (ibid.). The problem with this sampling strategy was that it resulted in higher margins of error than a simple random sample (Wiseman, 1986). It also resulted in the omission of whole sections of the country (the North, for example). Similarly, because the investigators were forced to select their respondents from a limited cluster of ridings, voters in only a handful of ridings in the smaller provinces were sampled (ibid.). Despite these criticisms, the studies' principal researchers argued that the sampling frame nevertheless enabled them to encompass between 90 and 95 per cent of the population (see LeDuc et al., 1974: 704, n. 4).[6] The recent adoption of CATI has meant that the main potential threat to the randomness of the sample lies in the number of Canadians who do not have access to a telephone. And since over 98 per cent of Canadians have a telephone in their home,[7] this threat is relatively limited.

One of the continuing concerns of behavioural researchers is the validity of the measures upon which conclusions are based. As others in this book have noted, question wording and question ordering can have important consequences for survey results. Because of the need to ensure that researchers are actually measuring what they think they are measuring, survey questions must be highly structured yet relatively simple. The cost and time constraints of conducting large-scale public opinion studies frequently require that respondents be provided with a small number of answers to choose from, limiting researchers' ability to explore the nuances and subtleties that might be revealed in more open-ended approaches. The trade-off between the amount of manageable information to be gained by limiting responses and the degree of validity of the data is one that continues to confront survey researchers. In the past this has tended to restrict explorations of the calculations and motivations behind various attitudes or behaviours. However, the introduction of embedded experiments in studies such as the Charter Study and more recent CES suggests that greater attention is now devoted to the question of instrument validity. Researchers such as Sniderman et al. (1996) and Johnston et al. (1992) have shown that minor changes in question wording can alter support for civil rights and policies such as free trade. Others, such as Bassili and Fletcher (1991), have looked at response-time measurements as a means of understanding non-attitudes.

Furthermore, researchers are becoming more cognizant of factors that may lead different groups to respond to survey questionnaires in different manners. Blais and Gidengil (1993), for example, noted that the translation of questions from English to French may produce very different connotations, and David Northrup's (1995) analysis of interviewer effects reveals that men's and women's answers to questions on affirmative action vary with the gender of the interviewer. These and other studies have drawn attention to the complexity of the process of measuring attitudes and beliefs and to the need for researchers to consider all factors in their interpretation of survey questions. While this stands as an important development in survey research and suggests that we have come some way in addressing criticisms such as those levelled by Elkins and Blake, there is admittedly work that remains to be completed.

Along with questions about the quality of research instruments employed to gather data, Elkins and Blake also raised concerns about the degree of theoretical development occurring in early studies. Research up until that point was dominated by the use of simplistic analytical approaches, which tended to be exploratory and descriptive rather than more complex analyses useful for establishing relationships among variables. This limited theoretical development was attributed to the 'lack of cumulative learning which characterises the field, including the lack of textbooks, the primitive use of control variables, the general lack of multivariate analytic techniques, and the inadequate and infrequent revision of research instruments' (Elkins and Blake, 1975: 317). Subsequent research has become increasingly sophisticated, and a quick review of the techniques employed in the research—many of them included in this book—makes it clear that this criticism is less valid than in the past. While scholars must take care to avoid using statistics simply for their own sake and sheltering poor theoretical work with sophisticated statistical techniques, it is clear that the development and use of advanced quantitative methods are helping to further the theoretical arguments being presented. Indices and scales, interaction variables, factor analysis, regression analysis, and even time-series analysis are now considered important means for conveying an argument, even in introductory texts designed for undergraduate students. Unfortunately, while advances in technology have improved the study of political behaviour, the discipline has not been as successful in taking advantage of them. Undergraduate and graduate students alike are often not required to take methods or statistics courses to complete degrees in political science. This situation is worrisome, for it means that students are unlikely to understand the procedures behind the statistics and, as a result, will be unable to critique their use or the conclusions drawn from them.

Political Behaviour: An Americanization of Canadian Political Science?

The behaviouralist approach has also been subjected to criticism that its adoption represented an Americanization of Canadian political science. There is no question that the study of political behaviour is stronger in the United States than anywhere else in the world. The largest number of political scientists teaching and researching on these topics are located there along with a number of specialized associations and conferences,[8] the most significant journals,[9] major data archives,[10] and key summer school programs offering courses in data analysis, political psychology, or campaigns and elections.[11] The consequence is that American research dominates the field, causing concern that Canadian political behaviour may import research agendas and methodologies that are inappropriate north of the border.

Indeed, early Canadian behaviouralist studies were frequently based on American models, due partly to the fact that these projects were conducted by American scholars or by Canadian academics trained in American graduate programs. Efforts to test American arguments in a Canadian context can be found in studies of Canadian political culture (Horowitz, 1968), voting behaviour (Clarke et al., 1979), and political participation (Mishler, 1979). However, the conclusions in many instances were distinctly Canadian, reflecting the importance of history, ethnicity, regionalism, and institutional structures in creating a political system different from that to the south. Thus, it would be wrong to argue that Canadian research has simply mirrored US work or that it simply transplants American models to Canadian soil. Canadian scholars have looked to the United States for theoretical arguments and methodologies designed by American scholars. Yet rarely has this occurred without significant modification, as it became clear that their explanatory value was weak when they were used to account for the Canadian political environment.

While the field never dominated the discipline of political science in Canada to the degree as in the United States, graduate programs with a specialization in political behaviour appeared at a number of Canadian universities. By 1971 a special section for the presentation of behaviouralist research was established at the annual conferences of the Canadian Political Science Association. The result is a significant development of the field of political behaviour and the small 'incestuous' community of scholars[12] in the 1960s and 1970s has grown to include a significant number of researchers trained in behavioural methods. The resultant broadening of the scope of the research questions has helped to provide a distinctively 'Canadian' approach to the field.

Research Trends

Research on voting and citizen participation in elections dominated early Canadian studies of political behaviour. Scholars such as John Meisel (1962, 1972), Jean Laponce (1969), Peter Regenstreif (1965), and Vincent Lemieux (1964), along with those contributing to early collected editions on voting (Meisel, 1964; Courtney, 1967), helped to define the field and secure its focus on elections as the primary means for citizen participation in the Canadian political system. Although some early scholars explored political attitudes (Schwartz, 1967) and the transformation of social movements to political parties (Pinard,1971), they were more the exception than the rule. Today the term 'political behaviour' still evokes images of voting studies, and important research continues to be conducted in this area (Nevitte et al., 2000; Clarke et al., 1996; Johnston et al., 1992). As this book has shown, however, the field has progressed beyond its focus on the ballot box to research in such areas as political culture, public opinion, political élites and activists, participation, and interest groups and social movements.

Driving much of this research are questions of how behaviour and attitudes are linked to territory, whether at the national, provincial, or local level. Even the concern about the role that language and ethnicity play in Canadian politics has traditionally been closely connected to Quebec's large French-speaking population and the predominantly English-speaking population in the rest of Canada. Elkins and Blake (1975: 314) argued that this initial preoccupation with region tended to limit research agendas since many questions are problem-oriented and not bound by locale. They further emphasized a need to focus less on 'existing political boundaries and be more attuned to relevant comparisons of groups of individuals wherever located'. This shift in attention has been slow to develop. In 1985, Bashevkin again characterized Canadian behavioural studies as giving primacy to the role of region, and Gidengil (1992) found that there was a dearth of Canadian studies exploring the impact of psychological factors, such as personality traits, and sociological factors, such as gender and ethnicity, on attitudes, voting behaviour, or participation.[13]

Changes are occurring, however, and as this book has shown, the past few years have seen an expansion in research with topics such as political sophistication and opinion formation, the development of non-territorial identities based on gender and ethnicity, value change, and political participation outside of the boundaries of political parties and elections. While regional identities continue to be important to analyses of Canadian political behaviour,[14] other sociological and psychological factors are also recognized as primary forces shaping attitudes and behaviour. In part, this has resulted from the broadening in the discipline of the definition of political activity to encompass involvement in social movements and civil society. It also reflects the larger and more mature Canadian scholarly community and the interests of new generations of scholars, which together have contributed to a growing diversity in the focus of research.

At the same time, there continue to be important theoretical developments in the literature on political parties and voting and elections.[15] Studies such as those included in this book highlighting the democratic implications of party organization, partisan ideological consistency, and the impact of media coverage on campaign dynamics are some examples of areas in which scholars have furthered our understanding of Canadian political behaviour. This research has helped our understanding of the relationship between behaviour, the political environment, and the opportunity structures provided by important Canadian political institutions such as the electoral system, the parliamentary system, and the Charter of Rights and Freedoms. Despite its breadth, this text has exhibited only a fraction of the research currently being conducted on Canadian political behaviour.

Challenges for the Future

At a recent gathering of Canadian researchers interested in the study of political behaviour there was considerable optimism about the future of the field. Exciting new work was being discussed by highly regarded senior scholars, new academics, and graduate students. Yet, while there has been significant development in the Canadian study of political behaviour over the past few decades, serious challenges still face the field.

First among these challenges is the need to ensure that research addresses questions of relevance to those beyond the ivory towers of academe. For behavioural studies to have any real significance for students and those in the non-academic community, researchers need to demonstrate the practical, social, and political implications of their work. This is not to suggest that behavioural researchers abandon the objectivity expected by the logical positivist approach and instead become political advocates. Rather, continued effort needs to be made to justify the applied value of this form of research. Studying the career paths of politicians or the relationship between political parties and social movements is interesting, particularly for those who have chosen the study of politics as a career, and there is a sound argument for conducting research that simply advances knowledge. But the relevance of this research also lies in its implications for the participatory and decision-making opportunities found in Canadian democracy.

A second challenge is the continuing necessity of questioning the appropriateness and validity of the methodologies employed. Do the research instruments accurately measure the concepts under examination? What is the impact of question wording or interviewer effects? And what alternative measures or approaches can be created to improve our ability to answer new and old research questions alike? While innovation in election surveys and the development of new research instruments by individuals or teams of researchers have resulted in significant methodological development over the years, there remains room for improvement.

A related challenge is the difficulty of conducting research in an environment of fiscal constraint. In the past decade governments have dramatically reduced the funds available for academic research, particularly in the arts, humanities, and social sciences. The resulting budget reductions have necessarily meant that research is often limited to employing the most cost-effective methods, which are not always those most appropriate for ensuring its success. While this poses obvious challenges, the problem of limited funding for large-scale survey projects might provide an incentive for expanding the methods adopted for examining research questions beyond the familiar. Researchers (CES teams and individual academics alike) may need to tackle those projects that do receive funding with new questions and new analytical approaches. The current budget restraints may also lead to a greater reliance on data collected by private polling companies, governments, and think-tanks, which are currently available in many instances through data archives across the country. Alternatively, limited funding may entail a move beyond traditional survey research towards alternative methodologies such as macro-level analysis, case studies, and content analysis.

Finally, one of the ongoing challenges facing the field is the fear of 'numbers' on the part of many students in political science. This fear often results in the avoidance of courses where they might be confronted with tables of numbers, which they feel they cannot interpret, or with readings based on statistical procedures that strike terror into their hearts. We would argue that students will only overcome this fear by learning how to analyse statistics and to 'do numbers', and that departments around the country should rethink the requirements for a political science degree. Such a policy, hopefully, would increase the number and quality of resources available to academics teaching courses designed to introduce students to the study of political behaviour and its methods. Many excellent monographs and articles are available on these subjects, but many of these are academic explorations not specifically designed for use in undergraduate courses. The numerous introductory texts available for students studying political parties, public policy, or Canadian federalism are not matched by those available for use in courses on political behaviour, public opinion and voting, or political participation. In having drawn together a selection of accessible articles reflecting some of the most important work currently being conducted in the field, we hope to fill that void.

Conclusion

As noted in the introduction of this text, the study of political behaviour is inextricably tied to the democratic project, which views informed citizen participation as necessary to its success. Individuals represent the most basic unit within democracies, and understanding how they relate to their government and participate in its decisions is necessary for a valid assessment of the democratic nature of these governments. As political scientists, it is important for us to untangle the many complex factors affecting the choices citizens make, including those related to support for an issue, to acts of participation, and even to acts of non-participation.

The subject matter of political behaviour (political culture, public opinion, voting, participation, élites and activists, and interest groups and social movements) helps us to do this. A broadening of the field of inquiry over the past few decades —to examine questions of particular importance to Canadian politics, to explore the roles within the polity of women and other groups whose experiences have traditionally been ignored, and to consider new forms of political participation—has meant that we now have a much better understanding of the determinants of political behaviour. However, many important and interesting questions remain to be answered.

The behavioural method, built on scientific, objective, and reasonably unbiased assessments of political activity, is critical to our ability to answer these queries. Improvements in recent years in sampling and data collection, the development of new research instruments and measurements, and the use of more sophisticated analytical techniques have enabled us to provide the necessary empirical support for theoretical arguments about the relationships between various factors. Only after we answer the questions of *how* and *why* citizens actually engage with their governments can we then move beyond description and explanation to an informed discussion of how they *should* or *ought* to be able to interact.

Notes

1. Prior to and including the study of the 1984 election the studies were referred to as the Canadian National Election Studies. Since 1988 they have been referred to as the Canadian Election Studies. The 1965 CNES was conducted by Philip Converse, John Meisel, Maurice Pinard, Peter Regenstreif, and Mildred Schwartz. The 1968 survey was conducted by John Meisel. The 1972 election was studied privately by Canadian Market Opinion Research and the survey has received little academic attention. The 1974, 1979, and 1980 CNES were conducted by Harold Clarke, Jane Jenson, Lawrence LeDuc, and Jon Pammett. The 1984 CNES was conducted by Ronald Lambert, James Curtis, Steven Brown, and Barry Kay. The 1988 CES was conducted by Richard Johnston, André Blais, Henry Brady, and Jean Crête. The 1992 Referendum Study and the 1993 CES were conducted by Richard Johnston, André Blais, Elisabeth Gidengil, and Neil Nevitte. The 1997 and 2000 CES were conducted by André Blais, Elisabeth Gidengil, Richard Nadeau, and Neil Nevitte.

2. Examples of such surveys include the World Values Surveys (1981 and 1991), the Charter Study (1987), and the Ethics Study (1996). A growing amount of data gathered by private companies such as Gallup, Pollara, Environics, Decima, and Angus Reid is now available through data archives. For examples of major studies that have not relied on CES data, see Schwartz (1967), Elkins and Simeon (1980), Sniderman et al. (1996), Nevitte (1996), and Mancuso et al. (1998).

3. The principal investigators of studies in this period were Warren Miller, Philip Converse, Donald Stokes, and Angus Campbell.

4. Since 1977 the American National Election Studies have been funded by the National Science Foundation.

5. The Canada Council and the Laidlaw Foundation helped fund the 1965 study. The 1968 study was funded by the Izaak Killam Memorial Fund of the Canada Council. As noted above, the 1972 study was a private survey conducted by Canadian Market Opinion Research.

6. American studies conducted in presidential election years continue to be conducted in this manner.

7. This figure is based on 1998 Statistics Canada data, available at http://www.statcan.ca/english/Pgdb/People/Families/famil09b.htm

8. For example, the International Society of Political Psychology, the American Association of Public Opinion Research, the Society for Political Methodology, and the Mid-Western Political Science Association are all specialized organizations that focus on behavioural research.

9. For example, see *American Journal of Political Science, American Political Science Review, Public Opinion Quarterly, Political Psychology, Political Behaviour, Press/Politics*, and *Political Analysis*.

10. The Inter-University Consortium for Political and Social Research, which houses many of the world surveys and data sets, is located at the University of Michigan. All of the Canadian Election Studies can be retrieved through the ICPSR.

11. For example, the ICPSR offers a regular summer program in Quantitative Methods of Social Research, Ohio State University offers a summer institute in Political Psychology, and the private organization Campaigns & Elections regularly offers seminars for political practitioners.

12. Elkins and Blake (1975: 323) chose the term 'incestuous' to argue that the small number of Canadian scholars in the field of political behaviour resulted in the greater likelihood that they would '(a) know each other well and therefore hesitate to criticize each other honestly, (b) sit on review boards for each others' grant applications and (c) do secondary analysis of each others' data.'

13. Gidengil's review article focused solely on studies using Canadian Election Study data.

14. The most recent study of Canadian elections has concluded that 'the vote is more strongly regionalized in Canada than in any other Western democracy, except perhaps Belgium' (Nevitte et al., 2000: 13).

15. For recent studies on Canadian political parties, see Carty et al. (2000) and Bickerton et al. (1999). For recent studies on Canadian elections, see Nevitte et al. (2000), Clarke et al. (1996), and Johnston et al. (1992).

References

Arscott, Jane, and Linda Trimble, eds. 1997. *In the Presence of Women: Representation in Canadian Governments*. Toronto: Harcourt Brace.

Bashevkin, Sylvia. 1985. *Canadian Political Behaviour: Introductory Readings*. Agincourt, Ont.: Methuen.

————. 1993. *Toeing the Lines: Women and Party Politics in English Canada*, 2nd edn. Toronto: Oxford University Press.

Bassili, John N., and Joseph F. Fletcher. 1991. 'Response-Time Measurement in Survey Research: A Method for CATI and a New Look at Non-Attitudes', *Public Opinion Quarterly* 55: 331–46.

Bay, Christian. 1965 'Politics and Pseudopolitics: A Critical Evaluation of Some Behavioral Literature', *American Political Science Review* 59, 1: 39–51.

Bickerton, James, Alain-G. Gagnon, and Patrick J. Smith. 1999. *Ties That Bind: Parties and Voters in Canada*. Toronto: Oxford University Press.

Blais, André, and Elisabeth Gidengil. 1993. 'Things Are Not Always What They Seem: French-English Differences and the Problem of Measurement Equivalence', *Canadian Journal of Political Science* 26, 3: 541–55.

Bourque, Susan, and Jean Grossholtz. 1974. 'Politics an Unnatural Practice: Political Science Looks at Female Participation', *Politics and Society* 4, 2: 225–66.

Cairns, Alan. 1975. 'Political Science in Canada and the Americanization Issue', *Canadian Journal of Political Science* 8, 2: 191–234.

Carty, R.K., William Cross, and Lisa Young. 2000. *Rebuilding Canadian Parties*. Vancouver: University of British Columbia Press.

Clarke, Harold D., Jane Jenson, Lawrence LeDuc, and Jon H. Pammett. 1979. *Political Choice in Canada*. Toronto: McGraw-Hill Ryerson.

———, ———, ———, and ———. 1996. *Absent Mandate: Canadian Electoral Politics in an Era of Restructuring*, 3rd edn. Vancouver: Gage.

Courtney, John, ed. 1967. *Voting in Canada*. Scarborough, Ont.: Prentice-Hall.

Dahl, Robert. 1961. 'The Behavioural Approach in Political Science: Epitaph for a Monument to a Successful Protest', *American Political Science Review* 55, 4: 763–72.

Elkins, David, and Donald Blake. 1975. 'Voting Research in Canada', *Canadian Journal of Political Science* 8, 2: 313–25.

——— and Richard Simeon. 1980. *Small Worlds: Provinces and Parties in Canadian Political Life*. Toronto: Methuen.

Erickson, Lynda. 1997. 'Entry to the Commons: Parties, Recruitment, and the Election of Women in 1993', in Tremblay and Andrew, eds. (1997: 219–56).

Everitt, Joanna. 1998. 'The Gender Gap in Canada: Now You See It, Now You Don't', *Canadian Review of Sociology and Anthropology* 35, 2: 1–29.

———. 1999. 'Public Opinion and Social Movements: The Women's Movement and the Gender Gap in Canada', *Canadian Journal of Political Science* 31, 4: 743–65.

Gidengil, Elisabeth. 1992. 'Canada Votes: A Quarter Century of Canadian National Election Studies', *Canadian Journal of Political Science* 25, 2: 219–48.

———. 1995. 'Economic Man—Social Woman? The Case of the Gender Gap in Support for the Canada-US Free Trade Agreement', *Comparative Political Studies* 28, 3: 384–408.

Horowitz, Gad. 1968. *Canadian Labour in Politics*. Toronto: University of Toronto Press.

Johnston, Richard, André Blais, Henry Brady, and Jean Crête. 1992. *Letting the People Decide: Dynamics of a Canadian Election*. Montreal and Kingston: McGill-Queen's Press.

———, ———, Elisabeth Gidengil, and Neil Nevitte. 1996. *The Challenge of Direct Democracy: The 1992 Canadian Referendum*. Montreal and Kingston: McGill-Queen's University Press.

Laponce, Jean. 1969. *People vs. Politics*. Toronto: University of Toronto Press.

LeDuc, Lawrence, Harold Clarke, Jane Jenson, and Jon Pammett. 1974. 'A National Sample Design', *Canadian Journal of Political Science* 7, 4: 701–8.

Lemieux, Vincent. 1964. 'Election in the Constituency of Lévis', in Meisel (1964).

Mancuso, Maureen, Michael Atkinson, André Blais, Ian Green, and Neil Nevitte. 1998. *A Question of Ethics: Canadians Speak Out*. Toronto: Oxford University Press.

Megyery, Kathy, ed. 1991. *Ethno-Cultural Groups and Visible Minorities in Canadian Politics: The Question of Access*. Toronto: Dundurn Press.

Meisel, John. 1962. *The Canadian General Election of 1957*. Toronto: University of Toronto Press.

———, ed. 1964. *Papers on the 1962 Election*. Toronto: University of Toronto Press.

———. 1972. *Working Papers on Canadian Politics*. Toronto: University of Toronto Press.

Mishler, William. 1979. *Political Participation in Canada*. Toronto: Macmillan.

Nevitte, Neil. 1996. *The Decline of Deference: Canadian Value Change in Cross-National Perspective*. Peterborough, Ont.: Broadview Press.

———, André Blais, Elisabeth Gidengil, and Richard Nadeau. 2000. *Unsteady State: The 1997 Canadian Federal Election*. Toronto: Oxford University Press.

Northrup, David. 1995. 'Gender-of-Interviewer Effects and Level of Public Support for Affirmative Action', in François-Pierre Gingras, ed., *Gender Politics in Contemporary Canada*. Toronto: Oxford University Press.

O'Neill, Brenda. 1998. 'The Relevance of Leader Gender to Voting in the 1993 Canadian National Election', *International Journal of Canadian Studies* 17: 105–30.

Pinard, Maurice. 1971. *The Rise of a Third Party: A Study in Crisis Politics*. Englewood Cliffs, NJ: Prentice-Hall.

Regenstreif, Peter. 1965. *The Diefenbaker Interlude: Parties and Voting in Canada*. Toronto: Longmans Canada.

Schwartz, Mildred, 1967. *Public Opinion and Canadian Identity*. Berkeley: University of California Press.

Sniderman, Paul, Joseph Fletcher, Peter Russell, and Philip Tetlock. 1996. *Clash of Rights: Liberty, Equality and Legitimacy in Pluralist Democracy*. New Haven: Yale University Press.

Tremblay, Manon. 1998. 'Do Female MPs Substantively Represent Women? A Study of Legislative Behaviour in Canada's 35th Parliament', *Canadian Journal of Political Science* 31, 3: 435–65.

——— and Caroline Andrew, eds. 1997. *Women and Political Representation in Canada*. Ottawa: University of Ottawa Press.

Wiseman, Nelson. 1986. 'The Use, Misuse, and Abuse of the National Election Studies', *Journal of Canadian Studies* 21, 1: 21–35.

Contributors

Yasmeen Abu-Laban is Assistant Professor in Political Science at the University of Alberta. Her research interests relate to the Canadian and comparative dimensions of gender, ethnic, and identity politics. Her publications include articles in the *Canadian Journal of Political Science*, *Canadian Ethnic Studies*, *Canadian Public Policy*, *Canadian Review of American Studies*, and *International Politics*.

Keith Archer is Professor of Political Science and Interim Vice-President (Research) at the University of Calgary. His research centres on political parties, voting, and elections. Recent books include *Quasi-Democracy? Parties and Leadership Selection in Alberta* (with David Stewart, 2000); *Parameters of Power: Canada's Political Institutions* (with Rainer Knopff, Roger Gibbins, and Leslie Pal, 2000), and *Political Activists: The NDP in Convention* (with Alan Whitehorn, 1997).

Jerome H. Black is an Associate Professor of Political Science at McGill University. Over the years, he has published in the areas of women and politics, the political participation of ethnoracial minorities, Canadian immigration and refugee policy, strategic voting, and comparative voter turnout. Currently, his main project centres on ethnoracial minorities in Canada as both office-seekers and parliamentarians.

André Blais is Professor in the Department of Political Science and research fellow with the Centre de recherche et de développement en économique at the Université de Montréal. His research interests are voting and elections, electoral systems, and public opinion. He is the principal co-investigator of the 1997 Canadian Election Study. His most recent book is *To Vote or Not to Vote? The Merits and Limits of Rational Choice Theory* (2000).

Donald E. Blake is Professor of Political Science at the University of British Columbia. He specializes in the study of public opinion and elections in Western democracies. Previous work on environmental issues has appeared in *BC Studies*, the *Canadian Journal of Political Science*, and *Canadian Public Policy*.

Sandra Burt is a member of the Political Science Department at the University of Waterloo. Between 1999 and 2002, she is the English Co-editor of the *Canadian Journal of Political Science*. Recent publications include a study of women legislators in Ontario and a review of the federal government's policies on male violence. She is currently working on a third edition of *Changing Patterns* (with Lorraine Code) and a review of the Women's Program in the federal government.

Louise Carbert is an Assistant Professor of Political Science at Dalhousie University. Her research has centred on rural political economy, political attitudes, and participation, including women's election to public office. She has recently completed a focus-group series with rural community leaders across Atlantic Canada, supported by a grant from the Indo-Canadian Shastri Institute. She is the author of *Agrarian Feminism* (1995).

William Cross is Director of the Centre for Canadian Studies and a member of the Department of Political Science at Mount Allison University. He is co-author of *Rebuilding Canadian Party Politics* (2000).

David C. Docherty is an Associate Professor of Political Science at Wilfrid Laurier University. His current research interests include constituency and legislative behaviour of parliamentarians in Canada, Great Britain, Australia, and New Zealand. He is the author of *Mr. Smith Goes to Ottawa: Life in the House of Commons* (1997) and numerous chapters and articles on Canadian political careers.

Munroe Eagles is an Associate Professor of Political Science, and Associate Dean for Graduate Studies, at the State University of New York at Buffalo. His current research with Ken Carty is focused on local parties, election campaigning, and the political ecology of party financing in Ontario and New Brunswick.

Joanna Everitt is an Associate Professor of Politics at the University of New Brunswick, Saint John. She researches topics in political behaviour, including: gender differences in public opinion; women, media, and leadership evaluations; and voting behaviour. She has published in journals such as *Press/Politics*, *Women & Politics*, the *Canadian Journal of Political Science*, and the *Canadian Review of Sociology and Anthropology*.

Patrick Fournier is a post-doctoral fellow in the Department of Political Science at the Université de Montréal. His research interests in political behaviour include public opinion, elections and voting, citizen sophistication, and political psychology. He has published in journals such as the *Journal of Politics*, *Public Opinion Quarterly*, the *Japanese Journal of Political Science*, and the *Canadian Journal of Political Science*.

Elisabeth Gidengil is Professor of Political Science at McGill University. She co-directed the survey of Canadians' opinions on electoral democracy for the Royal Commission on Electoral Reform and Party Financing (the Lortie Comission) and was a member of the 1992 Charlottetown Referendum/1993 Canadian Election Study and the 1997 Canadian Election Study teams. She is co-author of *Making Representative Democracy Work* (1991), *The Challenge of Direct Democracy: The 1992 Canadian Referendum* (1996), and *Unsteady State: The 1997 Canadian Election* (2000).

Richard Jenkins is a visiting Assistant Professor and SSHRC post-doctoral fellow at Queen's University. His research focuses on election campaigns, news coverage, political parties, and voting behaviour. Previous publications have appeared in the *American Review of Canadian Studies*, *Political Communication*, the *Journal of Politics*, and a number of edited books.

Mebs Kanji is a PhD candidate in Political Science at the University of Calgary. His research interests are in Canadian and comparative politics, focusing on the study of political and electoral behaviour. He is the co-author of *Governing in Post-Deficit Times: Alberta in the Klein Years* (with Barry Cooper, 2000) and has published in journals such as the *International Journal of Public Opinion Research*, the *American Review of Canadian Studies*, and the *International Journal of Comparative Sociology*.

Lawrence LeDuc is Professor of Political Science at the University of Toronto. His publications include *Comparing Democracies: Voting and Elections in Global Perspective* (1996), *Absent Mandate: Canadian Electoral Politics in an Era of Restructuring* (1996), *How Voters Change* (1990), and *Political Choice in Canada* (1979, 1980), as well as articles on voting and elections in a number of North American and European political science journals.

Pierre Martin is Associate Professor of Political Science at the Université de Montréal, where he is also an associate fellow in the Centre de recherche et développement en économique. In 1999–2000 he was the William Lyon Mackenzie King Visiting Associate Professor of Canadian Studies at Harvard University. His work is in the areas of international political economy, international relations, public opinion analysis, and Quebec politics. His articles have appeared in *Comparative Politics*, the *Canadian Journal of Political Science*, *International Journal,* and the *British Journal of Political Science.*

Richard Nadeau is Professor of Political Science at the Université de Montréal. A specialist of electoral behaviour, political communication, public opinion analysis, and political methods, he has published widely in the foremost journals of his discipline, including the *American Political Science Review*, the *American Journal of Political Science*, the *British Journal of Political Science*, the *Journal of Politics*, and *Public Opinion Quarterly*. He is a member of the 1997 Canadian Election Study research team and a co-author of *Unsteady State: The 1997 Canadian Federal Election* (2000).

Neil Nevitte is Professor of Political Science at the University of Toronto. He is Principal Investigator of the Canadian component of the World Values Surveys and a member of the 1997 and 2000 Canadian Election Study research teams. His recent publications include *Unsteady State: The 1997 Canadian Federal Election* (with André Blais, Elisabeth Gidengil, and Richard Nadeau, 2000); *The Decline of Deference* (1996); and *The North American Trajectory* (with Ronald Inglehart and Miguel Basanez, 1996).

Jacquetta Newman is an Assistant Professor in the Department of Political Science at King's College, University of Western Ontario. Her research focuses on social movements, political subjectivity, and identity politics, looking at phenomena such as the peace movement, women's movement, and subnationalism. Current research projects include the globalization of social movement politics and civil society, and the development of feminist peace campaigns in Canada. Her publications include work in *Peace Research: The Canadian Journal of Peace Studies* and a review of social movement literature for Amnesty International's (London) Global Trends Seminar, 'Social Movements in the Context of Globalisation'.

Brenda O'Neill is Assistant Professor of Political Studies at the University of Manitoba. Her research has examined gender as a defining factor in public opinion and political behaviour. Recent publications can be found in the *International Journal of Canadian Studies* and the *Canadian Journal of Political Science.*

Anthony M. Sayers is an Associate Professor of Political Science at the University of Calgary whose research encompasses political parties, election campaigns, theories of representation, and federalism. He is author of *Parties, Candidates and Constituency Campaigns in Canadian Elections* (1999) and has published in a number of journals, including the *Australian Journal of Political Science*, the *Canadian Journal of Political Science*, and *Electoral Studies.*

Lorna Stefanick is the Associate Director of the Government Studies Unit at the University of Alberta, Faculty of Extension. Her research has focused on environmental policy, process, and actors and has appeared in *Canadian Public Administration*, *How Ottawa Spends*, and various edited collections. Her current research focuses on regional governance and the creation of virtual communities for local administration.

David K. Stewart is Associate Professor of Political Studies at the University of Manitoba and Dean of Studies of St John's College at that university. His research interests focus on political parties and he is the co-author (with Keith Archer) of *Quasi-Democracy: Parties and Leadership Selection in Alberta* (2000).

Ian Stewart is a Professor of Political Science at the Acadia University where he has taught since 1982. His major research interests are in the party politics and political culture of the Maritime provinces. He is the author of *Roasting Chestnuts: The Mythology of Maritime Political Culture* (1994).

A. Brian Tanguay is Associate Professor of Political Science at Wilfrid Laurier University. His research focuses on the organization, ideology, and electoral activities of political parties, as well as the interaction among parties, interest groups, and social movements. He is the co-editor (with Alain Gagnon) of *Canadian Parties in Transition* (1988, 1996) and has published (with Barry Kay) articles on the political activity of local interest groups for the Royal Commission on Electoral Reform and Party Financing and in the *International Journal of Canadian Studies*.

Lisa Young is Associate Professor of Political Science at the University of Calgary. She is author of *Feminists and Party Politics* (2000) and co-author of *Rebuilding Canadian Party Politics* (2000). Her research interests include women in politics, political parties, and electoral law and regulation.